THE
PEOPLE'S
MACHINE

THE
PEOPLE'S
MACHINE

Arnold Schwarzenegger
and the Rise of
Blockbuster Democracy

JOE MATHEWS

PublicAffairs
New York

Published in the United States by PublicAffairs™,
a member of the Perseus Books Group.
All rights reserved.
Printed in the United States of America.

Photographs of Arnold Schwarzenegger appear with permission
from the *Los Angeles Times*, Zuma Press/*Sacramento Bee*, Ringo Chiu, and the
George Bush Presidential Library. The photograph of Hiram Johnson appears with
permission of the Bancroft Library.

Library of Congress Cataloging-in-Publication Data
Mathews, Joe.
The people's machine:
Arnold Schwarzenegger and the rise of blockbuster democracy /
Joe Mathews—1st ed.
cm.
Includes bibliographical references and index.

ISBN 13: 978—1—58648—272—5
ISBN 10: 1—58648—272—6

1. Schwarzenegger, Arnold.
2. California—Politics and government—1951–.   1. Title.
F866.4.S38M38 2006
979.4'054092—DC22
2006045004

FIRST EDITION
10   9   8   7   6   5   4   3   2   1

Text set in 12 point Centaur MT

For Anna, for Grandma Oops,
and in memory of Edith LeFrancois

I SHOULD HAVE WISHED to be born in a country in which the interest of the Sovereign and that of the people must be single and identical; to the end that all the movements of the machine might tend always to the general happiness.

—Jean-Jacques Rousseau, from the dedication to Geneva in his *A Discourse on the Origin of Inequality*

H E DID NOT CARE ANYMORE. Life and death the same. Only that the crowd would be there to greet him with howls of lust and fury. He began to realize his sense of worth. He mattered.

—The Wizard, in *Conan the Barbarian*, speaking of Conan the Barbarian

Contents

CONTENTS

ACKNOWLEDGMENTS

THIS BOOK IS A TESTAMENT TO MY two great loves: my wife, Anna, and the state of California. Anna supported us for more than a year while I took an unpaid leave from the *Los Angeles Times* to pursue this project. After she moved to Washington for her job, she allowed me to work and spend most of my time in Los Angeles and Sacramento. She tolerated muscle magazine subscriptions, bookshelves full of political surveys, and my poor attempts to speak with an Austrian accent. My parents, Jay and Linda Mathews, read the first draft and offered constant encouragement.

Two of the most generous people I've ever met, Peter Nicholas and Clea Benson, made this adventure possible. Peter, who was Hans to my Franz in covering Schwarzenegger for the *Times*, and Clea, a reporter at the *Sacramento Bee*, allowed me to live in their guest house in Sacramento. Clea even helped edit the manuscript. Bob Salladay, another *Times* colleague and Schwarzenegger watcher, read drafts, housed me on occasion, and handled the driving to Fresno and Redding so I could write in the back seat. Together with my grandmother in San Mateo, Peter, Clea, and Bob formed a Northern California network of support. In Southern California, Charitie and Brendan McArthur allowed me to make a home in theirs. The DeWees family gave me shelter in the Inland Empire and Orange County, and Tony Mariniello and Hollie Heatherley provided parking. My late, great aunt Win Cole encouraged this project early on. I miss her.

Peter Osnos of PublicAffairs saw immediately that the story of Schwarzenegger and direct democracy needed telling, and he put his faith in this project and in me from the beginning. Our publisher, Susan Weinberg, and the entire PublicAffairs team supported the book with a ferocity that surpassed all my expectations.

David Patterson, my editor, patiently guided me through the entire process and magically managed to make the manuscript shorter and more complete. My agent, PJ Mark, handled all the important details. Thanks to Marcia Hawkins and Carol Grant's whole team for transcription. Ringo Chiu helped out with pictures. Walt Mossberg offered technical advice. Julian Barnes, Nick Riccardi, Dan Weintraub, Hal Wilde, Lou Cannon, Miriam Pawel, Gady Epstein, and Margaret Talev, among others, read drafts and offered excellent suggestions. As much as possible given very limited time, people I interviewed for this book were given relevant quotes and sections to check for errors. Any mistakes remain my responsibility. Conversations that I did not hear or see have been reported as the participants remembered them, with emphasis on those elements found in more than one account. Some sources provided information on the condition it not be attributed to them by name.

This book flowed from my work for the *Los Angeles Times*, my hometown paper, covering the recall campaign and Schwarzenegger's first year in office. I am honored to work for the *Times* and its editor, Dean Baquet. The *Times'* former editor, John Carroll, gave me my start in journalism, and was one of many *Times* people who made this book possible. Janet Clayton gave me the time to report and write this properly. Miriam Pawel assigned me to cover Schwarzenegger in August 2003 even though I didn't want the job. The Sacramento bureau and its chief, Virginia Ellis, treated me as one of the gang, even though I root for the wrong basketball team. Thanks to Patti Williams, Donna Reith, Nancy Vogel, Bob Durell, Eric Bailey, Jenifer Warren, Bill Stall, Jordan Rau, and the incomparable George Skelton. Special thanks to Evan Halper, Dan Morain, and Marc Lifsher for reading chapters. The two finest political reporters anywhere, Michael Finnegan and Mark Z. Barabak, offered good company and advice. The editors in Los Angeles, including Bill Nottingham, David Lauter, Pat McMahon, Cathleen Decker and Linda Rogers, often saved me from myself.

California has the best group of Capitol and political reporters of any state, and I had many talented competitors whose work informed this book. Among them were Erica Werner, Gary Delsohn, Kate Folmar, Jim Hinch, John Gittelsohn, Dion Nissenbaum, Carla Marinucci, David Drucker, Soraya Sarhaddi Nelson, and Ann Marimow.

I interviewed more than 250 people for this book. Governor Schwarzenegger, although he was under no obligation to do so, made himself available for interviews and conversations during his many campaigns. He granted me two long interviews at the conclusion of my research. The governor also opened a few doors that led to friends, associates, and important documents. He asked for nothing in return.

For all of that, for his good humor in the face of my most obnoxious questions, and for his thoughtful if unsolicited advice on matters of dress, exercise, and marketing, I thank him.

Governor Pete Wilson, Mayor Richard Riordan, Leon Panetta, and George Shultz offered their insights. So many members of the governor's team were helpful that it is difficult to thank them all here. Thanks to Bonnie Reiss, David Crane, Donna Lucas, Cassandra Pye, Pat Clarey, Richard Costigan, Peter Siggins, Cynthia Bryant, Moira Topp, Garrett Ashley, Margaret Fortune, Donna Arduin, Tom Campbell, H. D. Palmer, Mike Murphy,

Don Sipple, George Gorton, Marty Wilson, Jeff Randle, Todd Harris, and Sean Walsh.

Rob Stutzman, the governor's communications director the first two years, was full of good baseball stories even in the heat of hack-flack combat. The governor's advance operation—Fred Beteta, Will Fox, Ed Reno, Eddie Kouyoumdjian, Jonathan Coors, Elaine Jennings, and so many others—and his CHP detail treated me with professionalism, even when I did not deserve it. I'm particularly grateful to press secretary Margita Thompson and the governor's current and former press aides, including Julie Soderlund, Jennifer Scoggins, Vince Sollitto, Rob McAndrews, Leigh Thomas, Katherine McLane, Sheryl Main, Terri Carbaugh, and Ashley Snee Giovannettone. Darrel Ng merits a special note of thanks for his kindness. Thanks also to Clay Russell and Walter von Huene for their good humor.

John and Judy Cates took me through Schwarzenegger's fitness work. Danny Hernandez did the same for the Inner City Games. Chip Nielsen and Maryann O'Sullivan explained the development of Proposition 49. Joel Fox was an invaluable resource on many subjects.

Literally dozens of supporters and opponents of the recall provided me their memories. A special word of thanks must be said for Ted Costa and the folks at People's Advocate, as well as Tom Bader, Shawn Steel, Mark Abernathy, Howard Kaloogian, Sal Russo, Bill Simon, Jr., Pat Caddell, Dave Gilliard, Melanie Morgan, Buck Johns, Phil Paule, Scott Taylor, Ken Khachigian, Fred Kimball, Rick Arnold, Angelo Paparella, the Arno brothers, Tom Hiltachk, and Colleen McAndrews.

Speaker Fabian Núñez made himself and his staff available. Thank you, particularly to Steve Maviglio and Rick Simpson. Two dozen legislators granted interviews, among them John Burton, Kevin McCarthy, Darrell Steinberg, Dick Ackerman, Jim Brulte, Keith Richman, Ray Haynes, John Campbell, Tony Strickland, Bonnie Garcia, Gilbert Cedillo, and John Laird.

The reporting for this book required travel to fourteen states and four foreign countries. In Washington, D.C., David Dreier, Bill Thomas, Darrell Issa, Orrin Hatch and Rod Paige granted interviews. In Ohio, Jim Lorimer and the staff and competitors of "the Arnold" answered every question I asked. In Michigan, An-Me Chung and Bill White of the C. S. Mott Foundation educated me about after-school programs.

In Austria, Alfred and Heidi Gerstl welcomed me into their home. Josef Krainer explained Austrian politics and introduced me to Styrian asparagus. Peter Urdl provided a personal tour of Thal. Albert Kaufmann, Heinz Anderwald, Kurt Marnul, Reinhold Lopatka, Herwig Hösele, Andreas Bernhardt, and Martin Eichtinger gave generously of their time. Michael Steiner and Oliver Rathkolb corrected my history. Danny Dailey turned German into English. I have never felt more inspired about journalism than after a long conversation with writer Werner Kopacka. Thanks to Barbara Gasser for her friendship and to her brother Chris for housing me in Vienna.

The staff of the Bancroft Library at UC Berkeley helped me access the papers of Hiram Johnson and his contemporaries. The George Bush Presidential Library in College Station, Texas, and the Jim Dan Hill Library at the University of Wisconsin–Superior, each hosted me for research through their Schwarzenegger-related files. Thanks also to Bill Deverell for sharing his thoughts.

The California Teachers Association, president Barbara Kerr, and staffers John Hein, Joe Nunez, and Bob Cherry were generous with their assistance. Jack Gribbon at UNITE HERE, Mike Jimenez at the California Correctional Peace Officers Association, Lou Paulson and Carroll Wills at the California Professional Firefighters, Dave Low and Rob Feckner at the California School Employees Association, and everyone at the California Nurses Association provided indispensable information.

Contrary to their reputation, political consultants are wonderful people. Thanks to Gale Kaufman, Wayne Johnson, David Townsend, Rick Claussen, Ray McNally, Richard Temple, and others. Pollsters—among them Jan van Lohuizen, David Binder, Mark Mellman, and Frank Luntz—allowed me to put faces to the cross tabs. A quick note of gratitude to Roger Salazar, Andrew Acosta, Bob Chitester, Don Novey, Shelley Zalis, Charlotte Parker, Steve Poizner, and Dan Schnur.

Many people provided inspiration: the Wilde family, Kurt Streeter, Peter Hong, Cara DiMassa, Conan Nolan, Laurence Leamer, Kate Marsh, June Shih, Josh Gerstein, Bruce Murphy, James Cham, the Thorell family, the Rev. Brian Ellison, John Fairhall, Rafael Alvarez, Sarah and Ken Cooper, Greg Feldmeth, Roger Ipswitch, John and Molly Aboud, Joshua Wolf Shenk, Raj Shourie, Alessandra Galloni, Conrad Nussbaum, Andy Vollero, everyone at Pasadena Southwest Little League, Danny Cunningham, Jordan Wallens, John Borovicka, Jim Ho, and Jim Mathews.

A final thought: the governor likes to say that he owes everything he has to California. I feel the same way. This book is a journalist's attempt to record one piece of the history of the state. The research offered me the opportunity to take a long and eventful journey without ever really leaving home.

"Day One"

I'm a peee-pull person.

It's supposed to be an explanation. It's the only explanation he ever bothers to give. His friends, his wife, his team of consultants and policy advisors, and Hollywood marketers use it, too. It explains everything: why he left behind his home and village and family; why he ended up in California; why, despite the "name problem" and the "accent problem" and the "talent problem," he always knew he wanted to be in pictures.

It's why today he is in this Progressive-era auditorium.

It's why he is about to take power using a democratic tool a little older than the room.

He has always wanted to see how many folks he could convince to follow him into the gyms and into the theaters, and now into the voting booth.

How did he get here? Why is he running? Why are we here?

The peee-pull.

The peee-pull.

The people.

He's a people person.

The advance man whispers to the assorted aides and friends. The words are his way of clearing some space for the candidate, who is rehearsing backstage at the Sacramento Memorial Auditorium. It's also an apology.

Arnold wants to see you. He wants to know you. But he needs you to stand far away. It doesn't matter if you're the press, the event host, or even one of his aides. The candidate needs his privacy. He doesn't mean to be rude or standoffish.

He's a people person.

There wouldn't be an election in this fall of 2003 without the people. Back in the spring of 2003, voters began signing petitions to remove Governor Gray Davis from office. Their signatures triggered a special election. Now, in six days, Californians will decide whether to recall the governor of an American state for only the second time in the country's history, and for the first time in more than eighty years. They will also vote on a successor. A new poll has the recall winning and the candidate eight points ahead.

The world's media portrays this as the beginning of another strange show from one of the world's stranger places, a movie star making an abrupt career change for unknown reasons. The star, who has awakened on this day feeling certain of victory, sees this as the culmination of years of quiet preparation for a mission that seems to him entirely natural: rescuing the largest state in his adopted homeland.

Both are right, to a point. Yes, a new governorship is coming and yes, this new career marks a rise to power of a one-of-a-kind American political figure. But today really marks a middle point in a far grander tale of a form of government that is not quite republican and not purely democratic, and of a method of politics in which the very act of lawmaking is a public spectacle and mass entertainment. This is the story of blockbuster democracy.

THE CANDIDATE is calling today's speech "Day One." His campaign advisors are worried that the people don't have a clear idea what he'll do as governor.

How can the people not know?

They already know more about Arnold Schwarzenegger than any political figure in the world. They have seen him naked. They have seen him give birth (in the movie *Junior*). They have seen him kill. They have fallen asleep to his voice on TV. They have imitated his accent.

They know him. They've seen him in action for years.

But what do the people really know? They have never seen him run a government. He has campaigned for less than eight weeks. He hasn't said what programs he'll cut, how he'll balance the budget, or how he'll handle recalcitrant legislators. They have laughed when he declared gay marriage should be "between a man and a woman" and promised everyone "a fantastic job." They, again, have imitated his accent.

They don't know him. They've never seen him in action before.

He has reveled in the confusion. He seems utterly comfortable with contradiction.

He is running the most public of campaigns for a statewide office—with a dedication to secrecy so severe that his spokesmen have been required to sign confidentiality agreements. He says he is making an offbeat, inspired attack on the status quo, even as he mouths cautious, centrist political statements. He distrusts power and special interests, even as he takes millions in political donations from corporate executives. He is a Republican, even though most of the people close to him are Democrats.

He swears he is not a politician, but he has been around politics all his life. His candidacy is a joke told to the world, a joke he himself enjoys telling, and it's as serious as a $40 million opening weekend or a $38 billion budget shortfall. He is running as an American icon, even as he retains his citizenship in a small European nation.

He made his reputation with his body, but physically he is awkward: his trunk seems built for a much taller man; his shape is all chest and shoulders and arms. As he walks around backstage, his small legs seem to groan under the weight of his torso like an old flatbed truck carting a load too heavy for its own wheels.

He will tell you that he's not much of an actor. But he is a brilliant performer. His voice is no prize. But it is unforgettable.

He poses as one of the people everywhere he goes. When boasting about his strength in handling a challenge, he is the ex–pro athlete, a seven-time Mr. Olympia. On *The Howard Stern Show*, he is a comedian. On *Oprah*, he is a dutiful father. To Central Valley alfalfa growers, he is a farm boy from Austria. To the chamber of commerce, he's a real estate investor. With the media, he's the understanding husband of a journalist.

None of these poses are really him.

All the posing is.

HE NEEDS to be alone now.

The advance man is chiding an aide who lingered too close.

The candidate, as he rehearses alone, must have his space.

How can such a man ever be alone?

Just out of earshot hover more than a dozen aides, the Republican leader of the state senate, a bodybuilder, a friend from Austria, two public relations people, a make-up woman, two sound guys, a lighting consultant, a personal photographer, and his dialogue coach. On the other side of the curtain are two dozen TV cameras representing eight countries, four local TV affiliates, and three national news networks. Fifteen hundred people fill seats in the hall.

In one section of the auditorium sit about fifty academics, entrepreneurs, and government officials who have given him policy advice. Most are volunteers who have dropped everything at the mention of his name to drive to his home in Brentwood or his office complex in Santa Monica. There they have marveled at the mural of the Terminator, shooting through a brick wall, in the elevator landing.

Schwarzenegger University, the sessions were called. It was a private school, enrollment of one. In less than six weeks, the sessions have produced the most detailed policy platform of any candidate in the race, a platform that the candidate has largely hidden from public view. The people, the candidate says, aren't interested in details and numbers. The people want to know only that their governor will do as they wish.

Today, though, the candidate will give a glimpse of how he would rule. His top political consultant, sick and feverish in a hotel room at the other end of the state, has insisted on the speech. Opponents are attacking from right and left, arguing that Arnold is not ready to govern. Outside the auditorium, some 150 union members protest. Being a governor is not like being a movie star or even like being a political candidate, the protesters say.

The candidate's whole life tells him that this criticism is wrong. The people are the pee-pull, whether they sit in the dark of a movie theater, stand behind a voting booth curtain, or squeeze into a giant crowd at a rally.

Schwarzenegger has agreed to give the speech. But he balked at a plan to put bleachers on the stage behind him and fill them with the aides who would serve in his administration. Their faces would be too familiar, too elite, too distracting.

Soon Arnold Schwarzenegger will take the stage alone.

THE SACRAMENTO MEMORIAL AUDITORIUM occupies a full block that was donated to the city of Sacramento by John Sutter for use as a public square. Sutter, born in 1803 in Germany to Swiss parents, came to North America as a young adult to seek a fortune. In California, he turned a land grant from the Mexicans into his own private agricultural kingdom at the intersection of the American and Sacramento rivers. He built a fort to defend it.

Sutter was one of the first men to cross an ocean to secure a great private fortune in California. He would not be the last. When gold was discovered on Sutter's land, people came from all over the world to seek it. They destroyed his crops and stole his herds in the process. The Gold Rush established California as the state that "has not grown or evolved so much as it has been hurtled forward, rocket-fashion, by a series of chain-reaction explosions," as the historian Carey McWilliams would put it. California remade itself overnight, through thrill-seeking, risk-taking, and popular action. The whole damn place was a special effect.

The Sutter land at the corner of 15th and J Street became an elementary school. The idea of building an auditorium was first offered in 1910, another year of explosive change in California. Political reformers around the state needed a candidate for governor. These businessmen and newspaper publishers, frustrated that their individual money and moxie carried so little weight with a state legislature dominated by the railroad interests, believed they could change California only by electing a leader who would allow the people to legislate directly.

The man they chose, a charismatic lawyer named Hiram Johnson, had grown up in Sacramento, five blocks from where the modern state Capitol would be built. He had attended the grammar school on Sutter's land at 15th and J. After a falling out with his father, Johnson left town and became famous as a lawyer in San Francisco.

Johnson had never run for office before. After what was then the longest campaign in the state's history, Johnson won. Once he was sworn in as governor, he convinced the legislature to put before voters twenty-three revisions to the state constitution. Among them were the initiative, the referendum, and the recall. The initiative allowed citizens to make laws or amend the constitution at the ballot. The referendum permitted citizens to overturn laws passed by a city council or legislature. The recall gave citizens the power to throw out an elected official at any point in his term. Each instrument of direct democracy required citizens to gather a certain number of signatures to place a proposed law, amendment, or elected official on the ballot.

Johnson promoted these reforms before some of the largest crowds ever to attend California political speeches. "The man who talks today of checks and balances is talking against popular democracy," he said in Berkeley. "No man is better able to govern than all others, no man is better in government than any other man." In an October 1911 special election, Californians approved nearly all of his changes, including the three pillars of direct democracy.

Johnson and the state's newest lawmakers—the voters—then constructed much of California's modern system of government. His governorship, which lasted six years, saw the establishment of a workers' compensation system, the regulation of utilities and railroads, prison reform, the first real state budget, and a building boom. In Sacramento alone, the Progressive era brought some thirty new major buildings.

One was the auditorium. The project stalled for a while as materials, money, and attention ran short in World War I. At the dedication in 1925, Johnson, by then a U.S. senator, greeted his seventh-grade teacher and gave the keynote speech.

"When in the future skillful, clever ministers of propaganda shall assail or seek to undermine The People's rights, here the voice of righteousness and fair play shall answer in trumpet tones," he said. "I leave you with the vision that is ours of the future of the Sacramento Auditorium: here no money changers shall ever dwell . . . free speech it shall foster, within it justice and fair play shall abide. It shall be the temple of The People, sacred to the right of The People."

SCHWARZENEGGER MIGHT HAVE been more at ease giving his speech in a mall, at the fairgrounds, or at some place where he could interact with a huge crowd. An old auditorium isn't his first choice, and his staff knows nothing of the building's history. But his consultant insists that the event look gubernatorial, indoors, bland, and reassuring.

Johnson's temple will have to do.

The people from Hartmann Studios, based in the Bay Area, have spent two days preparing. The candidate prefers to have the same production team for as many events as possible. If nothing else was consistent, at least his appearance would be. Today, to present the candidate as an emblem of the state, the production team arranges small palm trees behind the podium. They darken the rest of the room but light the trees and the podium from the back and the front. Television cameras will have nothing else to shoot but the next governor of California and the palms.

Light is the candidate's friend. When he is on stage, the light turns his orange-tinted hair a natural, sandy color that makes him look a decade younger than fifty-six. Light gives his orange tan a rich, sun-earned glow. He favors light-colored suits, mostly grays and tans, with pastel-colored ties. There is little risk in this feminine styling—no one questions the Terminator's manhood—and plenty of visual reward. The suits signal he is not another dark-suited politician. Put him in a group picture of other pols, and the light colors give him a sartorial halo.

"YOU KNOW, NEXT TUESDAY, the people of California will vote on the direction of this state. In the days ahead, there will . . . ," he begins the speech, then pauses. He has the early stages of hoarseness and coughs to clear his throat. "In the days ahead, you will hear a lot of talk about the campaign. But I am not here to talk about campaigning. I am here today to talk about governing."

A sly, shy grin comes over his face. It is new to his political appearances. On the stump, he has a repertoire of expressions and gestures: the fist pump, the thumbs up, the Terminator glare, the hand held up like a stop sign, the pointed index finger, and the big, boxy, self-satisfied smile recognizable to anyone who saw *Twins*. But now he grins like a man offering a glimpse of a secret.

"One survey found that California has the worst economic climate of all fifty states in the nation. We have the worst deficit, the worst credit rating, and the worst money management," he says. "The problem though is not California. The problem is Sacramento." With that, he points to the ground, a cue that gives broadcasters an excuse to remind viewers this speech is taking place in the state capital. "If the people give me the authority to act, I will do so decisively. Here is what I will do in the first days, the first one hundred days in office," he says. With that, a giant screen turns on above his head. The plan is broken down into ten steps.

He says he will freeze spending and suspend new state purchases, though it will prove difficult to enforce such measures on California's giant union-ized bureaucracy. He promises an audit of the entire government; that has the potential to offend most interest groups in the capital.

It gets dicier. He says he will repeal the tripling of the state's vehicle license fee. Governor Davis has raised the fee in a complex scheme to cover the state's obligations to local governments. Reversing the "car tax" increase might be popular, but a repeal will blow a $4 billion hole in the finances of the state's cities and counties. Mayors and county supervisors likely will howl, and the legislature probably won't bail him out.

Each step of the plan poses greater challenges. He promises to call a special session of the legislature, which will still be controlled by hostile Democratic majorities. "On the agenda will be spending cuts, streamlining government and constitutional amendments to get control of the budget," he says. The constitutional amendment to restrain spending is a non-starter with Democrats. And Republicans could block a compromise meas-ure. In the next breath, he says he will restructure the state's current debt. But how? He has said himself that the state's credit rating is poor.

He vows to force the legislature to repeal legislation that grants California driver's licenses to undocumented immigrants. And he promises new reforms of the state's workers' compensation system to help California employers, who pay premiums nearly twice as high as those in other states, even though lawmakers have passed a workers' comp fix in recent weeks.

He does not stop there. Schwarzenegger says he will renegotiate compacts with Indian tribes that own casinos. But those compacts are only a few years old and run for two decades. What interest will they have in renegotiating?

He rounds out the speech with a pair of proposals. He wants to reform education, perhaps by consolidating the state's ninety educational pro-grams—each with its own constituency—into a few large block grants. The goal is to get more money into the classroom. He pledges to ban political fund-raising during the budget process and enact an open records law.

Each proposal is a blast at interest groups. Each interest has the means to defend itself. On these issues, he will have few allies in the legislature.

He is smiling that Cheshire cat grin again.

Schwarzenegger moves immediately into a few applause lines that his con-sultant has written in hopes they will be quoted on TV and in newspapers.

"They say no on the recall. They would take us back. I say yes to California. I will lead us forward."

The entire speech lasts just twelve minutes, short enough to fit between commercial breaks. The plan is easily summarized by the campaign on a single sheet of paper.

Before he leaves town, the reaction comes in, quick and cold from the establishment political figures who run the state and from the major newspapers that have endorsed them for years. The candidate is dreaming, they say. He might be able to reinvent himself as a politician, but he will not be able to transcend the realities of government. They argue that the California dream—the Progressive one at least—is dead, that the state is no longer a blank slate upon which the ambitious can write their own screenplays, that even the most successful and resourceful and famous of self-made men will have to resign himself to the fact that the experts, not the people, know best how to keep the machine humming.

Bill Carrick, a Democratic political consultant who doesn't have a candidate in the recall race, predicts that if Schwarzenegger were to pursue even one of the proposals, the state government would be gridlocked for years. The *San Jose Mercury News*, in a bit of understatement, calls the speech full of ideas that "could be hard to get past the legislature and unions." The *Los Angeles Times* publishes my story under a headline that says: "Acting as if it's in the bag." I write that the plan is pie in the sky.

John Burton, the Democratic president pro tem of the state senate and California's most powerful legislator, says: "Fuck him. He ought to read the Constitution of the United States. He isn't being elected king. He's being elected governor, which is only one-third of the government. It's called checks and balances."

It will not be the last time that a California lawmaker invokes the American system of checks and balances when discussing Arnold Schwarzenegger.

WITHIN TWENTY-FOUR HOURS, the speech is forgotten. The very next day, October 2, the *Los Angeles Times* publishes a lengthy story saying Schwarzenegger, in the last thirty years, touched six women "in a sexual manner without their consent." *ABC News* and the *New York Times* report a different scoop: Schwarzenegger during the 1970s said that he admired Hitler, according to a book proposal circulated some years earlier. Both stories create worldwide media attention and dominate the campaign, but neither damages his election chances.

The book proposal's author disavows it. Schwarzenegger apologizes immediately for his conduct toward women. TV stations show pictures of

Schwarzenegger's four-day bus tour to close the campaign. No one bothers to wrestle with the implications of Schwarzenegger's ten-step plan.

AN ADVISOR TO SCHWARZENEGGER calls to protest my story. There is a way the government can tackle those issues—driver's licenses, budget finance, workers' comp, local government, Indian gambling, and political reform. Burton is reading the wrong fucking constitution, the advisor says. It's not the American one that counts. It's the constitution of the state of California—Hiram Johnson's playbook. Schwarzenegger could sponsor his own initiatives, go around the legislature, and push his agenda through the ballot box.

The strategy sounds outlandish, over-the-top, too expensive and confrontational. Who would even attempt such a thing?

He's a people person.

LEGISLATING AT THE BALLOT BOX has been a tradition in California since Johnson's day. It became commonplace again in the late 1970s. That's about the same time Schwarzenegger was launching his film career and beginning to dabble in politics.

Over the past twenty-five years, citizen groups, businesses, unions, the rich, the eccentric, and the famous have sponsored ballot initiatives in which they propose laws for voters to enact. Most of these initiatives have failed.

But every so often, a ballot measure captures public attention. Whether it is Proposition 13 and its restrictions on taxes, a limit on representatives' terms, or the "three strikes" law for convicted felons, these blockbuster measures not only win, they change the political narrative in the state in a way that no mere candidate can. So many people have tried to sponsor initiatives—to search for that blockbuster—that a California-based industry of signature-gathering firms, election lawyers, and consultants has developed. These are the producers, directors, and marketers of blockbuster democracy.

It is a system that no political leader, no matter how popular, has ever managed to tame. In several cases, popular politicians have sponsored ballot measures in order to get pet projects turned into law. Typically, these ballot initiatives are timed to coincide with their own campaigns for office. But most of these efforts falter and some backfire. Once in office, most statewide politicians govern so as to avoid challenges from interests that have the money and power to sponsor initiatives.

But Schwarzenegger sees ballot measures as opportunities. He sponsored a ballot initiative in 2002. Proposition 49 was a measure to fund after-school programs, but it also served as a dry run for a future gubernatorial candidacy. He has learned that ballot measures play to his strengths. He has been selling movies and winning opening weekends for years. A ballot initiative is just another tale he can sell to the public.

Now, from the Sacramento Memorial Auditorium stage, he is putting in motion a governorship so different from what Americans normally expect from a state chief executive that it would be difficult to call him merely a governor.

Here he is, less than a week before election day, and already he is setting the stage for more ballot measures, more campaigns, more elections. Sequels.

He will have to exploit his celebrity, to provide enough entertainment to keep public attention focused on himself and his proposals. He will need to understand policy well enough to tease out the issues that could be turned into good stories for the ballot. To finance so many initiative campaigns, he will be forced to become the most prolific fund-raiser of any governor in American history. He will need to demonstrate a political veteran's sense of timing in his negotiations with the legislature. He will have to be a manager of extraordinary skill, meshing the state's executive branch with a network of political entities he will build himself.

To succeed will require constant momentum. If he loses standing with the public, he will lose his special power and his entire strategy will be at risk. He might not be making movies anymore, but he will need to keep making hits.

It might be nothing but a show.

It will have to be some show.

Schwarzenegger will have to harness California's century-old system of direct democracy to build precisely the thing it had been designed to counter: a political machine. Of course, this will be a political machine run not on patronage but on stardust—fueled by money, fame, polling, TV ads, direct mail, signature gatherers, malls, and even a few stunts.

But won't it still be a political machine? Won't it rob him of his special promise as a political outsider and turn him into an insider? Won't it distort the decisions of his government? Won't it cause him as many problems as it solves?

"Trust me," the governor-elect of California will say to that question a few weeks later. "It's the people's machine."

PART I

THE VOICE OF GOD is the voice of the People. The people cry out "Let us, the People, God's people, go." You, our masters, you, our kings, you, our tyrants, don't you hear us? Don't you hear God speaking in us? Will you never let us go? How long at length will you abuse our patience? How long will you drive us? How long will you harass us? Will nothing daunt you? Does nothing check you? Do you not know that to ignore our cry too long is to wake the Red Terror? Ramses refused to listen to it and perished miserably. Caesar refused to listen and was stabbed in the Senate House. The Bourbon Louis refused to listen and died on the guillotine; Charles Stuart refused to listen and died on the block; the white Czar refused to listen and was blown up in his own capital. Will you let it come to that? Will you drive us to it? We who boast of our land of freedom, we who live in the country of liberty?

—Frank Norris, *The Octopus*

CHAPTER 1

"As Entertaining
as a Nickelodeon"

WITH A LONG OVERCOAT AND A NEW HAT, the saloonkeeper disguised himself as a lawyer. Surely, no one would pay him any mind. He would blend into the courtroom audience.

Two years earlier, in April 1906, a massive earthquake and fire had leveled San Francisco. Americans had sent whatever dollars they could scrape together for relief. In the aftermath, some of the city's leading citizens finally lost patience with the cronyism, misappropriations, and greed of the political, union, and railroad bosses who ruled San Francisco. One newspaper editor prevailed upon a sugar magnate to post $100,000 for the prosecution of local villains. On November 13, 1908, a team of prosecutors for hire had the city's top political boss, Abe Ruef, on trial. Getting that far had been no easy task. Ruef, a lawyer, had statewide influence, both legitimate and illicit. In 1906, he had all but named the new governor. He had tried to fend off an earlier attempt at prosecution by making himself San Francisco's district attorney.

Just as a recess was called, the saloonkeeper slipped through the swinging gate separating the prosecutors from the audience. He carried his hat in one hand. The other hand he stuffed deep into his overcoat.

By the time he pulled out the revolver, he was standing next to the lead prosecutor, Francis Heney. The saloonkeeper pushed the muzzle of the weapon against the right side of Heney's face, just in front of the ear. He fired.

No one will ever know for sure why Morris Haas pulled that trigger. The next day, the saloonkeeper was found dead in his jail cell with a bullet through his head and a gun by his side. He appeared to have killed himself, though there were rumors of foul play. Not long after, the chief of police disappeared off the end of a launch as it crossed the bay. These mysteries gripped the state and then the nation. More than a century earlier, a single bullet fired in Lexington, Massachusetts, had started an American revolution, bringing a new form of government into the world. With two bullets, the

3

saloonkeeper—and his assailant, if there was one—had touched off another political revolution, one that would fundamentally alter that same form of government in America's largest state. This second revolution would pave the way for the governorship of Arnold Schwarzenegger nearly one hundred years later.

HENEY WOULD LIVE. The bullet somehow squeezed between the prosecutor's jaw and skull, embedding in the back of his mouth. But the trial of Abe Ruef needed a new lead prosecutor. The natural choice was Hiram Johnson.

Johnson could be a difficult man. Born and raised in Sacramento, he was the son of Grove Johnson, who did the railroad's bidding in the state legislature. Hiram Johnson's brother had died an alcoholic's early death, and Johnson himself was prone to black moods and depression. Years earlier, he had escaped his father's grip, moved to San Francisco, and started a law practice. In the courtroom, he had proven to be a fantastic performer. In one case, he pulled a dagger out of the waistband of a witness during cross-examination. In defending a Chinese organized crime figure, he brought six Chinese men wearing yellow overcoats into the courtroom and placed his client among them. The witness identified the wrong man.

Johnson had lost his home and office in the earthquake of 1906. He detested the city bosses, and had signed up—for a hefty fee—to help Heney with the prosecutions. Now he would reap glory as well as cash.

Private detectives told Johnson that the jury was fixed; at least four jurors had taken bribes. Johnson did not report this to the judge. He had Ruef in the defendant's chair, and the entire country was watching. He would not let a few crooked jurors stop the show.

Johnson's summation to the jury was reprinted all over the state. He reminded jurors of the earthquake's destruction. "At that time when all of us were down in the dirt and in disorder, crawling through our streets, begging for aid, standing in the bread line, fighting indeed for life, it was at that time that Abe Ruef and the United Railroads sold our town and sold out you!" He all but called for public retribution against jurors who would let Ruef go free. "We know this man is guilty. You know he is guilty," he thundered. "Dare you acquit him? Why, if you don't convict this man, may God in his infinite mercy, or worse, call upon you the consequences of your act!"

The jury convicted. Hiram Johnson was suddenly one of the most famous names in California. He took care to be photographed regularly with his arms flexed or his fists up, the poses of a strongman.

Within a year, a group of rich men called on Johnson. Dissident Republicans in the north, a newspaper publisher in Fresno, and a socialist doctor from Los Angeles wanted to argue their own case—in the court of public opinion. What bound together the men who would become Johnson's political backers were a hatred for the state legislature, a distrust of parties and factions, and a willingness to do whatever it took to win. These characteristics led them to embrace direct democracy.

By the fall of 1910, when Johnson was the Republican nominee for governor, he confessed to a friendly journalist that he knew little about referenda, initiatives, and recalls. He did not immediately understand their implications for a country founded as a republic. But the concept sounded fine to him. Johnson trusted his audiences. If a fixed jury could reach the right verdict, surely the people could govern themselves.

THE SOUTHERN PACIFIC RAILROAD and its owners had no intention of allowing direct democracy to flourish statewide. The SP was the machine that couldn't be beat. The railroad controlled more than 85 percent of the track in the state and leveraged that power mercilessly. The railroad's shipping rates could make or break merchants. The railroad was the real government in the towns and cities that relied on it for their connections to the world.

At the end of the nineteenth century and the beginning of the twentieth, two national movements confronted the power of the railroads. The Populists, many of them farmers, laborers, and debtors, rose first, protesting that elected representatives had been captured by railroads and other moneyed interests. As the Populists faded with the turn of the century, the Progressive movement rose. Led by journalists, professionals, and businessmen, Progressives saw republican government as corrupt and inefficient. With more democracy, the government could operate in a just, businesslike fashion, not only meeting public needs, but elevating public life itself.

The Progressives in California, many of them dissident Republicans, disliked both the railroad and the labor unions. Their strongest faith was in public opinion, a "jury that could not be fixed," as the journalist Lincoln Steffens called it.

The Progressives looked around the world for democratic structures. At that time, many American political thinkers were studying the democratic advances being made by Switzerland. In 1848, the Swiss adopted a new constitution that allowed citizens to overturn laws. One of the first targets of referendum was a direct national subsidy to the Swiss railroad. In the 1850s, Swiss cantons had adopted the recall. Later, the Swiss added the initiative to the national constitution.

In 1888, James W. Sullivan, a member of the New York typographers' union, took a leave of absence and visited Switzerland. His 1892 book,

Direct Legislation by the Citizenship Through the Initiative and Referendum, was read closely by Progressives. In practice, Swiss direct democracy, which allows citizens to vote at least four times a year, proved to be a stabilizing force, a way to create a conversation between legislators and the public. But the Americans who read about Switzerland tended to be people who were at war with the status quo. They fashioned direct democracy as a weapon. The Populists and the Progressives worked to bring the initiative, referendum, and recall to the Western states, with their first success in South Dakota in 1898. Over the next twelve years, ten more states would follow suit. California's Progressives watched with envy. They wished for direct democracy, too. But the Southern Pacific wouldn't allow it.

LELAND STANFORD, ONE OF THE "BIG FOUR" railroad barons, was governor of California from 1861 to 1863. After that, he served as president of the Southern Pacific and founded a university named for his deceased son. Stanford also had a fondness for making large bets and funding expensive research on questions of interest to him.

In 1872, he had wanted to know: Do horses fly?

To be more specific: is there ever a moment when all four of a galloping horse's hooves leave the ground? He hired the English photographer Eadweard Muybridge to research the question. Six years later, after the photographer's acquittal at trial for the shooting of his wife's lover (justifiable homicide, the jury ruled), Muybridge produced an answer. At a track in Palo Alto, a wheeled cart was hooked up to one of Stanford's horses. As the horse ran, the wheels tripped a dozen different wires, each connected to a camera. The multiple pictures, in a series, captured the equine motion.

Horses do fly.

The Muybridge-Stanford collaboration ended, as so many motion picture success stories do, in disputes over who should get the credit. But Muybridge's reputation was made. Thomas Edison, inspired in part by Muybridge's device, developed a primitive motion picture machine of his own in 1891. An assistant made the first films, using vaudeville performers. Among them was a Prussian strongman named Eugene Sandow, who had been promoted by Florenz Ziegfeld, creator of the stage spectaculars known as Ziegfeld's Follies. Sandow became a star of sorts, publishing books, dating actress Lillian Russell, and serving as personal fitness instructor to King George V. He fancied himself a political man and advocated for health care, sanitation, and prenatal exams for women. From the earliest days of motion pictures, it was clear that an extraordinary body could lead to bigger things.

Although other inventors would soon produce far more advanced devices for making and showing movies, it was Edison who filed the first patents, and he enforced them ruthlessly in and out of court. In December 1908, he joined with some of his competitors to form the Motion Picture Patents Company, which came to be known as the Trust. The Trust soon controlled all the licenses for projection machines as well as the films themselves. Independent, non-Trust productions in New Jersey and New York found their prints stolen and their sets busted up. The Trust even created its own censorship board, a New York organization with a misleading name, the People's Institute.

The only way to beat the Edison machine, independent filmmakers decided, was to move as far away as possible.

DIRECT DEMOCRACY AND THE MOVIES would find fertile soil at the same time and in the same place: Los Angeles, a wide-open town with weak unions and warm weather. Even in the middle of a Los Angeles winter, one could shoot an outdoor scene—or walk the streets gathering signatures on an initiative petition—without the slightest discomfort.

Hollywood, where the movie colony would eventually camp, consisted mostly of gardens and churches. Most of the action was downtown, where the new theaters were. A doctor originally from Pennsylvania had already made a fortune in real estate there and was turning his attention to politics. John Randolph Haynes was a utopian, a Christian, a millionaire, and a Socialist. He had read what he could find on Switzerland, and in 1895 formed the Direct Legislation League.

"I believe I am a fundamental Democrat and I believe it is only through the proper physical, mental, and moral education of the masses of the people who will be, and should be the rulers of the government under which they live, that we will in time achieve the best known government," he wrote in an autobiography that he never completed. (Haynes also was a committed eugenicist, who argued for forced sterilization of criminals and "the degenerate.")

In 1902, a year before the first movie producers arrived, Haynes financed the successful campaign for a new Los Angeles city charter that included the initiative, referendum, and recall. From the beginning, direct democracy was not a tool for grass-roots idealists, but a club for those with the inclination and resources to practice power politics.

Haynes, joining forces with the Lincoln-Roosevelt League, a collection of disenchanted Republicans who would become Progressives, lobbied the state legislature to pass similar amendments to the state constitution. Haynes and his allies won several commitments from legislators, but the railroad's attorney, William F. Herrin, manipulated the legislative schedule to prevent a vote.

Dismayed, Haynes and the Progressives decided that only a governor with popular appeal could beat the railroad.

HIRAM JOHNSON'S WIFE did not want to leave their comfortable home on Russian Hill in San Francisco. But it seemed that every day during the winter of 1909, another newspaperman or Progressive businessman would arrive on their doorstep and ask Johnson to run.

The Southern Pacific had ever so slightly loosened its grip. In 1909, its lobbyists had permitted a bill to pass that created primary elections. Before, easily controlled party conventions chose the nominee of the dominant Republican Party. It was the perfect opening for Johnson. He was no party man, but Californians knew his name from Ruef's trial two years earlier. And no one could match his way with a crowd.

Johnson started six months before the election, launching the longest, loudest political campaign the state had seen. He gave as many as sixteen speeches a day. Refusing to ride the Southern Pacific, he toured the state in sporty red cars, sturdy and expensive Locomobiles that could go one hundred miles per hour. The cars became the symbol of his effort. In this new era, the people could steer for themselves.

People found it impossible to listen to Johnson for five minutes without wanting to join him in the fight. His speeches had the same theme: one man against a giant enemy, the railroad, which he alternately described as a "monster" and a "creature." In Petaluma, Johnson asked residents to ring the old bells in the Baptist church as they once had done to call out the vigilantes. For some speeches, he organized fireworks displays and car parades. In San Jose, teams of yell leaders, placed strategically in different corners of a theater, shouted in sequence to create a ringing effect. He arranged for a cannon to be fired upon his arrival at a Sacramento rally.

In San Francisco, rival campaign managers watched in despair as Johnson roused a crowd of ten thousand at a speech at Dreamland Rink.

"Johnson's surely as entertaining as a nickelodeon," one campaign manager grumbled to the *Examiner*, "and the people didn't have to pay a cent."

The newspapers led the counterattack. The *Los Angeles Times* called him a "political Delilah . . . fair to look upon, but a treacherous deceiver." In the final days of the campaign, the *Times* suggested—falsely and without naming its sources—that Johnson was secretly in league with the railroad. "Americans love a circus," the paper wrote. "While they are a serious people in the main they are possessed occasionally by a trivial mood and while that mood prevails they seek the frivolous as a momentary diversion. Hiram Johnson as an exponent of reform in politics rivals Barnum's best performers."

Meyer Lissner, the Los Angeles attorney who was Johnson's main handler, responded to such objections by noting the size of Johnson's crowds. By putting on such huge spectacles, Johnson could get his message out without newspapers, which often suppressed his words. "Out of one hundred points in the publicity game," wrote Franklin Hichborn, a journalist who aided Johnson's campaign, "I would not give the newspapers much more than ten." Johnson saw it as part of his duty as a political figure to entertain. "I have found as I ever found," he once wrote to his daughter, "when an issue is divorced from personality it lacks the heat of enthusiasm which stirs the electorate."

Johnson kept speeches short. As much as possible he avoided offering positions on the issues of the day and instead stuck to denunciations of the railroad. "I am not a politician, so I am not trying to pose as one," he told a Palm Springs audience on May 25, 1910. "And that is one reason why I expect to be elected governor. I think, and the people seem to think, that California has been ruled long enough by politicians." The three other Republican candidates—and the Democratic nominee—soon competed with the outsider to denounce the Southern Pacific.

Johnson's overwhelming victory on November 8, 1910, did not end his campaign. Within months, the new governor called an election and asked voters to adopt twenty-three amendments to the state constitution, among them the initiative, referendum, and recall. Johnson campaigned for three consecutive months for his measures.

Grove Johnson denounced his son's effort: "The voice of the people is not the voice of God, for the voice of the people sent Jesus to the cross." President Taft suggested the application of the recall to judges might be unconstitutional. Newspapers denounced the amendments as contrary to the tradition of Republican America. The *Federalist Papers* were often quoted. "A dangerous ambition more often lurks behind the specious mask of zeal for the rights of the people than under the forbidding appearance of zeal for the firmness and efficiency of government," Alexander Hamilton wrote in *Federalist Number 1*. "History will teach us that the former has been found a much more certain road to the introduction of despotism than the latter, and that of those men who have overturned the liberties of republics, the greatest number have begun their career by paying an obsequious court to the people, commencing demagogues and ending tyrants."

Johnson responded that truly righteous public officials had nothing to fear. "You can't make a coward by putting a pistol to his head," the governor said. "You can only prove him a coward."

The amendments passed. The direct democracy measures were by far the most popular. Seventy-six percent of voters approved the initiative and referendum. The other amendments established the structure of California government. Counties and cities were given new rights and new control over their finances. A workers' compensation system was established. A board of control was founded to draft and monitor the state budget. A century later, some of the very same subjects would occupy much of the time of a new governor, a political outsider with a flair for the dramatic and a devotion to direct democracy.

FOR JOHNSON, THE BALLOT ALSO PRODUCED HEARTBREAK. In 1912, he served as vice presidential nominee on Teddy Roosevelt's "Bull Moose" ticket for the Progressive Party. They lost to Woodrow Wilson. After Johnson was re-elected governor in 1914, he called a special election so voters could cast ballots on eleven separate measures, most notably his own plan to make state offices nonpartisan. But the public was "sick of campaigns and probably sick of the campaigner," Johnson wrote in a letter to an ally. In 1915, all eleven measures went down in defeat, with nonpartisanship losing by 18 percentage points. Nevertheless, the *San Diego Union*, observing the Johnson phenomenon, editorialized that Johnson's ways promised a flood of democracy: "California appears doomed to be continually in the throes of politics. As soon as one election is over, long-range campaigning for the next one will begin. This sort of political endless chain is not alluring."

Johnson's political base shifted during his governorship from San Francisco to Southern California. He scheduled long vacations in the south, invested in property there, and kept in touch with the growing movie colony, which included some of his supporters.

By the end of Johnson's first term, Colonel William Selig had set up his permanent movie operation in Los Angeles, where he could film three thousand miles from Edison's lawyers. And Carl Laemmle, the founder of Universal Pictures, had acquired a ranch in the San Fernando Valley and began building a studio on it.

Governor Johnson eagerly made use of Hollywood know-how. His 1914 re-election campaign commissioned a twenty-minute film in which children showed off free textbooks and women celebrated shorter working hours—both the results of ballot measures Johnson had championed. (Johnson received a half-dozen letters from voters complaining that such a blatant mix of the political and the cinematic was inappropriate.) The governor was ahead of his time, though. The following year, Universal offered President Woodrow Wilson the opportunity to deliver a message on its movie screens; he turned down the chance, saying such a forum would be disrespectful of his office.

Johnson went out of his way to associate himself with the movies. He denounced the Edison Trust, which would be dissolved in 1918 after a ruling by the United States Supreme Court. The governor praised D. W. Griffith's groundbreaking, explicitly racist *The Birth of a Nation* so lavishly that the film's producers used his comments in their national publicity. His devotion to Hollywood was such that, after his time as governor, Johnson was offered $40,000 a year by the motion picture industry to head a new law firm to combat censorship and other movie bugaboos. He declined.

As the Edison trust broke up and the Southern Pacific Railroad lost its stranglehold in the state, those who had mounted the successful challenges formed new machines that derived their power from the public.

Between 1910 and 1912, the number of Americans who regularly attended motion pictures doubled from ten to twenty million. By 1928, the Hollywood studios would bring in $1.5 billion a year and account for 90 percent of the films made. Hollywood was a machine built on a certain kind of democracy, as William de Mille wrote while on his way to join his brother Cecil in California. The movies were "a new theater which the people themselves would control by sheer force of numbers, since dictatorship, while frequently controlling the intelligentsia in their patronage of the so-called 'higher arts,' has never been able to influence popular drama," de Mille wrote.

Before long, critics complained that art was suffering for commerce. Even Karl Brown, camera operator for *The Birth of a Nation*, said: "Bigger meant better and a sort of giganticism overwhelmed the world, especially the world of motion pictures."

Direct democracy, too, offered new opportunities to build bigger machines. Governor Johnson himself erected one of the first. His political machine, the critics claimed, was more powerful and ruthless than the Southern Pacific's lobby had ever been. They had a point.

Violating an early promise, Johnson hit up his appointees for campaign contributions. He used private investigators to build files on members of the legislature and conduct surveillance on a San Francisco man, Alva Udell, who filed a recall petition against him. In his search for popular themes, the governor exploited anti-Japanese racism and signed into law the Alien Land Act, which prohibited noncitizens from owning land.

Johnson reached into the ranks of advertising experts, particularly Albert Lasker, a partner in the giant advertising firm of Lord and Thomas, for political advice. Lord and Thomas, in turn, found plenty of business in the new, Johnson-created field of initiative and referendum politics. The firm guided the initiative campaign that repealed a tax on chain stores—at the time the most expensive campaign in the history of California.

Johnson denied having a political machine. He merely appealed to the public, he claimed. "Let us assume that a governor was anxious to build up a tremendous and powerful political machine which would perpetuate him in power. How would he do it? Would he do it by trying to build that machine in the affections of the people at large? Or would he do it by endeavoring to control with party machinery a faction of the people?"

To Johnson, the answer was obvious. No one could control the people.

ALTHOUGH JOHNSON WOULD NOT ACKNOWLEDGE IT, direct democracy required a new sort of political organization. The sponsor of a ballot measure needed money and muscle to qualify measures and to put on a show to attract the attention of voters.

From its earliest days, the process of gathering signatures for initiatives and referenda had been a business. It was a way for young women, college students, derelicts, and sandwich men (who carried small billboards on their chests and backs) to earn cash. In 1912, paid gatherers in Los Angeles earned three cents for every signature they collected. By 1914, the practice had been professionalized, and a new firm, Robinson & Company, formed to gather signatures. In 1916, so many signatures were being gathered on so many petitions that Johnson worried aloud about the ability of the fifty-eight county clerks to verify the names properly.

In 1923, a special committee of the state senate would conclude that "campaign methods and practices" associated with initiatives and referenda "constitute a menace to our electoral system." Among the chief complaints was that, combined, the campaigns for the seven propositions on the 1922 ballot had cost in excess of $1 million.

With so much money to be made, California saw the first of a new breed: the professional political consultant. Ballot measures required that political campaigns be conducted outside the traditional apparatus of parties. There was no candidate on the ballot whose friends could be prevailed upon to help out. If there were to be initiative and referendum campaigns, someone would have to run them.

The first political consuting firm in the United States, Campaigns Inc., had its roots in the initiative process. Clem Whitaker, a reporter and the son of a Baptist minister, and his wife Leone Baxter founded and ran it. One of their first big contracts was a referendum on a Central Valley water project in 1933. Campaigns Inc. typically handled a half-dozen ballot measure campaigns in each election. They ran the campaign against "ham and eggs," the 1938 initiative that would have paid $30 every Thursday to each unemployed Californian over fifty years of age. One of their campaigns involved the distribution of 1 million pamphlets, 4.5 million postcards, 50,000 targeted letters, 3,000 radio spots on 109 stations, and hundreds of cinema slides.

"The average American doesn't want to be educated, he doesn't want to improve his mind, he doesn't even want to work consciously at being a good citizen," Whitaker wrote. "But every American likes to be entertained. He likes the movies, he likes mysteries; he likes fireworks and parades. So, if you can't put on a fight, put on a show."

By the time Whitaker and Baxter were running campaigns, Johnson had left California for Washington. In the U.S. Senate, Johnson came to be known not as a populist or anti-railroad crusader, but as one of America's foremost isolationists. Describing himself as a defender of popular sovereignty around the world, he opposed the League of Nations, the World Court, and all manner of treaties. He spoke against American participation in World War I, saying the United States shouldn't help "a little group of unpronounceable races."

He dominated the Republican primaries in his 1920 presidential run, but was outmaneuvered by Warren Harding at the convention. Johnson turned down the vice presidential spot on the ticket. Calvin Coolidge accepted, and became president after Harding's death in 1923.

Johnson died on August 6, 1945, the day an atomic bomb was dropped on Hiroshima. His passing drew little notice. His wife buried him in his own above-ground crypt in Cypress Lawn cemetery just south of San Francisco. A stanza from Rudyard Kipling is engraved in the marble:

> *This single faith in Life and Death and to Eternity:*
> *"The people, Lord, Thy people, are good enough for me!"*

Over time, Hiram Johnson's name would be invoked often when an issue was taken directly to California voters. No one would do this more than Schwarzenegger, but he would not be alone in claiming the mantle. Democrats would lionize Johnson as one of their own, a fighter against business abuses. Long-forgotten were the campaign coffers Johnson filled with money from grocers, canners, dairymen, bankers, wine and liquor merchants, and oilmen. Republicans, noting that Johnson had been a member of their party, conveniently ignored his advocacy of workers' compensation and eight-hour work days.

Most of those who invoked Johnson assumed him to be an idealist. But he understood better than anyone that initiatives, referenda and recalls were not the stuff of grass-roots dreams. Direct democracy was a gun in a man's hand. It came out of a time and place of vicious fights, political bosses, and crooked juries. If a man could handle this weapon, he stood a better chance of defending himself against the old machines. And he might be able to make a new one of his own.

CHAPTER 2

"Mad as Hell"

On a June morning in 1978 in the Venice area of Los Angeles, an elderly woman walked out of her home and embraced Arnold Schwarzenegger, the thirty-one-year-old retired bodybuilding champion. He was visiting the home of a friend who lived next door. Tears ran from the woman's eyes as she approached Schwarzenegger. "This is the happiest day of my life," she explained. "I don't have to sell my home."

Proposition 13 had passed the previous day. Property taxes, which had been soaring along with Southern California property values, would be returned to 1975 levels. Future increases in the taxes would be limited.

"I remember that woman very clearly," Schwarzenegger said.

It was not just Prop 13 that made an impression on him. One of Prop 13's proponents, Howard Jarvis, the executive director of the Apartment Association of Los Angeles County, was the sort of blunt iconoclast Schwarzenegger admired. Jarvis had taken the satirical howl from the movie *Network*, stripped it of its irony and made it his own: "I'm mad as hell and I'm not going to take it anymore!"

A year later, in the fall of 1979, Schwarzenegger traveled to Detroit on a tour to promote his new book about weight training for women. Waiting to be interviewed at a Detroit TV station, Schwarzenegger spotted Jarvis, who was there touting his own manifesto, *I'm Mad as Hell*. Both men were early for their appearances, so Schwarzenegger invited Jarvis to the station cafeteria. The two men—a bodybuilder and a taxpayer advocate—spent an hour chatting about taxes, real estate, California, movies, and Prop 13. Jarvis did most of the talking.

The term blockbuster, originally a name for the two-ton bombs the Royal Air Force used to smash German cities in World War II, has been applied since to a movie that "busted" competing theaters because of its success. In California in the late 1970s, politics and cinema were becoming contests to produce the biggest show possible.

Jarvis and Schwarzenegger's breakfast in Detroit may not have been Ben Franklin bequeathing his walking stick to George Washington, or Teddy Roosevelt whispering in his cousin Franklin's ear at Oyster Bay. But in California's emerging blockbuster democracy, it was the closest thing to a passing of the torch. Jarvis, for better or for worse, had just touched off a new era of politics. A quarter century later, Schwarzenegger would do the same.

IN THE YEARS AFTER WORLD WAR II, direct democracy had fallen into disuse. Seventeen initiatives had qualified for the ballot in 1914, the first general election after voters added direct democracy to the state constitution. In all of the 1950s, there were just ten initiatives; and in the 1960s, nine.

Plebiscites had been discredited internationally by their association with Hitler, who had used a vote of the people to endorse his decision to withdraw from the League of Nations in 1933 and to gain approval for merging the offices of president and chancellor. There was also less pressure for initiatives during an era of popular, productive governors such as Earl Warren and Pat Brown. But proponents of ballot measures faced a more fundamental obstacle. It was getting harder to qualify an initiative, a referendum, or a recall for the ballot.

The standards for qualifying measures are based on percentages: 5 percent of the voters in the most recent gubernatorial election for a referendum or an initiative to change a statute, 8 percent for an initiative to amend the constitution, 12 percent for a recall. Before 1940, the state's population had been just less than 7 million, and a measure could qualify with as few as 100,000 signatures. By 1970, California had more than 20 million residents. To get a half million signatures was an expensive undertaking.

The state's rules also discouraged petitioners. Initiatives were limited to general election ballots, so the public could make law only once every two years. After the war, local ordinances restricted where signatures could be gathered, putting off limits the shopping centers where more and more Californians spent their free time. The state also forced signature gatherers to include the precinct number of each person who signed a petition. Since few voters could recite their precinct number, signature gatherers spent long hours in county clerks' offices looking up the numbers by hand.

In 1968, however, the legislature allowed initiatives and referenda to appear on primary ballots. By 1976, the precinct requirement itself was eliminated. Court rulings declared malls to be the functional equivalent of town squares and opened them to signature gatherers.

It was a liberal activist who first figured out how to exploit this system. Ed Koupal, a failed bar owner who sponsored environmental initiatives, created the "table method" for gathering signatures that is still the standard today. Koupal instructed signature gatherers to work in pairs and set up a table outside a supermarket or mall, preferably one with a single entrance.

One gatherer sat at the table with the petition. The other approached shop-pers to ask: Are you a registered voter? If so, are you registered in this county? Anyone answering yes to both questions was directed to the table and the petitions. Koupal urged gatherers not to discuss the issue raised by a particular initiative.

"Don't debate or argue!" Koupal said. "Why try to educate the world when you're trying to get signatures?" If this method didn't produce eighty signatures an hour, gatherers should move their table to another store.

The table method transformed signature gathering into a highly orga-nized, competitive, and mobile business.

DIRECT DEMOCRACY WAS THE LAST, and by far the most successful, of several vehicles through which Howard Jarvis sought to make a name for himself.

He had owned weekly newspapers in Utah. After moving to California, he befriended J. Paul Getty and wrote a book about the Getty family. He produced a television show for the Republican Party called, *What's Ike Like?* and ran unsuccessfully for the U.S. Senate in 1962. He arranged a cosmetics endorsement deal with Hedy Lamarr and, through his job managing a man-ufacturing business in Hollywood, struck up friendships with Gary Cooper and Clark Gable.

"I got to be star struck and I wanted to be a part of the film business my-self," Jarvis later wrote in his autobiography. He put up some money to make a movie called *Ten Little Indians*, which he would later call "undoubtedly the worst picture in the history of the world."

Jarvis had neither looks nor polish, but he was perfectly cast as a colorful leader of a citizens' revolt. Pressed to defend his use of direct democracy to change California's tax system, Jarvis would reply: "Better government by the masses than government by the asses!"

He tried and failed to qualify initiatives to limit taxes four times before Prop 13. California's rising population had created a surging demand for homes—and a subsequent increase in real estate values. Property taxes rose so quickly that seniors and others complained of being forced to sell their homes to pay the taxes.

Prop 13 capped property taxes at 1 percent of a property's market value. Some owners didn't have to pay even that much. The tax-assessed market value of a property could not increase by more than 2 percent a year. Less noticed but most important, Prop 13 extended California's requirement of a two-thirds vote by the legislature—already in place for passage of the budget—to govern tax increases as well.

Governor Jerry Brown and the legislature fueled Jarvis's campaign by sitting on a huge budget surplus instead of providing tax relief. Opponents of Prop 13 issued warnings so dire—Schools will close! L.A. County will take its paramedics off the streets!—that Jarvis was able to attract more attention and make his show bigger. Turnout for the June 1978 election surpassed 70 percent. Prop 13 received 65 percent of the vote.

Prop 13 proved to be an important factor in the decline of public services and infrastructure in California. But the measure received more credit for keeping taxes low and more blame for California maladies than it merited. Two trends for which Prop 13 was often cited as a cause—legislative gridlock and poor performance of the state's schools—had their roots in government decisions that pre-dated the initiative. Much of its impact, while profound, was indirect. By limiting the ability of local communities to tax themselves, Prop 13 led to the centralization of budget authority in Sacramento.

Local governments retained control over one piece of revenue: local sales tax went to the jurisdiction in which a sale occurred. The result: localities offered incentives to build retail establishments, huge malls often anchored by movie theaters, and giant auto dealerships. In effect, Prop 13 started a competition between cities. The winners were the places that could draw the biggest crowds of shoppers.

It was an appropriate irony that these huge new crowds were ideal targets for signature gatherers bearing initiative and referenda petitions. Like any blockbuster hit, Prop 13 would inspire sequels.

PROP 13 CERTAINLY SHOWED a new way to political stardom. If Howard Jarvis and his face made for radio could end up on the cover of *Time* magazine (and in the movie *Airplane!*), then anyone could attract attention this way. If you could draft an initiative that told an interesting story and would garner publicity, the money it would cost to pay the signature gatherers—about $1 million per measure—was a bargain.

California had sixty-two direct democracy propositions in the 1980s. The legislature, which also had the power to put measures on the ballot, caught the mania and added 114 measures of its own. Prop 13 spurred interest in the direct democracy business in the other twenty-two states that then had the initiative. (Twenty-four states have the initiative now, and three others have popular referenda.) In the 1980s, 289 ballot initiatives appeared across the nation on state ballots. In the 1990s, a record 396 initiatives made the ballot.

Candidate campaigns required a choice between two people, the lesser of two evils. That was product sales—everyone needed toothpaste and a state senator. But a ballot measure was event promotion, not unlike convincing people to see a movie or attend a concert. To go or not to go? Yes or no? Certain stories sold better than others. Prop 13 had the classic plot: a people's revolt against heavy-taxing politicians. Preventing some scourge—be it taxes, cuts in services, immigration, or crime—was also popular. Occasionally, the ballot measure was a love story, a heartwarming appeal for new funds to benefit suffering seniors or adorable animals. Or, best of all, the children.

Just as most movies failed, most ballot measures lost. A large, well-funded "No" campaign usually guaranted defeat. ("Yes" campaigns that were outspent by a margin of two-to-one prevailed only 20 percent of the time.) By the same token, money could not buy a hit. And some initiatives that won the approval of voters never went into effect. Of the seventy initiatives to pass in California between 1960 and 2005, more than two-thirds were challenged in court. A majority of those were struck down by judges either in whole or in part. Although the state constitution says plainly that a law instituted by initiative may only be changed by another vote of the people, the reality was far more complicated. Legislators, governors, judges, and regulators often found ways to suspend or subvert measures.

In nearly a century of California direct democracy, just over one hundred initiatives have passed out of the more than three hundred that have reached the ballot. Since 1960, fewer than three dozen initiatives have been approved by voters and been successfully implemented. Many of the measures made significant changes: eliminating inheritance taxes, raising taxes on cigarettes and millionaires, adopting a state lottery, reforming campaign finance, guaranteeing a certain percentage of funds to schools, and regulating auto insurance rates. But with those kinds of odds, attracting publicity—not changing the law—was often the main reward of sponsoring a ballot measure.

Motion pictures are based on a phenomenon called persistence of vision. When film is flashed in front of a light at a speed of twelve or sixteen frames per second, the illusion of movement is created. Direct democracy operated on a similar principle. Ballot initiatives made for big campaigns and a big show. The impact of most measures was found in the stories they taught voters and politicians, and how those stories changed public opinion and political dynamics. Only a few initiatives changed the government itself.

BALLOT INITIATIVES PROVED IRRESISTIBLE to interest groups that had enough money they could afford to lose. In theory, a state with direct democracy should be subject to the whims of the majority. In practice, ballot measures proved more useful as a tool for unions or industries to carve out special protections for themselves. The California Teachers Association union wrote an initiative that reserved nearly half of the budget for education. Contractors sponsored an initiative dedicating gas taxes to transportation.

Advocacy groups found that by sponsoring initiatives in California, they could create national publicity and momentum for their movements across the country. The Humane Society of the United States managed to pass initiatives protecting animals in California and in several other states. Supporters of term limits won an initiative campaign, Prop 140, in 1990 in California. It imposed limits of three two-year terms for the state assembly and two four-year terms for state senators. Rather than creating a new class of citizen politicians, the measure kicked off a never-ending game of musical chairs in which the same old careerists jumped between the assembly and the senate—and then moved down to city councils and county boards of supervisors. Still, the California victory was followed by the adoption of legislative term limits in fifteen other states.

In 1990, U.S. Senator Pete Wilson, a Republican, helped sponsor an initiative on crime victims' rights and embraced the term limits initiative during his run for governor. He won. Before Schwarzenegger, no California politician immersed himself as deeply in direct democracy as Wilson.

"I used it more than any other governor," said Wilson, "because I knew it was a way to achieve reform that I could not get through the legislature, reform that I thought the public needed and, with a little education, would want." His campaign consultant, George Gorton, believed the initiatives were an important way for Wilson to get attention. "Voters could remember two, maybe three things about Pete Wilson, and that was it. And so we needed to decide what the two things were and then we needed to hammer those," recalled Gorton. "Initiatives helped us do that."

In 1992, Wilson sponsored Proposition 165, an initiative to reform welfare and grant the governor more power in the budget process. The Democrats called it a power grab by "King Pete" and the measure lost. In his run for reelection two years later, Wilson embraced two initiatives, both politically popular. One, the so-called "three strikes" initiative to guarantee life sentences for three-time violent offenders, was so popular that the legislature passed a bill adopting it before it reached the ballot; Wilson and other politicians continued to campaign for the measure anyway. The other measure, Proposition 187, proposed to deny undocumented immigrants access to public schools and other public services. Wilson said he did not particularly like the way Prop 187 was written, but believed it would help him press his case for the federal government to reimburse California for the costs of illegal immigration. Critics argued that Wilson's embrace of the initiative was at best a politically motivated bid for attention and at worst a way to exploit racial fears. The governor's media consultant, Don Sipple, made one ad in which a narrator ominously intoned over scenes of immigrants crossing the border illegally, "They keep coming."

During his second term, in 1996, Wilson promoted another initiative, Prop 209, which sought to end all race- and gender-based preferences in public education, contracting, and employment. It passed. In 1998, he tried two more—one to limit political contributions by labor unions, the other to reform education. Both lost. After two terms in office, Wilson was barred from returning to the governorship, but his political advisors had eight long years of experience trying to use direct democracy for the benefit of a California governor. In the new century they would have a chance to put that experience to work.

DIRECT DEMOCRACY'S ADVANTAGES did not accrue only for political insiders. Rich outsiders found they could use initiatives to make an outsized impact, achieve a quick notoriety, or try to bend some piece of policy to their personal interest. As the 1990s progressed, these personal narratives had a stronger impact on California politics.

Tim Draper, a venture capitalist, sponsored a school voucher initiative amid rumors he might run for office; the measure's defeat ended talk of a candidacy. Reed Hastings, founder of a software firm and CEO of the movie service Netflix Inc., sponsored an initiative to lift the state cap on the number of charter schools. After he gathered enough signatures to qualify the measure, the legislature passed a bill lifting the cap, and Hastings dropped his initiative. He later was appointed to the state school board.

Ron Unz, a Silicon Valley magnate who sponsored a successful 1998 initiative to end bilingual education, said, "One thing that amazed me was how much of this kind of politics has really merged with the entertainment business. The best background for someone running an initiative would be someone with financial resources and a name who comes from the media or entertainment."

By that standard, the film director and former TV actor Rob Reiner was perfect for the initiative business. Reiner was best known as Mike "Meathead" Stivic, Archie Bunker's sanctimonious, liberal son-in-law on *All in the Family*. After a divorce and remarriage, Reiner had started a family and become engaged in Democratic politics. Tipper Gore urged him to study early childhood development.

Reiner met brain scientists and read academic reports. He concluded that money spent on health care and prevention programs for children from birth to three years—when brains grow fastest—was essential.

Reiner first pushed federal legislation to give $11 billion over five years to such programs. After that didn't pass, Reiner decided instead to produce a model program in California. Political professionals advised him to use a ballot initiative. Reiner's initiative, which appeared on the ballot in 1998, raised cigarette taxes by fifty cents a pack to fund early childhood programs.

Reiner's own celebrity, and his ability to call on famous friends, provided Prop 10 with far more TV coverage than most measures. His campaign spent $9 million. The tobacco industry spent more than $40 million against Prop 10. Reiner won a narrow victory.

Unlike most ballot measures, Prop 10 had a direct financial impact. The proposition established commissions on early childhood development in each county through which the tobacco tax revenue—more than $650 million a year—would be distributed. Twenty percent of the money was reserved for a statewide commission, which Reiner chaired. By sponsoring a ballot measure, Reiner, a private citizen, gained control over hundreds of millions of tax dollars. He had converted his Hollywood cachet into real power.[1]

JUST AS CALIFORNIA DEMOCRACY CAME to resemble the movies in the years after Prop 13, the motion picture business turned downright electoral.

Traditionally, movies had opened slowly, building audiences over several weeks as they moved from city to city. The Hollywood studios, the outposts that had defeated Thomas Edison's Trust, became a machine that controlled production, talent, and theaters. By the 1940s, the federal government could no longer tolerate that arrangement and forced the studios to sell off their theater circuits. By 1970, motion picture attendance had reached an all-time low. The studios had to find a way to lure audiences back.

In the early seventies, an independent producer named Tom Laughlin showed them the way with his movies *Billy Jack* and *The Trial of Billy Jack*. The films starred Laughlin himself as an anti-establishment, half–Native American settler of scores. Rather than open his movie piecemeal, starting in big cities and slowly spreading the picture over the heartland, Laughlin promoted his movie as an event and opened it on the same day in theaters all over the country. "It was like running an election campaign," said Laughlin, who would later make an eccentric run for president.

---

[1]In the spring of 2006, facing criticism that the commission had used public money to advance a different initiative, Reiner resigned his post.

Billy Jack ushered in a new era of blockbuster movies, films such as *Jaws* and *Star Wars*, big productions designed to make enormous profits. Opening weekends were promoted as events, with movies competing against each other. To win these weekly contests, movie studios and producers availed themselves of the same kind of public-opinion research employed by political campaigns. In 1977, Joe Farrell, a pollster with the political research firm Lou Harris and Associates, came to Hollywood to convince the film industry to use his services. "My pitch to people was, 'This is like a campaign for a candidate or an issue that no one knows much about that needs to build awareness,'" said Farrell. He and a partner soon had enough customers to launch their own company, NRG.

Polling allowed the studios to test their marketing campaigns and to predict both the size and demographics of the audience for a particular movie. "Unaided awareness" became the key question in such research. How many people had heard of a movie even before the person conducting the survey asked about it?

Movie campaigns developed a rhythm that resembled that of ballot measures. Like an initiative or other types of "events," a movie might be years in the making, but the ad campaign typically started about six weeks before the opening.

Polls allowed producers to test casting decisions or excise certain story lines. Once the picture was made, the campaign to sell it almost always began with an extensive public opinion work-up called a "positioning study." Political campaigns often started with something similar—a "benchmark" poll—that posed dozens of questions. And movie marketers and political consultants alike tested audience response to potential messages. Would you be more likely to see the movie if you knew it was being produced by Jerry Bruckheimer? Would it matter if the film was "from the director of *Independence Day*?" Would the tort reform initiative attract more voters if it was advertised as saving businesses money—or if the emphasis was on the reduced litigation costs to school districts and non-profit organizations?

To win such competitions required a different kind of movie star, someone with a persona big enough to cut through the clutter of multiple advertising campaigns. Stars who could do that would be far richer than the actors or actresses of earlier areas. Their contracts often gave them a share of the revenues, making them partners with the studios and producers. This system, with no permanent alliances, meant that each film was a separate enterprise. The successful star had to sell himself. Acting skills would be less important than a presence that could be conveyed with few words—say, "I'll be back"—in a sea of special effects. The star's commitment would be to make the most accessible piece of commerce, to create a persona compelling enough that, grafted into any script, it could sell tickets. The successful star of the blockbuster era needed to be a pretty good politician.

Arnold Schwarzenegger fit this era. He disliked actors who "think this craft of acting makes the world go around. They're pseudo-intellectuals," he once said. He bragged that his movies had more action than art. "In our business it's like in the political arena—you have to find out what the audience really wants," he said during the promotional tour for *Last Action Hero*. Before the blockbuster era, it was not clear Schwarzenegger would succeed in motion pictures. In the 1970s, he had played a bit part in Robert Altman's unconventional take on Raymond Chandler's novel, *The Long Goodbye*. He had a supporting role in *The Villain*, a sort of Western farce, which flopped. Tellingly, his first cinematic successes came when he played versions of himself. As an Austrian bodybuilder who played the bluegrass fiddle (Schwarzenegger himself played the violin in one scene), he won a Golden Globe for best newcomer in Bob Rafelson's film *Stay Hungry*, released in 1976. And he was a critical hit as the star of the 1977 bodybuilding documentary, *Pumping Iron*. The movie told the stories of the bodybuilders in the 1975 Mr. Olympia competition. Schwarzenegger won, then retired from the sport.

Schwarzenegger broke out in a B-movie epic, *Conan the Barbarian*, released in 1982. The movie gave him a lasting persona—the indomitable warrior—that would carry him through his career. Conan was the first of many characters Schwarzenegger would play who took matters literally into their own hands.

Two years after Conan, Schwarzenegger starred as the Terminator, a killing machine from the future. It was the role that would define him as a movie star and, to a lesser extent, as a political personality. "He's never gonna play a character where he sits around in an office and wrings his hands," James Cameron, the writer and director of *The Terminator*, would say. "He is about direct action."

Many of Schwarzenegger's characters used strength or violence or humor to cut through a politicized, hierarchical, or bureaucratic environment. He played commandos, firemen, and police officers who ignored superiors and laws in order to take action. Conan was a king, but he was also an orphan and slave who swung his own sword. The greatest joy in life, Conan declared, was "to crush your enemies, to see them driven before you, and to hear the lamentations of the women." Two decades later, the governor of California would quote that line in describing his political philosophy to the *New York*

Times. Tongue in cheek, he would pause for a moment and then explain that he had briefly mixed up his movie persona with his political one.

SCHWARZENEGGER HAD BEEN IMPRESSED by Charlotte Parker, the publicist who handled the 1984 sequel to *Conan the Barbarian.* He made her his personal publicist; Parker would stay with him for fourteen years.

Parker carefully considered the ramifications, political and otherwise, of each public appearance. At first, she simply advised Schwarzenegger to stand next to stars who were more famous than he was at premieres. But as Schwarzenegger became more prominent, she kept other performers out of the frame. She advised him not to stand next to Charlton Heston because she feared that people would associate Schwarzenegger, a Republican who supported gun control, with the far more conservative Heston, who would later serve as president of the National Rifle Association. When Schwarzenegger visited Washington, Parker tried to have him photographed alongside Republicans with bipartisan reputations.

"I could sense his political ambition, even though he never overtly talked about it," said Parker, who in the 1980s jokingly addressed her client as "governor."

Parker helped Schwarzenegger build an image far larger than those of other movie stars. Schwarzenegger wanted to connect his personal brand to as many parts of American life as possible. In his service, Parker would get him on the cover of cigar magazines, car magazines, science fiction glossies, foreign magazines, even *Soldier of Fortune.* Parker wanted to convey with each story that Schwarzenegger was more than a muscled star. Parker and Schwarzenegger played up the star's cleverness in selling his movies. A key part of their movie marketing was, remarkably, about Schwarzenegger's skill at movie marketing.

Schwarzenegger ravenously consumed the polling and focus group research produced for his movies. He had *Daily Variety*'s various box office charts and data faxed to him. A *Los Angeles Times* reporter interviewing Schwarzenegger in 1989 described being deluged with questions about a competitor's film. Why had it opened weakly? Did the studio fail to promote it? How had the trailer tested? "He was very, very involved in the ad buys and very interested in the amount of money that was spent on the marketing," said Parker.

Schwarzenegger attended studio marketing meetings and previewed the trailers and ads personally. While making one movie, he spent his down time selling the previous film. Schwarzenegger at times seemed more interested in the marketing of his films than the studios did. During the shooting of *Total Recall*, Schwarzenegger invited studio executives to the set in Mexico so he could brief them on how to promote the movie. "A lot of these stars, they've got this attitude, you know, 'I'm an artist and I'll do the thing and then forget it.' But that's not where he was at all," said Jim Lorimer, his friend and business partner in a Ohio fitness convention and bodybuilding tournament. "He'd say, 'I'm a businessman. I made a product here, and how can I help sell it?'"

SCHWARZENEGGER THOUGHT IN PICTURES. "When people come to me with a script or concept, I tell them, 'Before we shoot the first frame, we have to shoot the poster. What is the image? What are we trying to sell here?'" he told the *Los Angeles Times* in 1991.

Before deciding which project to do, Schwarzenegger would conduct an elaborate "bake-off" for his services. He might be in touch with a half-dozen different production companies about as many projects. This "Arnold Sweepstakes" became his dominant method of decision-making.

"I don't make that mistake that some people do, that they sign contracts for two, three years in advance," Schwarzenegger told Larry King. "I like to keep it open in case a director—a good director—has a good project and comes to me. I don't want to miss that opportunity."

Often, Schwarzenegger insisted on changes to make a script more audience-friendly. The discussions Schwarzenegger had with writers were specific. Young men were a core audience for his movies. How could he attract young girls or older women without losing his base? Schwarzenegger tweaked the films if certain elements did not test well with audiences. Such re-shoots were a fact of Hollywood life, but few stars embraced the process like Schwarzenegger: "What I always like to do is let the audience tell us the way they feel, so we don't waste time. So you go in and you have what they call a 'focus group' and you ask them: 'What is it that you liked here? What is it that you liked there?' And then you go according to that."

At its most effective, the bake-off allowed Schwarzenegger to make careful, patient decisions after examining all his options. The downside became clear when Schwarzenegger himself was a main driver of a project. *Last Action Hero*, a flop, was a prime example. Schwarzenegger filled it with literally dozens of ideas—too many ideas, as it turned out, to please critics or audiences. Ultimately, he made a movie about a movie within a movie. Schwarzenegger starred as an actor playing an action star—in the contemporary reality of Hollywood—but also as an action star inside the movie reality of car chases and explosions. The plot shifted back and forth between the two realities. If it sounds a bit confusing, it was. As Tom Shone, former film critic for the *London Sunday Times*, wrote: "The movie didn't need releasing, still less reviewing. . . . It needed finishing."

AS EACH OF HIS MOVIES' RELEASE DATES grew near, Schwarzenegger turned from behind-the-scenes strategist to star of the publicity campaign. In their early years together, Schwarzenegger and Parker analyzed each gesture and word of his public appearances. Schwarzenegger even studied videotape of himself being interviewed. Parker and Schwarzenegger tried to strike a balance between controlling the terms of each interview and allowing the star to improvise a few racy or even off-color comments. The trick was to avoid gaffes while being unpredictable and colorful enough to stand out from other stars.

His accent and long name—which had once looked like detriments to a movie career—helped. "I felt my uniqueness worked to my advantage," he explained to one interviewer. "I wanted to make sure that if I go on an elevator, before people ever saw me coming around the corner, they would say already, 'That sounds like Arnold.'"

A creature of habit, Schwarzenegger preferred to promote movies in settings he had used in the past. His belief in repetition was almost religious: if a marketing tactic had worked before, why change? After his friend Tony Nowak, a Polish immigrant, made special jackets for his *Terminator 2: Judgment Day* promotion tour, Schwarzenegger had Nowak make similar "message jackets" for future movies.

He worked the press in a careful pecking order. He liked to start with a *Tonight Show* appearance. Then he would make the rounds of the national network morning shows and sit down with Larry King. Finally, as opening weekend approached, Schwarzenegger would talk to fifty or more media outlets a day—local TV reporters, entertainment media, and international journalists—at five- or ten-minute intervals. He did all of this without complaint. If Schwarzenegger had a weakness as a marketer, it was his taste for self-agrandizing stunts that were often more trouble than they were worth. In 1993, he arranged for a seventy-five-foot blow-up of himself to appear at the Cannes Film Festival, in France; the stunt drew huge press attention but did not make *Last Action Hero* a hit. Schwarzenegger even tried to have his name painted on the side of a NASA rocket. Once a movie had been released in America, Schwarzenegger would leave the country to promote openings all over the world. Even when the domestic box office of his films slumped in the late 1990s, he continued to attract large audiences overseas.

In the process, Schwarzenegger created "the template for film promotion in the blockbuster era," Jonathan Bing and Dade Hayes wrote in *Open Wide*, their study of movie promotion.

Spending so much time on camera taught the star how to stay on message. He could turn any question into a soliloquy on the action wonders of his latest picture. Schwarzenegger could be prickly in private about tough reviews, but like a good politician, in public he managed to sound unconcerned. "What makes you be in the position you're in as an actor or a star, or as a politician, as far as that goes, is the people, no one else," he said in 1993. "In the end we have to make movies not for the press but for the people."

SCHWARZENEGGER TALKED FOR YEARS about making a transition from star to producer and director. He took a producer credit on two movies in which he starred. He did a little directing—a *Tales from the Crypt* episode for HBO and a 1992 TV movie remake of *Christmas in Connecticut*, based on the 1945 film starring Barbara Stanwyck. In spite of his power in Hollywood, Schwarzenegger never took the next step. He did not produce the movies of others or become a director in the mold of one of his heroes, Clint Eastwood. He seemed to prefer the life of a free agent for whom each movie was a new campaign. Schwarzenegger had chosen a politician's life long before he entered politics.

CHAPTER 3

"Free to Choose"

Politics had long intrigued Schwarzenegger. George Butler, the director of the 1977 bodybuilding documentary *Pumping Iron*, once wrote that Schwarzenegger had a "master plan" since he was a young immigrant: to get an education, invest in real estate, become a star, marry someone glamorous and intelligent, and get into politics. Schwarzenegger himself had mused publicly and privately about a political career, but not until much later in his life would he think about it in a focused way. At various times, he dated his interest in government service to the state's budget crisis in 2001, his work with inner-city children in the 1990s, or to his meetings with Republican politicians in the 1980s.

There were signs that the thought occurred to him much earlier. In 1977, he told the German magazine *Stern*: "When one has money, one day it becomes less interesting. And when one is also the best in film, what can be more interesting? Perhaps power. Then one moves into politics and becomes governor or president or something." The bodybuilder Reg Park, a Schwarzenegger idol, recalled a twenty-year-old Schwarzenegger visiting Park's home in South Africa in 1967 and talking about a run for office.

Or did it begin in Austria, when he was a young boy intrigued by stories of Caesar and Charlemagne and other famous rulers?

In post-war Austria, a child could see the best and worst of governments. Arnold Alois Schwarzenegger was born on July 30, 1947, in the southern province of Styria, then occupied by the British in the post-war partitioning of the country. The Americans, who occupied Salzburg and Upper Austria, provided "Truman's care packages" of dried milk, cheddar cheese, and corned beef to hungry Austrian children in all parts of the country. Millions of dollars from the Marshall Plan built new Styrian factories, which produced cars, motorcycles, and steel. Decades later, as a Republican politician, Schwarzenegger would criticize the "Socialism" he had left in Austria. He was right—Austria had state-owned industries and a commission that set prices and wages. But many Austrians argued that socialism, combined with a protectionist trade policy, had allowed Austria to rebuild herself.

During the occupation, the Soviets controlled the northeastern part of the country. When young Arnold Schwarzenegger went to visit his relatives in the far northern reaches of Styria, the family had to negotiate Soviet military checkpoints near the Semmering mountain pass. Rumors abounded that the Soviets would take men prisoner, and he worried for his father and uncle. Schwarzenegger would publicly recall those brief encounters with Soviet soldiers and their nearby tanks as among the scariest moments of his life.

Schwarzenegger was only eight in 1955 when the Soviets left. Taking advantage of Stalin's death, the Austrians negotiated a treaty under which the Soviets, Americans, and British ended the occupation in return for a pledge of Austrian neutrality in international politics. Neutrality remains a sacred tenet of Austrian political life today.

SCHWARZENEGGER WAS THE SECOND of two boys born to Aurelia Jadrny, a young widow, and Gustav Schwarzenegger, a veteran of the Second World War. They had married in 1945, when Gustav was already thirty-eight. Arnold would travel so far in life that one day, Gustav Schwarzenegger's time as a police officer in the Nazi war machine would be the subject of political debate on the other side of the world in a state he would never see.

Gustav Schwarzenegger was a military man. He had served in the Austrian Army from 1930 to 1937, achieving the rank of section commander. That year, he left the army to try to make a living as a police officer. But in 1938, Hitler annexed Austria. Austrian men were automatically inducted into the German army, but Gustav Schwarzenegger went further. He joined the Nazi Party in 1938. A year later, he volunteered for the Sturmabteilungen, the SA, or "storm troopers," who six months earlier had attacked Jewish homes and businesses throughout Germany and sent thousands of Jews to concentration camps, an event known as Kristallnacht. Within the SA, Gustav Schwarzenegger became a master sergeant in the military police unit 521 of the Feldgendarmerie, otherwise known as the Chained Dogs. (The full extent of this war record was unknown to his son until the *Los Angeles Times* reported it in 2003; a decade earlier, when reports surfaced that Arnold Schwarzenegger's father had been a Nazi, the star asked the Simon Wiesenthal Center, a Los Angeles–based organization devoted to Holocaust remembrance and human rights, to investigate his father's record. The center, with Wiesenthal's personal help, found Gustav's Nazi Party membership, but failed to turn up the fact that he had served in the SA.)

Military records on file at the state archives in Vienna showed Gustav Schwarzenegger spent much of 1940 in France and Belgium, where the military police were supposed to subdue populations conquered by the Nazis. By

September 1941, Gustav Schwarzenegger had been transferred to the Eastern Front, scene of the bloodiest and most destructive fighting of the war. A military evaluation form from July 1943 described Gustav Schwarzenegger as a "quiet and dependable person not especially forward." Military records suggested he was wounded somewhere in Russia around this time, though details of the injuries were scant. He contracted malaria and by year's end had returned to Austria, where he was assigned to work as a postal inspector. There is no evidence that Gustav Schwarzenegger or his police unit ever participated in war crimes. The de-Nazification process in 1947 cleared him to work as a federal police officer.

Police work took him to Thal, a village on the other side of a hill from the provincial capital of Graz, the second largest city in Austria. He served as police chief there for more than fifteen years. Gustav Schwarzenegger was a difficult father. Arnold had to keep his own clothes extremely neat—the standards were military style—and polish his father's belt and shoes. After family outings, Gustav required Arnold and his older brother Meinhard to write reports. Schwarzenegger himself has said that discipline could be meted out with belt or stick. His father often drank too much.

His father's job, and the small size of Thal, gave Schwarzenegger a close-up view of government. Thal was in some sense a border town—Yugoslavia was thirty miles to the south, and Hungary an hour to the east—and Schwarzenegger said he once helped his father hand out food at a refugee camp for Hungarians fleeing their country after the Soviets crushed the uprising of 1956. The Schwarzeneggers lived on the second floor of a three hundred-year-old house that was reserved for families of officials (the local forest ranger occupied the first floor). Arnold's elementary school was part of the small town hall where his father and two deputies worked. Across the road stood the Catholic church. Thal was governed in effect by four people: the priest, the school director, the police chief, and the mayor. Some small towns nursed political feuds, but not Thal.

"Despite all the different institutions and political directions they came from, these four individuals always sat together and always made mutual politics," said Schwarzenegger's elementary school classmate Peter Urdl, who later became mayor of Thal. "They were careful to show the town they got along."

The province of Styria was governed by the more conservative party, the Austrian People's Party. But Thal was a Socialist town. Every mayor since the war has been a Social Democrat. As near as his friends could tell, so was the teenage Schwarzenegger. He expressed admiration for Bruno Kreisky, the Social Democrat foreign minister who had traveled to America, talked politics with the Kennedys, and would become chancellor. "I remember we were talking on the bus about Kreisky," said Urdl. "Both of us were of the opinion that he was the man of the future." Schwarzenegger, in truth, had few strong political views at that young age. In time, bodybuilding would shape his politics.

AFTER THE OCCUPATION ENDED IN 1955, Austria's two largest political parties—the Social Democrats (the reds to Austrians) and the Austrian People's Party (the blacks)—ruled in a coalition government. Elections determined the number of patronage positions granted to each party. With little money in private hands, institutions affiliated with one party or the other to survive. This was true for clubs, pubs, and even gyms.

Kurt Marnul, one of the country's leading bodybuilders, trained at a Graz gym affiliated with the reds. But when the gym's managers objected to his American training methods, which he had learned from magazines and brochures, he bolted. The Austrian People's Party agreed to help him find space for a new gym. As part of the deal, Marnul had to field a team of weightlifters, officially the youth representatives of the party.

One of his recruits was a boy, already six feet tall, whom Marnul had seen around Graz. Schwarzenegger had lifted some weights as part of his soccer training, but he had soured on soccer. "I didn't get the credit alone if I did something special. I just avoided team sports from then on," he would tell an interviewer decades later. Since Thal had only an elementary school, Schwarzenegger attended Fröbel, one of Graz's weaker secondary schools. At fifteen, he joined a vocational program through which he apprenticed at a construction materials company. Schwarzenegger sold wood.

In his teens, Schwarzenegger was seized by a feeling that he wanted more than Austria could offer him. He made a point of avoiding the ordinary activities his classmates and friends enjoyed. "When I make decisions, whatever it might be, I always consider, is what I am deciding on now different from everybody else? That's very important for me," he said in an interview for the film *Pumping Iron*.

Bodybuilding was certainly unconventional. By the time he turned sixteen, Schwarzenegger was working out obsessively. The People's Party youth weightlifting team was one of the best in the country, and Marnul coached him in bodybuilding as well. The gym was open five days a week. One weekend, Schwarzenegger and a friend broke in so they could use the equipment. On summer days, he showed off his muscles at the Thalersee, the small lake in Thal where people came to swim and dine at the Kling family restaurant.

The lake was small enough that Schwarzenegger, doing push-ups along the shore or chin-ups on nearby trees, could be seen by everyone else on the Thalersee. The place was his first stage. Twenty years later, he would bring Maria Shriver to the lake to propose to her.

One of his fellow weight lifters, Karl Gerstl, often invited Schwarzenegger home. There, Karl's father Alfred, who was active in the People's Party, held court. In time, Schwarzenegger would call Alfred Gerstl his second father and his first political mentor.

Alfred Gerstl was a conservative, someone who stood out in Graz for, among other things, his Jewish heritage (his father had married a Catholic woman and converted to get a job with the railroad) and his participation in the resistance during World War II. (He worked with Tito's partisans in nearby Yugoslavia to smuggle supplies, medicine, and deserting soldiers across the border.) After the war, Gerstl established a club within the People's Party for those who had been wounded or persecuted during the war. He involved himself in local politics after the city fathers wouldn't let him sell his tobacco shop. He had heard one official boast: Now we've destroyed the Jew. By the early 1960s, he had won election to the city council.

Gerstl hosted barbecues for Schwarzenegger and the bodybuilders at the Thalersee. In the evenings, Gerstl convened free-spirited political meetings at his home. Attendance was not limited by party or age. There were Socialists, conservatives, and a few radicals. Many were businessmen and entrepreneurs. They shared a concern that Austrians were in denial about their war role and that neo-Nazis were gaining influence. Gerstl often talked about the pre-war years. Party strife and civil wars had "paved the way for forces which led our country into disaster." He argued the only way to prevent a recurrence was to make Austria's system more democratic, capitalist, and open. "Democracy is the way you fight extremists," Gerstl would say.

"Arnold didn't talk. Sometimes he had other things on his mind, but he was listening," said Albert Kaufman, a contemporary of Schwarzenegger's who came to Gerstl's sessions. "Arnold inhaled everything." No subject was out of bounds at Gerstl's home. Helmut Knaur, who had been imprisoned by the Nazis in North Africa and later fought for the British, was an anarchist who routinely offered up the most outrageous comments. Knaur even insulted his host, Gerstl, by calling him a *knecht*, a word meaning "serf" or "slave to the system." Schwarzenegger perked up whenever Knaur opened his mouth. Knaur, a big bear of a man, spoke English and tried to teach Schwarzenegger the language by having him read copies of *Playboy*. "He was a very important influence to inspire me to learn, to speak languages, to be more worldly," said Schwarzenegger. "He said, 'Think big.'"

Gerstl and his friends organized a campaign against a group of young right-wing students who were protesting against the director of a local teachers' academy. The academy director had lectured against Nazism and encouraged school field trips to the site of the Mauthausen concentration camp. In 1965, the right-wing students had a demonstration in the Hauptplatz, the square in front of city hall in the old historic center of Graz. Gerstl staged a counter-demonstration with a group of young members of the People's Party, including the bodybuilders. Schwarzenegger punched one right-winger in the face and the bodybuilders chased the group down the Herrengasse, Gerstl recalled. An assault charge was filed against Schwarzenegger, Gerstl said, but a pair of friendly police officers arranged for the matter to be dropped.

Two months after his eighteenth birthday, Schwarzenegger entered the army to complete his compulsory service. But he went AWOL during basic training to compete in—and win—the junior Mr. Europe bodybuilding contest in Stuttgart, Germany. He was caught while sneaking back onto the base and spent a week in the brig. When news of his victory spread, he was ordered to focus on his bodybuilding training. He completed his service in October 1966, and was more determined than ever to leave Austria. "I kept thinking, 'It's not big enough, it's stifling,'" he wrote in his autobiography. "Even people's ideas were small. There was too much contentment, too much acceptance of things as they'd always been."

Schwarzenegger's vocational high school degree was not enough to secure a government or civil service job, so Gerstl wanted to put Schwarzenegger in charge of running the biggest city swimming pool in Graz. Although the job came with a pension and allowed time for his training, Schwarzenegger declined. "I didn't want a safety net," he said.

BODYBUILDING WAS THE "FOUNDATION" of his life, Schwarzenegger has said. It gave him more than just twenty-two-inch arms and a fifty-seven-inch chest. It provided a way of thinking about and preparing for any contest. It gave him a philosophy and an approach to politics. "Bodybuilders are the ultimate self-made men," wrote Charles Gaines, author of the novel *Stay Hungry* and coauthor of the 1974 book *Pumping Iron*, which led to the movie of the same name. "If you are as gifted a student as Arnold was, bodybuilding will teach you a muscular self-honesty and how to maximize your strengths and improve your weaknesses."

There were many lessons. Pain was pleasure, evidence that you and your muscles were growing. Surrounding yourself with good people was critical. A training partner with poor workout habits dragged you down; a diligent partner could push you to new heights. Bodybuilding taught Schwarzenegger the importance of elders and the power of mentors. There were the photographers who showed him how to make his muscles look best in their shots. There were gym owners who sponsored him at tournaments. And there was the bodybuilding promoter Joe Weider, who brought Schwarzenegger to America. From Weider's example, Schwarzenegger saw how to build one's name into a lucrative brand. Weider transformed his influence over bodybuilding and bodybuilders into a platform to sell products—magazines, T-shirts, workout equipment, and nutritional supplements, all bearing the Weider name—and ultimately into a business empire worth hundreds of millions of dollars.

From bodybuilding, Schwarzenegger learned the same lesson in many different ways: size was the prize. "People listen much more to bigger guys," Schwarzenegger wrote in his autobiography. "The bigger you are and the more impressive you look physically, the more people listen and the better you can sell yourself or anything else."

He trained his body with lighter weights and more repetitions, which allowed him to build a "showman's body" that dramatically expanded when he flexed. Schwarzenegger also learned how to read crowds. "I find out which poses" the audience likes, he said in the book *Pumping Iron*. "That's why I don't have a specific posing routine, because you never know what they like and what they don't."

This was a democratic sport decided by a vote of the judges. "Bodybuilding is Nation Building," was one motto of the International Federation of Body Building during the 1970s. With enough discipline and work, even flesh and blood could be transformed. Anybody could do anything.

Or go anywhere.

When Schwarzenegger landed at Los Angeles International Airport for the first time in 1968, he spotted a sign that read, "The government of the United States welcomes you." Two bodybuilding journalists had come to pick him up.

The new arrival barely spoke English but he had a question.

"What is 'government'?"

Schwarzenegger immediately took an interest in the politics of the country. He could not understand what the two candidates for president, the Republican Richard Nixon and the Democratic vice president Hubert

Humphrey, were saying when he watched their speeches, so he had a friend translate. Humphrey and the Democrats sounded too in love with the government, too Socialist—too Austrian for him. Schwarzenegger preferred Nixon's talk of free enterprise and declared himself a Republican, an identification that would wax and wane but never be discarded.

But it was bodybuilding, not politics, that defined Schwarzenegger. It was his good fortune that Joe Gold, born in East Los Angeles, had decided to set up his gym near Venice Beach, where Schwarzenegger and other top bodybuilders held their workouts. It only took one year to convert Schwarzenegger to the idea that this was paradise. The area around Gold's Gym would remain his enduring base. Here he would live, work, invest, and, one day, in his very own building just over the border from Venice in Santa Monica, hold meetings as governor.

Most of all, bodybuilding gave him a persona, an image that he could tweak and manage but, for better and for worse, never really shake. Schwarzenegger was bodybuilding personified, the man who would do anything, say anything, become anything, to sell himself. "I was meant to do revolutionary things, to break records, to just do things that nobody else can do," he told *Rolling Stone* in 1976. This image served its purpose. In a 2002 interview marking the twenty-fifth anniversary of the documentary *Pumping Iron*'s release, he said, "I believe that the more sensationalistic you are, the more outrageous things that you say, the more you get quoted, the more you get in the papers, and the more the sport of bodybuilding will benefit."

A man who would say anything was destined to be trailed by neverending rumors. His own life was improbable enough. But Schwarzenegger was doomed—in the fevered imaginations of others—to be dying of cancer he had never contracted, flashing secret Nazi codes that never existed, and bedding women he had never met. He had taken steroids, as had his competitors, under a doctor's supervision and without long-term health effects, he said. But as a public figure, he was the bodybuilder who would be asked about steroids for the rest of his life.

Early on, politics was part of this bodybuilding persona. In 1974, at a tournament, a fan shouted: "Arnold, when are you running for president?" He wasn't even a U.S. citizen yet, but he yelled back without missing a beat: "When Nixon gets impeached." In the movie *Pumping Iron*, the director George Butler portrayed him as the king of the bodybuilders. In 1991, at the height of his stardom and while serving on a presidential council, Schwarzenegger bought the rights to all the *Pumping Iron* outtakes, including anything that might be "embarrassing" or "reflect negatively" on him, according to the purchase agreement. The transcript of one interview suggested the *Pumping Iron* director wanted to present, for dramatic purposes, this native German-speaker with a heavy dose of authoritarianism and a whiff of Nazism.

"I think that we can't live without authority," Schwarzenegger said, according to the interview transcript. "Because I feel that a certain amount of people who were meant to do this and control, and a large amount like 95 percent of the people who we have to tell what to do and how to keep in order." In the transcript, Schwarzenegger was asked again and again about politics. He tried to steer the conversation to the physical pleasure of pumping one's muscles and the way body oil reflects stage lights. Eventually, he played along.

Schwarzenegger was asked three times to explain his feelings about Hitler. Is he your hero? "I admire him for being such a good public speaker and for his way of getting to the people and so on. But I didn't admire him for what he did with it." Schwarzenegger quickly added: "It's very hard to say who I admire, who are my heroes. And I admire basically people who are powerful people, like [John] Kennedy."

The questions continued. "Do you think the feeling that a politician has, that Kennedy had, or a Hitler had—I'm sure they are different people but the feeling regarding when the whole stadium at Nuremberg is cheering, and he's the leader, is that anything like the feeling you have when you've just won a contest?"

Schwarzenegger: "It's probably a thousand times as good. Their feeling, than mine. But, and I wish I could experience it sometime, the feeling like Kennedy had, you know, to speak maybe to 50,000 people at one time and having them cheer, or like Hitler in the Nuremberg stadium, and have all those people scream at you and just being in total agreement with whatever you say. But I experience a certain percentage of that. Which is already fantastic. Being up there on stage and having people scream at you and just going crazy over you."

The question was asked again: Is there a system or government that you know that you admire? "In a way I admire, well I would say for me the greatest country in the world right now is America. Except there's only one thing I don't like here—and that people go on their own little trips too much. The unity isn't there anymore. And I don't think it's too much the people's fault. I think it's because we don't have a strong leader there."

Schwarzenegger explained that he felt he had been an American in a past life.

"You mean," he was asked, "you were an American, let's say—not a Gestapo or that kind?"

"Maybe not, who knows. But I feel like, you know, that's where I lived before, because I cannot explain why. It's just . . . like destiny."

"I think your feelings about America are stronger than your feelings about Germany," the questioner continued.

"Oh definitely. I think that I like America because—well there are a lot of reasons why I like America. From the economic system it has here, from the freedom it has here, and everything else. Money. A rich country. It has the most open-minded people and so on."

When he ran for office, critics would charge that these statements exposed Schwarzenegger as a Hitler admirer. This was the same man who had chased neo-Nazis down the Herrengasse, who had gone AWOL from the Austrian army to win a bodybuilding tournament. He was a libertarian, an iconoclast, irreverent. "That was bodybuilding. We would say explosive things to each other, then we went to lunch," said Rick Wayne, a bodybuilder who wrote articles under Schwarzenegger's name for muscle magazines in the 1970s and who would publish a newspaper on the Caribbean island of St. Lucia. "I've never known Arnold to be a conservative. I've known Arnold to be a chameleon."

Pumping Iron revealed not hatred, but a different flaw, a habit of speech he could never fully overcome. In the heat of making a sale, Schwarzenegger would say almost anything if he thought it would stir his audience. In *Pumping Iron*, he had dismissed his best friend, the Italian bodybuilder Franco Columbu, as a "child." He had made up a story about his reasons for not attending his father's funeral (he borrowed the tale from another bodybuilder). His true beliefs weren't scary. His ambition was. "Let's create a villain," Schwarzenegger would say years later in recalling his attitude during *Pumping Iron*. "Let's create that guy that has the psychological power over people. . . . How can I sell the idea that I'm a machine that has no emotions, that doesn't care about any of my competitors, not even my best friend that was living with me at the time, Franco Columbu?"

SCHWARZENEGGER KNEW WHAT WOULD SELL. America loved the character it saw in *Pumping Iron*. Schwarzenegger, with the help of a publicist, used his newfound celebrity to introduce himself to all sorts of people. He met Andy Warhol, was painted by Jamie Wyeth, and was interviewed by Barbara Walters. At a Boston screening to raise money for *Pumping Iron* in the fall of 1976, Butler introduced him to John Kerry. Twenty-eight years later, the Republican governor of California could say the Democratic nominee for president was an old friend.

Bodybuilding also gave Schwarzenegger a lifelong friend and business partner with Republican instincts and a head for politics. Jim Lorimer had run the Mr. World bodybuilding tournament in 1970 in Columbus, Ohio, as a way to raise money for an Olympic weightlifting tournament he was obligated to put on. Schwarzenegger had never seen a better-organized event, and the twenty-three-year-old bodybuilder told Lorimer that eventually they would go into business together. As soon as Schwarzenegger retired from competitive bodybuilding in 1975, the two became partners in staging a bodybuilding tournament. Together over thirty years, they built the contest into a massive annual fitness convention, dubbed "The Arnold," that in 2006 would boast thirty sports, fifteen thousand athletes and more than one hundred thousand attendees.

In his day job as vice president of government relations for Nationwide Insurance, Lorimer started one of the first corporate political action committees and met some of the country's best-known politicians. At home in the Columbus suburb of Worthington, he would serve as both mayor and vice mayor for more than thirty-eight years.

Lorimer kept his eyes open for ways that Schwarzenegger might involve himself more directly in political life. "Politics was something we talked about," said Lorimer. "I knew that was always a goal of his. I felt that that was eventually one of the directions that he was going to go."

IN THE SUMMER OF 1977, with *Pumping Iron* still in theaters, Schwarzenegger had his publicist wrangle an invitation to a New York charity tennis tournament honoring the late Robert F. Kennedy. While there, Schwarzenegger chatted up Kennedy's niece, Maria Shriver.

"It was about to break up, about four o'clock," her father Sargent Shriver would recall, "and my daughter Maria said, 'Daddy, we're all going back on the airplane, aren't we, up to Cape Cod?' And I said, 'Yes,' and she said, 'Do you think it would be okay if we asked Arnold Schwarzenegger to come along on the plane and spend the weekend with us?'" Shortly after his arrival in Hyannisport, Schwarzenegger told Eunice Shriver that her daughter had a "great ass." Eunice laughed. Schwarzenegger spent the weekend playing sports and offering exercise advice to the Kennedy women. He even suggested an exercise program for eighty-seven-year-old Rose Kennedy.

It would be nine years before Schwarzenegger and Maria Shriver married. As in many of his major life decisions, Schwarzenegger took his time. Maria Shriver cast her marriage publicly as something of a rebellious act, a commitment to someone whose interests ran far away from politics. "Everyone assumed that I was supposed to marry someone like a John Kerry, some preppy that had gone to Harvard or Yale," Maria Shriver would tell *Vanity Fair.* "I didn't want to marry those boys—I did not like them. . . . I wanted someone different. I married my authentic self."

Schwarzenegger may have come in a different package, but his political ambitions were already a matter of public record. And Shriver, her protestations to the contrary, had more than a passing acquaintance with politics. She developed her interest in journalism in 1972 while sitting with reporters on the campaign plane of her father, the Democratic vice presidential nominee. And she would cover many campaigns herself as a TV reporter.

The Shrivers became a second family to Schwarzenegger, who had lost most of his own. Schwarzenegger's father died in 1972. Meinhard, his older brother, died in an alcohol-related car crash at the age of twenty-five. His mother lived in Austria. Perhaps as a result of this distance and the warmth of the Shrivers, he had an unusually close relationship with his in-laws. "I would say certainly the biggest influence in Arnold's life has been Daddy and Mummy, which is kind of ironic," Maria told her father's biographer. "Arnold is interested in ideas and creation and dreaming. He's a force that way, like my dad."

Sargent Shriver had a long career in public service. He chaired the Chicago school board, worked in business and law, and started the Peace Corps, Job Corps, and Head Start, among other programs. After running on the ticket with George McGovern in 1972, he ran unsuccessfully for the presidency himself in 1976. Shriver might have been governor of Illinois, but decided not to run in order to fulfill family responsibilities. Schwarzenegger said his father-in-law was skeptical of him at first and thought he should be doing more than bodybuilding and acting. Schwarzenegger would later call his father-in-law "one of my heroes."

Sargent Shriver often conversed with his son-in-law in German. Shriver had spent parts of 1934 and 1936 as an exchange student in Germany, not far from the Austrian border. Sargent Shriver, who would serve in the Navy reserve while attending law school, knew the horrors of Nazism, but also came to oppose American entry into World War II. (In 1940, Shriver was among the Yale law students who founded the anti-war organization America First. Its founding documents read: "American democracy can be preserved only by keeping out of the European war.")

OVER THE YEARS, SARGENT SHRIVER shared his perspectives on government and politics with his attentive son-in-law. While Shriver had a reputation as an unreconstructed liberal, his impatient attitude toward bureaucracy and his publicity-seeking style matched Schwarzenegger's instincts. In starting new programs, Shriver preferred to circumvent existing departments and create organizations outside the usual flowcharts. This put him on the wrong side of other government officials, but allowed him to build big programs quickly.

Most of all, Sargent Shriver had what his biographer described as "a showman's desire to entertain." He loved a relentless, exhausting publicity campaign. In one example, he came to California in 1963 for what he called a "blitz recruiting" of Peace Corps volunteers that included twelve speeches in four days. During the discussions that led to the establishment of Head Start in early 1965, he pushed to make the program bigger so more people would know about it. "We're going to write Head Start across the face of this nation so that no Congress and no president can ever destroy it," he declared. Schwarzenegger understood that marketing philosophy. It was his own.

His father-in-law "always called me 'the sponge' because I would go in there and pump him for information for hours," said Schwarzenegger, who recalled asking, "How did you set this program up? How did you get people together? And how did you get away with this?"

Schwarzenegger had an even stronger chemistry with his mother-in-law Eunice Shriver, the sister of former President Kennedy. "Eunice was always probably hoping that her children would go into politics. Now I come along," said Schwarzenegger. "She would give me a different type of advice than Sarge. Hers was, 'This is how you get in there. Jack always picked one issue and ran with it for months.' Sarge's advice was always, 'This is what you do for people.'" Eunice Shriver would send Schwarzenegger notes on his movies, faxes full of ideas, and religious books. Eunice Shriver had founded the Special Olympics to give people with intellectual disabilities an opportunity to compete in sports. Schwarzenegger would make dozens of trips all over the world on behalf of Special Olympics.

One of his first trips was to Wisconsin, where a professor at the University of Wisconsin satellite campus in the small city of Superior subsequently invited Schwarzenegger to join the faculty as a lecturer on physical fitness. Sure, I'll come, he said, but I'd like to be able to leave with a degree. A deal was reached, with the university agreeing to accept dozens of credits Schwarzenegger had accumulated from taking English and economics classes at Santa Monica City College and UCLA Extension. Schwarzenegger completed a science class by correspondence and took a mandatory swim test in Superior. (Schwarzenegger's swim test drew so many curious students that the pool doors had to be locked to control the crowd.) He would earn a degree in international marketing and business administration in November 1979.

In return, Schwarzenegger spent a few weeks at the university in fall 1979, holding a dinner with faculty, speaking at student luncheons, and giving four ribald seminars on such topics as fitness for women and fitness for winter sports. "After the movie bit," he told students at one lunch, according to the campus paper, "I would like to try politics."

ON SEPTEMBER 16, 1983, Schwarzenegger took the oath of U.S. citizenship at the Shrine Auditorium, across the street from the campus of the University of Southern California in Los Angeles. The Shrine was a frequent site for Oscar ceremonies. Schwarzenegger dressed in a pinstriped suit and red tie, and when he returned home, he wore an American flag around his shoulders for the rest of the day. "I always believed in shooting for the top, and to become an American is like becoming a member of the winning team," he told reporters.

Before becoming a citizen, Schwarzenegger had taken an unusual step. He asked his old friend Alfred "Fredi" Gerstl to look into the possibility of his retaining Austrian citizenship. Dual citizenship could only be approved by the governor of a citizen's home province, and Styria's governor, Josef Krainer, was a friend of Gerstl's. Krainer decided that while dual citizenship was a rare privilege, typically reserved for diplomats, Schwarzenegger qualified as an unofficial envoy of Austria.

"Arnold is an American," said Gerstl. "Perhaps some of this citizenship is an illusion. But it was an illusion that was good for our country."

Even as he became an American, Schwarzenegger built new ties to the leaders of his native country. His conduit was Gerstl, a People's Party leader and a city council member in Graz. By 1987, Gerstl would earn a seat in Parliament. He eventually served twice as head of the Bundesrat, a position akin to being the majority leader of the U.S. Senate. After Gerstl took office, Schwarzenegger arranged for the donation of much of the exercise equipment in a gym used by members of Parliament.

Through Gerstl, Schwarzenegger developed a close relationship with Governor Krainer, a member of Styria's dominant political family. Krainer's father had been governor for twenty-three years after World War II. Krainer himself would spend more than fifteen years in the same office. He and Gerstl would serve as mentors and political sounding boards for Schwarzenegger. This was an invaluable resource—two wise old pols on the other side of the world who could give their frank assessment of any question. "I am familiar with, in contrast to many American politicians, both political worlds,"

Schwarzenegger told an Austrian newspaper after he entered politics. "That is a huge advantage."

Krainer was a useful mentor not only because of his position as governor, but also because he knew America. In the 1950s, he had spent a year studying at the University of Georgia on a Rotary Club scholarship. Whenever Schwarzenegger went back to Graz to visit his mother, he would drop by the Burg, the fifteenth-century imperial palace that is home to the provincial government. Sometimes Schwarzenegger and Krainer had a meal at Fredi Gerstl's apartment. "I recognized his incredible political talent, but I didn't know how interested he was," said Krainer. "I asked Fredi about it and he would say, 'Geez, I don't know.'" Krainer loved the craft of politics, and he and Schwarzenegger discussed the finer points of speechmaking. Krainer advised Schwarzenegger that it was often better to speak extemporaneously, without text or notes. Sometimes during his visits, Schwarzenegger would tease Krainer and Gerstl about being such incorrigible politicians.

Schwarzenegger did not confine his contacts to Gerstl and Krainer. One day at the Schlossberg, the mountain castle with a clock tower that dominates the center of Graz, he met the journalist Werner Kopacka, a reporter for the *Kronen Zeitung*, the biggest daily newspaper in Austria. Kopacka, also an accomplished novelist, had been a foreign exchange student in Southern California. After he and Schwarzenegger struck up their friendship, Kopacka would fly to the U.S. to receive the first Austrian interview for many of Schwarzenegger's movies. Schwarzenegger would spend hours smoking cigars with Kopacka and pumping him for the latest political tidbits from Austria. Said the journalist, "He wanted to know everything, all the scandals, all the political news, and why this politician or that one lost the elections."

As a dual citizen, Schwarzenegger showed a new willingness to involve himself directly in Austrian public life. He convinced Austrian newspapers to run long stories encouraging physical education in school, a cause he was campaigning for in the United States. He wrote letters to Austrian parents warning them of the popularity of a horrific video game called *Concentration Camp*, in which players could gas Jews, pull out gold teeth, and build empires of gas chambers.

Schwarzenegger even issued endorsements in Austrian elections, including one for Alois Mock, the leader of the People's Party, in 1983 and for Josef Riegler, a People's Party member whose pro-environment views some in his party found too extreme. But the primary beneficiary was Krainer, whom

Schwarzenegger backed in each of three re-election campaigns. In 1991, the star sent postcards to voters across Styria. "Many greetings out of LA," the cards read in German. "I'm right in the middle of a shoot for my movie and I cannot come on September 22. So therefore I am asking you for a personal favor. Please do support Governor Josef Krainer. And therefore also for a secure future for our Styria."

Given Schwarzenegger's interest in Austrian politics, a few operatives talked him up as a possibility for the Austrian presidency in 1992 and 1998. (One party official even wrote him to say he would win if he ran, Schwarzenegger recalled.) In the mid-1990s, the People's Party commissioned polls that asked about Schwarzenegger and a handful of other famous Austrians, including the tennis star Thomas Muster, as potential candidates for office. One party poll taken in Styria found Schwarzenegger was the most popular person in his home province and would be second only behind his friend Krainer, the incumbent, if he ran for governor. A Schwarzenegger candidacy "was more a story than reality," said Reinhold Lopatka, a member of Parliament and a People's Party official who promoted the idea. "But I would have liked to see it."

ONE OF SCHWARZENEGGER'S AUSTRIAN endorsements would cause him a lasting political headache. In September 1985, Schwarzenegger published a letter to Austrians supporting former United Nations Secretary General Kurt Waldheim in the 1986 presidential elections. The letter received little notice at the time. But in March 1986, an Austrian magazine and the World Jewish Council published details of Waldheim's war record. Waldheim had claimed he spent World War II studying law in Vienna while, in fact, he had been a member of a unit of the SA that had committed atrocities in wartime Yugoslavia. On April 24, 1986, the Justice Department recommended barring Waldheim from the United States.

Two days later, Schwarzenegger married Maria Shriver in Hyannisport, Massachusetts. Schwarzenegger had sent invitations to hundreds of dignitaries, including Waldheim, who did not attend but sent a gift. According to the diaries of Andy Warhol, who was there, Schwarzenegger gave a toast to Waldheim: "My friends don't want me to mention Kurt's name because of all the recent Nazi stuff and the U.N. controversy, but I love him and Maria does, too, and so thank you, Kurt." Later that summer, Schwarzenegger visited Waldheim near Salzburg, where the two men had breakfast and went for a walk, according to Austrian newspaper reports.

By then, Waldheim had won the presidency with 54 percent of the vote. After the election, Austrians closed ranks. The opposition Social Democrats defended Waldheim, saying he had been elected democratically. But Austria's president held a largely ceremonial position in which the chief responsibility was to represent the country to the world. Waldheim was an international pariah, and did not stand for re-election in 1992. Schwarzenegger would eventually disavow his toast and support of Waldheim, offering the explanation that he had not known about Waldheim's Nazi past at the time. It was true that he had originally endorsed Waldheim six months before the revelations of his record, but Schwarzenegger's disavowal did not explain his toast or his visit in the months immediately after Waldheim's record became known.

At the very least, Schwarzenegger learned a political lesson. In the 1990s, he was quick to distance himself from Jorg Haider, a provincial governor who led the far-right Freedom Party and had praised the Third Reich for its "orderly employment policy." By 1995, Haider was displaying in his office a picture of Schwarzenegger and himself that had been taken at a movie premiere, where the star was photographed shaking hands with or smiling beside dozens of people. Schwarzenegger denounced Haider's comments and declared that they were not friends. Schwarzenegger's publicist, Charlotte Parker, even began to advise the Austrian government on how to handle the public relations fallout from Haider and improve the country's image in America.

When the Museum of Tolerance in Los Angeles—affiliated with the Simon Wiesenthal Center—included Haider on a watch list of demagogues, Haider contacted Schwarzenegger, a financial supporter of the museum and the center, to protest. Schwarzenegger told Haider he belonged there and urged him to change his ways. (The Simon Wiesenthal Center had investigated his father's war record at Schwarzenegger's request. Schwarzenegger took the relationship further and became friends with Wiesenthal, the famed Nazi hunter, whom the movie star made a point of visiting when he was in Vienna.)

Even after his experiences with Waldheim and Haider, Schwarzenegger did not reduce his involvement in Austrian politics. In November 2002, the star appeared in newspaper ads supporting Wolfgang Schüssel of the People's Party for re-election as chancellor. Schwarzenegger's Austrian friends believed his continuing ties to politics in his native country whetted his appetite for such a career in America. "It is not very astonishing, not very surprising that he would think about a political career," said Albert Kaufmann, his childhood friend who ran a school in Graz for training union stewards. "He grew up around all these people who were involved. To go into politics would be almost like coming back to his roots."

SCHWARZENEGGER DID NOT LIMIT his political mentors to Shrivers and Austrians. In 1980, he had watched and admired the PBS television series *Free to Choose*, a popular primer on free market economics. Its star, the 1976 Nobel economics laureate Milton Friedman, talked extemporaneously about various economic principles while standing in settings all over the world—a tobacco field, a train station, a factory. Friedman was the leader of the Chicago School of Economics, which stressed that business cycles and inflation were determined in large part by the money supply. He had served as an informal advisor to Barry Goldwater, Richard Nixon, and Ronald Reagan—both when Reagan was governor and when he was president. Friedman knew direct democracy, having campaigned for Reagan's unsuccessful Prop 1, a budget and tax initiative, in 1973 and for the victorious Prop 13 in 1978. Friedman and his wife Rose, also an economist, turned their TV series into a best-selling book.

The Christmas of 1980, Schwarzenegger gave copies of the book, *Free to Choose*, as presents to his politically liberal friends. The gambit annoyed them and attracted the notice of *Newsweek*, which ran a short item. Bob Chitester, the PBS station manager in Erie, Pennsylvania, who had produced the series, called up Schwarzenegger and invited him to meet the Friedmans.

One evening in the spring of 1981, Schwarzenegger dropped by the Friedmans' apartment in San Francisco. From there, the couple, Schwarzenegger, and Chitester went to dinner at a tiny French restaurant and talked for three hours. "What we did discuss in detail was the logic of a free society," how markets worked, how government and politics could be best conducted, Friedman recalled. "I know we came away with a very favorable impression—the impression was about the quality of his intellect."

The economist and the movie star stayed in touch. Schwarzenegger later joined the board of directors of Chitester's non-profit organization, which produced TV programming and videos about freedom and economics. When the Friedmans and Chitester decided to update the *Free to Choose* series in the late 1980s and bring it out on videocassette, Schwarzenegger volunteered to film an introduction to Part I. He wrote the text and arranged the taping himself, sending the final result to Chitester.

Sitting at a desk in his office, with Warhol's portrait of Maria Shriver visible, Schwarzenegger talked directly into the camera. It was one of his earliest and most important political statements, using phrases that would become staples of hundreds of future addresses:

. . . Being free to choose for me means being free to make your own decisions. Being free to live your own life, pursue your own goals, chase your own rainbow without the government breathing down on your neck or standing on your shoes. For me, that meant coming here to America. Because I came from a Socialistic country where the government controls the economy. It's a place where you can hear eighteen-year-old kids already talking about their pension. But me, I wanted more. I wanted to be the best. Individualism like that is incompatible with Socialism. I felt I had to come to America. I had no money in my pocket but here I had the freedom to get it. I've been able to parlay my big muscles into big business and a big movie career. Along the way I was able to save and invest. And I watched America change. I noticed this: The more the government interfered and intervened and inserted itself into the free market, the worse the country did. But when the government stepped back and let the free enterprise system do its work, then the better we did, the more robust our economy grew, the better I did, and the better my business grew. And the more I was able to hire and help others.

Schwarzenegger's public embrace of Friedman served as a coming-out for the star among Republicans and conservative activists. He was deluged with political invitations. At first, he limited himself to a few political fund-raisers and to brief appearances at the 1984 and 1988 Republican National Conventions. "When you promote a movie, you want to win over everybody," Schwarzenegger said in explaining this early political reticence. "You try not to make political speeches. No matter what you say, there's a percentage out there that is against it. So why turn them off?"

Schwarzenegger made an exception for the Reason Foundation, a libertarian non-profit based in Los Angeles. When Reason announced a banquet to honor the financier Michael Milken with the foundation's "Free Markets and Free Minds Award, Schwarzenegger called Reason's founder Bob Poole and offered to co-chair the event. Milken, famous for using high-yield junk bonds to finance corporate takeovers, spent two years in prison after pleading guilty to securities fraud charges. But the libertarians at Reason saw him as a genius who "made possible entrepreneurship in ways unparalleled before the invention of some of his financial tools," according to the award citation. Schwarzenegger was also an admirer.

At the dinner, Schwarzenegger gave a speech about his affection for Milton Friedman, and how his own life had been possible because of America's economic freedom. The foundation sent him a subscription to *Reason* magazine and invited him to other events. Schwarzenegger later attended a handful of "Reason Forums," small luncheons of between fifty and one hundred people at which a policymaker or academic would speak. (A picture from one luncheon showed him taking notes.)

Schwarzenegger said he sought Friedman out of personal interest and praised him because of deep belief. But connecting with the economist also opened doors politically. It allowed fiscal conservatives to claim one of America's most famous movie stars as their own. Friedman himself would become one of Schwarzenegger's most persistent backers, talking up the star's intellectual prowess and political potential to anyone who would listen. "Milton sang his praises," said George Shultz, the former secretary of state to Ronald Reagan.

Friedman's blessing served as a seal of approval among Republicans. And it raised Schwarzenegger's political profile as he sought his first government post.

"Pumping Up"

On the Thursday before the 1988 presidential election, Schwarzenegger flew to Columbus, Ohio. Vice President George H. W. Bush planned to hold a rally downtown in front of the Nationwide Insurance headquarters. Jim Lorimer, a Nationwide executive and Schwarzenegger's partner in the Arnold Classic bodybuilding tournament, had invited Bush to speak. Knowing that Schwarzenegger wanted to make political contacts, Lorimer arranged for his friend to introduce the future president.

That weekend would prove crucial to Schwarzenegger's political future. "I only play the Terminator in my movies," he told a crowd of ten thousand. "But when it comes to America's future, Michael Dukakis will be the real Terminator." The vice president was impressed, though a little miffed when half his audience drifted away once Schwarzenegger finished speaking.

Bush asked Schwarzenegger to accompany him to campaign stops in Illinois and New Jersey. On Air Force 2, the vice president, a fervent sportsman, chatted with Schwarzenegger about the sad state of American physical fitness. Schwarzenegger told him: If I can be of any help, let me know.

After a New York City doctor published a headline-making study in 1955 showing that European children were far fitter than their American counterparts, President Dwight D. Eisenhower established what would become the President's Council on Physical Fitness and Sports to do something about it.

Schwarzenegger wanted to be the council's chairman, and, after Bush's election in 1988, lobbied discreetly for the post. He sent a congratulatory telegram to the new president and scheduled a meeting with political consultant Bob Teeter at the Bush transition office. When Teeter didn't show, Schwarzenegger sat down with Jim Pinkerton, the aide running the domestic policy operation. Pinkerton thought Schwarzenegger was bright, and pressed for the star to get the post. Pinkerton, however, was not Schwarzenegger's foremost advocate.

Shortly after the inauguration, Eunice Shriver began her own personal letter-writing campaign on Schwarzenegger's behalf (but without his knowledge, he said). On March 13, 1989, Shriver wrote President Bush "to suggest that Arnold Schwarzenegger be appointed as the chairman" and to point out he was the "number one star" in the United States. Bush, well-known for connecting with people through notes, replied four days later with a letter thanking Schwarzenegger's mother-in-law for "recommending our man Conan," though he made no promises.

Some in the White House worried about Schwarzenegger's past. In June, a White House aide tracked him down in Mexico City to ask if he had used steroids. Schwarzenegger explained matter-of-factly that he had done so during his bodybuilding career. Later, an official in the White House personnel office flagged a January 1988 profile in *Playboy* that mentioned Schwarzenegger's love of cigars. (Schwarzenegger temporarily adopted a new policy: no cigar smoking when cameras were around.)

Seeking to stop the appointment, the National Coalition on Television Violence sent the White House a "full accounting of his violence"—Schwarzenegger averaged a staggering 109 violent acts per screen hour. The Texas Annual Conference of the United Methodist Church called him "a very poor role model for children, considering the genre of movies in which he has starred where violence and bloodshed abound and violent retribution is the standard resolution of human conflict." Letters opposing the appointment outnumbered letters in support by a ratio of five to one.

But Eunice Shriver also kept writing letters. On June 15, she sent a handwritten note singing Schwarzenegger's praises and enclosing a resume that included his fitness books and his travel for the Special Olympics. A few weeks later, she contacted White House Chief of Staff John Sununu to suggest Schwarzenegger could be co-chairman with the tennis player Chris Evert.

When no announcement was forthcoming, Shriver wrote Sununu on November 20, 1989: "Over a year has passed since serious positive feelings were expressed by Arnold to the president that he would like to perform a significant public service." After that letter, President Bush himself stepped in and ended the internal debate. On January 22, 1990, the president appointed Schwarzenegger as sole chairman. The star would treat the unpaid position not as a post to be held, but as a campaign to be won.

A WEEK AFTER THE ANNOUNCEMENT, Schwarzenegger called University of California–San Diego physical education professor John Cates at home on a Saturday morning. Schwarzenegger asked if Cates could immediately drive to Los Angeles to talk.

Schwarzenegger knew Cates only by reputation. In 1980, Cates had taken a sabbatical and driven around the country in a twenty-one-foot camper to conduct a comprehensive study of American fitness. His main finding—twenty years before childhood obesity became a hot topic—was that schools were reducing physical education requirements at a time when 50 percent of American children were showing cardiac risk factors by the fifth grade.

In Schwarzenegger's offices, the star greeted Cates in a Hawaiian shirt and flip flops. What can I do as chairman of the president's council to make a national impact? What, he asked, can the president do?

Nothing, Cates replied firmly.

Education, Cates explained, was a local and state function, not a federal concern. And most states didn't even bother to test and compile results on the fitness of their students. If Schwarzenegger was serious about making an impact, he would have to reach out to all fifty states, Cates said.

Schwarzenegger pointed out that the council had a small budget: just $1.5 million a year, which paid for a staff in Washington. Where would the muscle come from to make a difference in the states? Cates said that the natural partner would be the American Alliance for Health, Physical Education, Recreation and Dance, an organization of physical education and other teachers. This teachers' alliance had a chapter in each state, but its leaders did not get along with the president's council.

Cates told Schwarzenegger that PE teachers thought the fitness award given to students by the president's council was antiquated. Cates did not mention that some of these teachers were already mocking Schwarzenegger's appointment and the exercise advice he'd given in his books. (Physiologists didn't believe in deep knee lunges anymore.) Cates said that if Schwarzenegger wanted to improve the council's reputation, he should go to the alliance's national convention in New Orleans at the end of the month.

"OK, we're going to do this," Schwarzenegger declared. "And we're going to go to all fifty states."

Cates wasn't sure at first how seriously to take Schwarzenegger. A week later, the star called and said he wanted to hire Cates as his assistant. The professor turned him down. He had just completed a two-year leave. Within hours, Cates had a phone call from the University of California–San Diego Chancellor Richard Atkinson. You'll never guess who I just heard from, Atkinson said. Schwarzenegger had offered to pay Cates's salary, and do just about anything else the university needed. Cates could not refuse.

THREE WEEKS LATER, Schwarzenegger took the stage at the alliance convention in New Orleans. Cates, an alliance member, had to make a special request to get the star added to the schedule. In the politics of physical education, it was a Nixon-goes-to-China moment.

Schwarzenegger said the president's council would bury the hatchet with the alliance and cooperate with the teachers in developing a single fitness test for all children. "It doesn't make sense if we go in different directions, or have different programs, or have different testing or different awards," he said. "All this is going to hold us back. What we have to do is sit down and talk about the ways we are going to do all those things together." He promised publicly to visit all fifty states to push for more physical education. Then Schwarzenegger got a standing ovation.

Schwarzenegger outlined his vision for the tour in a July 24, 1990 memo, a useful illustration of how he plans. He wanted to follow a similar schedule in each state so he could hone his message through repetition. He wanted to meet each governor, preferably in a relaxed setting. He wanted to lead a public rally on behalf of youth fitness and hold a closed-door meeting with the state school superintendent and other education leaders. During this "youth fitness summit," he would ask those in attendance to commit to daily, mandatory P. E. with a trained teacher. And, he added, "it is important that we derive a high media visibility throughout this trip."

The president's council couldn't afford such a trip. Schwarzenegger wanted to hit two states a day. So he would fly in his own jet and pay the food and lodging costs of his own staff.

SCHWARZENEGGER TREATED these visits with the care of a diplomat negotiating an arms control treaty. He had Cates research personal details about each governor so he could start off on the right foot. Schwarzenegger insisted that the meetings had nothing to do with any political ambitions of his own, but the opportunity to sit and talk with forty-nine of the fifty governors—the governor of Arkansas was too busy getting elected president to see Schwarzenegger—would prove invaluable. He had breakfasts in the homes of Governor John Ashcroft of Missouri, Governor Mike Hayden of Kansas, and Governor Tommy Thompson of Wisconsin.

Schwarzenegger hit it off with Indiana Governor Evan Bayh, who followed up with a detailed letter and ultimately added fitness testing in the state. Governor Ann Richards of Texas simply could not contain herself around the star. "Look at those buns," she said into an open microphone, when Schwarzenegger bent over to pick up a note card he had dropped. With New York Governor Mario Cuomo, Schwarzenegger talked about teen pregnancy, Cuomo's habit of playing basketball with local kids, and the perils of being a Kennedy in-law. (Cuomo's son had recently married a Kennedy.)

A few governors did not click with Schwarzenegger. Virginia's Douglas Wilder seemed condescending. Nevada's Bob Miller, who enjoyed basketball, took Schwarzenegger out to play in his driveway even though the star wasn't much of a hoopster. Cates told Schwarzenegger later that the governor meant no offense and that Miller was just an old ballplayer who wanted to show off his skills. "But I don't take you into the weight room," Schwarzenegger told Cates.

SCHWARZENEGGER HAD INFORMED President Bush of his plans for a fifty-state tour during an afternoon meeting in the Oval Office on February 27, 1990. Bush made one suggestion: In each state, he should try to visit a school in a poor neighborhood.

Schwarzenegger wanted to bring the governors along on these school visits. To lure them, he agreed to do a press conference with each governor only if it was at a school. He invariably used the opportunity to force the governor to commit publicly to expanding physical education; Cates tracked down tapes of the event so Schwarzenegger had video evidence he could use to enforce these gubernatorial pledges.

His stop at Rosecrest Elementary in Salt Lake City, Utah, was typical. As Schwarzenegger led students through fitness stations that tested strength, balance, agility, coordination, cardiovascular endurance, eye-hand coordination, and flexibility, he asked reporters, "Now how could you expect an English teacher to set up exercises like this? Wouldn't it be better to have a trained physical education teacher?"

Schwarzenegger held a rally after each school visit. A Pump Up With Arnold fitness festival in Indianapolis drew four thousand youngsters. He attracted fifteen thousand to a rally at Joe Louis Arena in Detroit, eleven thousand to the Vanderbilt University gym in Nashville, and fifty thousand to Independence Stadium in Shreveport, Louisiana. Before concluding a state visit, Schwarzenegger would convene an hour-long summit of twenty-five leaders of state agencies and non-profit groups. Schwarzenegger began each meeting by reciting statistics Cates had turned up about the particular state's lack of physical education. Then he asked the group to lobby the legislature to mandate youth fitness tests and hire more physical education teachers. Schwarzenegger was careful to follow up. As his plane departed from each state, Cates would draft a letter with a list of five things the governor could do to boost health and fitness. Cates would send the missives by FedEx so they would arrive the very next day.

Schwarzenegger also sent surveys to officials who attended the fitness summits. In about a quarter of the states, Schwarzenegger's visits had little measurable impact. But in most of the states, the groups continued to meet. Some legislation resulted, much of it requiring more fitness testing. In a dozen states, Schwarzenegger's visits prompted the formation of a Governor's Council on Physical Fitness & Sports. In effect, Schwarzenegger had established lobbying groups for physical education.

THE TOUR SEEMED TO CONFIRM Schwarzenegger's political potential in Bush's eyes, and the president went out of his way to promote his fitness chairman. When Schwarzenegger asked the president to write a letter of welcome to the Arnold Classic bodybuilding tournament, Bush fulfilled the request against the advice of the White House counsel's office. (One lawyer made a note on a copy of the outgoing letter: "Is this presidential?") Bush sent personal notes and photographs to Schwarzenegger's mother back in Austria. At one point, the president objected to a *Parade* magazine piece on his workout routine because it did not include a picture of Schwarzenegger exercising with him.

Twice Schwarzenegger joined the president at Camp David—in March 1989 and January 1991. At the White House, the president let Schwarzenegger have the run of the South Lawn to put on a fitness promotion, the Great American Workout. Schwarzenegger hired his own team of event producers, a decision that annoyed White House staffers who believed they knew how to put on a massive party. Bush himself showed up on the South Lawn to run through the eleven fitness stations and greet athletes such as Chicago Cubs Hall of Famer Ernie Banks and Schwarzenegger celebrity friends such as comedian Kevin Nealon, who played the Arnold-worshipping bodybuilder Franz on *Saturday Night Live*.

In classic Hollywood fashion, the star treated the workout as a tent pole to which he attached a variety of deals and corporate sponsorships. The White House expressed concern about the event's sponsors. Did Coca Cola, which provided fruit juice for the occasion, represent fitness? Reebok paid $250,000 to sponsor the first workout, but the White House stopped the shoe company from distributing Great American Workout warm-up suits on the lawn because the clothing came with a Reebok logo. For the 1991 and 1992 Great American Workouts, the White House counsel blocked Schwarzenegger from allowing Planet Hollywood, a restaurant chain in which he had shares, to add its logo to Great American Workout T-shirts. The shirts also included the presidential seal, which could not be associated with a commercial entity.

IN THIS WAY AND OTHERS, Schwarzenegger's tenure at the fitness council offered a preview of the politician he would become. In attacking any problem, Schwarzenegger looked for ways to use his marketing skills to forge compromises. When he ran into trouble, it often was because he had gone too far, either in marketing or in compromising.

Schwarzenegger's biggest disappointment at the fitness council demonstrated this weakness. He had taken on the ambitious goal of creating a single fitness test that would be used by all schools around the country. To do that, he had to combine the fitness test administered by the alliance of the PE, dance, and recreation teachers, and the president's council's test. Their differences might seem minor, but the two groups sat on the opposite ends of a philosophical divide. The more liberal teachers' alliance rewarded students who demonstrated they were healthy, while the more conservative members of the president's council gave their awards to students who showed physical excellence.

Schwarzenegger, playing a centrist role, tried to forge a single, compromise test. One common test for children could be promoted more easily than two competing tests, thus raising awareness and convincing more children to have their fitness tested, he argued.

After more than a year, Schwarzenegger signed an agreement under which the teachers' alliance would help administer a single fitness test. The test would use some of the exercises of the president's council, but base awards on improvement. Both an elite athlete and a disabled child could take the same test. It was a compromise he planned to announce in the spring of 1992.

But, as part of the deal, Schwarzenegger granted the teachers' alliance the right to create brochures and products using the seal of the president's council. The sales of such products would help defray the costs of administering the test. That bit of marketing went a step too far. He had licensed the use of the president's name to physical education teachers.

Ash Hayes, a former physical education instructor at UCLA who had served as executive director of the president's council, called White House Chief of Staff Samuel Skinner to protest Schwarzenegger's new deal. Hayes followed up in late March 1992 with a two-page, confidential letter.

In the letter, Hayes argued that the council would "be entering into an agreement with a private corporation which will use the identity of the president of the United States to let that corporation sell publications, materials, and awards." That last objection broke up the deal, as Schwarzenegger's nemesis—the White House counsel's office—challenged the arrangement. Schwarzenegger and the teachers' alliance tried to revive it, but could not.

THAT WAS NOT SCHWARZENEGGER'S only disappointment with the administration. The U.S. Department of Agriculture had rebuffed his efforts to remove fatty foods from the federal school lunch program. Schwarzenegger also complained to the president that Bush's education policy, called Goals

2000, did not include physical education among its stated objectives. Schwarzenegger told Bush that he had met with Secretary of Education Lamar Alexander, who said the omission was an oversight and would be corrected. "We have yet to see any evidence of that and our frustration is mounting," Schwarzenegger wrote to Bush on October 29, 1991.

The White House did not add physical education to the education goals. But Bush's policy aides suggested ways for Schwarzenegger to sell the administration's policy on education and health care. A January 21, 1992, memo by White House policymakers suggested that Schwarzenegger give speeches on behalf of legislation Bush supported to expand access to health insurance. "An upbeat policy needs upbeat messengers," the two-page memo said. "There is of course the possibility that the Schwarzenegger touch on a weighty issue such as health care will seem jejune and unserious—too Hollywood. But it is possible to worry too much about courting ridicule or diminishing the seriousness of our health care proposals by using the Terminator as one of our spokesmen."

On education, Jim Pinkerton and Roger Porter, domestic policy advisors to the president, drew up a plan to create "Arnold's Corps." The corps would visit communities and schools that adopted Bush's Goals 2000 strategy and would encourage middle schools to remain open after school hours and provide a venue for fitness activities. As part of the effort, laid out in a memo on August 28, 1992, Schwarzenegger would participate in developing a pilot school voucher program called the "GI bill for kids." He also would take part in a daily Department of Education conference call. Pinkerton and Porter argued that Schwarzenegger could reach inner-city audiences without interference from liberal members of Congress.

Schwarzenegger agreed to participate, but never got the chance. These education and health care policies were to be rolled out in the second term Bush didn't win. In 1992, Schwarzenegger campaigned for Bush in New Hampshire and in Columbus, Ohio. "The *Terminator* star stirred much more excitement than the liberator of Kuwait could evoke," David Broder of the *Washington Post* wrote about the New Hampshire appearance. "Bush normally looks and sounds like a vigorous leader, but next to Schwarzenegger he—like most mere mortals—seemed a shrimp." (Both men were officially listed at 6 feet 2 inches.)

Schwarzenegger did not like the socially conservative rhetoric of the party and correctly predicted Bush's defeat. After hearing of Vice President Dan Quayle's May 1992 speech denouncing the TV show *Murphy Brown*, whose lead character had a child out of wedlock, Schwarzenegger called up Pinkerton and said, "with real conviction, 'This is a terrible speech. This is going to destroy you in California,'" recalled Pinkerton.

SCHWARZENEGGER WAS EAGER to continue his fitness work, even as the Republican president left office. Bush was the first major politician to understand Schwarzenegger's potential. His fitness chairmanship helped bring him to the notice of the second.

During his tour of the states, Schwarzenegger had done a press conference with California's new governor, Pete Wilson. That night, Wilson's chief of staff Bob White arranged for Biba, an Italian restaurant in Sacramento, to open late to host a private dinner for Schwarzenegger, Wilson, the governor's wife Gayle, and White.

"I have to tell you I have increased respect for your new job as Governor of California," Schwarzenegger wrote Wilson two days later. "It sounds very difficult and complicated and makes me all the more appreciative of the time you and Gayle gave me to express the issues and my concerns surrounding the youth fitness problem in our state. Thank you again, Pete, for your time, your energy, and your dedication. Keep pumping!"

Schwarzenegger asked Wilson to start a Governor's Council on Physical Fitness and Sports in the state, but the governor said the state didn't have the money. Schwarzenegger said he would provide the funds. In 1993, he launched the governor's council as a private, non-profit corporation, sponsored by Disney and two health-care concerns, Kaiser Permanente and Blue Cross of California. Cates agreed to become the new council's executive director. Schwarzenegger was chairman.

The job taught Schwarzenegger some of the basics of Sacramento, including the difference between budgets and appropriations. State law required fitness testing in three grades, but the state department of education—citing a lack of funds and staff—had stopped compiling and disseminating the test results. Schwarzenegger spent three years pushing for a $750,000 appropriation to pay for processing the data. He did better with a series of public events that promoted fitness and benefited the governor. During one event, the Great California Workout on the west steps of the Capitol, Schwarzenegger drew Wilson's attention to the state seal on the ground.

"That's it, governor," Schwarzenegger whispered. "That's the photo op."

Within seconds, Schwarzenegger had coaxed Wilson, an ex-marine, into a push-up contest on the state seal. The governor's aides looked mortified. But the picture appeared in newspapers across the state and all over the world. Schwarzenegger even had the good grace to lose. Wilson had been mayor of San Diego, a U.S. senator, and he would serve two terms as governor. But he envied Schwarzenegger's political talent and the star's love of political glad-handing. At one fund-raiser, Wilson turned to apologize to Schwarzenegger after the star was stuck greeting guests for more than two hours.

"Why are you sorry?" Schwarzenegger asked. "I enjoyed it."

"What the hell is the matter with you?" the governor asked.

Schwarzenegger familiarized himself with the state's political elite. (Spotting the skinny, light-haired lieutenant governor Gray Davis inside the capitol, Schwarzenegger remarked, "He looks like a piece of chalk.") Wilson talked up the possibility of a Schwarzenegger candidacy for governor. In 1994, at the eightieth birthday party for the fitness pioneer Jack LaLanne, Wilson told guests including Schwarzenegger: "I'd like to see you run for governor, Arnold. Someone who has played *Kindergarten Cop* already has the requisite experience to deal with the legislature."

DURING HIS CHAIRMANSHIP at the President's Council on Physical Fitness, Schwarzenegger met Danny Hernandez, the director of Hollenbeck Youth Center in Boyle Heights, a Latino neighborhood east of downtown Los Angeles. Hernandez had been raised by his mother in the streets and neighborhoods around his center. After the passage of Prop 13, the Los Angeles Police Department, whose officers ran the youth center, could no longer spare the bodies to staff it. Local businesses in Boyle Heights hired Hernandez to take over the center, which consisted of a gym and a boxing ring on First Street. Hernandez steadily raised money to expand, building offices, computer labs, and more gym space.

Over the objections of publicist Charlotte Parker, who thought the star was over-committed, Schwarzenegger agreed to be Hollenbeck's 1991 Man of the Year. As part of his duties, Schwarzenegger attended the opening of the Inner City Games—a brand new venture for Hernandez. In an effort to diminish gang violence and feuding, he had brought children together from various neighborhoods of East Los Angeles. Hernandez wanted to make the Inner City Games an annual event. Early in 1992, he invited Schwarzenegger to serve as commissioner for the games. The star did not respond at first.

On April 29, 1992, a jury in suburban Simi Valley acquitted three white Los Angeles police officers of using excessive force in the 1991 beating of motorist Rodney King. A fourth officer was acquitted of all but one charge. Within hours of the verdict, rioting began throughout greater Los Angeles. Over five days, fifty-four people died and more than two thousand were injured. It was the deadliest urban race riot since the Civil War.

When the rioting broke out, Schwarzenegger was on his way from Ohio—the last stop on his fifty-state tour—to Washington for a promotional workout and a speech to the National Press Club. He called Hernandez and invited him to a meeting the following week at his new Main Street office in Santa Monica. Schwarzenegger asked if it was possible to make the Inner City Games a citywide event. Hernandez said he would find out. He spent the next few weeks securing written commitments from the mayor, police department, and the University of Southern California to help put on citywide games.

Schwarzenegger gave the Inner City Games $25,000 of his own money and helped Hernandez raise another $400,000. Tens of thousands of children took part in the October 1992 games. Afterward, Schwarzenegger began to spend more time in the neighborhoods around the Hollenbeck Youth Center. He showed up at community award dinners, hit ceremonial pitches at softball tournaments, and played Santa Claus in a Christmas parade. Informal in private, Schwarzenegger seemed stiff by the standards of the barrio. Hernandez encouraged him to hug people on the street rather than shaking hands. "I would tell him, 'People around here want to touch you to know you're real,'" Hernandez said.

Schwarzenegger convinced Hernandez that the Inner City Games had potential as a national movement. In December 1992, they formed an Inner City Games Foundation.

In 1994, Schwarzenegger asked his friend Bonnie Reiss, an entertainment lawyer and environmental activist, to lead the expansion. Reiss would be the first major hire of his new career in public service. Schwarzenegger and Reiss had good chemistry, which was based on their different personalities. Where Schwarzenegger projected Austro-Californian cool, Reiss talked like a New York express train.

A Democrat, Reiss had met Maria Shriver in the late 1970s while working for Senator Teddy Kennedy. In 1979, when Kennedy's presidential campaign brought her to Southern California, Reiss met Shriver's boyfriend, Schwarzenegger. He was a Republican, but that did not stop Reiss from using him to help the campaign. Late in 1979, Shriver and Reiss were trying to build a crowd for a "young people's fund-raiser" at a roller disco club in Hollywood. "We talked him into walking down Venice Beach and gathering a crowd," recalled Reiss. "He let us walk twenty feet behind him and try to sell fund-raiser tickets to the people following him down the beach."

Using celebrity for political ends was a Reiss specialty. While practicing entertainment law in Southern California, she helped found the Hollywood Women's Political Committee. She later gave up her law practice to start the Earth Communications Office (ECO), which she called the "media component of the global environmental movement." Through ECO, Reiss labored to convince actors, directors, producers, writers, musicians, and the media to embrace environmental causes. She had environmental story lines slipped into TV sitcoms, produced trailers with environmental themes for movie theaters, and pushed the studios to establish recycling programs. (A typical triumph was convincing the makers of the TV show *Beverly Hills 90210* to put a "Save the Rain Forest" poster on the bedroom wall of one character.) Reiss's five years as ECO's president made her an expert on leveraging celebrity power and entertainment marketing in the service of political causes.

To fund the Inner City Games expansion, Schwarzenegger and Reiss decided to start affiliates in cities with high poverty—and a Planet Hollywood. The restaurant openings were turned into Inner City Games fund-raisers. By 1997, twelve cities had organized Inner City Games. There would eventually be fifteen in all.

Each Inner City Games affiliate signed a two-year licensing agreement with the Los Angeles headquarters and received about $200,000 a year. Much of that money came from the $15 million donated by General Motors in return for Schwarzenegger's promotion of the Hummer, the street-legal model of the military's four-wheel-drive Humvee. (In the late 1980s, Schwarzenegger had traveled to Indiana to convince Humvee's manufacturer to make a version he could drive legally on the streets of Los Angeles, sparking the design of the civilian Hummer.) Schwarzenegger insisted affiliates be free to fashion their own programs. When Reiss asked at a dinner with Eunice Shriver and him if there should be more central control, Reiss recalled, "he started in with me, 'That's your Democratic way of thinking.'"

But when some affiliates launched after-school programs that combined sports with education, Schwarzenegger liked that direction so much he embraced it. By 2000, the Inner City Games was attaching a key condition to the license renewals of its affiliates: they had to start after-school programs. Ironically, Danny Hernandez, the Inner City Games founder, declined to sign the agreement and instead focused his program on sports.

Within three years, the national Inner City Games would transform itself into a provider of after-school programs and take on a new name: After-School All-Stars. The program developed evaluations and tracked the students' grades and test scores. To expand, many of Schwarzenegger's affiliates came to depend on government for funding and sites.

Schwarzenegger felt the pull of government himself. Even if much of the public did not realize it, he had nurtured his own sideline career in politics and public service for more than a decade. If he wanted to run for office himself, the time had arrived to plan a transition.

CHAPTER 5

"Authenticity"

SCHWARZENEGGER HAD TWO hours before he had to confront the devil. That left time enough to stare down one of California's most experienced political operatives.

Bob White, the longtime right hand of former Governor Pete Wilson, had come to know Schwarzenegger when the star created the governor's council to promote physical fitness on Wilson's behalf. When Wilson departed the governorship after two terms at the end of 1998, Schwarzenegger asked White to stay in touch. A few months later, in early 1999, Schwarzenegger got a note from White about the new political strategy company he'd put together. The star responded by inviting White down from Sacramento for a visit on the set of *End of Days*, which was filming in Los Angeles.

End of Days was Schwarzenegger's first film after two difficult years. He had heart valve replacement surgery in 1997, and in August 1998, his mother collapsed and died while visiting his father's grave in the Austrian town of Weiz, north of Graz. In this comeback role, Schwarzenegger, slimmer and less muscled, played Jericho, a suicidal security guard with a drinking problem. In the final hours before the new millennium, he ends up in a battle against Satan, played by Gabriel Byrne, who seeks to mate with a young woman who will give birth to the Antichrist and usher in the end of civilization. Schwarzenegger alone stands in the devil's way.

White and a longtime associate, Camden McEfee, were ushered into Schwarzenegger's trailer, parked outside the St. Vincent de Paul Roman Catholic Church near the University of Southern California campus. Schwarzenegger took a seat in a chair next to a small table while his guests sat on the trailer's small sofa.

"So what's going on?" Schwarzenegger asked.

The previous year, Californians had elected a Democrat as governor for the first time since 1978. That governor, Gray Davis, was relatively popular. The state had a massive budget surplus, the product of a strong economy and the taxes that Silicon Valley executives were paying on huge profits.

White began by covering the state of Republican politics nationally. The consultant also laid out how California was governed and the structure of the state legislature, and he named some of the key players. White was trying to start a conversation about Schwarzenegger's political future. The actor stayed silent for more than fifteen minutes. "It was not clear to me: what was his agenda?" Schwarzenegger recalled. "Was he trying to say that we need you to run?"

The Republicans are in trouble, Schwarzenegger finally declared. To understand why, consider the movie business. Politics is not unlike marketing a movie, Schwarzenegger said. Politicians need to ask themselves these questions: What is their story? What is their concept? Now, the Monica Lewinsky scandal was a story, Schwarzenegger said, but it was not something the party could sell. "It was politically motivated rather than organic," Schwarzenegger said. Impeachment had nothing to do with people's aspirations and dreams. His own movies, Schwarzenegger said with a note of pride, reached young people because the stories appealed to the imagination.

If Schwarzenegger believed that the party had lost its way, White asked, what was he prepared to do about it? Did the actor want to make a difference in California? The state needed new leadership. Schwarzenegger couldn't sit on the sidelines. He had already done so much public service and political work that his name was on the lips of Republicans across the state.

"California needs you," White said.

Schwarzenegger could run for office, White suggested. He could sponsor initiative campaigns. White could put together a plan to accomplish his political goals. For most politically ambitious men, such an offer from a leading political powerbroker would be impossible to resist. Schwarzenegger balked. He suggested instead that the state Republican party could conduct polling to better understand its troubles.

White pushed back. To change California, Schwarzenegger would have to build his own organization, whether he ran for office or not. After ninety minutes of discussion, Schwarzenegger still would not commit to any future plans.

The actor was due on the set soon, but he offered his guests a quick tour. They walked through the church, which was wired with special effects. In the climactic confrontation of Arnold versus Devil, candles would explode like firecrackers. Statues would come to life. The roof would cave in.

White and McEfee walked back out into the Los Angeles sunshine. Schwarzenegger would stay and face the devil alone.

LATER IN 1999, White sent Schwarzenegger a reading list on California politics, a copy of the *California Political Almanac*, and a *Los Angeles Times* story summarizing twenty-one ballot measures facing state voters in March

2000. The actor began a subscription to *California Journal*, a magazine about state history and government, through his company name, Oak Productions. (His bodybuilding nickname had been "the Austrian Oak.") Occasionally, Schwarzenegger would call White or former Governor Wilson to chat about politics, but the discussions were rarely serious. He spent the end of the year relentlessly promoting *End of Days*, a box office disappointment that nonetheless made him $25 million by independent accounts. He devoted 2000 to the *The Sixth Day*, a cloning picture in which Schwarzenegger battled himself—literally. Its box office take was less than that of *End of Days*.

SCHWARZENEGGER FELT A GROWING frustration as he read about new problems with California's budget, economy, and electricity grid. "It was like wherever you turned you heard one bad news after the next," he said. "I just had this feeling all of a sudden where I started thinking, 'We need change, we can't continue this way.'" In press interviews, he kept talking like a potential candidate. He told *Talk* magazine: "The possibility is there. Because I felt it inside. I feel there are a lot of people in politics that are standing still and not doing enough. And there's a vacuum. Therefore I can move in." He appeared on the cover of *George* magazine dressed as George Washington riding a motorcycle. Schwarzenegger sent copies of the magazine to friends with a note that read, "What now?"

Schwarzenegger seemed to believe that by broadcasting his interest in politics, he would prepare the public for a possible run. But political professionals saw this as loose talk that invited attacks. Why would he make himself a target?

White got an answer on January 2, 2001. Schwarzenegger's office called to invite him to lunch the following week in Los Angeles. White met Schwarzenegger at 1 p.m. at Shutters on the Beach, a hotel in Santa Monica.

Schwarzenegger, in an open-collared shirt and sunglasses, ordered grilled fish and vegetables. White ordered a cobb salad. All that bacon, cheese, and avocado brought a look of disapproval from Schwarzenegger, who displayed what would become a minor political liability. He could not stop himself from commenting on the health habits and bodies of others. Look at what you just ordered, Schwarzenegger said as he gestured in the general direction of White's gut. That's why you look like that.

Nutritional advice aside, Schwarzenegger picked up the conversation right where he had left off more than a year earlier on the set of *End of Days*. Schwarzenegger said he wanted to see a plan for how he might enter politics. He said he was unhappy with the direction of the state, which had an electricity shortage that would worsen in the coming summer. Governor Davis had taken the symbolic step of turning off the capitol Christmas tree lights just minutes after he lit them.

White replied that while he had managed campaigns, he was not a campaign strategist. To go forward, Schwarzenegger would need advice from other political professionals with expertise in media relations, advertising, polling, and creating a message.

THE NEXT DAY, White was on the phone to George Gorton. "Would you like to meet Arnold Schwarzenegger?" White asked. White had known Gorton for more than thirty years; together they had handled nearly all of Wilson's campaigns. Gorton understood public policy better than many consultants and was careful not to run cookie-cutter campaigns. He would craft a plan that fit Schwarzenegger's unique attributes, White was sure.

Gorton stood out among the clean-cut young men and women who had surrounded Wilson. The consultant sported a goatee, fashionable clothes, and at times sought the spotlight. After the failure of Wilson's presidential campaign in 1995, Gorton had jetted off to Moscow on what was supposed to be a secret mission to help Russian President Boris Yeltsin win re-election. The story would be turned into a movie in which the beanpole Jeff Goldblum played the far shorter Gorton.

Gorton had at least two things in common with Schwarzenegger. Both men had lived briefly in Munich during the 1960s—Gorton as a college student and Schwarzenegger as a gym manager and young bodybuilder. And each had been attracted to politics by the speeches of Richard Nixon. As an eighth grader in Redlands, sixty-five miles east of Los Angeles, Gorton had played Nixon in a reenactment of the Nixon-Kennedy debate. Through high school and college, Gorton rose high in the ranks of young Republicans. He came to the attention of Nixon's camp, which hired him as national college director on the 1972 re-election campaign. Gorton, then twenty-five, won notice for his organizational skills and his flair. After the election, Bob Woodward of the *Washington Post* reported that Gorton had paid college students and others to infiltrate radical groups that demonstrated at the Republican convention in Miami as well as a contingent of Quakers who maintained a twenty-four-hour-a-day vigil in front of the White House. Woodward's disclosure ended Gorton's career in Washington politics.

By the late 1970s, Gorton had returned to California and reinvented himself as a Republican fund-raiser. In 1982, Wilson put him in charge of the then–San Diego mayor's campaign for a U.S. Senate seat. Gorton helped Wilson pull off an upset of Governor Jerry Brown, who was seeking to leave Sacramento for Washington. Gorton worked for Wilson for years, both in candidate races and in the various initiative campaigns Wilson supported. As much as any strategist in the country, Gorton knew how to use direct democracy to help candidates for higher office.

Within a week of White's call, Gorton was sitting in Schwarzenegger's Santa Monica offices. Less than five minutes into the meeting, the phone rang. "I better take it," Schwarzenegger told his guest. "It's Nelson Mandela," whom Schwarzenegger had met while traveling on behalf of the Special Olympics.

Gorton immediately recognized Schwarzenegger's greatest political asset. In a state of more than thirty-five million people speaking more than one hundred languages and scattered over rural areas and a half-dozen major cities, the international icon was one of the few names every voter knew. The consultant saw drawbacks, too. The actor was smart, but held strong opinions on issues about which he knew little. Gorton realized that Schwarzenegger wasn't interested in developing a conventional set of political principles. What he did have was an elaborate and detailed philosophy of life. In a nutshell, Schwarzenegger thought that anyone could do anything if given the opportunity. He believed that his philosophy, based on his experiences as an immigrant, bodybuilder, businessman, and movie star, could be applied to governing the state.

When Schwarzenegger asked for advice, Gorton stalled and said he wanted to observe the star speaking in public before making suggestions. Gorton later tagged along to a Schwarzenegger appearance at Danny Hernandez's Hollenbeck Youth Center. Gorton arrived to find nineteen television camera crews.

He was overwhelmed. "With Pete it was three cameras, you're hot! Five—unheard-of! Six? Never happens!"

The TV reporters wanted Schwarzenegger for their live reports at *Live at 5!* Most political figures dream of such coverage. Gorton approached Schwarzenegger, who was watching a youth basketball game on the gymnasium court.

Come on, come on, Gorton beckoned to Schwarzenegger. It's time to do your interviews.

The kids aren't finished with the basketball game, the star replied.

Arnold, Gorton said desperately, these TV crews want to broadcast your message to millions of people right now.

"They'll wait."

They did, breaking into the middle of their broadcasts to show Schwarzenegger. Gorton watched the press conference from the side of a bank of TV cameras, mesmerized by Schwarzenegger's skill in answering questions without deviating from his message. Gorton decided then and there he would advise the star.

As it turned out, Schwarzenegger was at least as interested in giving advice as receiving it. When he found out Gorton's wife Kiki was an actress, he offered her a small part in a movie. And George, Schwarzenegger thought, could improve his personal style. He should calm down. And stop taking everything too seriously. "George," he commanded, "lighten up."

OFFICIALLY, Schwarzenegger was working with Gorton and White. That did not mean they could control him. During the first week of February 2001, the strategists sent Schwarzenegger negative press clippings on Governor Davis to whet his appetite. The tactic worked a bit too well. From his trailer on the set of *Collateral Damage*, a movie in which he played a Los Angeles firefighter whose family is killed by terrorists, Schwarzenegger called *Los Angeles Times* political columnist George Skelton to suggest he might challenge the governor in 2002.

"I've thought about it many times because I love politics," he told Skelton. "The bottom line is if Davis goes on the way he is . . . if he doesn't keep his promises on all those issues—energy, environment, schools, health care—then you've got to say, 'OK, there's room for someone else.'"

Skelton's scoop was picked up by newspapers, radio stations, and TV networks around the world. Historians recalled not just Reagan but the California political careers of Upton Sinclair (who lost the governor's race in 1934); the actress Helen Gahagan Douglas, who served in Congress before losing a Senate race to Richard Nixon in 1950; and the song-and-dance man George Murphy, who served one term in the U.S. Senate from 1964 to 1970.

Garry South, Davis's top political consultant, was unnerved by the column. He had asked about Schwarzenegger in polls testing a theoretical 2002 gubernatorial match-up with his client. Davis won easily, but South was worried Schwarzenegger could become a political phenomenon if left unchecked. "If we did not provide instant and very powerful blowback on this guy, he could get started and we could never stop him," South said.

South had noticed an item on the Internet previewing an upcoming exposé on Schwarzenegger in the March issue of *Premiere*, an entertainment magazine. South had never heard of the magazine before. But after the Skelton column, South bought a copy of the March issue at his neighborhood newsstand.

The article was a gossipy compilation of allegations about Schwarzenegger's foul mouth, groping of women, and use of steroids, based mostly on anonymous sources. Schwarzenegger's lawyer and friends pointed out in letters to the magazine that *Premiere's* story was uncorroborated.

The accuracy of the allegations was not South's concern. Schwarzenegger had attacked his client, the governor of California, in the pages of the state's largest newspaper. The *Premiere* piece was, he would say later, a turd that could be thrown in the Schwarzenegger punch bowl. South faxed the *Premiere* article to political reporters around the state with a note: "This piece lays out a real 'touching' story—if you get what I mean." South later followed up with a fax of a similar piece in the *National Enquirer.*

Gorton wisely advised Schwarzenegger not to respond. But Schwarzenegger took the bait. Like many stars, he employed a lawyer whose portfolio included knocking down rumors before they spread. That lawyer, Marty Singer, faxed South a letter threatening a lawsuit and ordering him to stop circulating the article. Singer closed the letter by saying the letter itself was copyrighted and could not be disclosed. According to South, one page of the letter did not come through his fax machine. When one of South's assistants called Singer to ask that it be faxed again, Singer's office faxed over the original letter with a new letter saying he had confirmation that the first fax had been received. Within an hour, there was a knock on the door of South's office. A hard copy of the letter had been hand-delivered just to be sure.

"Bananas," South thought. "Who the hell are these people?"

Such letters were how Singer dealt with tabloids. But Singer now represented an aspiring politician. The letter was a serious political miscalculation. South faxed reporters a synopsis of Singer's letter, with a mention of the copyright. Political reporters had been reluctant to write about the *Premiere* article. But Singer, by threatening South, had created a new story that political reporters would write: The war of words between Schwarzenegger's attorney and the political advisor to the governor.

Each newspaper story and TV broadcast on the letters included a synopsis of *Premiere*'s allegations. "It was a major mistake by their side," South said. "It demonstrated that at that point, Arnold was not ready" to run for public office.

DURING THE SAME TIME PERIOD, Schwarzenegger authorized Gorton to conduct a political poll. Over four nights in February 2001, callers from Public Opinion Strategies, a firm with offices in Los Angeles and Washington, surveyed eight hundred registered voters across California. Davis remained popular, but 45 percent of Californians believed the state was on the wrong track. If the gubernatorial election had been held that week, Davis would have beaten Schwarzenegger 59 to 30 percent.

One question on the poll repeated the charges from *Premiere* magazine and asked if such allegations would make voters less likely to vote for

Schwarzenegger. Forty-six percent of the voters surveyed answered yes, the allegations would hurt—but at the same time, the news did not change these voters' views of Schwarzenegger as a good person. Sixty percent of the voters surveyed had a favorable opinion of him; only 18 percent viewed him unfavorably. The poll tested possible responses to the charges. One answer seemed to test particularly well with voters: that "during his career as a movie star, like most movie stars, he was flamboyant and not always a perfect gentleman, but he and his wife are happily married, most of the accusations are either made up or greatly exaggerated, and he and his wife agree they shouldn't discuss their private life any further than that."

The challenge was clear from the polling. People liked Schwarzenegger so much that they would take allegations against him in stride. But they were far from ready to make him their governor.

ONE AFTERNOON THAT MARCH, as Schwarzenegger was driving home to Pacific Palisades, he listened to a debate on the radio between the candidates for mayor of Los Angeles. Soon he was thinking of answers to each question. For a few minutes, he imagined himself there at the debate.

The radio cast a spell. As he neared home, he realized that he had been speaking out loud to himself, as if he were a candidate in the debate.

SOMETIMES WITHOUT telling Gorton or White, Schwarzenegger called up politicians who interested him.

By March, Schwarzenegger had scheduled political meetings almost daily. On Thursday, March 15, California Secretary of State Bill Jones met with Schwarzenegger to discuss the governor's race. At 11 a.m. on March 16, he met with the state Republican Party chairman Shawn Steel and a deputy, Tim Clark.

"Well, Shawn, you should know that I'm pro-gay, pro-lesbian, pro-transgender, and pro, pro. . ." Schwarzenegger paused to think for a second. "Pro-bisexual, pro-reasonable gun control, and pro-choice."

"Well, what are you against, Arnold?" Steel replied.

Steel assured Schwarzenegger that, despite his views on social issues, he would have the party's support if he took a strong stand against tax increases. Steel also told the potential candidate not to let politics get in the way of making *Terminator 3*. He wanted to know where the killing machine's story would end. "There are questions that must be answered," the Republican chairman joked.

WHITE SCHEDULED the first official strategy session of Schwarzenegger's political career for St. Patrick's Day, which fell on a Saturday in 2001. The meeting would take place at Oak Productions at 11 a.m. Oak's offices were inside the business complex Schwarzenegger had developed on Main Street in Santa Monica, just north of Venice and the old site of Gold's Gym. The complex held other offices—Johnny Carson had been a tenant—as well as a Starbucks, a salon, and Schatzi's on Main, the Austrian restaurant founded by Schwarzenegger and owned by his old friend Charly Temmel, a gourmet ice cream maker back in Austria.

To enter Oak was to step into a museum of Schwarzenegger's life, career, and interests. There was the first-floor elevator landing mural of the Terminator shooting through a wall, replicas of his movie characters in a reception area, Andy Warhol and Jamie Wyeth paintings, the Golden Globe he won for the movie *Stay Hungry*, legs from a five hundred-year-old Hercules statue he encountered in Italy, and busts of Reagan, Kennedy, and Lenin—the last a trophy given to him by visitors from the former Soviet Union. Schwarzenegger also kept a simple Austria room, with wood paneling and an etching of his home village, to remind him of his roots.

Schwarzenegger arrived early and took a seat at one end of the conference table. Three of the attendees—White, Gorton, and White's associate Camden McEfee—were by then familiar to Schwarzenegger. Two were new.

Don Sipple, a longtime strategist and creator of political messages and ads, had driven down from his home in Montecito. Larry Thomas, a onetime newspaper reporter who had been the spokesman for Governor George Deukmejian during the 1980s and for Wilson when he was San Diego's mayor, had come up from Orange County. Thomas now headed communications for the Irvine Company, a giant Orange County real estate firm, and worked closely with its politically connected chairman, Donald Bren. All five men had ties to Governor Wilson that reached back at least twelve years. Schwarzenegger was courting a team that was out of power.

At a quarter past eleven, Wilson himself walked in and took charge of the meeting. The former governor had no trouble being blunt. Wilson announced that he hoped Schwarzenegger would run for governor and that, although he did not know the actor's thoughts, he understood he had some interest in the position. Wilson said he had only one question. "What are you inspired to accomplish?"

Wilson warned that before Schwarzenegger could answer that question, he needed to be sure this was a transition he could make, in his life and in his career. If he decided to seek office, Wilson told Schwarzenegger, the people around this table could help him set up a fund-raising network and find people to teach him the issues.

Wilson asked each person to discuss what Schwarzenegger would face if he ran. Sipple went first. He had brought a yellow legal pad filled with notes about other famous men who had jumped into politics. Sipple urged Schwarzenegger to think of General Dwight D. Eisenhower. He talked about Reagan for several minutes as well, and then offered two examples of what could go wrong. Ross Perot, Sipple argued, had never committed himself to a political life. And Jesse Ventura, a friend of Schwarzenegger's for years, had been an accident of history and a gadfly.

Thomas discussed the press. You have to view politics like a play, he began. Politicians are actors on a stage. The press behaves like the audience, judging the quality of the performance more than its substance. As a movie star, Schwarzenegger didn't need handlers to teach him how to perform on stage. What he needed was to educate himself on issues.

Gorton spoke last. His subject was campaign strategy. Schwarzenegger had a dangerous combination: fame and scant political history. The opinion voters formed of him at the beginning of a campaign could be decisive. A Schwarzenegger campaign would start out like a blank chalkboard. Schwarzenegger would have to write on that chalkboard before his opponents did. A key way to fill that chalkboard would be to sponsor a ballot initiative ("Initiative as transition vehicle," read the meeting agenda). An initiative would convey his intentions more clearly than any speech could. Schwarzenegger would have to decide whether he wanted to make a substantive change to the state law or constitution, or if he wanted something more symbolic. "Until he is associated with something voters perceive as qualifying him to be governor, he will have a glass jaw," Gorton wrote in a memo following up the meeting.

A successful initiative campaign would require more than a year of planning. But it would also provide a vehicle for him to build a political organization, learn the ins and outs of fund-raising, and meet with interest groups. Gorton discussed the possibility of sponsoring an initiative in 2002 to coincide with a race for governor. If Schwarzenegger decided to wait before running for office, he could sponsor ballot initiatives in 2002 and 2004 as a way to build his political profile, Gorton suggested.

Schwarzenegger was pleasantly surprised by the enthusiasm for him as a candidate. "I thought they were going to say, 'Look, you're a great guy. Why don't you try to do something else? Why don't you try to be an ambassador or something? This is not the right thing for you,'" he recalled. "That's what I heard in the movie business at first. But that's not what happened. They said, 'There's meat on that chicken.' I could see it from the look on their faces."

"THIS IS ALL GREAT, GUYS," Schwarezenegger said, then asked, What are we going to do about it?

He said he had moments when he daydreamed that he was already governor, and shared the story of how he had thought he was a participant during the mayoral debate. He asked if someone in the room had tapes of past debates, perhaps even Nixon-Kennedy. He would like to have copies.

Schwarzenegger wanted a political plan. It was past 1 p.m.; Thomas and Wilson left. Sipple, Gorton, White, and McEfee scooted downstairs for a late lunch at Schatzi's. The actor had not given them a deadline, but they had better hurry. He sounded like a man running for governor.

WITHIN A WEEK, the consultants had cobbled together a plan. "You are and will continue to be a public/political figure, who has the potential to wield enormous influence as a public policy advocate and/or candidate for elective office," the undated document, headlined "Assessment and Preparation Plan," began. "It is obvious that you will forever be a force in the national and state political arena."

The plan laid out a timetable. First, Schwarzenegger needed seventy-five days to assess whether to run and to prepare in case he did. During that time, the consultants would conduct an "indepth self-exam of Arnold Schwarzenegger the person." They would produce a full biography and resume, investigate his personal and financial dealings, and examine a lifetime worth of public statements.

There would be surveys to find out how voters might receive a Schwarzenegger candidacy. The consultants wanted to produce a study to examine how the entertainment and international media might cover a campaign. There had to be a forecast of the candidate's schedule to show Schwarzenegger if his political career could fit with his movie and business commitments.

The plan called for omitting certain steps typical of most politicians. There would be no exploratory committee. The forming of such a body would be international news. Gorton also injected a call for a study of President George W. Bush's statements on whether he had ever used cocaine. Gorton wanted to present them to Schwarzenegger as a case study of how politicians can put personal peccadilloes behind them. The consultants also discussed assembling a kitchen cabinet of party heavyweights, modeled on the group that advised Reagan during his transition to politics.

With all this in hand by June 15, 2001, Schwarzenegger could make a decision whether to go forward in 2002 with a ballot initiative, with a gubernatorial campaign, or with both. "I was really testing how this would work," recalled Schwarzenegger.

In their e-mails, the consultants were circumspect. They referred to Schwarzenegger as "our friend." The choice was not just one of operational security. They still couldn't believe that this might be their candidate.

By early April, Schwarzenegger had seen the plan and signed off on many of its elements. On April 7, Schwarzenegger called his old friend and confidant, the Austrian reporter Werner Kopacka, back in Graz. "The world needs new political heroes, honest human beings with a heart, humans with power to persuade," he told Kopacka. "It is now almost certain that I will enter politics." But he added two caveats: He would have to find a way to get out of his *Terminator 3* commitment, and he needed to get his wife on board.

The question became whether to challenge Davis in 2002 or wait for a gubernatorial race in 2006. Gorton urged him to run in 2002. "One mechanism to do this is an initiative," Gorton wrote Schwarzenegger on April 10. "You don't have to make up your mind on running for governor until the legal announcement date in early November if you use this device because you can write on the chalkboard by talking with the press about, and appearing in TV ads for, the initiative." Gorton proposed to begin a TV ad campaign by fall 2001 for an initiative that would appear on the March 2002 ballot. "As the manager of your initiative," Gorton wrote, "I would make a few calls and let the appropriate people know that if they arrange calls and letters to you urging you to run, you probably could be persuaded. It would be a genuine draft."

Gorton struck one note of caution. "An initiative is not a perfect solution. A mistake or misstep in the initiative can be highly detrimental to a gubernatorial campaign."

AFTER THE ST. PATRICK'S DAY meeting, Governor Wilson began calling veterans of his administration. "I have a friend who is thinking about running for governor, and I'd like you to spend some time with him," Wilson would say.

Joe Rodota, Wilson's former cabinet secretary, flew to Los Angeles to meet Wilson's friend. Schwarzenegger wanted an explanation of how a campaign would put together a policy agenda. "He was interested in all the details, all the mechanics," said Rodota.

Over the first two weeks of April, Rodota reviewed all of Schwarzenegger's public statements, with tapes and clippings from Oak Productions. On the afternoon of April 16, 2001, Rodota delivered to Schwarzenegger a political biography, a statement of Schwarzenegger's philosophy, a reading list on policy, and a list of questions he might be asked as a candidate. The final piece of the presentation was a document called *Arnold A to Z.* It laid out, alphabetically, Schwarzenegger's publicly stated views—many from interviews he had conducted while promoting movies—on dozens of issues.

In doing the review, Rodota was struck by a published comment made by Milton Friedman: Schwarzenegger was one of the few people in America who knew exactly why he was successful. Like a politician, he knew he had a constituency for his movies and who they were—the young, NASCAR fans, and people who are "either the little guy or for the little guy," as he liked to say. On the issues, Rodota concluded that Schwarzenegger was well versed on immigration, movie violence, and trade (he'd lobbied Congress for most favored nation trade status for China, then a priority for the Hollywood studios). He had strong views on drugs, energy regulation, and taxes. Rodota determined he might be vulnerable in a Republican primary because of past remarks in favor of gun control, abortion rights, gay rights, and cloning. (He had indicated support for this last idea during his promotion of *The Sixth Day,* in which his character was cloned.)

THREE DAYS LATER, on the afternoon of April 19, Sipple sat down with Schwarzenegger and a camera. The schedule called the session an "authenticity interview." Schwarzenegger wore a white dress shirt, open at the collar, and a dark blue sport coat. From off camera, he was asked a series of straightforward questions about his childhood, his career, his beliefs, and his views on government and politics. The idea was to allow Schwarzenegger to speak his mind, providing a view of the potential candidate that was as authentic as possible. Tape of the authentic Schwarzenegger could then be shown to focus groups of voters. Those focus group tests would help the consultants determine which of Schwarzenegger's views were popular and should be highlighted in a campaign and which opinions he ought to keep to himself.

The exercise demonstrated what entertainment journalists who interviewed Schwarzenegger had long known. The Terminator, who used few words in the movies, simply could not shut up in real life. He talked expansively about his childhood in Austria, his process of visualizing goals, and his Harley Davidson motorcycle. He went into considerable detail in describing his difficulties getting into show business.

"I couldn't find an agent . . . . The simple thing was, 'Arnold, you have a Mr. Universe body, looks great. Why don't you go into nutrition? . . . I can get you parts to play a bouncer or some evil guy or something like that. But if you want to work your way up to be a star, to be a leading man like you have explained to me, it won't happen. . . .'"

At times during the authenticity interview, Schwarzenegger seemed a bit out of touch. Although he lived in a huge house in the elite neighborhood of Pacific Palisades on the west side of Los Angeles, he declared that "what we did with our kids is to bring them up in a very normal setting. Our house is a moderate house. It is not a huge Beverly Hills mansion . . . We wanted to have it much more normal, still extraordinary for other people's standards but for us it's normal." The star of violent movies proudly explained how he shielded his own kids from such fare. "I say this to Maria always, 'The children are an empty bucket.' And you know, I feel there are many different people who can fill up this bucket and I want to be the one who fills it up, and she should be the one. Rather than other people. Rather than MTV. Rather than television, movies or all the other kind of things, or other kids."

He said the state should help by providing better schools, more after-school programs, and health insurance for every child. He acknowledged that he sounded like Hillary Clinton, but declared: "I have learned firsthand that there is no such thing as a bad kid . . . there's no kid that is born and fills out a paper and says, 'I want to be a bad kid. I want to kill somebody, I want to rob somebody, I want to steal, I want to lie all the time.' It doesn't exist."

As the interview continued, Schwarzenegger's comments grew more impassioned and populist.

"I think in order to really be a good leader you have to ultimately always represent the people," Schwarzenegger said, clearing his throat. To him, the people meant "the consumer. Everyone out there. Rather than a specific interest group. To me this is a disastrous situation the way it has gone in politics. The way certain politicians go in there because they are supported by interest groups. I think the interest groups—it should never be allowed that any interest group participates in the campaign where they contribute money, where the politician takes money from them. Then you have to, you're obligated to help them rather than the people who vote out there. Rather than the average American."

He composed his thoughts for a few seconds. "You have to represent everybody. If you're a political leader you cannot represent the Republicans. You cannot represent the Democrats. You cannot represent an interest group. You have to represent the people . . . And number two, I think it is, that the more you are the typical career politician that is dug in there like an Alabama tick, that you can't get out, that is in there for five terms and six terms and the seventh term and all this. To me I'm against that. I think still in the traditional way, the way it was meant to be, where the community can reach out to somebody in the community. 'We would like you—you have displayed leadership in the community—we would like to send you to Washington to represent our state or something like this' . . . You will have people who think from outside the box much more rather than do the traditional kind of finagling like government does."

Schwarzenegger added that if he got into politics, he would bring humor and new language to the world of public affairs. People might not like what he had to say, but he would entertain them.

BY MID-APRIL 2001, Schwarzenegger was canvassing his close friends. Should he change careers? And if so, when should he make the jump?

Gorton outlined eight questions Schwarzenegger had to ask himself. What can I accomplish? Are there issues I could campaign on? Will I be a good campaigner? Can I raise money to win? What is my image now with the voting public and can that image be molded to fit the image the public has of a governor? Is there anything in my past that would make it difficult for me to be elected governor? What would my life be like as a candidate and as a governor? And can I win? Gorton wrote in a memo circulated among Schwarzenegger's consultants that the actor could answer all eight, but "he needs training in handling a hostile press (these ain't show biz reporters, baby—these guys advance their careers by destroying politicians) and he needs a deeper education in the issues."

Getting that education would be a full-time job, and Schwarzenegger had other commitments. He said a particular issue emerged as he talked to his friend, Andy Vajna, one of the producers of *Terminator 2*. Schwarzenegger was widely reported to have given some encouragement to a series of movie sequels: *King Conan*, *True Lies 2*, and *Terminator 3*. *Terminator 3* had seemed a longshot. Vajna and his partner had lost their rights to the sequel and had to buy them back in bankruptcy court. But Vajna had begun to find financing for the movie. Vajna's backers had commissioned a survey that showed people wouldn't pay to see another Terminator movie unless Schwarzenegger was in it.

When Schwarzenegger told Vajna he was considering a run for governor, Vajna told him he had already put together a script and sold some of the foreign rights. "Don't even think about it," was how Schwarzenegger recalled Vajna's end of the conversation. "He said, 'I almost have a script, I sold the movie already overseas, and I sold the different rights for merchandising, and this and that.'"

SCHWARZENEGGER TOLD HIS political team that he had little choice but to honor his commitment to the movie.

The financial lure was also huge. Schwarzenegger would not conclude contract negotiations on *Terminator 3* until December 2001, but it was clear that a big payday awaited him. Ultimately, he received a $29.25 million fixed fee, then believed to be the largest such fee ever paid to an actor for a single movie. The contract included another $1.5 million in perks and 20 percent of gross receipts from all sources, including DVDs, television, and other licensing. Such money had political value. It could take away the financial sting of moving into politics and provide cash so he could fund some of his campaigns himself. "I knew that my life hasn't yet in the movie business played out," Schwarzenegger recalled. "Number two, I felt like no matter what, I gotta do *Terminator 3*. I thought, 'If you ever want to go into politics, go out on a high note rather than a low note.'"

Finally, the transition to a political run would have been difficult for Schwarzenegger's family. As he debated whether to run in April, the *National Enquirer* was preparing yet another story, this one accusing him of an extramarital affair. Schwarzenegger's Hollywood team denounced it as a fabrication, and the woman herself later denied an affair. (In a subsequent interview with the author Laurence Leamer, the woman described an off-and-on relationship that included erotic touching but not intercourse.) Schwarzenegger maintained that the *Enquirer* story had nothing to do with his decision to stay out of the race. But the story also made clear that if he ran, he would have to contend with reports about his personal life.

Bonnie Reiss, his friend and advisor on after-school programs, believed that Schwarzenegger had long known he wasn't going to run in 2002, but went through the process of creating a plan in order to learn firsthand what a race would eventually entail. "He was smart enough to act like that was a possibility, and that accomplished a lot," she said.

On April 24, 2001, Sean Walsh, a former Wilson deputy chief of staff, faxed to the Oak offices a list of state and national political reporters who should be contacted with the news that Schwarzenegger might not run. That same day, Sipple cut short the second part of the authenticity interview. Schwartzenegger seemed tired. The next day, Schwarzenegger released a six-paragraph statement to the press. Headlined "Schwarzenegger will not run this year: will expand youth activities," the statement said he was "not available" to run because of family, business, and charity commitments such as the Inner City Games. He also mentioned *Terminator 3*. "I gave my word that this year I would undertake certain projects if the sponsors could put them together," he said. "They have, and I will keep my word."

With the announcement, Schwarzenegger appeared to take himself out of politics. But the actor told Gorton he wanted the preparations for a political career to continue. He still wanted to do something in 2002.

That meant a ballot initiative campaign.

The consultants were skeptical at first. How could a person make a movie and run an initiative campaign at the same time? Schwarzenegger didn't think there would a problem. He had successfully linked his pursuits before. He had cast bodybuilders in movies, turned premieres into benefits for after-school programs, held meetings for his charity work on movie sets, and formed a friendship with President George H. W. Bush through his business partner in an Ohio bodybuilding tournament.

A movie and a ballot initiative campaign—perhaps the two enterprises were not so different after all.

CHAPTER 6

End of Days

The focus group began with a bit of deception.

A few minutes after 6 p.m. on May 1, 2001, twelve registered voters from the San Fernando Valley gathered in a windowless room in Encino. They had been paid $65 each to express their opinions for two hours. Seven were men and five were women. They all identified themselves either as independent voters or as Republicans or Democrats who voted for political candidates of the other party. At the head of a glass conference table sat a balding man wearing a white dress shirt and dark slacks. He introduced himself as Fred Steeper and said he had just flown in from Michigan.

Steeper did not mention that he was one of the most prominent Republican pollsters in the country. Nor that he had helped pioneer the use of dial tests, in which voters in focus groups watched clips of politicians and registered their feelings, second by second, on an electronic counter. Nor that among Steeper's clients was the president of the United States.

Steeper told the focus group that he was studying people from different walks of life who might have potential as leaders on "public policy issues." That was the deception. Steeper did not tell the focus group that he was focused on one potential leader, his new client Arnold Schwarzenegger.

Schwarzenegger had announced he would not join the 2002 governor's race only the week before. But Gorton had scheduled four focus groups—two in Encino and two in the Bay Area community of Sunnyvale. California political consultants liked to survey people in the San Fernando Valley because it was full of middle-of-the-road voters who had a middling knowledge of political affairs. The Valley might be ideologically average, but its voters had a taste for populist uprising and ballot measures. The anti-tax rebellion that led to the passage of Proposition 13 began here. The Valley was the ideal place for Schwarzenegger's team to determine what sort of initiative Schwarzenegger should sponsor to introduce, politically, himself to the public.

"Hopefully, you'll find this whole thing, if not educational, at least entertaining," Steeper said as he handed out electronic dials to the group. At first, the dozen voters registered their views on political matters and key figures such as President George W. Bush and Governor Davis. Then, Steeper asked how favorably they viewed Arnold Schwarzenegger.

Giggles filled the room at the mention of the name. Steeper paused and continued.

"If Arnold Schwarzenegger sponsored a ballot initiative and was the main spokesperson for it, would that make you more or less likely to vote for it?" Turn your dial to zero, and that meant you'd defeat the initiative because of it. One hundred meant it would guarantee your support. Setting your dial at fifty meant you were neutral. All the dials but one turned north of fifty. Steeper then began to throw out adjectives, asking the voters to rate how well certain adjectives described Schwarzenegger. Tough. Likable. Exciting. Confident . . .

For a final question, Steeper asked the group to rate themselves, zero to one hundred, on how much they liked Schwarzenegger's movies. Then he opened up the floor to a discussion of Schwarzenegger's "potential to speak out on public issues."

In spite of the giggles, most of the people presumed he already was a political figure. Steeper seemed particularly surprised at how much the voters knew about Schwarzenegger—or thought they did. They knew of his ambition to be governor. They knew he was a Republican who had liberal views on social issues. Most had heard of his work for the first President Bush's fitness council. They knew he had married Maria Shriver, and that she was the niece of John F. Kennedy. Several volunteered that the marriage made him a natural for public office.

There were gaps and inaccuracies. One man insisted incorrectly that Schwarzenegger was a Scientologist. (He's Catholic.) There was some question in the group whether he was an Austrian or an American citizen. Three members of the group had seen the *National Enquirer* story the week before about an alleged mistress. Asked if that compromised Schwarzenegger as a leader, a young man named Max answered: "Not if he can get away with it." The rest of the group nodded in agreement.

"How do you think the public in California would accept him as a leader?" Steeper asked. "To what extent would people think it's a joke?"

Donald: Some Democrats, maybe. Moderates wouldn't think so.

Steve: He's a nice guy to have on your side.

Carol: California would like him. He has to be a likable character to get the box office hits he gets.

After nearly half an hour, Steeper cut off the conversation and asked them to pick up their dials again. Schwarzenegger's authenticity interview had been edited into six clips of about three minutes each. For the next hour,

Steeper showed those clips one by one, pausing in between so the group could record their ratings of each and hold a brief discussion.

The first clip, which showed Schwarzenegger talking about his difficulty breaking into Hollywood, received a warm reception. A pony-tailed man in his thirties, Joseph, said it inspired him. "You can become much more than people think you are," he said.

Two subsequent clips didn't play nearly as well. A segment with Schwarzenegger denouncing violence while saying his movies didn't cause violence was considered hypocritical by most in the group. The fourth clip, in which Schwarzenegger claimed his children were raised in a "normal" lifestyle, drew guffaws. There was head-scratching during still another clip showing Schwarzenegger discussing his view that the government should provide all children with health insurance. One woman, Joanne, objected that the program would cover undocumented immigrants. Others pointed out that the government already funded the health care of many poor children.

But the response turned electric when Steeper played the shortest of the clips—1 minute and 53 seconds of Schwarzenegger talking in populist terms about his distaste for interest-group donations, his dislike of partisanship, and his desire to serve the people. For a few moments, the chart monitoring the group's reaction went above ninety on the one hundred-point scale. "I'd like to see him run," said a middle-aged man. "The people come first.

("Populism has a long history as a successful campaign theme in American politics," Steeper would write in his focus group report. "It is somewhat ironic, but Schwarzenegger's personal wealth may be what ultimately gives him the credibility to champion this theme.")

Steeper continued questioning the group. "Pretend you're an advisor to Arnold Schwarzenegger and he has three styles he could present to the people," he asked. "He could present himself as the tough action hero. He could go for a white shirt and tie image—respected mainstream leader. Or third, he could show his caring, compassionate side." The focus group members wanted to see the compassionate Schwarzenegger.

As Steeper stood up to leave, he was deluged with questions. Are you his campaign manager? Is he going to run?

Steeper looked dumbfounded. When Schwarzenegger had hired him, he had been more than a little skeptical. In years past, he had tested the political potential of Penn State football coach Joe Paterno in Pennsylvania and Dallas Cowboys quarterback Roger Staubach in Texas. People didn't accept either as a public policy figure.

Steeper wondered if the next focus group, beginning at 8 p.m., would be different. It was. This second group of thirteen voters was even more intrigued. The only sour note was a man who claimed that thirty years earlier he had a dispute with Schwarzenegger over the price of a statue of the body-builder Eugene Sandow.

The dial tests showed an overall average of seventy-one on the one hundred-point scale. Anything above fifty-five is considered great for a politician. Gorton worried in a note circulated among the consultants that the results were so strong that Schwarzenegger "will erroneously assume from the high dial numbers he got that he is already ready for prime time." The star had to improve his self-presentation. "We need language to tell Arnold's story," Gorton wrote, "without seeming to be self-centered and without making others feel inadequate by comparison."

After the focus groups, Schwarzenegger rarely discussed his children pub-licly and never suggested that his lifestyle was "normal." He would talk about his achievements as something California, America, and the people had given him. Finally he would learn to avoid engaging in discussions about violence in movies. An argument about that subject was an argument that Schwarzenegger, of all people, could not win.

He would build his political persona on his populist views, which had tested so well. The focus groups liked Schwarzenegger personally and they liked his movie persona. In politics, they wanted him to play a more compas-sionate version of the character he played in the movies. He would be a po-litical action hero who would fight for them all the way.

That made him a perfect sponsor for a ballot initiative. He still had to fig-ure out exactly what it would be.

SCHWARZENEGGER HAD HIS own idea: a state subsidy for health insurance for all children. He had talked about that in the authenticity interview, but the focus groups hadn't taken to it. The consultants didn't like the idea at all.

Bob White, the former Wilson chief of staff who was advising the star, wasn't convinced that Schwarzenegger needed an initiative. An initiative car-ried with it all the difficulties of a piece of legislation—with the added bur-den that the process took place in public. Too much could go wrong, White worried. If voters rejected Schwarzenegger's initiative at the polls, where would that leave him?

Gorton argued an initiative was essential. His quarrel was over its subject. The costs of covering all children would scare off many voters, including the economic conservatives that Schwarzenegger, with his liberal social views, would need in the 2006 gubernatorial election if he wanted the Republican nomination.

At the same time, Gorton believed Schwarzenegger needed an initiative that showed he was compassionate. "There were people who didn't like violent movies and didn't know him in any other way," recalled Gorton. "Part of the strategy was to show his concern for kids." In a May 15 email to the other consultants, Gorton urged a united front in convincing Schwarzenegger to drop the concept of a health care initiative: "We mustn't make this quagmire sound like a good idea."

If not children's health care, then what?

THE ANSWER CAME from Schwarzenegger. By June 2001, he was planning to open after-school programs at four Los Angeles middle schools in 2002. There was not nearly enough government money for such programs, and Schwarzenegger was closely following an unsuccessful effort in the state assembly to win major increases in funding. Perhaps after-school programs could be an initiative. Gorton was skeptical at first. After-school programs had been part of the Clinton crime bill that Republicans had criticized in the mid-1990s. Was this the best way to introduce a Republican into state politics?

On May 31, Gorton called Chip Nielsen, an election lawyer in Marin County whose firm, Nielsen Merksamer, specialized in the drafting of initiatives. Nielsen also had handled legal work for Pete Wilson's campaigns. Gorton asked the attorney to see if an initiative was feasible.

A lawyer handling initiatives was part legal counsel, part political strategist, and part policy maven. Nielsen made a short study of after-school programs and wrote back to Gorton three weeks later. An initiative to provide more money would be workable, but it would not be an easy campaign, Nielsen said. No strong interest group championed after-school programs. The programs themselves required the cooperation of a wide variety of interests—law enforcement, education, and health care—that would oppose the measure if they weren't carefully consulted. The surest route to success would be to let interest groups participate in the drafting of the measure.

"If the interests we care about don't like our first suggestions, we can drop or modify it for the final draft," Nielsen wrote to Gorton on June 21. "I think [Schwarzenegger] need not apologize for not knowing all the answers in this subject area, and in fact I think he will be complimented for being open to suggestions. It's also a way to draw in allies and supporters."

"The Schwarzenegger Initiative," as Gorton outlined it in a memo, had several strategic objectives: to build a broad-based coalition that knew Schwarzenegger, to begin "to brand" Schwarzenegger politically, "to create a fund-raising base responsive to Arnold that includes major donors and at least 10,000 small donors," and to "create a team of top political professionals loyal to Arnold."

"Here he is over in this side of his life trying to make his after-school program go," recalled Gorton. "Over here at this other side of his life, he's trying to put his toe in the political water . . . So you put his reasons together with our reasons and it just screamed—this is a good movie. It all comes together."

THE MAN ON THE PHONE identified himself as Camden McEfee and said he represented a "major California philanthropist" who was prepared to make an investment in after-school programs. Steve Fowler, a public relations consultant, wasn't sure if the call was for real. But he represented the Afterschool Alliance, a non-profit awareness campaign funded by the C. S. Mott Foundation, J. C. Penney, and George Soros's Open Society Institute, and he agreed to a meeting the following Monday. McEfee, who worked with Bob White, and Gorton spent two hours with Fowler, a one-time Nebraska legislator, who quickly outlined the politics of after-school programs. Only at the meeting's end did Gorton identify his client. "They said they were playing catch up with Arnold. He knew more than they did," Fowler recalled.

Fowler arranged for the consultants to meet the next day with the California affiliate of the national non-profit Fight Crime Invest in Kids, which had been founded in 1996 by law enforcement officials and crime victims to research ways to prevent children from becoming criminals. The group had established two priorities: child care and after-school programs. Fight Crime's state director, Maryann O'Sullivan, a self-described "old-fashioned lefty, progressive Democrat," watched few movies and knew almost nothing about Schwarzenegger. But she and Schwarzenegger shared a key bit of biography: their fathers had been cops. And she and Schwarzenegger had separately reached the same conclusion about California's legislature: it would never fund after-school programs of its own volition.

At a meeting on June 27, 2001, Gorton and O'Sullivan each brought lists of what should be in an after-school ballot initiative. When they compared lists, the two documents were strikingly similar. Gorton, half-jokingly, exclaimed: This isn't subversive after all!

"George was suspicious—as if this was going to establish communism in California," O'Sullivan said. "We were lucky. Arnold just fell into our lap."

SCHWARZENEGGER WAS SCHEDULED to speak at a September 21, 2001, Perspectives conference, held by the Sacramento Metro Chamber of Commerce, as a way to build his political profile. After the address, Bob White would host a party at his home to introduce Schwarzenegger to Sacramento lobbyists, government officials, and other dignitaries. The speech was to be the culmination of a summer during which Schwarzenegger had added a number of political events to his usual diet of promotional and charitable appearances.

The week after he dropped out of the governor's race, Schwarzenegger had kept a breakfast appointment arranged by Wilson and White in Beverly Hills with a group of Republican governors. He tagged along with Los Angeles Mayor Richard Riordan, who was running for governor, to a meeting of two dozen California political figures with Enron chairman Ken Lay. (Schwarzenegger shook Lay's hand and listened as the chairman presented Riordan with a plan detailing his solution to California's energy crisis.) In July, Schwarzenegger sat on the dais at the inauguration of Jim Hahn as mayor of Los Angeles.

Schwarzenegger did not adjust easily to the rigors of a political schedule. As a bodybuilder and movie star, he was among the most independent of men. With a private jet at his disposal, he controlled his own schedule and often rearranged appointments and itineraries at the last minute. He resisted scheduling events far in advance, preferring to stay "flexible" and "organic"—the latter was one of his favorite adjectives. While he became more sensitive to the trouble his freewheeling ways created, he couldn't quite kick the habit.

After each public appearance, Gorton gave Schwarzenegger a memo with suggestions. Some of the suggestions had to do with crowd control, always a problem for Schwarzenegger. Gorton also tried to disabuse him of the notion that much of politics was suspect. "Those that attempt to govern without politics soon find themselves in the minority and therefore do not govern," Gorton wrote.

As summer turned to fall, Schwarzenegger made a national tour to stump for his own after-school programs, visiting San Diego, San Jose, San Antonio, Dallas, and Miami. In the midst of all that traveling, the Perspectives speech in Sacramento was slow to come together. A session to give Schwarzenegger practice with Teleprompters—the see-through screens that allow politicians to read speeches while looking at their audience without the audience knowing—failed to come off as scheduled. The September 11 terrorist attacks delayed preparations.

Bill Whalen, a former Wilson speechwriter, had drafted a twenty-five-minute speech for Perspectives. But as the date grew closer, Maria Shriver threw herself into the effort. She invited Whalen to the house in Pacific Palisades and described in detail what she saw as her husband's strengths. She wanted more in the speech about the self-made man who now wanted to give back to the country that had done so much for him. Eventually she wrote part of the speech herself. Shriver had an appealing conversational voice, but it clashed with Whalen's style. Schwarzenegger himself insisted on certain additions. The resulting speech was a dreadfully long mishmash that sounded part Shriver, part Pete Wilson, and part Austrian.

In Sacramento, Schwarzenegger began with a brief word about the September 11 attacks. Then he joked about the long list of speakers, including Henry Kissinger, who had addressed the conference. He said he had at first been intimidated, "But then again I said to myself, 'Hey, who of those guys ever had 22-inch biceps? And who of those guys has ever made a movie with Sharon Stone?'"

Early on, the address offered a few good yarns. Schwarzenegger described the lack of flushing toilets in his childhood home, the economics of strudel, and his parents' fears when he began to put pictures of naked male bodybuilders on his bedroom wall as a teenager. He cleverly made clear his gubernatorial ambitions without stating them outright: "I haven't been in Sacramento in some time, so I spent the morning walking around downtown. I also stopped by the state capitol. Looking at that majestic building, I couldn't help but think: 'I'll be back.'"

But the speech was full of cornball asides and real clunkers. "I wanted to weave myself right into the fabric of America," he said. He said that children in the Inner City Games were now "shooting hoops instead of shooting dope or shooting guns." Some members of the audience groaned audibly when he transitioned from recounting a meeting with Nelson Mandela to the following: "Mandela said that the most important thing was reconciliation, bringing his nation together, and he became a living message of love, inclusion, and tolerance. He's what I would call a true action hero. Making a difference beyond the mirror, that is my new measure of greatness today. It's what makes me feel good about myself, and I can tell you, it makes me feel much better than going out and buying another $20 cigar."

Schwarzenegger's delivery also failed him. Uncomfortable with the Teleprompter, he read his speech from typewritten pages. He seemed uncertain what to do with his hands. By the time he mentioned Nixon in the speech's second half, he was sweating like the thirty-seventh president.

When Schwarzenegger was done, he wiped his brow and headed offstage. Gorton greeted him with an unflattering remark about the speech. Schwarzenegger knew as much, but disliked being told so and snapped back.

Gorton convened two focus groups in the San Fernando Valley and showed a tape of the speech. Even after the terrible performance, focus group members were willing to consider him as a potential governor. Asked if people would say Californians had lost their minds if Schwarzenegger was elected governor, one focus group was unanimous.

Woman: No, I don't think so.
Man: I don't think so.
Woman No. 2: I think he has enough substance.
Woman No. 3: Clint Eastwood. He's mayor of Carmel.
Man No. 2: And Sonny Bono.
Woman No. 3: Was the mayor of Palm Springs.
Woman No. 4: He's kind of a narcissist, but at the same time he's kind of like laughable, too. He's cool.

The speech was cut almost in half before Schwarzenegger delivered it again at a business conference in Bakersfield. There it was a hit.

BETWEEN GIVING SPEECHES and preparing for *Terminator 3*, Schwarzenegger had allowed the drafting of the initiative to fall behind schedule. Gorton invited Chip Nielsen, the election lawyer who was writing the measure, down to Santa Monica to discuss his work directly with Schwarzenegger.

Over the summer, Nielsen had taken a two-page concept paper Gorton sent him and worked through seven drafts of an initiative. Instead of creating a brand new law, his initiative built on existing statutes. Schwarzenegger would quadruple funding, from $117 million to nearly $500 million—about a third of the estimated $1.4 billion cost of funding after-school programs in every single school in the state. Schwarzenegger also wanted non-academic programs such as fitness, computer programming, and arts to be eligible for state after-school money. Before the meeting, Nielsen sent Schwarzenegger his eighth draft, but labeled it Draft No. 1.

By the time Nielsen entered the Oak Productions offices, the actor was presiding over a meeting with his team. Nielsen, who at six feet four inches towered over Schwarzenegger, was introduced as "Arnold's election lawyer."

No, this isn't my lawyer, Schwarzenegger said. "I never hire lawyers taller than me." He said he would make an exception in Nielsen's case.

Gorton thought the initiative was ready to go.

"Wait a minute, George," Schwarzenegger interrupted. The star explained that he didn't like how the funding worked as a matching grant, with schools putting in one dollar for every one dollar they got from the state. It should be fifty cents from the school for every dollar from the state.

Nielsen was surprised. Gorton had said this would be a quick meeting, that everything was set. But the suggested change raised another point. The initiative as drafted would provide money to every school in the state. Why help rich districts?

"There's going to be some criticism, Mr. Schwarzenegger," Nielsen said.

"Call me Arnold."

And don't worry, Schwarzenegger said. Beverly Hills isn't going to take the money.

Nielsen replied that the draft would give every school a grant.

But they're not going to take it, Schwarzenegger said.

Who, Schwarzenegger seemed to ask, would cross the Terminator when it came to his own signature program? He would go to the superintendents of rich districts who applied for the grants and say, "You might want to think about withdrawing that request."

Schwarzenegger ran through a list of other changes before posing his own question: Where is the campaign kickoff going to be?

"Shit, Arnold," said Gorton. Once we get a final draft, then maybe we can start thinking about a press conference.

No press conference, Schwarzenegger replied. He wanted to do a "fly-around," going to five or six cities around the state in one day. In each place, he would go to a school. The mayors, superintendents, and police would be invited. It was the template he had used as chairman of the president's council.

Schwarzenegger then asked about the "next phase."

Well, after this, Arnold, we're going to run an election, Gorton said, referring to the initiative campaign.

"George, George, George. We're going to win the election," Schwarzenegger said. He would take care of that. Schwarzenegger wanted to know what they were going to do with the program after the victory. "Where is the implementation plan?" he asked.

In his twenty-five years working in initiative politics, Nielsen had never before heard the proponent tell his political professionals: Don't worry about winning, I'll handle it.

Nielsen, a bit stunned, flew back to Northern California to update his staff. You won't believe this guy, he told them.

THE DRAFTING PROCESS was still closer to the beginning than to the end. Now that Schwarzenegger was involved daily, he began to circulate drafts to after-school providers, labor leaders, even the California Medical Association and the state AARP.

Gorton used polling not only to guide the initiative's contents, but also to decide which endorsements to seek and what to call the initiative—which became the After School Education and Safety Act.

In a survey and in focus groups, Steeper tested thirteen potential components of an initiative. The idea was to tease out which ingredients might inspire support among voters and which might repel them. Steeper found that the initiative had to include two elements to win. Democratic women wanted the after-school programs funded by the measure to have a strong educational component. Republicans, conservatives, and men wanted the programs to focus on crime prevention and were wary of using taxes to provide the funds. So, to succeed with voters across the spectrum, the initiative would have to provide education, include an anti-crime component, and not raise taxes.

Fortunately for Schwarzenegger, 72 percent of those surveyed thought he would make a "great sponsor" for an after-school initiative.

"Arnold Schwarzenegger has substantial potential for leadership on public issues," Steeper wrote in a six-page memo to the campaign summarizing the focus groups and the poll. "In California his sponsorship of the initiative is a credible point for him to join the public arena. Though he is not yet a credible candidate for public office, this will lead to it."

Steeper found that most arguments against the initiative would gain little traction. But the poll had one major note of caution. Support for the initiative would be highly sensitive to endorsements by interest groups. Republicans and conservatives wanted to see endorsements by taxpayer groups and police chiefs. And the stance of the California Teachers Association could decide the election. Half of the sample in the poll was told the CTA endorsed the measure. The other half was told the CTA opposed it. That second half became opposed to the overall initiative as a result. Taxpayer groups and the teachers' union were bitter rivals. If he wanted to win, Schwarzenegger would have to draft an initiative that appealed to both.

AT 10 A.M. ON NOVEMBER 8, 2001, Schwarzenegger entered the temporary offices of the California Teachers Association on S Street in Sacramento; a gleaming new facility for the union was being prepared on 10th Street, a block from the capitol. Schwarzenegger's consultants had advised him, correctly, that the CTA was the most politically powerful organization in California.

Much of the public did not understand the extent of CTA's influence. The press dwelled on the political donations of Indian tribes and how those gifts paved the way for new casinos. Some thought the prison guards were the political colossus. California's wealthy business community had the cash to wield major influence, but was often politically divided. CTA had the edge on all these interests. The union spent more than $1 million a year on public opinion research, for which it employed the top Democratic and Republican polling firms, including one of President Bush's own pollsters. Democrats kowtowed publicly and grumbled privately about the union's arrogance. Even Republicans did their best not to provoke CTA's anger.

The CTA dominated in large part because its leaders knew how to use direct democracy. In 1988, the union had sponsored Proposition 98, a ballot initiative that added a minimum funding guarantee for education to the state constitution. CTA's goal was to make sure that school funding, at the very least, kept increasing along with the cost of living and enrollment. Prop 98 consisted of a complicated multipart formula for education funding, including a provision that required at least 40 percent of the state's general fund be devoted to public schools and community colleges. John Mockler, a cantankerous longtime education official who wrote Prop 98, called it "bad procedure" and said he didn't vote for it because he didn't like using the initiative process to make budget policy. "I've written a couple initiatives. I've never voted for one," he explained.

The fact that voters had approved Prop 98 very narrowly—with less than 51 percent of the vote—was mostly forgotten. Narrow as its victory was, Prop 98 firmly established CTA as the interest group champion of direct democracy. After fighting off a school voucher initiative in 1993, the CTA created its own separate fund for initiatives. In 1998, CTA beat back two of Governor Pete Wilson's initiatives. In 2000, the union spent more than $20 million to defeat another voucher initiative: Prop 38. Over the three election cycles, the teachers' union would convince voters to pass a total of $25 billion in state school bonds. Between 2000 and 2004, the CTA would spend more than $46 million on ballot campaigns—twice what it would spend on lobbying and on candidate campaigns during the same period.

Before approaching CTA directly, Schwarzenegger went to Sacramento to meet with Mockler, the Prop 98 author. Bob White, who played bridge with Mockler, sent him an early draft of the initiative. "For one thing, this is a piece of shit," Mockler recalled saying to Schwarzenegger. "Second, it doesn't do what you want. It needs more specific language to make sure the money ends up in after-school programs." And third, by carving out $500 million for after-school programs, Schwarzenegger would be taking money from the amount guaranteed by Prop 98. If he did that, Mockler warned,

Schwarzenegger would spend millions on the initiative only to have the CTA spend its millions and defeat it.

Well, said Schwarzenegger, they told me you would be blunt.

Mockler suggested a dozen different changes in the initiative's language, mostly to make it more precise. He also urged Schwarzenegger to see John Hein, the CTA's official in charge of politics and government relations. Hein was a straight shooter, Mockler advised, and liked after-school programs.

On the morning of November 8, Hein waited in the CTA conference room for Schwarzenegger to arrive. Hein himself felt no excitement, but CTA staffers had brought their cameras and children. It took Schwarzenegger fifteen minutes to negotiate the well-wishers on his way to the conference room. "Maybe it's because I was raised in Nebraska and everyone puts on their pants the same way, but I couldn't believe it," Hein said. "I could see right away if the guy made up his mind to run, he was going to be a real factor."

Schwarzenegger took a seat next to Hein and chatted about the Inner City Games. Then he shifted gears. He knew that schools in California needed more money and he didn't want to get in the way. He was determined to draft an initiative that did not disturb the education funding guarantee under Prop 98. As Gorton and O'Sullivan took turns talking, Schwarzenegger and Hein whispered in each other's ears. The actor asked Hein: Is there any way we could work together?

There was. In recent years, the legislature had added funding to after-school programs by using money that was counted as part of the Proposition 98 guarantee. That meant taking away millions that would have been allocated for schools. It also left CTA in a bad political position: to defend education money, it was opposing popular after-school programs. Hein believed the initiative could provide CTA a way out of this annual quandary. If Schwarzenegger included a separate funding guarantee for after-school programs apart from the Prop 98 money, CTA could support such programs.

Hein also saw that a deal would allow CTA to build a relationship with a future Republican leader. Just listening to Schwarzenegger convinced Hein that the star would run for office someday. And Schwarzenegger had been smart enough to come to CTA while the initiative was still being written. Hein said that he would like to put CTA's own election lawyer, Joe Remcho, together with Nielsen. Remcho and Nielsen, who were friendly, would exchange twelve drafts of language to ensure after-school money wouldn't come out of Prop 98 funds.

It was an extraordinary deal. Schwarzenegger, the best hope for Republicans in California, agreed to let the lawyer for the state's most powerful

Democratic interest group help write the initiative that would launch his political career.

Schwarzenegger worked hard to cultivate Hein. "Given the number of
people I've worked with who have been governors or elected officials, he was
much more appropriately attentive at the right times than anyone else," Hein
said. CTA eventually would donate $500,000 to the campaign. The union's
support did not guarantee victory, but it came close.

No relationship would be more important to Schwarzenegger's political
career than the one with the California Teachers Association. The state of
the bond between the star and the CTA would become the most reliable
barometer of his standing with the public.

WITH CTA ON BOARD, anti-tax groups expressed concern. Even though education funds would be protected, the after-school funds would have to be
taken from money previously bound for other popular programs—health
care, higher education, local government, and various entitlements. That
might create pressure for a tax increase.

Schwarzenegger's team spent a couple hours with Joel Fox, the former
president of the Howard Jarvis Taxpayers Association, who suggested some
tightening up of the financial oversight provisions in the initiative. Fox, for
his trouble, received two tickets to the premiere of Collateral Damage, a movie
starring Schwarzenegger as a Los Angeles firefighter who battles the terrorists who kill his family. Its release, originally scheduled for shortly after September 11, had been delayed until February 2002.

Conservatives argued that Schwarzenegger should take the money for after-school programs out of future increases in state revenue, not from a tax
hike and not from other programs. To figure out how that would work,
Schwarzenegger engaged state budget experts with ties to Governor Wilson.
The initiative was revised to say that once non-education spending had
grown by $1.5 billion, after-school programs would get their $500 million.
That was as much a political judgment as a budgetary one. The hope was
that health, transportation, and other advocates would not object to funding
after-school programs if they first received funding increases of their own.

ON DECEMBER 6, 2001, Nielsen wrote the nineteenth and final draft. With
all the additions, the measure ran thirteen single-spaced pages. Nielsen sent
it off to three different proofreading companies as a final check.

On December 9, Schwarzenegger broke six ribs when he fell off his motorcycle and was hospitalized for four days. He did his own final review from
his hospital bed. Although in pain, Schwarzenegger invited aides and politi-

cal advisors to the hospital for meetings. Shriver had to shut down the sessions so Schwarzenegger could rest.

To keep Schwarzenegger's involvement secret a little while longer, Paul Miner, a former Wilson policy advisor who had been hired as research director for the initiative, took the measure to the attorney general's office. Miner paid the $200 filing fee with a personal check and was listed as the official proponent. Schwarzenegger's name would be added later as co-proponent.

As a piece of politics, the proposition was a wonder. "The initiative has been pre-sold," Gorton said. As legislation, the measure was limited. It was full of caveats and delays and restrictions. It was lowest-common-denominator law. In a way, the initiative was less legislation than the script to a movie, one that wouldn't offend any interest group or scare off any part of a potential audience.

SCHWARZENEGGER hired two signature-gathering firms—one Republican-leaning, the other more Democratic—to circulate the initiative. If they could gather 373,816 valid signatures, or 5 percent of those who had voted in the most recent gubernatorial election, the initiative would qualify for the November 2002 general election ballot.

The California secretary of state assigns numbers to propositions in the order in which they qualify. Every ten years or so, they start over at number one. The after-school initiative would draw that most fortuitous of numbers for a California measure: Proposition 49. Schwarzenegger had joined the initiative gold rush.

CHAPTER 7

The Trailer Campaign

SCHWARZENEGGER KICKED OFF his public campaign for Proposition 49 on the morning of February 20, 2002, with a rally at Hart Street Elementary School in the San Fernando Valley. He hit three poll-tested themes: "This is an education issue, a crime issue, and a working family issue. Every child who wants and needs one should have a safe, educationally enriching, and fun place to go after school," Schwarzenegger said. The ceremony concluded with a teacher holding an initiative petition against Schwarzenegger's back and signing it.

What was unusual about the kickoff was the timing. Initiative campaigns typically lasted six weeks. This initiative would appear on the November ballot, nine months away. Signatures were still being gathered to qualify the after-school initiative officially for the ballot. Schwarzenegger had arranged for life-sized cardboard cutouts of himself, holding a child in each arm, to be distributed to signature gatherers. He gave away signed movie memorabilia to those gatherers who produced the most signatures.

Schwarzenegger's duties as a movie star forced him to re-adjust the normal political calendar. By February, pre-production on *Terminator 3: Rise of the Machines* had begun. In April, Schwarzenegger would disappear to the set, his schedule determined by the studio and the movie's director. He was due to be shooting until September, and it was unclear how much initiative work he might be able to do while making the movie. Schwarzenegger told the consultants that since most of the movie had to be shot at night, he would have to spend part of the day sleeping.

Schwarzenegger had contractual control over the script. It showed. In the new movie, the machine that gunned down Los Angeles police officers in the first 1984 film had the new strategy of shooting only to maim. For his initiative campaign, Schwarzenegger needed law enforcement endorsements. *Terminator 3*'s director, Jonathan Mostow, joked publicly that he had signed up to direct a movie only to walk into a political campaign.

That campaign was not merely for an initiative. It was designed to embed Schwarzenegger as a political figure in the public mind.

Schwarzenegger himself designed the launch not as one event but as a two-day "fly around," hitting six cities across the state. At each stop, he was met by at least ten television cameras. He would take a few questions and answer them easily. During a planning meeting at Spago, the well-known Beverly Hills restaurant of the Austrian-born Wolfgang Puck, Schwarzenegger's team of consultants developed forty-three possible questions that Schwarzenegger might be asked about the initiative, and scripted forty-three responses. To the question, "Is this just a platform for an eventual run for public office?" Schwarzenegger's scripted reply was: "Absolutely not! This initiative is the logical outgrowth of work I started a long, long time ago." In practice, Schwarzenegger's answers didn't match the script word for word. He couldn't resist ad-libbing asides that referenced bodybuilding or his films, but he got across the intended message each time.

Schwarzenegger thought the tour went well enough, but he did not like the somber aides and advance men who staffed the trip. "I came home that night and I said to Maria, 'I don't like this. I don't think I will be good for politics because these guys, they're not fun,'" he recalled. The star later brought his complaint to Gorton. The advance men act like something's wrong, said Schwarzenegger. "Make them happy, George!" It was not an idle request. Schwarzenegger insisted on living in a zone of good humor. Hence this early order in his first campaign: Smile or else.

PUBLIC EVENTS DID NOT happen without money. Schwarzenegger was prepared to put his own money into the campaign, but the actor's donations would cover only $2.2 million of the $10 million budget.

To fill out the rest, he set up lunch and dinner meetings with potential donors. The campaign worked from a list of people from whom Schwarzenegger hoped to raise as much as $1 million each. He knew many of them personally. George Soros had a vacation home near Schwarzenegger's getaway in Sun Valley, Idaho. Schwarzenegger had struck up a friendship with Warren Buffett and even attended a conference in England with him. The only two people to match the $1 million goal, according to secretary of state records, were Dallas-based tech entrepreneur Todd Wagner, who worked with the Inner City Games there, and Jerrold Perenchio, head of the Spanish language TV network Univision.

Schwarzenegger was a reluctant fund-raiser at first. "All my life I tried to make money so I didn't have to ask anybody for anything . . . All of a sudden, there you are, 'Can you help me with this?'" But Schwarzenegger hired a professional fund-raiser, Renee Croce, who would become a fixture in his political campaigns. Croce introduced Schwarzenegger to Paul Folino, the

CEO of an Orange County–based networking technology company, in what would prove to be a fortuitous meeting.

Folino had almost no history of political activity and only recently had switched his registration from "decline to state" to Republican. But Folino was active in educational charities. At the requests of friends from these non-profit boards, Folino had joined the New Majority, a new Orange County–based group of moderate businessmen who wanted to pull the Republican party to the center. Among the founders of the New Majority was Donald Bren, the chairman of the Irvine Company, the huge Orange County real es-tate company that would provide critical behind-the-scenes support for Schwarzenegger's political career.

Schwarzenegger and Folino had some things in common. Folino had risen from working-class roots in Seattle. Schwarzenegger, to Folino's ears, sounded more like a CEO than a movie star, and he liked the fact that Schwarzenegger's wife and business associates openly disagreed with him. After a dinner at the Schwarzenegger home, Folino decided to serve as fi-nance secretary for Prop 49.

Folino, it turned out, had a knack for organizing fund-raising events, at which Schwarzenegger felt at ease. Initially Folino kept events small, holding a dinner at his own home where the comedian Sinbad performed. When the campaign needed a bigger event, Folino arranged for Chapman University in Orange, where he sat on the board, to host a premiere of Schwarzenegger's movie *Collateral Damage* that would double as a Prop 49 fund-raiser. The movie studio agreed to the premiere on the condition that each guest be searched for video cameras and piracy devices before entering the fund-raiser. Schwarzenegger toured the campus and talked with donors "about some of the kooks in the Republican party and how far right they were," according to one donor. The event raised more than $600,000.

The New Majority and its members would ultimately donate more than $2 million to the initiative campaign. Folino gave more than $750,000, enough to fund all the signature gathering for the initiative. Schwarzenegger reciprocated by donating to Folino's charities. At Chapman University, he helped Folino raise $30 million to build a new film school.

AFTER THE CAMPAIGN KICKOFF, Schwarzenegger worked to lock up more endorsements. During a brief vacation in Hawaii, he arranged for a satellite linkup so he could speak to the board of the California Taxpayers Associa-tion. In person, he addressed the California Medical Association, the Cali-fornia State PTA, the Service Employees International Union, the Los Angeles City Council, and the California School-Age Consortium. If

Schwarzenegger's only goal had been an initiative victory, all these speeches and meetings would have been overkill. But for a potential governor, such events were essential political legwork.

Schwarzenegger also added state legislators to the guest list for his monthly cigar night at Schatzi's. For years, Schwarzenegger had used cigar night like a CEO servicing his company's vendors. Partners in his real estate deals, screenwriters touching up a movie to his specifications, and exhibitors at his Ohio fitness convention all stopped by.

At one cigar night, Schwarzenegger huddled with a half dozen of Sacramento's most conservative lawmakers. He even convinced a straight-arrow assemblyman from Orange County, John Campbell, to drink a bit of peach-flavored schnapps, an Austrian favorite. Campbell wouldn't support Prop 49 ("I saw it as just more spending," he said), but he would become a key supporter on the right. Assemblyman Russ Bogh, who was also in the room, said: "I remember having a conversation afterwards and we just agreed, 'This guy, he's no novice.'"

On March 26, seven months before Prop 49 would be voted upon, Schwarzenegger's political consultants held meetings on "building a political organization for the future," according to a meeting agenda. The team of consultants also debated possible slogans for Prop 49 and future endeavors. Scott Mednick, a marketing and entertainment executive who was on the board of Schwarzenegger's charitable foundation, suggested "Join Arnold." It stuck.

ON APRIL 15, *Terminator 3* began production in the Los Angeles Center Studios on the western edge of downtown. The original plan had been to film in Vancouver, British Columbia, where Schwarzenegger had shot *The Sixth Day* three years earlier. At that time he had called Vancouver "the greatest city I have ever worked in" and pledged to return. Now, shooting in the midst of a California political campaign, Schwarzenegger insisted that the production be kept in Los Angeles.

Almost as soon as Schwarzenegger left his Santa Monica offices to make the movie, the after-school campaign confronted its first serious opposition. At the end of April, the League of Women Voters balked at giving the campaign what consultants assumed would be an easy endorsement, and instead opposed Prop 49 as "ballot box budgeting." That is, voters should not be able to lock in spending increases because such decisions should be left to the legislature. The league's opposition meant very little by itself. But its argument quickly caught on among police chiefs and sheriffs. If law enforcement opposed an initiative that was being advertised as a way to save children from crime, Prop 49 would be in trouble.

Bob McDonell, the police chief of the Orange County city of Newport Beach, was particularly concerned. At the time, McDonell was serving a term as president of the California Police Chiefs Association (Cal-Chiefs). McDonell had nothing against after-school programs. What McDonell could not abide was Prop 98, the state's education funding guarantee.

To win the support of the CTA and protect Prop 98, Schwarzenegger had agreed to fund Prop 49 from growth in the non-education half of the budget—the half on which police departments depended for funding.

Cal-Chiefs voted to oppose the measure. After word of that decision leaked, the state sheriffs' association rejected Schwarzenegger's request for an endorsement and said it would stay neutral.

Schwarzenegger was stunned by the loss of law enforcement support. From the set, he called police chiefs and sheriffs and asked them to reconsider. He mentioned to a few chiefs that his late father, back in Austria, had been a cop. The chiefs and sheriffs told him the opposition was not personal.

Schwarzenegger's political team met at the Ritz Carlton Hotel in the Marina del Rey section of Los Angeles to plot strategy. The state sheriffs' association and Cal-Chiefs were well-respected, but they were small groups of managers. If their doubts spread to the California Peace Officers Association, which included rank-and-file officers from around the state, Prop 49 might be in trouble. It seemed possible the peace officers would formally oppose the measure at their convention in Sacramento on May 20.

It was time to call Jeff Randle.

SACRAMENTO HAD PLENTY of politically ambitious young men and women who attracted attention wherever they went. Jeff Randle was not one of them. He was a mechanic, a grind who excelled at the painstakingly detailed work of political operations: coalition building, endorsements, events. At UCLA, he had worked as an intern for U.S. Senator Pete Wilson and later got a job doing immigration casework for the senator. He did not mind menial tasks. When he started helping Wilson with his campaigns, he graduated to the grueling behind-the-scenes work of winning endorsements. "I found this niche in politics," he recalled.

Randle had worked on all of Wilson's initiative campaigns. When the governor left office, Randle tried corporate public relations and decided he'd rather be his own boss. Randle Communications kept its offices on 21st Street, not in the office buildings near the capitol where most political strategy firms located, and focused on interests that matched his own: criminal justice and education.

By May 7, the day after receiving a call from Bob White, Randle and his business partner, Mitch Zak, were running a campaign to limit the law enforcement damage to Prop 49. Each member of the California Peace Officers board received four pieces of mail from the Proposition 49 campaign. One of those letters came from Governor Wilson. Schwarzenegger himself called the peace officers' president.

McDonell, the Newport Beach police chief, was still raising questions with his colleagues about the measure. Randle called McDonell directly. The chief's objections were honorable but, Randle asked, what would his opposition accomplish? Schwarzenegger is going to be a "very important political factor in this state, and you might want to consider how vocal you are," Randle told him.

Randle worked to isolate McDonell. As the Schwarzenegger team lined up endorsements from dozens of individual police chiefs, Randle would call McDonell and quietly inform him of his progress. Not everyone appreciated this direct style. Los Angeles County Sheriff Lee Baca would become the first—but not the last—to accuse Schwarzenegger and his political team of bullying opponents. "Arnold wants to have everyone on board, but in politics you can't have that," Baca said. "I think they overreacted. You let people have their point of view. Randle pushed too hard." But pushing hard was what Randle was paid to do.

The campaign for law enforcement support proved effective. CalChiefs would remain officially opposed to Prop 49, but with so many individual chiefs backing the measure, the news media assumed that police chiefs endorsed Prop 49. Schwarzenegger did even better with the California Peace Officers' Association. Rather than stay neutral, the peace officers endorsed the initiative. Randle followed up by securing an endorsement from the narcotic officers association. Schwarzenegger flew by helicopter from the *Terminator 3* set to Lake Arrowhead to clinch the endorsement of the California State Sheriffs Association. Randle joined the flight, and for the first time met his new client, who teased the wiry political consultant about his puny arms.

Schwarzenegger had won the war. Whenever a reporter asked Schwarzenegger about the opposition of the League of Women Voters and other groups, he would pull out a huge, single-spaced list of organizations endorsing Prop 49 and would threaten to read the whole thing unless the reporter withdrew the question.

SCHWARZENEGGER HAD DODGED the last serious threat to the campaign. But the near miss with the cops put a scare into his team. The consultants bought more TV time and added more fund-raisers to the schedule.

All this required scheduling more meetings on the *Terminator 3* set. The director of a Mexican civil rights institute, a representative of the Christian Coalition, and the president of the powerful state prison guards' union all met Schwarzenegger in his trailer. Schwarzenegger greeted Mike Jimenez, the guard union president, while wearing green Lycra makeup over half his body and face; the other half of his face had been made up to look like he had been wounded. Jimenez found the experience of hearing a political pitch from the Terminator a little unsettling.

Donors jumped at the chance to meet Schwarzenegger at the set. Noting the reaction, the campaign auctioned off visits and a bit part in the movie to raise money. Even journalists were happy to play along. *Los Angeles Times* columnist George Skelton questioned Schwarzenegger about his gubernatorial ambitions as the candidate's face was covered in heavy make-up showing wounds, blood, and a metal skull. "I'm going to make this initiative succeed," Schwarzenegger told Skelton. "It's absolutely important. That is my mission right now . . . It is like the, you know, the Terminator mode."

As SHOOTING ON THE MOVIE CONTINUED, Schwarzenegger cleared a few hours on consecutive Saturdays that summer to produce Prop 49 commercials. Don Sipple, the media consultant who would produce these and future political ads for Schwarzenegger, had filmed governors, senators, and even presidential candidates. But no one understood ads as well—or had as many thoughts on how they should look—as Schwarzenegger. The star not only reviewed the script but made Sipple produce a series of storyboards.

For a set, Sipple used one of the four schools where the star's local after-school program operated—Mulholland Middle School in the San Fernando Valley. For the shoot, Schwarzenegger had a trailer and a crew of thirty so he could move immediately from shot to shot without waiting. Adam Greenberg, the cinematographer from *Collateral Damage* and *Terminator 2: Judgment Day*, agreed to serve as director of photography for the commercial.

Sipple produced a sixty-second ad that opened with dramatic black-and-white footage of teenagers committing crimes, from vandalism to smoking crack. After that montage, the screen shifted to Schwarzenegger in color, walking through the middle school and talking about the importance of after-school programs. In most of his future political ads, Schwarzenegger would deliver his message while walking. Even in politics an action star should not stand still.

Schwarzenegger's hair was unnaturally dark and slightly spiked—exactly like the Terminator's, since he had to return to the set when the commercial was over. On the following Saturday, Sipple shot the ad's conclusion in the

Oak Productions offices in Santa Monica. Surrounded by his collection of historic busts, Schwarzenegger talked about Prop 49's funding provisions. Before the ads debuted on September 3, Schwarzenegger showed them to his wife, a final check he had used with movie scripts and would employ with political texts as well.

THE INCUMBENT GOVERNOR, Gray Davis, was running for re-election on the same November ballot on which Prop 49 appeared. He had grown deeply unpopular as energy shortages and the state's budget crisis grew more serious. But Davis still led in the polls as his challenger, Bill Simon, Jr., a Republican businessman making his first run for office, struggled to get his message out. Gorton, who still wished Schwarzenegger had run for governor, added a question to one of the Prop 49 polls asking if voters would support Schwarzenegger as a write-in candidate. The poll results showed that the actor, while far more popular personally than either candidate, would likely lose such a contest.

On September 10, Schwarzenegger presided over a meeting at a Sacramento hotel of the coalition of more than eighty organizations backing Prop 49. The meeting was put together to create a unified message about the initiative—and to allow Schwarzenegger to cement his ties to interest groups that could help him in the future.

A slide show listed "voter-perceived negatives," including "this is just babysitting," "kids at risk won't attend," and "Arnold is using this to run for governor." If confronted with this last objection, Prop 49 coalition members were advised to list his record of charitable work on after-school programs. Coalition members also received a set of suggested questions that they should ask Schwarzenegger at town hall meetings. Among the questions were, "Why are you so passionate about after school programs?" and "Are you surprised that Proposition 49 has received such broad-based bipartisan support?"

The carefully solicited support was broad, but not as deep as the campaign would have liked. Prop 49 barely clung to the majority needed for passage—it registered 51 percent support in a Field Poll in September. The public backed after-school programs, but worried about spending hundreds of millions of dollars on a new program as the state budget fell deeper into deficit.

WITH POLLS SHOWING a narrow lead for 49, Schwarzenegger added touches to his speeches that went beyond after-school programs. He told the League of California Cities that the state government had been wrong to raid their money for so many years. He attended a meeting with insurance companies and a fund-raiser with Sacramento lobbyists.

Schwarzenegger appeared at schools with law enforcement officials, educators, and "as much as possible, flanked by numerous children." That last phrase came from the campaign's "earned media" plan, a strategy for public events and media interviews drafted by Sean Walsh, a former deputy chief of staff and press secretary for Governor Wilson.

"Arnold Schwarzenegger is an independent-minded individual who represents a new kind of politics," read the plan. Schwarzenegger should avoid the print press and use national TV and entertainment programs that were inaccessible to other candidates, but available to him as a movie star. He should exploit his celebrity advantage, but avoid public appearances with his celebrity friends.

Schwarzenegger did even more interviews than Walsh suggested. With *Terminator 3* production winding down, Schwarzenegger added extra rallies and public events to the schedule in the final six weeks of the campaign. (At an event in Contra Costa County, he showed up with his Terminator makeup still on.) He talked about the election as if it were a movie opening.

"November 5," he said, "is Judgment Day!"

ON JUDGMENT DAY, voters in the twenty-four states that had direct democracy cast ballots on a total of twenty-eight initiatives and more than eighty other measures that had been referred to the ballot by their state legislatures. In California, voters faced seven measures, numbered Propositions 46 through 52.

The California Republican Party would have been happy to have Schwarzenegger attend its election night party. But he decided to have his own election night event at the Hollenbeck Youth Center, where Danny Hernandez had founded the Inner City Games. The party was held on the basketball court.

An easy win had been expected. Instead, early returns showed a close race, and further results came slowly. Schwarzenegger sent out for food for the neighborhood children among the well-wishers at Hollenbeck. It was nearly midnight when he declared victory.

In the final tally, Proposition 49 won comfortably, with 4,024,904 votes out of more than 7 million cast, for a total of 56.7 percent. That was not overwhelming in normal times. But for California Republicans, Schwarzenegger's initiative was the only victory to which they could lay any claim. In the state that had propelled Ronald Reagan and Richard Nixon to the presidency, the 2002 elections had seen Democrats win every statewide office and maintain large majorities in the legislature.

SCHWARZENEGGER HOSTED a party at Schatzi's for the campaign team and donors. He sent bottles of wine to key backers. The campaign was not entirely over. Gorton had bought additional airtime for Prop 49 TV ads in the final weeks, pushing the initial $10 million campaign budget more than $1 million higher. Prop 49, like *Terminator 3*, had come in over budget. Schwarzenegger personally looked through the campaign expenditure reports and couldn't believe the size of the consultants' fees. He would have to hold more fund-raisers just to retire the campaign debt.

Gorton and his associate, the political consultant Mitch Mulanix, continued to work out of Schwarzenegger's Santa Monica office building after the election. But Schwarzenegger kept his distance. After a busy year, he wanted his life back. He planned to spend 2003 working on his after-school charities and pursuing various movie projects. Two sequels were being talked about— *True Lies 2* and *King Conan*—that would bring him back to the screen in his most popular roles.

In 2002, Schwarzenegger had learned how movie production and direct democracy could be combined. But California politics had no single director and would not accommodate his schedule. He would find himself starring in another blockbuster far sooner than he thought.

PART 2

On account of being a democracy and run by the people, we are the only nation in the world that has to keep a government four years, no matter what it does.

—Will Rogers

CHAPTER 8

"A Thing of Beauty"

"THIS THING would be perfect for Schwarzenegger."

The phone pressed to his ear, Ted Costa reached for a copy of the California constitution. His friend in Bakersfield, Mark Abernathy, might be right.

Costa and Abernathy had been having conversations about political strategy for more than thirty years. When they first met, the two had been members of a group of Sacramento Republicans who got together for cocktails on Fridays. Now Abernathy, a political consultant, worked closely with Republican Congressman Bill Thomas. Costa ran People's Advocate, the political organization of the late Paul Gann, co-author of Prop 13 with Howard Jarvis, from an office in a rundown building behind the Krispy Kreme donut shop on Sacramento's Arden Road. Inside the office, Costa hung pictures of Abraham Lincoln in so many places that the only way to escape the sixteenth president's gaze was to retreat to the bathroom. On the rare occasions when slick pollsters, ambitious legislators, or curious reporters made the fifteen-minute drive from the capitol to see him, Costa, a college dropout, would take them to the $5 all-you-can-eat Chinese buffet across the parking lot. He paid himself $38,000 a year, drove a twenty-year-old Ford compact and wore ill-fitting suits. Costa spent his evenings at his home in the suburb of Citrus Heights, kept company by his wife, a yard full of live animals, and a two-ton bust of Lincoln.

Arnold Schwarzenegger, the man Costa wanted to star in the political production he was cooking up, did not yet know Costa's name.

Only two weeks before Costa and Abernathy's conversation in November of 2002, Gray Davis had been re-elected governor of California. It was not an impressive victory. Davis collected just 47 percent of the vote, narrowly defeating an unknown Republican, Bill Simon, Jr., despite Simon's obvious handicaps. (The Green Party candidate drew just more than 5 percent.) Simon had never before run for office. He was a conservative in a socially liberal state. "And on television," he said, "I'm a little bit stiff."

Davis emodied the California political establishment. He had served as Governor Jerry Brown's chief of staff, spent two terms in the state assembly, and held the statewide offices of controller and lieutenant governor before winning the governorship in 1998. Early in his term, when Silicon Valley was minting millionaires, record state revenues allowed Davis to cut taxes, spend more on education, and give raises to state employees. By the time he was sworn in for his second term, he had come to embody something else: overly cautious leadership in the face of crisis. Davis had been slow to respond when California communities began to experience power outages in the summer of 2000. Out-of-state energy companies and traders in the wholesale market—most infamously Enron—took advantage of the situation. The utilities, which had paid $31 per megawatt hour in 1999, were being charged $1,000 per megawatt hour at peak times in the summer of 2000. Davis protested that the crisis was not his fault. That was true, but he failed to take quick action to solve it. It was not until 2001 that he signed long-term energy contracts with the wholesalers to ensure a stable energy supply. In doing so, he locked in exorbitant rates that were passed on to homeowners and businesses. It was a political double whammy. Davis had failed to prevent the crisis and had raised electric bills.

Simultaneously, the national economy went into a recession, and state revenues from personal income tax dropped. California's budget had had a record surplus in 2000. By the spring of 2002, the state was projecting a deficit. Shortly after his re-election in November 2002, Davis disclosed that the state, with a general fund of $75 billion, faced a shortfall that could top $30 billion.

Davis's political fund-raising also became a lightning rod. He solicited a $1 million donation from the California Teachers Association in his capitol office. He received $251,000 from the state's prison guards' union after giving them a 37 percent raise over five years. Davis's fund-raising, while heavily criticized in the state press, was rational. With California's wide-open politics and direct democracy, one rich person writing one big check could change the political dynamics of the state. A governor who wanted to defend himself had to keep his campaign coffers full.

While Davis kept a condo in West Hollywood, his professional life had been spent in Sacramento, and he did not like to toss major political decisions to the people through direct democracy. After the teachers' union threatened a ballot initiative requiring the state to match the national average for per-pupil spending, Davis added $1.8 billion for education to the already bursting budget. He similarly boosted workers' compensation benefits after attorneys representing injured workers talked of an initiative. "Every single Democratic constituency group threatened ballot initiatives against him," said Lynn Schenk, his chief of staff. "In retrospect, maybe we should have gotten in front of a couple of real populist initiatives that would have cemented his approval rating."

Ironically, Davis's uninspiring re-election campaign left him especially vulnerable to direct democracy. Hiram Johnson established qualifying standards for initiatives, referenda, and recalls based on the percentage of total votes cast in the most recent gubernatorial election. A referendum or an initiative changing the law could get on the ballot with a number of signatures representing 5 percent of the votes cast in the last election. The recall of a statewide elected official required 12 percent. In a state as large as California, collecting a number of signatures equal to 12 percent of votes cast was usually a prohibitively expensive proposition. But Davis's tactics helped push turnout in the governor's race so low that a recall could get on the ballot with fewer than 900,000 signatures. The price of making a blockbuster was suddenly cheap.

AS LUCK WOULD HAVE IT, Ted Costa was sitting on $200,000 left over from a 2000 initiative to take the power to draw Congressional and legislative districts away from the legislature. The money wasn't much to the political consultants on L Street in downtown Sacramento, but it was a fortune to Costa's organization.

Costa saw himself as a taxpayer rights advocate with a good government bent. His critics called him everything from a crank to a political terrorist. Neither his description nor his critics' explained Costa's true calling. In California's system of direct democracy, he was the most prolific, if hardly the most successful, screenwriter. When Costa had an idea for an initiative or referendum or even a recall, he wrote it down as quickly as he could. It didn't have to be his concept. He would hear something on the radio or pick up on a popular idea the legislature had ignored—and reduce it to an initiative within days. Some years, he filed a dozen initiatives. He rarely had the money to gather signatures on any of them. But that was not the point. Costa set down markers and thus claimed first right to a whole series of political stories.

With qualifying standards so low after Davis's re-election, Costa believed the time was right for something that would "excite the masses" and encourage people to pay attention to California's problems.

One such idea was beginning to circulate. After Davis's re-election, many pundits argued that the governor had deserved to lose. On November 15, two days before the conversation between Costa and Abernathy, Democratic pollster Pat Caddell had suggested a Davis recall on a cable TV public affairs show in Los Angeles. A journalist who appeared on the show, Tom Elias, wrote a column that appeared in newspapers around the state. Elias called for political reform and, without mentioning anyone by name, said the state needed a "Hercules" to lead a "new Progressive movement."

"Who, then, might be the next Hiram Johnson?" Elias wrote. "A Davis recall drive might be one way to find out."

Even before the column appeared in print, a similar thought had occurred to Costa. But it was not until that phone conversation with Abernathy that Costa first asked the question: "Why don't we recall him?"

Abernathy was quiet for a moment on the other end of the line.

"Well, that'd be a thing of beauty," Abernathy replied. "A thing of beauty for Arnold."

RECALLS HAD BEEN USED in local government since Hiram Johnson's day. Dozens of city councilmen, mayors, and school board members had been removed from office by the voters during their elected terms. In the 1990s, recalls had been carried out against Republican state legislators who voted for a Democrat as speaker of the assembly.

But no statewide elected official had ever been recalled in California. Even though some eighteen states allowed for recalls, only one governor—Lynn Frazier of North Dakota in 1921—had ever been removed from office in this way. (He was the victim of a political dispute involving a state-owned bank.) Several California governors had faced recall petitions, but none ever received enough signatures to qualify for the ballot.

As he studied the California constitution, Costa learned a recall would be a two-part ballot question. First, voters would be asked whether to recall Davis. Then, on the same ballot, voters would be asked to pick a replacement in the event the recall succeeded. There would be no party primaries, and the requirements for getting on the ballot were quite low. It would be a free-for-all with as many as twenty candidates, Costa guessed, and the winner would likely be a charismatic outsider, someone who stood out in a crowd.

SHAWN STEEL, the chairman of the state Republican Party, was due to leave his post in February. He decided not to go quietly. A lawyer who represented chiropractors and acupuncturists from his office in Los Angeles, Steel was an unconventional party chairman. On December 9, 2002, a month after Davis's re-election, Steel gave a speech to the Sacramento Press Club in which he pledged to work for the recall of any Republican legislator who cooperated with Davis on a tax increase to close the budget deficit. Other party leaders were furious. The very next day, the California Republican Party board of directors voted to censure Steel for his comments.

Costa, though, loved Steel's threat. He spotted Steel outside the capitol and asked: "Hey, Shawn, what do you think of recalling Davis?"

"Ted," Steel replied, "that's about the goddamndest, nuttiest idea I've ever heard. I'll have nothing to do with that." Except that Steel, as he did his Christmas shopping, could soon think of nothing else. Steel's friend Pat Caddell, the Democratic pollster who had once worked for Jimmy Carter, told him a recall could win.

The morning of January 20, 2003, Steel kept an appointment to call into KSFO-AM in San Francisco. The show's conservative cohost, Melanie Morgan, had risen from thirty-eighth in the Bay Area Arbitron ratings to the top five by taking issues and flogging them every day. The idea was to give listeners a story they could follow uninterrupted for months. The year 2003 was shaping up as a slow one. Morgan needed a hot topic, a new campaign that galvanized listeners.

Steel was nearly finished with his appearance on Morgan's show when the subject turned to SUVs. Morgan joked that her "Dump Davis" bumper sticker—a relic from the 2002 re-election campaign—was the only way she could find her SUV in the parking lots of Marin County. "I've got to tell you, I'm getting more honks and beeps from people now than when I had it on from the beginning of the campaign," Morgan said.

"Now that's very, very good news," Steel said, pausing. The possibility of a recall had yet to be discussed publicly by any party or government official. He didn't understand yet how the recall provision of the constitution worked. But now he thought, what the hell? Steel said:

> You know what? There's been some serious talk. Davis has of course done all the worst things, and much worse than what we said in the campaign. The deficit is worse. The tax hikes are real. People are really beginning to get fed up. And if anything, Bill Simon and the party underplayed how serious the crisis would be in California. Think about this, folks. I think that our party is going to be looking very seriously at a recall movement.

Morgan had to break for a traffic report, but asked Steel to hold the line. Morgan's e-mail box started to fill. There were two dozen e-mails by the time commercials for mattresses and home refinancing were over.

Back on the air, Morgan said: "Shawn, you were talking about something that really just got our attention. And that is talk of a recall of Governor Gray Davis. Could you elaborate on this once again for us?"

"So what do we do? Take it for four years?" Steel said. "We just simply do nothing? And let him change the California dream and opportunity? I don't think so. And I think if we start talking about recall with Davis, it's focused, it's specific. It's not some pie-in-the-sky dream."

Morgan pressed for details. How would it work? Steel stalled. Give me a week to figure it out, he said. Steel gave his e-mail address over the air so potential supporters could contact him.

He was deluged by emails. Radio stations begged him to appear. Steel called a political fund-raiser, Tim Macy. "How much money could the party make if it did a mailing on a recall?"

You'd make a fortune, Shawn, was Macy's reply.

Steel flew off to Washington to attend regularly scheduled meetings of the Republican National Committee. During the trip, Steel visited a number of the nation's most prominent conservative activists, talking up the idea. He handed out copies of the recall provision from the California constitution at the Wednesday morning meeting of Grover Norquist's Americans for Tax Reform, which draws economic conservatives from all over the country. At Paul Weyrich's Free Congress Foundation, social conservatives liked the idea, too. At the Conservative Political Action Committee meeting on January 30, Steel ran into the *Wall Street Journal* opinion writer John Fund, a Californian who soon wrote a column championing it. Steel was a pariah to California Republicans, but the recall was a hit in conservative Washington.

ON MONDAY, JANUARY 24, the manager of Bill Simon, Jr.'s failed gubernatorial campaign, Sal Russo, invited an old friend to lunch at the Sutter Club in Sacramento. A private club a block west of the capitol, Sutter was a good place for a quiet conversation. Russo promised to keep the identity of his dining partner confidential.

Russo's guest was John Hein, the California Teachers Association political strategist, who had advised Schwarzenegger during the drafting of Proposition 49 and had stayed in touch since. Russo and Hein, despite their political differences, got along well. At the Sutter Club, Russo drank iced tea and Hein sipped water as they talked about polls. The CTA had done some post-election surveys and found that Davis was still losing popularity, Hein told Russo.

"The easiest election to win today in California would be a recall of Gray Davis," Hein recalled saying.

Russo remained cool, but his mind raced. Why the hell was the CTA polling on Gray Davis? Why was the political advisor to the most powerful Democratic interest group in the state telling a Republican consultant that the Democratic governor was ripe for the taking?

Russo countered that he was not sure he believed it. The election results, just two months old, indicated that while people disliked Davis and his policies, they weren't ready to remove him from office. Hein replied: If you did the polls today, Sal, they would look different. Hein said he thought Democrats might support a recall if the group behind it was bipartisan.

Hein later would say he merely mentioned the polling to an old friend as a joke, and did not mean for Russo to take him seriously. But that was not Russo's impression. "He was so pointed," Russo said. "When we started the conversation, I thought we were just shooting the shit. But then I realized that he wanted me to go do it."

When Davis ran for governor in 1998, CTA had helped him. But once Davis won the office, the new governor took rhetorical jabs at the union and pushed through legislation the CTA opposed. The union encouraged primary challengers to the governor in 2002, though none stepped forward.

Schwarzenegger, by contrast, had worked closely with the union and even let a lawyer for the CTA draft Prop 49. Hein was close to Schwarzenegger's political consultant George Gorton. That said, there was no evidence of any direct contact or collusion between Schwarzenegger's team and the teachers' union to spark the recall. Officially, CTA would oppose the recall. At his Sutter Club lunch, which was never publicly disclosed, the CTA's political strategist gave at least an inadvertent push to the effort that would dethrone Davis and make Schwarzenegger governor. By February, a few weeks after the lunch, the teachers' union was distributing the surveys by Washington, D.C.-based pollster Mark Mellman to which Hein had referred in his conversation with Russo.

Returning to his office after lunch with Hein, Russo did not call Simon. The consultant thought if the previous year's Republican nominee was involved, a recall would seem like sour grapes. That afternoon, former assemblyman Howard Kaloogian, a probate lawyer in San Diego, happened to call Russo. Kaloogian, a part-time talk radio host, immediately agreed to become the recall committee's public face. Russo would handle operational details.

On January 30, Kaloogian and Russo filed papers to establish the Recall Gray Davis Committee. Kaloogian put the Web site up a few days later and began writing fund-raising appeals. The two thought this would give them some time to build an organization and determine the opportune moment to file a recall petition. But their time was already up. Costa was about to file.

WITH THE PROPOSITION 49 initiative behind him, Schwarzenegger had turned to another campaign: the selling of *Terminator 3*, which would open on July 2, 2003. He had declined dozens of invitations to speak at political events, though he was quietly keeping his ear to the ground. Richard Riordan, the former Los Angeles mayor who had lost the 2002 Republican gubernatorial primary to Simon, flew with Schwarzenegger to Kitzbühel, Austria, in late January to attend the International Hahnenkamm, a famous downhill ski race. There, Riordan mentioned that if the recall materialized, he would face a choice of whether to run again. "If there's nobody else, I could run, but to be quite honest, I don't have fire in my belly the way, you know, most people have when they want to take over an office," the seventy-two-year-old Riordan told Schwarzenegger.

"Well," Schwarzenegger replied. "I have fire in my belly."

ON SATURDAY, FEBRUARY 1, the Columbia Space Shuttle disintegrated upon re-entering the earth's atmosphere. On Costa's television, pieces of the shuttle were shown falling all over the Western states, but he kept his eyes on his work.

For weeks, Costa's friends told him to take his time. They wanted him to line up some Democratic support so the recall wouldn't look like a project of a nut with an office behind the Krispy Kreme. His lawyer, Tom Hiltachk, advised: "You don't want to be a gadfly for a change."

If political types wanted him to wait, Costa thought that meant he needed to hurry or he would be cut out of the recall action. He spent much of the morning writing the formal legal notice listing the grounds for the recall. By law it could be no more than two hundred words in length.

"Mismanagement of California finances, threatening public safety by cutting funds to local governments, and failing in general to deal with the state's major problems until they get to the crisis stage," he wrote, having tried a half-dozen versions by day's end. He e-mailed his work Saturday night to Abernathy, who called Sunday morning to suggest Costa add a few words. "Mismanagement of California finances" became "gross mismanagement of California finances and overspending taxpayer money."

Costa kept the statement short so it could be easily downloaded from the Web, signed, and sent back. A downloadable petition would reduce printing costs and make it less expensive to get signatures. Ever since Steel had mentioned the recall on Morgan's show, the idea had dominated talk radio. Talk show hosts could direct listeners to the Web site, assisting the recall effort without Costa having to spend one dime.

On Tuesday morning, February 4, Costa rose before dawn to appear on Eric Hogue's radio show on KTKZ-AM in Sacramento. To file his notice of recall, Costa needed the signatures of one hundred registered voters. He asked listeners to drop by his office on their way to work. By 8 a.m., 275 people had found the out-of-the-way offices of the People's Advocate.

Sal Russo and Howard Kaloogian were furious. Kaloogian would publicly accuse Costa of stealing his idea. The two recall groups would war for the rest of the year, but by being first Costa had legal control of the petition.

Costa left the first line on the recall petition blank so Shawn Steel could sign it. The Republican party chairman invited every Republican legislator to join a press conference outside the capitol. Only Dennis Mountjoy, a back bencher from Los Angeles's San Gabriel Valley, attended. The California Democratic Party had two men with signs saying "Shawn Steel Is Nuts" on hand for the occasion. Steel signed the formal notice, and he and Costa walked it over to the governor's office, where a receptionist accepted it.

The state's political wise men and women did not take the recall seriously. It took the *Los Angeles Times*, the state's largest paper, five days to note that the petition had been filed. Davis's formal response, issued February 13, received more coverage than the initial petition.

As politicos and pundits began to pay more attention to the recall submission, many of Steel's and Costa's fellow conservatives denounced it. "California is not a Circuit City store," George Will wrote. "A democracy with periodic elections should not have, regarding elected officials, a liberal exchange policy—anytime for any reason—for voters experiencing buyer's remorse." Dave Cox, the Republican leader in the state assembly, said, "Frankly, I don't think it's a good idea."

Some Republicans took the most cynical of views: with an ineffective Democratic governor in office, President Bush might be able to win the state in 2004.

The Republican reaction was so fierce that Costa himself harbored doubts. The legislature's approval rating had dropped to 21 percent in polls. Perhaps now was the time to revive his initiative to change the way legislative districts were drawn. Costa sent Davis a letter offering a deal. He would drop the recall if the governor would support such an initiative. "I could have been bought for redistricting," Costa said. He never heard back.

ON HIS LATE JANUARY TRIP to Washington, Shawn Steel had dropped by the Capitol Hill office of Congressman Darrell Issa. The stop was obligatory for the outgoing party chairman. Issa, who represented a district in San Diego County, was both a political and financial power in the state's Republican party. The grandson of a Lebanese immigrant, Issa grew up in working-class Cleveland, dropped out of high school, and joined the army. When he came home to help his ailing father, he began to hang out with his older brother, who had been in trouble with the law. In 1972, Issa was arrested for car theft. Although the charges were dropped for lack of evidence, revelations from that period of his life had been a constant in political campaigns against the congressman.

After college and a four-year stint as an army officer, Issa moved to California and built a business selling car alarms and other anti-theft devices. He also took an interest in the state's initiative politics. He made Proposition 227, the initiative to end bilingual education, a key plank of his run for Barbara Boxer's U.S. Senate seat in 1998. Issa spent $10 million of his own money, but lost in the primary. He was elected to Congress in 2000.

In Washington, Steel and Issa talked about challenging Boxer again in 2004. As he got up to leave, Steel mentioned offhandedly to Issa's chief of staff, Dale Neugebauer, that he was headed to a meeting to discuss a recall of Gray Davis. "The light bulb went on in my head," Neugebauer said.

Three weeks later, Issa flew to California to attend the Republican party convention in Sacramento. There, Issa did a series of interviews with the press, all of which focused on a Senate race. But behind the scenes, he sounded out supporters on whether they thought a recall of Davis was legally and politically possible.

Issa asked Ray Haynes, an assemblyman from Temecula who led meetings of conservative activists around the state, how much it would take to qualify a recall. Haynes guessed $2.5 million. "Nobody has the juice to make it happen," Haynes said. Russo's group and Costa's organization will just "mine this thing for money."

Issa asked, "Do you think if I financed the recall, people would consider me as a candidate for governor?"

Haynes was stunned. "I will guarantee you, if you don't write the check, people won't even care that you're running for governor," he said.

Issa said he was thinking of a run, but that he wouldn't make a move before the war in Iraq was over. The two men shook hands, and Haynes left. The assemblyman would later say of the conversation: "That was the weirdest thing I'd ever heard."

ON MARCH 20, the United States launched a predawn missile attack on what President Bush called "select targets of military importance in Iraq." The next day, American and British troops seized the southern Iraqi port city of Umm Qasr.

For Costa, Steel, and the recall's small band of proponents, the buzz over the Iraqi invasion provided a cover for their failures; they had not built a coalition. Costa had been battling with the secretary of state's office over the format and language of the petition. When he finally got his petition approved on March 25, Costa had a new problem: no signature-gathering firm would agree to circulate it. Arno Political Consultants, the state's leading Republican petition firm, at first had told Costa it would handle the recall. But Mike Arno, one of the two brothers who headed the firm, was urged by leading Republicans to stay out of it. The Silicon Valley Manufacturing Group, which had close ties to Democrats, hired Arno to collect signatures on a transportation ballot initiative. David Townsend, a political consultant close to Davis, told Arno that if he accepted the initiative contract, he couldn't work on the recall. Since Costa had no money at the time, it was a business decision for Arno.

When Costa turned to other signature-gathering firms, he learned that they all had accepted a contract from Democratic groups to circulate a non-binding petition opposing the recall. There had been one condition of getting the contract: the firms couldn't work for the recall. It appeared that Davis's allies had locked up all the signature-gathering companies in California.

Abernathy, the Bakersfield consultant, called a lawyer in Washington he had known for years. Was there anyone who could handle such a task? The lawyer replied that he knew someone who used to work in California two decades years ago. This fellow knew all about the signature-gathering game, but he had feuds with the other California signature-gathering companies.

Perfect, Costa thought.

IN MARCH OF 2003, Tom Bader was living in a small apartment with his wife, Joy, in his hometown, the St. Louis suburb of Hazelwood. In 1979, Bader had launched a signature-gathering company in California, but he found the competition to be vicious. In 1986, he sold his company and moved out of state.

Costa tracked down Bader and offered him $12,000 to return to a state where he hadn't worked in seventeen years and to a business he had abandoned. Bader, without many other prospects, drove his tan 1994 Ford Escort to California. He signed a short-term lease in an office complex next to John Wayne Airport in Orange County and wrote out a plan for a signature-gathering effort. Bader called up old friends from his California days, asking for leads on gatherers and regional coordinators who had quit the business or fallen out with the signature-gathering companies. Those calls produced a network of twenty-nine coordinators throughout the state. In Fresno, Bader signed up a farmer who had been blackballed by the signature-gathering firms for circulating school voucher petitions on his own. He would produce two thousand signatures a week.

Bader couldn't get many signatures without money to pay the gatherers who worked the malls and supermarkets. Costa had reason to believe the money would come from Schwarzenegger. George Gorton e-mailed frequently with Mark Abernathy's wife, Cathy, who worked for Congressman Bill Thomas, to ask about Costa's search for both signatures and money. Gorton never promised that the star would come through with cash, but his e-mails and calls raised hopes. On April 3, Costa signed a provisional contract with Bader to produce between 7,000 and 10,000 signatures a day. The attached e-mail noted that the contract would kick in "when Gorton gets us some money."

"Real financial support is still needed—can't get away from that in a state with this size," Cathy Abernathy emailed Gorton on April 4. "Instead of $1.5 million we will only need 750K to guarantee that Arnold can be sworn in by Thanksgiving. With $1.5 mil he could be sworn in by Columbus Day." Gorton said he would relay the message to his client.

Gorton thought the recall was a huge opportunity for Schwarzenegger. By running in a recall election, Schwarzenegger could win office without going through a Republican primary, where his liberal views on abortion and gay rights could hurt him.

But Gorton couldn't get his client's attention. For all his populist beliefs, Schwarzenegger sometimes showed too much deference to elite opinion. Through the Proposition 49 campaign, Schwarzenegger had met nearly all of the main players in California politics, Democrats and Republicans. These people told Schwarzenegger the recall was crazy.

Gorton nevertheless printed up a "Recall Gazette" for the star, a collection of stories he pulled off the Internet. But the newspaper Schwarzenegger read most closely, the *Los Angeles Times*, reinforced the elite view. "George, the *L.A. Times* says it isn't going to qualify," Schwarzenegger told Gorton when the two men discussed the possibility of funding the recall in April.

Schwarzenegger had taken an interest in a political subject, but it was not the recall. The Bush administration had proposed to cut $400 million out of $1 billion in federal funding for after-school programs. Schwarzenegger met first with U.S. Secretary of Education Rod Paige in Palo Alto to discuss the cuts. On April 8, as Baghdad was falling to coalition forces, Schwarzenegger traveled to Washington to lobby Congress to restore the money. During his visit, the star stopped by the Capitol Hill office of Bill Thomas, who chaired the House Ways and Means Committee.

Arnold, Thomas began, we can either bullshit and talk about after-school stuff, or we can get right to the point and talk about the recall.

You're my kind of guy, Schwarzenegger replied.

This is a once-in-a-lifetime event, Thomas said, taking out a pad of paper. Thomas outlined a normal election cycle for a Republican gubernatorial candidate, which would require a candidate to raise $18 million in a primary and $50 million for a general election. Schwarzenegger might not make it through a primary. But a recall, Thomas explained, would be a shorter campaign—about two months—and would cost half the money. Thomas told Schwarzenegger he needed to step up, put $100,000 behind the signature gathering and finance the recall. The congressman also reminded Schwarzenegger of a story from the 1980 presidential campaign, when Ronald Reagan, protesting the exclusion of other candidates from a debate in New Hampshire, famously asserted, "I paid for this microphone." If Schwarzenegger put up the money for the recall, he would own the movement and have first claim on the governorship if Davis was removed. Caesar, Thomas said, had taken the crown and crowned himself.

Schwarzenegger enjoyed Thomas's company, but he did not commit to putting up the money or to running for governor. If he were to do as Thomas suggested, it would look "too obvious," Schwarzenegger thought. The recall had to be, in the star's word, "organic," and stand on its own.

The next day, Schwarzenegger stopped by the White House to see Bush's political strategist, Karl Rove. Schwarzenegger arrived on time. He was accompanied by his after-school advisor, Bonnie Reiss, and Mitch Mulanix.

It was a courtesy call. But Rove was late, forcing a slightly annoyed Schwarzenegger to wait. When he arrived, Rove asked about life in Hollywood. Schwarzenegger talked briefly about after-school programs and said he would be happy to visit troops or help the war effort in any way the White House saw fit. Rove listened for about five minutes and then abruptly excused himself, saying he had to talk to the president about something. Just like that, the meeting was over.

The recall itself had not been discussed. It was not clear that the recall would even qualify. But the 2006 governor's race was a subtext of their meeting. Condoleezza Rice, then the National Security Advisor, had been talked about as a candidate for California governor. In one poll on Republican prospects, she won easily, with Schwarzenegger a distant second. On his way out, Schwarzenegger passed Rove, who pointed to Rice down a hall. There, Rove said, is your competition.

THE FALL OF BAGHDAD PROVIDED the recall with a boost. The war seemed to be over, and California's conservative radio hosts turned immediately to the recall to keep listenership high. If Americans could topple a failed regime across the globe, why couldn't they do the same in their largest state?

The talk radio hosts behaved as activists and entertainers. Melanie Morgan in San Francisco kept in touch with Eric Hogue in Sacramento and Roger Hedgecock in San Diego. Each host organized "drive-bys" to gather signatures on the recall petition. On April 15, Hogue gathered 1,056 signatures during one four-hour morning show. Morgan broadcast her show from in front of subway stations across the Bay Area so she could gather signatures. In San Diego, Hedgecock's rush hour drive-by caused a half-mile backup on a nearby road. Said Hedgecock, a former San Diego mayor: "It was a huge, huge ratings bonanza."

Bait and tackle shops volunteered to offer the recall petitions to customers; Davis's environmental policies had led to a decline in fishing licenses, fishermen argued. Operators of gun shows at the Del Mar Fairgrounds in San Diego, the Cow Palace in San Francisco, and the Orange County Fairgrounds in Costa Mesa distributed the petitions. An anti-abortion group added recall petitions to its monthly newsletter. These conservative organizations produced a steady stream of signatures—90,130 in the first month of gathering—but not at a fast enough rate to gather the required 897,158 valid signatures by the September 2 deadline. Meeting that deadline would guarantee a recall vote in March 2004. The signatures would have to be collected even sooner—by the end of July—to trigger a special election in the fall of 2003.

CONGRESSMAN DARRELL ISSA had spent several days in April in the Middle East. As an Arab American, he said he went to keep the dialogue open with leaders in the region, including Syria's Bashar al-Assad. After his return, he told aides that he wanted to devote some of his personal fortune to the recall effort.

Issa's plan was to put $100,000 into the signature gathering. He thought that would spark other donors to give the approximately $2 million needed to qualify the recall. To which group should he give the money? Issa had long distrusted Sal Russo, the political consultant working with Kaloogian. While Issa liked Costa personally, he didn't believe the activist had a large enough organization to use the money efficiently.

Issa called Dave Gilliard, a low-key Northern California native who had run Issa's successful Congressional campaign in 2000. "If you form an organization, I think you would probably find yourself with the resources to do it," Issa told Gilliard. The new group would be called Rescue California.

Issa's allies began talking to GOP donors about chipping in, but most resisted. Some would only back the effort if Schwarzenegger was the candidate. Issa was further hamstrung by the new federal campaign finance law, commonly known as McCain-Feingold. As a member of Congress, Issa was prohibited from raising "soft money"—that is, cash for accounts other than candidate campaigns.

Before he wired the first $100,000 to Gilliard's Rescue California, Issa called Davis's chief of staff Lynn Schenk.

What are you doing, Darrell? Schenk asked. A former congresswoman from San Diego, she knew Issa from her failed 1994 re-election campaign. He had backed her challenger.

"I'm not doing it," Issa replied. "Your office and the governor are doing it."

Are you serious about this? she asked.

"I'm serious, but the governor can stop it today and be out of this," Issa replied. He said if Davis took immediate action to improve the business climate in the state, he would not fund the recall. Schenk called the recall a horrible assault on democracy. Issa never heard back.

AFTER ISSA TRANSFERRED THE MONEY, Rescue California took over Costa's signature-gathering contract with Tom Bader. Phil Paule, a consultant who had worked with Issa for years, was put in charge of overseeing the signature security. The signatures collected on the street were brought to Bader's office in Orange County, where they were sorted by a staff of thirty. In Sacramento, Gilliard set up an office two blocks north of the capitol where volunteers integrated direct mail signatures with Bader signatures. Once processed, these petitions were driven to Costa's office. As the recall's official proponent, Costa had the right to screen the petitions himself. To staff Gilliard's office, five college students were hired at $10 per hour to open the packages and sort the petitions. At first, Paule insisted that all hires come from the college Republican club at UC Davis. That meant any spies would immediately stand out.

Paule worried most of all about how to get petitions safely to Sacramento from Bader's office in Newport Beach, 450 miles to the south. At one dollar per signature, a shipment of eighty thousand was worth $80,000, and their political value was incalculable. Issa insisted that Paule personally account for the petitions every step of the way. Even with electronic tracking, Paule refused to hire UPS or FedEx. A truck, he worried, could be hijacked. So Paule decided to do the job himself. In his closet, he found two big black Samsonite suitcases he'd bought for a safari trip to Kenya. For every delivery, Paule would take the suitcases to Bader's office, fill them with petitions, and fly them up himself to Sacramento on Southwest Airlines. He did this about two dozen times. One day he made the round trip twice.

His wife was accompanying him on one flight when birds were sucked into the plane's engines on takeoff. Such "bird strikes" have caused crashes. The pilot announced he would have to return to the airport for an emergency landing. "Oh, no," Paule thought as he grasped his wife's hand. "We could lose the signatures."

BADER STRUGGLED TO GATHER signatures at first, even with Issa's money. He had been forced to shut down San Francisco operations after several signature gatherers reported being attacked. One had hot coffee poured on him, according to a police report. Bader brought in 74,805 signatures the third week in May and another 99,245 the week after. That pace would qualify the recall, but was not fast enough to trigger a special election in the fall.

The Lincoln Club of Orange County and its leader Buck Johns agreed to kick in $100,000 on May 16. But the Lincoln Club was the only major donor group to rally to Issa's cause. By the evening of May 28, Bader was out of cash to pay signature gatherers. He prepared to shut down his operations. Costa desperately emailed Issa through his political consultant Scott Taylor: "My concern is we have worked so hard to pick up a good momentum and if we shut down now, we will be hard pressed to regain it."

Issa sent another $350,000. He made weekly money transfers for the rest of the recall. The payments not only supported Bader's efforts, but paid for a direct mail appeal to 1 million households with at least two registered Republicans. The mailing included a recall petition and a postage-paid envelope for sending it back.

Davis supporters quickly formed an anti-recall political committee, Taxpayers Against the Recall, which circulated the non-binding "no-on-the-recall" petition to occupy the other signature-gathering companies. It turned out that Davis, in supporting the legally meaningless petition to keep himself in office, had outfoxed himself. While the governor's allies had bought off the signature-gathering companies, the individual signature gatherers on the street were independent contractors who could not be easily controlled. Out to make as much money as they could, many carried both the recall and the anti-recall petition. Some gatherers discovered a synergy between the two. Outside a mall in a heavily Republican area of Riverside, signature gatherers pitched the recall petition and Davis's counter-measure as a package deal. "Here, sign the recall," shouted one gatherer, holding the recall petition in one hand. In the other, he waved the anti-recall measure: "And if you sign this other one, too, it costs Gray Davis two bucks!"

IN AN ESPECIALLY POOR POLITICAL DECISION, Davis provided a late boost to the signature gathering by issuing an executive order in June to triple the fees Californians paid for licensing their cars. He might have been better off raising taxes on sunshine. In a state of sprawl and long commutes, Californians saw the automobile as the very essence of personal freedom. Davis needed the money to cover the budget deficit, and he argued correctly that he was merely restoring the vehicle license fee to the same level it had been before he and his predecessor Pete Wilson cut it. But no matter how good his reasons were, Californians took the fee increase personally. No single act could better unite the state politically.

By June 12, Bader's signature gatherers carried signs that read: "Stop the Car Tax—Recall Davis." After Davis tripled the vehicle license fee, the recall organizers turned in 150,000 signatures in two days. Even the political establishment now realized the recall would go forward.

DAVIS HAD MISFIRED on the car tax, but his aim was devastating when it came to Issa. The congressman had formed a team of consultants, and by May was making campaign-style appearances around the state. The governor's supporters began a sharp counterattack against Issa. Opposition researchers revisited his past, from his thirty-year-old arrest for car theft to various business disputes, and got the information out to the state's newspapers.

Issa's campaign was slow to respond. Ken Khachigian, a former Reagan and Nixon aide and one of Issa's political advisors, could not get Issa to tell him the full story of his past. The result was that each new revelation caught the congressman's campaign team off guard. Issa also refused to go on TV with ads to answer the charges and to introduce himself to the state's voters. Larry McCarthy, Issa's media consultant, worried that the *Terminator 3* opening over the July 4 weekend might provide a window to launch a Schwarzenegger campaign. "We should be on the air in the pre-July 4 window," McCarthy wrote in an e-mail. But Issa wouldn't pull the trigger.

The attacks on Issa destroyed his chances of being elected governor, but may have guaranteed the success of the recall. Davis, by making the recall personal, missed an opportunity to look like a statesman rather than a partisan. A better strategy would have been to admit failure and make amends. A recall was more like a ballot initiative than a candidate campaign. The choice was yes or no, and Davis could not run as the lesser of two evils as he had in 2002.

By June, Issa had dropped in the polls. But the recall had a majority.

IN WASHINGTON, Schwarzenegger could claim political momentum. He had returned to D.C. in May to testify against the Bush administration's proposed cuts to after-school programs. Gorton and White had wondered about the wisdom of challenging the Republican president, but Schwarzenegger convinced Congress to reverse the cuts.

As the recall neared qualification, Schwarzenegger devoted most of his energy to promoting *Terminator 3*. His movie publicity had a strong political undercurrent. One premiere of the film doubled as a fund-raiser to retire debt from Prop 49. On *The Tonight Show* on June 26, Jay Leno asked Schwarzenegger whether he would run for governor. The audience applauded wildly as Schwarzenegger smirked: "In a few days from now, I do have to make a very, very—probably one of the most difficult—decisions of my life: what to wear on my opening day of *Terminator 3*."

In the weeks before *Terminator 3*'s July 2 debut, Schwarzenegger appeared on six magazine covers in the United States alone. He taped more than fifty TV interviews. In interviews with *Esquire* and *Entertainment Weekly*, he openly flirted with the idea of running for governor in the recall election. The *Esquire* cover, which was a surprise to his political advisors, carried the headline: "The Next Governor of California. Really." The producers of *Terminator 3* briefly discussed a "Terminator for Governor" ad campaign, but it never happened.

Schwarzenegger and his Hollywood publicists handled all of this. The political consultants weren't sure what to make of it. Was he using the recall to promote the movie? Or was he using the movie to promote a candidacy?

Gorton moved forward with plans for a possible campaign, using cigar nights at Schatzi's to recruit a staff. In an attempt to get Schwarzenegger's attention, Gorton commissioned two focus groups of independent voters and ticket-splitting Democrats. After the initial giggle from the focus groups upon hearing the star's name, the group members made plain that they took Schwarzenegger seriously as a political candidate and believed his fame and money would shield him from political corruption. In each group, at least one member reported having seen tabloid reports about philandering or sexual harassment by the star. Few said the issue mattered. "Most people shrugged, 'That's the way things go in Hollywood,'" Sean Walsh, who would handle the campaign's media communications, would later say.

The focus group findings were used to write a comprehensive statewide poll in late June. Schwarzenegger led among possible candidates in that survey, but drew just 21 percent. Asked for the general characteristics of the person they would like to see as governor, voters in the poll described an outsider. Sixty-eight percent thought it was very important that the replacement governor "be someone who can rise above partisan politics." Experience or even a clear plan to fix the state's troubles was not essential. Fifty percent said they would prefer a candidate who said "the situation is too complicated to make promises at this point," rather than a candidate with a plan for cutting spending or raising taxes.

The poll showed public respect for Schwarzenegger's rags-to-riches story, but he could not be elected on his biography alone. His wife, Maria, widely assumed to be a political benefit to him, appeared to hurt him slightly in the poll. Far more important was the impression among those surveyed that he had been a successful businessman. Sixty-two percent liked his work with the Inner City Games, and 61 percent were impressed by his campaign for Proposition 49—a higher percentage than had voted for the initiative. Pollsters also asked whether Schwarzenegger would pick up support if he ran as an independent rather than as a Republican. Sixty percent said his party affiliation would make no difference. He remained a Republican.

The survey concluded by testing Schwarzenegger's vulnerabilities. His past did not seem to make any difference. The fact that his father had been a Nazi party member made no impact. Bizarrely, 41 percent of those surveyed said they would be *more* likely to vote for him because he took steroids.

In one question, the survey put a variety of his pecadilloes together: "Now suppose you learned that Arnold Schwarzenegger had been accused of marital infidelity in the past, had smoked marijuana twenty-five years ago, used steroids in the 1970s for bodybuilding, and recently was quoted in *Esquire* saying that people assume he lacks intelligence in the same way they assume a blonde with great tits and a great ass has no brain, would you still consider voting for him?" Fifty-six percent said yes, 26 percent said no.

The poll then tested four different possible responses to questions about his history with women.

- Don't even bother asking me questions about my private life. It's private. Maria and I have a strong marriage, and we plan to keep our private lives private.
- It's just Hollywood gossip, and my focus is on the challenges facing the people of California.
- These attempts to destroy people on a personal level are ruining American politics and causing good people not to run for office. These kinds of attacks should not be part of the political process.
- I haven't always been a perfect gentleman. As a movie star, I behaved differently than I would have as a public servant.

NONE OF THE ANSWERS hurt him in the poll. And by using the third answer—that such attacks on personal character should not be a part of politics—Schwarzenegger might gain support. Far more respondents expressed concern about Schwarzenegger's support for gay rights (he was for domestic partnerships and adoption rights) than about anything he might have done in the past.

ON A TUESDAY NIGHT IN JUNE, Schwarzenegger made time for one political appearance. He gave the keynote speech at the twenty-fifth anniversary party for Proposition 13. It would be his first political address of the recall. Schwarzenegger, as always, began with jokes. ("Twenty-five years—just to show you how long ago that was, at that time I still had an accent.") He segued to pushing *Terminator 3*, which he had just seen for the first time with all the special effects complete. "I swear to you, it is fantastic. I want to put that plug in there right away. Selling, selling, selling is very important." From there, Schwarzenegger sought to link himself to Jarvis: "Howard Jarvis was the early Terminator, the tax Terminator." Schwarzenegger recast Jarvis's victory not as a blow against taxes but a victory for direct democracy. "He finally took the decision-making away from the politicians and put it squarely into the hands of the people," said Schwarzenegger.

Schwarzenegger then delivered the money line of the evening. "This is so embarrassing," he said, grabbing his head and looking puzzled. He claimed to have forgotten the name of the governor of the state. "But I know you will help me recall him," he said.

Schwarzenegger raised his right index finger and thundered: "The American people are the luckiest people on earth. Because they live in a country where we the people have the right to decide if our leaders are doing their job or not. And if they don't, then we have the right and the obligation to rise up, to take back the government, and to do the job ourselves. We owe it, we owe it to ourselves, and we owe it to future generations of California, to keep the spirit of the people's revolution alive. Forever vigilant, forever watchful, and forever willing to take charge. Our elected leaders will either act decisively or we will act in their place."

The standing ovation lasted more than a minute. Art Laffer, the conservative economist famous for the "Laffer curve" illustrating the relationship between tax rates and tax revenues, grabbed the microphone as Schwarzenegger left. "Wasn't he great, Schwarzenegger? Imagine what he'd be like in German! Wow!"

BUT SCHWARZENEGGER still had no plan in place if he chose to enter the race. And there was jockeying between some of the political consultants who had been involved in Prop 49 over what their places would be in a

Schwarzenegger campaign, if there was one. Schwarzenegger himself, busy promoting his movie, did not seem interested in sorting out the confusion.

Don Sipple, the media consultant who had made the Prop 49 ads, sat down to compose a memo to Schwarzenegger. He feared that the star wasn't ready to run. On June 29, he faxed Schwarzenegger's office with a strategy memo for a campaign that might never take place.

Left to his own devices, Schwarzenegger might have done many of the things Sipple suggested. But in two short pages, Sipple outlined not only the guiding philosophy of a Schwarzenegger campaign, but also the ethos of a new epoch in California politics.

Dated June 28, 2003, and labeled "Some Thoughts," the memo said that Schwarzenegger should launch his campaign only after the recall had qualified for a fall election. "No reason to put a bulls-eye on Arnold's back before we have to. (Issa is taking all the punishment right now while Arnold builds important momentum and excitement outside the political maelstrom.)" Sipple turned next to preparations. "The basics should be in place BEFORE we launch," he wrote. Schwarzenegger needed themes and messages, a fundraising plan, a staff, a Web site that "should be a conduit for young voters and mechanism for national small donor fund-raising (a la Howard Dean)," the Democratic presidential candidate who was then raising millions in small contributions over the Internet.

That would be only the beginning. "Unique circumstances and a unique candidate require a unique campaign that fits the circumstances (populist revolt) and unique candidate (non-politician/unconventional leader)," the memo said. The campaign needed to "eschew the traditional 'play to the press' mentality . . . Instead play to the people." Sipple called for big rallies at "malls, schools, colleges, athletic events," and media appearances should be on lighter shows—"*Larry King, Hardball, Entertainment Tonight*, Leno, Letterman, etc." Late in the campaign, "just as the press begins to conclude that AS and his campaign is devoid of substance . . . we schedule three high profile speeches . . . and AS with prepared text on Teleprompter goes into super substantive depth on his three issues that comprise his governing agenda."

Sipple outlined the message. "Preamble: There is a disconnect between the people of California and the politicians of California. We the people are doing our job—work hard, pay taxes, raise our families . . .. They, the politicians, are not doing their job—they fiddle, they fumble, and they fail. Governor Davis has failed the people of California . . . and it is time to replace him."

Sipple suggested that the campaign focus on three "big items." "Overhaul California's economic engine," was one. "Children have first call on state treasury," was another because "this allows us to talk about education, after-school, health care, preschool, etc., good outreach to Democrats and women." Finally, Schwarzenegger would discuss the subject that had emerged naturally during the "authenticity interview" back in 2001: "Public interest versus self interest and special interests."

"There must be some structural reforms to our political system that has become a self-perpetuating system of self-interest and special interests . . . i.e., part-time legislature, and other items," Sipple wrote.

The consultant concluded with bullet points:

- Arnold needs to be perceived as a leader with a reform agenda and massive public support.
- Campaign needs to be about BIG things that people will buy into. If we allow this campaign to be about solving a $38 billion budget deficit . . . then we might as well interview only folks who wear green eyeshades.
- My sense is that Arnold would embrace this kind of a campaign concept . . . because it is HIM.

Schwarzenegger did not immediately acknowledge the missive. But he would adopt Sipple's language almost word for word in making the most important announcement of his life.

TERMINATOR 3 opened on Wednesday, July 2, 2003, on 3,504 movie screens around the country. In California, some of the drama was outside the theaters. Tom Bader had encouraged his signature gatherers to approach the lines of moviegoers at cinemas showing the film. *Terminator 3* launched and the recall petition campaign closed at the same time and place. If it's possible to pinpoint the exact moment when California's direct democracy and the business of blockbuster moviemaking merged fully into a new political force, the Fourth of July weekend was it.

"Awesome," eighteen-year-old Jason Levine of Tarzana told the *Los Angeles Times* as he emerged from a *Terminator 3* showing in the San Fernando Valley. "He'd be way better than Gray Davis." Two men outside Grauman's Chinese Theatre in Hollywood held a homemade petition asking Schwarzenegger to keep making movies. In Sacramento, a Bakersfield assemblyman named Kevin McCarthy grabbed other Republican legislators and headed to a theater in the suburb of Natomas. On his way out, McCarthy began asking other moviegoers, "Would you vote for that man for governor?"

Schwarzenegger spent the weekend overseas campaigning for the movie. He attended the Tokyo premiere, and then flew to Kuwait. By July 4,

Schwarzenegger stood in the 115-degree heat of Baghdad. A longtime U.S.O. speaker, Schwarzenegger showed the new movie to troops and kept up the political tease. "It is really wild driving around here," he said. "I mean the poverty, and you see there is no money. It is disastrous financially and here is the leadership vacuum, pretty much like in California right now."

By Sunday night, July 6, *Terminator 3* had grossed $72.5 million. A few movies had had bigger openings over July 4, but it was by far the biggest opening ever for a Schwarzenegger film. The recall petition had done even better. Costa had 998,008 signatures at the beginning of the long weekend, though he wanted 1.2 million so that there would be a big enough cushion if a significant percentage of petitions was ruled invalid. By the end of the weekend, a total of 1.6 million people had signed or mailed in recall petitions.

On Monday, July 7, Rescue California and Costa pulled all petitions off the street. The next two weeks would see lawsuits, disputes between the Secretary of State and county clerks, and a prescient vow by Davis to "fight like a Bengal tiger," an endangered species. On July 23, the secretary of state certified the recall for the ballot. A day later, the lieutenant governor, Cruz Bustamante, set the election for October 7.

Issa stopped making payments after 1.6 million signatures were collected. He started calling his aide Phil Paule "Mr. 300,000" because the congressman had paid for $300,000 in signatures that had been unnecessary. But people kept signing even after the paid signature gatherers shut down. All told, the recall would attract 2.2 million signatures, more than any petition in the history of California's direct democracy.

ON THE EVENING OF JULY 21, Schwarzenegger flew home from the London premiere of *Terminator 3*. Gorton had prepared a day of political meetings for July 22. Schwarzenegger cancelled them.

Gorton and the consultants saw that as a sign that the Schwarzenegger candidacy might end before it began. That was just what the star wanted them to think.

CHAPTER 9

"Fiddling"

SCHWARZENEGGER LEFT EARLY for the taping of *The Tonight Show* on Wednesday afternoon, August 6. It was a case of traffic, not nerves. Outwardly, he seemed completely at ease, even blissful. At the studio, he was greeted by George Gorton, Mitch Mulanix, and Sean Walsh, who had been handling press questions for more than a month.

Gorton had a copy of a statement from Schwarzenegger announcing he would not run for governor. The star would endorse his friend, former Los Angeles Mayor Richard Riordan. Gorton had asked Schwarzenegger to check over the statement, which Walsh planned to release as the star went on the air.

The document is fine, Schwarzenegger told his aides. But don't give it to the press until after the show.

There was a reason why he didn't want the statement released. Minutes before he was to go on stage, he still had not decided whether he was running for governor.

RIORDAN AND SCHWARZENEGGER lived a little more than one mile apart in Brentwood, a tony enclave on the west side of Los Angeles at the base of the Santa Monica Mountains. The Riordan home was near Sunset Boulevard, making it an easy venue for meetings. Schwarzenegger's new home—he was in the process of selling his old compound in Pacific Palisades—required a drive up a narrow winding road to a gated community's guard shack. With an invitation, one could drive past the guard, up a hill, and arrive at the $11.9 million gated mansion with five bedrooms, eleven bathrooms, and sweeping views.

It was a supreme irony that of all the potential beneficiaries of the people's revolt Ted Costa had launched, these two rich and renowned men stood to gain the most. A newspaper poll released July 16 showed Riordan to be the first choice of voters to replace Davis, with 21 percent of the vote. Schwarzenegger was second, with 15 percent. If both ran, they could harm each other. If they joined forces, the two moderates would command a centrist block large enough to triumph in a multicandidate race.

Beginning on July 23, the day after Schwarzenegger returned from a European tour for *Terminator 3*, the mayor and the star met or talked almost every day. Often they sat in Riordan's den or backyard. The two men had a little more than two weeks to decide who would run. The deadline for candidates to declare themselves for the October 7 election was Saturday, August 9.

Schwarzenegger was a fastidious man who had every fingernail manicured. Riordan had met few tables on which he would not put his feet. But in other ways, the two had much in common. Both were Catholics who attended the same church, St. Monica's. Both men were married to Democrats who preferred their husbands not run. Both men would have liked to be governor. Both had turned their attention to politics later in life.

A lawyer, Riordan had been one of Los Angeles's best-known political moneymen for years, giving to Democrats and Republicans. But he had not run for office until after his sixtieth birthday. Under the banner "Tough Enough to Turn L.A. Around," Riordan had won the mayor's job a year after the 1992 riots and served two terms. The 2002 Republican gubernatorial primary was the first election Riordan had lost.

AFTER TWO DAYS OF DISCUSSIONS with Riordan, Schwarzenegger flew to Mexico City to promote *Terminator 3*. He refused to answer questions about the governorship, though he sparked a minor furor by declining to eat a hot chile offered him by a reporter during a press conference there. "I am going to be very cautious about what I put in my mouth down here," Schwarzenegger said.

When he returned, Schwarzenegger told political associates he wanted to back Riordan. Mulanix, the consultant who worked on Prop 49, told the star he would have been a great governor and went home to San Diego. Other staffers were left in the lurch. The day before, Paul Miner, the research director for Proposition 49, had quit his job in the legislature at Gorton's insistence to join the campaign. Miner had to ask for his old job back.

Schwarzenegger continued to meet with Riordan over the weekend of July 26 and 27, offering suggestions for the rollout of the former mayor's campaign. It appeared the mayor would announce his campaign for governor as early as Tuesday, July 29. But by Monday, July 28, Riordan was wavering, saying he needed more time to put a team together. Schwarzenegger told Gorton that until Riordan announced, it was best to keep the possibility of his own candidacy alive. That would pique public interest and benefit the mayor.

When they weren't sitting on couches in Riordan's den, the two men chatted by phone. Without telling his own political team, Congressman Darrell

Issa sometimes joined the phone chats. Issa wanted to be governor but believed Riordan was the strongest candidate. Issa was disappointed by Riordan's lack of enthusiasm. Riordan still said he planned to make the race, but kept adding a caveat: Arnold, I'd love to see you run. After a call with all three potential candidates on Friday, August 1, Issa was convinced that Riordan couldn't pull the trigger. (Neither could Issa. Just before the deadline, he would walk into the San Diego county clerk's office to file his papers, only to walk back out and tell reporters he wasn't running.)

AS THE REPUBLICANS DITHERED, the Democrats battled over how to respond to the recall. Davis and his advisors desperately wanted to keep big-name Democrats from entering the replacement race. To defeat the recall, the governor needed to give Democratic voters only one choice: they could keep him or have a Republican governor. But the party's union backers, chief among them the California Teachers Association, wanted to rally behind a Democratic replacement to ensure the party kept the governorship if the recall succeeded.

A Democratic pollster working for CTA had performed extensive surveys to determine which politicians would be strongest in the race to be Davis replacements. The poll made one point clear: if Riordan or Schwarzenegger—but not both—entered the race, either Republican would likely become governor. The polls were designed to determine if there were Democratic candidates who could clear the field by their presence. Only two politicians came close. One was the state's most popular politician, U.S. Senator Dianne Feinstein. The other was Leon Panetta, a former Monterey congressman and chief of staff to President Clinton.

Neither Feinstein nor Panetta was tempted. Feinstein detested recalls. (As mayor of San Francisco in 1983, she had survived a recall attempt by a group called the White Panthers, pro-gun leftists who objected to a strict handgun control measure she supported.) As the CTA quietly encouraged the Democrats to find a replacement, Feinstein called Democratic politicians asking them to stay out of the race. Several, including Lt. Governor Cruz Bustamante, publicly pledged not to run, although Bustamante would reconsider.

Davis shifted strategy from day to day. His aides privately touted a series of town halls, but the governor cancelled them. He announced that he would put together a group of distinguished Californians to attack the budget deficit, but never made the appointments. Following the advice of his pollster, Paul Maslin, the governor by early summer began attacking the recall itself. In a memo circulated among California Democrats, Maslin had suggested an "ideal sound bite": "The recall will cost taxpayers an additional

$30 [million] to $60 million, and is a partisan effort by Republicans to pursue their conservative agenda." The governor argued that the recall was part of an organized Republican plot to steal elections, dating back to the 2000 presidential election in Florida.

The recall effort was partisan, but hardly organized. Instead of unifying, the Republicans splintered. Tom McClintock, a conservative state senator from the suburbs north of Los Angeles, joined the race the day after the recall was certified. Bill Simon, Jr., the defeated Republican nominee from 2002, also got in. Even exbaseball commissioner Peter Ueberroth, a Republican, announced he would run as an independent.

IN THE MIDST OF THIS BIPARTISAN CHAOS, Schwarzenegger booked himself on *The Tonight Show* for Wednesday, August 6. He did not consult with his political advisors on the decision. Since Schwarzenegger had given every indication he wasn't running, the advisors agreed that the show offered a great venue to talk up the recall and Riordan.

The advisors had not known Schwarzenegger long enough to understand that he was always full of mystery and misdirection when it came to big decisions. For more than a month, he had been sounding out his worldwide network of friends and business associates. He even took the temperature of his lifelong Austrian friends. Peter Urdl, his elementary school classmate and the mayor of his hometown of Thal, said he warned Schwarzenegger that "in politics you cannot pick your roles. If you do it, you're going to see what kind of bullshit you have to deal with."

In Schwarzenegger's mind, the question was not merely whether to run for office or not. This may have been the ultimate Schwarzenegger bake-off: he appraised the future of his movie career, his investments, and his charitable enterprises. Through this methodical yet flexible style, he found he had no shortage of options.

New Line wanted him for a comedy, *Big Sir*, about a man traveling cross-country with his future stepchildren. There continued to be talk of sequels, *True Lies 2* or *King Conan*. And he was still in the midst of transforming his national Inner City Games charity into a provider of after-school programs. As always, he had an abundance of business opportunities.

There was another factor to consider. It seemed inevitable that the old allegations of womanizing that had appeared in the tabloids and entertainment press in 2001 would resurface. Polling conducted both for Schwarzenegger and for Democrats showed the political impact of new disclosures on this front would be negligible. People assumed stars behaved badly. But that wouldn't make living through the reports any more pleasant.

On that front, Schwarzenegger suddenly had an opportunity. In November 2002, Joe Weider, the bodybuilding promoter who had brought Schwarzenegger to America, had sold his empire of fitness and bodybuilding magazines and nutritional supplement brands. The buyer was American Media Inc., publisher of the *National Enquirer* and other supermarket tabloids.

Part of the value of the bodybuilding magazines was Weider's close relationship with Schwarzenegger. The star still had a column, Ask Arnold, published in *Muscle & Fitness*, and American Media CEO David Pecker sought a meeting with Schwarzenegger to make sure that association would continue.

The second week of July, as it became clear the recall would qualify for the ballot, Pecker met Schwarzenegger at Oak Productions in Santa Monica and proposed that the star become executive editor of two muscle magazines: *Muscle & Fitness* and *Flex*. Schwarzenegger did not commit immediately to Pecker's proposal. It was another option in the giant bake-off.

Both Pecker and Schwarzenegger later told interviewers that there was no discussion of how the tabloids might cover a gubernatorial campaign, if there was one. But it was obvious that making a deal with Schwarzenegger might be better if the tabloids went easy on the star. In the days leading up to the campaign—and during the run to come—American Media and its publications not only ignored Schwarzenegger's peccadilloes, they protected him. Early in the campaign, a reporter for American Media signed Gigi Goyette, an actress and bodybuilder who reportedly had a relationship with Schwarzenegger while he was married to Shriver, to a $20,000 contract. The document, titled "Confidentiality Agreement" and dated August 8, said Goyette could only tell her story to American Media. (A friend of Goyette's was paid $1,000 to sign a similar agreement.) But the company's tabloids didn't tell Goyette's story. Instead, American Media ran stories praising Schwarzenegger and published a special commemorative magazine dedicated to his career and campaign.

SCHWARZENEGGER'S POLITICAL advisors knew nothing of the American Media talks. Schwarzenegger not only kept Gorton and the other consultants at a distance, he also sought political advice from experts outside his employ. He invited the GOP pollster Frank Luntz to brief him on the results of focus groups he had done for the pro-recall organization, Rescue California.

One afternoon, Schwarzenegger invited Pete Wilson to his home. Wilson believed Schwarzenegger had decided to back Riordan, and was surprised to learn a candidacy was still possible. The two men, joined by Maria Shriver, talked for nearly three hours.

"I'm not concerned about you winning; I'm concerned about you making a decision without knowing what you're getting into," Wilson said he told Schwarzenegger. "Do you want this job badly enough to work at it as hard as you're going to have to work in order to do it right? Arnold, it is going to mean from early morning till late at night, day after day, month after month. It will change your life, your family's life." And what do you want to do with it? "You don't want to wear the office like a boutonniere," Wilson said. The former governor said he did not want to hear an answer right away. He just wanted Schwarzenegger to think about such questions.

A governor can do many things, Wilson said. Much of his power is to stop bad things. Sometimes, a governor can convince a legislature to act, but that would be extremely difficult in this era. In 2001, lawmakers of both parties had drawn their own districts to protect both Democratic and Republican incumbents, virtually eliminating competitive legislative elections in the state. Legislators had little incentive to challenge the status quo. To make changes in California, Schwarzenegger would have to use ballot initiatives. That would mean a lot of campaigns.

Wilson mentioned a conversation he had with Richard Nixon forty years earlier about a variety of career options Wilson was then considering including a run for a state assembly seat. Nixon's advice had been direct: You better do it because if you don't, you'll always question yourself about it.

Schwarzenegger thanked Wilson, and the former governor went home. His wife, Gayle, greeted him. How did it go?

"I don't know," Wilson said. "I'm afraid I talked him out of it."

ON FRIDAY, AUGUST 1, Schwarzenegger called friends and supporters with what appeared to be the final word. He was out. Paul Folino, the Orange County tech executive who had helped him raise money for Prop 49, got the call on his cell phone. "Paul, I'm calling a few of my supporters," Schwarzenegger said. "I want you to know I'd like to do it, but I just can't find a way there. It's too much for my family."

Schwarzenegger also touched base with Jim Lorimer, his business partner in the Arnold Classic in Ohio and a longtime supporter of the star's political dreams. Schwarzenegger would recall Lorimer advising him not to run; California was not governable, Lorimer argued. But later that day Lorimer faxed his friend a memo with ten reasons why he should go for it anyway.

Lorimer concluded his memo with a bit of verse by the nineteenth-century poet John Greenleaf Whittier from "Maud Muller," a poem about a love between a judge and a maid that was never consummated.

> *For all sad words of tongue or pen,*
> *The saddest are these: "It might have been!"*

ON SUNDAY AFTERNOON, August 3, the Schwarzenegger family drove out to a beach house that Riordan owned in Malibu. The star seemed resigned to his decision. But over barbecued burgers and chicken, the mayor started to talk. Even now, Riordan's heart was still not in the race. Raising money in such a short time would be hard, he said. The mayor wondered how conservatives would treat him.

"I said, 'Dick, you've got to make up your mind, because if you don't make up your mind and miss the deadline [of August 9], then we are both screwed and the Republican party is screwed,'" recalled Schwarzenegger. "So he said again, 'OK, I run.' But then we're walking out of the beach house, and he said to me again, 'I tell you one thing, though, you should run, Arnold.'" The conversation opened the door again for Schwarzenegger. He felt a need for a departure, a new challenge. He had everything he wanted. He could smoke a cigar, sit in his Jacuzzi, put his kids to bed, and make more movies. It all felt a bit too comfortable.

BY THIS TIME, the only debate that still mattered was taking place inside Schwarzenegger's house in Brentwood. Schwarzenegger said that when he first told his wife weeks earlier, as they sat in the Jacuzzi, that he was interested in running, she started to shake. She would later say she worried about the effect on their lives, their careers, their family. But Schwarzenegger had two crucial allies urging him to run: his wife's parents.

Eunice Kennedy Shriver had been her son-in-law's biggest booster, and she urged her daughter to get behind a campaign. "He's gonna run. Let him go," Eunice Shriver told her daughter. "Don't complain. Get out there and help him." Sargent Shriver also loved the idea. "You're making me very happy," Sargent Shriver wrote in a July 11 letter to his son-in-law. "I can't think of any person today that I would rather have in office. If I were a resident of California, I hope you realize that I'd be voting Republican for the first time ever!"

Schwarzenegger had put his wife in a difficult position. If he didn't run, much of the world would think it was her fault. Schwarzenegger said that he would not run without her blessing. "I don't want to do this if you and the kids don't feel it's OK," Schwarzenegger recalled saying. The two went back and forth until the final day. At a couple of moments, Shriver encouraged him to run, but was generally opposed. Schwarzenegger went to bed on the night of August 5, believing he would tell Jay Leno the next day that he was not making the race.

SCHWARZENEGGER AND SHRIVER, on Wednesday morning, went over the decision one more time. "She knew I was going to say I'm not going to run," Schwarzenegger recalled. "She said to me that morning, 'Look, I just want you to know, if this really means a lot to you, you should do it.'" Shriver picked up a page full of talking points for an announcement that he had withdrawn from the race. "This is me," she said, according to her husband. She pointed to the list of reasons to run for governor. "This is you. You can't be me, she added, and I totally support you in being you."

He had his wife's permission. But Schwarzenegger was still not certain he should run.

DON SIPPLE, the media consultant for Prop 49, answered his phone around 11 a.m. Wednesday. It was Schwarzenegger's executive assistant, Kris Lannin Liang. If you have thoughts about what he should say if he decides to go for it, fax them to the house, Liang instructed. And don't tell anyone.

Sipple took out his June 28 memo and reworked it. He looked back at the polling. He wrote that the people are "working hard, paying taxes, raising our families" while politicians were "fiddling, fumbling, and failing." He sent the fax along with his cell phone number. No one called back.

Schwarzenegger sorted through Sipple's fax and others as he got dressed. He received dozens of phone messages, many of them from his political consultants, but he didn't return them. "Everyone wanted to call whoever they were obligated to in the journalistic world and be the guy who breaks the news. I was not going to fall for any of that," said Schwarzenegger. "And I didn't know myself. I didn't want anyone to know. And to do that, you can't tell anyone the final decision. Not Maria, either." Shriver would learn whether her husband was running for governor at the same time as the rest of the world.

Through lunch and the early afternoon, Schwarzenegger still couldn't decide. "I tried to play it out and I couldn't," he said. So, with less than two hours before the taping, he resolved to let the moment seize him. "Finally, I said to myself, 'Well, something will come out on *The Tonight Show*. Just let it come out naturally when you're on the show. It will be judgment time.'"

THAT SAME MORNING, Senator Dianne Feinstein issued a written statement confirming her decision not to enter the race. But Feinstein's effort to unite her party against the recall had failed. By day's end, Bustamante would announce he was running. The Democrats had the worst of both worlds: a Democratic candidate in the replacement election who was not Dianne Feinstein.

THE TONIGHT SHOW appeared on NBC at 11:30 at night, but the show was taped shortly after 4 p.m. each afternoon in Burbank in the San Fernando Valley. To Schwarzenegger, NBC Studios felt like home. He had appeared on the show more than thirty times, usually to kick off his movie campaigns. His wife, an NBC journalist, worked in the complex, and he was friends with many of the network's leading lights, from the anchor Tom Brokaw to Leno, who had made appearances on behalf of Schwarzenegger's Inner City Games charity.

That afternoon in August 2003, Schwarzenegger arrived at the complex in a navy suit and white dress shirt, with no tie. Eager to show off a motorcycle with a Rolls Royce engine, Leno greeted Schwarzenegger in the parking lot. The consultants—Gorton, Mulanix, and Walsh—met their noncandidate off stage in *The Tonight Show*'s green room. There Leno and Schwarzenegger improvised a series of jokes about the star deciding not to run. "It would have been funny if Arianna and I had debated," Schwarzenegger said of the Greek-born Arianna Huffington, a Democratic commentator who was getting into the race. "No one would have understood anything we were saying."

Leno left to do his monologue. Gorton, who had Schwarzenegger's statement that he was getting out of the race in his pocket, sidled up to Schwarzenegger and confessed his disappointment in the decision not to run. Gorton reminded him that Feinstein was not running and asked if there was any way he might reconsider. Schwarzenegger gave no indication he had changed his mind. "Inside, I was thinking, 'Beats me,'" he said.

On stage, Leno went right to the decision: "Let me ask you about this now. I know it's been weeks and people going back and forth, and it's taken you a while and you said you would come here tonight and tell us your decision. So what is your decision?"

"Well, Jay, after thinking about this for a long time, my decision is . . ."

The loud bleep of a censor obscured the answer. It was a planned prank. The crowd laughed.

Walsh didn't like it. He had wanted Schwarzenegger to run. The recall was serious, and B-level jokes and gags seemed inappropriate.

Leno tried again.

"We've joked about this and thank you. It's been in my monologue. It's been a slow work week. It's been good for like a thousand jokes. But seriously, what are you going to do? You said you were going to come here tonight and tell us. What are you going to do?"

"My decision obviously is a very difficult decision to make. It was the most difficult decision to make in my entire life except the one in 1978 when I decided to get a bikini wax."

During the laughter, Schwarzenegger took a deep breath. In that moment, he knew his decision was final. What flashed through his mind were the doubts he had heard expressed by so many people about whether he was capable of being a governor and about whether California could be governed at all. "Whenever people said it can't be done, that was actually the thing that motivated me most," he would remember. Wouldn't it be fun to prove them wrong?

Schwarzenegger faced Leno.

"No, but I've decided that California is in a very disastrous situation right now. When I moved to California in 1968, California was a fantastic place. It was the greatest state of the greatest nation in the world. It was absolutely spectacular. Everyone could come here and have opportunities and come here and really grow up and enjoy life here. Now it is totally the opposite. The atmosphere is disastrous. There is absolutely no connection, there is a total disconnect between the people of California and . . . the politicians of California," Schwarzenegger said.

Off stage, Gorton stood stunned. These weren't the talking points from the announcement that he was bowing out. Mulanix realized immediately what was happening.

"He's going to fucking do it, George," Mulanix said.

On stage, Schwarzenegger continued riffing from the language that had been in Sipple's June 28 memo and in the fax sent again that morning: "What that means basically is that the people are doing their job. The people are working hard. The people are paying their taxes, the people are raising the families, but the politicians are not doing their job. The politicians are fiddling and fumbling and failing!

"And the man that is failing the people more than anyone is Gray Davis. He's failing them terribly and this is why he needs to be recalled and this is why I am going to run for governor of the state. . ."

The roar of the studio audience swallowed the rest of the sentence. Leno did a double-take. This bit had not been rehearsed.

"WHAT CHANGED YOUR MIND?" Leno asked. "Did you change your mind?"

Schwarzenegger described his family debate. He spoke as a certain victor—"then there will be the move to Sacramento." But soon he turned to the petition gatherers. Months earlier he had declined the chance to help the signature gathering drive for the recall. Now he embraced it as his own.

"One-point-six million people in California signed the petition that said they wanted to remove Gray Davis. And they basically said—1.6 million people said—'We are mad as hell and we're not going to take it anymore.'"

The last line was a nod to conservatives. He was using Howard Jarvis's battle cry, a slogan that Jarvis had taken from the movie *Network!* that satirized populism and television.

"And that message, that message is not just a message for California. That is a message that is from California all the way to the East Coast, for Republicans and Democrats alike to say to them: 'Do your job for the people and do it well or otherwise you are *hasta la vista*, baby!'"

The rest of the appearance was tactical. Schwarzenegger tried to pre-empt any skeletons that might come rattling out of his closet. "I know that they're going to throw everything at me and they're going, you know, to say that I have no experience and that I'm a womanizer and that I'm a terrible guy and all this kind of things are going to come my way," he said. But, he added, "I want to clean up Sacramento. I want to go in there and reform the system so it's back in the people's hands. The people should make the decisions, rather than special interests."

Leno tried to set up him up for the Arianna Huffington joke, but he wouldn't bite. "She is a very bright woman," Schwarzenegger said.

SCHWARZENEGGER, with a huge smile on his face, bounded off stage and approached Gorton, who looked overwhelmed. The star laughed.

Schwarzenegger walked into a press room that had been set up for his appearance. He shook hands with all thirty journalists in the room. "It is the most difficult decision I have ever made in my life," he said. Once he was done with the print reporters inside, Schwarzenegger walked outside to take questions from TV journalists. From a podium with *The Tonight Show* sign attached to the front, he argued that the transition from cinematic salesmanship to politics would be easy.

"I always said when I finished with my *Terminator* promotion, I would deal with the issue of whether I would run or not," he began. "You all know that I know how to sell something, right? . . . I had to sell bodybuilding when no one even knew what bodybuilding was in this country and we did it."

One reporter asked if his announcement on an entertainment show had made a mockery of the political process. The question amused Schwarzenegger. He thought that American politics could use more humor, though he didn't say that. "*The Tonight Show* has been really helpful to my career—it's been part of my career so much, so therefore I felt this would be a good way of doing it," he said.

Schwarzenegger answered questions about his plans in broad strokes, and immediately got himself into trouble. "I don't need anyone's money," he said. "Special interests—we will listen to them, but we will not be swayed by their money." That sounded like a promise to finance the campaign himself. Within days, Schwarzenegger's aides would say that he planned to donate some of his own money, but also would accept contributions from others as he had for Prop 49. As a result, Schwarzenegger would repeatedly face the accusation that he flip-flopped on fund-raising.

As Schwarzenegger walked back to his SUV, he shook hands with a group of fans assembled on the other side of a brick wall. Police escorted the vehicle off the NBC lot.

A reporter asked Gorton what would happen next. "I haven't a clue," he said. "I have to go make a plan." He couldn't make an outgoing call on his cell phone. Too many calls were coming in. He jumped in his car, still holding the press release announcing Schwarzenegger would not run for governor, and drove to the star's home in Brentwood.

The Tonight Show would not air on NBC until 11:30 p.m., but other outlets reported the announcement as soon as it was made. Congressman David Dreier, a Republican who was close to the White House, learned from Fox News that Schwarzenegger was running. Dreier called up Riordan, with whom he had just finished lunch an hour earlier, to relay the news. "Oh, really?" said the mayor. An hour later, Schwarzenegger was on the phone to Dreier, asking for help.

Mulanix rode with Schwarzenegger back to Brentwood and dialed the phone numbers of anyone he could think of who needed to hear of the decision. Mulanix juggled three cell phones, handing one to Schwarzenegger as he tried to reach people on the other two.

Schwarzenegger called donors from Prop 49: Republican officials, legislators, even Werner Kopacka, the reporter for the *Kronen Zeitung* back in Graz. "I am a moderate conservative who possesses a strong social conscience. That I brought with me from Austria and it is definitely my Austrian half that will help shape the Politician Arnold," he told Kopacka.

The Republican leader of the state senate, Jim Brulte, congratulated Schwarzenegger by saying: "I see you've mastered the first rule of politics."

What is that?

"Never tell your staff anything."

THIS WAS A LESSON that Schwarzenegger may have learned too well. Because he waited until the last second to make a decision, his aides had few campaign plans and little idea what he wanted done. The first night, consultants and friends gathered at Schwarzenegger's home. Many ideas were floated, some of them silly (one consultant wanted to change the way the candidate said "California"), but few decisions were made. Schwarzenegger, wearing shorts, hung out at the pool and smoked cigars. A campaign meeting, which took place the next day at Schatzi's restaurant, wasn't much better.

Schwarzenegger had left his neighbor and political ally Riordan in the lurch. The mayor, despite his reluctance, had been putting together a campaign team. Mike Murphy, a Republican consultant who advised John McCain's "Straight Talk Express" presidential campaign in 2000, was considering whether to work for Riordan. Murphy had been sitting by the pool at the Four Seasons in Beverly Hills when he heard about Schwarzenegger's announcement. Realizing that Schwarzenegger's entry would shut out Riordan, Murphy and two young colleagues went out to dinner where they joked bitterly about running the bodybuilder-turned–Incredible Hulk Lou Ferrigno instead.

The next morning, Murphy kept an appointment with Riordan. The mayor seemed annoyed that the star had not taken him into his confidence. But Riordan had called Schwarzenegger earlier that morning to pledge his help. After meeting with Murphy, the mayor took the consultant to see the new candidate. Murphy presented the polling that had been done for Riordan's campaign to Schwarzenegger, who thanked him. It was clear Murphy could join the campaign if he wished. But he had a vacation planned in Mexico. He left.

It was a sensible decision. The Schwarzenegger campaign had no phone banks, no computers, no cell phones, no Blackberrys, and no campaign Web site. In the twelve hours after the announcement Wednesday afternoon, the star's entertainment Web site, Schwarzenegger.com, had 70 million hits. It crashed.

In a normal election cycle, such start-up difficulties would not have mattered. There would be months before a primary election to get everything up and running. But the recall election was scheduled for October 7, just sixty days away. There were no position papers on issues. There was no "vulnerability study," political speak for the research that politicians routinely run on themselves to figure out how they might be attacked. The most recent polls were a month old. The campaign leadership included only Gorton and close associates, including his wife Kiki. Many of the political professionals who had committed to join a Schwarzenegger campaign had scattered to the wind. Paul Touw, a Silicon Valley multimillionaire who had supported Prop 49, sent a plane around the state to pick up some of them.

On one matter Schwarzenegger was efficient. Campaign staffers had to sign confidentiality agreements. Such agreements were typical on movie sets and in corporate suites, and Schwarzenegger had used them for years with members of his own staff. But they were rare in political campaigns. The agreements ran five pages and were designed to protect Schwarzenegger from having details of his personal life sold to the tabloids, or personal mementos swiped and hawked on eBay. Any letter, contract, or photograph from the campaign was controlled by Schwarzenegger, the agreements claimed.

BY FRIDAY MORNING, the chaos caused by Schwarzenegger's announcement caught up with him. The consultants booked the star on all three network morning shows, which began broadcasting at 7 a.m. eastern time—4 a.m. on the West Coast. Schwarzenegger had to rise at 3 a.m. after less than four hours sleep. For nearly any other candidate for governor at any other time and place, being able to appear on three TV networks in a single morning would be a huge coup. For Schwarzenegger, it was a strategic mistake. He could attract international attention anytime he wanted. There was no reason for him to lose sleep in order to appear on television.

Schwarzenegger did his first interview just after 4 a.m. Pacific time on NBC's *The Today Show*. After he answered two questions about how he had made his decision, host Matt Lauer pressed him on exactly how he would bring back the California economy. That led to a nonsensical exchange between the two men and, eventually, an abrupt end to the interview:

"Are you going to make your tax returns for the past several years available to the press?" Lauer asked.

Schwarzenegger fiddled with his ear piece. "Say again?"

"Are you going to make your tax returns for the past several years available to the press?"

"I didn't hear you."

"Apparently we are losing audio with Arnold Schwarzenegger in Los Angeles," Lauer said, sarcastically. NBC said it could find no technical problem with its audio equipment.

BONNIE REISS, the former entertainment lawyer who had run Schwarzenegger's Inner City Games foundation, spent Thursday and Friday canvassing the consultants and trying to put a stop to the chaos. On Thursday, she had sat in front of the fireplace at Schatzi's with Sipple and Paul Miner, the research director from the Prop 49 campaign.

What do we do to fix this? Reiss asked.

Sipple responded that a bigger team was needed. Schwarzenegger had to avoid specific issues while a campaign was built. "Don't shoehorn him into a traditional campaign and traditional appearances," Sipple warned Reiss. "It will diminish him."

At Schwarzenegger's offices in Santa Monica, Maria Shriver pulled Sipple into a closet to have a conversation. Sipple said they badly needed more bodies and soon. Shriver pressed: Who's good? And, just as Governor Wilson had suggested on his visit to the Schwarzenegger home two weeks earlier, Sipple said the campaign needed Bob White to provide some stability. Shriver would make phone calls to friends and contacts around the country asking for more names.

After the TV appearances on Friday, Shriver joined a meeting of the campaign consultants—including Gorton, Mulanix, Walsh, Sipple, Miner, and Jeff Randle—along with Reiss and the star's investment advisor, Paul Wachter. Shriver, Reiss, and Wachter all knew how to play bad cop to Schwarzenegger's good. The presence of all three was a sign that changes were coming.

Shriver began by saying that she had met leaders all over the world, and her husband could hold his own with any of them. She listed fifteen adjectives that described him, among them "courageous" and "intellectual." The campaign needed to convey that sense of Schwarzenegger, and the best way to do that was to let her husband be himself.

Shriver did not raise her voice. Her preferred method was to fire questions rapidly, creating a Socratic shooting range that staffers would call the "full Maria." Her target in this meeting was Gorton. What is your plan? Where is the staff? What is your message? What was the point of these TV appearances? What direction is the campaign going in?

Gorton responded by explaining his approach to politics. He said he couldn't answer many of Shriver's questions without up-to-date polls and focus groups. The campaign should wait until it had new research before putting together the plan. He hadn't had any polls in the field because Schwarzenegger's candidacy had been a surprise. Shriver pushed back, saying she didn't believe in polls and asking why there wasn't a clearly defined slogan for the campaign. She suggested that Schwarzenegger would want to be known as "The People's Governor." Gorton replied that he would have to poll on that—an answer that may have proved to be the last straw. By day's end, Schwarzenegger's campaign would have a new leader.

The meeting made plain that Shriver would have considerable authority in the campaign. For his films, she had read scripts and offered her advice on the marketing. In politics, she would do something similar. "The People's Governor" line would show up in TV commercials. For the bumper sticker, Schwarzenegger would use his slogan from Prop 49, "Join Arnold."

The next week, Shriver would take the children to Hyannisport for several days. But she stayed in the loop, calling senior campaign advisors as early as 5 a.m. Pacific time. When she was busy, the consultants would find themselves talking on the phone with Eunice Kennedy Shriver, who also faxed ideas to her son-in-law.

Maria Shriver made suggestions but did not give orders. And she lost arguments. She wanted Schwarzenegger to campaign in poorer neighborhoods of the state. He visited only two: one in Fresno and another in Los Angeles —Boyle Heights—where the Inner City Games began. The campaign pros said that with just sixty days to campaign, a Republican who wanted to win couldn't spend time on Kennedyesque appearances in the inner city.

Bob White had taken Friday off. When he turned his cell phone back on late in the afternoon, he was deluged with messages from the Schwarzenegger camp, one of the last from Shriver, who urged him to return her call first. White had run Pete Wilson's campaigns but thought he had gotten out of the business for good. He was an institution in Sacramento, where he made his living offering strategic advice to companies but did not, at least according to California's hard-to-understand laws, lobby the government. Newspapers would point out that for someone running against special interests, Schwarzenegger's hiring White as campaign manager did not fit the script. But by late Friday night, he had agreed to take over.

During a meeting that first Saturday morning at Oak Productions, Governor Wilson walked in unexpectedly, carrying a list of suggestions for policies Schwarzenegger might adopt. White quickly realized the freewheeling campaign needed order and routine. He called Pat Clarey, a deputy chief of staff to Wilson who was now an executive of HealthNet Inc. She, in turn, reached Marty Wilson, another old Wilson hand (no relation to the former governor) as he drank a martini on a train from San Francisco to Sacramento.

By Saturday night, Clarey, Marty Wilson, and White were meeting in Brentwood with the Schwarzeneggers. When Shriver asked questions about strategy, Wilson explained that he and Clarey were operations people. Clarey would run the campaign day to day. Wilson would coordinate the fund-raising, coalition building, and the campaign budget. Clarey and Wilson would retain some version of those roles—Clarey as the inside chief, Wilson as the operational captain of the team of outside consultants—well into Schwarzenegger's governorship.

Clarey and Wilson oversaw the process of turning offices in Schwarzenegger's Santa Monica building into a headquarters. Clarey assembled a campaign team, calling the employers of some recruits to request two-month leaves. White instituted staff meetings at 8 a.m. and 6 p.m.

White made the campaign more businesslike and happier. But he never gained full control, in part because Schwarzenegger himself enjoyed a little drama. Continuing to manage by bake-off, he liked to have advisors competing to give him the best ideas. Schwarzenegger's style might sow chaos, but it meant that when decisions got made, he was the one who made them.

Gorton stayed on as a strategist who oversaw the campaign's polling. He put up a sign in one of the second-floor windows. "Lighten Up," it said.

In shielding his campaign's start-up difficulties from the public, Schwarzenegger had 134 unwitting allies—the other declared candidates for governor. To qualify for the ballot, all one needed was $3,500 and the signatures of sixty-five registered voters. With the recall receiving news coverage worldwide, running for governor had become a marketing opportunity. At the polls, one's name might be seen by 10 million people.

Schwarzenegger himself made two trips to the Los Angeles County registrar-recorder's offices in the suburb of Norwalk. First on Thursday, August 7—the day after he announced his candidacy on Leno—he picked up his candidate papers. On the Saturday, August 9, deadline to declare, he returned to file them. Schwarzenegger was overshadowed by a much larger and stranger parade of lesser-known competition. There were the porn star Mary Carey and the former TV actor Gary Coleman. Several of the candidates claimed to be running as a form of performance art. Kelly Kimball, whose brother ran a leading signature gathering firm, and Scott Mednick, a marketing executive who thought up the slogan "Join Arnold" for the Prop 49 campaign, ran for governor to promote a brand of beer. The last person to file in Los Angeles was Kurt E. "Tachikaze" Rightmyer, 39, a sumo wrestler from West Covina. "As a sumo wrestler, I am uniquely prepared to take on this 800-pound gorilla of a government and big spending from every level," he said.

After installing White, Schwarzenegger flew East for two days. Some of his aides objected that this was no time to leave the state, but he had a long-standing commitment in Harlem for his After-School All-Stars charity. He used the long plane ride to begin drilling on policy with Reiss and Miner, the Prop 49 research director who would accompany him on the road as his designated wing man and policy tutor. On this trip, Reiss brought along copies of Teddy Roosevelt's speeches on conservation for Schwarzenegger to read. Before hitting New York, he stopped in Hyannisport and huddled with his Democratic in-laws. Robert F. Kennedy, Jr., agreed to help with the environmental platform. From there, Schwarzenegger flew south. At an award ceremony for the After-School All-Stars at City College of New York, thirty-three camera crews trailed him.

He took no questions. The New York media left unimpressed. "He couldn't last one round with Hugh Carey!" the legendary columnist Jimmy Breslin bellowed, in reference to a New York governor of yesteryear.

Money was a much larger concern than an agitated press corps. Schwarzenegger's New York trip included a lunch at the Four Seasons with eight prominent Republican political donors, many of them contributors to the Empire State's governor, George Pataki. No money changed hands, and the Schwarzenegger campaign denied at first that the lunch had taken place. But Schwarzenegger needed campaign funds and fast. Colleen McAndrews, his campaign treasurer, had taken the job on the understanding that there would be little fund-raising and easy compliance reports. Gorton had said Schwarzenegger would fund much of the cost of the campaign himself. But it was not in Schwarzenegger's best interests to turn down funds. By accepting donations, he would likely be taking some money that otherwise would go to his rivals.

At the time, Schwarzenegger also told me that the fund-raising would be "good practice." He did not explain what he meant by the comment. But as Pete Wilson had made clear to Schwarzenegger, to make policy changes in California would require him to take his proposals directly to the people. Ballot initiative campaigns were expensive. If it was to be effective, a Schwarzenegger governorship would require many campaigns. Even the star was not rich enough to fund such campaigns entirely by himself.

Schwarzenegger did, however, want to avoid taking money from people or groups who might negotiate with him as governor. He wasn't sure at first which contributions that might eliminate. A fund-raising policy approved by the candidate on August 21 laid out four rules. Schwarzenegger promised that, as governor, he would not use his appointees to solicit campaign funds or participate in campaign finance events. He pledged not to take money from political action committees, trade associations that represented only one industry, public employee unions, or "individuals, companies, or corporations that are engaged in gambling or tobacco." That notably excluded money from the state's Indian tribes. Although Schwarzenegger imposed more restrictions on himself than other candidates, those rules did not stop him from accepting millions in donations from individuals and groups with interests in government decisions.

Schwarzenegger's statement at *The Tonight Show* studio that he needed no money deterred some donors. The candidate also was reluctant to make phone calls to potential donors. He continued to dislike asking for money and hated the sense that he might owe someone as a result. Marty Wilson had to delay the campaign's first payroll for five days.

To make fund-raising easier for Schwarzenegger, Wilson conducted conference calls, with Schwarzenegger on one line and Wilson on another. Schwarzenegger would talk about the campaign and his goals for the state. Then Wilson would ask for money. Wilson tried to be in a different room during the calls so he wouldn't have to see the candidate's face.

Much of the money that was given to the campaign went to the purchase of TV time. Sipple filmed the first TV ad on Friday, August 15, nine days after Schwarzenegger joined the race. The set was Schwarzenegger's old compound of homes in Pacific Palisades. The opening scene showed the candidate walking outside and talking about the "historic election." The ad then switched to an office setting, where Schwarzenegger continued talking. "I am running for governor to lead a movement for change and give California back its future," he said, as the camera pushed in tight until his face filled the whole screen and his eyes stared directly at the viewer. "I want to be the people's governor. I will work honestly, without fear or favor, to do what is right for all Californians."

With the media starved for any new footage of Schwarzenegger, the advertisement was shown on TV news and entertainment programs more often than it appeared in purchased sixty-second spots—yet another way that his celebrity gave him an advantage over his opponents.

SCHWARZENEGGER SOUGHT high-profile campaign advisors, the bigger the name the better. On Wednesday, August 13, a week after he entered the race, he announced the billionaire Warren Buffett as cochair of his campaign's economic team. Schwarzenegger had attended a Buffett speech years earlier and introduced himself. Buffett had become concerned about California's economic crisis in June, when he learned of the state's need to borrow $11 billion in short-term notes to cover its deficit. The state had had to pay $84 million to convince a syndicate of investment banks to guarantee repayment of the money; California could no longer borrow large sums on its own word.

The choice of Buffett, a Democrat, drew rebukes from several Republicans. Two days later, the rebukes became screams when, in an interview with the *Wall Street Journal*, Buffett criticized Proposition 13.

Buffett's argument was anecdotal. Because the growth of California property taxes was limited by the 1978 ballot initiative, Buffett paid annual taxes of $14,401 on his $500,000 home in Omaha and just $2,264 in property taxes on a Laguna Beach vacation house valued at $4 million. In the last year, his Nebraska property taxes rose $1,920, while taxes on his California beach house increased just $23. "It makes no sense," Buffett told the *Journal*. "You have got to get [the budget] in balance . . . and they have to do whatever is necessary on spending or taxes to get it in balance."

Urging a tax hike was bad enough. But Buffett also had criticized the most powerful symbol of direct democracy in California. The Howard Jarvis Taxpayers Association, which had been preparing to endorse Schwarzenegger, backed away. "It was a disaster," Gorton recalled. "We needed that anchor on the right. I thought the campaign was in danger of coming apart then."

It took a day for the campaign to produce its first statement. "Warren and I have talked about Proposition 13, and he clearly understands my strong unequivocal support for the initiative," Schwarzenegger said. When that wasn't deemed strong enough, Schwarzenegger released a more detailed letter. Gorton and the former Howard Jarvis Taxpayers Association president Joel Fox spent two weeks trying to win back the Howard Jarvis endorsement. They called every board member. Schwarzenegger sent two letters to the Jarvis association, and finally clinched the endorsement after meeting with Jarvis's widow, Estelle.

BUT SCHWARZENEGGER was stagnant in the polls. While the star had led in the first surveys conducted after his announcement, a current newspaper poll showed Bustamante with a lead of 25 percent to Schwarzenegger's 22 percent.

The campaign's own first poll, completed on August 16 by Jan van Lohuizen, a pollster for President Bush and the CTA, painted an only slightly brighter picture.

The recall looked strong. Fifty-eight percent of Californians would vote to remove Davis. And the poll showed Schwarzenegger to be personally popular, with 62 percent of Californians having a favorable opinion. But Schwarzenegger had only 28 percent of the vote in this internal survey, the same as Bustamante. The star's challenge was clear: many of the people who liked him didn't plan to vote for him.

Seventy-two percent of voters who believed Schwarzenegger would make a bad governor cited his lack of experience as a reason for not supporting him. But the poll also showed the way Schwarzenegger could change those impressions. Once people learned about Prop 49, it became an invaluable political credential. For those who liked Schwarzenegger, the most common reason was his "record of supporting kids."

The survey determined that Buffett was not a popular economic advisor to Schwarzenegger. Only 30 percent had favorable opinions of him. The pollster also discovered that 46 percent of Californians had never heard of the other co-chair of Schwarzenegger's economic team, former secretary of state George Shultz.

WHEN, JUST DAYS after entering the race, Schwarzenegger called Shultz in his office at the Hoover Institution on the Stanford campus, Shultz gave the candidate thirty seconds to explain why he should back him. Schwarzenegger said he wouldn't spend more money than the state had. It was the right answer. Shultz, an economist, read to the candidate from a memo about the California budget that he had written with another Hoover scholar, John Cogan. In April 1998, Shultz and Cogan had given a private tutorial on economics to the governor of Texas, George W. Bush, who was thinking of running for president. They would perform a similar service for Schwarzenegger.

Headlined "Defining the Problem: Operating Deficit and Inherited Debt," the memo suggested breaking the state's budget crisis into two separate problems: the annual operating deficit and the accumulated inherited debt. The total inherited debt amounted to $21.5 billion and could be refinanced by issuing a large new bond to pay off the old borrowing. That bond could be paid off with a lower interest rate.

Cogan and Shultz argued that the operating deficit could be eliminated by slowing spending growth. State revenues had grown 27 percent during Davis's term in office, even with the economic collapse in 2000 and 2001. The problem, as Cogan and Shultz saw it, was that spending had grown by 36 percent.

Two days after Schwarzenegger's conversation with Shultz, the candidate called Cogan and invited him to his home in Brentwood. Joined by Pete Wilson's former finance director Russ Gould, Cogan and the candidate met on Saturday, August 16. As they drank lemonade, Cogan and Gould lectured on the state of the budget. Schwarzenegger asked questions.

After about an hour, Schwarzenegger took to the idea of rolling previous state obligations into one bond. Such a bond would require the approval of voters, so Schwarzenegger was already committing himself to at least one campaign if he were elected governor.

The session went so well that Schwarzenegger asked Joe Rodota, the campaign policy director, to put together similar study hours on other issues. Gould and Cogan had led the first class of what would come to be called the Oak Institute by some aides, Schwarzenegger University by others.

By 10 a.m. the next day, Schwarzenegger was sitting on his porch with former Governor Wilson, Assemblyman John Campbell, Gorton, and Miner to talk about taxes and spending. The economist Art Laffer, accompanied by his son, showed up to argue for a flat tax, a longtime conservative idea. (He also attacked Wilson for raising taxes when he was governor and said he wished Schwarzenegger had named Jimmy Buffett—instead of Warren Buffett—as an advisor.) Campbell argued that Schwarzenegger should convince voters to approve a constitutional amendment capping state spending. Laffer responded that such caps were too easy to get around. It was an important argument. In time, proposals for spending caps would spark long-running disputes among Schwarzenegger's advisors.

Schwarzenegger told Laffer and Campbell that he appreciated their ideas, but that he was still putting together his own thoughts on the subject. That worried Laffer. "I personally thought a live, real-time governor's race is probably not the best environment to do basic research on one's views as to how the world works," Laffer would later say.

SCHWARZENEGGER'S ONLY INSTRUCTION to Rodota about Schwarzenegger University was that he wanted the best briefers in the world. He did not care whether his instructors were Democrats or Republicans, or even whether his instructors intended to vote for him.

The candidate resisted both external and internal pressure to cut these briefings short so he could attend to other campaign needs. For most of August, Schwarzenegger faced daily criticism from reporters, including myself, for failing to describe his platform or answer questions from journalists. The campaign's communications staff pressed internally for more public events. And finance staffers wanted more fund-raisers scheduled. Schwarzenegger argued that he needed to know the issues first. Schwarzenegger University would remain in session for another two weeks.

Schwarzenegger University included a course in the "Powers of the Governor," laid out initially in a nine-page memo that had been produced by Rodota. "The office of the governor of California is second only to the presidency of the United States in scope and authority," the memo began. The only two elected officials in the United States with greater authority to make appointments were the president and the mayor of Chicago. Schwarzenegger learned that he could make four thousand appointments in one term, including 850 appointees to the executive branch. He learned how to veto a bill, how to call a special session of a legislature, and how to submit government reorganization plans. He discovered a governor can declare a state of emergency to suspend any regulatory statute. He also can call a special election. These last two powers would prove to be Schwarzenegger favorites.

Most of the Schwarzenegger University briefings were oral. The university's lone student kept the tone of the sessions light and personal. In an early briefing on gun control, Schwarzenegger was asked if he owned any guns. "As a matter of fact, I own a tank," he said, explaining how he had the Austrian government find his old army tank so he could have it shipped to Columbus, Ohio, where it sat in a military museum.

David Crane, a Democrat and friend of Schwarzenegger's since the 1970s, came down from San Francisco, where he was partner in a financial services firm, to lead two sessions, one on workers' compensation and one on energy. Terry Tamminen of Santa Monica Baykeepers, who would become a thorn in the side of the candidate's more conservative advisors, conducted a lunchtime briefing with Schwarzenegger on the environment. Harvard professor George Borjas, an expert in the economics of labor, flew out from the East Coast to lead "a very academic presentation" on immigration. "He didn't need my help," said Borjas. "From his own experience and the experience of his friends, he knew more about the subject than any politician I ever met."

After Schwarzenegger seemed bored by his first briefings on education and water, Rodota convinced Bill Lucia, a dynamic Californian who worked at the U.S. Department of Education, to do an additional education briefing. Lucia, instructed to be as energetic as possible, jumped out of his chair. Schwarzenegger liked him so much that Shriver tried, in vain, to hire him.

The candidate kept his Schwarzenegger University studies secret. He and his strategists believed the public wanted to vote for an outsider who could sweep Sacramento clean, not a man with a five-point plan.

SCHWARZENEGGER OFFERED one brief, but crucial, early glimpse behind the curtain. On August 20, he convened a meeting of his "economic recovery team" at an airport hotel in Los Angeles. Working with Rodota and his investment advisor Paul Wachter, Schwarzenegger had recruited two dozen people, mostly academics and businessmen, including Oracle president Ray Lane, National Semiconductor chairman Brian Halla, the venture capitalist Arthur Rock, and David Murdock, the billionaire owner of Dole Food Co. The only no-show, a minor embarrassment, was Schwarzenegger's agent Bryan Lourd. Lourd declined to explain his reasons publicly, but published reports speculated that supporting a Republican politician, even a client, was too big a risk in Hollywood.

Photographers and reporters were allowed to view only Schwarzenegger's welcome to the team. Once journalists had left, Warren Buffett took over the early discussion. He said California had lost such credibility with the markets that the state, the fifth-largest economy in the world, was having trouble selling its bonds. California would have to pay off $14 billion in short-term debt in June 2004, and had no plan to avoid default. Without a plan, the state might require a federal bailout by the following summer.

The group then reviewed the approach to the deficit that Cogan had first outlined for Schwarzenegger. The only person to challenge this strategy of borrowing and slowing spending growth was UCLA economist Ed Leamer, who had met privately with the candidate in one of the Schwarzenegger University sessions a few days earlier. Leamer believed that the economy could turn soft again and foil the strategy. The only way out of the budget trouble was a temporary tax increase, he said. Schwarzenegger did not agree with the argument, but his aides invited Leamer to the meeting to see what kind of reaction the economist's idea would get.

"That is the worst thing you could possibly do," George Shultz interjected, according to notes taken by two participants. It would be the pivotal point of the meeting. Shultz warned that by raising taxes, Schwarzenegger would lose any ability he had to control spending growth. Schwarzenegger agreed with him. If you're training for a bodybuilding competition and you cheat even a little on your diet, you won't win, the candidate said.

Outside the meeting, more than 160 members of the media representing five continents waited in a hotel ballroom for the first official press conference of the Schwarzenegger campaign. There were fifty-nine TV cameras. Congressman Dreier, who was advising Schwarzenegger, had never seen so many cameras, not even in the final days of a presidential campaign. Schwarzenegger, flanked by Shultz and Buffett, joked as he entered the room, "I would have wished for this kind of turnout when I did *Last Action Hero*."

The candidate gave a brief statement about California's budget troubles. He promised to hire an accounting firm to conduct a sixty-day, line-by-line audit of the budget, but claimed he had no plan for balancing the state's books.

Schwarzenegger opened it up to questions.

Would he ever consider raising taxes?

The candidate had planned a response. He said, as quickly and quietly as he could, that an earthquake, natural disaster, terrorist attack, or some unforeseen circumstance could require a tax increase. Then, having left the door carefully ajar, he delivered a sound bite that would be irresistible to TV directors and would make him sound like an implacable foe of tax increases.

"The people of California have been punished enough. From the time they get up in the morning and flush the toilet, they're taxed. Then they go and get a coffee, they're taxed. They get into their car. They're taxed. They go to the gas station. They're taxed." The rhythm built. "They go to lunch. They're taxed. This goes on all day long. Tax tax tax tax tax. Even when they go to bed, you can go to bed in fear that you may get taxed while you're sleeping. There's a sleeping tax."

A reporter asked whether Buffett's comments that California property taxes were out of whack "made sense."

Schwarzenegger smiled. "First of all, I told Warren if he mentions Prop 13, he has to do five hundred sit-ups."

Even reporters laughed. With one quip, the candidate had distanced himself from his famous advisor. But he had done it without insulting Buffett. Schwarzenegger, with a touch of humor, could put even a billionaire in his place. The clip would be replayed so often that California voters in surveys came to associate Prop 13 more closely with Schwarzenegger than any other politician. With one joke, Schwarzenegger had turned a liability into a strength.

SCHWARZENEGGER'S ADMONITION to Buffett ended Bill Simon, Jr.'s, campaign. Simon's campaign had conducted a comprehensive statewide poll in which 48 percent of respondents said they knew Schwarzenegger had an advisor who suggested raising property taxes. Yet when the same survey asked which candidate would fight property tax increases, the majority answered Schwarzenegger.

The survey also presented voters with a nameless candidate who shared Schwarzenegger's qualifications and policy views. The poll "showed us that there was no way they would vote for somebody that held all of these positions that Arnold held," said Wayne Johnson, Simon's strategist. But when the pollsters said these were Schwarzenegger's positions, those surveyed said they would vote for him anyway. Three days after the Schwarzenegger press conference, Simon dropped out of the race.

Schwarzenegger, despite his early missteps, now possessed real magic. But he would find it harder to make other rivals disappear.

CHAPTER 10

"Not Gonna Take It"

Two days after his press conference with Buffett and Shultz, Schwarzenegger campaigned in public for the first time. The day's schedule called for him to have lunch with businessmen on the open-air patio of a restaurant on Main Street in Huntington Beach, a city in Orange County. From there, he would stop in various shops on a two-block walk to the pier.

He would never get that far. By 11 a.m., thousands of people descended on Huntington Beach, seeking a glimpse of the candidate. Police closed down streets to control the size of the mob. It was too late. Old men in electric wheelchairs, surfers, parents with babies, women in bikini tops, and young men in black "Terminator for Governor" T-shirts all pressed as close as they could to Schwarzenegger.

The candidate was jostled after he walked out of a surf shop on Main Street. A reporter assigned to follow him was knocked to the ground. When Schwarzenegger waded into a group of media people to give a brief statement, he had to use a bullhorn to be heard. Rob Stutzman, one of the campaign's communications directors, was reduced to using his body to prevent the crowd from surrounding the candidate's SUV. "Please stand back," Stutzman begged. "Don't get run over."

As soon as Schwarzenegger was gone, Stutzman and other aides held an emergency meeting on the sidewalk. Many of these advance men and communications experts had spent their careers trying to build crowds for politicians. Schwarzenegger posed a new problem. How could the crowds be managed so no one got hurt?

The campaign responded by keeping the candidate's schedule a secret until mere minutes before future events. Pat Clarey, the campaign's operations chief, asked Republican politicians all over the country to loan aides to Schwarzenegger for crowd control. Finally, Clarey arranged to rent hundreds of metal bicycle racks to serve as barriers between Schwarzenegger and the public at his appearances.

Schwarzenegger had enjoyed the mayhem in Huntington Beach and at first resisted the changes. Reporters complained, too. The bike racks made it impossible for them to approach the candidate and ask follow-up questions after his speeches. For the rest of the campaign, Schwarzenegger would never appear without a barrier between himself and the voting public.

DON SIPPLE HAD RECEIVED A LITTLE uncredited assistance in preparing Schwarzenegger for the economics press conference. Mike Murphy flew in and met with the candidate in a room at the hotel where the summit was held. To avoid detection by the press, Murphy left through the hotel kitchen.

Bob White was managing the campaign, but Shriver also wanted a big-name consultant to take it in hand. Between her journalistic work and her family connections, she had as good a Rolodex as anyone in American politics, and she made calls all over the country to ask for suggestions. Shriver had a run-in with adviors to John McCain's presidential campaign, including Murphy, when she was covering his presidential campaign for NBC in 2000, but Sipple and other political professionals kept bringing up his name. Murphy had a long record of helping Republican governors get elected in Democratic states, among them John Engler in Michigan, Christine Todd Whitman in New Jersey, and Mitt Romney in Massachusetts.

To encourage Murphy to join, Shriver and Bonnie Reiss arranged a secret meeting with him on a private plane parked at the Santa Monica airport. Murphy said yes, for reasons that went beyond the immediate campaign. Murphy was a talented photographer and writer who wanted to make films, and he believed a high-profile California campaign for a movie star would provide an introduction to Los Angeles and a platform to enter the business.

It would be a week before Murphy joined up full time. After helping Schwarzenegger get ready for the economics summit, he flew off to Tblisi in the former Soviet Republic of Georgia, where he was advising a political party. In the campaign, Murphy would have no specific title. Schwarzenegger assigned people areas of responsibility, not titles. Murphy would not do a bloodletting, but he brought in two young policy aides, Trent Wisecup and Rob Gluck, as well as Florida Governor Jeb Bush's spokesman Todd Harris to join the communications operation. At first, Murphy was stunned by the free-flowing nature of Schwarzenegger's operation. He preferred a more controlled, disciplined shop. But Schwarzenegger put him at ease.

Don't be intimidated, the star warned. "I like directors who tell me what's not working. Just look me right in the eye and tell me."

THE LAST WEEK OF AUGUST, Murphy found a spot on the second floor of Schwarzenegger's Santa Monica office complex. He kicked the campaign's Internet team out of their large office at the end of a hall and built a war room there. A huge new calendar on the wall listed Schwarzenegger's public events, a theme for the day, and a schedule of TV ads. To Murphy, setting up this infrastructure was Campaign 101. It was a measure of the chaos in the campaign that no one had done this before.

Murphy turned his attention to the policy shop that was next door to the war room. While Schwarzenegger University sessions relied on visiting lecturers, the policy chief Joe Rodota also had recruited a group of full-time aides: Cynthia Bryant, a top legislative aide in Sacramento; John Schilling, who came west from a Washington education group that promoted charter schools; Viet Dinh, a Georgetown law professor and an architect of the Patriot Act; and Joel Fox, the former Howard Jarvis Taxpayers Association president.

The Schwarzenegger University sessions had produced a better-informed candidate, but few Schwarzenegger policies had been committed to paper. Murphy assigned Trent Wisecup and Rob Gluck, the two consultants he'd brought with him, to write up everything over the Labor Day weekend. When Murphy walked into the war room Tuesday morning to check on the exhausted Wisecup and Gluck, he bellowed, "I love the smell of policy in the morning!"

The exercise produced a white binder, the Join Arnold Policy Binder, that Schwarzenegger carried as he campaigned. By campaign's end, it had twenty-three pages on "Putting California's Fiscal House in Order," seven on "Fixing the Runaway Workers' Compensation System," twelve pages on "Meeting the Needs of California Students," and four on "The People's Reform Plan."

In most campaigns, these documents would be called position papers. But Schwarzenegger objected that he did not hold positions, he took actions. So the policy documents began, "As governor, I will. . . ." The candidate himself reviewed the new policy documents to check for active verbs.

At Schwarzenegger's insistence, his aides gave the policy binder an unusual appendix that recorded every promise he made. The list eventually ran to six single-spaced pages.

JUST BEFORE LABOR DAY, the campaign had asked Republican pollster John McLaughlin to conduct a new "benchmark" poll. The poll asked voters their views not only of Schwarzenegger, but of other candidates, of Governor Davis, of the condition of the state, and of a dozen different issues. The results would be used to shape campaign messages, write scripts for ads, and decide which issues to emphasize.

McLaughlin, who was close to Sipple, had experience overseas working for, among others, the Tory leader Ian Duncan Smith in Britain and the Likud Party's Benjamin Netanyahu in Israel. The multicandidate, multiparty races in those parliamentary democracies were more like the recall than most American campaigns, and they had taught McLaughlin a crucial lesson. When there were more than two candidates, the center was the last place you wanted to be. Such elections were won by building a devoted base on one side or the other.

Completed on September 7, McLaughlin's benchmark poll showed the recall would pass with 54 percent of the vote. But Schwarzenegger and Bustamante were in a dead heat to succeed Davis, with about 25 percent each. McLaughlin, who lived in New York, caught a plane from Newark to Los Angeles to deliver these results in person to Murphy, Sipple, and the rest of the campaign team.

McLaughlin had pointed advice for the strategists. The recall was far more popular than any of the candidates to replace Davis. Schwarzenegger received votes from only 34 percent of voters who viewed Davis unfavorably—and from only 41 percent of voters who favored the recall. For Schwarzenegger to gain, he had to *become* the recall in voter's minds.

Who were the recall supporters? McLaughlin's benchmark survey showed they were against raising taxes. They were ferocious in their disdain for the tripling of the vehicle license fee. And they believed the state was controlled by interest groups.

These voters included Democrats and independents, but the balance was conservative Republicans. Schwarzenegger could build a base on the right without alienating other recall supporters by focusing his campaign on those issues—taxes, workers' comp, Indian gambling—on which recall supporters of all stripes agreed. An internal campaign memo, headlined "The Winning Candidate for Conservatives," outlined the strategy. "While AS will have broad appeal, he must nonetheless forge a base of support within the California GOP . . . If AS can give them the tax issue, it can go a long way toward seeing conservatives give great credence to the 'winability' factor"—the notion that a moderate movie star had the best chance to win. Schwarzenegger should also avoid talking about social issues that divided the coalition of recall voters.

To create this GOP base, Schwarzenegger needed to give his candidacy a more Republican feel. He began daily appearances on local talk radio shows hosted by conservatives. His first call was to former San Diego Mayor Roger Hedgecock. Schwarzenegger found talk radio matched his freewheeling style. On one show, Schwarzenegger called Bustamante "Gray Davis with a receding hairline and mustache."

Talk show hosts seemed thrilled to have a chance to talk with the star. There were as many questions about movies and bodybuilding as politics.

Even those who challenged Schwarzenegger's views still praised him, especially the Fox News Channel's Sean Hannity, who forced Schwarzenegger to recite his views on social issues on his nationally syndicated radio show.

Hannity: Do you consider yourself, for example, pro-life or pro-choice?
Schwarzenegger: Pro-choice.
Hannity: Do you support partial-birth abortion?
Schwarzenegger: I do not support partial-birth abortion.
Hannity: Are you in favor of parental notification?
Schwarzenegger: I am, but in some cases where there is abuse in the family or problems in the family, then of course not.
Hannity: Do you support the Brady Bill or the assault weapons ban or both?
Schwarzenegger: Yes, I do support that and also I would like to close the loophole on the gun shows.
Hannity: Do you support gay marriage?
Schwarzenegger: I do support domestic partnership.
Hannity: But not gay marriage?
Schwarzenegger: No, I think gay marriage is something that should be between a man and a woman.

That last line was an all-time classic malapropism, but it didn't slow down Schwarzenegger. Before the show was over, he had come out against school vouchers, for the decriminalization of marijuana for medicinal purposes, and against offshore oil drilling. Hannity agreed with almost none of this, but praised Schwarzenegger for his honesty. He would host a town hall for the candidate later in the campaign.

Schwarzenegger followed up his talk show appearances by going on the road for the first rallies of the campaign. Murphy went with him. It was a crucial decision. The events had been difficult to arrange because Schwarzenegger was slow to agree to proposed schedules. By joining Schwarzenegger on the road, Murphy became the campaign's liaison to the candidate.

White and Maria Shriver had recruited Landon Parvin as campaign speechwriter. A former aide to Reagan, Parvin made his reputation by authoring a humor column for the Congressional newspaper *Roll Call* as well as many of the self-deprecating speeches given by presidents and politicians at Washington roasts. (He wrote Nancy Reagan's well-known "Second Hand Clothes" song for the Gridiron Dinner in 1982 when she lampooned her own taste for opulence.) Parvin worked out of his house in Fredericksburg, Virginia. But he was ahead of schedule on a book and decided he needed to shake up his life. Parvin knew little about California politics and had not followed the recall closely. Upon arriving in Santa Monica and taking a desk in Schwarzenegger's campaign headquarters, he poured over Internet Web logs to try to understand what was happening in the offices all around him.

When he wrote speeches for other politicians, Parvin would sit down with them and find out what they wanted to say. Schwarzenegger had neither the time nor the inclination to do that. He wanted his speeches to sound natural—the way he talked. So Parvin became a fly on the wall. He sat in on Schwarzenegger University sessions. He read transcripts of Schwarzenegger's media interviews. He listened in on fund-raising calls. He ate egg-white omelets for breakfast at the Firehouse restaurant, where the skinny speechwriter stood out among a clientele heavy in bodybuilders. On some nights, Parvin would go to Schwarzenegger's home, listen to him talk to friends, and take verbatim notes to capture his vocabulary and cadence.

Eventually Parvin characterized Schwarzenegger as a variation on Reagan. The two had similar messages, but Schwarzenegger's language was more staccato. Reagan had an air of reserve. Schwarzenegger craved a closer connection with the audience. And while most politicians tried self-effacement, Schwarzenegger preached the gospel of self-improvement. In his speeches, Schwarzenegger would unabashedly talk about how he achieved his wealth. "It's populist in a way," said Parvin. "It's genuine . . . People realize they didn't have it and he's got it. And he's quite happy about it. And they would be, too."

Before starting a speech, Parvin received an outline from Murphy detailing the elements that had to be included. Once Parvin completed a draft, Murphy added one-liners that would make the newspapers and the TV broadcasts. Then Schwarzenegger read through the text with his dialogue coach and friend, Walter von Huene.

Schwarzenegger kept von Huene's role a secret. A former acting coach on *Happy Days* and a TV director, von Huene had gotten to know Schwarzenegger while working with the child actors in the star's 1996 Christmas comedy, *Jingle All the Way*. The two men had strong personal chemistry. Born in Germany, von Huene came to California in 1952 when he was just three years old; he learned German from his grandmother and parents. He took small parts in several Schwarzenegger films. Von Huene worked with Schwarzenegger on *Batman & Robin*, *The Sixth Day*, and *Terminator 3*, going over Schwarzenegger's lines one by one to improve the actor's delivery.

Von Huene would perform a similar service in Schwarzenegger's political life. Which words should he emphasize? When should he pause? If some phrases written by Parvin and Murphy did not work, von Huene and Schwarzenegger sent the speech back.

When Schwarzenegger balked at Parvin's first few efforts—the speeches sounded too conventionally political—von Huene provided the speechwriter with important feedback. Parvin learned that he had to write speeches not only to match a political campaign, but also to fit the Schwarzenegger that the public knew from the movies. "He doesn't want to diminish the brand," Parvin said. "You couldn't write a normal political speech for him."

"I COME TO YOU TODAY not as the Terminator or the guy who fought the Predator," Schwarzenegger began his speech at the campaign's first rally. Truth be told, he came to the rally, in front of a mall and movie theater in Fresno on August 28, as a politician having a rough afternoon. On his way to the speech, he had toured a local factory while reporters pestered him about an interview he'd given to a skin magazine, *Oui*, in 1977.

Mickey Kaus, a journalist who produced a Slate.com column, had been lamenting online the lack of scandalous news on Schwarzenegger when he learned that a copy of the magazine was for sale on eBay. Kaus broke the news of the 1977 interview, which dominated the campaign for two days. In the interview, Schwarzenegger described engaging in group sex at Gold's Gym and receiving blow jobs backstage at Mr. Olympia contests.

Schwarzenegger said at the factory in Fresno that he didn't remember the interview. He later suggested he had made up the stories in 1977 to sell bodybuilding. "I said a lot of things that were not true," Schwarzenegger recalled. "It was only to dramatize situations—to dramatize things in order to make people . . . say, 'I am interested to watch this guy. This is an interesting personality.'"

In saying that he had lied at the time to sell himself and bodybuilding, Schwarzenegger was almost certainly telling the truth. The campaign began to trot out this defense against any provocative quote that emerged from Schwarzenegger's past. This was an unusual approach for a political candidate: He lied—so what? But it defused the issue.

When Schwarzenegger arrived at the rally and saw the crowd of more than two thousand, his worries seemed to vanish. Some people had been waiting since lunchtime for the 5 p.m. speech. The candidate was driven up to the stage in a dark SUV. He exited to a tape of the 1980s metal band Twisted Sister singing "We're Not Gonna Take It."

We're not gonna take it
No we ain't gonna take it
We're not gonna take it anymore
We've got the right to choose
And there ain't no way we'll lose it.
This is our life, this is our song.
We'll fight the powers that be just
Don't pick our destiny cause
You don't know us, you don't belong

Twisted Sister had named the 1985 album on which "We're Not Gonna Take It" appeared after an early Schwarzenegger film, *Stay Hungry*. A few conservative taxpayer advocates thought the song was a nod to Howard Jarvis's old cry: "We're mad as hell and we're not going to take it anymore."

The song matched perfectly the over-the-top feel of the recall campaign. California was hot and dry, its citizens angry and agitated. Schwarzenegger crowds wore light, loose-fitting clothes. The sixty-day race was about the length of a decent summer fling, the amount of time a huge hit movie stuck around in theaters.

Schwarzenegger talked for seven minutes. The crowd was so loud that, even speaking through a microphone, Schwarzenegger was difficult to hear. A group of a dozen ROTC cadets chanted the candidate's name. Schwarzenegger walked along the edge of the stage, signing Terminator action figures and old bodybuilding magazines.

The TV stations had cut away while Schwarzenegger shook hands and signed autographs. So Murphy figured out a simple, ingenious way to keep the cameras on the candidate even when he wasn't speaking. "I want a box of T-shirts wrapped up tight like footballs," he told Fred Beteta, who was in charge of campaign events.

At future rallies Schwarzenegger would finish his speech and throw T-shirts into the cheering crowd. TV stations might cut away from handshaking, but Arnold Schwarzenegger throwing T-shirts like a quarterback? That was action. The T-shirt throw bought him a minute or two of extra time on camera. When he saw news coverage of his first throw, Schwarzenegger said, "Give me more T-shirts." For the price of a couple dozen T-shirts, Schwarzenegger could get hundreds of thousands of dollars worth of air time.

EVEN WHEN SCHWARZENEGGER faced a tough crowd, the live television coverage conferred enormous advantages on his campaign. At the California State University campus in Long Beach, Schwarzenegger was hit in the shoulder by an egg thrown by a person who was never identified. The candidate got off a good line in response—"This guy owes me bacon"—but he rushed through the speech, which Parvin had written a bit too long for an audience of college students. Back at Oak in Santa Monica, campaign staffers watching on TV improved the look of the event by sending e-mails via Blackberry to the team onsite. A banner was shifted to the left so it looked better on screen. A yawning student was moved.

Schwarzenegger's ubiquity on television obscured the fact that he was avoiding interviews with newspaper reporters. The candidate instead devoted interview time to talk radio and national TV personalities such as Oprah Winfrey and Larry King. He gave one interview each to major newspapers and local TV stations. But he organized the sessions as he did his publicity for movie premieres. TV reporters were ushered into a room for ten minutes each, leaving almost no time for difficult follow-up questions. Schwarzenegger even tried to direct camera crews as if he were the star on a movie set. During one TV interview, the candidate chastised a cameraman who was standing behind the reporter. Schwarzenegger knew that his eye might follow anyone in his line of sight and make him look shifty-eyed.

Schwarzenegger's print interviews were only slightly more revealing. On September 4, with a few minutes' warning, one of the campaign's communications strategists, Sean Walsh, ushered me into a room in the historic Mission Inn in Riverside. This would be my only official interview during the campaign with the candidate I was covering daily for the largest newspaper in the state, the *Los Angeles Times*. Schwarzenegger spent the first six minutes politely criticizing a story I had written about his lack of an education policy. As it turned out, he was right. He had developed education policies during Schwarzenegger University, but had yet to disclose them. For the rest of the interview, he filibustered, reciting talking points as I tried to interrupt.

He offered almost no news. He did pledge to protect Proposition 98, the state's education spending guarantee: "There are certain fundamental things, I would just say, not over my dead body," he said to my question of whether he would change or suspend Prop 98. It seemed like boilerplate then, but the answer would prove to be one of his more important promises.

"Twenty minutes is up," Walsh said. I invited Schwarzenegger to visit with the paper's other political reporters before the campaign's end. He said he would. He did not. As I was escorted out of the hotel, Walsh called after me: "Make sure you write that the *Times* got its interview."

AS THE CAMPAIGN PROGRESSED, Schwarzenegger made his own news by seeking endorsements from groups that typically did not give them to

Republicans, or anyone at all. Swinging for the fences, the candidate struck out at first. He called prominent Democrats, but a "Democrats for Arnold" coalition never took off. Schwarzenegger appeared to have pulled off a coup with an endorsement from the state firefighters association (public employees rarely backed Republicans), but a rival firefighters group aligned with Governor Davis attempted to replace the leaders of the association.

Schwarzenegger turned next to the state's business community. Local chambers of commerce were opposing the recall; the Los Angeles Area Chamber, chaired by Maria Shriver's personal attorney, opposed the removal of Davis. The California Chamber of Commerce, the statewide group, had a policy of not issuing endorsements in state races. The chamber nevertheless had invited Schwarzenegger to speak.

Jeff Randle, the consultant who headed the campaign's political operation, saw the invitation and tried to use it to win an endorsement. "We'll come and speak," Randle told the chamber's Cassandra Pye when she called. "Just give me an endorsement."

Pye laughed at first, but she mentioned the request to the chamber's president Allan Zaremberg, who to her surprise did not dismiss it entirely. The chamber executive committee was reluctant at first. But that reticence vanished when Lieutenant Governor Cruz Bustamante announced his budget plan, which included tax increases on businesses to close the budget deficit.

Schwarzenegger made a point of leaving the campaign office by six o'clock each evening to go for a workout. But with Randle begging, the candidate stuck around for an early evening phone call with the chairman of the chamber's board, Raymond Holdsworth, a Los Angeles technology executive. Holdsworth said he would take the matter to his board at a meeting on Friday, September 5, at the Ritz Carlton Hotel in Dana Point in southern Orange County.

The board meeting offered genuine suspense. Forty reporters had gathered in a hotel courtyard. Randle felt ill. If the chamber chose not to endorse, the journalists were sure to call it a defeat.

Schwarzenegger gave a brief speech about the high cost of doing business. He told the story of his ten-year-old son Patrick's business selling milk and cookies to construction crews remodeling homes in Brentwood; "I'm worried about him, because every day I'm prepared to come home and find his workers' compensation is going to close him down," Schwarzenegger joked. He took a few questions and left to wait for the verdict in a hotel room.

Schwarzenegger did not receive unanimous support. And chamber members said the decision did not change their policy of avoiding endorsements in statewide races. But the recall was a historic event. The endorsement was front-page news in many of the state's papers.

The chamber's decision effectively ended former baseball commissioner Peter Ueberroth's campaign. Ueberroth had stayed in the race on the theory that Schwarzenegger would flop, and Ueberroth would emerge as the centrist, political outsider the state could rally around. After the chamber endorsement, Ueberroth's consultant, Dan Schnur, told his candidate that the only way he could win was by attacking Schwarzenegger. Ueberroth quit rather than do that.

As SCHWARZENEGGER DROVE yet another Republican from the race, he began to look more like a candidate. He once favored leather jackets and short sleeves. By September he was sometimes wearing suits (48 regular), dress shirts (17/35), and solid-color ties. He still favored gaudy rings. He had a boxing championship ring given to him by Muhammad Ali and a huge silver ring with a lapis lazuli stone that had been a gift from a Navajo man. He still had a habit of plugging products he liked—LifeCycle exercise equipment, Indian Chief motorcycles, certain brands of cigars—in his political speeches. Schwarzenegger's campaign was still looser than most. He appeared on *The Howard Stern Show* after Stern received an exemption from the FCC over the equal time rule so that he wouldn't have to give air time to the other 134 candidates. One afternoon, after receiving the Farm Bureau endorsement in Sacramento, Schwarzenegger unveiled a surprisingly good Nixon impression.

At Sipple's suggestion, Schwarzenegger started holding his own town halls, called "Ask Arnolds," in each major media market. Ask Arnolds were not open to the public. The campaign invited only members of supportive groups and local volunteers. The levels of the stage on which audience members sat were customized to the candidate's height so that Schwarzenegger was looking up at his questioners—a more attractive pose than looking down. (The teams that built town hall stages were told that Schwarzenegger, officially six feet two inches tall, was an even six feet.) At the San Diego "Ask Arnold," the invited guests enlivened the event by quarreling with one another over how close they could sit to Schwarzenegger.

As the election approached, the timing of "Ask Arnolds" was determined by fund-raising. The campaign needed cash. At one of the first fundraisers, a cocktail reception at the Century Plaza Hotel in Los Angeles, the crowd swelled so quickly that the candidate got trapped in the mass of donors. After that event, staffers took the metal bicycle racks that had been used to protect him from crowds in public and put them between donors and the candidate.

The campaign sometimes scheduled two or three fund-raisers in a single night. On an evening in September, Schwarzenegger had events at the home of venture capitalist John Hurley in the Russian Hill neighborhood of San Francisco, where guests smoked cigars on the roof and admired the views of Alcatraz, and at the Blackhawk Automotive Museum across the bay in Danville. At the museum, Schwarzenegger went upstairs to a private dinner for donors who had given more than $10,000.

The campaign press office had arranged for a TV reporter to ask Schwarzenegger a quick question on his way out. The candidate exited a side door and walked straight to the reporter, whose cameraman had the tape rolling. As the reporter asked his first question, Schwarzenegger stopped him.

"You know what? I didn't like the look of the exit. I walked right to you. Boring. It should seem like I didn't know, like you just grabbed me on the way out," he said. Schwarzenegger went back inside the museum and exited the same side door, but this time he walked away from the camera. After a few steps, Schwarzenegger turned around and came over to take a few questions. The candidate had produced the picture he wanted.

SCHWARZENEGGER NOW had only one rival remaining on his right: Tom McClintock. The campaign's polls suggested that McClintock was the only person standing between Schwarzenegger and the governorship.

McClintock had little money. He had spent twenty years in the legislature, but did not hold leadership posts. He had routinely voted against the budgets of governors of his own party. But he was eloquent and familiar to the conservative talk radio listeners who fueled the recall. In 2002, he had shown surprising strength in a run for state controller. With other Republicans out of the race, McClintock was running a strong third, with support in the double digits. He had many of the state's most conservative voters in his camp. Schwarzenegger held a narrow lead over the only major Democrat in the race, Bustamante.

How to react to this set of circumstances was a matter of constant debate in the Schwarzenegger campaign. Shriver and Reiss, both Democrats, had long argued for a centrist campaign that would transform California politics and the Republican party in the process. George Gorton had some sympathy with this position. Bustamante, he felt, had moved so far to the left by embracing tax increases and immigrant rights that a campaign could be won in the center. The other consultants disagreed. It might be nice to change California politics. It would be nicer to win. The only sure way to do that was to pry conservative voters away from McClintock.

Jan van Lohuizen, the pollster in charge of the nightly tracking surveys for the campaign, was adamant. He produced a memo on September 12 arguing that Schwarzenegger badly needed McClintock's conservative voters. Van Lohuizen's surveys of Democrats suggested that no more than 20 percent of them would vote for Schwarzenegger. If Schwarzenegger didn't continue to court conservatives, the Republican vote would be split. The result: Governor Bustamante.

Publicly, Schwarzenegger was full of praise for McClintock. Privately, he signed off on a strategy designed to push the state senator out of the race. Schwarzenegger's conservative supporters asked McClintock backers to stop donating to his campaign. This was a war of attrition. McClintock did not have the resources to keep up with the movie star's endorsements or ads. His team did not have its own polls in the field; Schwarzenegger had two of the nation's top Republican pollsters. McClintock raised $2.4 million in his campaign. Schwarzenegger would spend nearly ten times that.

McClintock never seriously considered dropping out. He loved to talk about his conservative ideas, and now cable network producers and syndicated radio hosts wanted to interview him. He had no desire to give that up.

GOVERNOR DAVIS TRIED EVERYTHING to survive the recall: apologies, attack ads, town halls, a visit from former President Clinton. Nothing worked, and some of his campaigning backfired. The governor made a major mistake by off-handedly criticizing Schwarzenegger for not being able to pronounce the word "California." (Schwarzenegger's version was "Cull–eee–fornia," which to some ears sounded close to the original Spanish pronunciation.) Even Democrats denounced Davis for this comment and demanded he apologize. The governor had mocked one of the most imitated and beloved accents in the world.

IN THE BATTLE for conservative votes, Schwarzenegger adopted much of McClintock's economic platform as his own. At the beginning of his campaign, McClintock had identified five issues on which he, as governor, would draft ballot initiatives to allow voters to enact new laws directly. Schwarzenegger embraced all five issues—workers' compensation, protection of local government funds, making lawsuits more difficult to file, the contracting out of some state government services, and a constitutional amendment to give the governor more power to cut spending.

In his effort to co-opt McClintock, direct democracy would prove to be Schwarzenegger's strongest political ally. A few days before the state Republican convention scheduled for September 12–14, Schwarzenegger sent a letter to all the delegates. The letter avoided policy statements and instead emphasized Schwarzenegger's support for ballot initiatives. "Dear Republican leader," the letter said, "Our campaign for governor represents a movement to return California government to the people . . . I believe that when Americans rise up united behind a cause, they can overcome any obstacle. It happened twenty-five years ago with Proposition 13."

Even in California, conservatives believed that when push came to shove, the people agreed with them. The history of direct democracy supported this view. California had two electorates. Californians chose more Democrats than Republicans for legislative and congressional seats, which were based on total populations of residents, not citizens or voters. But when forced to make decisions on certain issues through initiatives, California voters often cast ballots more like Republicans: against taxes and for tougher penalties against criminals.

In a recall, running as the embodiment of direct democracy made all the sense in the world. Schwarzenegger did not consider the problems that a strategy based on ballot initiatives might create for a governorship. The candidate made a point of not dwelling on negative thoughts, and there was little time for deep thinking of any kind in a sixty-day campaign. Schwarzenegger had officially been in elective politics for five weeks. He hadn't even won office yet. But he already was pledging himself to future campaigns.

CHAPTER 11

"A Time for Choosing"

On Friday, September 12, Schwarzenegger received a memo from his consultants about the California Republican Party Convention, which would take place that weekend at the LAX Marriott hotel. The 1,400 delegates, the memo explained, were more conservative than party voters, and their conventions usually were of interest only to political junkies. This weekend, the memo concluded, you are going to change that.

The party was unlikely to officially endorse either candidate at the convention itself, but the weekend offered a chance to win the backing of Republican regulars and set the stage for the party's endorsement in the weeks ahead. In this contest, Tom McClintock had left Schwarzenegger a huge opening. Knowing that the convention delegates were his natural ideological allies, the conservative state senator would give a speech, but not otherwise have much of a presence. Jeff Randle had a plan to fill the vacuum and push the party to endorse Schwarzenegger. The strategy was "shock and awe." Fred Beteta, who oversaw campaign events, reserved the parking lot outside the convention hotel for an outdoor rally of more than 2,500 people. A high school marching band was brought in to play the campaign theme song, "We're Not Gonna Take It." As the convention opened Saturday morning, September 13, the rally began. Delegates looking down from their hotel rooms could not miss it.

For Republicans—or anyone—watching on TV, the rally provided pictures of thousands of people at "the state Republican convention" screaming for Schwarzenegger. The fact that few in the crowd were delegates did not matter.

Landon Parvin, the former Reagan speechwriter, had put together Schwarzenegger's convention address after a long evening on the star's patio, listening to him talk about his political development. Schwarzenegger had spoken with Parvin about Styria, the Hungarian refugees who escaped communism and arrived in Austria when he was nine, the Soviet tanks he'd seen on family trips to Mürzzuschlag in northern Styria, his embrace of America's opportunities, his after-school programs, and the bust of Reagan he had commissioned.

After being introduced by Congresswoman Mary Bono, Sonny's widow, Schwarzenegger began his lunchtime speech.

"Why am I a Republican?" he said. "I am asked this thirty times a day. And that's just from Maria!"

Schwarzenegger rattled off a list of reasons why he was not only a Republican, but a conservative one at that.

"I'm a conservative because I believe communism is evil and free enterprise is good. I'm a conservative because Milton Friedman is right and Karl Marx was wrong. I'm a conservative because I believe the government serves the people; the people don't serve the government. I'm a conservative because I believe in balanced budgets, not budget deficits. I'm a conservative because I believe the money that people earn is their money, not the government's money."

Each line drew a huge roar. Not one offered a specific policy. But the language was a way of expressing sympathy with conservative ideals without making any pledges. His only promise was to take his bust of Reagan with him to Sacramento.

Schwarzenegger also echoed Reagan's well-known October 1964 speech, "A Time for Choosing," given as part of a TV program on behalf of Barry Goldwater's presidential campaign. Goldwater lost, but the speech propelled Reagan into the governor's office two years later. Reagan's speech had been profoundly conservative and ideological. He was picking a side. Schwarzenegger invoked the speech but in almost the exact opposite way. His message was: ignore ideology and get behind me for the sake of the party.

THE REAL ACTION of the convention came after Schwarzenegger's speech on the upper floors of the hotel. He had reserved adjoining suites, Rooms 1738 and 1740, as a base of operations from which he could lock down endorsements.

In this peculiar time and place, the fact that Schwarzenegger was not as conservative as conservatives would have liked gave him a special appeal to, of all people, conservatives. Jon Coupal of the Howard Jarvis Taxpayers Association laid out the strange logic in an e-mail to Shawn Steel, the former state party chair who had worked with Costa to promote the recall: "Supporting Arnold is, in fact, the more principled thing to do. As movement conservatives, endorsing Tom would be easy. It's what everybody expects us to do. BUT TAKING THE HEAT BY ENDORSING ARNOLD TO KEEP CRUZ OUT IS THE MORE RESPONSIBLE COURSE OF ACTION. In short, I am not about to sacrifice Prop 13 nor my children's future lives in California on the altar of ideological purity."

In one room of the hotel, George Gorton led a meeting with twenty prominent conservatives. Among them were the economist Art Laffer and a half-dozen talk radio hosts. Shawn Steel attended and savored the irony: by bucking the state party with the recall, he was now on the inside. One of the attendees, Steve Moore, the founder of the Club for Growth, which promoted cutting taxes and reducing government, had supported primary challenges in other states to moderate Republicans with views not unlike Schwarzenegger's. When it came to California and movie stars, the rules were different. "Arnold is a very seductive individual," Moore conceded.

Gorton gave the conservatives select glimpses of the policies that had been produced by the Schwarzenegger University sessions and said that a Governor Schwarzenegger would be open to all sorts of fiscally conservative ideas. But Gorton's main point was that Schwarzenegger, unlike McClintock, could fight and win ballot initiative battles. With Democrats controlling huge majorities in the legislature, any other Republican governor would be hamstrung. "That was the conversation," said San Francisco talk show host Melanie Morgan. "Arnold could overrule everyone else. He was going to govern by initiative."

While Gorton worked his room, Schwarzenegger smoked a cigar with Congressman David Dreier and cemented a bond that would make Dreier his top ally in Washington. Midafternoon, Schwarzenegger walked up to the eighteenth floor to meet with young Republicans and touch base with his group of Orange County donors, the New Majority.

From there, he headed down a short hallway to Executive Suite 1, where more than fifty of the Republican chairmen from California's fifty-eight counties were meeting. Schwarzenegger's first two meetings had been warmups for this third and most important session. If the chairs went for Schwarzenegger, the infrastructure of the party would follow.

Before Schwarzenegger arrived, the state Republican chairman Duf Sundheim asked for a show of hands. How many of the chairs think Schwarzenegger should drop out and McClintock should be the candidate? Four hands went up. How many think McClintock should drop out and Arnold should be the candidate? More than forty agreed. Many had wanted to back Schwarzenegger, but were too afraid to admit it to their fellow conservatives. Sundheim had revealed the chairmen to each other.

After listening to Schwarzenegger talk forcefully about the recall, the county chairs decided to spur the party to action. Mike Harvey, the chairman in Humboldt County on California's far north coast, tore a sheet of lined paper out of a notebook and drew up a petition to call a special meeting of the county chairs in a week's time. An endorsement would follow. In a single weekend, Schwarzenegger, the Hollywood moderate and perceived novice, had outmaneuvered McClintock, a politician for twenty years.

SCHWARZENEGGER HAD reserved the California State Railroad Museum for a September 18 press conference on political reform and government ethics. He had picked the venue as an homage to the long fight against the Southern Pacific Railroad, the battle that had midwifed direct democracy in California.

Schwarzenegger had received an education on the origins of California's direct democracy from Tom McEnery, the former mayor of San Jose, during the Schwarzenegger University sessions on political reform. McEnery's family had roots in California politics that dated to Hiram Johnson. One of his grandfathers, "Honest" Ben Sellers, had been a San Jose mayor and a Johnson supporter; his other grandfather was a Progressive newspaper editor. McEnery, a Democrat, had done his best to live up to that tradition. As mayor, he had championed limits on the gifts local politicians could accept, fought against expansion of gambling, and chaired a statewide initiative to promote campaign finance reform. (It lost.)

At each of three meetings with Schwarzenegger, McEnery brought up Hiram Johnson. Schwarzenegger had heard the name, but not much more. McEnery told his version of the Johnson story in broad strokes (fighting the special interests, the power of the railroad) and Schwarzenegger took to it. Johnson was the kind of governor Schwarzenegger imagined he could play. He asked his campaign staff to give him more information on Johnson. Joel Fox, the former Howard Jarvis Taxpayers Association president who worked as a policy aide, produced a five-page report for the candidate.

The athlete in Schwarzenegger understood the fight against political bossism—an ancient battle, to be sure—as yet another competition. He asked McEnery what the state could do to "be number one in political reform." Redistricting was McEnery's first answer. The former mayor explained how the legislature's Democratic and Republican incumbents had conspired to create safe districts for each other. With no real political competition for seats, few moderates could win election. Common Cause, the national non-profit that tried to make politics cleaner, had a model plan for redistricting that would allow independent panels of citizens or judges to draw the lines. Schwarzenegger should consider it, though McEnery warned that both parties would oppose reform. "Don't worry, Tom," Schwarzenegger replied, "you and I and the people like it."

Schwarzenegger and McEnery discussed other topics: politicians who broke campaign finance rules needed to be punished, and the state's system of boards and commissions had been turned into a patronage tool. The candidate offered ideas of his own. Schwarzenegger said he understood that it was impossible to eliminate money from politics. But was there a way to take money out of the process for a limited time, when the most important decisions were made? Joe Rodota, the policy chief, asked Viet Dinh, the legal scholar, to find out. Ideally, fund-raising would be banned at the end of the legislative session in the late summer, when bills were passed and signed into law. But that was deemed too close to the fall election season. Dinh's plan instead banned fund-raising earlier, when the budget was being debated. The campaign policy team made a few other additions to the package, including a requirement that all campaign contributions be disclosed within twenty-four hours and a provision to end a loophole that allowed some bills to pass through the legislature without a hearing.

Schwarzenegger's planned remarks for the railroad museum were circulated six times inside the campaign. An early draft called for him to take on Sacramento lobbyists, a group so powerful that they were called—accurately—"The Third House" of state government. "I want to burn the Third House down," Schwarzenegger was to have said. Some aides, particularly those with experience in government, argued that the Third House offered valuable institutional memory.

At the railroad museum, Schwarzenegger released his plan, ad-libbed a line about Hiram Johnson being his hero, and pointed to the trains for the cameras. McEnery and former Secretary of State Bill Jones, a Republican, stood next to Schwarzenegger. Jones suggested that if the legislature balked, Schwarzenegger could turn some of the proposals into ballot initiatives.

That seemed a likely prospect. Although Schwarzenegger drew the most positive newspaper coverage of the campaign with his reform proposals, legislative leaders dismissed the package bitterly. "We've got enough trouble with overcrowded prisons," the Democratic leader of the state Senate, John Burton, said in reference to the idea of tougher campaign finance laws. "He's so fucking full of shit I can't believe it."

By the next day, September 19, Schwarzenegger had a small lead in internal polls but still needed a final boost. The CTA tracking polls, done the week the reform package was announced, showed Bustamante and Schwarzenegger in a statistical tie. Schwarzenegger had a little momentum because conservatives were slowly leaving McClintock for him.

Most political campaigns in a similar bind would attack their opponents. But Schwarzenegger often boasted that he would run a positive campaign.

In truth, the Schwarzenegger campaign had launched a few surreptitious attacks, with Bustamante as the primary target. An opposition researcher affiliated with the campaign distributed information about the lieutenant governor's voting record, donors, property ownership, and membership in a left-wing Latino rights group. Republican attorneys made an issue of how Bustamante raised campaign money. A new law had put a $21,200 limit on donations to candidates, so Bustamante directed huge donations from public employee unions and Indian gambling tribes—including $1.5 million from the Viejas Band of Kumeyaay Indians—into a political account that predated the limits. Bustamante, whose brother managed an Indian casino in the state, then transferred the money to his gubernatorial account and to a ballot measure committee he controlled. A judge eventually ordered Bustamante to stop using the old account. News of the controversy dominated coverage of the lieutenant governor's campaign, making it difficult for him to gain ground in polls.

Attacking McClintock would be a trickier project. The weekend after the state Republican convention, the Schwarzenegger campaign convened two focus groups in the San Fernando Valley. One included only McClintock voters. The other consisted of Schwarzenegger and McClintock supporters. The findings of the focus groups were a pleasant surprise. McClintock's appeal had less to do with his ideology than his experience. McClintock voters liked Schwarzenegger, but did not understand why he was running. If ideology had been the problem, Schwarzenegger would have had few options. Perhaps Schwarzenegger simply needed to talk more about his reasons for wanting to be governor, and distinguish himself from McClintock in some way that wouldn't offend conservatives.

One issue offered an opportunity.

FOUR YEARS EARLIER, California's Indian tribes had used direct democracy to gain a monopoly on casino gambling in the state, but their public image had suffered since. Many voters thought they had authorized small casinos. But the tribes erected huge casinos throughout inland California. Their estimated total take surpassed $5 billion a year, more than Atlantic City's annual gambling revenues. The tribes paid few taxes and offered only a tiny fraction of their earnings to local governments. Some tribes had used their profits to become political kingmakers. Between 1998 and 2003, tribes donated more than $120 million to campaigns in the state.

Schwarzenegger had decided not to accept campaign money from tribes or other gambling interests. He said this stance was based on principle, but it also had strategic value. The campaign's polls showed that the public believed tribes spent too much on politics and should share more of their profits with the state. And in refusing to accept tribal donations, Schwarzenegger distinguished himself politically not only from Davis and Bustamante but also from McClintock.

Indian gambling offered a huge opportunity, if Schwarzenegger chose to take it. He could attack all his rivals with one single issue. And by associating McClintock with his Democratic rivals, he could subtly question McClintock's loyalty to the party. Doing all this, however, would break his promise to avoid negative campaigning.

No issue would be debated longer or harder in the Schwarzenegger campaign. For all the attention on Schwarzenegger's personality, this narrow political question of Indian gambling would prove politically decisive.

The campaign had to form both a policy and a political strategy. Sipple strongly advocated an attack on tribal casinos and the willingness of other politicians to take their money. He thought the tribes were "a symbol of what Arnold is against" and that an attack would dovetail well with the campaign's message that Schwarzenegger represented "change versus status quo." If Schwarzenegger was going to convince voters that he could change politics, he had to take on one of the big political players. Randle and Gorton worried about how the tribes might respond to an attack. The tribes could drop $20 million in negative advertising against Schwarzenegger (or in positive ads for McClintock) in a manner of days. But pollster Jan van Lohuizen found that if the tribes attacked Schwarzenegger, "that would be good, that was the proof we needed" that he would stand up to interest groups.

The campaign team debated even the smallest of Indian issues. Should Schwarzenegger talk to the tribes? The candidate placed calls to the leaders of two leading tribal organizations. Schwarzenegger talked briefly to one and left a message on the cell phone of another, Tribal Alliance of Sovereign Indian Nations Chairwoman Lynn "Nay" Valbuena. But when Valbuena called back, another debate ensued within the Schwarzenegger campaign and the candidate did not take the call.

Several Schwarzenegger allies offered their services as go-betweens with the Indians. Curt Pringle, a former assembly speaker, was among those who reached out to the tribes to no avail. Gorton sought out Gene Raper, a consultant for the Agua Caliente Tribe in Palm Springs, to find out if the tribes planned an attack on Schwarzenegger. There was little hope for peace.

The constant debate on tribes troubled Schwarzenegger. As he learned more about the tribes and their political power, he grew more wary of his own advisors and consultants. Had the whole political world gotten in bed with the tribes?

For help in figuring out a policy, Schwarzenegger turned to his own investment advisor Paul Wachter and after-school advisor Bonnie Reiss. Both had had huge roles in the campaign, with Wachter helping out on economic policy and watching the campaign budget (it had grown to more than twice what was first promised), while Reiss offered strategic advice and worked on education, environmental policy, and outreach to Hollywood.

As a managing director at Schroeder & Co., Wachter had overseen investments in hotels and gambling. And Reiss stayed in close contact with Maria Shriver's brother Tim, who ran the Special Olympics and had spent years living in Connecticut. The Pequot Tribe, which had started the Foxwoods Casino in Connecticut a decade earlier, was a donor to the Special Olympics, and Tim Shriver relayed to Reiss that the Pequots shared 25 percent of their net win from slots with the state. That was far more than California tribes gave the government. Reiss talked to the Pequot chairman and also to a Connecticut official. The campaign policy staff suggested that with California tribal gaming expected to grow to $6 billion in revenues, the state should get nearly $1 billion from the tribes annually. Schwarzenegger set an ambitious goal of 25 percent, or about $1.5 billion. Making that demand publicly would guarantee war with the tribes.

Murphy and Sipple drove to the Schwarzenegger home in Brentwood to make a pitch directly to the candidate. They asked Schwarzenegger to let Sipple film an advertisement on the Indian gambling issue. If the candidate liked it, they could run it. "Let's do it," Schwarzenegger said.

The ad began with a slot machine labeled California Indian Casinos. The machine showed $120 million, the amount tribes had donated to California political campaigns since 1998. Schwarzenegger, wearing a tan sport coat and no tie, looked into the camera. "Their casinos make billions but pay no taxes and virtually nothing to the state. Other states require revenue from Indian gaming, but not us. It's time for them to pay their fair share." The ad pivoted to attack the competition. "All the other major candidates take their money and pander to them—I don't play that game," Schwarzenegger said.

If Schwarzenegger had any lingering doubts about running the ad, they disappeared the third week of September when the Morongo Band of Mission Indians, owners of a huge casino near Palm Springs, began airing ads in support of McClintock. The ad argued "independent polls show that McClintock has the momentum to win." That ran counter to Schwarzenegger's efforts to convince Republican voters that Bustamante would win the election if they voted for McClintock. "This is war," the legal counsel to the California Nations Indian Gaming Association said in a memo to tribal leaders. "We're going after Arnold Schwarzenegger." Before the recall was over, the tribes would spend more than $10 million supporting Schwarzenegger's opponents to his left and to his right.

Schwarzenegger's ad debuted on Monday, September 22—fifteen days before the election. It was devastating to his opponents and to the image of the Native American tribes in California. Garry South, the strategist for Governor Davis, marveled: "I have never seen any campaign fund-raising issue penetrate as deeply down to the bottom of the electorate as this one did. People in focus groups began bringing it up of their own volition." In the first two nights after the ad went on the air, Schwarzenegger soared in the campaign's tracking polls.

Schwarzenegger finally had McClintock in a box. "I think that as far as Tom McClintock is concerned, the question for him is: Does he represent the Republicans? Or does he represent Bustamante?" Schwarzenegger said in one town hall.

MURPHY HAD CONVINCED Schwarzenegger to skip all the debates save one, scheduled for Wednesday, September 24, at the California State University campus in Sacramento. In doing so, Murphy had set a trap for reporters and opponents alike. They criticized Schwarzenegger for missing earlier debates and suggested that the former bodybuilder was not ready to lead the state. By publicly dismissing Schwarzenegger, his critics lowered expectations, just as Murphy wanted. Even a mediocre debate performance would look like a triumph.

Although Schwarzenegger had begun to tout the event as the "Super Bowl of debates," as a debater he needed to improve. He was a movie star, not a theater actor. There, he would get only one take.

Three days before the debate, Schwarzenegger rented a production studio near the Santa Monica airport where Ridley Scott shot movie scenes. Tables and chairs were arranged in the same V-shape that Schwarzenegger would encounter on the Sacramento stage. Walter von Huene, Schwarzenegger's acting and speech coach, played the moderator. Some of the preparation was videotaped so Schwarzenegger could study his own performance. After each practice of his closing statement, he would watch how he had done on tape and rehearse again. Schwarzenegger repeated this exercise a half-dozen times before he was satisfied.

The campaign arranged for stand-ins to play each of Schwarzenegger's four opponents. Rod Pacheco, a former Republican legislator now working as a prosecutor in Riverside, played Bustamante. Assemblyman John Campbell played McClintock. (Campbell, a clothes horse, wore the plainest suit and tie he could find to portray the senator, who bought off the rack.) Rob Stutzman, one of the campaign spokesmen, was Green Party candidate Peter

Camejo. Colleen McAndrews, a campaign lawyer, accepted the challenging role of commentator Arianna Huffington. Each of the stand-ins had met the person he or she played, and each received a briefing book with exact quotes from their candidate's speeches and a tape of an earlier debate that had not included Schwarzenegger. Murphy asked them to memorize the language of their candidate so Schwarzenegger would be prepared for the words he heard Wednesday. Murphy said he didn't want the stand-ins giving Schwarzenegger advice. That was his job. Rather, he asked them to do whatever they could to provoke the candidate.

Campbell, as McClintock, was fiercest. He mocked Schwarzenegger's Hollywood values by saying: You're not a moral example of anything. Pacheco, as Bustamante, was less personally insulting but still strong and aggressive. Stutzman, as Camejo, provided comic relief.

John McLaughlin, one of the campaign pollsters, had called Murphy beforehand with a warning. He had been on a panel at the Conservative Political Action Conference with Huffington when she was a Republican. He knew how caustic she could be. Under no circumstances could Schwarzenegger look weak in his exchanges with Huffington. Treat her just like a man, McLaughlin advised. If she attacks, hit back. Voters perceived Schwarzenegger as strong; he couldn't afford to look weak.

McAndrews, wearing a suit that looked just like the one Huffington wore in a picture on her campaign Web site, did her best to harangue Schwarzenegger about his finances, his Republicanism, his Hummers. She attempted a Greek accent when taunting him with the name of the president, "Arnold's friend Booooosh." Murphy wanted more.

Ramp it up, Colleen. Be more obnoxious.

She tried. But no one could get a rise out of Schwarzenegger. The only time the stand-ins unnerved the candidate was when they ignored him.

In anticipation of attacks against his character, Schwarzenegger memorized several one-liners, a few of them suggested by the comedian Dennis Miller. Some consultants and stand-ins said the one-liners were too Hollywood. "But Mike Murphy thought, 'No, Arnold is Arnold and let him be Arnold in this particular moment because that's what the people like,'" recalled Schwarzenegger, who sided with Murphy. To a personal attack from Huffington, Schwarzenegger would answer by mocking the deductions Huffington had claimed on her tax returns: "Arianna, your tax loophole is big enough to drive my Hummer through it." Murphy programmed in a few of his own Huffington ripostes. "Switch to decaf," was one.

When rehearsals began on Monday morning, Schwarzenegger had a set of note cards, each with a talking point, on the table in front of him. As he mastered each one, he removed that note card from the table. After five hours of work Monday and another four hours on Tuesday, the table was empty. Schwarzenegger's performance in the mock debate Tuesday was, by all accounts, powerful.

The Wednesday debate was scheduled for early evening. Murphy had a final rehearsal Wednesday morning, but Schwarzenegger appeared tired and tight. The rehearsal ended, and Schwarzenegger's jet headed north out of Santa Monica, bound for Sacramento.

THAT SAME MORNING, the *Wall Street Journal* published a long article under Schwarzenegger's byline on its editorial page, a major coup for any candidate seeking conservative support. He wrote that the "endless litany of taxing schemes" offered by Davis and Bustamante reminded him of the androids he battled in his *Terminator* movies, "which I keep shooting dead but keep coming back to life."

The piece represented another missed opportunity for McClintock. Steve Moore, who headed the Club for Growth in Washington, had suggested that McClintock write a piece in the *Journal.* Moore even called the editorial page editor on McClintock's behalf. The editor was receptive, but McClintock never produced the piece.

After a week, Moore called Schwarzenegger instead. Two days later, Gorton returned the call.

Steve, Arnold loves this idea, Gorton said. When can you write it?

Moore took old interviews with Schwarzenegger and cut and pasted them together to create the article, which he sent back to Gorton. It took nearly a week to receive the okay. Schwarzenegger insisted on deleting personal swipes at Governor Davis. The "author" thought they were gratuitous.

The article produced several new endorsements for Schwarzenegger. Bill Simon, Jr., the 2002 Republican nominee for governor, would cite the piece in endorsing Schwarzenegger the very next day.

"WHAT DO YOU THINK of this recall, Mr. Schwarzenegger?" asked the debate moderator.

"I think it is a great idea, and I thank God every day that we have Hiram Johnson that created this more than ninety years ago."

Schwarzenegger, like the other candidates, had received the debate questions in advance. Because the format was so open, that proved less helpful than one might imagine. Candidates could interrupt each other as they pleased. As early as the second question—what should the new governor's priority be?—decorum began to break down. When Schwarzenegger said he would improve the business climate and reform the workers' compensation system, Bustamante replied that Davis had just pushed through legislation to do that very thing.

"What you guys just did was total pre-election bogus and you know that," Schwarzenegger retorted. Huffington pounced. The business climate Schwarzenegger was discussing, she said, was "the same kind of business climate that brought us Enron and Global Crossing and Adelphia. And it's cost millions of jobs and we're still paying the price. And one more thing, Arnold, you know you talk about . . ."

Schwarzenegger unveiled his first one-liner. "Your personal income tax has the biggest loophole. I can drive my Hummer through it. That's how big your loophole is."

Huffington knew the line was coming. Schwarzenegger had been so proud of it he leaked it beforehand to a reporter. Still, she seemed flummoxed. "You know very well that I pay $115,000 in property taxes and payroll tax. And you know what? I'm a writer. In these two years, I was writing and researching a book and I wasn't making $20 million violent movies. I'm sorry."

The exchanges with Bustamante were nearly as unpleasant. The lieutenant governor talked under Schwarzenegger, in a low monotone, as the star said the state should settle an ACLU lawsuit accusing California of neglecting poor schools.

> Schwarzenegger: The ACLU has sued the Los Angeles Unified School District because they have no toilets there that are flushing, paint is peeling.
> Bustamante: Yes, Arnold.
> Schwarzenegger: If you call this equality in education, I think it is outrageous. You know what you guys do, you politicians . . .
> Bustamante: Yes, Arnold, go ahead.
> Schwarzenegger: You go into the classroom, you do the photo op. You do the photo op, and then you leave and we may never see you again . . .
> Bustamante: You're one to talk about photo ops, Arnold.

In the process, Bustamante managed the self-defeating combination of sounding both tired and condescending.

McClintock decided he couldn't compete with Schwarzenegger in one-liners and stuck to meaty, straightforward answers. In instant polls, most viewers would say McClintock won the debate. But for long stretches, McClintock, Camejo, and Bustamante served mainly as witnesses to the Huffington-Schwarzenegger smackdown. So many barbs were traded (Schwarzenegger even told her, as he had rehearsed, that she should switch to decaf) that the moderator, a former legislator named Stan Statham, declared: "This is not Comedy Central."

A question about taxes led to still more personal insults. The consultants had wanted Schwarzenegger to stand up to Huffington, but he went too far. After Huffington raised her voice and was interrupted by Schwarzenegger yet again, this exchange followed:

> Huffington: Let me finish. Let me finish. Let me finish. You know, this is completely impolite, and we know this is how you treat women and we know that, but not right now.
>
> Moderator: On that point, excuse me, excuse me, excuse me. Candidates, please let me take control of this for a moment. I'm going to decide it is my privilege as moderator that that was a direct and personal attack on Mr. Schwarzenegger, so would you respond?

Schwarzenegger was out of one-liners. In less than ten minutes, he had run through everything he had rehearsed.

The star made something up on the spot.

"I would like to say that I just realized that I have a perfect part for you in *Terminator 4*. That's it."

In *Terminator 3*, Schwarzenegger had battled another machine in female form; in one scene, he slammed her head into a toilet. By the next morning, Arianna Huffington was claiming Schwarzenegger in effect had threatened to do the same thing to her. The star would explain he meant to compliment Huffington for her relentless nature. "In *Terminator* we always had powerful women," he said. Whatever his meaning, the one-liner would dominate TV coverage of the debate for days.

Schwarzenegger had not been at his best, but he had tripped up Huffington and Bustamante in the most fundamental of ways. The two Democrats had been so caught up in the exchanges with Schwarzenegger that they failed to point out Schwarzenegger's weakest point: he was not directly answering the policy questions posed by the moderator. Schwarzenegger had succeeded in turning a debate into an entertainment, which was the star's turf. As if to reinforce his domination of the evening, Schwarzenegger sent Dennis Miller out to conduct post-debate spin with reporters.

Even members of Schwarzenegger's own campaign were slow to recognize his victory. At headquarters in Santa Monica, some aides despaired that their candidate had lost. The advisors who had seen the rehearsals knew that Schwarzenegger could perform better, but the candidate had far surpassed the public's low expectations. By the following week, the campaign's tracking polls had him approaching 40 percent support, with a fifteen-point lead over Bustamante. A week earlier, the difference had been within the margin of error.

To SHAKE UP THE RACE, Davis challenged the star to a one-on-one debate; he declined. On the stump, Schwarzenegger fought back overconfidence. "I am the kind of governor . . ." he told a crowd in Santa Maria on September 28, before correcting himself: "I will be the kind of governor . . ." Schwarzenegger toned down his anti-Sacramento rhetoric: "I don't see anyone as a villain," he said of legislators. "I think everyone there is trying to do something good."

To inoculate himself against last-minute attacks, Schwarzenegger preemptively blamed Davis for any dirt thrown at him, and suggested the press was in league with the governor's operatives. (On Fox News' *The O'Reilly Factor*, he went so far as to claim, falsely, that the *Los Angeles Times'* editor had admitted to favoring the governor in placement of stories.) Davis's long record of negative campaigning made him the perfect stooge. The Democratic attorney general Bill Lockyer had earlier warned Davis publicly against engaging in "puke politics" during the recall. Schwarzenegger's campaign adopted the puke politics warning as its own.

"Desperate Davis is going to do all kinds of tricks," Schwarzenegger told a crowd of two thousand in Redding. "He's going to start a dirty campaign now." A cell phone rang out in the audience. "That is Gray Davis calling to say goodbye," Schwarzenegger quipped.

DEMOCRATS WERE PEDDLING information on Schwarzenegger's financial dealings. Code Pink, a feminist and antiwar group whose members saw Schwarzenegger as a California stalking horse for President Bush, sent repeated emails to reporters demanding stories on Schwarzenegger's treatment of women, his use of steroids, and his endorsement of Kurt Waldheim.

The people inside the Schwarzenegger campaign were attempting to track more than a dozen separate media investigations of the candidate. They believed the *San Jose Mercury News* was examining his immigration record and tax history. CNN was looking at his finances. ABC News had been chasing a story about Schwarzenegger praising Hitler in an outtake of *Pumping Iron*. The *Los Angeles Times* had assigned a team of reporters to investigate allegations of sexual harassment by Schwarzenegger. The team worked separately from the rest of the newsroom. Women, many of whom worked in Hollywood, had told stories for years of offensive come-ons and physical advances at gyms, on movie sets, and in public places.

In these waning days, the campaign cut down what little press access had been allowed. Schwarzenegger was running out the clock. When he flew to small cities around the state, no press plane was provided. His lone press conference in the next-to-last week took place in a cramped San Francisco hotel room. Just as he started to answer questions, the comedian Dana Carvey marched to the podium in the character of Hans—one half of the body-building team Hans and Franz from *Saturday Night Live*—to take questions.

The one scrap of information the campaign would release was the itinerary for the closing four-day bus tour, running from Thursday, October 2, through Sunday, October 5—two days before the election. The buses would be named for movies. *Running Man* would carry the candidate. VIPs would ride on *Total Recall.* The four press buses? *Predator 1, Predator 2, Predator 3,* and *Predator 4.*

On Wednesday, October 1, as Schwarzenegger laid out his policy agenda in his "Day One" speech in Sacramento, his campaign received a call. The *Los Angeles Times* was asking for a comment on a story that would appear the next day. The story would detail allegations by six women who said Schwarzenegger had touched them without their consent in separate incidents between 1975 and 2000. Two of the six women were named in the account. Not one had filed any type of legal claim against Schwarzenegger. According to the *Times*, he had reached under the shirt and grabbed the breast of one woman at a gym in 1975; propositioned and squeezed the breast of another on a Santa Monica street in 1980; grabbed the butt of a movie studio secretary in the late 1980s; repeatedly tried to remove the bathing suit of a *Terminator 2* crew member in 1990; pulled another *Terminator 2* crew member onto his lap while asking a crude sexual question, also in 1990; and touched the breast of a British TV host in 2000. The campaign frantically tried to find people who could discredit the accounts. Sean Walsh issued a denial to the *Times* on behalf of the candidate, arguing, "We believe Democrats and others are using this to try to hurt Arnold Schwarzenegger's campaign."

Schwarzenegger spent Wednesday evening at home while aides worked through the night to draft a response that the candidate could deliver at the kickoff of the bus tour the following morning in San Diego. The idea was to craft a statement that put the issue behind Schwarzenegger. At dawn Thursday, the campaign advisors held a conference call to finalize it.

Murphy and Sipple went to the Santa Monica airport to meet Schwarzenegger and join him on a flight to San Diego. What do we do about damage control? Schwarzenegger asked.

Murphy handed him a short statement on a note card and explained how the statement could put the issue to rest. The candidate studied the card for a few moments and began rehearsing.

"I KNOW THAT THE PEOPLE of California can see through the trash politics," Schwarzenegger said after taking the stage at the San Diego Convention Center. This was the official kickoff of the bus tour. But for the five days between Thursday and the election, Schwarzenegger would be running two campaigns. One consisted of a series of huge public rallies along the bus route. The other was a fight against personal attacks that drew on the entire history of his life and seemed to come from everywhere.

"Let me tell you something, a lot of those, when you see those stories, it's not true," Schwarzenegger told the crowd. "But at the same time, I have to tell you that I always say that wherever there is smoke, there is fire." The idea of expressing sorrow for his past actions (the candidate could be seen by other rally participants practicing the words, "I'm sorry," backstage) was part of the strategy, but the line—"where there is smoke, there is fire"—had not been on Murphy's note card. A few members of the crowd gasped at those words. Some told reporters they had wanted to hear Schwarzenegger fire back at the *Times*.

Instead, Schwarzenegger continued with his regrets. "And so what I want to say to you is that, yes, I have behaved badly sometimes. Yes, it is true that I was on rowdy movie sets, and I have done things that were not right, which I thought then was playful, but now I recognize that I have offended people. And those people that I have offended, I want to say to them, I am deeply sorry about that and I apologize, because this is not what I tried to do. When I am governor, I want to prove to the women that I will be a champion for the women. And I hope that you will give me the chance to prove that. Now, let's go from the dirty politics back to the future of California."

It was a clever apology. The campaign had polling going all the way back to 2001 that showed Californians would not be shocked by revelations from Schwarzenegger's personal life. There was nothing to be lost, and perhaps political points to be scored, by acknowledging the behavior. Schwarzenegger's admission was carefully phrased. He had not been specific about what he had done and reporters never managed to pin him down. And he had set up the campaign's counterattack on anyone who might try to keep the subject alive.

In San Diego, Schwarzenegger boarded the bus to head north to a huge rally at the Orange County fairgrounds. Each hour brought new attacks. By the afternoon, ABC News and the *New York Times* were quoting a six-year-old book proposal in which George Butler, the director of *Pumping Iron*, claimed Schwarzenegger, as a bodybuilder during the 1970s, had admired Hitler. The candidate's friends counterattacked. The bodybuilding promoter Joe Weider, who is Jewish, declared: "He's always made fun of Hitler. He didn't admire Hitler at all." In Austria, Schwarzenegger's old friends called reporters and recounted the story of how a teenage Schwarzenegger chased the nascent neo-Nazis down the Herrengasse. By the next day, Butler would retract part of his book proposal, saying that *Pumping Iron* interview transcripts showed he had misquoted Schwarzenegger.

In the evening, the campaign invited a handful of reporters to the Century Plaza Hotel in Los Angeles. Schwarzenegger, breaking away from his bus tour for a fund-raiser in the hotel, appeared along with his wife. The candidate offered another apology to women and a firm denial that he had ever admired Hitler in any way. "I always despised everything Hitler stood for. I hate the regime, the Third Reich, and all of those whole Nazi philosophy, I have always fought against that," he said. His wife praised him for apologizing. They took a question from a radio reporter and another from one of Schwarzenegger's own aides who stood with the reporters. But Shriver and Swarzenegger walked out of the room when I—the only *Los Angeles Times* reporter there—asked a question.

Butler's retraction and Schwarzenegger's denial muted the Hitler story. Schwarzenegger's quick blanket admission blunted the impact of the *Times'* piece on women.

THE RESULTS OF THURSDAY NIGHT's tracking polls had good and bad news for Schwarzenegger. More than 90 percent of those surveyed said they had heard about the allegations in the *Times* story. Schwarzenegger's supporters were sticking with him—his favorable ratings dropped only a point, from 59 to 58 percent—but the percent of people who did not like him jumped ten points to 40 percent. The recall vote was unaffected—55 percent supported removing Davis from office. The tracking suggested that the news might have hurt Schwarzenegger with younger women but, for reasons the poll did not explain, helped him with older women and voters in rural areas and San Diego.

The revelations, oddly, finished off McClintock's campaign. The state's conservative voters were furious at the media for what they saw as politically motivated attacks by liberal journalists on a Republican within days of the election. Some saw the *Times* attack as license to vote for Schwarzenegger. "It became a rally point for our audience," said Melanie Morgan, the San Francisco talk show host who had championed the recall and supported

McClintock. "It made it acceptable for people to vote for Arnold Schwarzenegger."

Only a clever, levelheaded politician could turn such personal bad news to his political advantage. From the day the story hit, Schwarzenegger and his supporters stoked the anger against the stories to achieve his political goal of attracting more conservative voters. At each rally on his bus tour, Schwarzenegger would be introduced by a conservative talk show host. In several cases, these hosts railed against Davis and the *Times*, treating the newspaper as another political opponent.

Newspaper columnists, Internet bloggers, and radio hosts friendly to Schwarzenegger took up the cause. Without offering any evidence, they alleged that the *Times* had been duped by Davis operatives and that the paper had manipulated the timing of the groping story to hurt Schwarzenegger. None of these claims had any basis in fact, and Schwarzenegger himself admitted to the pattern of behavior in the story. There were journalistic questions that could be asked about the *Los Angeles Times* story's use of allegations made anonymously. But the people criticizing the paper were more interested in the political outcome than the truth.[1]

By Friday night, the campaign believed it had weathered the groping story. Tracking polls were typically conducted only on weeknights, since so many voters were out of the house on Friday night and the weekend. But for the fi-

---

[1] The clearest defense of the newspaper came from Mark Z. Barabak, a *Los Angeles Times* political writer. He said that a postelection seminar at UC Berkeley, "This is a pretty politically sophisticated audience, and I think a lot of people realize that if you want to work with the premise that the *LA Times* set out to destroy Arnold Schwarzenegger's candidacy, we would have published these articles two or three weeks earlier, before people had really made up their minds and opinions had settled. It's obviously a lot harder to turn people back when they're supporting Arnold Schwarzenegger than when they were kind of sitting on the fence. The second thing, and the most important point I will make, is that the electoral results validated precisely what we did. The stories were published not a minute earlier or later than when they were ready to be published, and we did what newspapers do, we put the information out there and people could then decide: 'I think it's a hit piece and it's irrelevant.' 'I'm really bothered about this, I'm not going to vote for him.' Or 'It bothers me, but I dislike Gray even more, so I'm going to vote for him.' That's what newspapers do. We put the information out there, and the notion that it was a late hit, you know, we don't live in the day of the pony express, where Arnold Schwarzenegger had to write out his response by hand, put it in a saddlebag, ride it across the country to a telegraph office in New York. He had five days. Five days, plenty of time to respond to it. And I would lastly say he didn't deny it. He said it was true."

nal weekend, van Lohuizen did tracking polls even on Friday and Saturday. The Friday night results showed Schwarzenegger had slipped slightly—from 42 to 39 percent—but maintained a healthy lead.

THE STORIES ABOUT WOMEN did not go away. After the *Times'* front-page story recounting tales from six women first appeared, several other women called the paper to recount past instances in which Schwarzenegger had either touched them or said inappropriate things. On Saturday, the paper ran a story with allegations from three more women. Rob Stutzman, one of the campaign's three key communications aides, said the *Times* was not fit to own a printing press, and in Santa Monica, the campaign staged a press conference devoted to criticizing the *Times* for "totally, totally irresponsible" journalism. The paper did not relent. On Sunday, the *Times* reported allegations from four more women. One said Schwarzenegger had spanked her three years earlier at a postproduction studio. Three others said he had fondled them: one at a bar in the late 1970s, another outside a gym in the mid-1980s, and a third on the *Predator* set in 1986. The campaign denied three of the allegations and said Schwarzenegger had no recollection of the gym incident.

Schwarzenegger and his allies managed to make one particular claim stick in the public consciousness: that Governor Davis was somehow behind the *Times* stories. There was no evidence of that, though the governor's political team certainly worked to fan the flames once the news was published. (Garry South, a lead campaign strategist for Davis, said there was so much information publicly available about Schwarzenegger that the governor's team never did formal opposition research on him. "Well, we did Google him," South conceded.) The Schwarzenegger campaign nevertheless blamed Davis. "I think they're part of the trying to derail my campaign," said Schwarzenegger to a question about the *Times* during his bus tour. "I think that it's part of the puke campaign that Davis launched now."

The campaign distributed a memo called "The Smear Campaign" that showed connections between Democratic politicians and two women who made allegations. In one case, the campaign distributed an e-mail suggesting that a woman who had claimed mistreatment by Schwarzenegger had a record of arrests. As it turned out, that record belonged to a different woman of the same name. The woman who had complained about Schwarzenegger filed a lawsuit that was dismissed the following year, with a ruling that the campaign's mistake had been unintentional.

In these closing days, Schwarzenegger did more than just counterattack. His campaign made sure that he was surrounded by female supporters during his appearances. Two Republican assemblywomen, Bonnie Garcia and

Sharon Runner, took prominent places onstage. Volunteers held banners reading, "Women Joining Arnold."

Shriver also joined the effort, denouncing the stories as "gutter journalism." Inside the campaign, Shriver engaged in damage control. She offered names of people who could rebut specific allegations and bucked up her husband's advisors. But the situation took a toll. One politician traveling with the campaign noticed Shriver had a nervous habit of scratching her palms with her nails; by weekend's end, her palms looked raw.

Privately, Schwarzenegger reacted to each new allegation almost philosophically. "Is this crazy or what?" he asked aides about one *Times* story.

THE CAMPAIGN'S MOST effective response to the stories was the bus tour itself. Schwarzenegger drew thousands to each rally. Campaign officials would answer questions about the latest allegation by referring to the size of the crowds. The implication was clear: Schwarzenegger had pulled off a blockbuster. Who cared what the movie critics were saying in the papers?

In Modesto, Schwarzenegger addressed a crowd in front of a movie theater on 10th Street Plaza. In Bakersfield, the campaign had planned for five thousand people. Nearly twice that many showed up. Schwarzenegger used his Hollywood know-how to make each stop a spectacle. For the bus tour rally at the Orange County fairgrounds, the candidate wanted to blow up a car to symbolize his intention to reverse the tripling of the vehicle license fee. To pull it off, Pat Clarey, the campaign's operational chief, talked with an explosives expert who had worked in Schwarzenegger movies. When aides decided that an exploding car might evoke thoughts of terrorism, Clarey made alternative arrangements.

"I was twenty-five years in show business," he told the Orange County crowd. "In the movies when I played a character and I didn't like someone, you know what I did? I destroyed it. I'll show you exactly what we're going to do to the car tax." With that, a crane dropped a 3,600-pound weight on top of an Oldsmobile Cutlass. "*Hasta la vista*, car tax," he bellowed.

Like many blockbuster productions, the bus tour went over budget. The campaign had planned to spend $80,000, but the four-day operation cost more than $1 million. And there was a bit of movie illusion to the notion that Schwarzenegger himself was actually on a bus tour. A private jet shadowed his route so that, at the end of each day, Schwarzenegger could fly back to Los Angeles where he huddled with advisors and slept in his own bed. Early each morning, he got back on the plane and rejoined the bus before anyone knew the difference.

The bus tour finished up in Sacramento on Sunday, two days before the election. Schwarzenegger waved to a crowd at Raley Field, a minor league baseball park, and boarded the bus, which led a caravan of antique cars and trucks on a short drive to the capitol.

Schwarzenegger gave a brief speech and then demanded a broom. "Please bring me the broom, please bring me the broom now. We are here to clean house! We are here to sweep out the bureaucracy. We are here to sweep out the special interests . . . . They know I'm here to kick some serious butt!"

Dee Snider, lead singer of Twisted Sister, had flown to Sacramento to sing "We're Not Gonna Take It" live. For a few moments, Snider gave Schwarzenegger an electric guitar, and the candidate pretended to play.

TRACKING POLL NUMBERS for a Saturday were notoriously unreliable, but the results that final weekend caused nervousness in the campaign. Schwarzenegger's support had dropped from 39 to 33.5 percent. Bustamante remained at 26. The vote on the recall dipped just below the required majority—to 49.8 percent—for the first time. By Sunday night, the news was better. The tracking showed the recall returning to majority support with 53 percent. Schwarzenegger was gaining voters again on the second question.

As he flew around the state on Monday, Schwarzenegger carried a picture of Hiram Johnson given to him by McEnery, the former San Jose mayor. In San Bernardino, young women walked through the crowd wearing T-shirts that read, "Davis Groped My Wallet."

In Huntington Beach, Arnold Schwarzenegger's strongest political supporter showed up unannounced. "I'm Eunice Shriver," she declared to an advance man who at first did not believe her. Soon, she was working the beach to win a few more votes for her son-in-law.

SHORTLY AFTER NINE on Tuesday morning, Schwarzenegger and Maria Shriver entered their local polling place—the Brentwood house of a UCLA business professor—as the director Sydney Pollack left.

By 2:30 p.m., the campaign's consultants had exit poll data in hand. Schwarzenegger would win easily with nearly 50 percent of the vote. He had actually picked up votes in the final weekend of attacks.

Schwarzenegger held his election night party at the Century Plaza Hotel, where Ronald Reagan had celebrated his victories. Upstairs in a suite, Shrivers from all over the country mingled with the campaign's mostly Republican leadership. Former Governor Pete Wilson and former Los Angeles

Mayor Richard Riordan accepted congratulations as if they had won. Darrell Issa stopped by. Ted Costa was not even invited. He spent the evening at a party with friends in Sacramento.

Landon Parvin had written three election night speeches: one in case of victory, one in case of defeat, and one if the outcome was unknown. But the contest was over the moment the polls closed. By 10 p.m., the party had moved to the huge ballroom in the hotel basement. With so many VIP guests and international media, many campaign staffers could only attend the party if they bought tickets. The Shriver clan was supposed to wait offstage as Schwarzenegger gave his speech, but the family rebelled when they were told that by campaign aide Garrett Ashley. The Shrivers assigned themselves a spot behind Schwarzenegger. "What have we done?" two Republican consultants asked themselves, as they looked at all the Democrats onstage. In the chaos, the actor Gary Busey somehow made his way onstage as well.

JAY LENO INTRODUCED the victor, a confirmation that the election was as much a pop culture milestone as a political triumph. In his own speech, Schwarzenegger thanked California voters for their trust. "I will do everything I can to live up to that trust. I will not fail you. I will not disappoint you and I will not let you down." All over the world, the media hailed the rise of an Austrian farm boy to the governorship of America's most populous state.

Much of the world misinterpreted the election as a purely personal victory. Voters liked Schwarzenegger and most had enough confidence in him to risk voting for the recall. But Californians were not yet sold on the star as a political leader. He had not even won a governor's race in any conventional sense. He had won a two-part ballot measure campaign.

The true winners of the night were the recall and California's system of direct democracy. A *Los Angeles Times* exit poll asked voters why they had come out to vote. Eighty-nine percent said the recall question was first and foremost in their mind. Less than 10 percent came to the polls primarily to vote for a specific candidate. People showed up for the movie, not the star.

Schwarzenegger's campaign had spent $22 million in sixty days. He had received 4,109,743 votes, or 48.6 percent of those cast. He had spent almost five dollars per vote. The recall, in contrast, had qualified for the ballot with less than $2 million. It had drawn 2.2 million signatures and 4,976,274 votes, or 55.4 percent. The recall had no campaign dedicated to convincing Californians to vote "yes." Gray Davis, other Democrats, unions, and trial lawyers had spent tens of millions of dollars attempting to defeat it. Still, the recall had won.

Californians had intervened more directly than ever before in the governance of the state. One poll showed that 99 percent of the state's residents had followed news of the recall. There had never been a bigger, faster-paced campaign in the history of the country's largest state. The election made news in most of the world's countries.

Once and for all, democracy in California had gone blockbuster.

CHAPTER 12

"Makeup, Please"

Schwarzenegger took the oath of office on November 17, 2003, on the west steps of the capitol. He had cut the budget for this "people's inaugural" from $1 million to $750,000. But holding back the media hordes was impossible. A five-story tower had to be built to accommodate more than two hundred members of the press from five continents. Vanessa Williams, his costar in the film *Eraser*, sang the national anthem. A choir warmed up the crowd with tunes from *The Sound of Music*, including "Edelweiss" (but not "How Do You Solve a Problem Like Maria?"). There were so many invited celebrity guests that the public could only catch fleeting glimpses of the stage through the trees. The inaugural ended up costing $1 million anyway.

Landon Parvin, with a copy of Hiram Johnson's 1911 inaugural address by his side, had produced three drafts. Parvin had talked not only with Shriver and Schwarzenegger, but also with the state librarian, Kevin Starr, author of a series of books on California history. In 1911, Johnson had spoken of the "absolute sovereignty of the people." So would Schwarzenegger.

"I enter this office beholden to no one except you, my fellow citizens. I pledge my governorship to your interests, not to special interests," Schwarzenegger declared.

The speech, just twelve minutes long, offered a brief recasting of American history to fit the new governor's personal story. Schwarzenegger spoke of the test on U.S. history and government he had passed to become a citizen in September 1983. "What I learned—and what I've never forgotten—is that in a republic, sovereignty rests with the people—not the government," read the text of the speech. Schwarzenegger, in his delivery, omitted the words "in a republic." Although the new governor's aides would say he meant nothing by it, the omission served as a forecast. Schwarzenegger would help make California less of a republic and more of a democracy.

After the ceremony, Schwarzenegger headed into the capitol for his first official act: signing an executive order to repeal the tripling of the state's vehicle license fee. "Makeup, please," he quipped before signing the order. With his pen, Schwarzenegger had fulfilled a key campaign promise and added $4 billion to California's projected budget shortfall of more than $30 billion.

Schwarzenegger treated the day as the launch of yet another campaign. In the afternoon, he gave a talk at the Sacramento Convention Center, where a giant cocktail party for the new governor's supporters had been put together. There would be no inaugural balls—too ostentatious for a fiscal crisis—so this would be the biggest party of the day, with several hundred people mingling in a dark room while bands played. Schwarzenegger entered through a rear door and stood on the small stage, metal bicycle racks separating him from well-wishers.

"If you thought the campaign was tough, and that we were in the trenches and we were fighting then, there is much more to come," the new governor said. Californians were scheduled to return to the polls in less than four months for the March 2, 2004, primary. They would vote again in November 2004. Most governors in their first hours in office would be thinking of anything but the next election, but Schwarzenegger saw the two 2004 elections as an opportunity to push his agenda through ballot measures, though he wasn't certain of the exact details. Perhaps budget reform, workers' compensation reform, or political reform could be put before the people.

"All of those kinds of reforms we want to put on the ballot," he told his supporters. "And it will take some pushing. It will take TV spots on there, which of course cost millions of dollars. So I will be coming back to you and saying open your wallets again."

THROUGHOUT THE TRANSITION, ballot measures had been on the minds of Schwarzenegger and his advisors. Joe Rodota, the campaign's policy chief, had begun working on the transition on September 11, four weeks before the recall election. A campaign memo written by Rodota that day specifically contemplated the use of direct democracy—particularly the referendum—to overturn bills Davis had signed or might sign. Schwarzenegger thought ballot measures would give voters a sense of action. "Everything is psychological," Schwarzenegger recalled thinking. "It's not just enough to know you're doing something, you have to make sure the people feel things are happening."

Two weeks before the election, campaign manager Bob White had told Schwarzenegger he needed to select staff, develop a theme for the new administration, plan a swearing-in, nominate cabinet secretaries, put together a budget, resolve his personal matters (including where he would live), and prepare a state of the state speech for January. Such work had to begin immediately, White wrote, "creating the perception and fact that you know what you are doing, that you are in charge, and that you have a direction and a plan." White ruled out running the transition. He worried about creating a perception that this would be a third term for Pete Wilson.

So on a Sunday morning nine days before the election, Schwarzenegger and Shriver invited Congressman David Dreier to join them for services at the Crystal Cathedral in Orange County. For the Schwarzeneggers, who attended Mass on Sunday mornings in Santa Monica, this was a political visit. The televangelist Robert Schuller presided over the glossiest of Christian services; his Easter and Christmas pageants used live animals and had angels who flew (from wires). After the service, Schwarzenegger, a creature of habit, made his daily stop at Starbucks. There, the candidate and his wife asked a disbelieving Dreier to run his transition team.

Dreier was an unconventional choice. Well-known politically, the congressman was an outsider to Sacramento. Dreier reacted to Schwarzenegger's offer by telling the candidate that he had been to the state capital fewer than ten times in his life and knew little about state government. Schwarzenegger said that a little distance from Sacramento was what he wanted.

He wanted the congressman to find people for three roles: the auditor who would fulfill his campaign promise to perform a "sixty-day" examination of the state finances, "line by line"; the finance director who would put together his first budget; and the chief of staff. Before the election, Dreier had to keep his work completely quiet. Brad Smith, Dreier's chief of staff, was immediately dispatched to Santa Monica. He wore a badge identifying his responsibility as "research."

With help from Mike Murphy, Dreier first found an auditor, Donna Arduin, the budget director for Florida Governor Jeb Bush. But Schwarzenegger's own staff was hardly committed to the audit. One campaign memo had questioned whether such an audit was possible since the governor would have to have his new budget ready after less than two months in office. Arduin, arriving in Santa Monica, asked a table full of staffers at Schatzi's what Schwarzenegger meant by a sixty-day, line-by-line audit. "They all looked at me and said, 'We don't know,'" Arduin recalled. "'You tell us.'"

Within three weeks, Arduin agreed to stay on permanently as the director of finance, California's equivalent of budget director. She told Schwarzenegger that an audit of the type he promised—something that might be done by a consulting or accounting firm—would have little value. Instead, Arduin looked at every state program and service to see how much money was spent over the last five years, paying particularly close attention to those programs that had spending increases which exceeded the growth of state revenues.

The results, released in several pages of pie charts, showed that, if left unchecked, automatic increases in state spending required by law could produce a $62 billion deficit by 2006–2007.

This was an important exercise for understanding the trends in the state budget. It also produced a politically conservative conclusion: that growth in spending should be slowed. But it was not the audit of "waste, fraud, and abuse," Schwarzenegger had promised.

THE TRANSITION DID NOT always run smoothly. Dreier spent part of each week in Washington. Schwarzenegger's friends and donors, many of them unsophisticated about politics, felt empowered to make suggestions. Trusted campaign aides returned to the jobs they had held before joining Schwarzenegger, leaving the governor-elect to put together a whole new team.

Schwarzenegger had to adjust his own life, though he tried to change as little as possible. He and Shriver decided not to move to Sacramento. With no governor's mansion in California, Schwarzenegger would commute to Sacramento during the week, sleeping on the top floor of the Hyatt Regency across L Street from the capitol, while his family remained in Los Angeles. The governor-elect also had to shut down his Hollywood career and put his maze of business investments in a blind trust. He did not let go easily, and he tangled with one lawyer who was brought in to help restructure his affairs. Schwarzenegger had spent his life building up contacts, and he resisted modifying old relationships.

He ultimately did not achieve enough separation from his former life to avoid controversy. The governor appointed his longtime investment advisor, Paul Wachter, to oversee his blind trust. There was nothing illegal or unusual about having such a close friend manage a blind trust. But Wachter negotiated one deal during the transition that would later produce political embarrassment. On November 15, two days before the inauguration, Schwarzenegger signed a memorandum of understanding under which he agreed to serve in the honorary position of executive editor of *Muscle & Fitness* and *Flex*, two magazines owned by American Media, the company best known as publisher of supermarket tabloids. Those tabloids had gone easy on Schwarzenegger during the recall campaign. Now he would be a partner of their owner. In exchange for using Schwarzenegger's name in its muscle titles, American Media guaranteed Schwarzenegger at least $1 million a year—even more, depending on whether the company's various magazines increased their ad revenues. Schwarzenegger did not disclose the financial terms of the deal and it would be more than a year before the public learned the details through disclosure by American Media to the Securities and Exchange Commission. Schwarzenegger would say he signed the deal out of loyalty to bodybuilding, but politically, it would prove to be a mistake.

There were other ways Schwarzenegger would profit as he took office. A twenty-fifth anniversary edition of *Pumping Iron*, including outtakes to which Schwarzenegger held the rights, was released November 11, the week before his inauguration. Warner Brothers, the distributor of *Terminator 3*, timed its DVD release for the same day. (Before the October 7 election, the studio ran projections to determine how his election would affect DVD sales.)

DURING THE TRANSITION, Schwarzenegger formed four working groups, each of which handled an issue—taxes, spending limits, workers' compensation, and education—that in time would be taken to the ballot. Schwarzenegger asked for changes in the official state Web site (which would identify him as "The People's Governor," the slogan Shriver had suggested for the campaign). Schwarzenegger also requested that the "governor" box at the top of the flow chart of state government be superseded by one that read, "The People of California."

Filling out the rest of the flow chart with a staff was Schwarzenegger's most pressing problem. Of his closest partners and aides from business, bodybuilding, movies, and philanthropy, only Bonnie Reiss would follow him to Sacramento, where she would become his senior advisor.

For chief of staff, he briefly contemplated his brother-in-law Tim Shriver. A more serious early contender was Orange County Sheriff Mike Carona, who had become close to Schwarzenegger during the Prop 49 campaign. But Carona worried about the effect of a move to Sacramento on his young son.

The job was first offered to former Pete Wilson finance director Russ Gould, who took himself out of the running. The governor-elect turned next to Bob Hertzberg, a former Democratic speaker of the state assembly. Schwarzenegger had known Hertzberg, who represented the San Fernando Valley, since 1984, when they met through their mutual friend Gale Ann Hurd, the producer of *Terminator*. Hertzberg's wife, Cynthia Telles, was the daughter of a former U.S. ambassador to Costa Rica who knew the Shriver family well. But what drew Schwarzenegger's notice was a memo and *L.A. Daily News* op-ed that Hertzberg had written and sent to Richard Riordan, who shared them with the governor-elect. Hertzberg argued that Schwarzenegger should build a thoroughly bipartisan government. "Take the initiative to go and meet with members of the legislature, Democrats and Republicans alike," Hertzberg wrote in the *Daily News*. "Sit in their offices, meet them as human beings, and learn to work with them." At the same time,

Schwarzenegger should make constant trips around the state to hold town meetings, and keep pressure on legislators to act, the memo said.

Schwarzenegger invited Hertzberg to his home on Monday, October 13. Over a few hours of conversation, Hertzberg advised Schwarzenegger to think about what he wanted accomplished by the time he left office and, working backwards, figure out the steps that would get him there.

Schwarzenegger asked Hertzberg if he had any interest in being chief of staff. A lawyer with political ambitions of his own (he would run for mayor of Los Angeles in 2005), Hertzberg was not seeking the job and asked if the governor-elect had a backup plan. Schwarzenegger replied that he didn't make backup plans. By Thursday, Schwarzenegger had hatched a decidedly bipartisan idea. There should be cochiefs of staff—his own "joint chiefs"— one Democrat and one Republican.

On Saturday, October 18, Schwarzenegger invited Hertzberg and Pat Clarey, the campaign operations chief and a former deputy chief of staff to Pete Wilson, to his home, though the governor-elect did not tell Clarey what the meeting was about.

Clarey, a Republican, had been one of three people suggested by Dreier, who thought that Schwarzenegger needed a bureaucratic workhorse rather than a big name. She knew the direct democracy business well from working on Wilson's ballot measures and monitoring initiative campaigns during a long-ago stint at Chevron. But when Schwarzenegger had asked her a week earlier if she had any interest in being chief of staff, Clarey pointed out, correctly, that she didn't know the governor-elect very well. That comment stoked his interest.

Clarey was the last to arrive in Brentwood Saturday and was surprised to see Hertzberg. When Schwarzenegger offered her the job of chief of staff, Clarey was incredulous. She knew there was a catch.

There was. She would be sharing the job with the former assembly speaker. Schwarzenegger knew the arrangement was unconventional, but believed it fit the governorship he envisioned. On *True Lies*, no one but Schwarzenegger had wanted the comedian Tom Arnold in the movie, he told them, but the star's gut feeling had been right. Clarey, however, asked a series of pointed questions about the arrangement. Who would be responsible for screwups? What would happen when the cochiefs disagreed? Her reaction blew up the idea. Hertzberg said he didn't think the concept would work unless the two individuals were extremely close and had a history of working together. Clarey and Hertzberg were strangers. Each left without the job.

Schwarzenegger asked for five more names for chief of staff, but transition aides argued that the governor-elect was wasting his time. Two days later, Schwarzenegger called Clarey to offer her the job alone.

"Traditional chief of staff?" she asked.

Yes.

I'm completely in charge?

Yes.

She agreed, though Clarey would learn that in Schwarzenegger's world, no one was ever completely in charge.

CLAREY WAS EMBLEMATIC of the administration the governor-elect formed. Schwarzenegger had entertained ideas of putting together a team of out-of-the-box thinkers who would work in new and interesting ways. But when push came to shove, he made mostly safe choices and ended up with experienced, hard-working bureaucrats who believed in incremental change. In retrospect, the governor-elect felt his choices were limited by the calendar. "I chose who I chose because they were the best I could find in a short period of time," he later explained. With more time, he might have made bolder choices.

Schwarzenegger did what he could. He had George Kieffer, a politically connected Democrat who was also Shriver's lawyer, monitor appointments and do outreach to make sure "the best" possible aides were recruited, regardless of party affiliation. The governor-elect wanted ethnic and geographic diversity, as well as people who had open minds.

He did make a few nontraditional hires that raised eyebrows. Terry Tamminen, an environmentalist with an eclectic resume that included stints as a tugboat captain and manager of a sheep ranch, was named environmental secretary over Republican objections. David Crane, a Democrat who was retiring from a financial firm in San Francisco, came on as business czar. And although most of his aides were insiders and establishment figures, they did represent an unusually diverse, bipartisan cross-section of that establishment. The resulting team, however, was not a cohesive group. His appointees did not know each other particularly well or share a core set of beliefs. What they had in common was Schwarzenegger.

ON NOVEMBER 18, the day after he was sworn in, Schwarzenegger scheduled a press conference at the Sacramento Memorial Auditorium, the same building where he had outlined his agenda in the final days of the campaign. (The press room in the capitol was not large enough to hold all the reporters who wanted to come.) Schwarzenegger announced his California recovery plan. It included three planks: a general obligation bond of $25 billion to cover the state's deficit, a cap on state spending, and a reform of workers' compensation. The bond, by its nature, would require a statewide vote of the people. The spending cap, as a constitutional amendment, would require a similar vote. With workers' compensation, Schwarzenegger said he would seek to negotiate with the legislature to reduce premiums paid by businesses. But if he couldn't get a satisfactory legislative deal, he would sponsor a ballot initiative. On his second day in office, Schwarzenegger was committing himself to at least two and possibly three ballot contests.

There was a fourth item that also might require a ballot campaign. During the recall, Schwarzenegger had criticized Davis's decision to sign legislation granting California driver's licenses to undocumented immigrants. In the late days of the recall election, a conservative group had begun gathering signatures for a referendum to cancel the new law at the next statewide ballot in March 2004. In the transition, Schwarzenegger had embraced that referendum, though he did not actually want to see the measure reach the ballot. He instead planned to use the referendum campaign as leverage. At that first press conference, the new governor demanded the legislature repeal the driver's license bill, even though it had become law just two months earlier.

GILBERT CEDILLO, a state senator from a district including downtown and the east side of Los Angeles, had championed the driver's license bill for years. California driver's licenses had been available to undocumented immigrants until 1994, when Governor Wilson signed legislation taking away that right. In California's car-centric culture, immigrants drove anyway, risking arrest and the impounding of their cars—and thus economic isolation. While running for a state assembly seat in 1997, Cedillo had heard complaints about confiscated cars and promised to support legislation to grant driver's licenses to the undocumented. Governor Davis vetoed Cedillo's bill in two successive legislative sessions. But Cedillo did not give up. He promised his wife, who was dying of cancer, that he would secure the legislation, no matter what.

In 2003, during the recall, Cedillo's bill again reached Davis's desk. Latino leaders threatened to abandon him and support Bustamante if the governor vetoed the bill. His signing of the bill fueled the recall movement itself. Schwarzenegger called the legislation a "pre-election special" and accused the governor of a flip-flop.

Four days after the inaugural, Cedillo met with Schwarzenegger at the Oak Productions office in Santa Monica. (While there was a governor's office in downtown Los Angeles, Schwarzenegger would continue to use his movie offices.) As Schwarzenegger nibbled on strudel, he and the state senator talked in Oak's Austrian room—the wood-paneled room with benches—about Schwarzenegger's approach to leadership.

Finally, Cedillo changed the subject to the newly signed driver's license law. As Cedillo recalled the conversation, he said he didn't want to fight with the governor and was prepared to repeal his own bill. Before he did that, Cedillo needed Schwarzenegger's commitment to support a new bill. The senator had a number of requirements. Cedillo wanted all undocumented immigrants to be eligible. He said the licenses could be no different for immigrants—there should be no distinguishing mark. The governor replied that as an immigrant, he understood that a cop who saw a different license might be more inclined to discriminate. Schwarzenegger expressed concerns of his own. The governor said he could support a bill if there were safeguards to ensure that immigrants carried insurance, did not have criminal records, and posed no homeland security threat.

Do we need to put this in writing? Cedillo asked. "I give my word," Schwarzenegger said. Cedillo replied that, as a union official, he had signed seventy-five collective bargaining agreements and each had closed on a handshake. The immigrant-governor reminded Cedillo of his own maternal grandfather, an undocumented immigrant who worked the mines and spent decades with the Santa Fe Railroad. Schwarzenegger's word was good enough for Cedillo. In retrospect, the two men should have reduced their understanding to writing. Cedillo thought he had a firm commitment from Schwarzenegger to replace one law with a new one. Schwarzenegger and his aides said he committed only to bargaining on a new bill.

THE FOLLOWING MONDAY, Cedillo rose in the state Senate to call for repeal. "It's difficult for me to be here and ask you to do this," he said. "I have met with the governor; I believe him; I trust him. He has articulated a manner in which we can resolve concerns of mutual interest." The Senate quickly repealed the law, as did the assembly. The referendum soon was dropped.

Cedillo could have chosen a different path. If he had fought repeal in the legislature, the referendum against his law would have gone forward in March 2004. Polls showed the law almost certainly would have been cancelled by the people. Cedillo, in that defeat, would have become a political martyr in the cause of immigrant rights. Instead, the senator, by choosing to make a deal with Schwarzenegger, kept the issue alive. It was an accommodation for which Cedillo would be viciously attacked in the Spanish-language media as a sellout.

For a few months, Schwarzenegger lavished Cedillo with praise. The state senator was invited to the governor's home in Brentwood and Shriver gave him her personal cell phone number. The governor's aides huddled with

Cedillo on how to construct new legislation. But the polls continued to show widespread public opposition to granting driver's licenses to the undocumented. The governor's homeland security advisors questioned how effective even a criminal background check would be as a security device if the names submitted by undocumented immigrants were not real.

Cedillo, while attending a wedding in San Francisco, would receive a phone call in his hotel room from Pat Clarey. She would say there was no deal between the governor and Cedillo. The senator would insist there was. The staffs of both men would talk about compromise legislation, but nothing would be produced. Cedillo eventually pushed through another bill. Schwarzenegger vetoed it.

Schwarzenegger maintained that Cedillo did not drop his bill because of any deal. It was the threat of referendum—one of the three pillars of direct democracy—that moved him. That was true, but not the whole truth. Cedillo felt he had given the governor a quick political victory in his early weeks in office and was not subsequently repaid in kind. Some Democrats saw it as an early sign that Schwarzenegger would have trouble keeping his commitments.

IN EARLY DECEMBER 2003, right after the repeal of the driver's license bill, Schwarzenegger pursued his recovery plan with the legislature. He decided to delay the workers' compensation piece of the plan in order to focus on convincing lawmakers to add the two budget-related measures—a deficit bond and a spending cap—to the March ballot by the December 5 deadline. The proposed bond, at $25 billion, would have many uses, financial and political. It would provide money to help pay off $14 billion in short-term debt due in June 2004. It was too late to gather signatures and qualify the bond for the March 2004 ballot. To get the bond on that ballot, the legislature would have to act.

Schwarzenegger proposed to pair the bond with a constitutional amendment to cap state spending. Such a cap had been a campaign promise, but a vague one. The governor declared he was willing to negotiate the details, but he needed to have both a bond and a spending limit of some kind on the ballot.

Schwarzenegger, turning on the charm, invited every legislator into his office. Breaking with tradition, he also began a practice of walking around the capitol and dropping in on legislative offices. On these visits, he squeezed the arms of legislators to appraise whether their workouts were producing the right muscle development. Once the fitness talk was over, he would hand out cigars with his name on them as souvenirs. Making good first impressions was easy for him. Negotiating a deal to get the bond and the spending cap on the ballot would be harder.

Schwarzenegger, choosing to use his bake-off strategy, triple booked the negotiating job. Officially, Donna Arduin, the conservative finance director hired away from Jeb Bush, was the lead negotiator. His own senior staff, mostly Republicans from the Wilson administration, represented a second channel to legislative leaders. And quietly, he and Reiss constructed a back channel to the Democrats. Schwarzenegger invited Hertzberg, a Democrat, to fly with him up to Sacramento during the first week of December and to look for a way to reach a deal.

Within his own administration, these three channels—Democratic, mainstream Republican, and conservative—each tried to negotiate a deal. The internal competition created action. It also caused confusion.

Legislators of both parties complained of receiving mixed messages. Some members of his own staff were not sure if Schwarzenegger was backing their talks or some competing effort. But the governor said that, whatever the drawbacks, this method of negotiating allowed him to see the entire landscape of options. These multiple channels would remain the norm in any major Schwarzenegger enterprise.

SCHWARZENEGGER HAD simultaneously begun a public campaign for the bond and spending cap. His first such appearance, just four days after taking office, did not go well. Before he arrived at Galpin Ford, a huge car dealership in the middle of the San Fernando Valley, two TV cameramen departed. They had both gotten the same call: police were searching Michael Jackson's Neverland Ranch in Santa Barbara County for evidence the pop star had molested children. (To prevent future conflicts, a senior advisor to the governor began keeping a calendar with courtroom dates for the Jackson, Kobe Bryant, and Scott Peterson trials.)

The first week of December, after the assembly's budget committee refused to approve the bond and spending cap plans for the ballot, Schwarzenegger took to the road again. It was the Christmas shopping season, and the governor decided to hold rallies in malls. In Schwarzenegger's political life, the mall would assume the same iconographic importance that the fireside held for FDR, or the back of the train for Truman.

On Tuesday, December 2, Schwarzenegger gave a lunchtime speech outside Horton Plaza, a shopping center in the heart of San Diego. More than two thousand people filled a huge outdoor courtyard at the mall's entrance. A half-dozen men wore Santa Claus caps. Hundreds of shoppers peeked out of store windows and peered down from a walkway next to an upstairs food court. As the people waited for the governor, the mall's marketing director took the microphone to announce sales.

Schwarzenegger arrived a half-hour late, just as the crowd had started to get restless. His message was simple. He was grateful for the chance to be governor and was enjoying the new job. He talked about his early victories— how he had said, "*Hasta la vista*, baby" to the car tax and the driver's license bill. Then he spoke of his desire to put the bond and the spending limit on the ballot so the people could vote on them, up or down. He closed by talking of "cutting up the state's credit card." That was a strange argument on behalf of a huge new bond to cover state deficits, but Schwarzenegger made it nonetheless. He tore up a giant mock state credit card made of cardboard. The stunt got the second loudest applause of the speech. His closing line, "I'll be back," drew the loudest.

Schwarzenegger reprised the same show two days later outside Bakersfield's Valley Plaza mall, and he addressed a raucous crowd in an indoor mall in the Central Valley community of Tracy the day after that. Malls allowed Schwarzenegger to satisfy his conflicting political needs for wide-open publicity and tightfisted control. He could reaffirm his populist credentials by creating TV pictures of himself speaking to large crowds of people in a public space. At the same time, he could control the look and feel of the events because malls were legally private property. Schwarzenegger's team managed to keep off-camera union members and advocates for the developmentally disabled, who were protesting possible cuts in various state health programs.

Going to malls was highly unusual for a politician. The best customers of malls were people so young or politically apathetic that they didn't vote, so politicians typically picked more voter-rich targets. And mall owners had spent years, and millions of dollars in legal fees, fighting to keep groups or people who wanted to practice politics out of their stores. Politics, it was thought, could offend customers. But for a politician who was also an international celebrity, mall owners made an exception.

The governor, who was a partner in a large mall outside Columbus, Ohio, asked the managers of the malls in San Diego, Bakersfield, and Tracy for estimates of how his speeches increased their traffic. On average, he brought in three thousand additional people per stop. "They want me to have a little problem in Sacramento because they know I go out to the shopping malls and help their business," Schwarzenegger would later joke.

In these appearances, Schwarzenegger played a double game by attacking as "spending addicts" the same legislators he cozied up to in Sacramento. In another twist, when lawmakers objected to visits to malls in their districts, Schwarzenegger invited them to stand on stage with him so they could watch the crowds' rowdy reactions up close.

However, the roar of the audiences at the malls did not translate into a flood of calls to lawmakers in Sacramento. The speeches' chief impact was to fire up Schwarzenegger, who would return to negotiations in the capitol so full of populist fever that he was reluctant to compromise. The Democrats broke off talks on December 5. Shortly before midnight that evening, the governor left his first-floor offices in the capitol to speak to the assembly Republicans upstairs. Schwarzenegger declared that he would fight the Democrats and take his spending cap proposal to the voters in the form of an initiative on the November ballot. "We're going to war," Assemblyman Kevin McCarthy, a Republican, said gleefully.

EARLY SATURDAY MORNING, December 6, Schwarzenegger flew home to Los Angeles, accompanied by Reiss. Secretary of State Kevin Shelley, who administered elections, had declared the previous day—Friday, December 5—the absolute deadline for adding measures to the March 2 ballot. Even if Schwarzenegger could revive a deal, he would be out of time. Shriver and Reiss talked and wondered if there wasn't some way to extend the deadline and revive talks. By late Saturday morning, Reiss was busy trying to find out.

Effectively circumventing Chief of staff Clarey, Reiss got in touch with legal affairs secretary Peter Siggins, and together they reached out to Shelley to ask about the possibility of a deadline extension. He didn't immediately rule it out.

On Saturday afternoon, Schwarzenegger and Shriver flew to Palm Springs to attend a dinner of California's congressional delegation, a famously fractious group that was holding its first-ever bipartisan retreat at a resort in nearby Rancho Mirage. The coincidence that such a meeting had been scheduled on the weekend after the breakdown of talks in Sacramento may have changed the course of Schwarzenegger's political career.

Former President Gerald Ford, former Clinton White House Chief of Staff Leon Panetta, and Reagan's Secretary of State George Shultz also joined the delegation for dinner. In a discussion led by Panetta and Shultz, each man said that Schwarzenegger should attempt to restart talks and make a deal with lawmakers, at least on the bond.

"It's never too late to make a deal," Shultz remembered saying. "Keep working on it."

After his talk, Panetta took a seat near Shriver and Schwarzenegger and argued that the symbolism of Schwarzenegger reaching a deal with the legislature was as important as the substance of any agreement. "I said, 'You're going to have to cut a deal,'" Panetta recalled. "'You've got to get some things done. If you can begin to show that you have that ability to do that, that's the most important signal. It will create a momentum that will give you the ability to do other things.'"

Shriver and Schwarzenegger flew back to Los Angeles that night even more determined to try again. The governor and Shriver led a conference call Sunday with the governor's consultants and top aides to work through how a deal might work. There was plenty of skepticism. But Schwarzenegger wanted to restart the negotiations, if possible.

Reiss went to work on preparing her boss for those talks. She reached out to Paul Wachter for financial advice on how a deal might be structured. On Sunday night, Reiss led a three-hour-long practice negotiation at the Schwarzenegger home in which she played the roles of Speaker Herb Wesson and other legislative leaders. As Schwarzenegger negotiated deal points during this session, Reiss made extensive notes on a yellow legal pad. The governor would try to recreate this practice deal in Sacramento.

By Monday, there was so much momentum for a deal that when legislative moderates sent a letter to the secretary of state asking for an extension of the deadline, he agreed within hours, setting a new deadline for the coming Friday, December 12.

SHRIVER STAYED IN BRENTWOOD on Monday to tend to a sick child, but flew to Sacramento on Tuesday, December 9, and quickly made her presence felt. She talked extensively with Reiss and even sat for a briefing on the budget with Schwarzenegger's health secretary.

She also attended a luncheon in her honor, and used the opportunity to take a swipe at the legislature for failing to negotiate. "I always come back to parenting, because I say that if some of these legislators were children we'd give them a time-out," Shriver said. "I said to Arnold, 'Take away their play dates. Talk to them about conflict resolution. We will get something done if they behave that way.'"

Ready to fight the previous Friday night, Schwarzenegger now talked publicly of moderation. At the Christmas tree-lighting ceremony on the west steps of the capitol, Schwarzenegger claimed to have carried the tree down from the Sierras himself. "It's a real challenge to put this tree up, I tell you, to make it straight," he told the crowd. "Because you see here in the capitol things have a tendency of leaning too far to the right or too far to the left." Schwarzenegger went from the ceremony directly into talks, which he handled personally. At difficult points, he took Democratic leaders out of the room for one-on-one discussions. The outlines of a deal became apparent late Tuesday night.

Schwarzenegger spent Wednesday negotiating before flying to Orange County for an early evening fund-raiser to retire some of his campaign debt. Hertzberg drove down to meet him there and talk about how to close the deal. Schwarzenegger then flew back to Sacramento for more negotiations starting at 10 p.m. His main negotiating partner was the assembly speaker, Herb Wesson. Schwarzenegger served wine to the Democrats, though he himself did not imbibe.

Schwarzenegger and Wesson debated the period of time over which the bond should be paid back. Eight years? Ten years? Fifteen years? The governor decided to call Warren Buffett, who advised that a longer payback time was better for a host of financial reasons. Wesson and Schwarzenegger soon settled on fourteen years.

The bond would go on the ballot as Proposition 57. It gave the governor a chance to replace the costly short-term debt with cheaper, voter-approved borrowing. The governor agreed to reduce the size of the bond from $25 billion to $15 billion, which would cover the short-term debt due in June and leave a small cushion for future budget years.

At $15 billion, it still would be the single largest general obligation bond measure ever to face state voters, and it was a strange sort of bond at that. It wouldn't produce one school, road, or park. It merely would give the state a way to consolidate and pay off debt already accumulated. Fitch Ratings, the bond-rating agency, would downgrade the state's bonds from A to BBB, saying Schwarzenegger's strategy of putting the debt to the vote "injects another element of uncertainty."

REACHING AGREEMENT on a spending limit would prove even more difficult. Wesson would not accept the hard spending cap Schwarzenegger wanted. Instead, the speaker's staff, in meetings with legal affairs secretary Siggins and Schwarzenegger aide Cynthia Bryant, worked out language for what amounted to a balanced budget amendment to the state constitution. It would have four components. The state would be required to put aside money in a rainy day fund, not spend more than its revenues, put a limit on its debt load, and establish a process for correcting budget imbalances in the middle of the year. When Schwarzenegger pushed again for a tighter spending limit in the negotiations, Wesson and his staffers quoted the governor's own campaign platform—produced during the Schwarzenegger University sessions and later posted on his campaign Web site, joinarnold.com—back to him.

The final troublesome details involved how the rainy day reserve would be set up. Schwarzenegger wanted 10 percent of state revenue to go into the fund; Wesson proposed 5 percent. They ultimately compromised with a sliding scale. The resulting measure would go on the ballot as Proposition 58.

The two propositions, 57 and 58, were linked legally. If either measure failed to win the approval of voters, both would fail.

Shortly after 1 a.m., Wesson declared: "We have a deal."

"The speaker's right!" Schwarzenegger said.

The negotiators enjoyed celebratory glasses of schnapps.

Wesson went home and turned on the TV. There was the governor in *True Lies*, jumping into a harbor just as something colossal blew up. Wesson laughed. He had just helped Schwarzenegger with another escape.

BY THE NEXT MORNING, Thursday, December 11, Democrats exulted that they had forced the governor to drop his spending cap and endorse a proposal closer to their own. Many Republicans thought the governor was giving up his best chance to get a tougher cap, and the conservatives among the governor's own advisors agreed.

They believed a spending cap would help the governor get control of the budget and reduce pressure for tax increases. Mike Murphy argued that it was best to take on big, hard fights early in his term, even if it meant a considerable decline in popularity. Murphy told Schwarzenegger he had taken Governor John Engler of Michigan down so low in his first term that only 19 percent of voters in one poll said they were willing to re-elect him. (Engler eventually served three terms.) "You should have told me this before I hired you," Schwarzenegger responded, deadpan.

Schwarzenegger's Democratic partners could not put the measures on the ballot alone. He needed a two-thirds vote of the assembly and the senate and that meant getting the support of skeptical Republicans. Schwarzenegger called assembly Republicans into his office in small groups. One group of four—Russ Bogh, Rick Keene, Sharon Runner, and Bonnie Garcia—had agreed among themselves to deliver the message that they were unhappy. But they found it hard to get in a word as Schwarzenegger, wearing new cowboy boots with the governor's seal, demanded their support. Enough Republicans swallowed their doubts to assure victory.

After the vote was won, Schwarzenegger called Republican legislators down to the governor's first-floor suite of offices, known as the Horseshoe. The governor, who had been in the next room watching speeches on the floor, entered expressing frustration. He couldn't believe that Democrats were saying he had caved. The room of legislators was silent, because so many of them agreed with the Democrats. Among the frustrated Republicans was Assemblyman John Campbell. In a conversation a few days later, the governor reassured Campbell. As Campbell recalled the conversation, "What he said back to me was, 'Look, John, I probably should have done something different. I've been on this job three weeks, and I made some mistakes here. I won't make them again.'"

AS HE MADE HIS DEAL with Democrats, Schwarzenegger also walked away from a number of budget cuts his finance director, Arduin, had proposed. California's deficit was so large that Schwarzenegger could lay off every state employee and still be in the red. Arduin had cultivated an image as a bad cop so she could push unpopular cuts while Schwarzenegger remained above the fray. She walked out in the middle of her first hearing before the assembly budget committee, a calculated stunt that reporters wrote up as an example of her cold-blooded conservatism. Arduin thought that coverage was perfect. Burton, the Democratic leader of the state senate, called her "an ogre." Arduin, a funny and free-spirited person in private, proudly attached a sign a Republican legislator gave her to the door of her first-floor capitol office. "Ogre-Xing," it warned.

Arduin had drafted $1.9 billion in cuts for the current fiscal year. The cuts included the suspension of the Lanterman Act, which established an entitlement program for the developmentally disabled. She quickly ran up against Schwarzenegger, his wife, and his senior advisor, Reiss. They wanted the governor to be nice and conciliatory in public, *and* in reality. "I was willing to see how far we can push people," Arduin said. "He didn't want that." The governor, citing his mother-in-law's work with the disabled, abandoned the proposal.

And he didn't stop there. When Arduin flew home to be with her ailing father, Schwarzenegger changed the next year's budget on his own, removing $1 billion in proposed cuts. He filled that hole by claiming he would get more money from Indian casinos and the federal government.

For most of his adult life, Schwarzenegger had fancied himself an economic conservative, a devotee of Milton Friedman's small government philosophy. Now with a budget deficit providing the kind of opportunity for government retrenchment about which his theoretical heroes could only dream, Schwarzenegger couldn't pull the trigger.

Dropping his own proposals for budget cuts may have been the right thing to do, but it sent a message that would hurt his ability to govern. Democrats saw that he would back down if he was challenged. Schwarzenegger, used to being loved, simply didn't have the political pain tolerance for serious cuts. Other aides believed Schwarzenegger, never much of an ideologue, simply didn't want to cut children's programs. The governor also had a third factor to consider.

With Propositions 57 and 58 now on the March ballot, Schwarzenegger needed voter approval to advance his agenda. Politicians in other states might be able to handle a huge drop in popularity to do something difficult. A California governor who wanted to govern by ballot measure did not have the same luxury.

HAVING ABANDONED many of his own cuts, Schwarzenegger needed a way out of the budget bind that did not cripple him politically for the Prop 57 and 58 campaign ahead. He hit upon a strategy of negotiating temporary cuts directly with interest groups. The first one of these deals would come to define, first for better and later for worse, his governorship.

His first partner would be the CTA, the 335,000-member teachers' union. Schwarzenegger began by approaching John Hein, the CTA political director who had helped him with the Prop 49 campaign. One morning in early December, Schwarzenegger invited Hein over to the Hyatt for a meeting. I've got to have $2 billion from education funding, Schwarzenegger said. Can I do that?

"I told him, if we sit down and talk, we can probably figure out a way to do that," Hein said. "But the important thing will be . . . that you want to have a conversation with us about how to make that happen. I think you'll find that the organization is awfully good at solving problems when you talk to us early in that way." Hein arranged for Schwarzenegger to meet with Barbara Kerr, the Riverside kindergarten and first-grade teacher who was CTA's elected president. When the governor repeated his request, Kerr said that taking $2 billion out of the $44 billion education budget would be difficult, but "we'll sit down and see if we can find a way to make it happen."

At their session, Kerr and Schwarzenegger outlined a partnership between the governor and the CTA to look at ways to reform education. The two talked about class-size reduction, special education, the federal No Child Left Behind Law, and the lack of freedom teachers felt as they complied with state curriculum standards. "We talked about how we could get through this money crisis and we would go on to change education," said Kerr.

The CTA brought in John Mockler, the author of Proposition 98, to help with the technical details of the agreement with Schwarzenegger. Mockler was believed by some to be the only person on earth who understood the complex education funding formula Prop 98 created—even though that formula governed roughly one-half of the budget of America's largest state.

In brief, Prop 98 created a minimum funding guarantee for education. The guarantee was set each year based on a three-part formula that took into account tax revenues, school enrollment, and per-capita personal income growth. Prop 98 was a moving target. As each of those factors changed, the guarantee could go up or down, depending on the day it was calculated.

Under the Prop 98 guarantee as it stood when Schwarzenegger took office, education funding was expected to increase by $4 billion for the coming budget year. Under the agreement Schwarzenegger would reach with the CTA, he would get to hold onto $2 billion of that increase to help close the budget deficit.

The schools would still get the other $2 billion, which was supposed to be enough to pay for increases in the cost of living and student enrollment. In Schwarzenegger's mind, this was the essence of the deal he made: he would get some budget savings while making sure the schools received enough new money to keep up with growth.

Schwarzenegger did not agree—as some critics would later claim—to pay back the $2 billion he saved the following year. That $2 billion had been saved and would never return. But he did agree not to tinker with the guarantee level again, and to eventually restore the $2 billion to the education funding base upon which future budgets would be built.

Finally, instead of simply setting a figure for the education budget, Mockler and the CTA added a wrinkle that would become the most scrutinized provision of this most important deal. The schools would get whatever the Prop 98 guarantee was eventually calculated to be—minus the $2 billion Schwarzenegger wanted to save. In other words, the exact amount the schools would receive would be a floating number—based on Prop 98—rather than a fixed one.

It seemed like a narrow, complicated distinction. But it would make a profound difference.

If the state economy came back and revenues went up, so would the Prop 98 guarantee, and Schwarzenegger would have to give the schools this increase the following year. In time, the Prop 98 guarantee would soar, and the deal would prove to be very beneficial for the schools and the CTA. "Not that I mistrusted anybody," said Mockler. "But even in poker, I do cut the cards."

POLITICALLY, the deal was an immediate triumph for Schwarzenegger. CTA officials laid out the proposed agreement for other education interest groups—other unions, the California School Boards Association, and school business officers—at a December 19 meeting. Hein warned them that the deal would stand California politics on its head. In most years, the governor proposed a budget in January, and the education community spent the first half of the year lobbying the legislature to add more money to the budget.

Legislators loved this dynamic because they could champion education and make the budget fight with the governor apear to be about schools. But with this deal, the education lobby would be defending the governor's budget against the legislature.

Three days later, on December 22, representatives of the education groups met with Schwarzenegger and much of his senior staff at 3 p.m. in the Reagan cabinet room. The governor kicked off the meeting by thanking the education groups for working with him. He then turned the floor over to Hein, who outlined the deal. Hein went through a variety of particulars including the key element: the fact that if the Prop 98 guarantee grew, Schwarzenegger would make sure the schools got that increase. Notes kept by one participant read: "pledge that $2 billion hit on [Prop] 98 won't become a larger number even if the obligations to schools increase due to new revenue, more students . . ."

"I don't dispute those notes," Reiss would later say. "They understood the term of art that it meant. And he didn't. And I believe they knew that."

Schwarzenegger would later say he had no recollection of hearing such a clear commitment on Prop 98 growth at the meeting. It's possible, he would allow, that "I missed that because this was more a conversation where we all sat around the table and said, 'This is really great. I'm glad that we came to a settlement and blah blah blah.' There was all kinds of dialogue of making everyone feel good. That I remember." Schwarzenegger said he understood he had committed to a deal built around the Prop 98 guarantee, but added that he was not the only one who did not comprehend all the particulars. Even CTA president Barbara Kerr confessed to him some haziness when it came to Prop 98, he said.

In his own remarks at the meeting, Schwarzenegger talked about how the deal would be presented to the public. He emphasized that he did not consider the $2 billion in savings a suspension of Prop 98 (even though, as a legal matter, that's what the deal was). The governor had promised during the campaign that he would not suspend, Prop 98, and his political team found in a December poll that a suspension, while supported by half of those surveyed, could cost him the support of Democrats and independents. The education groups and the governor agreed to call the deal a "rebasing" of Prop 98. On their way out the door, some of the education lobbyists had their pictures taken with the governor.

Schwarzenegger and the education coalition had concluded an agreement in principle, but not all details were reduced to writing. Among other things, the exact timing under which Schwarzenegger would make good on his promises to restore the $2 billion to the funding base was not spelled out in the written agreement. Schwarzenegger and the CTA officials had decided to rely on each other's good faith. The governor stopped to view damage from an earthquake on California's central coast before flying to his vacation home in Sun Valley, Idaho, for the holidays. When he returned to Sacramento the first week in January, the governor and leaders of the education lobby announced the deal inside the library at Sutter Middle School.

Schwarzenegger praised CTA for "great vision and great leadership." Kerr, the union president, said: "The way he involved us in this budget is a first . . . He said he would protect school funding and he's doing that." A blue banner behind the speakers read, "Promise Made, Promise Kept."

"I'm absolutely convinced it will stick," Schwarzenegger said of the deal. "Trust me."

As with anything having to do with Prop 98, this was a confusing subject, and Schwarzenegger, after less than six weeks in office, did not immediately grasp what he had done. A few months later, in the spring, Mockler was walking over to lunch at the Esquire Grill when he ran into Schwarzenegger, who joked that the turtleneck Mockler was wearing made him look like a priest.

Projections of the Prop 98 guarantee for the 2004–05 budget year had already increased by more than $500 million. Under the deal, Schwarzenegger would achieve budget savings of $2 billion from whatever Prop 98 turned out to be. The state was thus on the hook for any growth in the Prop 98 guarantee, including this $500 million increase.

You cost me half a billion dollars, the governor complained, according to Mockler's recollection. (The governor would say he did not remember the details of the conversation.)

What are you talking about? Mockler replied.

Prop 98 minus $2 billion, Schwarzenegger explained, I didn't know what that meant. I know now.

Despite his promise, the education funding deal could be in jeopardy if Schwarzenegger did not convince voters to pass Propositions 57 and 58. Without the bond money in Prop 57, the state, facing default on its short-term debt, might be forced to make deeper cuts in education, raise taxes, or both. A governor who made policy at the ballot would have trouble honoring his deals if he could not earn the people's support.

PART 3

Laws are like sausages. It's better not to see them being made. —Otto von Bismarck

CHAPTER 13

"Back on Track"

SIX SLIDES INTO his presentation on December 30, 2003, pollster John McLaughlin delivered a dose of reality to Schwarzenegger's team of political advisors and gubernatorial staffers. Proposition 57, the $15 billion bond that Schwarzenegger had convinced the legislature to add to the ballot three weeks earlier, was in political trouble.

The governor would have to convince voters to pass Prop 57 and the balanced budget amendment Prop 58 on the March 2, 2004, ballot. If he couldn't, the state would have to find some other way to pay off $14 billion in short-term debt that would come due in June. But Prop 57 was backed by only four out of ten voters in McLaughlin's survey.

Even those who supported the measures in the poll were not enthusiastic. While Democrats in the legislature had provided most of the votes to put the measures on the ballot, Democratic voters preferred to raise taxes, and were still angry about the recall and suspicious of any plan with Schwarzenegger's imprimatur. Republicans, whose elected representatives had been reluctant to endorse the package, wondered why a governor of their own party would borrow rather than cut the size of government.

Prop 57 "has no base of support and has real opposition from Democrats, independents, liberals, and social issue voters," McLaughlin warned in his slide show.

The slides drew nervous looks from the consultants and staffers gathered for this secret strategy meeting inside the Golden State Room on the second floor of the Hyatt Regency in Sacramento. (The governor was spending the holidays at his Idaho vacation home and would be briefed later.) McLaughlin's poll made clear that Schwarzenegger would need to launch another major statewide campaign immediately. For this governor, ballot measures would come first. He was still two weeks away from hiring an appointments secretary to help him fill vacant posts.

Voters liked Schwarzenegger, but skepticism was high and so were expectations. Fifty-eight percent of the eight hundred voters in McLaughlin's survey, conducted between December 15 and 18, said they had a favorable impression of him. Twenty-three percent had an unfavorable impression.

Asked what they liked most about the governor, voters identified personal traits—that he's honest and sincere, that he's not a politician, and that he keeps his promises. "He is seen as a populist with integrity," McLaughlin explained in one slide. "Weaknesses which could hurt the governor's popularity are most related to character: not qualified and breaks promises," said another slide.

Voters remembered Schwarzenegger's promises. Six in ten knew that the governor had promised not to raise taxes. At the same time, the poll showed that a majority of voters believed the budget could not be balanced without raising taxes. Such a statistic made raising taxes look tempting, but, if Schwarzenegger did so, his popularity would likely plummet. And he needed to be as popular as possible to convince voters to pass Propositions 57 and 58.

This was the trap. Many political commentators were urging Schwarzenegger to raise taxes as part of a plan to eliminate the budget gap. They recalled how Ronald Reagan had reversed himself on a similar no-tax pledge. They did not understand Schwarzenegger's predicament. He could lose popularity even by doing a popular thing, and find himself unable to pursue the rest of his agenda.

PROPOSITION 57 was his way out of this fix, if the governor could get it passed. But winning a Prop 57 campaign did not look easy. One rule of thumb in direct democracy was that ballot measures should have at least 60 percent support at the beginning of a campaign to have any hope of passing. Most ballot measures lost and most late-deciding voters voted no, so the support for most measures usually dropped even during a well-run Yes campaign. Proposition 57 was polling at 42 percent in McLaughlin's survey even after voters were read a favorable description of the measure. By conventional standards, it was in trouble.

McLaughlin had tested possible messages in his poll. A campaign simply warning of big tax increases if Proposition 57 failed would not work, the pollster warned. Too many voters already believed a tax increase to be inevitable given the state's budget problems. McLaughlin's data suggested it would be better to play on voters' fears of cuts to education and health care. And despite Schwarzenegger's popularity, the governor was perceived as such a novice that endorsements would be important. The backing of the CTA would be crucial.

McLaughlin finished his eighty-slide presentation with a profile of voters who were undecided on Prop 57. The bond was weak among Democrats in the Bay Area—who had opposed the recall—and among Republicans in the Central Valley—a stronghold for Schwarzenegger in the recall. A campaign to attract such different groups of voters would test the skills of any political veteran.

SCHWARZENEGGER NEEDED to create a political entity to win such a campaign. What his team began to build at the Hyatt would become the political structure for waging all his campaigns.

This structure would benefit from his power as governor, but it would be deliberately separate from the government and his official role. Its goals would eventually include reforming the workers' compensation system, changing the structure of local government finance, renegotiating Indian gaming compacts, passing a state budget favorable to the governor, preserving a sentencing law for certain convicted felons, and, of course, protecting and enhancing the political power of Arnold Schwarzenegger.

This structure would consist of fund-raisers, political consultants, pollsters, multiple campaign committees, and non-profit organizations. None of these elements was new. But by combining such entities with direct democracy and the celebrity of a world-famous movie star, Schwarzenegger and his people would construct a new type of political machine.

THE DAY BEFORE the Hyatt meeting, Schwarzenegger's team had filed the paperwork to establish the linchpin of this political operation, the California Recovery Team.

The CRT was a political committee for promoting ballot measures. By itself, CRT was not unusual. Ballot measure committees were typically formed to pass one particular measure. In some cases, governors and politicians had raised money for such committees or established a committee to take on one particular issue. But the CRT was an all-purpose committee Schwarzenegger could use in campaigns for or against any measure. Major interest groups, most notably the teachers' union, had established similar committees. By setting up CRT, the governor was not merely trying to beat the interests at their own game. He was creating an outside lobby of his own.

The CRT for all practical purposes *was* Schwarzenegger. Marty Wilson, the consultant who had taken charge of the gubernatorial campaign's finances, would lead the CRT. The committee rented office space in Schwarzenegger's building in Santa Monica. It had a five-member board: Tony Russo, an executive of the Orange County real estate giant, the Irvine Company; Gary Hunt, a former Irvine executive and longtime force in Republican fund-raising; Schwarzenegger senior advisor Bonnie Reiss; the election lawyer Tom Hiltachk; and Donna Lucas, the deputy chief of staff who served as liaison between the governor's office and Schwarzenegger's team of political consultants.

Over the Christmas holiday, Marty Wilson sketched out a proposed budget of $10 million for ballot measure campaigns in 2004 and another $5 million for 2005, when no statewide election was yet scheduled. Schwarzenegger would begin furiously raising money for the CRT just days after the committee was formed. Schwarzenegger convinced wealthy individuals and businesses to give millions to the CRT, even though they could not be sure which individual ballot measures would ultimately be funded by the committee. In the world of political fund-raising, this was a considerable coup. Whether this sort of fund-raising structure was more corrupting than conventional ones was difficult to say. Schwarzenegger argued that his fund-raising was less compromising than direct donations to a candidate for office. An initiative, unlike a politician, could not be bribed. But at the same time, ballot measures brought donors more directly into the process. Schwarzenegger's contributors were not merely backers of a governor. They were direct investors in new laws.

To SCHWARZENEGGER'S CRITICS, the California Recovery Team amounted to an all-purpose (though legal) slush fund. Schwarzenegger incorporated the CRT as a non-profit organization so it could lobby the legislature, send mail at a discount and accept donations in stock as well as in cash. The non-profit also provided some protection from disclosure, allowing the governor to obscure his ballot initiative activities in the period before he began circulating petitions. This gave him a slight head start against potential opponents. And as a ballot measure committee, CRT was not subject to the same contibution limits as a political committee for a specific candidate. In fact, CRT could accept donations in any amount.

The governor's political consultants became CRT contractors. Don Sipple would produce the ads for all the ballot measure campaigns. George Gorton signed on to offer strategic advice. Jeff Randle agreed to build coalitions for the CRT, just as he had done for the gubernatorial campaign. Mike Murphy would serve as the quarterback for these strategists.

Murphy had lived in Washington, but the millions he had made from running campaigns gave him the financial cushion to give Los Angeles and a Hollywood career a try. So the irony: As Schwarzenegger left behind Hollywood for politics, the political advisor he trusted most was drawn to Hollywood.

After the recall election, Murphy bought a home in Los Angeles and found an agent. He talked of writing two scripts—one a thriller, the other a comedy. He got a paid gig as consultant to the comedian Dennis Miller's short-lived CNBC talk show, on which Schwarzenegger was the first guest. And Murphy's national consulting and strategy company, DC Navigators, established a Sacramento office across L Street from the capitol. Todd Harris, a political consultant who had come out to work with Murphy on the recall, ran it. Murphy visited Sacramento one day a week.

DC Navigators' new Sacramento office was only one example of how the consultants who were part of CRT expanded their businesses after Schwarzenegger's election. Randle increased his company's size and moved to new offices near the capitol. Marty Wilson launched a new public relations company of his own. George Gorton set up his own Sacramento office, sharing space with Wilson.

Each consultant would say that Schwarzenegger was their most important client, but he was not their only one. Most of the consultants made a point of accepting clients in public relations campaigns for policies that matched those supported by Schwarzenegger. Despite such precautions, the simple fact was that the strategists for the CRT—his permanent political operation—had clients whose businesses were affected by the decisions of Schwarzenegger's government. This was hardly a new phenomenon. Political consultants to previous governors also had outside clients, but the scale and permanence of Schwarzenegger's political operation put a greater spotlight on the arrangement.

CRT became the central hub of an expanding wheel of Schwarzenegger-affiliated political entities. Non-profits sprang up to achieve some of his goals: encouraging California tourism, convincing companies not to leave California, helping small business, promoting California agriculture, supporting charitable causes and conferences championed by Maria Shriver, and even finding an official governor's residence.

The governor maintained a policy that restricted his own fund-raising for political committees, though he received little praise and more than a few headaches for his trouble. A November 19, 2003, fund-raising policy memorandum written by Marty Wilson declared that Schwarzenegger would not accept donations from public employee unions, Indian gaming tribes, single-industry trade associations, or lobbyists.

The governor would sometimes raise money for his various ballot measures directly. In other cases, he would raise funds for the CRT, which would then transfer the cash into other committees set up for a specific ballot measure. That extra step helped Schwarzenegger obscure the sources of funding in some TV ads. California law required TV commercials to disclose major sources of funding. When CRT paid for commercials directly, the ads would mention leading corporations or wealthy people who were top CRT donors. By pouring money from CRT into the separate committees, the ads could list their major donor as "Governor Schwarzenegger's California Recovery Team."

The separate political committees also attracted donors who did not support Schwarzenegger or other parts of his agenda, but who agreed with the governor on a particular ballot measure. The governor could tap into the Democratic donor base this way. This was his plan for Propositions 57 and 58, which had a separate committee called Californians for a Balanced Budget, the Yes on 57 and 58.

RICK CLAUSSEN saw the advantages to this approach. At the December 30 meeting, the governor's team had decided to hire Claussen, a veteran initiative consultant, to handle the day-to-day management of the Yes on 57 and 58 campaign. The separate political committee for 57 and 58 would "provide some insulation for the governor and the California Recovery Team should we not be successful," Claussen wrote in a January 7, 2004, memo that was circulated to consultants and senior staff. "While I think this is highly unlikely, we need to consider the possibility."

Propositions 57 and 58 were complicated measures, and Claussen began the campaign by sketching out eleven different arguments on their behalf. Rather than dwell on each measure's details, Claussen argued for selling Propositions 57 and 58 as a way to send a message to the state's politicians. He wrote: "Just like families sometimes get into financial trouble and have to borrow, these propositions are needed because California's finances were mismanaged. Just like families have to live within their means, these propositions force state government to live within its means." Claussen also played up the unattractive alternatives if the measures didn't pass. "Everyone wishes we didn't have to resort to a bond to get us out of this budget mess. Unfortunately, the only alternatives are an $8 billion tax increase or even more spending cuts that will severely damage our schools and universities."

The two best arguments were contradictory. Schwarzenegger should say, Claussen wrote, that voting for 57 and 58 would show it was "time to stop pointing fingers and solve the problem." At the same time, the governor would need to argue that by voting for the measures, people were fighting back against politicians and taking back popular control of the state budget. This was, of course, pointing fingers. Schwarzenegger would use both arguments, often in the same speech.

Jan van Lohuizen, who also did work for the CTA, conducted a benchmark survey for the 57 and 58 campaign. His findings, received by Schwarzenegger's team on January 17, found the campaign "winnable" but warned, "The public suffers from bond and budget fatigue and voters are not thrilled by the prospect of another bond." Prop 57 still had less than the 50 percent support needed for passage in his poll, but the measure did have a lead of 48 percent yes to 33 percent no, better than it had shown in McLaughlin's survey. Prop 58 led more comfortably by 59 to 27 percent. According to van Lohuizen, the governor could win converts to the package by emphasizing a Prop 58 provision that required the legislature to stay in session until the budget crisis was resolved. The public is "very anti-legislature so slapping them around a bit should be helpful," van Lohuizen advised.

As Murphy and the rest of the governor's team poured over van Lohuizen's data, the state's newspapers published results of their first polls on the measures. Both the Field Poll and the survey of the Public Policy Institute of California in mid-January showed Prop 57 in much deeper trouble than van Lohuizen said. The measure had just 33 percent support in Field and 35 percent in PPIC. When they first saw those numbers, Murphy and Todd Harris, who would be communications director for the 57–58 campaign, erupted in joyous laughter. It was the ideal situation for political consultants. With expectations so low, a victory would be seen as a far greater triumph than it actually was.

SCHWARZENEGGER DEVOTED nearly all of his public appearances to the propositions. The first half of his first State of the State speech, delivered on January 6, 2004, consisted of an appeal for 57 and 58. The speech also made clear that, as Schwarzenegger governed and conducted direct democratic campaigns, he would continue to play a version of his usual cinematic character. In promising to reform the state government, he declared: "Every governor proposes moving boxes around to reorganize government. I don't want to move boxes around; I want to blow them up." He added jokes: "If I can sell tickets to my movies like *Red Sonja* or *Last Action Hero*"—two box office bombs—"you know I can sell just about anything."

The real news of the speech was that Schwarzenegger had found a Democratic cochair for his 57 and 58 campaign: the state Controller Steve Westly. It was a clever choice. The Democratic state Treasurer Phil Angelides had already declared his opposition to the ballot measures and just about anything else Schwarzenegger said or did. Angelides was already planning a run for governor in 2006. Westly would counter Angelides perfectly. "They have a Democratic financial guy against this," Murphy explained. "Let's create our own Democratic financial guy."

The move was not without political risk. Westly was a moderate Democrat whose wealth probably surpassed Schwarzenegger's. He had been an early executive of eBay, and his stock had made him tens of millions of dollars. He had gubernatorial ambitions of his own, so Schwarzenegger, by campaigning with Westly, would be giving a potential rival a huge boost in name recognition. Schwarzenegger did it anyway.

Westly said he had few doubts about joining up. In early 2004, Schwarzenegger looked and sounded like a Democratic governor. Shriver sent copies of a biography about her father to each state legislator, and she brought her mother around the capitol to meet legislators. "How can an Irishman be a Republican?" Eunice Shriver asked the new assembly Republican leader, Kevin McCarthy, during a visit. The governor even made peace with Gray Davis, who came over to the Schwarzenegger house for dinner, as well as for a few acting tips. Davis, world famous as a result of being replaced by a movie star, had landed a guest spot on a TV sitcom.

Back in Sacramento, Schwarzenegger was spending much of his time cozying up to the most powerful Democratic legislator, the irascible state senator John Burton. Much of the capital city wondered if Schwarzenegger was seducing Burton or if Burton was seducing Schwarzenegger. In truth, it was a little of both. Burton was the sort of older, wiser man that Schwarzenegger had spent a lifetime courting, from Joe Weider in bodybuilding to President George H. W. Bush in his earlier political life. As a young man, Burton had been stationed in Austria during the post–World War II occupation. "Arnold and I would talk about that," Burton said. "I could speak some pidgin Deutsch and would say a few words. And then he would go on for another minute. People would think we were having a big conversation in German."

Burton was finishing his last year in the senate before term limits would force him into retirement. He was an old-style San Francisco liberal, a champion of the poor, disabled, and homeless. He had been a lawmaker since Pat Brown's governorship and, to keep the state mental hospitals open, led the only override of a veto by Governor Reagan. Reagan, all but suggesting Burton himself could benefit from institutionalization, called him the "one man in Sacramento who has the most to fear from the squirrels in Capitol Park."

Burton had recovered from cocaine and alcohol addictions that led him to give up his seat in Congress two decades earlier. His older brother, the late Phillip Burton, had served in the assembly and Congress himself and crusaded for the same causes. John Burton was known not only for his liberal politics but also for his screaming fits and his filthy language. "When I met him," Schwarzenegger said, "he laid out very clearly how he operates: that he sometimes screams and I shouldn't take it personally." Burton took a liking to Schwarzenegger because the goevernor was fun. "I know he cares about people less fortunate than him," Burton told reporters. "Hell, we're all less fortunate than him."

One night, Burton showed up at the restaurant where Schwarzenegger was dining. A waiter came over and said the governor would like to send him a bottle of red wine. Burton told the waiter, "I don't drink, but I'll take the money." The waiter returned with a $100 bill from Schwarzenegger. Burton signed it and sent it back. All these games were fun, but the relationship also had political benefits for Schwarzenegger. Among the most crucial was that Burton would round up support for 57 and 58.

ONE AFTERNOON in late January, Schwarzenegger met with his political advisors to flesh out strategy for the 57 and 58 campaigns. The governor chomped on a cigar, with Claussen to one side and Murphy on the other. Schwarzenegger was interested in the campaign's ads and strategy, but what absorbed him was the look and feel of the public events. Schwarzenegger insisted on a bus tour, even though the consultants thought it was unnecessary. He believed a bus tour would build momentum.

The governor also insisted on a full campaign schedule. Claussen had budgeted only $50,000 for press events. Schwarzenegger burned through that in the first week. The relentless approach taxed Schwarzenegger's staff, but it got him and the propositions the attention he wanted. He had kicked off the campaign the third week of January with an "Ask Arnold" town hall at Duncan Enterprises, a ceramics packaging facility in Fresno, a three-hour drive from Sacramento and out of easy reach for the state's political press. This was like starting a show off-Broadway. The governor treated the event like a promotion for one of his movies. He insisted on starting with a string of jokes. "I love Fresno," Schwarzenegger began. "Do you know that I got 100 percent of the vote here? One hundred percent of all the Austrian-born bodybuilders voted for me. Actually, I got 70 percent of the votes. The other 30 percent just never forgave me for the movie *Hercules in New York*."

Schwarzenegger wore a black, bomber-style "message" jacket just like the ones he had used in his movie promotions. This new jacket read "Yes on 57 and 58" on the front and the back, so Schwarzenegger could turn his back to TV cameras and viewers still would see the numbers of the propositions.

"Flex your muscles," he told the crowd. "Flex your muscles like you did on October 7, when you elected me. You showed that you are in charge, that you have the power to make a change. This is again the way we make a change. I want to take all those initiatives directly to the people, because I don't trust the politicians in Sacramento . . . I don't want them to decide what happens in the state. You should decide what happens in the state."

In Fresno, Schwarzenegger insisted on warning of "Armageddon cuts" in the state budget if the propositions failed to pass. It was a classic Schwarzenegger overstatement, common to his movie campaigns, but it bought the governor more than he had bargained for. The *Los Angeles Times* ran my story under a five-column headline the next day, and Walter von Huene, his acting coach and friend, had to tell the governor he shouldn't refer to Armageddon anymore.

Westly, the Democratic state controller, would usually come on stage once Schwarzenegger finished his opening remarks. After jokes about *Twins 2*, Westly—playing the shorter, geekier counterpart to the governor—would praise Schwarzenegger's bipartisan approach and explain that without Propositions 57 and 58, the state would run out of money in June. "Now, is there a perfect solution?" Westly asked. "I hate to tell you this, but perfect doesn't exist in Sacramento. It's the best possible solution that can enjoy Democratic and Republican support. And does this guy ever lose at anything?"

WITH A BUDGET of $7 million, the campaign only had enough money for three weeks of TV ads. Schwarzenegger's road show filled the gap. He did Ask Arnolds in the middle of a Miller brewery in the San Gabriel Valley, in a huge senior community in the Bay Area, and at a school in San Diego. He appeared on more than fifty talk radio shows.

To pay for the 57 and 58 campaign, Schwarzenegger held fund-raisers nearly every day. Robin Leach of TV's *Lifestyles of the Rich and Famous* filmed one dinner for $100,000 donors at the home of Gavin Maloof, an owner of the Sacramento Kings. After dinner, Leach accompanied Shriver and Schwarzenegger to that night's Kings game; lesser donors paid $25,000 to watch the game with the governor in a private box.

In his first month of raising money for the propositions, Schwarzenegger pulled in a dozen six-figure contributions. But he never had enough money. The campaign delayed the start of the nightly tracking poll by ten days for lack of cash. On February 7, an internal campaign memo said it was unclear if the governor would have the money budgeted for the $1.5 million a week in TV ad buys. The next day, the governor's senior advisor in charge of his public events, Fred Beteta, indicated in a memo that he had designed the big push the governor wanted for the final days of the campaign, but didn't have the staff or money to put it all together.

In the meantime, Schwarzenegger campaigned everywhere he went. At the reopening of Frank Fat's, a Chinese restaurant that was a capitol hangout, the governor claimed to have made a deal on a napkin with the Democratic legislators who were on hand. "Yes on 57 and 58," the governor had written on the napkin with a black marker. "As you know, I'm like a machine," Schwarzenegger said. "I will not stop talking until we win."

To FILM ADS FOR 57 and 58, Schwarzenegger once again used Sipple and the facilities of the Cimarron Group, a Hollywood firm known for producing movie trailers. Schwarzenegger had worked with Cimarron in his previous campaigns and in his film career. When Westly showed up at the studio to film his part of the ads, he was overwhelmed by the scene. There was a crew of more than two dozen people, including a cinematographer from Schwarzenegger's movies. Sipple had sketched out an ad in which Westly and Schwarzenegger literally completed each other's sentences.

The ad began with a shot of Schwarzenegger, in a shirt and tie with no jacket, walking through a room full of plasma screens containing Yes on 57 and 58 messages. "For the first time in a long time, Republicans and Democrats . . . ," he began, before the camera switched to a shot of Westly, who finished the sentence, ". . . are working together in Sacramento to solve California's problems."

Westly's name and title would be flashed onscreen as he talked. There was no need to do the same for Schwarzenegger, which was another advantage of his celebrity. The two or three seconds that most politicians needed to introduce themselves could be used to drive home a message.

At the ad's conclusion, the camera panned back to show Westly and Schwarzenegger standing next to each other.

"Join us," Westly said.

"In voting yes on 57 and 58," the governor said.

Sipple tested the ads in focus groups on February 3. Voters liked them, but some expressed confusion about what the propositions did.

IN THE RECALL CAMPAIGN, Schwarzenegger's behind-the-scenes efforts had been aimed at Republicans who were supporting McClintock. But this first ballot measure campaign would be a contest for Democratic endorsements. Darry Sragow, a Democratic political consultant who worked closely with Westly, led this effort.

The opposition was the treasurer, Phil Angelides, who traveled around the state trying to convince Democrats to oppose the propositions. The governor was, in effect, caught in the middle of an early Democratic primary between Angelides and Westly, who also made the rounds of Democrats and union leaders to seek backing for the measures.

The most crucial endorsement was that of the state's most popular Democratic politician, Senator Dianne Feinstein. Angelides and Schwarzenegger both lobbied Feinstein personally. David Crane, a Democrat who served as Schwarzenegger's job czar, and Bob Denham, a bond expert and former chairman of Salomon Brothers who advised Schwarzenegger on Prop 57, appeared to seal the endorsement over a long phone call with Feinstein. When Feinstein first got on the phone, she seemed inclined to oppose it, but "she got it," said Crane. "She understood it was a refinancing of debt." Feinstein asked for a few days to tell allies who disagreed with her on the propositions. But Schwarzenegger simply could not keep such good news a secret, and he blurted out Feinstein's endorsement on a radio show. It was a rookie mistake—politicians let their colleagues announce their own endorsements— and Feinstein reacted by withdrawing her backing. Schwarzenegger apologized and asked Feinstein to come aboard again. She agreed.

THE GOVERNOR had spent so much time reaching out to Democrats that the consultants worried about turning away Republican voters.

Many Republicans disliked Prop 57's borrowing. Conservative voters preferred steep spending cuts. Schwarzenegger's consultants worried that the state Republican party, meeting at its convention in Burlingame the third weekend of February, might decline to endorse the governor's propositions. So his team put together a campaign. Conservative allies of Schwarzenegger wrote letters to all 1,400 Republican convention delegates. The letters barely mentioned the merits of 57 and 58 and focused instead on what a popular Schwarzenegger might do on other issues if he won a political victory on March 2.

Schwarzenegger came to the convention Friday night and gave a speech loaded with red meat for conservatives. The idea was to create goodwill for 57 and 58. He ripped Gavin Newsom, the mayor of San Francisco, for allowing gay couples to marry despite a voter-approved ban in the state constitution. The governor had no personal or moral objection to gay marriage, but he publicly cast Newsom's actions as a threat to the rule of law. The Republican crowd, full of conservative activists who disagreed with the governor on the morality of gay marriage, loved the denunciation of Newsom and gave the governor a standing ovation.

Schwarzenegger's advisors spent much of Friday and Saturday forcefully lobbying members of the party's initiatives committee before finally winning an endorsement for Props 57 and 58 on Sunday.

SENATOR FEINSTEIN announced her endorsement of 57 and 58 at a press conference inside a Santa Monica hotel on February 19. Afterwards, Schwarzenegger joined his consultants and some senior staff for a meeting at Oak Productions. With the fireplace roaring, Donna Lucas brought up a new public poll, released that morning by the Public Policy Institute of California, which showed Prop 57 in a 38–38 tie. Why, she asked, aren't we moving numbers?

Don Sipple came under the sharpest questioning. Were his TV ads, featuring Schwarzenegger and Westly, really working? Some advisors suggested cutting different ads, with a nurse or a teacher rather than the governor as the spokesman for the propositions. Sipple defended his ads and showed the governor's poll numbers to demonstrate that the "no" vote was falling. Gorton said the campaign simply needed to win over Democrats. Let's pick up some Democratic support, and we'll be fine, he said.

To that end, Sipple made an ad with Feinstein staring into the camera and delivering her endorsement. "Our state faces a massive fiscal crisis," Feinstein said. "Now that's the reality and we've got to deal with it. There is a solution . . . Now I've looked at these carefully. They're the right thing to do. So I urge you, vote yes on 57 and 58." It was an effective spot. Feinstein, a former San Francisco mayor, moved the demographics Schwarzenegger struggled to reach: Bay Area residents, women, and Democrats. Her endorsement gave people who didn't like Schwarzenegger a reason to vote for his ballot measures.

Propositions 57 and 58 had become such a Democratic campaign that Schwarzenegger felt comfortable jetting off to the East Coast for four days. He attended the National Governors Association meetings in Washington and raised money for the California Recovery Team there and in Manhattan. At social events with his fellow governors, Schwarzenegger adopted the role of class clown. As their group portrait was taken in Washington, the governor of California yelled: "Wait a minute. A lot of these guys need makeup!" When the governors visited the White House, Schwarzenegger—alone among them—had a separate hold room where his hair and makeup could be done.

Even as governor, Schwarzenegger led the star's life of private jets and luxury hotels. In New York, where, on the trip, he held a fund-raiser hosted by the owner of the New York Jets and attended by Donald Trump, Schwarzenegger stayed at the Four Seasons. His bill for hotel extras included twelve bottles of Evian, oatmeal cookies, and the rental of a cappuccino machine. While the rooms were non-smoking, hotel staffers told aides that the governor was free to light up a cigar.

WITH FEINSTEIN's ad on the air, the campaign's tracking poll on Monday night, February 23, showed Prop 57 had 51 percent support to 30 percent who planned to vote no. The Field Poll, sponsored by most of the state's major newspapers, put Prop 57 at 50 percent.

In a February 24 memo circulated among the campaign team, Claussen predicted a narrow victory on Prop 57 and a more comfortable win on 58. But he noted that 19 percent of voters were still undecided. "At this point, I think the greatest threat to the campaign is to allow ourselves to get off track—we have spots that work and all we need to do is to use Feinstein to reach voters that are not supportive of the governor," Claussen wrote. "We must be very careful not to overreact during these final few days."

Shriver threw herself into the campaign as well. She had briefly returned to work at NBC after the recall election, but news reports about how she advised her husband led to scrutiny of whether she could be both a journalist and a political player. In early February, she took a leave from NBC News. On the Thursday before the March 2 election, Shriver led a press conference at the Presidio in San Francisco for Democrats who endorsed the propositions. Even Dolores Huerta, a co-founder of the United Farm Workers who had protested at a Schwarzenegger town hall during the recall, showed up.

John Burton was there, too. Shriver said with a smile that Schwarzenegger had warned her, "Don't do anything to make him mad." The state senator was on his best behavior. Burton called Schwarzenegger "the most secure governor" he had ever met. "I go all the way back to Gov. Pat Brown, and the only one secure enough to change his mind was Gov. Schwarzenegger."

SCHWARZENEGGER returned to California in time for his bus tour on the last weekend of the campaign. Actor Rob Lowe emceed a kick-off rally at the Universal City Walk—an outdoor development of restaurants and stores outside the Universal Studios theme park—on Friday, February 27. "Governor Schwarzenegger is the people's governor," Lowe said. "Maybe that's because you don't get to be the biggest movie star in the world without knowing your audience." Schwarzenegger showed up and recalled approvingly how Universal had made "a little movie called *Conan the Barbarian*."

On Saturday morning, the governor visited Mulholland Middle School in the San Fernando Valley, where he had established an after-school program. The bus also stopped at the Valley Plaza Mall in Bakersfield and the Shops at River Park in Fresno. "I want you to be my power lifters for progress," he told the Fresno crowd. Feinstein joined him for the final bus tour stop at a San Jose library on Sunday.

Hiram Johnson, governor of California from 1911 to 1917, convinced voters to add direct democracy—the referendum, initiative, and recall—to the state constitution. Johnson was more showman than administrator. (Bancroft Library)

Arnold Schwarzenegger, age 17, poses in front of the Thalersee, the lake in his hometown of Thal. Alfred Gerstl, the father of Schwarzenegger's friend Karl Gerstl (right), was a politician who later served as president of the upper house of the Austrian Parliament, and became a mentor to the future governor. (Courtesy Alfred Gerstl)

Schwarzenegger, as chairman of the President's Council on Physical Fitness and Sports, meets with President George H. W. Bush in the Oval Office. (George Bush Presidential Library)

Schwarzenegger (at left), during his time as chairman of the fitness council, talks with John Cates (center), a University of California San Diego physical education professor who served as his assistant. Immediately to the right of Cates is longtime friend Jim Lorimer, Schwarzenegger's partner in a Ohio fitness convention and bodybuilding tournament. (Photo courtesy John Cates)

Schwarzenegger helps children carry bags of petitions for his after-school initiative into a county office in Sacramento on April 17, 2002. (Sacramento Bee, Zuma Press)

Schwarzenegger celebrates the victory of Proposition 49, his first ballot initiative, in November 2002, at the Hollenbeck Youth Center in Los Angeles, where Schwarzenegger and Danny Hernandez founded the Inner City Games. The triumph set the stage for his run for governor the following year. (Los Angeles Times)

The international media surround Schwarzenegger on August 7, 2003, outside a Los Angeles County office building in Norwalk where he would file to run for governor. The star's ability to get press coverage whenever he wanted was an enormous political advantage. (Ringo Chiu)

At the end of his recall bus tour on October 5, 2003, Schwarzenegger pretends to play a guitar outside the Capitol in Sacramento while Dee Snider, lead singer of Twisted Sister, belts out the campaign theme song, "We're Not Gonna Take It." (Los Angeles Times)

State Senate President Pro Tem John Burton, at a press conference with the governor, was Schwarzenegger's main negotiating partner in the legislature during his first year in office. Burton, known for liberal politics and foul language, tangled with the governor over policy but befriended him in private. (Los Angeles Times)

Pat Clarey, chief of staff for Schwarzenegger's first two years, talks with Schwarzenegger inside the Horseshoe, the governor's suite of offices on the first floor of the Capitol. The painting of First Lady Maria Shriver is by Andy Warhol. (Los Angeles Times)

Schwarzenegger prepares to tear up a mock "state credit card" during a rally at a mall in Tracy, California. The December 5, 2003, rally was designed to convince the legislature to put a bond and a balanced budget amendment on the ballot. The governor used malls as the setting for speeches to pressure the legislature. (Los Angeles Times)

Schwarzenegger asks shoppers at a Costco in the Sacramento suburb of Roseville for their signatures on his workers' compensation initiative petition in March 2004. Costco used its employees to gather signatures. (Sacramento Bee, Zuma Press)

Anthony Pico, chairman of the Viejas Band of Kumeyaay Indians (left), presents a blanket to Schwarzenegger during a ceremony to sign new gambling compacts on June 21, 2004. Paula Lorenzo, chairwoman of the Rumsey Band of Wintun Indians is at right. By some estimates, tribal gambling is a $6 billion industry in California. (Sacramento Bee, Zuma Press)

Former Governor Gray Davis, who was recalled in the 2003 election that put Schwarzenegger in office, joined Schwarzenegger in opposing Prop 66, an initiative to loosen the state's three strikes law, at a press conference on October 28, 2004, in Los Angeles. (Ringo Chiu)

Schwarzenegger, at the Beverly Hilton Hotel on election night in November 2004, celebrates the victory of most of his initiative choices, which are displayed on a screen behind him. (Ringo Chiu)

On March 1, 2005, Schwarzenegger kicks off signature gathering on reform initiatives by driving a Hummer from the Capitol to a Sacramento-area restaurant. Public employees protested at this and the governor's other media events and fund-raisers. (Sacramento Bee, Zuma Press)

Union members protest outside a Schwarzenegger town hall in San Diego on September 16, 2005, the day the governor announced he would run for re-election in 2006. A $164 million campaign by labor and its allies helped sink his initiatives in the 2005 special election. (Los Angeles Times)

Warren Beatty argues with Schwarzenegger aide Darrel Ng in San Diego on November 5, 2005. Beatty and his wife Annette Bening were blocked by gubernatorial aides from entering a rally for Schwarzenegger's initiatives. The stand-off drew media attention away from the initiatives. (Los Angeles Times)

Schwarzenegger, four days before the November 2005 special election, waves from his bus outside a helicopter manufacturing plant in Torrance. His initiatives lost, but he would be back for more ballot measure campaigns. (Los Angeles Times)

The campaign's tracking polls showed Prop 57 pulling over 50 percent of the vote, but Schwarzenegger kept campaigning. He went to downtown Los Angeles the day before the election to shake hands with diners at the Original Pantry, the restaurant owned by Richard Riordan, now his education secretary.

Most politicians never speak a bad word in public about their voters or their hosts. But Schwarzenegger had handed out tough advice on fitness for thirty years, and being inside a greasy spoon seemed to incite him. He asked a heavyset man at the counter what he was eating. The man's T-shirt hung low off his neck, and the governor noticed a surgical scar on the man's chest and pointed to it. "I see. Are you staying away from carbs?" the governor asked.

"Oh, yeah."

"Stay away from the potatoes, too."

"I stay away from that once in awhile."

"Better to stay out of this restaurant."

That afternoon, Schwarzenegger went to Burbank to appear on *The Tonight Show*. With Republicans supporting the propositions overwhelmingly, Schwarzenegger was still hunting for Democratic votes. He arranged for Gray Davis, who had endorsed 57 and 58, to join him on *The Tonight Show* stage. He then retreated from his comments to the state Republican convention on gay marriage.

"This gay marriage thing, what's your position on it, how do you deal with it?" Leno asked.

Schwarzenegger looked Leno over. "Are you trying to ask me something?"

"No, I'm not trying to ask you something."

"C'mon, admit it. Be honest."

"All right, I admit it, I'm in love with you."

"Finally!"

"But would you have any problem if they changed the law?"

Schwarzenegger then gave the answer that would win him friendly headlines in the Bay Area. "No, I don't have a problem. Let the court decide. Let the people decide." Voters in 2000 had approved a ballot initiative declaring marriage to be between a man and a woman. But "if the people change their minds and they want to overrule that, that's fine with me," he said.

As SCHWARZENEGGER took the stage at the Fairmont Hotel in Santa Monica on election night, he turned to Westly and apropos of nothing whispered, "I'm a major shoe queen." Westly laughed. The mood was light. Westly so enjoyed the company of his campaign cochair that he asked if he could attend the Oscars with Schwarzenegger. (The governor, never much of a contender for acting awards, would skip the ceremony.)

For a winning bond campaign, not usually a big news event, the governor had attracted twenty-five TV cameras. A fire marshal was hovering, worried that there were too many people in the room. Political commentators marveled at all the Democrats celebrating with the Republican governor.

Prop 57 exceeded the predictions of the most optimistic pollsters and won 63 percent of the vote. That was a twenty-five-point jump from the Public Policy Institute of California poll released just two weeks earlier. Schwarzenegger had faced little opposition, but he milked this comeback for all it was worth.

"You know something? Everyone wrote us off. Everyone said this is not going to happen. The Democrats and the Republicans will never work together. But you know something, we knew better.

"Together we have begun to restore the dream," he continued. "Together we have started to rekindle the flame of hope. So ladies and gentlemen, let's tell the entire world . . ."

Schwarzenegger paused. A sign behind the stage was supposed to open up to reveal the words, "California is back on track." But the sign seemed to catch on the word California. An aide scrambled to pull the rest of the banner down so the whole message could be seen.

IN CLAIMING the state was "back on track," Schwarzenegger had oversold his victory. The governor had done little to reduce the state's long-term deficit. But the passage of the bond led to a boost in the state's credit rating. By summer, all three of Wall Street's principal credit rating agencies had raised their ratings on California's debt by multiple steps. While Schwarzenegger had accepted his predecessor's decision to use debt to cover the state's deficit, the governor, by convincing voters to ratify that debt, had made the borrowing significantly cheaper. Proposition 57 was a modest policy success, but a considerable political triumph.

Schwarzenegger had won more than just Propositions 57 and 58. Voters had endorsed his preferences on two ballot measures—a $12 billion school bond, Prop 55, was narrowly approved, and Prop 56, a measure to make it easier to raise taxes, which he had opposed, was defeated. As they ate sushi and smoked cigars late into the night, the governor's advisors were quite full of themselves. Schwarzenegger had a 68 percent approval rating among likely voters. Fifty-two percent of Democrats approved of the job he was doing. His press secretary half-jokingly suggested that towns erect statues to the governor. (Even before the election, the governor's aides had arranged to have

Schwarzenegger's name put in gold letters above the engraved label "Governor" that graced the entrance to his office in the capitol. The letters were supposedly there to help tourists find the office, but no previous governor had put his name above the title.)

With the victory, Schwarzenegger had in effect created two pools of money that he could control. One pool was public. The $15 billion bond would not only pay off the state's short-term debt but also leave a cushion if Schwarzenegger encountered unexpected budget problems. The other pool of money was private: the cash collected by his California Recovery Team for his political activities.

In time, some Schwarzenegger aides would wonder whether, in devoting himself wholeheartedly to passing the Prop 57 bond, the governor had lost the opportunity to push through bolder reforms during his political honeymoon. But Schwarzenegger was proving to be a politician of unconventional means—a big, Hollywood-style campaigner for a bond measure—and moderate ends. He had little choice but to deal with the state's short-term debt, and he had spun that necessity into a demonstration of his strength at the ballot. Like so many successful ballot measures, Propositions 57 and 58 would spark more campaigns. By week's end, Schwarzenegger would be preparing to go to the people again.

CHAPTER 14

Costco and the Carrot People

THE TOWN OF ARVIN SITS ON the south edge of Bakersfield, north of the Tehachapi Mountains that separate urban Southern California from the state's Central Valley. The sandy loam soil and dry weather make this one of the few places on earth that can support two carrot harvests a year.

Grimmway Farms, the largest of the carrot companies, produces several million pounds a day. The Grimm brothers, Bob and Rod, had moved up to Arvin after their Orange County farm was purchased by the state for the 91 Freeway. Through acquisitions and the embrace of machines that harvested seventy-five tons of carrots an hour, the brothers Grimm built an agricultural giant that grew even after Rod passed away.

Bob Grimm, still trim at age fifty-one, while influential in local matters and in an association of growers, was content to build his business and ignore his state's initiative politics. But in 1999, Grimmway's workers' compensation costs soared, even though the company had improved its safety record and its workers were filing fewer claims. By 2003, the amount Grimm paid annually to insure his workers had more than doubled from $4.5 million to $10 million. He estimated that in 2004, the number would jump again to $12 million. Many of the state's employers—businesses as well as non-profits and local governments—faced similar predicaments.

In California, workers' compensation was as old as direct democracy itself. Governor Hiram Johnson had convinced Californians to permit a workers' compensation system in the same 1911 special election that added the initiative, referendum, and recall to the constitution. While many American states adopted workers' comp during the Progressive era, the concept had originated in Germany with Bismarck in the 1880s. Workers' comp was a no-fault system of insurance for workplace injuries. Workers gave up the ability to sue their employers in return for medical and other benefits. In California, employers were required to insure workers themselves or purchase policies from insurance companies or from a state fund.

Workers' comp had been a major issue in the recall. As Schwarzenegger took office, labor and business groups agreed that soaring costs had slowed job growth in the state. Workers' compensation premiums paid by California employers roughly doubled between 1999 and 2003. On average, businesses paid $4.81 in workers' compensation costs for every $100 in payroll in the summer of 2003. Without a change in the system, the costs were projected to surpass $6.50 per $100 by early 2006. California employers paid far more than any other state. The national average was less than $3 per $100 in payroll.

Workers' comp had been deregulated in the early 1990s, which, at first, led to predatory pricing and later a huge rise as the workers' comp insurance market consolidated. After the September 11 attacks, reinsurance rates soared and investment income plummeted, a reversal of two trends that had kept rate levels low for all kinds of insurance, including workers' comp. In 2002, Governor Gray Davis increased benefits for temporarily disabled workers after labor leaders threatened to put an initiative hiking benefits on the ballot. Some employers saw that increase as a reason for the rise in premiums. Davis, in the middle of the recall campaign, pushed through legislation to bring down premiums by imposing new controls on fees for outpatient surgery and doctors' visits. But those changes needed time to take hold, and Davis was out of time.

In the fall of 2003, Bob Grimm asked two of his lawyers, Jeff Green and Sean McNally, to find some way to reduce Grimmway's costs. McNally, a workers' comp specialist, and Green, who was well-connected in Bakersfield politics, called a local operative named Stan Harper and asked: What could Grimmway do to change the law? Harper said a statewide ballot initiative was a possibility, but it would cost $1 million just to get a measure on the ballot. If they wanted to win, the carrot farmers would have to raise as much as $50 million. Bob Grimm agreed to put in $1 million to get things started. He saw the money as a business investment since he could save far more than that by reining in his workers' comp costs.

Through Harper, Grimmway hired GOP pollster Frank Luntz to conduct a statewide poll. Focus groups were held in Santa Monica and Sacramento. At each, Luntz asked whether people knew anyone who had abused the workers' comp system. All the focus group members raised their hands.

Luntz told Grimm and his lawyers that a ballot initiative to reduce the costs of workers' compensation was a likely winner. There were two caveats: the initiative had to have the governor's support and it had to be drafted to protect the rights of workers to choose their own doctors. If workers had to go to physicians chosen by employers, that provision could sink the measure.

The political consultant had other advice, too. He chided Jeff Green for wearing a tie. "From now on, don't dress like that," Luntz told the men from Grimmway. "You're farmers. You might be standing out in the fields in commercials someday. Dress like you were out in the fields."

So Green and McNally headed to Sacramento without their ties. This would become their trademark as they walked the halls of the capitol.

Those guys without ties? Those are the Carrot People.

GRIMM AND HIS LAWYERS DID not understand at first that they were walking into the busiest season in the history of California's direct democracy, and right into the path of the new governor of California.

With workers' comp, Schwarzenegger would try to blend initiative politics with old-style backroom dealing. In the attempt, Schwarzenegger fashioned an approach to governing that would become his public trademark and a private touchstone. His devotion to this hybrid strategy—initiatives on the outside and negotiations on the inside—would become the source of much of his success, and of his greatest political troubles.

THE CARROT PEOPLE WERE NOT the only ones to draft a workers' comp initiative. When longtime initiative professionals learned there might be money to support a measure, they rushed to the attorney general's office to file their own. To register an initiative, the state required only a filing fee of $200, a fraction of the thousands of dollars in staff time that it cost the attorney general's office to write a title and summary for each measure. In the Schwarzenegger era, this small but important state subsidy to direct democracy would be exploited like never before.

Ted Costa, the original proponent of the recall, filed a workers' comp measure that had been drafted by Tom Hagerman, a furniture manufacturer in Pasadena who ran a small business group.

And another initiative had the new governor's fingerprints on it. This measure had been written by Nielsen Merksamer, the law firm that had drafted Schwarzenegger's after-school measure Proposition 49. Joel Fox, a policy aide to Schwarzenegger with a long history in initiative problems, and Chris George, a mortgage broker who had supported Schwarzenegger during the recall, served as official proponents. Fox had formed an advocacy group, the Small Business Action Committee, before the recall election with funding from businesses, among them the Irvine Company, the Orange County landowner and real estate giant that backed the governor's political activities.

Although Schwarzenegger had no official role in the Fox initiative, the governor had come to see workers' comp as a symbol of the dysfunction that had robbed the state of its promise. He saw an initiative as the way to force the legislature to make changes. Through staff and allies, he made it clear that it would be better to have one measure to use as a club, rather than three.

In December 2003, the Carrot People arranged a meeting in Sacramento with the governor's senior staff. To the visitors from Bakersfield, the reception felt hostile. Moira Topp, a Schwarzenegger aide who had long experience with workers' comp as a legislative staffer, grilled the Carrot People. Have you done polling? Do you know how much money your initiative would save? She all but suggested that the Carrot People drop their initiative.

Paul Miner, the policy aide during Prop 49 and the recall who was now chief deputy cabinet secretary to Schwarzenegger, walked in late. After listening to the conversation for a while, he slipped McNally a note that read: "We need to talk." Afterward, as they stood outside the capitol, Miner told McNally to keep pursuing the initiative. Eventually, the Carrot People and the governor would have to work together.

BY JANUARY, Schwarzenegger was working behind the scenes to dictate the details of a combined initiative. He had seen two extensive polls on workers' comp, each done by one of his recall campaign pollsters. In a December survey, John McLaughlin found that 79 percent of voters would support an effort by Schwarzenegger to reduce workers' comp premiums paid by employers to a rate "about the same as those in other states." The survey showed vulnerabilities as well. If the plan were opposed by labor unions, support would fall. And voters would oppose the initiative by an overwhelming 59 to 20 percent if it required workers to go to a company doctor.

On January 11, the governor invited Luntz, the pollster working for Grimmway, to meet with him in Sacramento. Schwarzenegger was adamant that, as a matter of policy, such an initiative had to include some sort of controls on employees' choices of doctors for their on-the-job injuries. It was the only way to get a handle on medical costs. Luntz warned the governor that that provision alone could drag down the initiative, but Schwarzenegger wouldn't budge. "He stared me down," the pollster said.

Luntz walked from the capitol to a meeting in the law offices of Nielsen Merksamer. McNally, the Grimmway attorney who oversaw workers' comp, was already there, fuming. As a representative of the Carrot People, McNally had been invited up to talk about joining forces with the Fox initiative. He felt he had walked into an ambush. The room was filled with Schwarzenegger aides and lawyers. Jim Gross, a Nielsen Merksamer lawyer, had begun with an evisceration of the Carrot People's initiative and praise for the Fox ballot measure.

After forty-five minutes of debate, it appeared there would not be enough unity to have the one initiative Schwarzenegger wanted. Paul Miner pulled

McNally out of the room and into partner Steve Merksamer's office down the hall.

What's it going to take for you guys to go away? Miner asked.

McNally explained that he didn't have the authority to drop the ballot initiative. Only his boss, Bob Grimm, could do that. And Frank Luntz believed that the Fox measure would go down to defeat.

My boss, Miner said in reference to the governor, told me not to leave this office until there is one initiative. What do you have to have?

McNally named several necessary changes.

Shit, Miner said, that's your initiative. You've got to give me more than that.

A bargain was reached.

The combined ballot initiative would run to fourteen single-spaced pages, making it unusually long and, because of the resulting weight of the petitions, expensive to print and circulate for signatures. But it suited the Carrot People. And the governor believed it gave him the leverage he needed to bargain for a bill with the legislature.

McNally added that Grimm would remain the proponent of the combined initiative, meaning the Carrot People retained the power to go forward or withdraw it. "We are not going to sign away our fate," McNally explained. "Nobody can pull this initiative unless Bob Grimm signs off on it."

SCHWARZENEGGER WAS NOT ENTIRELY satisfied with that last piece of the bargain. The next day, Miner called the Carrot People to ask them to take Grimm's name off the joint initiative. Grimm and McNally had left for Argentina on a dove-hunting trip that morning. Jeff Green took the call. Miner explained that to make a deal with the legislature, Schwarzenegger needed to convince lawmakers that he could make the initiative go away. The governor couldn't let the Carrot People keep control.

Green had been left behind in Arvin with orders to keep Grimm's name on the initiative at all costs. "But we don't know you," Green recalled saying to Miner. "We don't know how serious the governor is about this."

Miner said, bottom line, we can't go forward with Grimm's name on the initiative.

Green stalled for time. He told Miner he'd call back. He couldn't reach Grimm in Argentina. So Green called Miner and said Grimm would come off the measure, but the Carrot People wanted to meet with the governor.

When they gathered a few weeks later in Schwarzenegger's office, the governor thanked the Carrot People and said how much he admired them for filing the initiative. Guys, the governor asked, what's your bottom line?

McNally responded by asking the governor the same question. When the governor hedged, McNally asked again. C'mon, what's your bottom line?

Schwarzenegger laughed. He said employer medical control was important despite the political problems it might cause. The Carrot People agreed, though they worried the provision could defeat the initiative. As the Carrot People stood up to leave, the governor asked if Grimmway had any animals on its farms. Schwarzenegger fondly remembered growing up around animals back in Thal.

THE LAST WEEK OF JANUARY, the joint initiative was formally announced. In California, a ballot initiative required a maximum of fifteen days for review by the attorney general's office, which produced a title and summary, and up to twenty-five working days for legislative analysts to estimate the measure's fiscal impact. An initiative as complex as this would take the full forty days.

On March 5, three days after Propositions 57 and 58 passed, the initiative was approved for signature gathering. The governor announced a March 31 deadline for reaching a deal with the legislature, but the real final date would prove to be April 16: the last day for turning in signatures if the measure was to qualify for the November ballot. If no deal was forthcoming, the signatures would be submitted and Schwarzenegger would campaign for the initiative.

Schwarzenegger was using the state's direct democracy calendar to force the legislature to act quickly; there was no other reason to pass a legislative package so fast. Legislative leaders objected, but Schwarzenegger liked having a deadline. For a quarter century, he had watched movie projects go through years of development hell when nothing seemed to happen. But in a short shoot, movie people moved mountains. The governor believed politicians would behave the same way.

AS THEY WATCHED THE CARROT PEOPLE and the governor cooperate on the initiative, labor leaders decided to start negotiations themselves. The state AFL-CIO and the California Teamsters Union convened meetings with representatives of companies such as Costco Wholesale Corp. and the Walt Disney Company that had made reducing workers' compensation costs a priority. In February the governor invited the labor and corporate representatives to hold their sessions in his office. The governor could use these "Five and Five" meetings—there were five people on the business side of the table, and five people representing labor—to provide feedback on specific proposals. And by limiting the meetings to labor and business, he effectively barred from the negotiations the two interest groups that had the most to lose financially from reform: the insurance companies and the lawyers for injured workers.

In the Five and Five meetings, Allan Zaremberg, the president and CEO of the California Chamber of Commerce, led the corporate side. Tom Rankin, the president of the California Labor Federation, was top chair on the labor side. Rankin, who feared that the initiative would leave injured workers with far less in the way of legal protections, wanted a deal to keep the measure off the ballot.

Beginning in early March, Schwarzenegger also convened meetings of the "Big 5," the term for the five leading figures inside the capitol: the governor, the assembly speaker, the state senate pro tem (the top official of the majority), and the minority leaders of the assembly and the senate. The Big 5 meetings were cordial but unproductive.

The real negotiations were done at the staff level. Schwarzenegger assigned his chief deputy legislative secretary Cynthia Bryant and deputy cabinet affairs secretary Moira Topp to negotiate the details of the legislative package with Democratic staffers. The governor told the two women he wanted them working every day until a deal was reached. They took one Sunday off early in the negotiations, and made a pact not to tell Schwarzenegger.

These staff negotiations took place in a conference room in the far northwestern corner of the Horseshoe, under what was jokingly called the "cone of silence." (At one meeting, a staffer doodled a drawing of the cone, which included the staffers themselves, the governor, and the Senate President Pro Tem John Burton.) The silence allowed the staffers to deal with many issues themselves, without telling the labor or business representatives in the Five and Five meetings all they were doing. Burton often yelled at Topp and Bryant, calling them "Thelma and Louise." The implication was that, just like Susan Sarandon and Geena Davis in the movie of the same name, Topp and Bryant were driving off a cliff.

Schwarzenegger enforced the silence around the deal-making in part by playing mind games with Democratic and Republican legislators. This distracted them from the substantive staff negotiations going on right under their noses. In meetings with Democrats, the governor said he didn't think he could support regulating the rates charged by insurance companies, but was willing to study the issue. With a group of Republican assemblymen, he made the same point but with a different emphasis: "I'm thinking about rate regulation." Ray Haynes, a conservative assemblyman who had encouraged the recall, declared that competition was the best rate regulator and even offered to retrieve his copy of *Capitalism and Freedom*, by economist and

Schwarzenegger friend Milton Friedman. Provoking Haynes further, Schwarzenegger replied: What about greedy insurance companies?

The governor's clever posturing kept Republicans on edge. Their public statements made his position look more reasonable in comparison. And by at least discussing rate regulation, Schwarzenegger undercut arguments by labor and Democrats that the legislation would merely add to the profits of insurance companies.

At a dinner for major donors to the state Republican party, Schwarzenegger answered a question about the workers' compensation negotiations by pointing at Senate Minority Leader Jim Brulte and Assembly Minority Leader Kevin McCarthy. "Their job is to be the bad guys," the governor said. "And my job is to be the good guy." Brulte asked if he and McCarthy would ever get to be the good guys.

Schwarzenegger stared back and said firmly: "No."

PETITIONS FOR THE WORKERS' COMP initiative reached the streets the weekend of March 6 and 7. In the period ending with the April 16 deadline to turn in signatures for the November ballot, more than 15 million signatures would be collected on two dozen other potential ballot measures, including the workers' initiative. Never before had so many signatures been collected in so little time in California.

Ten of the more than two dozen initiatives in circulation had "full funding." Their sponsors would pay whatever it took to qualify. With so many possible initiatives on the street, backers of each measure were faced with a choice: raise the price they paid for each signature or lose signatures to a competing initiative that would pay more. A bidding war ensued.

For the workers' comp initiative, Schwarzenegger's team included Marty Wilson, who headed his California Recovery Team; George Gorton, his political consultant since early 2001; Rick Claussen, who had managed the 57–58 campaign; and Frank Schubert, a veteran initiative consultant who was close to the business community. Every Monday morning, the governor's team held conference calls, with the rising signature prices often a topic of the conversation. Schwarzenegger's advisors agreed to several increases, all the way up to $4.50 per signature.

Those price hikes indirectly helped the governor fight off a ballot initiative he opposed. The California's Teachers Association and movie director Rob Reiner had put together an initiative to remove the Proposition 13 limits on commercial (but not residential) property tax rates, creating a "split roll." The new revenue would go to education. Since Schwarzenegger and the CTA had been allies in putting together the state budget, the union held out some hope that Schwarzenegger would not oppose the split roll. But Schwarzenegger, during the recall, had pledged to defend Prop 13.

The governor had Jeff Randle, who handled coalition building and other political operations, run an early and aggressive effort against the split roll initiative. On April 8, CTA president Barbara Kerr announced the union was abandoning the initiative. Union officials suggested Reiner hadn't come up with enough money, and Reiner's allies said the union hadn't committed to the measure. What's indisputable is that the rising cost of signatures for the workers' comp initiative and other measures forced CTA to spend far more money than anticipated. Through direct democracy, Schwarzenegger had won one victory by pursuing another.

The governor faced the same financial pressures. He needed just under six hundred thousand valid signatures to qualify workers' comp for the ballot. Since so many signatures on initiative petitions are typically invalid—the voters aren't registered, addresses are wrong, etc.—the team really needed to collect 1 million signatures. After four weeks, the signature gathering lagged behind the pace needed to reach 1 million by April 16.

With prices rising, the individual signature gatherers on the street had more power than ever before. Many responded to the bidding war by holding on to petitions instead of turning them in. The longer a gatherer retained his signatures, the more valuable they became. In March and April of 2004, hundreds of thousands of signatures were being hoarded.

The governor's team set up a bonus program to encourage earlier return of signatures. Schwarzenegger prevailed upon the Republican party to give money to the signature-gathering campaign. The governor himself kept close tabs on the street price of signatures. With signatures costing more, Schwarzenegger would have to do more fund-raising. He was already being criticized in the press for raising more than $10 million during his first six months in office. As it turned out, the governor would soon receive a gift of signatures from an unexpected source.

"*PUEDE VOTAR EN CALIFORNIA?*" Christina Hernandez asked shoppers. "Are you a registered voter, ma'am?"

On most days, Hernandez worked a nine-to-five shift in the clothing section of the Costco warehouse in the Los Angeles County city of Hawthorne, south of LAX along the 405 Freeway. On March 23, Costco had asked employees in all ninety-eight of its California stores if they would volunteer to collect signatures on workers' comp petitions. Hernandez, twenty-four years old and three months pregnant, admired Schwarzenegger and had heard he was behind the measure. She volunteered.

Costco was a big-box retailer known for selling items in bulk at low cost. Customers were members who paid fees starting at $45 for the privilege of shopping there. Costco also was known for paying decent wages and providing full health benefits even in the face of criticism from Wall Street. (Hernandez made $14 per hour and had full health-care coverage.)

Costco had plans to open more stores in the state, but the company had seen an annual increase of $26 million in its workers' comp costs, a jump so extraordinary that Costco had circulated a nonbinding petition in its California stores in September 2003 calling for legislative action to reduce such costs. Costco members signed 521,838 petitions in twenty-six days.

The Carrot People knew about that effort and called Costco in March to ask if the company would gather signatures for the initiative itself. With the exception of its nonbinding petition, Costco had banned political activity in its stores. Signature gatherers in California who tried to work outside Costcos were typically asked to leave the premises. But for Schwarzenegger and workers' comp, Costco made an exception. The issue was crucial to the company, and taking on workers' compensation was good marketing. Approximately 1.2 million of Costco's customer-members were registered as "business members," and California's small business owners were furious about workers' comp costs. Although the governor's team offered to arrange for paid signature gatherers inside the stores, Costco insisted on using its own employees—who had to volunteer for the duty—to do the gathering.

At the Costco in Hawthorne, Christina Hernandez set up her table across from a display of four-pound bags of jelly beans selling for $12.99. The company gave her no script to follow. She decided to talk about how workers' comp was hurting businesses and costing California jobs. While Hernandez worked the table near the entrance, another employee, Joe Alarcon, wandered the aisles with a clipboard full of petitions. A new employee, he was making $10.40 an hour at Costco while he attended a nearby community college. Alarcon spent a lot of time in the books section, where he felt his chances of finding registered voters were better. When the lines at the cashiers got long, Alarcon walked over to get signatures from shoppers who were waiting.

"Sign this to help Arnold Schwarzenegger," he told customers.

When Schwarzenegger heard that Costco was helping, he visited the stores to gather a few signatures himself. The governor turned his appearances into media events. On March 24, he was mobbed at a Costco in the Sacramento suburb of Roseville by shoppers who wanted his autograph. The governor obliged and then asked fans for their signatures on a workers' comp petition.

"This is what the people want to see," Schwarzenegger boasted to reporters at the Costco. "They want to see an action governor, not someone who sits around the office in Sacramento, not doing anything."

The governor ended press conferences by reminding people to go to Costco and sign the petition. In the three weeks before the April 16 deadline, more than 190,000 registered voters visited Costco and did as Schwarzenegger suggested. It was a strange synergy. Costco received a free endorsement from one of the most famous men in the world. And the governor of California received crucial leverage as he negotiated major legislation.

THREE TIMES BEFORE APRIL 16, Schwarzenegger would leave talks over workers' compensation to head to a Costco, collect signatures, and then return to the capitol. From inside to outside to inside again, this was the governor's pattern in negotiations. He would rail publicly at the legislators for failing to fix workers' comp, while inside the Capitol he handed out cigars and worked with lawmakers on legislation to fix it.

Schwarzenegger wanted a legislative deal, not the initiative. With a deal in April, a workers' compensation law and related regulations would go into effect more quickly and would save California companies money much faster than a November ballot initiative victory ever could. In Schwarzenegger's mind, the initiative was not a bluff, but it was a hand he preferred not to play.

Mike Murphy, his consultant, counseled Schwarzenegger not to appear too eager to make a deal. By expressing a willingness to go to the ballot, the governor would get more of what he wanted in the legislation. Schwarzenegger conveyed that willingness the way he knew best: through a public campaign. Workers' comp, a technical subject, was an unlikely issue for the full movie-star treatment, but that did not stop the governor. He had a message jacket made. Red, white, and blue T-shirts were distributed. They read:

JOIN ARNOLD
FIX WORKERS' COMP
TERMINATE FRAUD

AS SCHWARZENEGGER STEPPED UP the public campaign, John Burton played an inside game. Burton would sabotage Big 5 meetings by having temper tantrums and walking out whenever there was a substantive discussion of workers' comp. The Democratic senate leader wanted to negotiate a deal on legislation directly with the governor, not with all the other legislative leaders. Clarey, Schwarzenegger's chief of staff, asked Republican leaders Brulte and McCarthy not to say anything to irritate Burton. Brulte was abrupt: "With all due respect, if he wants to act like a childish asshole, that's his problem, not mine."

Schwarzenegger often took the bait and went off to talk to Burton privately. Then the mind games began. Schwarzenegger tried to soften up Burton by getting Warren Buffett to autograph a box of See's Candies (See's is owned by Buffett's Berkshire Hathaway.) But Burton was even better at getting inside Schwarzenegger's head. When the governor suggested changing a legal requirement that the courts "liberally construe" workers' comp laws to the advantage of workers, Burton protested that his late brother Phil Burton, an assemblyman and congressman, had written that provision. "He put his hand on my shoulder, and his eyes were getting glassy," Schwarzenegger recalled. "He would look up to heaven and say, 'Arnold, that's my brother. Don't bring it up again.'" The comment threw Schwarzenegger.

The governor refused to meet with Burton for two days so he could plan his approach. "I was totally schvitzing about this thing," Schwarzenegger said. When the governor brought up liberal construction again with Burton, he made sure he had a copy of a 1995 book on Phil Burton, *A Rage for Justice*, sitting in a prominent spot on the table. "I said, 'John, your brother was a great guy. It's unbelievable the kind of guy he was. But liberal construction? I think it's wrong, just wrong.'"

Like the unions, Burton did not pursue a deal by choice. He feared the initiative would hurt workers and distract from his own top priority on the November ballot: expanding health care coverage. In 2003, Burton had championed a labor-sponsored bill requiring companies with twenty or more employees to provide health insurance for their workers. After the bill passed the legislature and was signed into law by Governor Davis, business groups gathered signatures to put it to a referendum on the November 2004 ballot. It was groundbreaking legislation that Burton and labor badly wanted to defend, but the unions' resources would be divided if they also had to fight a workers' compensation initiative.

So Burton's goal in the workers' comp negotiations was simple: "I was fighting to make something that I didn't like palatable, like when somebody gives you a shit sandwich, and so you put the ketchup on it, you put the mustard on it, you put on the Worcestershire and a couple onions." Labor leaders also mistakenly thought that Burton had extracted a promise from Schwarzenegger: the senate leader would help the governor on workers' comp, and Schwarzenegger would stay out of the referendum on health insurance. "I should have asked for that deal," Burton would later say. "I didn't."

THE GOVERNOR AND BURTON had long one-on-one meetings in the canvas tent Schwarzenegger had erected in the patio outside his office, twenty feet from the doors to comply with state laws prohibiting smoking in public buildings. Inside the tent, Schwarzenegger puffed on cigars as he pleased. (The tent's Astroturf floor was later blamed for blocking a drain pipe and contributing to the flooding of Horeshoe offices during a rainstorm.) The governor enjoyed the private negotiations, which allowed him to put his personal imprint on a deal. As a former bodybuilder with high tolerance for physical pain, he sought to boost benefits for workers with documented injuries, but force those claiming only pain to provide medical proof. Schwarzenegger also came up with the idea that an injured worker could get opinions from three doctors inside a network of physicians approved by employers. If the worker was still not satisfied after three opinions, he or she could seek medical care outside the network. The governor talked openly about how he had gotten three medical opinions after injuring his shoulder during *Terminator 3*. "Why shouldn't everyone else have the same privilege?" he said.

Burton did not care for Schwarzenegger's trips away from the capitol to hunt for signatures. He took to comparing Schwarzenegger's desire to appear before crowds to the drug addiction Burton himself had battled. The governor needs his fix, Burton would say of the Costco visits. After one contentious conversation over workers' comp, Burton stormed out of the governor's office. "Go take it to the people," Burton yelled. "I don't fucking care. Take it to your fucking people."

AS MUCH AS BURTON DISLIKED breathing cigar smoke, he and the governor were making progress in their talks. By the last week of March, the two men had the outline of a deal written out on a single sheet of paper. It included new ways to determine benefits for people who were partially disabled, a faster process to get injured workers back on the job, and an increase in benefits for the most severely disabled.

The Carrot People did not think such a deal would produce enough savings, and met with the governor to protest. "He was trying to make sure that we weren't straying off the reservation," McNally recalled. "He said, 'I'm not going to deliver everything I said I would deliver.'"

McNally countered that the devil was in the details, and so Schwarzenegger's understanding with Burton needed clarification. Schwarzenegger said, Okay, you're going to be vetting the legislative language. One staff member objected, but Schwarzenegger was adamant: I'll have it faxed to you.

On Sunday, March 28, Schwarzenegger flew to Sacramento for a night meeting with the Big 5 that he hoped would clinch a deal. The Republicans balked. Brulte said the governor had a deal with Burton, not him. Under this pressure from the right, Schwarzenegger talked tough. The governor called in print reporters (to whom he rarely talked) for one-on-one interviews in which he accused interest groups of manipulating the negotiations, even though he himself had invited labor and business representatives into his office. "I feel very strongly that special interests are running this building," he told the *Los Angeles Times*.

This harder line appeared to move the negotiations his way. By Friday of that week, April 2, Burton had offered a few new concessions, and the governor believed he had wrapped up a deal. The draft agreement had twenty-five parts. California's workers' compensation system would be remade into what amounted to a giant health maintenance organization in which injured workers would be funneled to pre-approved groups of doctors. The legislative language itself would still have to be drafted. But Schwarzenegger was comfortable enough with the deal to leave Sacramento and take his wife and children, who were on spring break, to Maui for a week's vacation.

Almost as soon as Schwarzenegger left the state, the deal blew up. The Carrot People and other business interests complained that this new HMO-style bureaucracy would not save employers much money on their workers' comp premiums. And the unions complained there was nothing in the deal to stop insurance companies from profiting.

As Schwarzenegger played with his kids in Maui, he fielded a steady stream of phone calls from California. On Monday, still on vacation, he put out a letter encouraging the initiative backers to continue gathering signatures. "Your extraordinary efforts to qualify the workers' compensation initiative for the ballot in November are keeping all parties who are engaged in seeking a legislative solution working around the clock," the letter said. The next day, Schwarzenegger and Shriver granted an interview to my *Times* colleague Peter Nicholas, who had been sent to Hawaii to track him down. The governor, noting that legislators seemed unable to negotiate in his absence, mused about busting the legislature down to part-time status.

Topp and Bryant, Schwarzenegger's designated negotiators, continued to meet each day in the governor's office with Don Moulds, a staffer for Burton, and Greg Campbell, a Democratic assembly staffer. Their negotiations had proceeded well, but now became a victim of the tensions. Moulds was at one point kicked out of the governor's office. A few days later, Burton, believing the governor's people were being unreasonable, called Moulds at the negotiating table and ordered him to "get the fuck out of there."

Working long hours and dealing with their bosses' machinations, the governor's staffers and their Democratic counterparts became close. By Thursday, April 8, they reached another tentative agreement. But business groups, Republican legislators, and the Carrot People objected to provisions that, they argued, left open too many loopholes for workers to exploit. The governor backed away.

The Carrot People were blamed for the breakdown. With a week before the April 16 deadline, the talks were stalled. It appeared that workers' comp would go to the ballot.

As APRIL 16 APPROACHED without a deal, Stan Harper's temp agency at Meadow Fields Airport in Bakersfield became the hub of California politics. Harper had first suggested an initiative campaign to the Carrot People in 2003. Now Harper, who combined political consulting with running his temp agency, had been hired to help manage the processing of petitions. The number of signed petitions inside the arriving shipments of U.S. mail and UPS and FedEx boxes was the leading indicator of the governor's political fortunes. With only six weeks to gather, collect, and process the signatures, Harper's office was deluged. The post office made deliveries twice a day to keep up with the volume.

Harper had the delicate task of handling the Costco petitions, which would provide a cushion if a high percentage of signatures were found to be invalid. Costco executives wanted to keep separate the signatures gathered by their employees, so Harper maintained a store-by-store record of how many signatures Costco produced. The biggest producer would be the store in Roseville that Schwarzenegger visited. More than three thousand signatures were gathered there. Other stores never got the hang of collecting signatures. One Costco store kept sending its daily receipts instead of petitions.

Harper had noticed that every time Schwarzenegger said a legislative deal was likely, the flow of signatures into his Bakersfield office slowed. When Schwarzenegger appeared at a Costco or publicly urged voters to sign, the office would be flooded with signed petitions. When the governor departed for Maui with a deal seemingly done, the signature flow again stagnated.

Fabian Núñez, a Democrat and the new speaker of the assembly, understood this dynamic, too. He announced on a few occasions that a deal was "95 percent there" or "95 percent certain." Staffers in the capitol—locked in the stalemate—wondered what Núñez was up to. The speaker was cleverly talking up the possibility of the deal in the hopes that it would dissuade people from signing the initiative.

The breakdown in talks sparked one last surge of signatures. When the governor left for Maui on April 2, Harper had worried that he would not get enough signatures. A week later, Harper knew he had more than enough. With this final push, the Carrot People and Schwarzenegger collected 1.2 million signatures when 1 million would have sufficed.

ON EASTER MORNING, APRIL 11, Bryant and Topp reconvened negotiations with Democratic staffers in the governor's office. The staffers were exhausted from weeks of work, and the final week promised to be even more tiring. Bryant had a bottle of champagne in front of her in hopes that a deal would quickly be reached. But by 9 p.m. that night, the bottle remained unopened. "Hello from Hell," Bryant said as she answered the phone.

Schwarzenegger, who had returned from Hawaii earlier in the weekend, met that same Easter night with Burton and other legislators in Sacramento. The governor flew back to Los Angeles so he could visit a Costco in Burbank Monday morning. Even though there were already enough signatures, Schwarzenegger wanted to keep the public pressure on the legislators. The deadline for turning in signatures to qualify the initiative for the November ballot was that Friday, April 16. If there was no legislative deal by then, the governor and the Carrot People planned to turn in the signatures. Once signatures were in, the initiative could not be withdrawn even if a deal was later reached.

Under pressure, Democrats and labor started to offer a variety of new proposals and concessions. Tom Rankin, the president of the California Labor Federation, concluded that the unions simply couldn't risk the initiative fight. Labor agreed to a two-year cap on the length of time workers could receive payments for temporary disabilities. The unions also agreed that injured workers would choose from networks of doctors, though there was still a dispute over how such networks would be put together. And labor asked that employers provide immediate medical care for any work-related injury. Business representatives agreed, arguing that quick care might save money in the long run.

On Tuesday, Schwarzenegger lifted the cone of silence, and his aides updated labor and attorneys for injured workers on the language Topp and Bryant had produced in their talks with Democratic staff. Rankin, the labor leader, was surprised and angry at the language he saw. Art Azevedo, the president of the association of attorneys for workers' comp applicants, declared: "It is not a compromise. The governor is absolutely intimidating the Democrats in the legislature. How he has gotten away with this I have no idea."

The answer to that question came at lunchtime. Schwarzenegger, pressing his advantage, left the capitol to appear at a Costco in Sacramento and ask for even more signatures. About fifty injured workers were protesting outside the store. "Get real quiet," Schwarzenegger hushed shoppers so they could hear the workers chanting. "You can hear the special interests." By Tuesday night, there was some hope the legislation could be drafted and passed on Wednesday, April 14. A conference committee with lawmakers from the assembly and the senate was scheduled for 11 a.m. that day.

Shortly before 11 a.m., Burton marched into the governor's office to declare there would be no deal until Schwarzenegger loosened the requirement that workers go to a doctor in an employer-controlled network. Two hours before that, the initiative's backers held a conference call during which one corporate executive gloated, "We got more than we could have imagined." The comment was relayed to Democrats, who pushed back. Schwarzenegger recited his position again, and Burton stormed out.

"Hey, man, no hard feelings," Burton said. "But I can't fucking do this." The conference committee was cancelled. The deal was off.

But, later in the day, Burton called Rankin, the labor federation president, who agreed to meet. Clarey, the governor's chief of staff, joined the session and soon huddled with Rankin alone. They worked out a face-saving agreement that would allow workers to opt out of the medical networks, but would cap the number of people who could do so. The deal allowed the unions to change their position on the bill from "opposed" to "neutral." Said Rankin: "It was a bogus solution because they wanted to cap the percentage of people and that's totally impossible to enforce."

The deal with labor did not end the activity inside the governor's office. Topp and Bryant led a group of staffers, Democrats and Republicans, who continued to draft language late into Wednesday night in a conference room inside the Horseshoe. It wasn't until late evening that the staff produced a full version of the proposed bill. No one else in the capitol had the language. Sacramento lobbyists, generally content to stay in their offices and favorite restaurants, roamed the capitol looking for copies of the bill, but the few that could be found showed huge blanks. A new conference committee was postponed repeatedly before finally being set for 2:35 a.m.

McNally, the Grimmway lawyer, ensconced himself in the office of the assembly minority leader McCarthy. Every fifteen minutes or so, he would get a phone call from the governor's office asking about a different piece of the bill. McNally was delighted at what he was hearing, but he resolved to look as angry as possible. He worried that if people understood how happy he was, the momentum might change.

Joel Fox, Schwarzenegger's policy advisor from the campaign, had the final say on whether to file the signatures and qualify the initiative. But Fox was depending on the Carrot People for guidance. At 3 a.m., McNally smiled for the first time as he read the bill presented to the conference committee. Shortly after three, Burton told the conference committee that he was supporting the bill to avoid the initiative.

Schwarzenegger received a call in his hotel room at the Hyatt to make sure he was okay with a few last-minute changes. He was. The conference committee passed the bill, by a six–zero vote, literally in the middle of the night.

The bill would be voted on in the assembly and senate Thursday morning, only a few hours later. No legislator had time to read the bill before the conference committee. A labor lawyer took it to a Denny's restaurant and read through the bill. He caught some mistakes.

Every photocopy machine in the capitol was used to run off copies of the bill. The last copies were handed out after 5 a.m.

THE ASSEMBLY APPROVED THE BILL seventy-seven to three. Every Democrat who spoke in favor of the legislation cited the initiative as a factor in his or her vote. State Senator Sheila Kuehl, a Los Angeles Democrat, explained her support in terms that Governor Hiram Johnson would have understood well: "We are voting on this with a gun to our heads." Rankin, the labor federation president, sent a letter to legislators urging the bill's passage: "The bill has to be viewed in the context of the pending initiative," which, he argued, would have been much worse.

Some Republican legislators feared the bill would not reduce costs enough. Two Schwarzenegger allies, assemblymen Keith Richman and Abel Maldonado, privately urged the initiative backers to file the signatures and qualify the measure anyway. Joel Fox and the Carrot People decided not to. But they did instruct Mike Arno, whose company had overseen the paid signature gathering, to hold onto the signatures as insurance. If Democrats tried to back away from the deal, the signatures could be filed and the initiative would appear on the ballot at the next election after November 2004. The workers' comp signatures would remain stacked inside Arno's loading dock until August.

As the Senate voted for the measure thirty-three to three, Schwarzenegger sat alone in his office, catching up on paperwork. He signed official letters and autographs that had been requested by voters and movie fans. With signatures, one could do anything.

SCHWARZENEGGER SIGNED THE BILL itself the following Monday, April 19, in an elaborate ceremony at a Boeing manufacturing facility in Long Beach. The governor's team wanted to put on a show that would awe legislators and encourage them to make more deals with Schwarzenegger. More than 2,700 people filled bleachers in front of a stage, which had been set up in front of a C–17 military cargo plane. The governor himself put together much of the staging.

Schwarzenegger had pushed an extremely complicated, politically explosive bill through the legislature quickly, even though a majority of the lawmakers had not seen a need for it. He had gotten labor to engage in extensive bargaining for a piece of legislation the unions could have done without. And by threatening the initiative and campaigning for signatures outside the capitol, Schwarzenegger found that he could control the details of the legislation.

At first, workers' comp seemed to be the type of complicated, technical issue that would elude a novice governor. But it was the perfect subject for Schwarzenegger. He enjoyed working out multifaceted equations, whether they appeared in the movie contracts he negotiated or the chess games he played. The governor also had the advantage of having studied workers' comp more thoroughly—and more recently, from his days at Schwarzenegger University—than the legislators with whom he negotiated. And he had been learning about the human body and how it ached and grew and was injured since he was a teenage bodybuilder.

SCHWARZENEGGER'S VICTORY WAS so complete that, paradoxically, he may have won too much. With the initiative and the Carrot People at his back, he had an enormous advantage that he had exploited. The governor delivered for employers. By 2006, the premiums paid for workers' comp insurance would fall to half of what they were at the beginning of the recall, and California would no longer have the highest workers' comp costs in the country. The insurance companies had won, too. There would be no rate regulation in the deal. But for labor, the deal was a mixed bag. The unions had secured higher benefits for injured workers who didn't get their jobs back, but the bill put more of the burden on employees for pre-existing injuries. The bill loosened the requirement that courts "liberally construe" workers' comp cases to favor the employee. (This was the provision that had meant so much to John Burton and his late brother.) These changes helped reduce costs and some of the incentives for fraud, but labor leaders felt they had been bullied and hurried into accepting them. The unions would be reluctant to make deals with Schwarzenegger again.

Workers' comp had been a hasty production, rushed by a deadline imposed by the calendar of ballot initiatives. The bill was full of technical errors that needed cleaning up and was vague on other key points, including how awards for workers permanently disabled on the job would be determined. Regulators in Schwarzenegger's administration used the ambiguity of the bill to draft regulations that contributed to a reduction of about 50 percent in the average payments to permanently disabled workers. That result would leave Burton feeling betrayed. "I believe I was fucked in workers' comp," he would later say.

Schwarzenegger's victory left him with an outsized view of his own power and raised his own expectations for the future. He would try to replicate his workers' comp strategy on a number of issues. While the governor saw himself as a fighter against special interests, his method of using ballot initiatives to pressure the legislature required him to grant considerable power to interest groups. He had brought the labor and business groups directly into the process through the Five and Five meetings. Simply by sponsoring a ballot initiative, the Carrot People had found themselves in the position of vetting language in the bill. And the costs of signature gathering required Schwarzenegger to raise and spend more than $6.4 million through the California Recovery Team and a separate workers' comp committee.

As a candidate, Schwarzenegger had railed against backroom deals and said there was "no such thing as democracy in the dark." But the workers' comp bill had been put together behind closed doors. The one public hearing on the legislation took place in the middle of the night. Schwarzenegger acknowledged the problem but said there was no other way. "We had to make decisions very quickly," he said.

None of these drawbacks would stop him from prodding the legislature with ballot initiatives in the future.

"It's kind of the carrot-and-stick method," he said. "I like the idea of using the stick."

CHAPTER 15

All Politics Is "Girlie Men"

By LUNCHTIME ON JULY 17, more than one thousand people had squeezed into the Ontario Mills Mall food court. Signs that read "Taxes" and "Special Interests"—with lines drawn through them—hung from the ceiling around the stage. The noise of the crowd echoed off the walls.

Ontario Mills, billed as the largest one-story mall west of the Mississippi, sat near the intersection of Interstates 10 and 15 in the growing suburban city of Ontario, thirty miles east of Los Angeles. The mall was a natural spot for a Schwarzenegger rally. It had two different movie theaters, was easy to find, and was located in a legislative district where the recall had won overwhelmingly.

The Schwarzenegger who appeared on stage at Ontario Mills was the political counterpart of the avenging characters he played in the movies. The governor talked about the cooperation he had gotten from lawmakers on Propositions 57 and 58 and on workers' compensation. But three months later, he said with a note of sadness, "all of a sudden we're at a standstill."

With that, he lit into the state legislators. They were selling out to unions. They were selling out to special interests. He threatened to campaign against those who opposed him. "I'm going now to pronounce each and every one of you as an official terminator," he shouted to the crowd. "Because I want you, I want each and every one of you to go to the polls in November, on November 2 when it is Election Day. That will be Judgment Day." The words "Judgment Day" echoed.

The governor had a speech in front of him, but he was freelancing, playing to the raucous crowd. His frustration came pouring out. "The legislators are playing games right now in Sacramento. We want action, not games. We want action, not the dialogue. We want action, not the promises. We want action and not the lies that are up there in Sacramento continuously. You all, all of you, sent me to Sacramento to represent the people of California and to fight for you and I can guarantee you, I am your warrior."

He spoke faster and faster, so quickly that it became hard to hear the details of his grievances. Finally, he uttered what became the most famous line of his early political career.

"I demand that the legislators go back to the table and start working on the budget and pass my budget," he said. "If they don't have the guts, I call them girlie men!"

The roar was loud enough to be heard in Rancho Cucamonga. Schwarzenegger did not immediately recognize "girlie men" as a mistake. In the aftermath, he would get a resolution to the immediate contest he faced in Sacramento. But what the governor didn't understand amid the cheers was how the phrase would come to define him as a politician. The speech at Ontario Mills Mall was not the beginning of the end, but it was the conclusion to one phase of the governor's use of direct democracy. "Girlie men" marked the end of Schwarzenegger's beginning.

THE TROUBLE HAD STARTED THREE months earlier, on April 16, the very day the legislature approved workers' comp legislation to head off his threat to qualify a ballot initiative. The governor had used the April 16 ballot deadline to force the deal. Hours later, the local governments of the state were using the same deadline to pressure him.

That afternoon, Schwarzenegger jumped on a phone call with an audience of mayors and city councilmen meeting four hundred miles to the south in Riverside.

"I'm with you," the governor said over the phone.

Lobbying groups for the cities, the counties, and special local government districts of California had collected enough signatures to qualify an initiative to restrict the state's ability to tamper with their funding streams. Since the 1970s, when court decisions and Prop 13 combined to rob California localities of the power to raise their own taxes, cities and counties had depended on the state for most of their budgets. They were subject to the whims of legislators and governors. The initiative was an attempt to end that uncertainty and lock in a certain level of funding for local government. If the state wanted to take away money that would otherwise support local government, the voters would have to approve the transfer.

This initiative, which would be numbered Prop 65, put Schwarzenegger in a difficult spot. The governor saw himself as a champion of local government. Behind the scenes, he had been talking about reforms similar to Prop 65 since the transition. Former Democratic Assembly Speaker Bob Hertzberg, with whom the governor conducted many of these conversations, had put together a ballot initiative that would protect local funds and change local funding formulas to de-emphasize sales taxes and thus reduce the competition among cities to build sprawling retail developments.

But Schwarzenegger was counting on making one last state raid on local government funding to reduce the budget deficit. Prop 65, if passed by the voters in November, would prevent that. Even though the passage of Prop 57 would allow the state to pay off its short-term debt, California still faced a structural deficit of $15 billion. (The state was scheduled to spend $90.5 billion in 2004–05 while revenues were projected to reach just $75.4 billion.) Schwarzenegger had few good options. On his conference call with the cities, he had to find a way to make Prop 65 go away.

YOUR INITIATIVE IS TERRIFIC, the governor began. He said he respected anyone who had a good idea and qualified it for the ballot. Without such people, he himself wouldn't be in office.

Forget about your initiative, Schwarzenegger declared. Work with me. We'll draft a ballot measure together to protect local government funds. It would be too late to gather signatures for the November ballot, but the legislature could still add measures to the ballot as late as August. Schwarzenegger said that he would negotiate the terms of a ballot measure with the local governments and then work to convince the legislature to put it on the ballot. All he needed in return was for the locals to agree to a "haircut," one last raid to help the governor fix the budget deficit.

It was an interesting offer: money up front from the locals in return for Schwarzenegger's support of a ballot measure to prevent future raids. The governor, hearing hesitation on the line, offered a little bit extra. "I'll campaign for the measure," he pledged, "just like I did for 57 and 58."

One gubernatorial staffer grimaced at the boss's pledge. His push for 57 and 58 had been an exhausting six-week sprint.

The local officials on the phone seemed a bit overwhelmed. They had already filed their signatures earlier in the day. Prop 65 would be on the ballot one way or another. But that did not end their interest in a deal. The next day, the cities decided to enter negotiations with the governor to design an alternative measure to their own Prop 65. The counties and a variety of other local bodies, including redevelopment agencies, would take part as well.

Schwarzenegger had bought himself a new set of talks, and a new headache. By linking a new ballot measure with a "haircut" for local government, the governor was further complicating one of the most difficult budget negotiations in memory. Now he would have to get the legislature to pass a budget—never easy in California, which required a two-thirds vote—and convince lawmakers to put the local government alternative measure on the ballot, too. John Burton, the Democratic senate leader, would later ask, "What the fuck is he doing?" Less profane versions of the sentiment would be heard around the capitol. Some of his own aides wondered why Schwarzenegger didn't simply oppose Proposition 65. It would be difficult for the locals to pass such an initiative against opposition from a popular governor.

But the governor thought of the situation differently. He agreed strongly with the policy of protecting local government. And he felt far more comfortable with ballot measures than most of his advisors did. It was not merely his election in the recall, or his successes with Propositions 49, 57, and 58, that led him to embrace the ballot. Schwarzenegger believed his outsider status allowed him to confront thorny problems. When the people around him expressed surprise at his tactics, he sometimes took their disapproval as a sign he was on the right path.

AFTER SIX MONTHS IN OFFICE, Schwarzenegger had developed a routine that was all his own. He insisted on keeping his official schedule flexible and resisted efforts to put meetings or events on his calendar more than a few days in advance. "It's important to keep things organic," Schwarzenegger said, "so you can react and respond as things change. I don't like to keep schedules. I have an improvisational style."

This approach had advantages. When Barbara Kerr, the president of the CTA, sent a message one morning in late April that she was unhappy about something, Schwarzenegger called her up within two hours and invited her to lunch that day. But the flexible scheduling presented plenty of headaches for his staff, who found it difficult to put together meetings and speeches in advance. And Schwarzenegger could be impatient when made to wait. "I'm the action governor," he sometimes complained to aides.

He spent nearly half his days on the stump, campaigning for one measure or another. While traveling, he had certain rituals, among them the daily stop at Starbucks for a macchiato, a tea, or a pastry. He went around the state by private plane; he owned a share in a plane, which entitled him to a certain amount of time in a Gulfstream jet or, when his traveling party was smaller, a Hawker. Since the state reimbursed governors for travel only at the rate charged by Southwest Airlines for its flights from LAX to Sacramento, the governor—or his collection of political committees—had to pay for the travel.

Schwarzenegger chose not to accept his salary as governor. He has declined to disclose his net worth, though public reports suggest the number is at least $100 million and probably far greater. His tax returns showed income of more than $13.8 million in 2003 and more than $16.7 million in 2004. But his investment advisor privately expressed concern about the spending required to maintain his movie-star lifestyle. In becoming governor, he had not only forfeited the cash flow of movie paydays, but also had put millions of his own money into his campaigns.

Most weeks, the governor spent Monday, Tuesday, and Wednesday nights in Sacramento, working out of the capitol through Thursday afternoon before flying home to Los Angeles. He often worked from his Oak Productions office on Fridays. He would wake up around six, read news summaries, and ride an exercise bicycle for forty-five minutes. His time on the stationary bike was an opportune moment for aides and friends to get his attention, either by calling or sending a fax so he could read as he pedaled. After breakfast, he would arrive in the office around nine and work until about 1, when he made a point of leaving the office for lunch. A creature of habit, Schwarzenegger often went to the lobbyist ghetto Esquire Grill, two blocks from the capitol, or Lucca Restaurant & Bar on J Street, where he sat at an outdoor table.

Schwarzenegger would be back in the office by two and work until around seven. After that, he liked to go to a public gym near the capitol for his second workout of the day. Fellow hardbodies reported that the governor had the same intense stare familiar from the movie *Pumping Iron*, but used much lighter weights. From there, he went out to dinner or ordered room service at the Hyatt. The governor occupied a two-thousand-square foot suite that included a living room, a dining room, TV lounge, a kitchen, a hot tub, and two bedrooms. He had spent months at a time living in hotels while filming movies, so the Hyatt felt familiar except for one thing: the studio was not paying. For his first year in office, campaign donors could pick up the tab. (After that, the newly formed Governor's Residence Foundation would help Schwarzenegger with the bills.) With a negotiated discount, the hotel bill ended up being about $6,000 per month. That was a good deal, but the entire arrangement added to the unsettled, campaign-style feel of his governorship.

Clay Russell, Schwarzenegger's personal assistant, provided some stability. He had worked for the Schwarzenegger family before the governorship. In politics, most such "body men" were twentysomethings aspiring to political careers, but Russell was a professional chef who had not worked in politics and cultivated a wry detachment from the hubbub around him. An openly gay man who wore a wedding ring and lived with his partner in Los Angeles, Russell was a registered Democrat. He answered the governor's cell phones, wrote thank-you notes, copied his speeches onto note cards, and served as a test audience for gubernatorial jokes. When Schwarzenegger was in Sacramento, Russell stayed in the other bedroom in the Hyatt suite. No aide spent more time with the governor.

Russell was part of an entourage of familiar faces around Schwarzenegger. The governor invited friends from his earlier careers, including the director Ivan Reitman and the producer A. C. Lyles, to shadow him for a day. His executive assistant from Oak Productions and a publicist who handled promotion of his movies followed him into government. His dialogue coach Walter von Huene joined him on the road, as did his movie stand-in Dieter Rauter, a native Styrian who also served as Schwarzenegger's personal videographer.

Schwarzenegger kept in touch with old friends, attending cigar nights at Schatzi's and stopping by his longtime haunt Caffe Roma in Beverly Hills. Early on many Sunday mornings, he and a group of friends, including the director James Cameron, rode motorcycles up the Pacific Coast Highway. (The governor never had the proper license to drive a motorcycle in California, but that fact was not disclosed until after he had an accident while riding in 2006.)

Maria Shriver served not only as first lady but as political consultant, companion, and foil. While Schwarzenegger sometimes forgot people's names, she made a point of thanking staff and even calling the spouses of aides whose work hours ran long. She had her own office in the Horseshoe, decorated with pictures of her children. Although Shriver spent only a day or so a week in Sacramento, Pat Clarey, the chief of staff, tried to brief her ahead of time on major announcements.

Shriver played to her strengths as a journalist. She made suggestions on communications plans in meetings with the political team and worked the phones to come up with names for appointments. When former Secretary of State George Shultz wanted the governor to hire someone, or when legislative Democrats needed a favor, they called Shriver. (Her uncle, Senator Edward Kennedy of Massachusetts, sent along jokes Schwarzenegger sometimes used on the stump.)

For Schwarzenegger, the most difficult part of life in office was being away from his four children—two teenage girls and two younger boys—on so many nights. Shriver established a "hotline," a special phone number to his Sacramento office that his children could use.

At work or on the road, Schwarzenegger spent downtime playing chess, often with von Huene, his coach and friend. The two played so often that Franco Columbu, the former bodybuilding champion and longtime Schwarzenegger friend, was moved to ask: Are you guys working in Sacramento or just playing chess?

SCHWARZENEGGER'S CHESS GAME WITH LOCAL government soon brought results. On May 12, three weeks after his call to the League of California

Cities board, Schwarzenegger's staff and local government representatives formally announced an agreement on both a budget haircut and a ballot measure that could be an alternative to Prop 65. Financially, it was a compromise. Schwarzenegger had wanted the local governments to agree to give up $1.3 billion in funds each of the next three years. The locals had wanted only one year of givebacks. The deal was $1.3 billion a year for two years. In exchange, the alternative ballot measure would protect locals from future state raids on their funds. The legislature, however, had to agree to put the measure on the ballot.

One facet of the deal made it novel in the history of California direct democracy. Schwarzenegger had convinced interest groups—in this case the cities and counties—to agree to campaign against their own measure, Prop 65, in favor of the new alternative measure that would appear on the same ballot. The local governments' coalition had spent two years and more than $3 million getting Prop 65 drafted and qualified for the ballot. The deal demonstrated once again the value of Schwarzenegger's celebrity and strength at the ballot box. The cities and counties were willing to give up billions in funding and their own initiative for the opportunity to have Schwarzenegger lead a campaign for their cause.

In his haste to put together an agreement to meet the timelines of budget and ballot, the governor missed an opportunity for deeper reform in local government finance. In particular, Schwarzenegger could have granted cities more control over their property tax revenues and thus encouraged home building and reduced incentives to build sprawling retail developments.

Even after the announcement of the haircut and the new ballot measure, a number of people friendly with Schwarzenegger, including Democrats (Hertzberg and the assembly budget chairman Darrell Steinberg) and Republicans (Anaheim Mayor Curt Pringle and Assemblyman John Campbell) urged the governor to add that reform to the alternative ballot measure. They won the support of the counties. But the cities were split. About four dozen cities objected because they had prospered under the current rules by building huge sales-tax bases.

Schwarzenegger supported the reform in principle. But as the controversy over the property and sales tax issue grew, he expressed concern that the growing divide among the cities could threaten his own deal. Rather than push for sales tax and property tax reform, the governor quietly asked aides to shut down the reformers.

"We felt it was a terrible opportunity missed," John Campbell, the Republican assemblyman, said. "Cities and counties wanted protection; this was the time to use that and get some reform."

SCHWARZENEGGER HAD SAVED MONEY by making deals with local government and the CTA, but those agreements would not be enough to close the budget gap. Although Schwarzenegger portrayed himself as a staunch opponent of tax hikes, in early May his pollster John McLaughlin looked at all budget options, including a tax increase.

Seventy-one percent of voters in McLaughlin's survey believed the governor generally kept his promises, and 59 percent knew that he had promised not to raise taxes. Both items were at the very foundation of his popularity. But some taxes were popular, too. McLaughlin tested the idea of raising $1.5 billion by creating a 5 percent personal income tax surcharge on Californians who earned more than $250,000 a year. Sixty-four percent supported such a move. The poll asked about raising the highest state income tax rate from 9 percent to 10 percent on Californians making $100,000 a year or more. Fifty-five percent backed the idea. And McLaughlin found that a twenty-five-cent-per-pack increase in the cigarette tax had the support of 69 percent of those surveyed. Increasing the state sales tax from 7.25 percent to 8.25 percent drew support from 52 percent of those surveyed.

McLaughlin polled not only on the popularity of tax increases but also on the effect tax increases would have on Schwarzenegger's standing. Voters were of two minds. A tax increase would be seen as a broken promise, but most voters preferred a tax increase to spending cuts, and half of the public believed the only way to balance the state budget was by raising taxes. At first glance, that looked like an opening for a tax increase, but McLaughlin found few voters were willing to pay higher taxes themselves. And the only spending cuts with any popularity were freezing state workers' salaries and cutting welfare payments to people who did not find a job within five years. Neither would produce enough savings to close the deficit.

All of the governor's options came with risks. About a third of the public was concerned that Schwarzenegger seemed too eager to make deals with Democrats. Another 37 percent of the public felt he had a tendency to be "too rigid in demanding his own way on policy questions." If he were to stage a public fight with Democrats, any fallout would hurt Schwarzenegger because his potential opponents in such a battle were virtual unknowns to Californians, the vast majority of whom did not closely follow state affairs. Two-thirds of state residents had no opinion of John Burton, an important figure in California politics for forty years.

In light of these poll results, Schwarzenegger's current budget strategy— campaigning in public while seeking deals and accommodations with interest groups in private—seemed as wise a course as any. He reached a funding agreement with the University of California and California State University systems under which those institutions agreed to take a cut of $1 billion in state aid in return for a promise of steady, predictable growth in funding for research, faculty salaries, and student enrollment in future years. Legislators, accustomed to scoring points by riding to the rescue of higher education, howled in protest. "The governor is trying to make the legislature meaning-less," said state Senator Jackie Speier, a Democrat from Hillsborough, on the San Francisco peninsula.

Schwarzenegger was far more involved in negotiating the details of the budget than many of his predecessors had been. Staffers would go out to work on budget issues at the beginning of the day and then circle back to Schwarzenegger, who would decide which legislators to bring in for private talks. The governor also had press aides patrol the hallways outside his office and listen in on reporters' interviews with lawmakers on their way in to see him. The aides e-mailed accounts of the conversations by Blackberry to staffers inside the Horseshoe so Schwarzenegger would know what legisla-tors were going to say before they arrived.

Some of his own aides thought that Schwarzenegger, by involving himself so directly, had a tendency to give too much away in talks with lawmakers. He dropped a proposal on welfare reform and restored money to health care and other programs he had proposed to cut.

To balance the budget, the governor turned to the kind of gimmicks and one-time fixes that he had once criticized as "special effects." He used a bond to push pension costs into the future. Without good reason, he as-sumed that more federal funds would come to the state. Throughout the process, his finance director kept a chart with two columns, one for reforms enacted and another for opportunities missed. The column of opportunities missed was longer.

THE GOVERNOR WANTED A BUDGET passed on time, before the start of the new fiscal year on July 1. He had done so much deal-making with interest groups and compromised so significantly on spending that he expected the Democratic majority to move quickly. Instead, Democrats stalled. On June 17, Schwarzenegger scheduled a speech at a mall in Chico, north of Sacra-mento, to press the legislature for action. There he bungled the name of the town, calling it "Chino," a Southern California suburb. The slip took much of the energy out of the crowd. A few days later, he complained of the legis-lators, "We cannot just hang. As I've said, I'm an action guy, I want to have action now. And if it means that we have to work during this weekend, stay here this weekend . . . work day and night, it makes no difference to me."

By the last weekend in June, budget negotiations gathered momentum. But it was Schwarzenegger's local government ballot measure that proved to be the key stumbling block. As irascible as he was, John Burton was a veteran dealmaker who wanted to reach an agreement and get out of town for the summer recess. The new Assembly Speaker Fabian Núñez, a former amateur boxer who was the leader of the far more liberal assembly majority, took a more pugnacious approach.

BECAUSE OF AN INITIATIVE PASSED IN 1990, assembly members were limited to three two-year terms. Legislators ran for leadership posts in their very first term so they could spend at least four years in charge. Núñez had won election as speaker at the end of his first year in office. The new speaker, while only thirty-six at the time, was a political pro who had come out of California's powerful labor movement. As political director for the Los Angeles County Federation of Labor, Núñez worked on the campaigns for as well as against several statewide ballot initiatives. He was known for organizing rallies in 1994 against Prop 187, which would have denied public services to undocumented immigrants. Those protests backfired because many of the participants waved Mexican flags, thus fueling the same fears about immigrants' loyalties that sparked the ballot initiative in the first place.

Núñez, like Schwarzenegger, used mixed messages. He talked of the need for the governor to be bipartisan, but did not always meet that standard himself. The previous summer, Núñez and a handful of other assembly Democrats had made plans to stall in responding to the state's budget crisis in order to make it easier to raise taxes. The lawmakers had not realized an intercom in the meeting room was on, and the exchange was broadcast around the capitol. Shortly after he became speaker, he gave an interview to a Mexico City paper in which he was quoted as saying in Spanish, "I have already personally declared war on Schwarzenegger." That was a natural sentiment for Mexico, where Schwarzenegger's opposition to driver's licenses for undocumented immigrants had hurt his popularity. In Sacramento, Núñez denied he'd ever said it.

Schwarzenegger, as was his habit with opponents, did his best to charm Núñez. When the new speaker was sworn in, the governor made a point of taking pictures with Núñez's entire family. During the Prop 57 and 58 campaign, the governor rearranged his schedule to attend a new gymnasium opening at the school attended by Núñez's daughter in Pomona.

Publicly, Núñez praised Schwarzenegger. Behind the scenes, he pressed Schwarzenegger hard and found the governor responded to pressure. Schwarzenegger put more money into higher education than the governor's deal with the universities required after Núñez and his caucus championed such a move. He pushed to close a loophole that allowed yacht owners to avoid taxes. The morning Núñez was prepared to drop the subject, Schwarzenegger agreed to it.

As the governor agreed to more Democratic demands, Republicans grew angry. One Republican lawmaker claimed the governor was treating his own party like a "potted plant." On Saturday, June 26, legislative Republicans began an effort to slow down the budget talks out of fear that in his rush to get an agreement on time, the governor was giving too much away.

Nevertheless, by Thursday, July 1, the governor appeared to have a budget deal. The last piece to be negotiated was the alternative ballot measure to protect local government funding. Núñez demanded a number of changes to the agreement Schwarzenegger had reached with the cities and counties. Local government would have some protection from state raids, but Núñez wanted the legislature, with a two-thirds vote, to be able to take that money back. The powerful CTA made plain it would oppose the measure if the local governments received greater protection than that provided to the schools by Prop 98, the education funding guarantee, which also could be suspended by a two-thirds vote.

AT 5:45 P.M. that Thursday, Schwarzenegger joined a conference call with League of California Cities officials, including the mayors of many of California's largest municipalities. Schwarzenegger acknowledged that the alternative ballot measure was no longer what he and the local governments had agreed upon. But he said it was the "best he could do" with the Democrats and that an agreement on the ballot measure would close the budget. The mayors thanked Schwarzenegger for championing the local government cause, but made their doubts plain. Fresno Mayor Alan Autry, like Schwarzenegger a Republican-actor-turned-politician (he played Sergeant Bubba Skinner on TV's *In the Heat of the Night*), advised the governor to tell Democrats, Burton in particular, to "kiss my ass." Schwarzenegger listened, thanked them, and asked everyone to "think about it" and give him an answer the next morning, when the state senate would take up the bill.

The governor would get his answer later that night. Since the state budget already required a two-thirds vote, city officials argued that the alternative measure didn't give any additional protection. By 7:30 p.m., the cities and counties had convened their own conference call to plot strategies to stop the compromise.

Schwarzenegger had reached two agreements on the same ballot measure: the first with the locals in May, the second with legislative Democrats. City and county leaders, feeling double-crossed, flooded lawmakers' e-mail in-boxes with messages and planned to fill the capitol Friday morning with po-lice officers and firefighters. Democrats angrily insisted they had a deal with Schwarzenegger and that the budget negotiations were over. And the Republi-cans had a new reason to slow down their own governor's budget. Before Schwarzenegger returned to the Hyatt for the night, the new senate Republi-can leader Dick Ackerman of Irvine and Assembly Minority Leader Kevin McCarthy marched into the governor's office to declare they would only ac-cept the original deal with local governments.

When city and county representatives told Schwarzenegger early Friday they could not support his deal, the governor replied, "Well, I'm going to be with you all the way. You are my partners." Before the morning was out, Schwarzenegger had pivoted away from the alternative measure he'd negoti-ated with Núñez and back to the original bargain he had struck with the lo-calities. The speaker was furious. In a phone conversation, Núñez asked the governor why he had flip-flopped.

I don't flip-flop, came the icy reply.

The governor asked Núñez to allow a floor vote on Schwarzenegger's original agreement with the locals. The speaker refused.

Suspicious that the Republicans were plotting something, Núñez called two of his top lieutenants and asked them to see if the Republicans were at-tempting to put the original local deal up for a vote. The Republicans were. At the same time, Núñez received an invitation to see Schwarzenegger in his office. Before Núñez went downstairs to the Horseshoe, he asked assembly-man Dario Frommer to quietly get the Democrats to the assembly floor. Once everyone is there, Núñez instructed, gavel the assembly to a close and adjourn. That would block any attempt by Republicans to get a vote on the original local government deal. While Núñez sat talking with Schwarzeneg-ger in his office, Frommer carried out the plan. Republicans, hearing that the assembly was being shut down, rushed to the floor but were too late.

As Núñez and Schwarzenegger talked in the governor's office, McCarthy, the assembly Republican leader, walked in and snapped at Núñez: "This is chicken shit. You shut down the assembly."

Núñez blasted back. "What are you saying, Mr. Indignant?" the speaker asked. "You're trying to jam us with a deal when we haven't finished negotiat-ing this thing." The governor, caught between these two angry, younger men, stayed quiet. McCarthy left, and Schwarzenegger tried to calm Núñez.

The governor would not get a vote on the original local government deal. Democrats announced the assembly would stay shut down until there was an agreement on the entire budget.

THE DEMOCRATS WOULD ARGUE THAT THE governor crossed a partisan Rubicon on that Friday afternoon, July 2. They felt he should have told Republicans, the cities, and the counties to accept the alternative ballot measure Núñez had negotiated. Schwarzenegger already had won plenty of victories. Even with a massive deficit, the governor in his first eight months in office had cut the car tax, reformed workers' comp, and secured a budget without a tax increase. In the Democratic view, it was greedy for the governor to demand his original deal on local government, too.

In truth, Schwarzenegger was frustrated with both Democrats and Republicans, whom he saw as more interested in fighting than in cooperating on the big changes the state needed. "What's this about?" Schwarzenegger recalled thinking. "Republicans are all of a sudden for local government? It's mostly Democrats in local government. There was a line drawn." But the lines made no sense to him. Did either side really mean what it said? They were behaving, in Schwarzenegger's favorite insult, like a bunch of foreheads.[1]

SCHWARZENEGGER'S MISTAKE was not one of partisanship, but of process. On the local government deal, he had reached two different understandings with two different partners, and each was understandably upset. The governor was equally disappointed. After all the concessions he had made to lawmakers and all the cigars handed out, he still could not get the legislature to address serious issues and pass a budget on time. If lawmakers would not set aside their differences in the aftermath of a recall and in the midst of a budget crisis, when would they ever behave responsibly? The legislative behavior hardened his attitude towards lawmakers and further confirmed the wisdom of governing through direct democracy.

"I never walked away from the negotiating table," he said later. "It was them who walked away from the negotiating table. I am an action governor."

What was his next move? He could have used the various levers of gubernatorial power to force both sides back to the table. For decades, California governors—who have the line-item veto—had threatened legislators with the veto of money for their districts in order to win votes for the budget. Schwarzenegger could have done extensive horse trading, offering to sign

---

[1]Schwarzenegger once explained the term. "You know how gorillas, the hairline goes down to the eyes? It means they have no forehead. So you know, the hairline, the lower it goes, the idea is the less intelligence and brain you have. I just say forehead rather than low forehead. I don't want to offend anyone. It's just a saying. It's a way to say to anyone, 'Hey, you're saying something stupid. Hey, forehead.'"

bills on legislative priorities in return for support on the local government measure he wanted. He could have threatened to withhold political support from recalcitrant Republicans.

In this moment, he did not use any of these levers of power. Instinctively, he did what he would do nearly every time his governorship hit rough water. He went to the people.

LESS THAN TWENTY-FOUR HOURS LATER, Schwarzenegger stood behind a microphone in the rear of a huge fire station in the San Fernando Valley. In this very same facility, just off Sepulveda Boulevard in Sherman Oaks, he had filmed scenes for the movie *Collateral Damage*. Seven TV cameras had shown up on a hot Saturday morning, July 3. "We are all here today calling on the legislators, and to tell them to go back to Sacramento and to vote for our local government agreement so that the people have their budget," he said. Afterwards, Schwarzenegger flew to Fresno, where he gave the same speech at a police facility there.

Núñez's response was harsh. What was Schwarzenegger doing campaigning when the budget was not done? "He flip-flopped on local government and now he wants to put the onus on the legislature," the speaker said. "I think there has to be a level of respect for the balance of powers. We are not on a movie set here."

Schwarzenegger did not agree. Campaigning two days later, July 5, in the town of Dixon west of Sacramento, the governor encountered a five-year-old girl, Ashley Everett, at the Chevy's Fresh Mex restaurant.

"You are the kindergarten cop!" she squealed as the governor passed.

"I am the kindergarten cop," Schwarzenegger replied. "And you know something, nothing changed because that's what I am in the capitol still. I have 120 children." There are eighty assembly members and forty senators.

SCHWARZENEGGER SPENT THE REST of that work week in meetings in Sacramento, trying to restart talks on local government. Los Angeles Mayor James Hahn and Fresno Mayor Alan Autry had been appointed to represent the cities in the capitol, and Autry, the former TV actor, sat in the smoking tent with Schwarzenegger. "It was an alternative universe, the Terminator and Bubba, to shape the future of the state," Autry recalled.

Schwarzenegger's longtime friend, Austrian president Thomas Klestil, an Austrian People's Party member whose campaigns he had endorsed, died that week, and President Bush sent the governor to Vienna to represent the United States at the funeral. Schwarzenegger flew all night Friday to get there in time for the Saturday morning Mass. After sitting near Vladimir

Putin at the service and walking in the burial procession, Schwarzenegger stopped by the apartment of the ailing Simon Wiesenthal. He and his aides then drove the two hours over the Semmering into his native Styria. They would spend the night in Graz, the provincial capital.

Standing in the city where he went to school, where he trained, his frustration spilled out. "There is a certain arrogance among the legislators, certain kinds of legislators in Sacramento, that they feel like they can run the cities and the counties better," he told me in the lobby of his hotel.

That night, the governor walked through the rainy streets, pausing in front of the Graz city hall on his way to dinner with friends at a restaurant under the city's Glockenspiel. He loved the old part of the town, and pointed to his favorite stores and hangouts. At the restaurant, he was joined by old friends, including Alfred Gerstl, his early mentor who had grown up to lead the upper house of the Austrian Parliament.

The next morning, Gerstl drove the governor over to the Burg, the office of the provincial governor, Valtraud Klausnic. Among the welcoming party was former Styrian governor Josef Krainer, with whom Schwarzenegger had long discussed politics. The three Austrian governors—Klausnic, Krainer, and Schwarzenegger—commiserated about dealing with lawmakers.

"I am giving him tips on the budget tonight," Krainer joked.

Schwarzenegger jumped at the offer. "You know, if I have a problem, he's going to come over and he's going to give me some insights."

"He doesn't need any," Krainer quickly replied. "Arnold has been learning for a long time."

THE GOVERNOR, STILL FULL OF FIGHT, flew back to California from Austria on Sunday afternoon. Schwarzenegger and legislative leaders continued to bargain, but the talks soon bogged down again. Republican legislators insisted on revisiting issues that had little to do with local government or the budget. They demanded that the Democrats agree to repeal the state's "sue your boss" law, which allowed workers to sue employers over labor code violations even if they weren't impacted by them. Republicans also called for the repeal of a legal prohibition on contracting out school services. Schwarzenegger agreed with the Republicans on both policy changes, and soon adopted their demands as his own.

The fights over these side issues obscured the lack of progress on local government. The legislators appeared willing to take a $1.3 billion haircut from the locals and give nothing in return. A few of Schwarzenegger's own aides, fearing a prolonged fight would hurt the governor, agreed. Why risk popularity and political capital on this of all issues?

But Schwarzenegger had made a promise to the locals and was determined to honor it. With talks at a standstill on July 15, he marched into capitol room 1190, the stage for official press conferences, and declared he would return to the campaign trail to demand a local government ballot measure. He pledged to "fight like a warrior for the people of California . . . There is no one that can stop me. Anyone who pushes me around, I will push back."

Núñez led the counterattack. He avoided blaming the governor directly, but instead blasted the Republican legislators. "Arnie's Army isn't Arnie's Army because the last time I checked, the privates follow the captain," the speaker said. Schwarzenegger didn't appreciate those comments. He reached Núñez on his cell phone and loudly accused the speaker of holding up the local government ballot measure and the budget. Núñez laughed in response and urged the governor to calm down. Schwarzenegger responded that he would campaign publicly for the local government deal—and go after Democrats in the assembly who opposed him. The people are going to be with me, the governor told the speaker.

The threat surprised Núñez. Getting involved in legislative races seemed like poor strategy for Schwarzenegger because there was so little to be gained. California's legislative and congressional districts were so thoroughly gerrymandered that removing an incumbent of either party from office was nearly impossible. And by engaging in partisan challenges to legislators whom most Californians could not pick out of a police line-up, the larger-than-life governor would be stooping to their level. At the same time, the governor's popularity was such that the mere rumor of a Schwarzenegger threat unnerved the handful of moderate Democrats who represented the few districts that could be considered even remotely in play. With his threat, Schwarzenegger drove the moderate legislators who were most likely to support him on key votes into the arms of the speaker.

IT WAS TWO DAYS AFTER HIS PHONE CALL with Núñez that Schwarzenegger went to the Ontario Mills Mall and gave his "girlie men" speech. The governor would say afterwards that the line had been a joke that he had used for years in promoting his movies. The phrase had originated with the old *Saturday Night Live* skit "Hans and Franz," in which the comedians Dana Carvey and Kevin Nealon played Austrian-accented bodybuilders who called anyone without huge muscles "girlie man." Schwarzenegger himself had appeared in one of the sketches.

But in the midst of a high-profile budget fight, the phrase had costs. Democratic lawmakers claimed that the "girlie men" jibe was sexist and homophobic, and it gave them an opening to argue that the governor was engaged in name-calling, not negotiating. "This is offensive for women," Senator Gloria Romero, a Los Angeles Democrat, told the *Sacramento Bee*. "It is offensive to gays and lesbians in the legislature because of the way that term historically has been applied." Núñez said his thirteen-year-old daughter was offended by it. "It's like we're replaying all his movies again here," the speaker said. "We've got to get back to Sacramento and sit down and negotiate a budget."

At least one Democrat, Burton, played the comment for laughs. He placed a "closed until further notice" sign on the espresso machine he used to make coffee when Schwarzenegger visited his office. Republicans generally loved the "girlie men" line and, after the speech, entrepreneurs scrambled to make T-shirts and bumper stickers with the phrase. The *Wall Street Journal* quickly offered a supportive op-ed. Reporters asked Schwarzenegger if he would apologize. He wouldn't. "Sometimes the jokes get me into trouble, sometimes not," he would say.

"GIRLIE-MEN" WAS THE LAST LOUD SHOUT of the budget battle. The resulting attention seemed to push all sides towards a resolution. Two days later, on Tuesday, July 20, Schwarzenegger had Reiss invite Núñez to resume negotiations. By Friday, the governor and Núñez had reached another compromise on the local government measure. The state could still raid city and county funds with a two-thirds vote of the legislature, but such raids could occur only twice every ten years. And any money taken by the state had to be paid back entirely, with interest, within three years.

It fell short of the protection Schwarzenegger had been willing to grant local governments. Some mayors resisted this new deal at first, demanding that the legislature be required to have a three-quarters vote before taking local money. The mayors enjoyed the attention they received for fighting alongside the governor on the issue. Autry, the Fresno mayor, begged the governor's staff not to give up. But that weekend, the governor's aides began calling city and county officials to urge them to declare victory and accept this version of the alternative ballot measure.

ON MONDAY NIGHT, JULY 26, Schwarzenegger joined conference calls with city and county officials. As he spoke, Burton peered in the window from the governor's patio. The senate Democrat badly wanted the budget fight to be over.

"This is as good as it's going to get," the governor told the local representatives. They agreed.

Republicans were not entirely happy. They had convinced Democrats to repeal the "sue your boss" law, but could not get other concessions they had sought. In a meeting later that night, Schwarzenegger made clear he could wait no longer. The governor got up and walked over to the door, held it open and said he planned to walk outside and tell reporters the budget was closed. Fixing his gaze on Republican leaders, Schwarzenegger asked, "Are you coming or not?"

In the press room, Burton was asked how the budget was resolved. "I think speaking for myself and my senate colleagues, when we accepted the fact that we were really girlie men, we just were able to get over that and get on with the budget," he said. Everyone laughed, and Burton later gave the governor a football jersey with the words "#1 Warrior." But Schwarzenegger's relationship with the legislature would never be the same. Lawmakers would not forget Schwarzenegger's confrontational tone, and, in time, they would respond in kind.

As part of the budget agreement, Schwarzenegger and the legislature had finally added an alternative local government measure to the November ballot. It would be called Proposition 1A. The cities and counties would support 1A and oppose their original initiative, Proposition 65, because, with Prop 1A, the locals had Schwarzenegger on their side.

On his way home to Southern California on Thursday night, July 29, Schwarzenegger stopped at the League of California Cities convention in Monterey to accept the thanks of local officials. A birthday cake was wheeled out for the governor. He would turn fifty-seven the next day. The local officials treated him like one of their own.

He was. In California, local officials did not run in party primaries. Mayors, city councilors, and county supervisors were officially nonpartisan. Schwarzenegger had been elected in a recall without a party primary, either. The son of a small-town police chief had found a political base among the local officials of California.

SCHWARZENEGGER WOULD CAMPAIGN in the fall for Prop 1A. The governor would hold a press conference outside Dodger Stadium, headline a fundraiser for the measure, and, at his own suggestion, even do a joint appearance with San Francisco Mayor Gavin Newsom, who had quarreled with Schwarzenegger over gay marriage earlier in the year.

But the campaigning the governor had done during the budget fight was all the support Prop 1A really needed. The combination of Schwarzenegger's celebrity and the controversy over what been an arcane issue had captured public attention.

Schwarzenegger had a tendency to oversell his victories. He told an Orange County rally that with the budget deal, "We said 'hasta la vista' to the special interests!" But he could claim some progress on policy fronts and a political winning streak. He had convinced voters to pass Propositions 57 and 58, he had pushed through a workers' comp package, and now he had a budget with new protections for local government.

With Prop 1A presumably on its way to an easy win in the fall, Schwarzenegger had time to take on some of the fifteen other statewide measures on the November ballot. For this governor, the opportunity to involve himself in more campaigns would prove hard to resist.

CHAPTER 16

"The Indians Are Ripping Us Off"

As ANTHONY PICO drove up and down the hills of the Viejas Indian Reservation thirty-five miles east of San Diego, most of what he could see was new. New driveways. New mailboxes. New homes replacing the trailers that had dotted the reservation when he grew up there. And a newly refurbished casino, with a tribe-owned outlet mall across the street. A few years earlier, the rate of unemployment was nearly 80 percent among the three hundred or so registered members of the Viejas Band of Kumeyaay Indians. (The Kumeyaay, of which a dozen bands survived, had been the original residents of San Diego.) Now, in 2004, most had new jobs. Tribal members received hundreds of thousands of dollars in casino profits. The tribe had money to restore its ancient wetlands.

Pico, the tribal chairman, said he had been the first member of the tribe to be born in a hospital. He was one of thirteen children. After being drafted, Pico in 1966 was sent to Vietnam. He recalled his days as an Army paratrooper as the most profound experience of his life. Back home on the reservation, he overcame post-traumatic stress disorder and alcoholism. He was first elected tribal chairman in 1983, when it was not much of a job because the Viejas Band had so little. These days, Pico worried about how to protect the new prosperity.

The governor of California had a different concern: how to convince the Viejas and other tribes to share more of their new gambling wealth with the cash-strapped state. In his attempt to do that, Schwarzenegger would once again combine populist rhetoric with backroom deals.

CALIFORNIANS would vote on sixteen statewide measures on the November 2, 2004, ballot, one of the longer ballots in state history. Only one proposition, the local government measure Prop 1A, was officially Schwarzenegger's. The governor was not entirely happy about this. Over the summer, he said he would have preferred to have a few of his own initiatives on the ballot to advance reforms he'd promised to pursue while running for governor. But Schwarzenegger had already done so much with ballot measures that some

advisors wondered: how many campaigns could one governor, and one political operation, handle?

Movie stars can become overexposed if they appear in too many films.
Was that true of governors and initiative campaigns? Schwarzenegger's team
endlessly debated how best to use, and preserve, his celebrity. Some consultants advised him to stay out of the fall initiative campaigns. Let the people
decide, they counseled.

The governor had little choice but to make a priority of defeating two
competing ballot initiatives that promised to change one of California's
fastest-growing industries: Indian-owned casinos. Schwarzenegger expressed
no worries about the morality of gambling. (Before entering politics, he was
involved in an effort to open a casino in Las Vegas, and two of his top aides,
Reiss, who served on the board of a company that owned casinos, and cabinet secretary Marybel Batjer, who had worked for Vegas impresario Steve
Wynn, had ties to the industry.) But he believed the two measures were af-
fronts to the power of the governor and abuses of direct democracy. He
didn't want to just beat the measures. He wanted to rout them and send a
message to interest groups.

The irony was that neither measure would have been on the ballot without Schwarzenegger. As a candidate, he had demanded tribal casinos share
more of their winnings with the state. Now, to catch some of the governor's
stardust, the proponents of each initiative claimed to be putting into law
Schwarzenegger's own gambling policy through his political tool of choice:
the ballot measure. In truth, one of the initiatives had been designed to give
Schwarzenegger political leverage. The other initiative represented the first
attempt by political opponents to counter his power through a ballot measure of their own.

IN 1988, THE UNITED STATES authorized tribes to conduct casino gambling
on their lands as long as they first reached agreements, or compacts, with
their home states. California tribes sought to negotiate compacts for electronic gambling devices and card games not permitted at the time under California law. When the state balked, Anthony Pico's Viejas Band and other
tribes opened casinos anyway. The dispute between the state and the tribes
ended up in court. In the meantime, the legal uncertainty made it hard to attract solid financing. Twice, the Viejas had to close down their gambling
business.

Direct democracy changed all that. In 1998, a group of tribes, including
the Viejas band, sponsored a ballot initiative to give Indians a monopoly on
Vegas-style gambling in the state. Proposition 5 would have forced the gover-

nor to sign a model compact prepared by the tribes. The initiative faced an onslaught of negative advertising funded by gambling corporations in Las Vegas, just a four-hour drive from Los Angeles. But the Indians, using proceeds from their unauthorized casinos, spent more than $60 million, mostly on TV ads starring the photogenic Mark Macarro, chairman of the Pechanga Tribe, wearing a bolo tie and his hair in a ponytail. The ads talked about past injustices against Indians and tapped a deep reservoir of good will among the California public. Prop 5 passed overwhelmingly. The measure was so poorly drafted that the courts quickly ruled it unconstitutional, but the public mandate from the victory was such that the new governor, Gray Davis, negotiated twenty-year compacts in 1999 with many of the tribes. A second ballot measure, similar to Prop 5 but more carefully drafted, was passed by voters in the spring of 2000.

The tribes were sovereign states. Like other governments, they did not have to pay taxes to federal, state, or municipal governments on their profits. As part of their compacts, they did agree to pay into funds to assist poor tribes, the ones too remote or too small to build profitable casinos. But under the Davis compacts, these payments turned out to be a tiny fraction of the tribes' enormous income. A month after signing their compact, the Viejas became the first tribe to offer Vegas-style games. The Viejas' 280,000-square-foot casino, which was decorated with tribal motifs, offered two thousand slot machines (the state limit set by the Davis administration), blackjack, poker, restaurants, a 1,500-seat Bingo pavilion, and an off-track betting operation.

By 2004, fifty-three of California's more than one hundred tribes operated casinos. The industry had an estimated annual take approaching $6 billion—Nevada's take was estimated at $9 billion—and employed more than forty thousand people. Some of the Las Vegas interests that fought Prop 5 were now partnering with California tribes to build and manage casinos. The tribes' profits, some of which were disbursed through payments to members, of which many tribes had fewer than five hundred, made many once-poor California Indians rich overnight.

This windfall turned the tribes into one of the state's most powerful political forces. The tribes spent more than $120 million on ballot measures and on candidates of both parties between 1998 and 2003.

In the recall campaign, Schwarzenegger had argued that Indians should pay more of their revenues—a "fair share," he said—to the cash-strapped state government. Pico had made a similar argument a year earlier in a plan circulated among other tribes. In an attempt to head off public relations problems, the tribal chairman had suggested sharing profits at a rate similar to the corporate income tax in California, 8.84 percent. Schwarzenegger had set the far more ambitious goal of 25 percent of the gambling revenues.

After he took office, he invited tribes to renegotiate their Davis compacts. Most tribes had little incentive to change those generous twenty-year agreements, but Schwarzenegger offered a few inducements. He would be willing to lift the two thousand–slot machine limit. And he might extend the compacts for longer than their twenty-year terms.

Few tribes jumped at the offer. More slots were attractive, but tribal leaders believed that Schwarzenegger's 25 percent policy was unreasonable. That percentage had been borrowed from the example of Connecticut, where two tribes shared a market from New York to Boston. California had more than fifty gambling tribes, many of them in remote locations. It appeared the governor would need more than the offer of expansion to draw tribes to the table. He also had to find something he could use as a stick.

No POLITICAL CONSULTANT had meant more to Schwarzenegger's entry into politics than George Gorton, who had guided his campaign for Proposition 49, the after-school initiative. He also led the gubernatorial campaign before Bob White joined as campaign manager. After Schwarzenegger took office, Gorton served as a consultant for the governor's California Recovery Team, the hub of the political operation.

Before Schwarzenegger joined the race for governor, Gorton had been retained by the owners of the state's largest horseracing tracks. The rise of Indian gambling provided competition for which they had no easy answer. Track owners claimed that without slot machines, they could not compete. The operators of the state's card rooms—gambling halls that could offer card games as long as there was no "house" (customers wagered against each other)—made the same argument. So with guidance from Gorton and a team of consultants, a ballot initiative was drafted, and Schwarzenegger, running for governor by this time, was briefed on the details. The measure, which would eventually be numbered Proposition 68, gave tribes a choice. They could adopt Schwarzenegger's campaign policy and turn over 25 percent of their "net win" (revenues after payout by machines) and keep their monopoly on Vegas-style gambling. Or they could refuse to accept those terms, and five horseracing tracks and eleven of the state's card rooms would be allowed to install up to 30,000 slot machines among them.

The horse tracks and card clubs put together a Schwarzenegger-friendly team to run the initiative campaign. In addition to Gorton, the governor's media consultant, Don Sipple, was retained. So was George Kieffer, Maria Shriver's politically influential attorney. Los Angeles County Sheriff Lee

Baca, an ally since Prop 49, signed on as campaign cochair. David Townsend, a Democratic consultant, managed the effort.

Gorton argued publicly that the initiative would force the tribes to rene-gotiate their existing compacts and provide more money to the state. For his part, Schwarzenegger played a double game. In private, he expressed frustra-tion that the initiative expanded urban gambling and directed new funds to local governments instead of the state. Publicly, he maintained throughout early 2004 that he had no stance on the measure. That mysteriousness was by design: by not committing to campaign for or against the initiative, he re-tained his leverage. If he opposed the measure right off, the tribes would have less incentive to come to the table and negotiate. If he announced his support, he would be declaring war against the tribes. "I let it hang out there for a while," Schwarzenegger would recall. "It's all about timing in those things."

Whatever the governor's ultimate position, the tribes knew they would have to fight the initiative. The question of how to do that would split the Indians by geography, politics, and their views of the nature of sovereignty.

One group of tribes, mostly the owners of large casinos in northern Cali-fornia and San Diego County, believed one way to beat 68 was to court Schwarzenegger and renegotiate their Davis-era compacts to get more slot machines. The attorney who represented many of these tribes, Howard Dickstein, had taught international law at Cambridge University and saw tribal issues in that context. Tribes had sovereignty, but in the modern world, sovereign nations became stronger when they had good relations with their neighbors. New compacts with an increased revenue share with the state, Dickstein said, "would give the state a stake in Indian gambling, to protect it, to enhance it, to be in some ways dependent on it."

Another group of more hard-line tribes, many of them from near Palm Springs and other areas east of Los Angeles, wanted to expand but were un-willing to pay more to the state. These tribes saw themselves as defenders of the principle of sovereignty, and were determined not to bend to pressure from Schwarzenegger.

One of these tribes, Agua Caliente, decided to fight Prop 68 with an ini-tiative of its own. The tribe owned two casinos and was the largest land-holder in Palm Springs, the desert city known as a refuge for Bob Hope, Frank Sinatra, and celebrities of similar vintage. Union and neighborhood activists claimed Agua Caliente had all but purchased the town.

On January 21, the day before Dickstein's tribes started negotiations with the Schwarzenegger administration on new compacts, Agua Caliente chair-man Richard Milanovich filed the counter initiative. The measure required the governor to offer a new ninety-nine-year compact to any Indian tribe that wanted one, and lifted all limits on gambling on Indian land. In return, Milanovich dusted off Pico's proposal for a "fair share": the tribes would pay 8.84 percent of their profits, an amount equal to the corporate income tax. But those payments would cease if horse tracks or card rooms or other non-Indian gambling establishments were permitted to have casino-style gambling, as Prop 68 proposed.

To make the tight deadline, the tribe paid the highest per-signature gathering prices in California history—$6 a signature, according to gatherers on the street. Milanovich believed his measure stood a good chance of winning, but that was not the main objective. The goal of Prop 70 was to defeat Prop 68. Prop 70 also provided a way to dilute the governor's leverage in negotiations. If Schwarzenegger drove too hard a bargain in negotiating new compacts, tribes might opt to support Prop 70 instead.

ANTHONY PICO flew to Sacramento on January 22 to join the opening session of compact renegotiations. The discussions took place in Dickstein's fashionable 16th Street offices, with their glass walls and contemporary art. A block north was the Sacramento Memorial Auditorium, where Schwarzenegger had laid out his plan to govern near the end of the recall. Renegotiating Indian gambling compacts had been one of the governor's promises that day. The pledge had seemed improbable at the time, but on this day, seven tribes sat in Dickstein's office, ready to bargain.

To handle the negotiations, the governor had hired a former judge, Dan Kolkey, who had negotiated the very first compact, with the Pala Tribe, while serving as Governor Wilson's legal counsel in 1998. Dickstein had been the Pala's lawyer in those talks, and the two attorneys liked each other. The governor's legal affairs secretary, Peter Siggins, would oversee the negotiations and meet with interest groups that wanted to influence them.

Before the negotiations got underway, Schwarzenegger invited Dickstein over to the governor's office for lunch. The governor told Dickstein that his attacks on tribes in the recall had been tactical, not personal. Schwarzenegger said he hoped the tribes would enjoy unprecedented success, but wanted to make sure that their good fortune was shared with the state. "Good for you, good for us," the governor said. When Dickstein asked what the governor intended to do about Prop 68, Schwarzenegger said he was not inclined to back it, but couldn't rule out the possibility.

Dickstein got the point. "It was apparent to me there was a connection between the governor's position on 68 and the success of the compacts and the success of the compact negotiations," he said.

VIEJAS WAS ONE of seven tribes at the first negotiation session. Of the six largest tribal casinos in the state, five—the Viejas and the Pala Band of Mission Indians, each from San Diego County; the United Auburn Indian Community from Placer County; the Morongo Band of Mission Indians from Riverside County; and the Rumsey Indian Rancheria of Yolo County—were represented. Some tribes sent lawyers to the sessions. Others sent their tribal chairs. The turnout, however, was only a fraction of California's more than fifty gambling tribes. At first the group met every other week in half-day sessions. By early spring, Kolkey and the tribes would meet as often as four days a week. "There was time pressure to get something before the ballot campaigns happened," Pico said.

Money was the most difficult, but not the only, subject of the talks, and would be negotiated first. Schwarzenegger's starting proposal of 25 percent of their net win was simply too much, the tribes argued. At times, Pico thought of walking out of the negotiations but decided to remain. By being first to negotiate a new compact with Schwarzenegger, Pico could establish the framework for future agreements.

Morongo and its chairman, Maurice Lyons, convinced many of the bigger, hard-line tribes to join the talks. By March, representatives of these tribes—the San Manuel Band of Mission Indians from San Bernardino County, the Pechanga Band of Luiseno Indians from Temecula, and from San Diego the Sycuan Band of the Kumeyaay Nation and the Barona Band of Mission Indians—began attending meetings in Dickstein's office. Some tribal leaders thought the hard-liners were merely stalling for time as they gathered signatures on Prop 70. Deron Marquez, the San Manuel chairman, thought Viejas and Dickstein's tribes were too afraid of Prop 68 and thus too eager to get a deal. "We would walk in and the first words out of their mouths were, 'We better sign this compact or else 68 is going to pass,'" Marquez said.

The hard-line tribes—including Agua Caliente, the sponsors of Prop 70—began having separate meetings with Kolkey. One such session at Kolkey's San Francisco law office ended badly when the lawyer, checking on schedules for a future meeting, told the assemblage of attorneys and tribal officials that he did not want to "haul you" back to San Francisco. Lyons, the Morongo chairman, turned his back to the table and started coughing. He seemed furious. He was the leader of a sovereign government and would not be "hauled." Kolkey tried to make clear that no offense was intended.

Kolkey also turned down an offer of a $1 billion up-front payment to the state from the hard-line tribes because they wanted a forty-year compact. (The administration believed that the lengthy deal did not provide nearly enough money on an annual basis.) The hard-line tribes also would not agree to the governor's demand for compact provisions that would protect casino patrons from being cheated, grant local governments the right to arbitrate disputes with the tribes, and give casino workers the right to bargain collectively. Milanovich, the Agua Caliente chairman, said he could not understand why a Republican governor wanted to encourage labor unions.

SCHWARZENEGGER BELIEVED THAT, because state and federal labor law did not apply to the Indian casinos, collective bargaining was the best way to protect the non-Indians who worked there. There was also a political fact of life. The governor would need the support of both Democratic lawmakers (since the legislature would have to approve any renegotiated compacts) and of Democratic voters (who would be casting ballots on Propositions 68 and 70 in the fall). Finally, Schwarzenegger's stance reflected his little-known but warm relationship with one of the country's most powerful unions.

In his first few weeks in office, Schwarzenegger had reached out to the Hotel Employees and Restaurant Employees International Union (HERE, later known as UNITE HERE). The move demonstrated that the governor did not hold many grudges. (During the recall election, HERE organizers had brought women whom Schwarzenegger had allegedly groped to rallies.) After an initial meeting with HERE's California political director, Jack Gribbon, Schwarzenegger sat down with John Wilhelm, president of HERE at the time. Wilhelm, a Yale graduate, knew the governor's Kennedy in-laws well. He and the governor hit it off, exchanging jokes and news about mutual friends.

There was serious talk, too. HERE had tried for years to organize the casino workers on California Indian reservations, with little success. Wilhelm and Gribbon pointed out that employees at many Indian casinos relied on state health programs for the poor because the profitable gambling halls offered so little in benefits. They argued that this was a hidden state subsidy to the tribes.

Wilhelm so impressed the governor that Schwarzenegger would ask him to join a jobs commission, one of several non-profits affiliated with the governor and his allies. The 5 foot 7 inch Gribbon, dubbed the "little union guy" by Schwarzenegger, proved a big ally in dealing with lawmakers. After Schwarzenegger told HERE officials that he would include collective bargaining rights in the compacts, Gribbon agreed to use the union's muscle to support the compacts in the legislature. Gribbon and Jay Ziegler, a political consultant who worked with the union, even joined meetings of the governor's advisors. Having a Democratic political consultant and a top union official on board throughout 2004, a year of intense partisanship in national politics, would prove invaluable.

CONTINUING TO PLAY the populist in public and the backroom deal-maker in private, Schwarzenegger opened communication lines with the more accommodating tribes. On the final day of March, the governor invited some of these tribes to his office for a friendly conversation. He talked about what compacts could mean for the state and for their businesses. "Why make $10 when you can make $100?" the governor declared.

The meeting turned out to be a prelude to an agreement. It would take more than two months to produce the final language, as Kolkey, Dickstein, and the attorney general's office created new standards for liability law, environmental regulation, and collective bargaining that could be applied to sovereign Indian governments.

On June 21, the governor signed compacts with five tribes, including the Viejas. The agreements said the state would get $100 million annually from the tribes, plus more money, on an increasing scale, depending on how many new gambling machines the casinos added. The total annual take was estimated at between $150 million and $200 million a year. That was more than the corporate tax rate but far less than the 25 percent of revenues that was Schwarzenegger's stated policy. The tribes liked the deal because it lifted the caps on expansion and because their annual payments to the state could not be adjusted upwards for inflation. The administration maintained that California would get more money from the tribes than most other states received from Indian gambling. The governor, for his part, expressed hope that with five compacts signed, more tribes would come to the table. The compacts passed the legislature with a push from the hotel workers' union.

BEFORE THE COMPACTS were signed, Gorton had met with Peter Siggins, the governor's legal secretary, to make the case for Prop 68. The political consultant argued that the initiative would produce more money than Schwarzenegger would be able to get in his compacts. Gorton may have been right. But the signing of the compacts changed the political dynamics.

If Prop 68 were to pass, the tribes would lose their monopoly on gambling and the renegotiated compacts would be voided. To defend his new compacts, Schwarzenegger had to oppose the initiative. And since Prop 70 would provide far more favorable terms to gambling tribes than his new compacts, Schwarzenegger had to run a No campaign against 70 as well.

Schwarzenegger's opposition created turmoil inside the Yes on 68 campaign, as several key players associated with the governor quit to avoid conflicts of interest. Sipple, who had made ads for Yes on 68, stepped away. By August, Sipple was offering advice to Schwarzenegger on how to beat 68 and 70. Gorton stepped down from the Yes on 68 campaign, but continued to work with one of the race tracks.

This back and forth resulted in yes and no campaigns on each measure that sounded the same: like Schwarzenegger. The tracks and card rooms called the Yes on Prop 68 campaign "A Fair Share for California." The Yes on 70 tribes established "Citizens for a Fair Share of Indian Gaming Revenues." And Schwarzenegger's team formed "No on 68 and 70, Governor Schwarzenegger's Committee for Fair Share Gaming Agreements."

Schwarzenegger was, of course, partly responsible for both initiatives: Prop 68 had provided him with leverage for the compact and legislative negotiations, and Prop 70 had been designed to counter 68. So, like Dr. Frankenstein, the governor would have to face his own monsters.

IN A FIELD POLL taken the second week of June—three weeks before the compacts were ratified—Prop 68 led among those surveyed, 57 percent yes to 26 percent no. Prop 70 had a 53 yes vote against a 26 percent no. Both measures had a chance. The horse tracks backing Prop 68 and the tribes behind 70 had deeper pockets than most initiative proponents.

After the compacts were passed at the beginning of July, Schwarzenegger's political team, joined by Gribbon from HERE, began meeting on Tuesdays, usually in the offices of Steve Merksamer, a former chief of staff to Governor George Deukmejian and now a lawyer whose practice was largely devoted to ballot measures. As Schwarzenegger spent July fighting with the legislature over the local government ballot measure, his team began a multifaceted attack on 68 and 70. The hotel workers' union, delighted that Schwarzenegger had championed collective bargaining, convinced state Democrats to oppose both initiatives, even though some hard-line tribes were donors to the party. And Merksamer successfully urged the attorney general's office to change the title and summary of Prop 68 to say the initiative could lead to an expansion of gambling. Lobbying and even litigation over titles and summaries was common and sometimes resulted in changes. In this case, the switch in titles ended up costing Prop 68 in the polls.

Schwarzenegger's immediate political problem was money. HERE agreed to spend $1 million to oppose the propositions, but it was not clear how much cash Schwarzenegger would have for his own No on 68 and 70 effort. The governor and his nest of political committees had raised $20 million, but most of that cash had been spent on the 57 and 58 campaign and the workers' comp signature gathering. Marty Wilson, the head of the California Recovery Team, said that if he was lucky, he might raise $4 million against

68 and 70. Even with that money, Schwarzenegger could be outspent ten to one on Prop 70 alone.

In an August 5 strategy meeting, the governor and his team debated how to wage such a campaign. Some consultants suggested that $4 million in TV ads would be of little use in confronting the expected deluge of spots from the tribes and tracks. The governor's team considered accepting donations from friendly tribes to fight the measures, but the governor refused to break his long-standing promise not to accept Indian gambling money. The consultants also discussed outsourcing the campaign entirely to friendly tribes aligned with Dickstein, whom Mike Murphy advised. But none of these proposals were acceptable to the governor, who wanted to keep control of the campaign. He asked his team for more options.

Despite the money shortage, there was good news for Schwarzenegger. A survey of six hundred California voters done for the governor found that more than 74 percent had heard about the renegotiated compacts. Schwarzenegger, by virtue of his extraordinary fame, had led an overwhelming majority of the public to learn about an issue that had once seemed arcane. Minds were changing. While Prop 68 still led with 54 percent of the vote, support for the measure was falling among independents and Republicans. And Schwarzenegger, through the compacts, had quickly collapsed support for Prop 70 down to 36 percent.

THE BUSH CAMPAIGN had invited Schwarzenegger to speak on August 31 at the Republican National Convention in New York City. Shriver, to no one's surprise, suggested he skip the event. To everyone's surprise, John McLaughlin, the governor's pollster and a conservative Republican, suggested the same thing. McLaughlin argued that Schwarzenegger needed to keep as much of his cross-party appeal in Democrat-dominated California as he could. Associating himself with the polarizing Bush could only hurt.

A McLaughlin poll taken in late spring showed that 52 percent of Californians thought Schwarzenegger was a moderate. On a separate question, 35 percent thought he was too conservative, and twenty-one percent believed he was too liberal. Those were good numbers. McLaughlin hoped to preserve them as long as possible.

Even though relations had not been particularly warm between California Republicans and the Bush White House, Schwarzenegger felt a strong personal loyalty to the Bush family. The first President Bush had given him a taste of politics with the chairmanship of the President's Council on Physical Fitness and Sports. Murphy, Schwarzenegger's top consultant, worried about the lack of enthusiasm for the governor among many conservatives and pointed out that 75 percent of Schwarzenegger's supporters in polls also had favorable views of George W. Bush. A convention speech might be one way to send a message to the base. Schwarzenegger's posture, however, was complicated by the fact that he had known the Democratic presidential candidate John Kerry for thirty years, since the then-aspiring politician had helped raise money for the movie *Pumping Iron*. "I promised myself that in this campaign I would never talk negative about him," Schwarzenegger explained in an interview with talk show host Tony Snow, who later became White House press secretary. But Schwarzenegger could not resist the opportunity to give a speech in prime time from Madison Square Garden. The Republican convention was too big a stage to miss.

Landon Parvin, the former Reagan speechwriter, employed his usual technique, listening to Schwarzenegger talk and turning the best bits into an address. By early August, Parvin had produced a draft that Shriver and Reiss argued was too partisan. Parvin pointed out this was a Republican convention and that Schwarzenegger, a Hollywood star with out-and-out liberal views on many issues, needed to establish his Republican credentials.

Parvin, Shriver, and Murphy each made changes to the address. Before the convention, the speech would go through fifteen drafts. The final draft was a compromise that closely resembled the speech Schwarzenegger had given to the state Republican convention in Los Angeles late in the recall. It contained full-throated praise for President Bush as well as nods to the value of dissent within the party. "Now, many of you out there tonight are 'Republican' like me in your hearts and in your beliefs," the speech read. It added: "And maybe, just maybe, you don't agree with this party on every single issue. I say to you tonight—I believe that's not only okay, that's what's great about this country. Here, we can respectfully disagree and still be patriotic, still be American, and still be good Republicans." The speech also contained references to the Peace Corps, which Maria's father Sargent Shriver had founded, and Nelson Mandela, whom Schwarzenegger had met through his volunteer work with Special Olympics. Parvin, at Shriver's request, removed a joke about Teddy Kennedy's weight.

CONVENTION SPEECHES had to be vetted by the Bush officials, who were nervous about Schwarzenegger's address partly because they did not receive a final advance copy until the night before. Parvin kept the Bush campaign up to date as the speech came together, and he responded to various objections. The Bush team even suggested Schwarzenegger drop the story of how he became a Republican, a tale he had told thousands of times. As a new immigrant to the United States in 1968, he had followed news of the presidential contest between Richard Nixon and Hubert Humphrey on TV. A friend translated the words into German, and, as Schwarzenegger described it, he found he preferred Nixon's talk of "free enterprise, getting government off your back, lowering taxes, and strengthening the military." Convention handlers were wary of how open support for Nixon would play. Schwarzenegger's aides responded that the story was true. It stayed in.

Schwarzenegger did not get his way when it came to the look of the speech. Long before the convention, the governor's team had considered having him make a huge Hollywood entrance, with a Schwarzenegger stunt double riding out from one side of the stage on a motorcycle in Terminator leather as the governor entered from the other side in suit and tie. The motorcycle plan was never that serious. But Schwarzenegger's aides did ask the Republican National Committee to let the governor walk through the audience on his way to the stage. This request was also turned down.

Schwarzenegger rehearsed more thoroughly for this speech than any he had ever given. To get over his limited experience working with Teleprompters, the governor had the machines moved into his hotel room. Friends listened to the rehearsals and interrupted Schwarzenegger frequently with screams and cheers so he could learn how to pause and wait for the cheers to subside, instead of talking over them. The rehearsal paid off. His delivery was easily the best of his political career.

Schwarzenegger talked about his fear when, in his childhood, his family was stopped at a Russian checkpoint near the Semmering mountain pass. He described Austrian socialism in terms so stark that leftist commentators in his home country would criticize him afterwards. He discussed his own immigration to the United States. And as he had done during the recall, he made his rhythmic case for Republicanism.

"How do you know if you're a Republican? I'll tell you how.

"If you believe that government should be accountable to the people, not the people to the government, then you are a Republican.

"If you believe a person should be treated as an individual, not as a member of an interest group, then you are a Republican.

"If you believe your family knows how to spend your money better than the government does, then you are a Republican.

"If you believe our educational system should be held accountable for the progress of our children, then you are a Republican.

"If you believe this country, not the United Nations, is the best hope of democracy in the world, then you are a Republican.

"And, ladies and gentlemen, if you believe we must be fierce and relentless and terminate terrorism, then you are a Republican."

More than a few Democrats would agree with those positions. But in Schwarzenegger's mouth, they sounded like fighting words. As was his habit, the governor delivered a couple of lines that weren't in the text distributed to reporters. He joked that the huge ovation for his entrance was "like winning an Oscar—as if I would know." And in what would become the most quoted line of the speech, he mocked assessments that America's economy was in the dumps. "To those critics who are so pessimistic about our economy, I say: 'Don't be economic girlie men!'" The speech drew huge cheers inside the Garden and genuine thank-yous from the Bush campaign. In the afterglow, newspaper stories were written and scholarly discussions were held about amending the U.S. Constitution to permit foreign-born citizens to serve as president.

Despite the reaction, Schwarzenegger, by taking sides in a hyperpartisan national election, had added a bit of partisan flavor to his populist governorship. There would be a lingering aftertaste. Long after the convention, Schwarzenegger would joke publicly that his wife had denied him sex for two weeks after his speech to the Republicans. (Like other Schwarzenegger jokes, it did not translate well, and newspapers on five continents reported this as fact.) In truth, Shriver, along with Parvin and the governor himself, could claim partial authorship of the address.

BEFORE LEAVING NEW YORK, Schwarzenegger addressed the California delegation at the Planet Hollywood restaurant in Times Square. In his remarks, the governor only mentioned President Bush briefly. He preferred to talk about ballot initiatives, and lashed out at the Indian tribes. The governor had been furious to learn that Yes on 70 tote bags had been distributed by the tribes to the California delegates, and he asked them to throw the bags away.

"Remember, we are going to demolish Prop 70," he said.

SCHWARZENEGGER returned to California with difficult work ahead of him. He could not spend September campaigning full-time because he had to review hundreds of bills passed by the legislature before the end of the session. Those bills were a political minefield.

In his one year in elected office, the governor had taken positions on many issues, but he had yet to stake out ground on specific policy details. Democratic leaders expected many of their bills to be vetoed. That was the point. They wanted to force Schwarzenegger to identify his positions so that the party could exploit any unpopular stances. Schwarzenegger claimed that Democrats had warned him of this tactic ahead of time. "It's Democratic leaders, okay? They said to me, 'Have you ever heard of the word *jamming?'* Well, we are jamming you so we can go out and say, 'You see, the governor will not want to help the people.'"

Schwarzenegger bucked Republican orthodoxy on some issues. He signed bills to cut greenhouse gases, allow over-the-counter sales of hypodermic needles for drug abusers, and grant food stamps to convicted felons. Each decision drew criticism from the right. But Schwarzenegger took the Democrats' bait on other bills. He vetoed an increase in the minimum wage, a proposal to allow Californians to buy cheaper prescription drugs imported from Canada, and a bill to impose more regulation of electricity. The Democrats would use some of those vetoes against Republican candidates in the November races for state senate and assembly seats.

Ever the entertainer, Schwarzenegger spent considerable energy making his signing and veto messages distinctive. His veto of a bill legalizing the keeping of ferrets as pets began: "I love ferrets. I costarred with a ferret in *Kindergarten Cop*. However, this bill is far too bureaucratic."

In his early months in office, Schwarzenegger had told Democrats he planned to stay out of the legislative races. But during the July battle over local government, he had vowed to take out Democrats who had stalled negotiations. A number of his consultants advised Schwarzenegger that he could build good will with legislative Republicans, many of whom had failed to vote for his budget and his gambling compacts, by supporting them in their races. He could not threaten the Democratic majority, but the consultants said that if the Republicans could take three seats from Democrats in the assembly, the Democrats might topple Speaker Núñez.

In fact, there was little the governor could do to change the makeup of the legislature. California's legislative districts had been gerrymandered to protect incumbents of both parties. Schwarzenegger campaigned only in ten districts, and those efforts lacked the relentless quality of his ballot measure campaigns. The governor declined to appear in TV ads for legislators, and by relying on the party to vet candidates, he ended up campaigning for a Republican with a long history of bad business dealings who was running against Nicole Parra, a Democratic assemblywoman who had supported Schwarzenegger on key votes. This was a strategic mistake. The governor put his prestige on the line, without full commitment, for races that almost certainly couldn't be won.

BY THE FIRST WEEK OF OCTOBER, the governor was back on the campaign trail, going all out against Propositions 68 and 70. The written campaign plan called for a five-week closing flourish that emphasized the supposed threat that Propositions 68 and 70 would pose to the environment, law enforcement, local government, and state taxpayers. Some of the arguments were contradictory. The governor was to criticize Proposition 68 for sending gambling revenues to local government instead of to the state—and Prop 70 for providing no money to local government.

A new poll conducted for the No on 68 and 70 effort showed that both propositions had declined rapidly as the public learned more about the compacts and Schwarzenegger's opposition to the initiatives. Prop 68 had just 39 percent support. Prop 70 was now stuck at 27 percent. But Schwarzenegger wanted even more emphatic defeats.

This impulse had less to do with Indian gambling as an issue than with Schwarzenegger's desire to position himself to pursue major political reforms the following year. He had been so willing to compromise in his first budget that legislators and interest groups were saying the governor would back down if pressured. He wanted to send a message: if you pushed him around, he would push back.

Schwarzenegger and his team took a tough stance with the tribes that backed Prop 70. Milanovich, the Agua Caliente chairman, was pulled out of a reception line at a legislator's fund-raiser attended by the governor. At a conference of Republican legislators near Palm Springs the first weekend of October, Schwarzenegger criticized the lawmakers of his own party for taking money from the tribes. The event was closed to the press, but the governor made sure that word of what he said reached the state's newspapers.

The second week of October, the tracks and card clubs backing Prop 68 officially gave up. Between the compacts and $33 million in TV ads run against the initiative by tribes, the measure was already dead. The governor's team, not in the mood for subtlety, put out a triumphant statement declaring Prop 68 "six feet under," though Schwarzenegger would campaign against it for another week.

Prop 70 also remained way behind in the polls. The three tribes supporting 70—Morongo, Agua Caliente, and San Manuel—were making huge ad buys in the last month, though to the governor's good fortune, the tribes had been unable to cooperate on a single, coherent message. Schwarzenegger responded by putting up ads that showed him walking through a nest of TVs displaying various Yes on 68 and 70 ads. With a snap of his fingers, the governor shut the ads off. He also kept to an intense schedule of town halls, which took him to Irvine, San Jose, the Fresno suburb of Clovis, and San Diego. The official subject was Indian gambling, but Schwarzenegger also talked generally about his desire to "reform" the state in the coming year.

By mid-October, all this campaigning had begun to feel like overkill. Schwarzenegger got himself into trouble during an October 14 campaign swing through San Diego. Greeting diners at the Old Town Mexican Café, Schwarzenegger declared, "The Indians are ripping us off."

This was a classic Schwarzenegger miscue: the governor, in his desire to fire up his audience, went too far. The tribes backing 70 accused the governor of racism and demanded an apology. Even Schwarzenegger's tribal allies criticized him. "I am just deeply, deeply hurt," said Pico, the Viejas chairman. "We made the governor look pretty damn good in my opinion." While the governor was careful not to use the "ripping us off" line again, he did not apologize.

Indeed, Schwarzenegger stepped up his attacks on the tribes, Agua Caliente in particular. Not content to defeat Prop 70, Schwarzenegger decided to involve himself in a local Palm Springs ballot question, called Measure U.

It was a referendum on Agua Caliente's development plan for a square-mile piece of Palm Springs land known as Section 14. Community groups and HERE, the hotel workers' union, which had long fought to organize Agua Caliente's casinos, qualified the referendum for the city ballot to void the development plan. Schwarzenegger had a stated policy of staying out of local ballot measure fights, but at HERE's request, he made an exception for Measure U. If Agua Caliente was going to challenge his compacts with a ballot initiative such as Prop 70, the governor would fight the tribe on every front.

The governor made unsolicited phone calls to reporters in Palm Springs and Riverside to suggest that Agua Caliente was trying to deceive Palm Springs voters and that the tribe's true intention was to build a third casino on Section 14. "They say, 'All we want to do is put a restaurant here, a hotel there.' But don't believe them," Schwarzenegger told the *Press-Enterprise* of Riverside. Agua Caliente leaders were stunned. "It was very disheartening to us as tribal people to have a governor of the state of California jump on the opposing side of a local measure," said Milanovich, the tribal chair. Raper, the tribe's consultant, denounced the move as "totally immature and vindictive."

San Manuel, one of the tribes supporting Prop 70, decided to respond to Schwarzenegger's tactics with new ads attacking the governor personally. The tribe's chairman, Deron Marquez, had been offended by what he saw as Schwarzenegger's use of the tribes as political whipping posts, and he resolved to oppose the governor, no matter what.

The San Manuel hired former Minnesota Governor Jesse Ventura, Schwarzenegger's costar in the film *Predator*, to film an advertisement. In thirty strange seconds of television, Schwarzenegger's "rip off" line was tossed right back at the governor. Filmed in a dark room, Ventura looked into the camera and said: "Tribal governments offered to share revenues with the state at the same rate other businesses pay. No less, no more. That's not enough for Governor Schwarzenegger. He demands tribal governments pay three times more than other businesses. That's not fair . . . I guess it's okay to rip off Indians."

Ventura would not disclose how much he was paid for the ad. Schwarzenegger, who had attended his inauguration as governor of Minnesota, laughed it off. "That's what friends are for," he quipped. But San Manuel would continue to run the Ventura ad and other TV spots attacking Schwarzenegger even after the election was over.

ON OCTOBER 19, Schwarzenegger finally abandoned his campaign against 68 and 70. Sipple argued in one meeting that fighting the two initiatives was like "killing a corpse."

The fight over Propositions 68 and 70 was an expensive spectacle, with more than $105 million spent on the campaigns for and against them. That was a record for two competing initiatives on the same subject. Schwarzenegger had achieved an important political victory by beating both initiatives while spending just $4.6 million.

In terms of policy, however, he produced a mixed record on Indian gambling. The governor and his aides had made some progress despite negotiating from a position of weakness. Schwarzenegger had convinced tribes with generous twenty-year compacts from the Davis era to renegotiate and provide the state with more money. And in Propositions 68 and 70, he had fought off policies that threatened these gains. The compacts also eased the way for the unionization of casino workers. By the spring of 2006, the hotel workers' union would have collective bargaining agreements with four tribal casinos.

But the governor's first five compacts gave the state roughly half of the 25 percent of revenues Schwarzenegger had promised in his campaign. Tribal lawyers argued that the long-term value of these compacts might be even less than that because the guaranteed payments to the state were based on gambling revenues in 2003 and could not be adjusted for inflation.

Schwarzenegger had managed to sign five more compacts in August 2004, and he would ink deals with four more tribes in 2005. But the legislature refused to pass the last five of those nine compacts. And most of California's gambling tribes did not renegotiate. Schwarzenegger would beat Propositions 68 and 70 at the ballot, but with their defeat, he would lose some of what little leverage he had over Indian gambling.

THERE WERE FOURTEEN other initiatives on the ballot and just two weeks until the November 2 election. Schwarzenegger wanted to jump yet again into the fray. His fall campaign was far from over.

"Behind Bars"

ON OCTOBER 20, the day after he concluded his campaign against Propositions 68 and 70, Schwarzenegger went to a hotel in Ontario, the same Southern California city where he had given the "girlie men" speech, to attend a
press conference on behalf of the No on Prop 66 campaign. The event,
which he scheduled around a fund-raiser in nearby Corona, appeared to be
an afterthought. TV reporters stayed away because a rainstorm was pound-
ing greater Los Angeles. Rain was such a major news event that it required all
available cameras for "Storm Team Coverage."

Proposition 66 was an attempt to loosen requirements of the state's three
strikes law, approved by California voters in 1994 after a twelve-year-old girl,
Polly Klaas, was abducted from her Petaluma home and killed by a parolee.
"Three strikes" allowed prosecutors to seek sentences of twenty-five years to
life for defendants convicted of a third felony if they had two prior convic-
tions for serious violent felonies. In a few celebrated cases, criminals had
been given lengthy sentences for such offenses as stealing a spare tire or
shoplifting a $70 electric drill from Sears.

Prop 66 sought to require life sentences be given only to criminals whose
third strike was for a serious or violent felony. If Prop 66 had stopped there,
the measure might have attracted little opposition. But 66 also reclassified
some crimes that had been considered serious or violent, including residential burglary and arson, as nonserious crimes under the three strikes law. Prop
66's provisions were retroactive, raising the prospect that thousands of convicted felons could win quick release if the measure passed.

Schwarzenegger, worried about just that scenario, had come out against
Prop 66 in early summer. But this Ontario press conference was at the time
his only scheduled event for No on 66. There appeared to be little he could
do. That very morning, just two weeks before Election Day, the *Los Angeles
Times* published a poll showing that Prop 66 had the support of 62 percent
of those surveyed with 21 percent opposed. Even Polly Klaas's grandfather
made TV ads supporting Prop 66.

With the gambling measures 68 and 70 headed for certain defeat and the
election two weeks away, the governor was looking to focus his energies on

another ballot measure campaign. Prop 66 was merely one of the candidates available for the full Schwarzenegger treatment.

THE GOVERNOR HAD already announced positions for or against fourteen of the sixteen statewide ballot measures. Most of the governor's advisors thought he had overdone it. "The wisdom says, 'Stay out of the initiatives. Or don't get involved until the last day, look where the poll numbers are and then get involved with the winners,'" Schwarzenegger recalled. Back in the spring and summer, before he let his preferences dribble out in e-mailed press releases, Schwarzenegger had his deputy chief of staff Donna Lucas put together long sessions during which he could hear the pros and cons of each November ballot measure. And despite his general distaste for memos or paperwork, Schwarzenegger kept a binder with extensive policy information on all the measures.

Of the sixteen propositions, eleven had been qualified via signatures from citizens, four had been placed on the ballot by the legislature, and one was the result of a court decision to split a legislative measure in two. There were proposals to collect DNA from criminals, put billions in public money into stem cell research, end partisan primaries, raise taxes to pay for mental health programs, limit lawsuits when plaintiffs could not prove an injury, and ease access to public records.

Once Schwarzenegger decided his positions on all these measures, he took the unusual step of printing and distributing his own guide to the ballot measures. (The state already had an official guide.) *Governor Arnold Schwarzenegger's Ballot Proposition Voter Guide* was a glossy, magazine-style publication that would be mailed to 5 million voters across the state, with the Republican Party picking up the costs. The governor personally reviewed the galleys, suggesting changes to the pictures and graphics.

As he headed to Ontario, Schwarzenegger was still trying to figure out which of his ballot measure favorites he would champion during these last two weeks. There appeared to be four options. Each had drawbacks.

The business community wanted him to campaign for a limit on lawsuits, Prop 64, and against Prop 72, a referendum on a landmark law requiring companies with twenty or more employees to offer health insurance. The governor agreed with the business positions on both, but was wary of doing too much. Some of Schwarzenegger's allies in the environmental movement opposed 64, and his Democratic ally John Burton considered the health care law in 72 a key part of his legacy.

Schwarzenegger could score points with his fellow moderates by getting behind Prop 62, an initiative to end party primaries. When Republican and

Democratic leaders denounced it in a joint conference call with him, the governor told them that if both parties agreed it was a bad idea, it must be good. But some of his own consultants worried that if he was too vocal in backing 62, he would divide his center-to-right coalition of supporters. The proponents of Proposition 71, a $3 billion bond to fund stem cell research, waged an extensive campaign for Schwarzenegger's support. The governor had endorsed the measure, and he liked the idea of making California a leader in such research, but he was not enamored of putting the cash-strapped state into more debt to fund it.

The No on Prop 66 campaign stood out among these choices both for its subject matter—crime, which had not been a focus of Schwarzenegger's governorship—and because it was a longshot. Not only did Yes on 66 have a huge lead in the polls, but with the backing of billionaire George Soros, who devoted part of his philanthropy to reforming criminal laws, the Yes on 66 effort appeared to have an overwhelming advantage in campaign funds. The No campaign had just $30,000 in the bank, and the California District Attorneys Association, which opposed the measure, had little in the way of money. And while the state prison guards' union had plenty of campaign cash, polls suggested donations from a union with an interest in keeping the prisons full might boomerang and create support for the measure.

Prison guards' union president Mike Jimenez would later say he told his board there was no point in fighting: Prop 66 would pass. Jimenez assumed that the governor would be blamed if Prop 66 led to the release of thousands of criminals. Schwarzenegger's aides feared the same thing. Jeff Randle, the Schwarzenegger consultant who handled political operations, had pushed for the governor to attend the No on 66 press conference in hopes that Schwarzenegger would meet crime victims and be moved to make the defeat of 66 his top priority.

By Schwarzenegger's standards, it was a simple, cheap event in a small hotel ballroom. The governor, Oakland Mayor and former Governor Jerry Brown, law enforcement officials, and a few crime victims stood in front of posters showing the faces of violent criminals who had been sentenced under the three strikes law. A woman employed by the No on 66 campaign gave me a DVD with a TV ad. She added one caveat: the ad was not on the air. There was no money for it.

The real audience for the event was Schwarzenegger himself. Three crime victims spoke, each addressing the press and the governor. One said the man who raped her could be released from prison if Prop 66 passed. Another, Sherry Souza, described how her nineteen-year-old son was killed while riding in the car of one Richard Keenan, who was driving drunk on a suspended license and crashed the car. Souza's son and a woman, also nineteen years old, died. A third passenger was injured. Keenan was convicted of killing the two passengers and sentenced to eight years. He might be released early if Prop 66 passed. His father, Jerry Keenan, an insurance company owner, had given more than $1.5 million to the Yes on 66 campaign.

On serious occasions, Schwarzenegger was usually stoic. But as the governor listened to the victims, he appeared to be fighting back tears. When he took the microphone, he criticized the Keenan family personally. "You shouldn't be able to buy some guy's freedom," he said.

Backstage, Schwarzenegger found Randle and communications director Rob Stutzman. "We have to do whatever we can to help this one," the governor told them.

JUST BEFORE MIDNIGHT the following evening, October 21, Randle received a call from former Governor Pete Wilson. Wilson had been a champion of the "three strikes" initiative in 1994, and had been searching for money to fund a campaign against 66. He told Randle, a former Wilson aide, that he had finally found a donor.

Wilson had just spoken with Henry Nicholas, the billionaire founder of the semiconductor company Broadcom Corporation. Nicholas's sister had been murdered in 1983 by an ex-boyfriend. His mother, Marcella Leach, was vice chair of Crime Victims United, a group closely affiliated with the prison guards' union. Only after talking with Wilson did Nicholas realize that 66 was likely to pass. "I was asleep at the fucking wheel," said Nicholas. Nicholas told Wilson that he would put in $1.5 million if Schwarzenegger would lead the effort.

The next morning, October 22, Schwarzenegger dedicated the state's first retail fueling station for hydrogen-powered vehicles. When the event near LAX was over, the governor joined a conference call with his political team. "It gave me heart failure," recalled Lucas, his deputy chief of staff. "I said, 'What? We have twelve days to the election. You're going to put your name behind that one?'"

As the governor thought about 66, the fact that the measure seemed unbeatable made a campaign against it attractive. If Schwarzenegger could not bring the initiative down, he would not suffer much political damage. And if he managed somehow to defeat 66, the turnaround would be a huge, dramatic story.

IT WAS A CLASSIC Schwarzenegger operation, with seat-of-the-pants planning and not enough time. Schwarzenegger's political committees converted

$500,000 of TV time that had been bought for ads attacking the two gambling measures into No on 66 spots. His team purchased another $1.5 million in the last six days. The ads could only be fifteen seconds long. At this late date, there was not enough available TV airtime for thirty-second spots.

By late afternoon on Saturday, October 23, Schwarzenegger was in a studio in Hollywood making a TV ad. Sipple filmed the governor walking through a room full of giant, blown-up mug shots of criminals sentenced under the three strikes law. At the end of the ad, bars slammed down dramatically over the mug shots as the governor's familiar voice echoed: "Keep them behind bars!"

The governor personally reviewed the details of the ad buy. He asked to be quoted the number of gross ratings points per market (the standard measure of how many people will see an ad). When Schwarzenegger flipped through the channels on his TV on Monday the 25th, he called Sipple. Where were all the ads? Relax, he was told. It would take until Tuesday morning to get the spots in rotation.

"Will I see a shitload?" Schwarzenegger asked.

"You will see a shitload," Sipple said.

SCHWARZENEGGER REMADE his political calendar in service of Prop 66. Campaign appearances with Republican legislative candidates were reinvented as No on 66 events. When talk radio hosts tried to draw him out on the Bush-Kerry race, Schwarzenegger turned the conversation to the state ballot initiatives and 66 in particular.

His rhetoric was fierce. He claimed 26,000 criminals would be let out on the street, an estimate from prosecutors. The likely figure was closer to 4,000. But the Proposition 66 supporters took the bait and accused Schwarzenegger of exaggerating the figures. That tactic played into the governor's hands by focusing media coverage on the issue of how many criminals might be released if 66 passed. Whether the accurate number was 4,000 or 26,000, to many voters, either figure sounded like too many.

On Thursday, October 28, Schwarzenegger and the state's district attorneys staged an endorsement of No on 66 by three of California's former governors in downtown Los Angeles. Even Gray Davis spoke. In the service of winning a campaign, Schwarzenegger was again happy to share the spotlight with the man he had bounced from office.

HENRY NICHOLAS, the Broadcom founder, was donating hundreds of thousands of dollars a day to pay for ads, but he wanted to do more. With sixteen measures on the ballot, there was not enough available TV time to buy on short notice. Nicholas called radio station ad reps at home to purchase time, though he did not yet have commercials to air.

The weekend before the election, Nicholas sent a private plane to pick up Jerry Brown in Oakland and fly him down to Long Beach, where Nicholas's friend Ryan Shuck of the band Orgy had a recording studio in his home. Brown, Nicholas, and musicians from Orgy and the band Korn stayed up all night making No on 66 ads. By Sunday, October 31, the spots blanketed the airwaves.

This last-minute flurry came so quickly and so late that there was no time left for the Yes on 66 side to respond, despite its resources.

SCHWARZENEGGER TOOK one day off from the No on 66 campaign: the Friday before Election Day. While the governor had resisted entreaties to tour the country with President Bush and other governors, he had privately agreed to join Bush for one rally in Columbus, Ohio, the site of his annual fitness convention. His business partner in the Arnold Fitness Expo, Jim Lorimer, had reserved the Nationwide Arena in Columbus back in August for such an event. In 1988 and 1992, Lorimer had arranged for Schwarzenegger to campaign for George H. W. Bush in the final days before the election. At Lorimer's suggestion, the governor would do the same for his son.

But Schwarzenegger seemed reluctant. At one point earlier in the year, the governor had talked of scheduling a trade mission to Japan during the last week of the campaign. In public, Schwarzenegger played coy, keeping up a game of "Will he or won't he?" with reporters until forty-eight hours before the trip to Ohio. The object was to signal Democrats in California that while the governor would go to Ohio, he was not making Bush's reelection a top priority.

Whatever the governor's reservations, in Columbus the standing ovation for the entrance by the governor and the president lasted more than six minutes. Schwarzenegger's speech was brief but energetic. He praised Bush's handling of the war on terrorism and the president's determination in the face of critics. But mostly he recycled lines familiar from his ballot measure campaigns about how "the greatest power comes from the people."

Schwarzenegger took a seat next to Laura Bush as the president rose to speak. When Bush talked about the war in Iraq and the economy, Schwarzenegger clapped heartily. But the governor's expression went blank when the president approached social issues. When the president talked about—in a clear reference to his opposition to gay marriage—"marriage is a sacred institution," Schwarzenegger did not clap at all.

Coming off the stage, the governor looked bemused, as if he was taken aback by all the culturally conservative red meat. "Fucking Republicans," he grumbled, loud enough for others to hear.

Schwarzenegger returned to California that night so he could campaign for his ballot measures the next day. Shriver's parents were visiting, and everyone spent hours talking about politics.

Bush would win the presidency by virtue of a narrow victory in Ohio. Schwarzenegger jokingly told reporters not to give him any credit. He was already in enough trouble at home.

THE MORNING AFTER his trip to Ohio, Saturday, October 30, Schwarzenegger kicked off a bus tour to promote his picks on all the ballot measures, with the first stop at a warehouse next to Del Mar racetrack north of San Diego. Some aides did not see the need for a costly bus tour on a weekend when the country would be paying more attention to the presidential election. But Schwarzenegger, while limiting this tour to just one day, insisted. A bus tour to end each initiative campaign was now his signature.

Schwarzenegger had named the bus the "Road to Reform Express." His picture was painted on it, along with his positions on ten of the ballot measures. The governor had his aides make poster-size placards—green posters for yes and red for no—for his stance on each ballot measure. He held these up during his speeches as he reviewed his positions one by one.

As he played chess and talked strategy with his team on the bus, the governor's political operation was sending three million emails asking California voters to check out his initiative ballot guide online. After a second bus stop in Anaheim, the tour headed over the Tehachapis to Bakersfield, where Schwarzenegger attended congressman Bill Thomas's barbecue, a tradition before each general election. Thomas gave the governor an apron, but Schwarzenegger, unlike other politicians who visited the event over the years, declined to work the grill or serve food. That ended the bus tour but not Schwarzenegger's day. From Bakersfield, he took a private jet to Las Vegas, where he attended the finals of the Mr. Olympia contest. Per tradition, Schwarzenegger handed out the trophy to the winner.

In his column in the muscle magazine *Flex*, Schwarzenegger would recall it as the perfect day: ballot initiatives, big rallies, and a bodybuilding tournament. At that moment, it seemed like his political honeymoon might never end. His life story and career and direct democracy still seemed an irresistible combination. Some of his supporters began to wear "Amend for Arnold" buttons, a reference to the national conversation about the possibility that he could become president. As a native Austrian, he was ineligible because Article II, section 1, clause 5 of the U.S. Constitution required presidents to be "natural born citizens."

Schwarzenegger spoke publicly in favor of an amendment to the Constitution, but downplayed his own interest in the office. One of the governor's donors, Lissa Morgenthaler-Jones, had formed a group called Amend for Arnold and was in the process of establishing a fifty-state volunteer network and setting up an office in Silicon Valley. Morgenthaler-Jones made ads that would air on cable TV after the election. "You cannot choose the land of your birth. You can choose the land you love," she said in the spots.

Schwarzenegger's team allowed Morgenthaler-Jones to use a picture of him in the ads. She said that when she told the governor of her plans, he replied, "It's about time."

SCHWARZENEGGER spent Sunday and Monday flying around the state like a presidential candidate trailing in the polls. On Monday, he made six stops, hitting six different media markets in eight hours.

He began the day by shaking hands with the customers and staff at Edie's Diner in Marina del Rey. People walked up to the governor to get his autograph or a picture. Schwarzenegger, while obliging, tried to talk about his propositions. The governor started off a conversation with Ryan Hodges, a twenty-two-year-old Loyola Marymount student and aspiring weightlifter who was eating egg whites, by denouncing Proposition 66. Within seconds, the governor was adjusting Hodges's training regimen.

Minutes later, the governor was on board his Gulfstream IV, with the wood paneling and plush seats and a huge back bathroom with a closet for his message jackets. (The No on 66 campaign effort had come together so quickly that there hadn't been time to make jackets.) He flipped through architecture magazines and a copy of Joan Didion's *The White Album*.

At each stop, he had his picture taken with a Republican legislative candidate and stumped against Prop 66. At a phone bank in Fresno, he said to incredulous voters on the end of the line, "Yes, it's really me. You didn't recognize the accent?" At a roadside restaurant in Monterey, he ditched the initiative talk for a few moments to convince one diner to eat her broccoli. At a big rally at the Santa Barbara Airport, he waved warmly to a group of protesters even as they shouted "Don't touch my breasts—it's sexual assault."

On the plane ride, he asked aides to point out the location of a past levee break near Stockton. He had ambitious plans to rebuild the infrastructure of the state, he said. But first, he had a big idea for a series of reforms that would change how politics would be conducted in California.

What would those be, governor?

"Now don't jump ahead to the next movie," he warned. "We are still in this one."

EVEN WITH THE PRESIDENTIAL election as competition, Schwarzenegger would draw a crowd on election night. Five risers were needed to accommodate the thirty-five TV cameras set up in the back of a Beverly Hilton ballroom.

Immediately behind the stage was a huge electronic screen. "Reform Scorecard," read the title on top. On the screen were running vote tallies on twelve of the fourteen ballot measures on which Schwarzenegger had taken a position.

Schwarzenegger could count on a few sure victories. As hard as it had been to negotiate, Proposition 1A, the ballot measure protecting local government, passed with 84 percent of the vote. Propositions 68 and 70, the two gambling measures, were being "demolished," with 68 getting just 16 percent of the vote and 70 receiving only 24 percent. (The Agua Caliente tribe had survived Schwarzenegger's attacks and convinced Palm Springs voters to approve Measure U, its development plan.)

Early in the evening, it was clear the voters had agreed with at least nine of Schwarzenegger's fourteen choices. Later, as the governor had hoped, Prop 72, the referendum on John Burton's health insurance mandate legislation, would lose 50.8 percent to 49.2—thereby overturning Burton's law. But the nonpartisan primary measure the governor backed, Prop 62, lost narrowly.

Prop 66 provided the final suspense. The measure jumped to an early lead, reaching 54 percent support in early returns from the secretary of state's office. Those reflected a strong absentee vote for 66 on ballots mailed before Schwarzenegger began his last-minute campaign against the measure. As the votes came in, the margin narrowed. Prop 66 slipped below 51 percent but was still ahead as the governor took the stage at eleven.

Schwarzenegger briefly mentioned Bush's apparent victory (Kerry did not concede until the next day) and turned immediately to the ballot initiatives on the screen behind him. "This wasn't a victory for me, it was a victory for the people of California," he said. The only rhetorical flourish that was not thoroughly populist was a thank you to his donors.

Just before midnight, Prop 66 lost its majority, which it would not regain. It may have been the fastest, deepest collapse of a ballot measure in the history of California's direct democracy. Leading 62 to 21 percent in the polls two weeks out, Prop 66 would lose with 53 percent voting no. By one estimate, about two million California voters had changed their minds during his twelve-day campaign.

Schwarzenegger's side had prevailed on ten of the twelve ballot measures on the screen behind his stage. In all, he would be on the winning side of eleven of the fourteen initiatives on which he had taken a position.

The governor's political advisors were exhausted. From his after-school initiative in November 2002 through the November 2004 election, Schwarzenegger had campaigned for or against twenty ballot measures, including the recall, in two years. It had felt like one relentless campaign to those who lived through it. His staff looked forward to a little rest. Schwarzenegger did not want to slow down.

THE AFTERMATH of victory can be a dangerous time for politicians. Overwhelming triumphs breed overreaching policies. Schwarzenegger would not prove immune. Voters appreciated the governor's work. But there were limits to his power. The governor had been unable to spread his magic to Republican legislative challengers. Every single Democratic incumbent won. Schwarzenegger's brand was no match for the gerrymandered districts of California, where not one legislative or congressional seat—out of 153 up for grabs—would change party hands.

Even on ballot measures, polls showed that voters overwhelmingly made up their mind regardless of the governor's opinion.

Schwarzenegger did not have extraordinary powers of persuasion. What he did have was a seemingly supernatural ability to get more attention than any other political figure—as a result of his fame and his hyperaggressive campaigns for even little-known or unexciting issues. It was when Schwarzenegger combined his ability to attract the limelight with a good message (and money to broadcast it) that he was most difficult to beat.

This was a particularly useful power for a governor in early twenty-first-century America. It had become harder and harder for anyone, politician or celebrity, to command the public's attention. The value of paid advertising had diminished. Newspaper readership was down. Direct mail had little shelf life. Schwarzenegger and his ballot contests were good entertainment, and thus effective politics.

The governor did not yet appreciate that the combination of his celebrity and ballot initiatives also left him more vulnerable than other politicians. His power to get attention could be used against him—if his opponents could find a way to get in the picture.

PART 4

The people are to be taken in very small doses.
—Ralph Waldo Emerson

CHAPTER EIGHTEEN

Deal Breaker

As he entered the conference room, Schwarzenegger held a cigar in his mouth but did not light it. The Sheraton in Sacramento, where his top advisors had gathered for a strategy session on the afternoon of November 18, 2004, did not permit smoking in its meeting rooms. On this day, the unlit stogie was the only concession Schwarzenegger would make to limits set by others.

The governor arrived at the Sheraton possessed by two seemingly contradictory feelings: lingering frustration and overwhelming optimism. Both sensations stemmed from the same belief: that he and his state had reached a turning point.

After a string of victories in his first year in office, the governor felt he had a once-in-a-generation opportunity to overturn California's current political order. "I mean we know that if I cannot change it, no one ever will," he would say later. Although there was no statewide election scheduled in 2005, as governor, Schwarzenegger had the constitutional power to call a special election whenever he wanted. He would be able to control the timing of his next campaign.

Paradoxically, the victories that provided this opportunity also fueled his frustration. Certainly, by the standards of most politicians, the triumphs of Propositions 57 and 58, workers' comp legislation, and the local government measure, and the defeat of Prop 66 were significant accomplishments, noteworthy in particular for the unusual political methods he used to achieve them. But for a governor with such a huge persona, incremental fixes to the state's problems did not seem nearly big enough.

The sheer spectacle of his 2004 campaigns not only obscured the state's problems and his own shortcomings, but also raised public expectations and heightened the danger of a political fall. In public, the governor had consistently oversold even modest achievements as historic reforms. In private, the governor talked frequently about all the things he had not been able to do, all the dramatic changes the state still needed, and all the ways the current political reality limited him. He wanted to invest billions in repairing California's infrastructure, but the state budget, while far healthier than when he took office, was still not balanced for the long term. He wanted to reform the political process, but legislators, protected by gerrymandering, would oppose him at every turn. Schwarzenegger sensed that lawmakers and interest groups, after working together with him during 2004, were prepared to use his pledges of wholesale structural change against him. As he faced 2005, Schwarzenegger knew it would be a struggle to reconcile his own promises to balance the budget, avoid a tax increase, and protect popular spending programs, particularly the school funding guarantee that was at the center of the deal he had made with the California Teachers Association.

As he looked for a way out of this predicament, Schwarzenegger thought he saw the answer in the same direct democratic tools that had brought him to power. He believed he could repeat his strategy of pursuing ballot initiatives to create leverage for deal-making behind closed doors. He could call a special election in 2005 and turn it into a sequel to the recall. He did not anticipate that the initiatives and ballot measures that made him could also break him. The governor was about to try to make new political history just as his own political history was catching up with him.

HE FELT ANOTHER FRUSTRATION. While the public strongly supported him and the idea of reform in the polls, Schwarzenegger was having trouble getting his staff to buy into the concept. For months before the November 18 meeting, the governor had been unsuccessfully pressing for a plan to turn the political capital from 2004 into major reforms in 2005. During the first week of August 2004, he had invited his advisors to Sacramento to celebrate the first anniversary of his *The Tonight Show* announcement that he would run for governor. Over two days of meetings, they produced a list of some three dozen reform ideas on education, health insurance, environment, economic development, and other subjects. Schwarzenegger's political consultants talked about creating a reform commission with big names, perhaps Democrats such as Leon Panetta and former Secretary of State Warren Christopher, to create a comprehensive reform policy Schwarzenegger could embrace.

But over the summer, Schwarzenegger's staff did not come up with an action plan. The governor again reminded his team of his reform goals during a staff and cabinet retreat the weekend of September 10 and 11, 2004, in Squaw Valley near Lake Tahoe. Schwarzenegger had asked those in attendance to bring "big ideas," and staffers suggested everything from major water projects to free telephone calls for California soldiers stationed overseas. But many of these ideas, aides said, would never be passed by the legislature. On the Saturday afternoon of the retreat, Schwarzenegger announced he wanted to have a special election in 2005 to push through these reforms. His communications director, Rob Stutzman, immediately asked skeptical questions. If there's a special election, Stutzman said, all your chips would be in the middle of the table. If your ideas flop, the defeat could threaten your re-election. Why not wait until the next statewide election in June 2006? Schwarzenegger responded emphatically that he didn't want to wait to make changes the state needed. But the conversation soon moved to other topics.

There were various reasons that a plan for a special election was not produced. Back in his transition into office, Schwarzenegger had picked a staff of competent, experienced managers who thought far more traditionally than he did. Without an unambiguous order from Schwarzenegger, they were preparing for a quiet year of incremental changes that would build on his high political standing and position him for an easy re-election in 2006. And throughout the fall of 2004, the governor's political consultants were preoccupied with his various ballot measure campaigns. In this way, Schwarzenegger's insistence on demolishing the Indian gambling initiatives and pulling out a victory in the No on 66 campaign cost him valuable time that might have been used to get ready for 2005. The fatigue of his team was also a factor. After an exhausting year, his aides seemed tired and easily distracted. In one fall meeting ostensibly to prepare for 2005, there was considerable talk about how to protect the lunch cold cuts from being eaten by the other hotel guests in the hall.

But Schwarzenegger's own multichannel management style was at the heart of his inability to get what he wanted from his staff. To do a single deal, Schwarzenegger negotiated simultaneously through two or three or four different channels, each staffed by a different group of aides or allies. This meant that his advisors were often competing against each other to bring the governor the best agreement. Schwarzenegger himself could be hard to pin down, and there was always a new wrinkle he wanted to explore. With so many channels, the governor kept control and got to make all the decisions, but it could be hard for staffers, who were never sure if the path they were exploring would be the one Schwarzenegger chose. The governor's method was healthy to a point, and worked for a while. But over time, his management style created an air of uncertainty about exactly who was in charge in the Horseshoe. Legislators and interest groups found themselves having to develop separate plans to appeal to the left, center, and right of Schwarzenegger's team. The administration was like a European parliament, or Noah's ark. Among his collection of staff Schwarzenegger had two of everything. The uncertainty discouraged long-term planning.

Most destructively, the governor's management style contributed to factions within the team. The deepest divisions among Schwarzenegger's staff had as much to do with access as ideology. The governor had what some aides called "the Posse," a group of advisors who were personally, as well as professionally, close to him: Shriver, Reiss, the new cabinet secretary Terry Tamminen, his business czar David Crane, his investment advisor Paul Wachter, and Paul Miner, the deputy cabinet secretary who had been a key policy tutor during the gubernatorial campaign. Most, but not all, members of the Posse were Democrats, and most had little experience in government. Some Posse members saw Clarey and other aides—mainly Republicans who had long experience in government, Sacramento, or both—as "the Cabal," allegedly more interested in preserving the status quo than in enacting Schwarzenegger's bolder ideas. The Cabal members saw the Posse as dilettantes who plotted overly ambitious schemes and had long meals with the governor while the Cabal did the hard work of holding the government together. The two groups had uneasily coexisted since the recall, but the differences were largely obscured by the need for both sides to keep up with Schwarzenegger during his first-year sprint of campaigns and deals.

These resentments revealed themselves most clearly whenever long-term policy planning was required. In the late summer and early fall of 2004, the Posse vs. Cabal split had been one factor in the failure of Schwarzenegger's first attempts at structural reform.

One key divide inside the staff was between Clarey, who ran the Horseshoe day to day, and Miner, who was a champion of big changes. Early in Schwarzenegger's term, Miner had been the administrative liaison to the California Performance Review, a vast government reform and reorganization plan Schwarzenegger had commissioned. CPR, as it was called, seemed to embody the spirit of the recall and Schwarzenegger's promise to turn the government upside down, as 275 state workers were detailed to revamp state government. But CPR's report was a sprawling, unfocused piece of work that filled two telephone book–sized volumes and called for consolidating the government into eleven departments and eliminating eighty-eight boards and commissions. To the Cabal, the report looked like it would create more problems for Schwarzenegger than it solved, and Clarey moved behind the scenes to scuttle it. To CPR's advocates among the Posse, the report was the launch of a grand project, and its best ideas should be refined and championed. In the end, Clarey prevailed, as most of the recommendations died as a result not only of internal opposition from the Cabal but also of public criticism. (Newspapers noted that the state workers who conducted the review had signed confidentiality agreements and that some corporations had managed to get pet ideas included in the report.) Schwarzenegger, who had touted CPR as part of his plan to "blow up the boxes" of state government, lost some credibility as a reformer in the process.

WHILE SCHWARZENEGGER ENJOYED debate and creative tension, he also put a premium on working in a positive, upbeat environment. The governor's optimism and action-oriented attitude worked against him in putting together a 2005 plan. Some aides were loath to challenge his ideas outright for fear of being labeled negative. The better strategy, many of his staffers felt, was to let his most outlandish dreams die of benign neglect.

Schwarzenegger understood his staffers were doing this. (He had become particularly frustrated earlier in 2004 when aides were slow to pursue his proposal to have one million solar roofs installed on California homes.) But, rather than confront these aides directly, Schwarzenegger worked around them to plan for 2005. He encouraged Assemblyman John Campbell, a policy advisor during the recall, to continue work on a ballot initiative to limit state spending. He sought advice from George Shultz and Anaheim Mayor Curt Pringle, the last Republican to serve as speaker of the assembly. Pringle, for one, received an invitation to meet Schwarzenegger at his Brentwood mansion in October. The governor began by asking: what did I do right and where did I screw up in my first year?

Schwarzenegger also spoke in detail with former Governor Wilson, who urged him to tackle a number of reforms that Wilson himself had pursued but never achieved. Wilson began quietly encouraging his old allies to pursue reform ideas in the event Schwarzenegger went forward with a campaign in 2005.

Critical to this early planning was the Irvine Company, the giant Orange County real estate concern whose chairman Donald Bren was an old Marine Corps buddy of Governor Wilson's. Bren, a billionaire who kept a low profile, had been one of the cofounders of the New Majority, the group of moderate Republicans who had been top supporters of Schwarzenegger's various campaigns since Prop 49. Irvine's current and former executives had assisted Schwarzenegger through every step of his political career. Larry Thomas, a senior vice president, had attended the March 17, 2001, meeting at Oak during which Schwarzenegger's transition into politics was first discussed. Gary Hunt, a former Irvine Company executive who had helped set up the New Majority, assisted Schwarzenegger with fund-raising. Tony Russo, a political consultant who was now an executive at Irvine, served as a board member of Schwarzenegger's California Recovery Team.

Russo did much of the earliest work to prepare for a potential special election. He commissioned polling on various reform ideas, mostly having to do with education. The public opinion research showed that passing reforms as ballot initiatives would not be a slam dunk. Pollster Jan van Lohuizen found that for a reform push in 2005 to have a chance with voters, the specific proposals had to represent a clear attack on the state's political elite. And a governor, even a popular celebrity one, was not a natural messenger for such an attack because he was part of that elite. Russo reached out to a variety of reform-minded organizations, from charter school advocates to the recall proponent Ted Costa, who had drafted an initiative that would allow a bipartisan panel of retired judges to define the boundaries of congressional, state senate, and assembly districts. Russo also stayed in contact with Reiss and Miner, as well as Joel Fox, who ran a small business advocacy group that received substantial funding from Irvine. Fox, who had helped put together the workers' comp initiative that the governor used to prod the legislature, quietly encouraged various groups to file reform initiatives to provide Schwarzenegger with similar leverage in 2005. "We did the groundwork," Reiss recalled.

This early work was thorough, but largely underground. Miner worried that if Schwarzenegger's other aides learned too early of this planning, the Cabal would try to block it. Russo and Fox, as yet another Schwarzenegger back channel, had a hard time determining exactly which reforms the governor and the rest of his team wanted.

THE NOVEMBER 18 MEETING at the Sheraton was Schwarzenegger's belated attempt to bring together his own team, both staff and consultants, and make clear that they needed to begin planning for a 2005 special election. More than two dozen advisors showed up. So did Maria Shriver, still limping after breaking her foot jumping up and down as she watched her beloved Boston Red Sox beat the Yankees in the baseball playoffs. The meeting started with a presentation from John McLaughlin, who had flown out from New York, on the results of his massive new poll. All told, the survey data ran more than 1,000 pages, which McLaughlin distilled into 112 slides.

The good news came first. Seventy-one percent of the voters surveyed had a favorable opinion of Schwarzenegger. Even 50 percent of Democrats gave him a favorable rating. "Enjoy it," McLaughlin told the governor as he chomped on his cigar. "We have no place to go but down."

McLaughlin followed up with results showing Schwarzenegger would have to be cautious in pursuing reforms. The poll had tested voters' views of Schwarzenegger's performance on a half-dozen issues. Although 80 percent approved of his handling of economic issues and 77 percent believed in his approach to the budget, Schwarzenegger was weak on crime and drugs (37 percent), health care (41 percent), and education (43 percent).

The education numbers were the most troubling. Only 29 percent of voters labeled him good or excellent at "reforming education," and only 35 percent gave him credit for "providing funds for our schools." Voters weren't wrong. Schwarzenegger had focused on the budget, workers' compensation, and local government in his first year. He had made enough progress on those problems that voters now saw education, not the budget, as the top issue. The governor was a victim of his own success.

But Schwarzenegger still faced a budget deficit of about $6 billion in the new year. Few options would allow him to balance the budget and increase education spending enough to satisfy voters. They supported the idea of a tax increase, 49 to 39 percent, but they did not support specific taxes. He was still a character politician, beloved for his style. By a 65 to 26 margin, voters believed Schwarzenegger kept his promises.

In the final slides, McLaughlin turned from the budget and Schwarzenegger to assessing the prospects of possible 2005 ballot initiatives. Although McLaughlin tested many other sorts of measures, education and political reform had the strongest backing. Eighty-four percent of those surveyed would support a measure to guarantee that 75 percent of all school funding was spent in the classroom. Sixty-six percent supported a measure that would limit tenure for educators and tie employment for government workers to performance goals. Sixty-four percent supported a redistricting proposal that would strip legislators of the power to draw district lines.

McLaughlin argued that by backing initiatives on education and health care, Schwarzenegger could improve his political standing on both issues. The pollster found that 86 percent of voters would support a proposal to make the cost of health insurance tax deductible. He also tested a proposal that would require the employers of uninsured Californians to take about $150 a month from their paychecks to pay for health insurance. Fifty-seven percent of those surveyed supported it.

Despite the popularity of structural reform, the public did not necessarily agree with Schwarzenegger about the urgency of making many major changes within a year. When voters in McLaughlin's survey were told that a 2005 special election would cost $60 million—a tiny amount in a state with a budget of more than $100 billion—support for the idea stood at just 56 percent, and Democrats opposed it by a 48 to 43 margin. And voters, while supporting many of Schwarzenegger's reform ideas, were not captivated by them. Asked to rate the importance of putting each reform idea on the ballot, voters—on a scale of 1 to 10—ranked no measure as high as 8. Schwarzenegger was undeterred. The governor told advisors that if he didn't go on offense by preparing initiatives and threatening a special election in

2005, legislative leaders would stall and make 2005 a lost year. If he ran for re-election in 2006, Democrats would paint "the super hero, the big star, the big Arnold Schwarzenegger" as a "do-nothing governor," he said.

The speechwriter Landon Parvin, who was taking notes at the meeting in preparation for drafting the State of the State address, marveled at how often Schwarzenegger mentioned the people's desire for reform. "If the government doesn't reform, the people will rise up and reform it themselves," Schwarzenegger said at the meeting, in a line he would be repeat in public.

The governor was convinced that if he applied enough pressure through initiatives, he would reach a deal with the legislature to place compromise reforms on a special election ballot in 2005. By seeking change immediately without a full consideration of the consequences, Schwarzenegger believed he was doing what voters always said they wanted from politicians: Stop being so cautious, do what you believe. He was not wedded to any particular proposal, but whatever the package was, it had to be big.

SCHWARZENEGGER'S POLITICAL consultants would later claim that they had argued against a 2005 special election at this meeting. In truth, most were torn between concern about the difficulties of such an enterprise and a shared belief that Schwarzenegger had a historic opportunity to change California. But interviews with eleven participants show only three people in the room dared object directly to his insistence on an immediate return to the campaign trail.

One was Shriver. She expressed concern that another election would be too much, and argued that the sixteen measures on the November 2004 ballot, two weeks earlier, had been an awful lot for voters, herself included, to digest. Another doubter was Clarey, who saw her top priority as getting the governor re-elected in 2006. Clarey had bad memories of working for Governor Wilson during the initiative fights at the end of his time in office, when he had been badly beaten by the very same public employees' unions that would likely object to Schwarzenegger reforms. The third dissenter, the recall campaign's policy chief Joe Rodota, said he didn't see the need for a 2005 election.

Miner, the chief deputy cabinet secretary who had championed CPR and had been working with Russo, argued most forcefully for a 2005 special election. Miner even suggested that, for symbolic reasons, the election be called on or close to October 7, 2005, two years to the day after the recall vote.

Gorton wondered whether it would be better to focus on one particular reform. Sipple asked whether Schwarzenegger might need to consider a temporary tax increase to balance the budget as part of his 2005 package of reforms. The consultants discussed a new state campaign finance regulation that would make it more difficult for Schwarzenegger to bring in money as he had in 2004. Previously, there was no limit on contributions to ballot measure committees. But the new regulation capped the amount of each individual's or company's contribution to any political committee controlled by an elected official, including the governor's California Recovery Team. Schwarzenegger would either have to spend more time raising money than ever before, or partner with a ballot measure committee that was not under his control. Either way, Schwarzenegger, facing multiple opponents, was certain to be badly outspent.

As usual, the talk of difficulties served only to convince him that he was right to take on the challenge. "I thought, 'The only way you find out if it can't be done is if you try it,'" he would recall. "Otherwise, you walk away and always wonder the rest of your life, could it have been done?"

After months of pushing for a plan, Schwarzenegger was more than a little impatient listening to the debate. When he was annoyed, he became quiet and the features of his face grew still. By midafternoon, he looked like a block of granite. "He didn't want to have an argument," recalled Reiss. "He wanted to make it work." After two hours, Schwarzenegger departed, thinking the meeting was useless. Shriver and some advisors stayed for the rest of the afternoon, but there was still no plan.

THE NEXT MORNING, SCHWARZENEGGER assembled his staff. Tell me if I need new advisors, the governor said, quietly but angrily. Tell me if I need new staff or consultants to get this done, because it's not getting done. Schwarzenegger said yet again that he wanted to move forward with plans for initiatives reforming the state in 2005. Why couldn't his team get the message?

Stutzman, the communications director, spoke up. Let's be perfectly clear, Stutzman said. You want a special election?

Schwarzenegger was amazed at the question. "Isn't it obvious?" the governor replied.

Nothing was ever entirely obvious amidst all the back channels of Schwarzenegger's world. Some staffers who had witnessed Schwarzenegger's earlier suggestions of a special election thought he was trying to start another discussion, not giving an order. "It is what it is," Clarey told the staff over and over again, when discussing the governor's decision making. But she felt terrible: she should have read him better. That it had taken until this morning, November 19, to rally his own troops did not bode well for selling the urgency of reform to the public at large.

Now, the entire team, some of them halfheartedly, would be playing catch-up, producing two packages of reforms on two parallel tracks. His senior staffers would have to come up with reform legislation that could be introduced in the legislature early in 2005. Outside the government, his allies would have to draft and file multiple ballot initiatives that resembled the legislation, in order to give him leverage with lawmakers. To ensure that such initiatives qualified for a fall election if lawmakers didn't agree to reforms, these new measures would have to be submitted to the attorney general by January 2005 so they could be on the street for signature gathering in March. Signatures would need to be submitted by early May.

The governor outlined some of the subjects he wanted to tackle—the budget, redistricting, education, and pension costs—but he and his team did not have clear ideas about the details of reforms. Schwarzenegger had launched a campaign, which would now go in search of its policies.

McLaughlin, the pollster, sent Schwarzenegger a box of Harry Truman brand cigars from a factory in Key West. The box came with a note: "Like Harry Truman, you have some tough decisions to make."

THE NEXT WEEK, SCHWARZENEGGER and his family flew back to Washington, D.C. to spend Thanksgiving with Sargent and Eunice Shriver, who lived in the Maryland suburb of Potomac. By the time he got back to California, the State of the State speech, at which he would presumably announce his agenda, was less than five weeks away.

Partly because Schwarzenegger had devoted his first year to public campaigns, he had not built a policy shop that could produce speedy and substantive proposals. Without up-to-date reform legislation that could be quickly introduced, Clarey divvied up the staff by subjects. Reiss and a legislative aide with deep education experience, Paul Navarro, looked at education proposals. Business czar David Crane and legislative aide Cynthia Bryant examined pension reform. The governor's new director of finance, Tom Campbell, would draft budget reforms. Each policy effort was separate. There was no quarterback who could make sure the reform proposals fit together. At a December meeting at Murphy's Sacramento office across the street from the capitol, Schwarzenegger's consultants had no policies to discuss or to test with focus groups. It was like trying to shoot a movie without a script.

The governor himself professed no worry. He remembered all the drama and panic of movie development, and how his films often came together quickly in the end. In politics, he had won his gubernatorial campaign in less than two months, and his defeat of Prop 66 had come together in twelve days. But the governor's staffers and political advisors recognized that this effort would be more complicated than any previous endeavor. Shriver privately expressed her concern, asking his advisors why they weren't further along. Gorton and Sipple argued the effort was too sprawling and ad hoc. Sipple, in a memo dated November 23, 2004, and addressed to Schwarzenegger, attempted to outline "how this movie plays out. . . . There should be one person in charge—a project manager, if you will—he/she should be highly organized, only have your best interests at heart, bring a command focus to development of policy and precise language of initiatives to be submitted, set timetables and deadlines for action, coordinate inside and outside advisors to achieve results."

Schwarzenegger saw himself as that project manager. And his primary concern was getting the best ideas for reforms. He considered dozens. There was talk of initiatives to contract out public services to private companies, to boost the governor's power to reorganize the government and build infrastructure and to make the legislature part-time. Some aides examined CPR, the nearly defunct government review plan, to see if any of its recommendations could be revived.

In each subject area, the governor conducted a bake-off within a larger bake-off, examining all the permutations of a policy. On redistricting, he wanted to blow up the 2001 gerrymander that protected incumbents of both parties. At times, he seemed to embrace separate proposals from the business community, legislative Republicans, and the good government group Common Cause, whose president Chellie Pingree he had met in the green room of comedian Dennis Miller's TV show.

A similar dynamic played out in education reform. Reiss held long dinners and meetings to consider dozens of ideas. Among them was a plan to make collective bargaining a statewide process so the unions could not buy off individual school boards to win favorable contracts, and a proposal to make it easier for city mayors to take control of school districts. Uncertain which reforms the governor would choose, members of the legislature resorted to filing their education ideas as ballot initiatives as a way to get the governor's attention. Assemblywoman Bonnie Garcia, a Republican, submitted three education ballot initiatives at the suggestion of the governor's ally Joel Fox. "I thought at most what it would do was pump the discussion," Garcia said. "And maybe he would pick one."

With time so short and campaign finance rules limiting his involvement, Schwarzenegger found it easier to latch onto proposals drafted by others than to produce his own. On pension costs, he embraced a legislative constitutional amendment by Assemblyman Keith Richman, a Republican from the San Fernando Valley, to offer 401(k) retirement accounts rather than pensions to new public employees beginning in 2007. An anti-tax group soon filed an initiative modeled on the legislation. At a morning staff meeting, Schwarzenegger's legal affairs secretary Peter Siggins pointed out that the initiative was so broadly worded that unions could call into question whether death and disability benefits for police officers and firefighters would be outlawed. Such an argument would be a stretch legally, but politically powerful. The governor wanted to personally review the details of the pension measure with the same care he had given Prop 49, his after-school initiative in 2002. But he didn't. By that point, he was "overwhelmed with a thousand other things," he recalled.

Siggins and Reiss suggested changes to the language to make absolutely clear that law enforcement wouldn't suffer. Others disagreed, arguing that pension costs were a problem with law enforcement employees, too, and that, as a technical matter, death and disability benefits would not be affected by reform. With his staff divided, the status quo—the Richman legislation and the related initiative—prevailed.

In this giant bake-off, one ballot initiative was filed with the expectation that Schwarzenegger could use it as a negotiating tool to get his way on other subjects. This was "paycheck protection," the requirement that public employee unions seek permission from their members before using dues money on political contributions. Schwarzenegger's allies hoped that the threat of such an initiative would convince the unions to make concessions on other reforms. In fact, the measure would unite the unions in opposition to the governor.

As HE REMAINED PREOCCUPIED with the unfinished task of putting his reform package together, the governor's administration made a number of regulatory decisions. One would have profound consequences for his entire reform effort.

Under landmark legislation signed by Governor Gray Davis, the staffing ratios in surgical and emergency units of California hospitals had been reduced to five patients to one nurse, from six-to-one. The state hospital association, whose members included donors to Schwarzenegger's ballot measure committees, said the change had forced hospitals to reduce the number of beds, to decline requests for patient transfers, and to increase emergency room wait times. In the long run, the association suggested, the ratios could force the closure of hospitals. Two days after the November 2004 election, Schwarzenegger, citing the hospitals' claims, declared a state of emergency and delayed the implementation of new ratios until 2008.

That put Schwarzenegger on a collision course with one of the more aggressive unions in the United States, the California Nurses Association. CNA had made the California law a showpiece of a nationwide organizing campaign in which the union had promised nurses not only better pay and benefits but a "voice in the legislative and regulatory arenas." The American Nurses Association, from which the CNA had split in 1995, also claimed that CNA destabilized its own bargaining units in this campaign. CNA denied that.

The governor did not meet with the nurses' union before issuing the order, a decision that Schwarzenegger himself came to believe was one of his worst mistakes in office. He did not immediately understand that a battle with the famous governor of California was an enormous opportunity for a union bent on expansion. The nurses soon filed a lawsuit challenging the governor's emergency order and accusing Schwarzenegger of "claiming an overarching but otherwise undefined and unjustified imperial authority." It was an appealing story line: nurses against a musclebound governor.

A fight with nurses was a political loser for Schwarzenegger. To his good fortune, the dispute drew little press coverage at first. The nurses, determined to do something about that, targeted a speech the governor was to give on December 7, 2004.

Maria Shriver had taken charge of an annual conference on women and turned it into an extravaganza that filled the convention center in Long Beach. CNA purchased fifteen tickets. Before Schwarzenegger's speech, the nurses wearing business suits found seats directly in front of the TV cameras. As the governor began to talk, the nurses pulled banners out of their suits. "Hands Off Our Ratios," one banner read.

Schwarzenegger could not read the banners, which were forty yards away in a crowd of more than 10,000. He would later say he had not known the protesters in business suits were nurses. "Pay no attention to those voices over there," Schwarzenegger said, as the nurses were escorted out. "They are the special interests, and you know what I mean. The special interests don't like me in Sacramento because I am always kicking their butts."

The moment, recounted again and again on television and newspapers, would be reduced to this: Schwarzenegger had boasted that he kicked nurses' butts. Union leaders were ecstatic.

For the next year, nurses would protest nearly every public event attended by Schwarzenegger, as well as many of his private fund-raisers. The CNA hired a plane to carry a sign criticizing the governor over Schwarzenegger's Brentwood home while he was throwing a party on Super Bowl Sunday. At the Vanity Fair Oscar party, to which Schwarzenegger had been invited, nurses in Arnold masks handed out mock awards for fund-raising. By spring, Schwarzenegger publicly conceded a grudging respect for the nurses' skills as performers in his traveling show.

The nurses won more than the public relations war. The courts would find that Schwarzenegger's emergency delay of the ratio regulations exceeded his authority. Some hospitals even began negotiating new union contracts that incorporated the ratios Schwarzenegger's order had delayed. "I'll tell you, screw the industry," said Stutzman, the communications director. "Absolutely screw the industry. They swear to God on a stack of Bibles this is going to crater us, this is going to close hospitals. Then they go ahead and start cutting bargaining agreements that bring in the new ratios." Schwarzenegger would lose the policy battle and earn an enemy that could hurt his reform push.

THE NURSES' PROTESTS SHOULD HAVE provided an early warning against taking on a union that represented a well-regarded, service-oriented profession dominated by women. But as he considered various reform proposals, the governor and his team came to understand that they were heading for a reckoning with the most powerful union in the state, the 335,000-member California Teachers Association. Through CTA, two of Schwarzenegger's most momentous decisions—one regarding the next year's budget itself, the other on the nature of the budget reform he planned to pursue—would collide. Taken together, his choices on these two issues would change the entire course of his governorship.

SCHWARZENEGGER HAD BUILT HIS relatively brief political career on three legs. The first was his celebrity, which enabled his run and his governing style. The second, direct democracy, provided him with a vehicle to enter politics (Prop 49), to get elected (the recall), and to govern (through various propositions). The third leg, less noticed but still critical, had been the protection of the CTA.

Before he ran for governor, Schwarzenegger had paid respect to the power of the teachers' union. Four years earlier, he had permitted a lawyer for CTA to help write Prop 49, the after-school initiative that launched him into California politics. And during the gubernatorial campaign, Schwarzenegger had sworn that the education funding guarantee of Prop 98—the source of the CTA's power over the budget—would be changed only "over my dead body."

Prop 98, passed by the voters in 1988, established a minimum funding guarantee for education. It consisted of three distinct formulas, or "tests."

Depending on school enrollment, per capita personal income and state revenues, one of the three formulas would go into effect each year. In years when the amount spent on education didn't match Prop 98's guarantee, the difference—called the "maintenance factor"—was established and had to be paid off in the future. Since the state almost always owed money to education under the maintenance factor, the education lobby, and CTA in particular, held a political sword over the governor and the legislature.

Accepting this reality, Schwarzenegger in his first weeks in office had approached the union and cut a deal that gave him a cushion during his first budget year. The deal was an extraordinary political accommodation between the state's most powerful Republican politician and its most powerful Democratic interest group.

Throughout 2004, relations between the union and the governor had been warm. Schwarzenegger even agreed to videotape a message praising CTA for the National Education Association convention in Washington. "With the leadership of Barbara Kerr, I know we can do it all," Schwarzenegger said on the tape. Kerr, the kindergarten and first-grade teacher in Riverside and the CTA president, had long experience in direct democracy. She had worked on the union committee that put together Proposition 98.

Kerr had been a Schwarzenegger skeptic, but during his first year in office, she was won over by the funding deal and his subsequent actions. The governor had settled a lawsuit brought by the American Civil Liberties Union against the state for failing to provide equal educational opportunity for inner-city school districts. CTA had been included in an education reform commission put together by Schwarzenegger's education secretary Richard Riordan. Behind the scenes, Kerr and other union officials expressed a willingness to embrace education reforms if they were collectively bargained. To lay the groundwork, Kerr established an "education change work group" inside CTA to re-examine the union's position on several ideas it had long opposed. Union officials said that by late 2004 they were prepared to support some forms of performance pay for teachers, policies to grant individual schools more freedom to make decisions, incentives to get more experienced teachers into poorer schools, and a change in funding called "weighted student formula," which would attach school funding to individual students.

By the fall of 2004, feelings were so positive that the teachers' union began making plans to endorse Schwarzenegger for re-election. Kerr said she discussed such an endorsement with board members.

The governor, however, was unaware of the possible endorsement. John Hein, the CTA political director with whom Schwarzenegger had formed a close relationship during Prop 49 and the negotiations for the funding deal, had retired in April 2004. With Hein gone, Schwarzenegger lost his best personal connection to CTA. And the governor had begun to feel trapped not only by his budget deal with the union, but by the Prop 98 formula itself.

As part of the deal between Schwarzenegger and the CTA, education was to receive $2 billion less than the Prop 98 guarantee for the current budget year, 2004–05. That guarantee was not a fixed number. It could swing up or down. By late 2004, with the economy recovering and a state tax amnesty program bringing in extra revenue, the Prop 98 guarantee was projected to be $1.8 billion higher than when Schwarzenegger first agreed to the deal.

According to the deal, Schwarzenegger had to include that growth in his budget for the coming year. And if the Prop 98 guarantee continued to grow as projected in 2005–06, he would be on the hook for another $1.3 billion in Prop 98 growth on top of the first $1.8 billion. He had not anticipated such an outcome.

Schwarzenegger was in a jam. Tax revenues had soared more than $5 billion over his year in office, but the combination of these new Prop 98 obligations and other state spending formulas would require him to increase spending by $10 billion. The governor had the power to stop some of these increases, but not without a debilitating political fight in which he would be accused of cutting programs even as the budget was increasing.

"You have to understand, it's nothing personal with me," Schwarzenegger would say of the predicament. "Gray Davis could not make it manage. No one could have made it manage under the political and budget system that we have. The system itself is dysfunctional."

Could he extricate himself? On the advice of George Shultz, the governor had recruited former congressman Tom Campbell, a Republican, to replace Donna Arduin as finance director. "When he approached me, he said, 'I not only want to fix the budget this year, but I want to fix the budget system,'" said Campbell, then the business school dean at UC Berkeley.

While the rest of Schwarzenegger's aides had been slow to create the plan the governor wanted for a special election in 2005, Campbell arrived full of proposals and ideas. The new finance director filled the policy vacuum created by the governor's divided staff. Over nine years in Congress and two in the state senate, Campbell had developed a reputation for integrity, intellectual independence, and creative policies that proved to be political bombs, among them proposals to relax drug laws and to replace the income tax with a national sales tax. By December, Campbell was advising that if Schwarzenegger wanted to get control of the budget, he would have to fix what the new finance director called "autopilot spending." And to do that, Schwarzenegger would have to change the terms of Prop 98 itself.

SCHWARZENEGGER AND CAMPBELL put together the January 2005 budget proposal at the same time they considered long-term budget reform. With Schwarzenegger facing a projected deficit in the coming budget year, the legislative analyst's office—a nonpartisan arm of the legislature that is the California equivalent of the Congressional Budget Office—produced a report that all but invited the governor to back away from his deal with CTA. Instead of making increases to reflect the growth in Proposition 98, Schwarzenegger should boost the education budget only enough to reflect changes in the cost of living and enrollment growth. This could reduce spending by $1.4 billion in the current and coming budget years, the legislative analyst estimated.

Schwarzenegger had three options, each of which posed a huge political risk. He could take the legislative analyst's advice and not provide the growth in Prop 98, turning the CTA against him and hurting his public standing on the very issue—education—on which his own polling showed him to be weakest. Or he could keep the deal and slice into the rest of the budget, which would mean cutting human services programs his wife's family had long championed. Or he could raise taxes and thus violate another promise, risking the political support of Republicans. McLaughlin had tested the possibilities in his November poll and found no easy way out. Voters opposed the idea of not paying the full Prop 98 growth by 49 to 40 percent.

Members of Schwarzenegger's council of economic advisors, who met on December 2, advised him to honor the education deal. So did Reiss—who had helped negotiate the agreement with CTA—and Campbell. Reiss and Campbell argued that if he gave schools the Prop 98 growth, he would be in a stronger political position to reform 98. Reiss further argued that if he were to give education all that money in his January budget proposal, the resulting uproar from health advocates would help the governor make his case about the difficulties of meeting the Prop 98 guarantee. The governor could say: I hate this budget, but it's what Prop 98 requires.

But Reiss and Campbell were in the minority. Both the right and left of Schwarzenegger's divided staff were in agreement. Conservatives argued that CTA was a pig at the budget trough and that paying back the Prop 98 growth would encourage a tax increase. Kim Belshe, the health secretary, argued that if Schwarzenegger provided the additional billions in Prop 98 growth, the governor would have to cut so deeply into health programs that the state would have to deny state-sponsored health insurance to tens of thousands of poor children.

The health secretary played yet another card. Since the early days of the administration, Belshe had developed a relationship with Shriver, keeping the first lady updated on her programs.

As a decision on the budget approached, Belshe called Shriver to warn her of the possibility of cuts in health programs. The first lady was soon on the phone to her longtime friend Reiss. Why aren't you protecting these programs? Shriver demanded of Reiss. "I said, 'Maria, in a zillion years, I couldn't advocate nor could your husband the governor sign a budget that had those kinds of health and human service cuts,'" Reiss recalled. But she explained to Shriver that by putting the cuts in the January budget proposal and fully funding the Prop 98 growth, the governor would make the case for Prop 98 reform. And the governor would still have time to restore the money to health programs when he revised the budget in May.

Shriver's views did not sink the education deal, but they did indicate the direction the governor was heading. For all his tough talk about holding the line on spending, the Terminator was susceptible to any argument that he was harming children. And he was not inclined to take Reiss and Campbell's advice. If he had taken $1.8 billion out of health and put it into education in January, only to reverse himself in May to protect health programs, he said, "there would have been a huge thing about 'The governor flip-flops again. Once again, he's changing his mind and he's under pressure and all that.'"

Schwarzenegger, after listening to Belshe and Campbell discuss the pros and cons in his presence in the early weeks of December, declared that the consequences to health care of providing the full Prop 98 funding were unacceptable. "I had a choice," Schwarzenegger would recall. "If we want to give education the $2 billion more they say they are owed, we have to take the $2 billion out of health care, and that means we would have to take it out of vulnerable citizens. I was not willing to do that." He saw no justification for raising taxes by $2 billion instead. The state's revenues had already increased by $5 billion, and "I promised the people of California that I won't raise taxes," he said.

Schwarzenegger took comfort in the legislative analyst's advice that he not provide education with the full growth in Prop 98. "Of course, I tried to make it work," he recalled. "We just couldn't make it work. It was impossible."

IN DIFFERENT CIRCUMSTANCES, Schwarzenegger might have approached the CTA earlier in the fall and tried to fashion a compromise. The CTA and the

California School Boards Association had contacted the governor's office in the fall asking if there was a problem; word went back that Schwarzenegger would abide by the agreement. Privately, education leaders wondered why isn't he reaching out to us? Schwarzenegger's aides debated how he could possibly call a meeting with the CTA when he was still figuring out the contents of his reform package. If the governor chose to amend Prop 98 as part of his budget reform, he would be in a fight with the teachers' union anyway. In addition, the governor was looking at education reforms and the "paycheck protection" measure on union dues, which the CTA was likely to oppose. As Sipple said in a December 9 memo to the governor and a top staffer, "We are going after CTA with a vengeance."

On December 15, three top Schwarzenegger aides, including Tom Campbell, told John Campbell (no relation to Tom), the Republican legislator who was part of a group of conservatives drafting a spending limit, that the governor wanted to amend Prop 98 as part of his budget reform. The group of conservatives had no problem with the idea, but worried politically about the CTA. "We weren't going to do this because we weren't going to take on the teachers' union directly," John Campbell said.

THE NEXT DAY, DECEMBER 16, Schwarzenegger invited Kerr and other CTA officials to a meeting in the Reagan cabinet room. Kerr brought along John Mockler, the author of Prop 98. The governor and his team had decided to make no mention of the budget reform proposal. Instead, Schwarzenegger used the meeting to try to figure out if there was any way he could renegotiate his original budget deal with CTA.

I'm having some trouble, Schwarzenegger confessed to Kerr. I can't keep the deal this year without hurting health care and other programs. Is there anything you could do to help us?

We have a deal, Kerr bluntly replied. We expect you to honor it. The CTA had agreed only to the one-time, one-year savings of $2 billion from the Prop 98 guarantee, she said. In the world of Prop 98, the governor was not really asking for a compromise. He was asking, in effect, for more savings from education. The union president also shared some polling that showed more than 60 percent of Republicans knew of Schwarzenegger's promise to education and wanted him to keep it. "I think he was startled that I didn't just say, 'Oh, OK.' I don't think he likes to be told no," Kerr said.

Eventually, each side —the teachers' union and the governor—would recall this meeting and claim the other had behaved in bad faith. The governor would describe the union as more interested in money than in what was best for the state or for children's health. The union noted the governor's failure to disclose the full extent of his reform plans, especially his work on a spending limit that would change Prop 98.

Kerr and the CTA officials left after ninety minutes. The following day, Tom Campbell talked with union officials by phone. Each side seemed to be waiting for the other to make an offer of compromise. Neither one did. "I remember saying, 'Is there anything you can give?'" Campbell recalled. "The answer was, 'No, we've got nothing to give.'"

The following week, Schwarzenegger left California for Christmas vacation. CTA leaders held a conference call. No one, least of all Kerr, could believe that Schwarzenegger would turn his back on the deal entirely. He might propose a tough budget in January, but make the final figure more generous in the official revision in May.

A governor would have to be crazy to break such a high-profile deal with the CTA.

SCHWARZENEGGER WOULD WAIT until immediately before the State of the State speech to break the bad news to the education lobby, and he wouldn't do the job himself. Instead, Reiss invited representatives of various education groups to the Horseshoe at 3:30 p.m. on January 5, 2005, less than two hours before the address. Tom Campbell greeted guests at the door of a conference room before taking a seat at one end of the table alongside Reiss and Riordan, Schwarzenegger's education secretary. The education lobbists thought the meeting was to provide a preview of the speech and coordinate the messages they would give the press.

Gubernatorial aides sat in chairs along the rim of the room as the education representatives took their seats. Everyone who worked for Schwarzenegger—save Campbell, a preternaturally upbeat person—looked grim.

Riordan began. The governor had faced "Sophie's choice," he said. "He had to live up to his promise and give the schools $2 billion extra or give health care to poor people," the education secretary recalled saying. "And God was going to punish him either way." Campbell took over and revealed the first piece of bad news: the governor would not provide the money in the budget as dictated by Prop 98 and the original deal. Reiss added a few remarks, and the floor was opened to questions.

There were a few moments of stunned silence.

Let me get this straight, asked Glen Thomas, who represented county school superintendents and was a friend of Riordan's. You're breaking the deal?

"I'm not going to argue with you over that characterization," Campbell replied.

Kevin Gordon, executive director of the California Association of School Business Officials, followed up. Campbell had said in his talk that Schwarzenegger would be "modifying Prop 98." It wasn't clear whether he meant the terms of the funding deal, or Proposition 98 itself.

Are you amending the state constitution? Gordon asked.

Yes, Campbell replied.

Rick Pratt, an assistant director of the California School Boards Association, asked about the nature of the changes to Prop 98. Campbell put the best face he could on the budget reform measure, but the trouble was that Schwarzenegger had made no final decisions on details of the proposal. The finance director told the education lobbyists that the governor would cushion the changes by not allowing the legislature to suspend Prop 98 ever again. (In time, the governor would drop even that provision from his spending limit.) Campbell also disclosed that the governor's spending limit would give him new authority to make cuts in government programs, including education, if the budget fell into deficit in the middle of the year.

That didn't sound so bad at first. The education lobbyists pointed out that under Prop 98, any money cut by the governor would have to be returned to the funding base for education in future years. That was the essence of Prop 98's "maintenance factor."

Campbell paused, then delivered more bad news.

We're getting rid of the maintenance factor, too, the finance director said.

That was the formal declaration of war. Scott Plotkin, executive director of the school boards association, said that most of the people in the room headed membership organizations—of school boards, school business offices, etc.—and had promised their members the deal with Schwarzenegger would stick. By breaking his word, Schwarzenegger would turn most of the people in the room into liars. Plotkin said he hoped he didn't lose his job.

One education advocate asked Campbell, Reiss, and Riordan if they understood the size of the fight they had just picked. The education lobby would have no choice but to attack the governor.

You have to do what you have to do, replied Reiss, looking grim.

WITH SO FEW OF THE POLICY details of the reforms finalized, Parvin, the governor's speechwriter, had found it difficult to put the State of the State together. There was such uncertainty that Parvin actually drafted a second speech Schwarzenegger could deliver to the legislature at some future moment when he had made up his mind on the specifics of the reforms.

As Schwarzenegger entered the assembly chamber to deliver the address, he felt calm and relaxed, despite all the uncertainty. After a few jokes and brief nods to his wife and the legislators, the governor began the speech by thanking the people of California for voting for so many of his ballot measures the previous year. Now he would ask the public to act again. "My friends," he said, "this is a time for choosing."

Parvin, a former Reagan aide, knew the reference better than anyone. "A Time for Choosing" had been the title of the televised speech Reagan had given in support of Barry Goldwater in the closing days of the 1964 presidential campaign. Goldwater had lost in a landslide, but Reagan's message was so compelling that two years later, he was elected governor of California. Schwarzenegger had mentioned Reagan's speech in an address to the Republican convention during the recall campaign, when he was battling state senator Tom McClintock for support. But the Reagan reference was wrong for this State of the State address. Schwarzenegger was now the governor, not the political outsider Reagan had been in 1964. By invoking Reagan, he struck a partisan note that did not serve him or his reforms well. And Schwarzenegger, having failed to settle on the details of his reforms, was still busy with his own choosing.

The governor, nevertheless, announced special sessions of the legislature to address "financial, educational, and government reforms" without clearly saying what he was proposing. "Now I'm going to tell you something that you know in your hearts to be true," he said. "In every meeting I attend in Sacramento, there's an elephant in the room. In public, we often act like it's not there. But, in private, you come up to me—Republicans and Democrats alike—and you tell me the same thing, 'Arnold, if only we could change the budget system. But the politics are just too dangerous.' . . . And now we can change that. My colleagues, I say to you, political courage is not political suicide. Ignore the lobbyists. Ignore the politics. And trust the people."

The rhetoric was powerful but did not explain what his budget reform would be. He made a similar mistake in introducing other reforms. He correctly mentioned the problem of pensions, and of how the state's annual payout to cover pension costs had grown from $160 million to $2.6 billion since 2000. But in outlining the solution he was considering—replacing pensions with 401(k)s for new workers hired after 2006—he failed to explain that no current employees would lose their pensions. In describing education reform, he said, "We must reward, we must financially reward, good teachers and expel those who are not." What did that mean? The words raised fears that he was launching an attack on the entire profession.

Only in describing his desire to remove the power to draw legislative districts from the hands of legislators did Schwarzenegger approach clarity. He recalled that not one of the 153 congressional and legislative seats up for grabs in California in 2004 had changed party hands. "What kind of democracy is that?" he asked.

Schwarzenegger suggested he would call a special election in early summer to push reform measures. Given that he didn't know exactly what those reform initiatives would say, having measures ready for a summer election was nearly impossible. Even a fall election would be a stretch.

The governor made plain that he expected a big fight. "The special interests will run TV ads calling me cruel and heartless," he predicted, correctly. "They will organize protests out in front of the capitol. They will try to say I don't understand the consequences of these decisions." The governor said he welcomed the alternative reform ideas of legislators, "but do not bring me small ideas, bring me big ideas that match our future. Bring me reforms that equal our problems."

Schwarzenegger and Shriver watched the Democratic response on a TV in the capitol and marveled at how conciliatory the speaker and senate president pro tem seemed to be. In truth, legislators weren't sure exactly how to respond. Schwarzenegger seemed to be too high in the polls for direct confrontation.

The governor went off to a party at Lucca, the restaurant where Schwarzenegger spent so much time that a new item had been added to the menu: the "governor's special salad," which was topped with three kinds of sausage. Schwarzenegger thanked his senior staff and political advisors, at least a few of them oblivious to the seriousness of the fight they had started. "Can you believe CTA?" one aide, monitoring emails to his Blackberry, reported to others outside the party. "They're going ape shit."

BARBARA KERR WATCHED THE SPEECH on the TV in her office at CTA headquarters in the San Francisco suburb of Burlingame. Word had already reached her of the education lobby's meeting with Tom Campbell, Riordan, and Reiss. She grew more and more furious as she listened to Schwarzenegger. After the governor declared that on the budget "we must have a new approach that overrides the formulas, that overrides the special interests," she knew that he was coming after Prop 98. Before the speech was over, Kerr turned over pictures she kept in her office of herself and the governor and put them in a drawer. She emailed CTA board members: "I guess I'm a wartime president."

In Sacramento, Gale Kaufman, the political consultant who worked for Speaker Núñez and the CTA, was supposed to provide postspeech spin, but the address seemed so outlandish she didn't know quite what to say. Joe Nunez, who had taken over for Hein as CTA political director, joined representatives of other education groups at the school boards association office at 10th and L Streets. Schwarzenegger's decision to drop the deal was so unexpected that some education officials argued for holding their fire for a day or two. Let's see if Schwarzenegger really meant this, they said.

Schwarzenegger wouldn't reverse course. The governor professed surprise at just how angry his former partners in the teachers' union were. The next afternoon the governor bumped into Joe Nunez at the Esquire Grill.

"We're stunned at what you said last night, governor," Nunez said.

"What are you talking about?" the governor asked. "I love teachers."

THE CTA WAS NOT THE ONLY GROUP taken aback by some of Schwarzenegger's rhetoric. His own allies and aides seemed caught off-guard by the magnitude of the speech, which had been kept under wraps.

The governor thought he would capture huge attention by springing his reform effort as another big surprise, just as he had in announcing his decision to run for governor on *The Tonight Show* sixteen months earlier. The address would achieve surprise, but little else. Schwarzenegger had no ads ready to go on the air, no coalition of endorsements, and no schedule of campaign events to capitalize on the speech.

Reiss said none of Schwarzenegger's advisors were ready: "I think—and I put myself as part of that group—his political team and his senior staff didn't do what we should have done. You have a governor who has told you he's declaring war on three continents and you don't have a plan on where your forces are."

To a public and a political elite who knew nothing of his months of preparing for a 2005 special election, Schwarzenegger seemed to be making a jarring change of course. For his part, Schwarzenegger believed he was merely providing the opening offer in what he expected would be months of talks on a grand compromise deal with the legislature.

But the governor had kicked off a bid to reform California's education, budget, and political systems by breaking a deal he had made over the education budget with the most politically powerful union in the state. Why would the legislature, why would the CTA, why would anyone make a big deal with Schwarzenegger after watching him change the terms of the biggest deal of his political career? And why would a public that valued education above all other government programs rally to his side?

WHEN HE LOOKED BACK AT THIS momentous set of decisions, Schwarzenegger believed he was a victim of his own impatience. He should have taken more time, perhaps a year or two, to lay the groundwork before pushing for such reforms. That was true, but there was more to his troubles than that. In retrospect, he would have been better off if he had been up front and informed the CTA of his budget problems and his reform goals far sooner than he did. With the deal still intact, Schwarzenegger would have been in a better position to negotiate a comprehensive understanding that included both the immediate budget and budget reform. Perhaps CTA might have declared war anyway, but disclosure would have been the more responsible course of conduct.

Instead, all of Schwarzenegger's problems—his conflicting promises on spending and taxes, his weak public standing on education, his bake-off style of management—conspired against him on the education funding deal. The consummate salesman, the governor did not even make time to develop a plan for explaining to the union or the public his change of heart on Prop 98. His staff problems did not help. Several senior aides, mostly members of the Cabal, had never cared for the education deal. Since Reiss and Schwarzenegger had negotiated it, why not let them clean up the education mess themselves? "It was the irresponsible part of me," said one staffer. "Bonnie had wanted to own it, so let her own it."

Rather than facing the fact that he had made a bad deal that no longer served him and then making amends, Schwarzenegger turned to direct democracy and embraced a budget reform measure to change the very basis of the deal. The measure was less a proposal to improve the governance of the state than a method to rescue the governor from a political mistake.

Direct democracy was a fantastic tool for many things: for telling a story to the public, for leveraging public opinion to force the legislature to act, for building coalitions. But Hiram Johnson's system was not a magic elixir for politicians to drink when they got into jams.

By biography and profession, Schwarzenegger was a manufacturer of magic. The governor seemed convinced he'd be able to conjure a compromise with the legislature and even the unions. He said that he always intended to provide the schools with the money they were entitled to under Prop 98, but he simply couldn't do it in this particular year and under this budget. "I always recognized that we owed them money," he would say. "The question is how do you pay it back." He believed that, too, with all his heart. "He never wanted to break that deal," said Reiss. "He never intended to break that deal." But the fact was that a delay in funding Prop 98 growth was not part of his agreement with the CTA.

Schwarzenegger was slow to recognize how a broken funding deal based on Prop 98 could combine with a budget reform amending 98 to produce something so toxic it could poison all of his plans. It would be a supreme irony of Schwarzenegger's career: the modern champion of direct democracy first tripped over a fifteen-year-old ballot initiative.

CHAPTER 19

Musclebound

ON JANUARY 17, 2005, TWO WEEKS after the State of the State speech, the California Teachers Association gathered fifteen political consultants and pollsters from around the country for a secret meeting in Sacramento. It was a national holiday—Martin Luther King, Jr.'s birthday—and the strategy session went undetected by the press corps.

Schwarzenegger, a strong partner and ally of the union since the after-school initiative Prop 49, had turned himself into CTA's enemy number one in less than two weeks. Joe Nunez and Bob Cherry, the CTA staffers who handled politics and communications, asked each invitee for ideas on how to confront the governor and his political operation. For the most part, the consultants and pollsters offered sympathy and suggested avoiding a fight with one of the most popular governors in modern California history.

One CTA pollster, Mark Mellman, shared the results of a poll taken right after the State of the State speech. Schwarzenegger's ratings had dropped slightly since November, but more than 60 percent of Californians liked him and thought he was doing a good job. The governor's turnaround on the education deal offered one potential avenue of attack. Mellman's poll suggested that once voters came to believe Schwarzenegger had reversed himself on potential education funding, the governor would decline in popularity.

Despite some of the consultants' doubts, Nunez and Cherry debated the strategy after the session and decided to move forward with an aggressive challenge to Schwarzenegger that would be guided by public opinion research. It was a gutsy decision, and one that few other interest groups in the state would have made. With 335,000 members and thousands of local politicians whose campaigns had been funded with donations from its affiliates, CTA possessed far more organizational infrastructure than the governor's administration. Simply by increasing the dues of its members, the union could surpass Schwarzenegger's fund-raising. And while the governor had his machine of political committees and non-profits to sell himself and his ballot measures, the CTA was one of the few interest groups with a separate fund of its own specifically dedicated to direct democracy.

The teachers' union would not be content to merely match Schwarzenegger with its own machine. CTA officials felt so threatened by the governor's new direction that they wanted to build something far broader and bigger than their existing political structure, a new entity to wage direct democratic warfare. It would be a people's machine that in money and organization would dwarf Schwarzenegger's own.

THE NEXT DAY, CTA AND THE REST of the education lobby announced a full campaign to condemn Schwarzenegger for breaking the education funding deal and for proposing to amend Prop 98. Meanwhile, CTA would order up extensive polling, focus groups, and other research by four different Democratic pollsters—Mellman, David Binder, John Russonello, and Diane Feldman. Over the course of the year, they would produce an average of three large statewide polls per month, an overwhelming amount of research for one election cycle. There would be focus groups at least every other week.

Russonello's first focus groups confirmed that forcing Schwarzenegger to reverse himself would be a daunting task. In the San Fernando Valley, focus group participants liked Schwarzenegger so much, personally, that they discounted questions about his policies. Few believed at first that he had broken his own deal on education. But when focus group leaders described in detail the nature of the deal, "even though they started out with a great deal of good will for the governor, they were hopping mad," Russonello said.

Still, Schwarzenegger's popularity in these first focus groups and surveys made clear that a personal, hard-edged attack would not work, at least in the beginning. So the union went with a relatively gentle approach in its first ads, which were on the air in the latter part of January and early February. One radio spot urged the governor and the legislature not to "balance the budget on the backs of our children." A follow-up radio ad quoted from a study by the non-profit think tank RAND that said California schools had declined in quality over the last generation.

CTA's strategists believed that to beat the governor, they would have to run not one campaign but several. First, they needed to let the public know about their education funding deal with the governor. Second, the CTA had to diminish his popularity so he would be a less effective advocate for making changes to Prop 98 and for his other reforms. Finally, once the governor was wounded, they could attack his reform proposals in detail.

Because elected officials had so little credibility with California voters, a message attacking the governor would have to come from classroom teachers themselves. The union wanted to move fast. If Schwarzenegger could be taken down quickly, he might reverse himself on the education deal or not call a special election in 2005 after all. The governor was up against opponents who knew him, understood direct democracy, and were intent on finding a way to use his best asset—his outsized personality—against him.

THE UNION HAD A NATURAL ALLY INSIDE the capitol: Speaker Fabian Núñez, the former political director for the Los Angeles County Federation of Labor. As CTA took on the governor with radio and TV ads, Núñez (no relation to the CTA's Joe Nunez) would play the good cop. Schwarzenegger had called special sessions of the legislature beginning in January in hopes of convincing lawmakers to pass reforms. The speaker responded by publicly talking of his desire to work with Schwarzenegger while quietly delaying hearings on his ideas.

The governor had spent considerable time and effort trying to build a relationship with Núñez. Their talks had given the speaker an opportunity to size up the former movie star. Noting the governor's affection for large cars, large watches, and even large cowboy boots (with the gubernatorial seal), Núñez decided that a major Schwarzenegger weakness was the governor's never-ending desire for "something big." Núñez decided to embrace the governor's big goals publicly while preparing to beat Schwarzenegger on details.

The speaker had assembled a tough-minded communications shop that included three former aides to Governor Gray Davis, among them Steve Maviglio, Davis's communications director. Maviglio read every book he could find on the governorship of the former wrestler Jesse Ventura in Minnesota, and learned that voters had grown tired of Ventura's Hollywood act and outsized persona. "I'm a big believer in fighting this guy with his own personality," said Maviglio. "That's what did Jesse Ventura in. Jesse Ventura took on everybody and came away with nothing. People get tired of even Hollywood acts after a while."

Maviglio launched a rapid-response effort with the intent of putting a spotlight on Schwarzenegger's foibles, and quickly got under the governor's skin. After Schwarzenegger spoke to the Sacramento Press Club at a local hotel on January 27, Assemblyman Dario Frommer—sent by Maviglio—responded outside the speech that the governor had been slow to offer details of his reform proposals. Taking the bait, Schwarzenegger called a press conference to respond to the attack. Núñez emerged the next day to play the statesman, claiming Democrats wanted to work with the governor, but their priorities were not political reform but education and health care, issues on which Schwarzenegger's approval ratings were weakest.

A game of cat and mouse ensued. When Schwarzenegger started recording a Saturday radio address for stations across the state, Núñez followed suit. After the speaker criticized Schwarzenegger for not getting more money for California from the Bush administration—cleverly reminding the state's Bush-hating majority that Schwarzenegger had campaigned for the president—the governor convened a summit of the California congressional delegation in Washington. Schwarzenegger would call Núñez before press conferences to ask the speaker, "Don't be tough on me" or "don't attack me personally." When Núñez claimed that Schwarzenegger's reform agenda bore the imprint of conservative think tanks, the governor was soon on the line. "I'm calling from a right-wing think tank," he said. Schwarzenegger told aides that he had looked into Núñez's eyes and was convinced the speaker, at heart, wanted to make a deal. Most of these aides saw the speaker as a partisan determined to stick it to Schwarzenegger every chance he got.

It was Núñez who in late January urged the CTA to bring back its retired political director John Hein to organize the larger effort against the governor and his reforms. Hein had put together the original education deal with the governor. Over several weeks in February and early March, Hein assembled a political committee that unified the state's various public employee unions, from the teachers to the more conservative police, fire, and prison guard representatives. In theory, this coalition building should have been difficult, since Schwarzenegger had worked with nearly every union during his various ballot campaigns. Other unions had long complained that the CTA, through Prop 98, controlled too much of the budget. But Hein found he had little competition from Schwarzenegger's advisors for the unions' loyalties. Labor officials didn't know what the governor's proposals were, and what they did learn frightened them. They also had grown weary of the governor's tactic of threatening ballot initiatives. As Bob Balgenorth, president of a council of building and trades unions, said: "Nobody thinks that you have a relationship with someone who bargains with a gun pointed at your head. That is not a relationship."

It took more than simply the governor's rough tactics to bring the union coalition together. Schwarzenegger's desire to eliminate pensions for new employees provided some glue as well. His plan, based on legislation submitted by Assemblyman Keith Richman, would replace pensions with 401(k)s for all new employees of the government. Schwarzenegger might have been able to isolate CTA and neutralize other unions by quickly backing away from this proposal or amending it so it would modify but not eliminate pensions. He didn't.

Instead, the CTA isolated Schwarzenegger by attacking Democratic politicians who lined up with the governor. When the new Democratic leader in the senate, Don Perata, suggested he might be able to work with Schwarzenegger on changing Proposition 98, the union sent 50,000 pieces of mail to voters in his Oakland district. "Senator Don Perata wants to cut funding for local schools," the mailers said.

By mid-February, the union coalition had started to take shape. The coalition would adopt Alliance for a Better California as its permanent name. Even the acronym, ABC, served to remind voters of Schwarzenegger's betrayal of education. Not all unions could join. Though the CTA would carry the financial load, the ABC alliance required a buy-in of $500,000 from each union. By combining forces, the ABC unions would be able to raise and spend more than twice what Schwarzenegger could. They would share staff, expertise, and financial resources. The teachers' union alone would come up with more than $50 million by raising dues on its members $60 a year. All together, the unions in ABC had more than 2.5 million members.

AT MEETINGS EACH THURSDAY AFTERNOON, the ABC unions debated strategy. Almost immediately, ABC began to make the case that a special election represented a costly abuse of direct democracy. This argument had also been used against the recall, but the public—taken with the spectacle of a populist uprising, Arnold Schwarzenegger's first run for office along with 134 other candidates—had ignored it. However, it was unlikely that Schwarzenegger's reform push could match the recall's entertainment value. The unions found that when they linked the cost of a special election to the education deal, the case against the governor took hold.

At the same time, the ABC unions decided that they had to do more than badmouth Schwarzenegger and a possible election. In the event that the governor went forward with such an election, the unions wanted to qualify initiatives of their own. The previous fall, Democrats had conducted polls on several bills Schwarzenegger had vetoed. These surveys covered such legislation as an increase in the minimum wage, a re-regulation of the state's electricity market, and discounts on prescription drugs. By February, new surveys by a Democratic pollster found these bills were still popular—and that voters did not know Schwarzenegger had vetoed them.

So ABC quickly filed the minimum wage increase and other popular, Schwarzenegger-vetoed bills as ballot initiatives. These measures were designed to do more than simply let the public know about unpopular vetoes. Three initiatives—one requiring pharmaceutical companies to offer discounts on prescription drugs, a "Car Buyers' Bill of Rights" to impose new regulations on car dealers, and a third to re-regulate the energy market—were aimed at industries that had provided financial support for previous Schwarzenegger campaigns.

The ABC strategy showed just how far Schwarzenegger had shifted California's political center of gravity in the direction of direct democracy. By the middle of 2005, the number of proposed initiatives filed with the attorney general's office—the first step toward the ballot—had surpassed all existing records. Ultimately, some 152 proposed initiatives would be filed in 2005, which of course had been scheduled to be an off-year for California elections.

The overwhelming majority of these measures would be abandoned before signature gathering was complete. ABC would drop most of its countermeasures, including the minimum wage initiative. But simply filing the initiatives gave the unions and their allies leverage over the governor's donors. Rather than fight the "Car Buyers Bill of Rights," car dealers agreed to support legislation that added some of the consumer protections in the initiative to the laws governing car sales. PhRMA, the Pharmaceutical Research and Manufacturers of America, approached the CTA to negotiate a legislative alternative to ABC's drug discount initiative, but those talks failed. The pharmaceutical industry instead filed its own initiative establishing voluntary drug discounts to counter ABC's measure.

This multifront contest of reform measures, countermeasures, and even counters to the counters, contributed to the slow pace of Schwarzenegger's own decision-making. The governor and his team seemed overwhelmed by the variety of threats. In January, he had formally embraced a package of four constitutional amendments introduced in the legislature: a spending limit for the budget, merit pay for teachers, the replacement of pensions with 401(k)s for new workers, and a plan to have retired judges rather than the legislature draw legislative districts. The legislature was only one-half of his strategy. Schwarzenegger still planned to back ballot initiatives on each of the four subjects. But by late February, he had not yet embraced specific initiatives.

As the unions united, Schwarzenegger's own team splintered. Some of his consultants were sidelined for legal reasons. The previous year, the state's Fair Political Practices Commission had approved a new regulation that required Schwarzenegger's ballot measure committees—and other committees controlled by office holders—to abide by the same donation limits that applied in candidate campaigns. (This was to prevent politicians from using ballot measure committees to get around the limits.) The regulation went into effect after the November 2004 elections. When the regulation was first adopted, Schwarzenegger's lawyers had advised him to challenge it in court because such limits would handicap the governor, who would have to fight initiative campaigns against interest groups that could raise unlimited money themselves. But Schwarzenegger, a supporter of campaign finance reform, declined to challenge the regulation in court when it was first approved.

Since the regulation barred unlimited donations to the governor's own committee, Schwarzenegger's allies and donors, mostly in the business community, decided to launch a new ballot measure entity, the Citizens to Save California. The CSC could raise money in unlimited amounts as long as the governor did not "control" the committee. A legal opinion provided to the governor's staff said the CSC could consider the governor's reform goals, but that Schwarzenegger's aides and advisors should avoid any unnecessary contact.

Establishing the CSC made legal and financial sense, and the committee would raise money quickly and deftly handle the mechanics of qualifying measures under trying conditions. But the move also had political costs. By allowing the CSC to be created, Schwarzenegger had made fund-raising in unlimited amounts a higher priority than controlling the drafting of the ballot initiatives that could shape the future of the state. In retrospect, the governor might have been better off living under the contribution limits while immediately challenging them in court.

The creation of the CSC also inspired a game of "gotcha" as the unions and the press scrutinized whether Schwarzenegger was attempting to exert control over the committee. He provided plenty of fodder, speaking at CSC fund-raising lunches and joining CSC conference calls to explain the need for reform. As a result, the governor's fund-raising dominated media coverage, and left the mistaken impression that Schwarzenegger was a fund-raising colossus when, in fact, he would be badly outspent by ABC. The governor said he needed to raise $50 million to have a chance. The unions could put together more than twice that. In a bit of chutzpah, the unions organized public protests outside CSC fund-raisers to highlight Schwarzenegger's fund-raising.

But the composition of the CSC reinforced the perception. Allan Zaremberg, the CEO of the California Chamber of Commerce, cochaired the CSC, and the board also included representatives of the California Business Roundtable, commercial property owners, and banks. "I am unexcited about the Chamber fronting for the Citizens to Save California . . . for two reasons," Sipple wrote in a January 23, 2005, memo distributed among

Schwarzenegger's advisors: "First, if this is to be a true anti-establishment effort to fix California, why have one of the pillars of the establishment at the forefront? Secondly, ultimately we should want this Year of Reform to be a bipartisan citizen-based cause—I think we may be unwittingly helping our opponents' framing effort by signaling this as a partisan, business-backed effort. Seems too Sacramento Centric."

But, after so many ballot campaigns, the governor, once a reluctant fund-raiser, had grown closer to the business donors who made his initiative work possible. The previous fall, he had vetoed all ten bills that the chamber labeled "job killers." And the consultants who made up his political team had other clients, many of them businesses that were part of the chamber or the business roundtable. In the previous fall, Murphy had been part of a chamber-backed effort to elect more pro-business politicians to the legislature.

With Schwarzenegger devoted to the ballot, a handful of his staffers began to moonlight for his various political committees. For example, Richard Costigan, Schwarzenegger's legislative secretary, was paid as much as $5,000 per month to do work for the California Recovery Team, Schwarzenegger's main ballot measure committee. (He and other aides also appeared at some fund-raisers, an apparent violation of Schwarzenegger's promise during the recall not to use his appointees in fund-raising.) The governor's chief of staff and communications director each received extra pay for political work through another committee, set up in the event Schwarzenegger chose to run for re-election in 2006. Such arrangements, while essentially allowing political donations to supplement the salaries of state workers, were legal. But they demonstrated how Schwarzenegger's practice of using the ballot to govern brought his team into closer contact with political donors.

THE CITIZENS TO SAVE CALIFORNIA held weekly Tuesday meetings in Sacramento, usually in the office of election lawyer Steve Merksamer. These meetings included the business representatives who made up the CSC board, as well as political consultants and lawyers such as Merksamer who specialized in ballot initiatives. These experienced professionals knew just how difficult it was to win a "yes" vote for one initiative, much less four at the same time. But the CSC advisors argued that "this governor" was special. This governor could get the California public to pay attention to complicated reform proposals. This governor could beat back more than $100 million in union attacks. This governor could leap tall buildings in a single bound.

To determine which initiatives to back, CSC commissioned a series of eight surveys by the Republican pollster Neil Newhouse between February 13 and 17. Some 4,400 people were surveyed. (Most political polls interviewed between 400 and 800 people.) Eight potential initiatives were tested: three education proposals, pension reform, the spending limit, a measure that would give the governor more power to reorganize the executive branch, an initiative to allow more contracting out of government services, and a so-called "paycheck protection" initiative that would require public employee unions to seek permission of members before spending dues on politics. The polls revealed effective arguments both for and against each possible initiative. The results also raised questions about the viability of a major reform push led by Schwarzenegger.

The governor, by getting into fights with the teachers' union, was losing the support of Democrats, who now viewed "the governor's agenda with heightened suspicion," the pollster Newhouse wrote in a memo to the CSC. More dangerously, Schwarzenegger had lost popularity across the board because of the broken education deal. Forty-seven percent of voters surveyed agreed with the following statement: "He is really cutting California's education budget this year because he did not give the schools all that was due them under Prop 98."

(Voters in related focus groups asked openly if the state itself was governable. "Indeed one of the more interesting findings from the focus groups was voters' sense that California's problems might be even too big for Schwarzenegger to handle," according to a report produced by Newhouse.)

Worse still, each of the eight reform proposals had vulnerabilities. The pension reform backed by Schwarzenegger and Richman was particularly weak. A slim majority, 53 percent, supported the measure, and there were three strong arguments against it that tested better than any argument in favor. A spending limit initiative would have 68 percent support on first blush. But when voters learned that the proposal would change the Prop 98 education guarantee, support dropped to 49 percent. Voters supported stripping legislators of the power to draw their own districts, but redistricting reform could be beaten by attacking the use of retired judges to draw the lines instead.

Of all the initiatives tested, the safest political bet was a proposal to require school districts to dedicate at least 75 percent of their money to the classroom. Even after voters were read arguments against the measure, this "75–25" initiative retained better than 65 percent support.

The concept of a reform package "is a much easier sell than the component pieces of the agenda," Newhouse wrote. Despite the governor's own baggage "we need to tie these proposals together and hitch them to his star." Read one way, the polls and focus groups suggested that Schwarzenegger's entire reform push should be reevaluated, but Newhouse struck an optimistic tone. "While it is unlikely that we could sweep all these measures in the fall, there is little doubt that the combination of a favorable political environment and Arnold's persona makes it likely that we can pass some meaningful and substantial reforms."

The polls left unanswered what would prove to be one of the most important political questions of the year: whether voters would be more or less inclined to support such measures if they had to vote on them in a 2005 special election. Newhouse's survey asked again and again if voters wanted to cast ballots on the reforms, and about two-thirds said yes. But he did not specifically gauge how support for the measures would be affected if they were part of a special election ballot. This omission would prove crucial.

THE POLL SEEMED TO HAVE LITTLE impact on the choices made by the CSC. The committee pressed forward with the unpopular pension reform measure, and did not pursue the most popular education reform, a guarantee that 75 percent of school funds would reach the classroom. Some wondered if such a rule was practical as policy, and putting together a 75 percent law that would be enforceable in large urban and rural school districts would take months. CSC and Schwarzenegger did not have that kind of time if they wanted an education measure on a 2005 ballot. Instead, CSC began collecting signatures on an initiative establishing a merit pay system for teachers. But that proved so unpopular in polls that CSC would have to drop it after spending $100,000 on signatures. It would ultimately embrace an education initiative extending the period California's public school teachers must wait to receive tenure from two years to five years.

In their bid to get the governor's and CSC's backing for their particular reforms, Schwarzenegger's allies began running behind-the-scenes campaigns against each other. Zaremberg, the chamber president, filed a redistricting alternative to Ted Costa's measure that would delay implementation until 2012. (Costa's measure ultimately received CSC's backing.) On spending limits, more than a dozen possible initiatives drafted by three separate groups were considered, touching off a bitter battle inside both CSC and the governor's office. Conservatives in the governor's camp wanted a strict spending cap that limited the government's ability to raise fees. Administration liberals, most notably the new cabinet secretary Terry Tamminen, pointed out that many of the state's environmental programs were funded through fees paid by individuals and businesses for government services. Some Republicans sided with Tamminen for a different reason. They feared that if the spending limit included fees as well as budget reform, it could be challenged legally for violating a rule requiring ballot initiatives to cover only a "single subject."

The CSC was prepared to back the spending limit of John Campbell, an assemblyman-turned-state senator. John Campbell and his allies had been vetting their measure for a year. But when he refused to remove the restrictions on fee increases from his spending limit, CSC board members said they wouldn't endorse his measure. Campbell made an appointment with Schwarzenegger to appeal the decision, but the governor's senior staff, including Clarey and Stutzman, intercepted him and wouldn't let him see the governor.

Schwarzenegger convened a long meeting with his top advisors in February so he could get a full briefing on all the various initiatives. He soon reached decisions on most, but by early March had not endorsed a specific spending limit. So Hauck and Zaremberg, the two business leaders of CSC, had yet another spending limit drafted, called the Live Within Our Means Act. It was a mixture of John Campbell's initiative and the legislative reform finance director Tom Campbell had put together. But this initiative was so rapidly and poorly drafted—it took less than ten days—that no one has ever publicly admitted to authorship.[1]

The measure misstated the funding formula that allocated money to community colleges. One provision would have allowed governors unilaterally to stop honoring contracts. At the same time, the initiative's spending restraints had been weakened to the point that, while they would smooth out fluctuations in tax revenues, the measure would not accomplish Schwarzenegger's goal of eliminating the state's structural deficit.

In one sign of the confusion, Schwarzenegger himself was unaware that a provision of the Live Within Our Means Act further violated his funding deal with the CTA. As part of that agreement, the governor had pledged to restore the accumulated "maintenance factor"—the shortfall in education funding from previous bad years when the money that went to schools did not match the Prop 98 guarantee—to the funding base for future years. While Schwarzenegger wanted to eliminate the maintenance factor provision as part of his amendments to Prop 98, he did not immediately understand that the Live Within Our Means Act would alter the previous maintenance factor he had promised to restore. Reiss said this fact was not mentioned when the governor was first briefed on Live Within Our Means in March. "If he had complete control of it from the beginning and had all his lawyers looking at it, he

---

[1]CSC records suggested that several people had a hand in the drafting of it, including Hauck, Zaremberg, and budget experts such as Loren Kaye, Steve Spears, and Russ Gould.

probably wouldn't have wanted" that, said Reiss. Tom Campbell said that Live Within Our Means was written more severely in order to pressure the legislature and the education lobby to agree to an alternative.

Schwarzenegger recalled that the provision was added late in the drafting process. By the time the governor spotted it, there was no time to refile and still qualify Live Within Our Means for a 2005 special election. "I was unhappy about that," the governor recalled.

The mistake was a striking example of how Schwarzenegger had lost control of his reform agenda. Publicly, the governor would call the Live Within Our Means Act the centerpiece of his reform effort. That centerpiece was a perfect mess. The spending limit offered little in policy and no shortage of political vulnerabilities that could be exploited. Live Within Our Means would take the unpopular step of altering the Prop 98 education funding guarantee while also failing to provide the tough limit on spending that conservatives wanted. And Live Within Our Means polled so poorly that union strategists believed they could use the initiative to discredit Schwarzenegger's other proposals.

CSC board members and their initiative consultant, Rick Claussen, rapidly gathered signatures on the Live Within Our Means spending limit and three other reform measures—teacher tenure, pension reform, and redistricting. Given the short time frame, it was difficult work. But they comforted themselves with the belief that the initiatives were a bluff to allow Schwarzenegger to secure a legislative deal. "At some point in sixty days," Claussen recalled thinking, "everybody would probably pack up and go home and, you know, whatever signatures were gathered would go into the dumpster. And we'd all be happy and have a nice rest."

SCHWARZENEGGER'S POPULARITY COULD not withstand his own mistakes and the union attacks on his education record. By late January, 73 percent of voters were expressing concerns about "cuts" in education, according to the Public Policy Institute of California. In February, the percentage of voters who had a favorable opinion of Schwarzenegger dipped below 60 percent, the lowest it had been since the beginning of his term in office. Publicly, Schwarzenegger taunted the unions and Democrats, and pretended his poll numbers weren't sliding at all. "Those poor little guys," he said at the state Republican Party convention the second week in February. "They're trying very hard. . . . They may have a wonderful dream about that. But the reality is very sad for them. The reality is that they're not going to get my numbers down."

Behind closed doors, though, Schwarzenegger was concerned. On February 7, he met privately with Barbara Kerr, the CTA president, and her top staffers. Kerr had asked for the meeting after her aides advised her to see if there was any way the governor might change his mind about the deal. Instead of sounding apologetic, Schwarzenegger took a wounded tone. Why don't you guys like me? he asked. He pointed out that education spending was going up on a year-to-year basis to keep up with the cost of living and enrollment growth. But as Schwarzenegger knew, that increase fell short of the growth in the Prop 98 guarantee. Kerr replied that it was nothing personal: she simply wanted the governor to stick to their original deal. The teachers' union president mentioned that she had heard Schwarzenegger was planning to make TV ads disputing that he had broken his deal with the unions. The governor then said icily: Barbara, I have listened to your radio ads.

These were the relatively mild ads that quoted from a RAND study on California education.

You are very dramatic, the governor said to Kerr. You should play the Shelley Winters role in *The Poseidon Adventure*.

It was an insult disguised as a compliment. Kerr and the late-career Winters were both full-bodied women. Kerr fixed him with a stare.

I have offended you, Schwarzenegger said. I should send flowers.

Diamonds won't do it, Kerr replied. The only thing that will solve it is if you keep your promise.

Kerr had been accompanied there by CTA political director Joe Nunez. He was furious. Reiss averted a confrontation by changing the subject.

As the meeting broke up, Kerr approached the governor directly. She was determined to find out whether he supported the paycheck protection initiative on union dues. The governor told her he didn't. That answer was technically true. But Schwarzenegger's allies had filed the measure as a bargaining chip that he could trade away to get other reforms. In time, Kerr would remember the governor's words that day as another broken promise.

Two days later, the teachers' union began broadcasting a new, tougher radio ad by the Washington media consulting firm Dixon/Davis. The spot consisted of a fictional phone call from a man to Schwarzenegger's office. The man complained to the operator taking the call that "when he was campaigning for governor, Schwarzenegger promised to protect Prop 98, a law passed by voters that guarantees minimum funding for our schools . . . . Well, now he wants to gut Prop 98 and stiff our kids for $2 billion every year."

"Sir, what were you expecting?" the operator asked.

"Well, I guess I expected the governor to keep his word to our students."

The operator laughed.

SCHWARZENEGGER WANTED TO RESPOND publicly to such claims, which he believed distorted the deal and his intentions. But his consultants, wary of causing any legal trouble for the CSC, were doing very little. When, on a Friday in late January, Schwarzenegger told aides he wanted a TV ad on education on the air by the following week, he learned that nothing had been filmed. His own political accounts had less than $1 million, not nearly enough for an effective statewide buy. (All the money was going to the CSC for signature gathering.) At the governor's direction, Sipple produced a spot showing Schwarzenegger talking about his reform plans on pensions and teacher merit pay. But the initiatives on those two subjects polled poorly. One version of the merit pay proposal inadvertently deleted a state law governing dismissal of teachers. The ad never ran.

Schwarzenegger advisors inside and outside the administration offered plenty of ideas for getting the governor out of his slump. Tamminen, the cabinet secretary, twice circulated a memo arguing that the governor needed to do themed events to highlight his policy accomplishments. Sipple circulated a memo in late January calling for meetings of the advisors, new focus groups and surveys, and a series of major policy speeches by Schwarzenegger on his reforms. Gorton warned in one missive that the governor was politically surrounded by the unions. We're Custer, Gorton believed. They're the Indians.

Schwarzenegger dropped by a meeting of his consultants in Century City on February 3 in an attempt to prod them. Although it was becoming conventional wisdom among California pundits that the governor was a creature of these consultants, in truth, he was furious with them.

What the fuck are you guys doing? he asked. Why is nothing happening?

Schwarzenegger went after Randle, his political operations guru. The governor asked: Why don't I have a coalition of teachers to defend me on education funding and reform? And where is our law enforcement support on pensions? Randle said he had been told that coalition building was supposed to be handled by the senior staff.

I don't care about that, Schwarzenegger responded. You've always done this for us.

OK, Randle said, I'll build a coalition. But there has to be a comprehensive strategy of TV ads and press events, not just endorsements.

The consultants then debated what that strategy should be. Schwarzenegger needed somehow to counter the attacks on his education record while at the same time define his reform measures. But he barely had enough money to achieve one of those objectives. Some consultants argued strongly for putting TV ads on the air to fight back on education. Others responded that such ads would play into the union attacks on the governor. He needed to put his proposals, not himself, at center stage.

Schwarzenegger listened to both arguments before weighing in. He didn't think the public was ready for a debate on the merits of his reform proposals just yet. After all, he was still sorting out the details himself. The governor wanted to see ads countering the education attacks immediately. Too many people thought he meant to cut education. He even had to explain himself to parents at one of the private schools attended by his children.

The meeting, while difficult, produced some results. Within two weeks, Randle put together a Coalition for Education Reform, consisting of principals, teachers, and school administrators who would defend Schwarzenegger's commitment to schools and promote his education reforms. Stutzman and Murphy produced a plan to win press and TV coverage over the next two months. Schwarzenegger began a new series of media events. In San Diego, he gave a short speech about pension costs while standing before an armored truck with piles of cash spilling out the doors as if the driver had been robbed. "Right now, our treasury is like this armored car with the doors kicked wide open," he said. "The money is just flying out and it's bleeding the state dry."

The governor's team also put together focus groups in the San Fernando Valley. Many of the participants were reassessing Schwarzenegger, primarily because of what they were hearing about education funding. Worse still, none of the reform subjects seemed to excite people. The consultants were dismayed. They thought Schwarzenegger's staff and the CSC had done more thorough vetting. Schwarzenegger himself did not attend the focus groups but he soon heard reports of the debacle.

When the governor joined a conference call of his consultants and top staff from his mountain getaway in Idaho at 8 a.m. on Saturday, February 19, he was angrier than any member of his team had ever heard him. His falling numbers, the constant union attacks, and his own inability to respond were beginning to unnerve him. One by one, Schwarzenegger lashed out at his advisors. He asked why Stutzman, the communications director who had taken over Donna Lucas's role as liaison between the Horseshoe and the political team, didn't have more of a plan for countering the CTA on education. Why couldn't Randle produce more teachers to appear in the TV ads? While some consultants defended themselves, others agreed with Schwarzenegger.

You're right, Gorton told the governor. We've all failed you.

Murphy took the brunt of Schwarzenegger's ire. Murphy had been on a cruise sponsored by a conservative magazine during the focus groups.

Schwarzenegger, from his own vacation home, started needling him about the cruise and other vacations. This was one of the governor's less attractive traits. He did not demand ideological conformity from aides, but he wanted them to build their lives around him. But Murphy had initially agreed to stay with the governor only for his first year in office. Even after signing up for another year, he balked at spending more time in Sacramento. It was a point of pride with Murphy that he did not know the names of all the Republican legislators. In his view, the political culture in Sacramento was based on whether or not your enemies were happy with you. All decision-making there was emotional, with too much of an emphasis on approval ratings. Murphy joked that if he was the head of North Korean intelligence and wanted to sabotage California politics, he would take $10 million and bribe the Field Poll, which produced surveys for most of the state's newspapers.

Murphy also believed the difficulties facing Schwarzenegger were not extraordinary. That perspective was born of experience Schwarzenegger did not yet have. Murphy had worked for governors all over the country. Making big changes required big fights, and big fights hurt politicians' ratings. That was a fact of political life, even if you were a movie star.

On that Saturday morning phone call, the governor's personal criticism crossed the line with Murphy, who said he would not accept that sort of treatment. Murphy wanted control of the political operation—real control, not the first-among-equals status he currently had—or he would walk. Schwarzenegger didn't offer it. As soon as the governor signed off the call, Murphy announced: "I've had enough." He quit. Randle indicated he might leave as well. With his tantrum, Schwarzenegger had effectively blown up his political team at the exact moment he needed his consultants pulling together in his defense.

THAT SAME PRESIDENT'S DAY WEEKEND, the unions put the finishing touches on their plans for a new wave of attacks on the governor. Labor leaders felt they had found a soft target: the governor's proposal to replace pensions for new state workers with 401(k)s.

In the weeks after the State of the State in January, a labor coalition, which was separate from ABC but included many of the same unions, saw its numbers grow so fast, from twelve to fifty organizations, that it had to move meetings to CTA in order to have enough space. The unions, following a strategy derived from polling, argued that by eliminating pensions, Schwarzenegger's proposal would also eliminate death and disability pensions for firefighters and police. Widows of police officers killed in the line of duty would argue publicly that death benefits are "the only barrier be-

tween them and the gutter," according to a memo by a public relations firm
working for a Los Angeles police union.

The unions had spent two months honing the attack. But in order to take
advantage of the calendar, they kept it under wraps until the last week of
February. By waiting to point out the mistakes, the unions made sure it was
too late for the governor to refile a corrected pension initiative in time to
qualify for a special election in 2005.

In point of fact, many pension experts agreed that Schwarzenegger's proposal would not touch the death and disability pension of any current employee. The ban on pensions would only apply to future employees, and it
would not preclude state or local governments from offering special death
and disability benefits.

Still, the future ban on pensions offered at the very least a political vulnerability. According to a four-page written account of their activities produced
by the coalition, the unions met with the state attorney general Bill Lockyer,
a Democrat, whose office soon gave their argument credibility by including
"elimination of death and disability benefits" in the official title and summary for the pension initiative. Lockyer's motives and role in preparing that
title and summary—and another title and summary of questionable accuracy for the governor's redistricting measure—would become a subject of
dispute. Lockyer maintained that the lawyers in his government law division
did the work and that he had no role. But in a speech to the state Democratic
convention, he boasted that he had contributed to Schwarzenegger's growing
political troubles.

Even longtime Schwarzenegger allies such as L.A. County Sheriff Lee
Baca criticized the pension measure. The League of California Cities and
the California State Association of Counties, which had worked with
Schwarzenegger to pass Proposition 1A the previous year, also opposed it.
Democrats in the legislature had been preparing an alternative to
Schwarzenegger's plan. But with the governor losing so much support, they
decided not to throw him a lifeline.

Schwarzenegger tried to ignore the attacks at first, but the unions soon
made sure he couldn't. The governor kicked off the signature-gathering drive
for some of his initiatives on March 1 by driving one of his Hummers
(dubbed "Reform One" for the occasion) from the capitol to a local Apple-
bee's, where he circulated a petition among diners. Union members protested
both outside and inside the restaurant. The next day, some three hundred
union members protested at Schwarzenegger appearances in Hayward, on
the east side of San Francisco Bay, and in Bakersfield.

The Arnold chase was on. Throughout 2005, wherever Schwarzenegger appeared in the state or the country, California union members greeted him. The unions' response was lightning fast. Less than two hours after learning of a Schwarzenegger appearance in Santa Ana in March, the unions had eighty people there. The California Nurses Association, which had begun protesting Schwarzenegger in late 2004 when he delayed the implementation of new nurse-patient ratios, even picketed the finals of the Arnold Classic bodybuilding tournament in Ohio on the first Saturday in March. As Schwarzenegger tried to raise money on the East Coast the following week, the California Professional Firefighters union picked up the trail. A Santa Clara firefighter managed to get inside the 21 Club in Manhattan during a Schwarzenegger fund-raiser with New York Governor George Pataki and ask Schwarzenegger, Why are you trying to take away our death and disability benefits? You're misinformed, the governor replied.

The next day, union protesters braved freezing temperatures outside a fund-raiser at the St. Regis Hotel in Washington.

The anti-Schwarzenegger protests became a traveling festival. The nurses tracked Schwarzenegger's movements while firefighters cooked to feed the protesting crowds. Teachers brought students. On March 16, three thousand people surrounded the Century City hotel where Schwarzenegger was holding a fund-raiser for donors who had paid between $10,000 and $89,200 for their seats.

These protests were not spontaneous. They were well-organized events sponsored by some of the largest, best-funded unions in the state, but they had an easy, celebratory feeling that made them both irresistible to TV cameras and fun to attend. The protests used Schwarzenegger's celebrity against him. Not only did the governor attract TV cameras, some protesters said they showed up in the hopes of catching a glimpse of him.

Criticizing Schwarzenegger became fashionable. Honoring a union request, U2 singer Bono made a brief statement of support for the nurses and other protesters during a concert in Los Angeles. Warren Beatty began conferring regularly with Speaker Núñez, and in March, he gave a speech denouncing the governor at a Beverly Hills dinner sponsored by a group that operated a Web site devoted to criticism of Schwarzenegger, arnoldwatch.org. This was the start of a new pastime for Beatty as a public critic of Schwarzenegger.

In March, the governor's popularity took a nose dive. By month's end, he was below 45 percent in his job approval rating in one union poll. With financial help from the state Republican Party, Schwarzenegger finally made the ad he had envisioned with teachers defending his record on education.

The TV spot concluded with Schwarzenegger walking into a classroom and saying: "$50 billion, almost half of our state's budget, will go into education this year. I want to make sure that money goes directly to the classroom for your kids and the teachers who care about them."

But Schwarzenegger had not adopted the education reform guaranteeing 75 percent of education dollars to the classroom. And the ad simply came too late to counter the popular impression that the governor, by failing to provide the Prop 98 growth as part of his budget deal, had cut education.

SCHWARZENEGGER WAS LOSING THE public relations fight on pensions, too. On March 14, the Citizens to Save California conducted focus groups in Concord, an East Bay suburb, to assess the damage sustained to Schwarzenegger's pension reform proposal and to the governor himself.

For all the media attention given to the union protests on the pension issue, few voters in the focus groups had heard much about the subject. Informed of the unfunded pension liabilities of the state and cities, the focus group members said they understood the need for reform. But as soon as they were told of the unions' arguments about death and disability, they turned against the pension proposal. "When voters become aware of this provision, it is a poison pill," the pollsters Neil Newhouse and Patrick Lanne, whose company Public Opinion Strategies ran the focus groups, concluded in a confidential memo to the CSC. "Quite simply, voters believed society has a moral obligation to provide these benefits to the families of our 'front line' public servants." By the end of each focus group, all participants said they would vote no on the measure.

The pollsters concluded: "The prospects of this measure passing were never very strong. . . . This measure could easily become the 'Death and Disability Elimination Act' and will almost certainly fail."

AFTER THE DISASTROUS PRESIDENT'S DAY weekend conference call among Schwarzenegger's advisors and Murphy's resignation from the political team, it fell to Clarey to soothe egos. This was not easy work. The team was roiled by rumors that President Clinton's one-time advisor Dick Morris, who wrote newspaper columns praising Schwarzenegger for his redistricting reform and his environmental record, was being hired. (The governor and the consultant talked once, Morris would say in an e-mail, but "we didn't get into political advice.")

Clarey helped talk Randle, who was still furious from the President's Day weekend call, out of resigning. And in the days after Murphy quit, Schwarzenegger placed a few calls to the consultant, who didn't immediately return them. Late one afternoon the following week, Schwarzenegger made a private visit to the set of Steven Spielberg's film *War of the Worlds*. From there, he departed for a secret meeting so he and the consultant could work out their differences.

Murphy arrived first in a downscale restaurant near LAX—complete with potted plants and surly waitresses—for a decidedly mob-style reunion.

I can tell the future, Murphy told a waitress. In about ten minutes, you're going to wish you had a camera. The waitress ignored him.

Ten minutes later, she did a double take as Schwarzenegger walked in with his California Highway Patrol security detail. Murphy again insisted on full control of the political team. Schwarzenegger said fine, but if you're going to be in charge, you need to be in charge. Murphy could make whatever changes in the team he wished, but the governor demanded what he had long wanted from Murphy: his full attention. Schwarzenegger also gave Murphy a watch as a gift. Murphy's brief departure from Schwarzenegger's employment was never publicly disclosed.

A court ruling issued in March gave Murphy even freer rein. A judge struck down the Fair Political Practices regulation that had required Schwarzenegger's ballot measure committee—or any such committee controlled by a politician—to abide by limits on campaign donations. (Schwarzenegger and the CSC had challenged the regulation in court after they were sued for violating it.) The governor could again use his California Recovery Team to accept unlimited donations. Murphy told the *Sacramento Bee*: "Any advantage the Democrats thought they'd have because of the bifurcated nature of the campaign has evaporated. Now they're going to face everything we've got. If I were them, I'd make a deal."

The decision came three months too late for Schwarzenegger. The CSC had already drafted his initiatives. He had suffered substantial political damage. The unions had a two-month head start in the fight, during a period when the money the governor raised went to signature gathering. The unions, rather than fearing Schwarzenegger's reform proposals, now saw some of them as weapons they could use against him.

Schwarzenegger and his operation were back in full control, but they seemed to be in denial, talking as if it were still November and Schwarzenegger were polling at 71 percent. One consultant suggested starting over and putting together another commission (call it the California Citizens Association or California First Committee) to look at reform. With the public and visitors to his office, the governor declared that with time, he could sell the public on his approach to changing the state. But in one conversation, Schwarzenegger blamed Murphy for convincing him to threaten the legislature with ballot initiatives. This was a rewriting of history: the idea had been Schwarzenegger's.

During his seventeen months as governor, Schwarzenegger had become accustomed to practicing politics from a position of strength, leveraging his popularity and direct democracy into deals. Now he would have to negotiate from a position of weakness.

MURPHY RECONVENED THE ENTIRE political team at Oak on Good Friday, March 25. Schwarzenegger did not join the meeting. The consultants had a narrow and urgent focus: they wanted the governor to dump the politically poisonous pension measure. The CSC had already spent more than $400,000 gathering signatures for the initiative, but it polled so poorly that if it wasn't dropped, it could bring down the whole reform package.

Schwarzenegger initially balked at the suggestion when it was presented to him the evening of March 30 in Los Angeles. This was a giant strategy session, attended by political consultants, senior staffers, and even fundraisers. They made clear that raising money would not be easy, and Schwarzenegger would need every dollar he could find if he wanted to compete with the unions on TV. (To save money, Schwarzenegger's consultants had their contracts adjusted to cap their annual earnings, and the California Recovery Team hired Steve Kram, a former chief operating officer of the William Morris Agency, to keep a close eye on political expenses.)

Schwarzenegger asked pointed questions at this meeting about his political predicament. When Stutzman left briefly to go to the bathroom, the governor stopped the conversation so the communications director wouldn't miss any part of what he was saying. Schwarzenegger wondered if there was any way to salvage pension reform. Randle explained that his options were limited. The governor had lost rank-and-file public safety employees. His only hope was to convince groups representing law enforcement managers to back him.

The next day, March 31, Schwarzenegger called in police chiefs, fire chiefs, narcotics officers and sheriffs for meetings on pensions. Each group said they were grateful for the chance to discuss the subject, but suggested he should have asked for their opinions when the measure was first being put together. As she sat through this day of law enforcement meetings, Clarey could have kicked herself for not having arranged such sessions sooner. "I think the biggest mistake that I made in serving him was not pushing those people in and hearing from the constituent organizations on pensions sooner," she said. "I take total responsibility for it."

After two days of eating humble pie with law enforcement, Schwarzenegger tried to see if he could start negotiations on a compromise measure with the legislature and unions. On an April 6 conference call with police chiefs, he was told plainly that such negotiations would go forward only once the initiative was abandoned.

The next morning, April 7, Schwarzenegger called a press conference to drop the pension initiative. It was the biggest setback of his eighteen months in office. He gave interviews to a dozen different radio shows to say he would continue to pursue pension reform, but would make adjustments first. "Exactly the way you rewrite your script, exactly the way you kind of retape a show," he said. "If the answer doesn't work or your performance doesn't work the same as we do in movies, you do take two, take three, take four. That's exactly what we're doing."

However, Schwarzenegger couldn't even surrender without a snafu. In dropping the pension initiative, the governor had pledged to halt any campaign activity on the issue. But his consultants didn't get the word and the next morning, April 8, they put a new pension ad on the radio. In the spot, the parents of a slain sheriff's deputy praised the governor for trying to reform pensions. (The unions had used the widow of the same deputy in an ad criticizing the pension initiative.)

That evening, Schwarzenegger called Marty Wilson, the consultant who authorized the buy, on his cell.

"What are you doing?" the governor asked. "I didn't authorize the radio ad."

Wilson pulled it off the air. "I realize my day is generally no match for yours, but this shit is starting to get to me," Wilson wrote in recounting the episode by e-mail to Stutzman. "To quote Lloyd Bridges, 'I picked the wrong week to quit sniffing glue.'"

The unions agreed to begin pension talks with Schwarzenegger aides the following week, but they resolved not to bargain. "I have no intention of negotiating or offering any proposals at the meetings," one union leader said in an e-mail to other labor officials before the April 14 talks. Schwarzenegger's aides told the unions they did not care if retirement money was paid out as a pension or a 401k as long as there was "stabilization" of costs for the government. At each of the first two sessions, labor negotiators objected that legislative leaders weren't present. When Schwarzenegger's aides brought out flip charts to start drafting potential legislation at a third negotiation session on April 19, the union leaders told the governor's team "that it would be counterproductive to conduct parallel negotiations on this issue because it is inextricably tied to the other initiatives," according to an e-mail account circulated by Dave Low of the California School Employees Association. The governor's staffers said "they were moving forward with discussions on specific proposals with those in the room, and if we didn't want to participate, that was our business," the e-mail report concluded. At that point, the unions walked out of the negotiations and did not return.

AT THE END OF APRIL, THE GOVERNOR returned to the stump to help signature gatherers meet their deadlines on the three remaining initiatives: teacher tenure, the Live Within Our Means spending limit, and redistricting.

A fourth measure, backed by gubernatorial allies but not endorsed by Schwarzenegger himself, also was heading to the ballot: the paycheck protection initiative. The signatures on all four measures needed to be turned in by the second week of May if they were going to qualify in time for a 2005 election. If Schwarzenegger were to call such an election, the most likely date would be November 8, when several cities and counties already had elections scheduled.

On the campaign trail, Schwarzenegger made uncharacteristic mistakes. During a speech to a convention of newspaper publishers, he suggested that the federal government "close the borders," a xenophobic comment for which he quickly apologized, saying that he had meant to say the borders should be better secured. Ten days later, he called a talk radio show in Los Angeles and praised a citizen militia group, the Minutemen, who patrolled the borders. President Bush had called the Minutemen vigilantes. The call was not part of any political strategy, and Clarey went through the roof when she found out about it. In polls, the percentage of Latinos who approved of his job performance dropped below 25 percent.

In his public events, Schwarzenegger leaned harder than ever on theatrics. He seemed to believe that bigger, flashier events would give him a better chance of pulling out of his rut. At a press conference in Sacramento, his team had a twenty-five-foot model of the capitol constructed along with a giant faucet spewing red water—"red ink"—so he could turn it off to illustrate how his spending limit would work. Schwarzenegger instead reaped negative publicity for the cheesy stunt and for using state government employees to build the model. In the Sacramento suburb of Elk Grove, he cut a ribbon down the middle of a street in one gated community to show how gerrymandering had divided neighborhoods. Democrats quickly pointed out the ribbon Schwarzenegger cut was a few blocks away from the real district boundary. After Schwarzenegger patched a pothole in San Jose to illustrate how his spending limit would free up more money for infrastructure repairs, the San Francisco Chronicle reported the pothole had been a crack in the road that was turned into a hole by city crews for the occasion.

Similar events had worked in previous campaigns, but did not match the reform effort. Whatever their flaws, Schwarzenegger's proposals were detailed and serious. He needed the public to pay attention to the initiatives, not to his persona. His ads failed on this score, too. One new spot, in the cafeteria setting he had used in some recall ads, received attention mainly because Schwarzenegger was pictured at a lunchroom table filled with products—Pepsi, Arrowhead water, Cheetos—made by companies that had donated to his campaigns. The governor's aides denied any product placement.

Schwarzenegger needed to talk about his reform proposals more than ever because he was suddenly less popular than his initiatives. At the end of April, Schwarzenegger's pollster John McLaughlin flew out to California from New York to present his latest surveys. McLaughlin was frank. Schwarzenegger had lost the public relations battle with the teachers' union over education funding. That defeat had cost Schwarzenegger crucial support from Democrats, independents, and some Republican women. The pollster urged Schwarzenegger to find some way to give the education lobby the money it wanted—but without raising taxes, which would be considered a betrayal by Republicans.

During the presentation, Schwarzenegger seemed strangely disengaged, as if he did not want the bad data to shake his optimism. He told the consultants that the year was unfolding like a movie script, and this was the second act when the hero struggled. Later, the governor told two advisors that polls were like muscles, all you had to do was pump them up a little.

On May 9, Schwarzenegger drove a truck full of signed initiative petitions to a rally at a paint company in Orange County. This event marked the end of the signature gathering. His three reforms—teacher tenure, spending limit, and redistricting—would qualify for the ballot (as Propositions 74, 76, and 77 respectively.) So would the paycheck protection proposal to limit the ability of unions to spend dues on political campaigns. It would be numbered Prop 75.

Shortly before signatures were submitted for Prop 75, Gale Kaufman, the political consultant for the ABC union alliance, joined a meeting with Murphy and Clarey to discuss a comprehensive deal on all measures. Kaufman warned that once Prop 75 qualified for the ballot, the ABC unions could not support a deal with the governor on that or the other measures. Since 75 was an attack on union power, the unions would have to run a full campaign and defeat it. "This is not a leverage point for us," she said.

Clarey and Murphy thought that was a bluff. Schwarzenegger, by failing to support or fund it, could make Prop 75 a dead letter, his advisors argued. Clarey and Murphy reminded Kaufman of Prop IA, the compromise measure on local government that Schwarzenegger had convinced the legislature to add to the ballot in the summer of 2004. Cities and counties had qualified an initiative on the same subject, Proposition 65, but agreed to drop their campaign for it and support 1A instead.

Kaufman thought that was ridiculous. She argued that dropping Prop 75 was a precondition to negotiations, since there was no compromise or alternative ballot measure that could replace Prop 75. Murphy concluded that Kaufman simply wanted to prevent a deal. As it turned out, Schwarzenegger did nothing to stop the measure's backers from submitting signatures. And the measure's qualification did not preclude talks with the unions.

In addition to paycheck protection and Schwarzenegger's three measures, two initiatives sponsored by ABC would be on the ballot: one initiative that required pharmaceutical companies to offer drug discounts to California residents (Proposition 79) and another to re-regulate the power market (Prop 80). The pharmaceutical industry, in turn, submitted signatures on an initiative for less generous drug discounts as a counter to the unions' counter. The industry measure would be Prop 78. An antiabortion activist had earlier qualified an initiative, Prop 73, requiring the notification of parents before minors have an abortion. It was unrelated to the larger war between Schwarzenegger and the unions. But if a special election was called, it would be one of the eight initiatives on the ballot.

Polls suggested that not one of the measures had stirred the public imagination. While an overwhelming majority of Californians wanted to vote on the initiatives, voters were content to wait until the next regularly scheduled election in June 2006.

IF CALIFORNIANS WERE TO VOTE ON his measures in November, Schwarzenegger would have to call a special election five months ahead of time—by the second week of June. Before he announced his decision on the election, the governor made one final, secret attempt to reach a deal on his reforms.

Two CTA officials, Joe Nunez and Bob Cherry, along with Prop 98 author John Mockler, had held informal discussions with Clarey and finance director Tom Campbell earlier in the spring to see if there was any potential for a legislative compromise. These sessions did not go particularly well, and the exchanges were at times sarcastic and nasty. When Mockler accused Tom Campbell of "sophistry" at one point, the finance director snapped back. Mockler, a cantankerous sort, called Campbell a sophist again.

But at the end of May, with prodding from Speaker Núñez, the CTA and its former political director Hein agreed to enter into new, secret negotiations with Schwarzenegger's top aides. On May 31, Hein, Mockler, and Joe Nunez met in a second-floor room at the Sheraton in downtown Sacramento with three top gubernatorial advisors, including Clarey. For nine straight days, CTA officials and Schwarzenegger's aides would trade proposals in a variety of secret locations outside the capitol.

The talks dealt with Schwarzenegger's Live Within Our Means spending limit, Proposition 76, which among other things would amend the Prop 98 education guarantee. The goal was to see if the union and the governor could reach a compromise on that limit, and on any changes to Prop 98. The CTA also pushed for Schwarzenegger to return to his original deal with the lobby. The meetings were agonizing, as every single word was parsed.

Clarey attended only the first session. As she left, Tom Campbell joined the negotiations. He would argue with Mockler, the Prop 98 author, about the details of the guarantee. Campbell claimed that the guarantee perversely hurt education funding because legislators knew that if they put more money into schools in one year, that cash would be locked into the Prop 98 funding base for future years. Mockler argued that increased spending on non-education programs and Schwarzenegger's cutting of the car tax, not Prop 98, were responsible for the state's budget problems.

The CTA offered to support a handful of changes to Prop 98 that would "smooth out" education funding. In effect, the union would cap increases in the Proposition 98 formula in good years and add a floor in years when spending would be less likely to grow. Hein would later recall, "We had told them, 'Here is a permanent change in Prop 98 that we can accept that helps you. The thing that is really hurting you is the peaks and the valleys. The thing we'll do is we'll make peaks shorter and the valleys shallower.'"

The governor's team saw these as minor changes. Schwarzenegger's staffers, including Campbell and legal affairs secretary Peter Siggins, said they wanted to cut the state's structural deficit, estimated at about $8 billion, in half. To do that, they said the Prop 98 provision called the maintenance factor—which guaranteed that if education was shortchanged in a given year that the money would be restored to the funding base in future years—had to be eliminated. The union objected that ending the maintenance factor would undermine the whole idea of having a minimum guarantee for education funding. The Schwarzenegger aides offered some concessions, but after nine days, there was still no agreement on specific proposals. The governor's team wanted a deal that gave the governor authority to make cuts in the budget in the middle of the year if revenues got out of line with expenditures. That was a deal breaker for the union.

Hein took the most hawkish attitude of the CTA negotiators in the talks. Privately, however, Hein considered circumventing CTA and the governor's staff and trying to cut a deal directly with Schwarzenegger. He decided against it, fearing that such an end-run would cause too much trouble.

CTA officials said they pressed the governor's office to keep talking, but Schwarzenegger staffers stopped calling. Tom Campbell recalled the final session ending on June 8 with Hein saying: We'll see you at the ballot box.

AT 5 P.M. ON JUNE 13, Schwarzenegger formally declared a special election for November 8, 2005. Despite the importance of the televised announcement, the governor's speech would be overshadowed by the biggest news in the state, the acquittal of Michael Jackson on child molestation charges. No Los Angeles TV station aired the governor's speech live.

Schwarzenegger delivered the brief address in the Reagan Cabinet Room, where busts of Reagan and Lincoln were visible. The room was also home to Conan the Barbarian's sword, and one member of the governor's team suggested in an email, half in jest, that Schwarzenegger swing the sword at the speech's conclusion. That was too theatrical even for this governor.

Schwarzenegger spent much of the speech defending himself. He talked about his record on education funding—"we are investing more money in education than ever in our history, $3 billion more for education this year"—before mentioning the election. Even his explanation of the election sounded defensive. "I know some people say, 'Arnold, why not wait until next year? Why have a special election now?' But how can we just stand around while our debt grows each year by billions of dollars? If you break your arm, you don't wait until your next physical. You get it fixed now." He dismissed the estimated $45 million cost of the extra election. "Do the math: for a buck and a quarter per citizen, you can fix a broken system and save the state billions of dollars. Now remember, this is your money. That is a fantastic bargain!"

EVEN WITH THE ELECTION NOW OFFICIAL and his initiatives on the ballot, Schwarzenegger still had time to reach a deal on compromise reforms that could be added to the ballot by the legislature. If such an agreement could be reached, Schwarzenegger would promise to campaign against his original initiatives and for the new compromises. The legislature could add measures to the November 8 ballot as late as August 15. Schwarzenegger, desperate for a deal, pulled back aides who criticized the unions or Democratic legislators. After Todd Harris, a consultant who worked with Murphy, criticized the CTA in the press for raising union dues to fund the campaign against

Schwarzenegger's initiatives, Harris received a warning from Stutzman. Rein in the rhetoric. The boss doesn't want it.

Calling the election had one immediate benefit. It helped Schwarzenegger prevail in the annual budget fight. On May 31, Nunez and assembly Democrats had announced a plan to raise income taxes on people making more than $300,000 a year in order to fund the $3 billion in Prop 98 growth that the education lobby said the schools were owed under their deal with the governor. By proposing taxes, the Democrats handed Schwarzenegger an issue that he quickly exploited in a thirty-second TV ad. The governor's advisors seemed to be wishing for a long budget battle that would dominate state news all summer and give Schwarzenegger an extended opportunity to show that Sacramento was dysfunctional and needed reform.

With their advantage in the polls and in money, the ABC unions did not want to give Schwarzenegger that chance. Pollsters for the unions worried that in a prolonged budget battle, Schwarzenegger could frame the special election as a choice between his opposition to taxes and the support of unions for tax increases. Under pressure from the unions, Democrats quickly abandoned their tax plan.

At first, Schwarzenegger did not want to declare victory. Assemblywoman Jackie Goldberg, a Democrat, said her party was looking for someone to accept its surrender. The governor's aides suggested he would not sign a budget unless he first negotiated a compromise ballot measure on his spending limit. But he dropped that demand by the July 4 weekend, when legislative leaders and the governor worked out the budget in the capitol.

The last point of contention was education funding. Schwarzenegger said he would be happy to restore the growth in Prop 98 if the Democrats could find the money. "I even gave them the budget and said you try to figure the extra money out," Schwarzenegger recalled. "You try to find it. If you find it, the $3 billion for education that you all say that I promise and I should pay back to education . . . let me know." They couldn't.

Schwarzenegger prevailed on most of his priorities. The budget had no new taxes and no new borrowing. There was even limited funding for one of the reforms he supported, an experiment with merit pay for teachers. None of this was enough to satisfy legislative Republicans, who complained that the governor had allowed the Democrats to boost spending on too many programs. Half of the Republicans in the assembly voted against their governor's budget.

The budget deal did trigger a brief period of good feeling. Schwarzenegger's children spent the final weekend in Sacramento, with Fabian Núñez's daughter Teresa joining them as they swam, took a boat ride, and worked out at 24 Hour Fitness. The governor made a point of spending some time with Núñez's son. With the budget complete, the governor and the speaker would make one last effort to reach agreement on compromise ballot measures. If the governor could not fashion such a deal, his badly battered machine would be in a full-scale campaign war with the unions, whose own machine was only growing in strength.

CHAPTER 20

One Big Enchilada,
Whipped

"He's pussy whipped!" the woman said, frustrated like the rest of the focus group members after watching clips of the governor's recent speeches. He seemed to spend too much time waffling on issues and praising his wife. The governor's political consultants, watching from behind one-way glass, laughed at the comment, perhaps a bit too hard.

This was an early session in the four hours of focus groups the governor's team was conducting in the early days of summer. The extent of Schwarzenegger's political troubles became clear almost as soon as the moderator began. The setting was the middle-class city of Orange, just east of the stadium where baseball's Los Angeles Angels of Anaheim play. Orange was chosen because it was more politically independent and less Republican than other parts of Orange County. The governor also had a high profile around town. He had done political events for years at Chapman University in the charming downtown. Orange should have been Schwarzenegger Country.

Except that it wasn't. The focus group members, who were mostly independents and Republican women, had soured on the governor. His political persona seemed stale. He was no longer a movie star, but not quite gubernatorial. The focus group members' reviews of taped Schwarzenegger speeches and appearances were harsh. Some wondered about the message jacket he was wearing in the clips. Did the state seal have to be quite so big? One person called the governor, one of the most incorrigible freelancers in American politics, stiff. He's a Manchurian candidate, another said. The focus group members either had forgotten or did not know of his political triumphs. Only one person in the group was aware that the governor was about to sign a budget that did not raise taxes. Opinions about what was wrong with Schwarzenegger were all over the map, but the discontent was unanimous.

Even his supporters in the group questioned the special election. What was the urgency? This line of argument particularly worried the governor's consultants. It appeared that some voters wouldn't consider the initiatives because they didn't like the vessel—the election—in which they were being presented. "The electorate is not engaged in this agenda and our research needs to figure out how to get them to buy in," read an e-mail report on the focus groups.

Schwarzenegger would not watch the focus group tapes. So Reiss asked for copies and watched all the tapes herself. She sat Schwarzenegger down and shared the comments with him, including the "Manchurian candidate" quip. Remember, she asked Schwarzenegger, when he would visit companies that sponsored the Inner City Games? The CEOs would invariably tell Reiss after the meetings: we did not realize he was that smart and quick. She told Schwarzenegger that he needed to be the freewheeling performer he'd been before running for office.

With his political standing so low, the governor would be better off if he could find a way out of the special election towards which he was hurtling. He needed a new campaign dynamic, he needed to remake his image, but most of all, he needed a bipartisan deal that would effectively replace his initiatives with compromise reforms supported by the legislature.

THE ENCHILADA MEETINGS BEGAN shortly after Schwarzenegger called the election on June 13. The governor dispatched his top staffers to sit down with Democratic legislative staffers in secret and hash out compromises on the various reform measures. The only requirement stated at the outset was that they negotiate, in Speaker Núñez's words, the "whole enchilada."

These new talks were partly the product of another Schwarzenegger back channel. In late April, the governor had asked the former assembly speaker Bob Hertzberg for his thoughts on compromise reform measures. On May 7, Hertzberg sent Schwarzenegger the first of several documents outlining the points of a possible deal to produce an "amicable November 2005 special election for negotiated constitutional measures." Hertzberg suggested an elaborate compromise that included some elements of Schwarzenegger's redistricting and spending limit measures and other ideas—for example, allowing the budget to be passed by a majority vote (rather than the current two-thirds) if it was passed on time—that would appeal to Democrats. On June 8, Hertzberg wrote Schwarzenegger and urged "a 'global approach' which preserves the essential elements of reform while you are attempting to meet some of the needs of the opponents." Hertzberg also marked up copies of Schwarzenegger's initiatives, deleted some sections, and added possible compromises, and shared the documents with the governor and one of the speaker's staffers. Hertzberg's drafts helped launch the Enchilada Meetings.

Schwarzenegger believed that if there was a deal to be had, it would come first with Núñez. The public employees' unions, the governor's chief tormentors, had told the speaker that they saw no need for negotiation since Schwarzenegger was ripe for defeat in the special election. But the speaker said he sincerely wanted a deal because he thought it would improve the image of lawmakers. Time for a compromise was running short. California Secretary of State Bruce McPherson had identified August 15 as the deadline for the legislature to add new compromise measures to the ballot, but lawmakers were scheduled to begin a month-long summer recess on July 15. Schwarzenegger told Núñez that sometimes the best deals were put together in a hurry; the contract for the movie comedy *Twins* had been drawn up on a napkin.

Aides to the governor and the speaker charted the progress of these talks in a large, grid-style document that was labeled "The Enchilada Chronicles." Over four long meetings that kicked off negotiations, the staff members touched on every reform issue: education, redistricting, even the pension measure Schwarzenegger had dropped back in April.

According to copies of the Enchilada Chronicles, there might have been compromises on most reforms, particularly redistricting. But with war raging with the CTA and the ABC unions, Schwarzenegger's team would not be able to get a formal agreement on these items without a deal on the most sensitive issue: working out an alternative to Prop 76, the spending limit initiative that would amend Prop 98.

By July, Democratic and gubernatorial staffers exchanged outlines of a deal. Schwarzenegger's team even had some legislative language prepared. Clarey optimistically told the governor, "I can see this. I can see how we get there." But Siggins, the governor's lawyer, said that on two occasions, Democratic staffers indicated "we had something approaching conceptual agreement," only to back away. "That's when I first thought, 'This is about keeping us at the table to keep the governor hopeful and essentially keep him off the campaign trail,'" Siggins recalled.

By the second week of July, the talks bogged down over how the Prop 98 spending formula might be amended and over what sort of authority the governor would have to make cuts in the middle of the budget year. The legislature left town on July 15 for a month-long summer recess, and, although the Enchilada Meetings continued into the following week, there was little movement. On Tuesday, July 19, Núñez held a press conference. "We are seas apart of where we need to be," Núñez said. "The type of power the governor is looking for here is the power that no democratic leader in any democratic society currently has, and it's too difficult to get there." The speaker headed off to Europe for the rest of the month to learn about preschool programs. The talks appeared to be dead.

IF SCHWARZENEGGER WANTED TO CALL OFF the special election, this would have been the moment. The governor could have argued that he had prevailed on his priorities by signing a budget with no new taxes and no new borrowing. His initiatives would simply roll over to the next statewide election in June 2006. That would give him another year to negotiate compromise measures and repair his political standing so he could better sell the plan to voters. But it also would likely prolong the fight with the ABC unions. Schwarzenegger said his wife asked him if he still wanted to go forward with the special election. Reiss, worried that Schwarzenegger would go home and hear too much talk about impending disaster, advised the couple that the special election should proceed, but that they should steel themselves for defeat. "I said, 'There comes a point where if you can't get a decent deal, it's way more honorable to walk away and try to do a dignified, honorable campaign even if you lose everything,'" Reiss recalled. "Having a dignified campaign to stand on principle to try to fight for the reform you believe in, even if you lose, history will reflect well on you."

Schwarzenegger's political operation was not yet in campaign shape. There was less than $2 million in his political accounts. The Citizens to Save California and other affiliates of the governor's political operation had raised $22 million so far in 2005, but nearly all of that money had been spent. One of the things that Schwarzenegger's divided staff agreed upon was the value of a face-saving deal on compromise measures so the governor could avoid going to the ballot in the fall with just the initiatives he had qualified. "I was ready to make a pile of shit a coconut cream pie in order to make that happen," said Stutzman of his desire for an agreement he could spin.

During a July meeting at the Sacramento office of his consulting firm DC Navigators, Murphy warned the team: nothing negative. Even the attack dogs at the Republican Party were told to stand down. The governor believed that public spats with the legislature or the unions would undermine any hope of reviving talks.

Shriver tried to help pull the team together and salvage the situation. She sought counsel from as many people as possible outside Schwarzenegger's immediate circle, from the former campaign manager Bob White to former Reagan consultant Stu Spencer ("Tell the son of a bitch to start governing," Spencer reportedly advised). In calls and meetings with the governor's consultants, she argued for a move away from big, B-movie style events—"boys with toys," she called them—towards speeches that would explain how reform would improve, for instance, the life of a mother stuck in traffic on her way to her children's soccer practice. She suggested turning the two-year anniversary of Schwarzenegger's *The Tonight Show* announcement into an event that would repair the perception of her husband. And she had a list of eleven slogans for a special election campaign e-mailed to the political advisors. Among them were: "Courage to make a change," "Battle for the soul of California," "Change needed," "Change isn't easy, but we have to have the courage to change," and "The strength to take us where we need to go."

Schwarzenegger did not adopt the slogans, but he modified his style. He ditched the message jackets. And he began to emphasize small acts of governance—new legislation he supported, regulations the administration had enacted—on the stump. Stutzman pulled together a list of Schwarzenegger accomplishments that could be incorporated into events. Consultants offered all kinds of ideas in e-mails: that the governor spend time working in different parts of the state, that he hold office hours for citizens, that he put on health care and regional transportation summits. Schwarzenegger was to make July and August of 2005 the "summer of governing."

These new events went well enough. But his team's focus on repairing his own image cost him an opportunity to start a public debate on the substance of the initiatives. As Schwarzenegger traveled the state talking about his plans to take junk food out of schools, the ABC unions continued to broadcast ads criticizing the governor and the special election. The nurses' union even protested inside Disneyland when he appeared at the fiftieth anniversary of the theme park.

The impact of the summer of governing was blunted by bad news. On July 14, the *Los Angeles Times* and *Sacramento Bee* revealed the details of the contract Schwarzenegger had signed with American Media, the publisher of supermarket tabloids as well as two muscle magazines for which the governor served as an editor. According to a filing with the Securities and Exchange Commission, Schwarzenegger was guaranteed $1 million a year, but his pay also was tied to the advertising revenues of all the company's magazines. This arrangement was not illegal, but as an ethical matter it was highly questionable. Many of these ad revenues came from companies that sold dietary supplements; the previous year, Schwarzenegger had vetoed a bill intended to restrict high school athletes' use of such supplements. After two days of critical newspaper and TV stories, he cancelled the contract. The unions pressed the legislature to hold hearings, but Speaker Núñez and other lawmakers declined. The political damage had been done. His approval rating, at 49 percent in July in a CTA poll, dropped to 45 by August and continued to fall.

The week after the magazine contract story broke, Schwarzenegger took another blow when a court threw his redistricting initiative, Proposition 77,

off the ballot. Ted Costa, the official proponent, had circulated for signatures a version of the measure that differed in a dozen places from the initiative that had been filed with the attorney general's office. Although the
mistakes were clerical and did not appear to change the meaning of the initiative, Attorney General Bill Lockyer argued that allowing the measure to
remain on the ballot would establish a precedent that could be exploited by
initiative proponents who wanted to deceive the public. A judge agreed.

By the third week of July, Schwarzenegger was down to two reform initiatives: a measure that would change teacher tenure, Prop 74, and his Live
Within Our Means Act spending limit, Prop 76 (which was in trouble in the
polls). Republican pundits suggested that the governor reverse his June announcement and call off the November special election.

Some of his political advisors agreed. In a conference call on Friday, July 22,
the consultants went through the pros and cons. McLaughlin, the pollster, was
particularly adamant, arguing that Schwarzenegger could cite his budget victory and get out. Randle said that Schwarzenegger didn't have the resources to
fight, and the team hadn't sold the idea of a special election. Sipple suggested
that Schwarzenegger could cancel the election, announce he needed time to develop a more thorough reform package, and create a bipartisan group of distinguished citizens to tackle health care, transportation, education, and other
thorny problems. The advisors also discussed whether Schwarzenegger should
make some kind of apology—"a sorbet to cleanse the collective palate of California," in the words of Sipple—for previous mistakes.

Within hours of the call, the fact that the consultants had discussed the
possibility of canceling the election had leaked to Gary Delsohn, a *Sacramento Bee* reporter who would later take a job as Schwarzenegger's chief
speechwriter. It was a disastrous leak. By letting ABC and Democratic legislators know that the governor's team wanted to avoid an election,
Schwarzenegger's consultants had undermined the governor's ability to
make a deal on compromise measures. Why bargain with a governor who
might surrender anyway?

Stutzman e-mailed the political team in disgust that weekend: "Fuck you
to all of you taking calls from the press about the political team consideration of delaying the election. Unbelievable." Gorton suggested bringing in
polygraph machines to identify the culprit, though that never happened. No
one was conclusively fingered for the leak.

RATHER THAN RALLYING HIS OWN staff and advisors again, Schwarzenegger
left them out of a last-ditch attempt to forge a deal on compromise measures. He felt many of his top aides and advisors were too close to Republican

legislators who wanted him to give up on negotiations and start campaigning for the initiatives. The first week of August, the governor decided to start a new, secret round of talks. With Clarey on vacation, he would handle all the negotiating himself.

These negotiations needed a mediator. So Schwarzenegger asked Hertzberg, who had the trust of both the speaker and the governor, to handle those duties. Hertzie, as the governor affectionately called him, was willing to help. A Democrat, he didn't agree with Schwarzenegger's politics, but said, "What I do like is his courage." Once the speaker returned from his European trip, Núñez and the governor talked by phone. "All of a sudden there was again some movement," Schwarzenegger recalled.

At three o'clock on the afternoon of Saturday, August 6, the speaker, the governor, and Hertzberg gathered at Schwarzenegger's house in Brentwood. Núñez came directly from the set of an HBO movie about a student walkout in East Los Angeles schools in 1968; the movie's director, Edward James Olmos, had given Núñez a small speaking role as a police officer. The speaker boasted that he had done it in one take.

The speaker and the governor each brought one aide. Núñez was accompanied by Rick Simpson, an education and budget expert who had worked in the legislature for much of the past quarter-century (and had once done an eighteen-month stint at CTA). Schwarzenegger invited his finance director, Tom Campbell, who brought along his wife Susanne, the head of a management program at UC Berkeley. While the negotiations took place, she worked out on the exercise equipment of the former Mr. Olympia.

The governor and the speaker were still trying to reach an all-encompassing "enchilada" deal. But they talked only briefly about most of the reforms. An agreement could be reached on other matters if they could find a compromise on the spending limit and Prop 98.

As the five men munched on finger sandwiches, fruit, and cheese, Schwarzenegger made plain that his real passion was to fix the state's structural deficit. He was tired of the annual budget fight, which consumed time that would be better spent on making plans for the future. The structural deficit had been reduced, but it was still estimated at about $7 billion for each of the next two fiscal years. Schwarzenegger said he was open to any reform that would eliminate that deficit.

So, with a push from Hertzberg, the speaker and the governor began working backwards from the budget. If the structural deficit was going to be eliminated for the next two years, what did they need to do? Soon the two men began the audacious exercise of negotiating the budgets for the next two fiscal years 2006–07 and 2007–08—by themselves.

They worked from copies of Prop 76, the Live Within Our Means spending limit, with Hertzberg taking notes on which pieces might survive and which might change. All this would be turned into a secret document (only Simpson, Hertzberg, and Schwarzenegger would have copies) that charted the progress of the talks. The document was given a title befitting a Middle East summit: "ROAD MAP TO PEACE IN OUR TIME." The Road Map listed each issue that was subject to the negotiations alongside three columns: one for the position of the governor on the issue, one for that of Democrats, and a third for a possible compromise position.

To get peace, Núñez and Schwarzenegger had to reach agreement on any modifications to Prop 98. Simpson, Núñez's aide, argued that Prop 98 did not represent the threat to the budget that the governor believed it did. Tom Campbell countered that the maintenance factor provision of Prop 98 was a contributor to the state's chronic deficit. The finance director advocated so strenuously for keeping provisions of Prop 76 in any compromise that, on two occasions, the governor had to ask his finance director to move on so negotiations could progress.

This discussion led to the first breakthrough of the afternoon. The speaker would not eliminate the maintenance factor as the governor wanted. But Núñez did agree that when the maintenance factor was restored to the funding base for education, those payments could be spread out over many more years with an annual cap. Schwarzenegger wanted to cap it at $300 million a year. The speaker proposed more than twice that. There was a tentative compromise at $500 million.

Shortly after 8 p.m. that evening, the meeting broke up as Simpson scrambled to catch a plane to Sacramento. The governor headed out of town on a vacation that included a stop in the Bahamas, but he continued to talk by phone with Hertzberg throughout the week. On Friday, August 12, the California Supreme Court overruled the lower court and put Schwarzenegger's redistricting reform initiative, Proposition 77, back on the ballot. The court ruled that the discrepancies between the version of the initiative filed with the attorney general and the version circulated among voters were too minor to be of consequence. The decision strengthened Schwarzenegger's political hand.

The very next evening, Saturday, August 13, Núñez and Schwarzenegger arranged to meet once again at the governor's home. Campbell learned of the session too late to join the talks. The finance director was celebrating his birthday on Clear Lake in Northern California, and was out of cell phone range when the governor called to invite him to Los Angeles. Schwarzenegger would negotiate alone with Núñez, Simpson, and Hertzberg.

JUST AFTER DUSK, THE FOUR men took seats on a patio next to an outdoor fireplace and ate chicken, beef, and vegetables on sticks. The governor even offered a brief tour of his home, lingering in a room where he had a framed thank-you note Bill Clinton had written him after Schwarzenegger denounced the president's impeachment. The governor seemed looser than he had been the previous Saturday. He talked openly about mistakes he'd made over the year, and he explained in detail why he had not given the education community the money he originally promised. He simply had not been able to abide the cuts in health programs that would be required to fund the growth in Prop 98 education spending. "That wasn't who I am," was how the governor put it.

It was striking how personally Schwarzenegger had taken the unions' attacks. He was particularly upset about being accused of cutting the budget after increasing spending it. "We added and added and added," Schwarzenegger recalled saying. "But when you go out to the people and interview them, they think we have cut." Simpson, the speaker's staffer, interjected the third time Schwarzenegger said he'd been treated unfairly: You volunteered for the job, governor, Simpson said. Schwarzenegger did not quarrel but pivoted into a discussion of how California needed to rebuild its infrastructure.

After three hours of talks, the speaker and governor had begun to whittle down the $7 billion deficit projected for each of the next two years. They resolved to ask the education lobby to forego a $1 billion increase to its funding base for one year. Another $2 billion would be covered from estimates of new revenues. That got the deficit down to about $4 billion.

To cut that hole in half, Schwarzenegger and Núñez then agreed to tap the approximately $4 billion in general obligation bond authority left over from Proposition 57, the $15 billion bond that Schwarzenegger had convinced voters to adopt in March 2004. Two billion dollars of that money would be used to cover half of the $4 billion remaining deficit in 2006–07. The other $2 billion of the bond money would be used in 2007–08. That reduced the deficit for each year to about $1.9 billion.

The next day, a Sunday, Hertzberg flew up to Sacramento on Schwarzenegger's plane. The governor, Tom Campbell, the speaker, Simpson, and Núñez's budget aide, Craig Cornett, continued negotiations inside the governor's capitol office. Three of Schwarzenegger's own staffers sat outside in the Horseshoe courtyard, where they received periodic reports about the talks. That meeting ended with Núñez and Schwarzenegger in agreement that the remaining $1.9 billion deficit for 2006–2007 and 2007–2008 would likely have to come from cuts. But the speaker balked at negotiating those cuts specifically. Hertzberg, still pressing for a compromise, took a room at the Hyatt, where Schwarzenegger lived when he was in Sacramento.

Núñez, Schwarzenegger, and staff members met in the governor's hotel suite on Monday. A chess board was set up with a game in progress. The speaker and governor agreed upon the framework for an enchilada deal that covered each reform, but could not agree on all its details. In particular, while the Democrats wanted Schwarzenegger to oppose Prop 75, the paycheck protection measure qualified by the governor's allies, the governor would agree only to go neutral. Hertzberg spent the rest of Monday conducting shuttle diplomacy, talking separately with Schwarzenegger and Campbell and taking their views back to the speaker.

The two sides had reached tentative agreement on changes to the maintenance factor piece of Prop 98. And they had a deal on how to cut the budget mid-year that would dismay allies on both sides. If the governor and legislature didn't agree on cuts, across-the-board cuts would be automatically triggered, though there would be exemptions for entitlements, salaries, and contracts.

These changes would be wrapped up into a new budget reform ballot measure, to be numbered Prop 1A. (When ballot measures were added late by the legislature, the late arrivals were typically numbered 1A, 2A, 3A, etc.) It would be the first of three new compromise ballot measures. While the details would still have to be negotiated, Prop 2A would be a redistricting reform that would go into effect in 2012, not immediately as in Schwarzenegger's Prop 77. Prop 3A would extend term limits for legislators, allowing them to serve twelve years in either house.

Even with this framework in place, it would still be difficult to make the deal work. The measure to extend term limits was designed to win votes in the state senate, whose leader Don Perata was not part of the talks. Even if support materialized in the senate, there was precious little time.

This particular Monday, August 15, had been set as the deadline for preparing ballots so they could be mailed to overseas voters on September 8, the required sixty days before the election. The speaker and governor asked Secretary of State Bruce McPherson for an extension, and he granted them four more days, until midnight on Thursday, August 18.

BY THE NEXT DAY, Tuesday the 16th, Schwarzenegger and Núñez were telling each other privately that they had a deal. "What I remember is we walked away and said, 'Okay, agreed,'" recalled the governor. In fact, the two had not agreed on the last $1.9 billion of cuts to close the budget deficit in each of the next two years.

Núñez was content to leave the specifics unanswered. If he committed to $1.9 billion in cuts, he would be in a horrible position with interest groups and his caucus. If he waited, he might be bailed out if rising tax revenues surpassed estimates. Núñez also secretly held out hope of another possibility: that he could find Republican votes for a tax increase to cover the gap. A Republican state senator, Jim Battin, seemed to be hinting that he might have votes for such a tax hike. But the governor and Tom Campbell insisted that this $1.9 billion in cuts be locked down. Ironically, such cuts would likely have had to come from health programs, the same programs Schwarzenegger had refused to cut back in December when he decided not to give the schools the Prop 98 growth. Nine months and thirty fewer job-approval rating points later, Schwarzenegger was in the same bind.

For all the deal making and secret sessions, Schwarzenegger and Núñez could not bridge this seemingly smallest of gaps: $1.9 billion out of a budget of more than $100 billion. The $1.9 billion did not end the talks. But it was an inconveniently open item.

Each man still had to take the deal back to his allies. On Tuesday morning, Núñez told Schwarzenegger that it was time to "test the water." So Núñez briefed the CTA leadership: president Barbara Kerr, vice president David Sanchez, and staffers Joe Núñez and Bob Cherry. As the speaker laid out the deal on flip charts, the CTA officials raised several objections. The union representatives disagreed with the changes in Prop 98 and the maintenance factor. Núñez and Schwarzenegger had agreed to mandate across-the-board, midyear cuts, which the CTA saw as a backdoor attack on Prop 98 that they could never accept. The union officials pressed Núñez: why do you want us to take our foot off his neck? Why make a deal with a governor who had broken his word before?

It was clear to the CTA and his own staff that Núñez, as close as he was to the teachers, was willing to buck the union. "He was trying to save the governor's ass at the end for reasons unknown to me," a Núñez staffer said. The speaker returned to the talks saying he felt like Nixon going to China.

"He came back and said, 'The deal has to be a little bit better than we worked out. I think we can make some adjustments,'" Schwarzenegger recalled. "But he and I needed some more time to figure that out."

Meanwhile, the governor asked his own staffers for their opinions. This was a difficult sales job since all but Campbell had been cut out of the talks. (Some aides were so angry at Hertzberg that they encouraged reporters to ask if his law practice would profit as a result of his access to the governor.)

A meeting on Wednesday between Schwarzenegger, Campbell, and Clarey proved critical. Campbell said a deal was possible, but did not think it was real without the speaker's commitment on the $1.9 billion in cuts. Clarey objected that the mid-year cut authority—the same provision the CTA had found too unyielding—was not tough enough. She did not think that union contracts should be exempted from midyear cuts while health programs could be slashed.

Others worried that if Schwarzenegger continued to pursue a deal and fell short, he would fatally damage his initiatives in the fall. By negotiating compromises, the governor was conceding that the initiatives already on the ballot were less than perfect. Longtime counselors, among them former Secretary of State George Shultz and former Governor Wilson, weighed in against the deal. Schwarzenegger listened to all this advice but quietly seethed. Rather than trying to make this deal happen, his team was trying to talk him out of it, he felt. He promised himself he would replace his top aides before the year was up.

Schwarzenegger told Hertzberg and Núñez that he still wanted a deal, but he sounded more skeptical than before. Hertzberg went home to L.A. on Wednesday. Núñez headed for an event in Monterey. The governor, speaker, and Hertzberg negotiated by phone all day Thursday, while trying to find a way to extend the deadline. Hertzberg tracked down a four-year-old legislative memo showing that there was precedent for extending the deadline. By statute, legislative measures should be placed on the ballot 131 days before the election—but in the past, the legislature had added measures as few as 68 days before an election. There were still eighty-two days until the scheduled election. In a last-ditch effort to buy time, a Republican senator put a bill in print that would have delayed the special election a month to give the governor and legislature more time to negotiate compromises.

On Thursday, after attending a fund-raiser for his California Recovery Team at the Sutter Club in Sacramento, Schwarzenegger returned to the Horseshoe in the early evening and convened a meeting of staff and Republican legislators to discuss a deadline extension. Núñez joined by phone. Hertzberg and Núñez had told the governor he needed to insist on an extension.

The governor called Bruce McPherson, the secretary of state, at home to settle the question.

Bruce, we're getting close to an agreement, the governor said.

That was not as firm as the speaker would have liked to hear.

"First of all, I commend you," McPherson recalled saying. "But I think you're threatening the integrity of the election if you extend it beyond this point." McPherson, so prepared that some people on the call thought he was reading a statement, made a narrow but politically explosive point. Some 62,000 of California's 16 million registered voters were overseas; many of them were military personnel.

It was true, McPherson noted, that in previous elections supplemental ballots had been printed for late-arriving measures. But McPherson said this would not work in this case. The new ballot measures Schwarzenegger and the legislature would add if they reached a deal might well contradict the original initiatives. That would be particularly unfair to these overseas voters, who could vote on their original ballots before they even received supplemental ballots. McPherson said that the governor and the legislators could push on with negotiations and try to extend the deadline. If the election went badly, "it would have been on their lap," he would later say.

In the face of McPherson's argument, Schwarzenegger did not push hard for an extension. The governor did not want to do anything that would limit the voting rights of soldiers overseas. His consultants and aides were clamoring for him to begin the campaign. He had fund-raisers scheduled in three different states over the next three days.

The governor would say publicly that Núñez was simply incapable of getting a deal through the legislature given the opposition of CTA. "That's the sad story of our capital," he would say. Privately, however, he blamed his own staff for delaying and derailing his deal-making.

That Thursday night, after his call with McPherson, Schwarzenegger emerged from his office at 10 p.m., just two hours before the midnight deadline. "Everyone has tried very hard," the governor told reporters. "And we were very close, very close. As a matter of fact, if we would have had another two, three days, we could have done it."

Schwarzenegger left the capitol, facing the most difficult campaign of his life. Usually, he loved a contest. But for months, he would rue the deal he couldn't make, the enchilada he never got to taste.

SCHWARZENEGGER'S BALLOT MEASURE committees desperately needed money if the governor was to have a chance in the special election. August was a lousy time to raise money, as the rich of the state were scattered to retreats all over the world. But the same week that time ran out for compromise ballot measures, Schwarzenegger began a seventeen-day fund-raising tour. He kicked it off with an event in San Bernardino and followed up with a $25,000-per-couple lobster dinner at Shakespeare Ranch on the Nevada side of Lake Tahoe. From there, he flew east for a Saturday fund-raiser in

New Jersey, hosted by the Republican gubernatorial candidate Doug For-
rester. On Sunday, August 21, he held a fund-raiser during a Rolling Stones
concert at Boston's Fenway Park.

These events went well, but not well enough. At Fenway Park, some of the
seats donated by mortgage lender Ameriquest were noticeably empty. The
nurses' union protested inside and outside the ballpark. In California,
Schwarzenegger made fund-raising calls almost daily, but found donors to be
reluctant. Since he had refused to commit to running for re-election in 2006,
some donors did not want to give to a campaign that would challenge union
power. If Schwarzenegger ended up back in Hollywood in 2007, who would
protect his donors from retribution?

SCHWARZENEGGER WAS DELUGED WITH contradictory advice over how to
stop his slide. Eunice Shriver, who had been visiting California and watching
the union ads, called and ordered him to "go out and talk about yourself, all
the great things that you have done for this state." He explained to his
mother-in-law, "Look, it's important for me to talk about the issues and to
talk about reforms and why we need to fix the broken system."

During the fund-raiser at the Rolling Stones concert in Boston, Republican pollster Frank Luntz showed up in the Ameriquest box and told
Schwarzenegger he wanted to help the campaign. Of his own volition, Luntz
had done private polls for the past two years he would show to the governor
in occasional meetings. His new poll found that Schwarzenegger's political
persona was obscuring the initiatives. The GOP pollster recommended a tactic that flew in the face of decades of Schwarzenegger marketing, from
movies to initiatives: that the governor avoid personalizing the election in any
way. "Better to focus on the issues than the politics," Luntz concluded in his
polling report, which urged "More Accountability, Less Arnold."

The pollster showed up two days later in Santa Monica at the Fairmont
Miramar Hotel, where the governor and his advisors were meeting. Luntz
did not make it inside the consultants' session, but his appearance infuriated
Murphy. The governor's team did not heed Luntz's recommendations. The
advisors sketched out a campaign strategy designed more to fit the needs of
a typical Republican politician than the unique circumstances of
Schwarzenegger and his initiatives. Two Republican Party officials joined
the meeting and agreed to fund a voter guide on the initiatives that would
be produced by Schwarzenegger's team. The party also hired a political consultant from the Religious Right to turn out more voters, and retained a
Virginia company to do "micro-targeting." The term referred to the technique of studying the purchasing habits and viewing preferences of voters

so that mail and phone calls and other political messages could be targeted to those most likely to support the initiatives.

Schwarzenegger's consultants assumed that turnout in the special election would be low and that an outpouring of Republican votes would provide a narrow victory. They were slow to realize that involving the governor so thoroughly in the campaign would draw the attention not only of Republicans, but also of voters who were sour on Schwarzenegger. The governor's stardom and his consultants' strategy of targeting Republicans were at war with each other.

Much of the discussion at the Fairmont was about the size of the campaign's budget for TV ads: $8.5 million, a paltry sum given the more than $100 million the unions had massed against Schwarzenegger. When the governor heard the figure at a post-meeting dinner at the Buffalo Club, he immediately declared: that's not nearly enough. With only $8.5 million, TV ads could not begin until the first week of October, only four weeks before the election.

If he wanted more ads, Schwarzenegger would have to do two things. First, he needed to let skittish donors know that he was running for re-election. Second, he would have to contribute money of his own.

Marty Wilson told Schwarzenegger that if he wanted to donate his own money, he should do that sooner rather than later. A last-minute expenditure would look desperate. Schwarzenegger asked if his own donations would dry up other donors. To the contrary, Wilson replied. The governor had been back to the well over and over with many of the same donors ever since Prop 49. Putting in his own money would show confidence and encourage others to give. Schwarzenegger would give $7.75 million to his California Recovery Team. All told, from Prop 49 through the special election, he donated $25 million to his own campaigns.

THERE WERE JUST TWO MONTHS until the election and Schwarzenegger's consultants did not seem able to get organized without prodding. Clarey took a leave from her chief of staff job, rented a campaign office in the Senator Hotel building across the street from the capitol, and put campaign staffers' names down on seats. Anyone who didn't show up in the office the next day, she announced, would not get paid.

The campaign team set up a popcorn machine and a life-sized cutout of Schwarzenegger in the office's entryway. Inside, Murphy, Clarey, and Fiona Hutton, a Los Angeles public relations consultant who had been brought in to help manage the effort, worked out of a room straight back from the reception desk. Down the hall and to the right was a war room where Stutzman and Todd Harris set up shop. The TVs were turned to cable news channels except for one screen, on which the aides played a few movie comedies starring Will Ferrell. *Old School* was a particular favorite.

Schwarzenegger had declared the special election would be the sequel to the recall, but running the campaign from Sacramento rather than Santa Monica was just one way 2005 would be different from 2003. The recall had been a major news story around the country and the world. In the fall of 2005, Hurricane Katrina and the war in Iraq dominated the national news. In 2003, Schwarzenegger's campaign team had reveled in the disdain of the state's political elite. Now they were obsessed with the Sacramento mindset. One night in September, the governor and his consultants even held a strategy dinner at the Hyatt during which, over filet mignon and crème brulee, Schwarzenegger listened for two hours to the ideas of Republican political operatives not currently in his employ.

IN THE RECALL, SCHWARZENEGGER had faced an unpopular governor and a collection of replacement candidates, whom he could outspend and outmaneuver. In the special election, he faced an alliance of unions that had more money, more organization, and more political firepower than his faltering machine could muster.

With the kickoff of the traditional campaign season after Labor Day, the ABC alliance had a daily tracking survey—six nights a week and during the day on Saturdays—for the nine weeks before the election. Schwarzenegger, with less money to spend, would not begin his own tracking until October 20.

The governor starred as the villain in the unions' massive TV ad campaign. ABC produced eighteen different spots, nearly all of them showing teachers, nurses, firefighters, or police officers talking directly into the camera in a work setting. Every single one of the ads mentioned the governor. "I voted for you because I trusted what you said," a police officer said in one spot. The ads primarily attacked Schwarzenegger for breaking the education deal and for backing Prop 76, the spending limit that amended the school funding guarantee Prop 98. By September, the ABC unions began using Prop 76, which had little hope of passing, to taint the governor's other initiatives in a direct-democracy version of guilt by association.

One ad against Prop 75, the paycheck protection measure, was pure chutzpah. The unions complained of being "silenced" by the governor in a spot that was part of a $100 million campaign that effectively drowned out the voice of one of the most famous men in the world. The alliance even produced test advertisements in favor of Prop 75, which they opposed, so they could test it in focus groups and refine their campaign against the measure. In the test Yes on 75 ads, a teacher of twenty years complained of her union, "I've always been a proud member, but I resent that some of my dues go to candidates and campaigns I disagree with. That's unfair. It's un-American." Focus groups found that the real Yes on 75 spots by Schwarzenegger's allies were not nearly as effective.

SCHWARZENEGGER WAS SO POLITICALLY wounded that he hurt almost any proposal he touched. Even supporters of two initiatives he favored asked him to keep his distance from their measures. Ted Costa, the author of the redistricting measure Proposition 77, asked Schwarzenegger's team to keep the governor from signing the official ballot argument in favor of the initiative. (Schwarzenegger signed it anyway.) A Republican donor, Bill Mundell, formed his own Yes on 77 committee and turned down a request to work more closely with the governor. "Proposition 77 is not Arnold Schwarzenegger," Mundell said.

Schwarzenegger himself asked Steve Poizner, founder of two technology companies—one of which had been sold for $1 billion in 2000—to start another, separate Prop 77 political committee. Poizner, a moderate Republican, had spent millions of his own money in an attempt to win a safe Democratic assembly seat in 2004, and had come up just short.

Poizner began talking frequently with Pat Caddell, a Democratic pollster who had been helping Mundell and Costa with the redistricting campaign. In a September 13 memo distributed to supporters of 77, Caddell argued for doing everything possible to disassociate the cause of redistricting from Schwarzenegger. Caddell wrote that public discontent with California politics was higher now than during the recall. Democrats were mad at the governor, primarily about education funding. Independents and Republicans hated the state's political status quo, of which the governor was part. Schwarzenegger "is a wounded and bloodied captain," Caddell concluded.

The proponents of Prop 75, the paycheck protection measure, agreed. In early September, Schwarzenegger told his team he wanted to endorse Prop 75. After learning this from Schwarzenegger's consultants, Lew Uhler, the initiative's author, asked them to reconsider. In a memo to the Prop 75 campaign, Republican pollster Neil Newhouse showed that the initiative needed to retain as much as 45 percent of the vote of union households to win. But the governor's approval rating among union members was only 36 percent. A Schwarzenegger endorsement was bad news because it would "galvanize the opposition," Newhouse wrote.

"Realistically," the pollster added in an e-mail to the Prop 75 campaign, the governor "could actually drain some needed crossparty and union support for the measure and hurt our chances of passing it in November."

Uhler, in a September 6 memo received by the Schwarzenegger consultants, wrote: "Frankly, we are fearful that if the governor comes in visibly and forcefully in support of Prop 75 and appears to take charge and make Prop 75 one of his initiatives, we are likely to lose. That is a risk we need not and should not take." The memo concluded: "Prop 75 is too important to California's and the governor's future to risk any other course of action."

But he would back it anyway. Some of the governor's donors wanted him to endorse the measure. And the unions and the press already were saying that he was behind Prop 75. Schwarzenegger by mid-September supported four consecutive ballot measures, Prop 74 (teacher tenure), Prop 75 (paycheck protection), Prop 76 (the Live Within Our Means budget reform), and Prop 77 (redistricting). Having such a slate made it easier for him to campaign, and far easier for the ABC unions to educate voters on which initiatives belonged to the governor.

THE GOVERNOR CONSIDERED other ways to change the dynamics of the race. As of the second week of September, Schwarzenegger had not yet declared whether he would run for re-election in 2006. His wife had made her feelings known. "I want him back home," Shriver had said earlier in the year during an appearance on *Oprah*. He had until March 2006 to formally declare his candidacy, and he seemed content to wait until after the special election so he could focus on the initiatives. Schwarzenegger had envisioned a re-election announcement on the *The Tonight Show*. But in the midst of his faltering campaign, he reasoned that he could help the initiatives by quickly settling the most burning question about his future.

His first town hall in a major media market was scheduled for September 16 in San Diego. It was Mexican Independence Day, and most spots in the country's largest border city were booked, so the campaign rented a small theater in a rough part of downtown. The theater's stage was not properly oriented for the event so the governor's advance team built its own. And the building had no air-conditioning, so portable swamp coolers (which remove heat by evaporating water) were placed on either side of the stage.

The governor's consultants wanted the re-election announcement to come in response to a question from a voter at the town hall. But Murphy and Stutzman, wary of fueling press reports that Schwarzenegger's town halls were scripted events, did not plan a moment for the re-election announcement. After forty-five minutes of questions about the initiatives, immigration, and even dairy farming, no one had posed the question. So Schwarzenegger turned to a bank of two dozen cameras in the back of the room and asked the question of himself.

"I got the question several times this last week from various different people, if I'll run again or not. Here's the bottom line," he said. "As I said, I'm a follow-through guy. I have learned that from sports. In every sport, you learn about following through, right?

"In golf, about swinging through," he said, swinging an imaginary golf club. "In tennis, with follow-through," he said, pantomiming a forehand. "In skiing, we finish the turn. It's all about follow through. I learned most of my lessons from sports. So, of course, I'm going to follow through with this here. I'm not in there for three years as I originally got into this. Because to finish the job, I'm in there for seven years. Yes, I will run for governor next year again."

It had none of the drama of his 2003 announcement on *The Tonight Show*, but making a media splash wasn't his intent. The announcement worked as a fund-raising appeal. Over the next month, Schwarzenegger would raise more than $10 million, compared to about $3 million in the previous month.

The surge in donations came late in the campaign. The ABC unions had already bought their TV time, locking in relatively low rates. Schwarzenegger, without the money for advance purchases, would have to pay rates more than 50 percent higher.

THE UNIONS HAD AN ACTOR on their team too: Warren Beatty, who had been criticizing the governor in public since early in the spring. Throughout the year, Beatty had talked frequently with Speaker Núñez, and union leaders, particularly the California Nurses Association executive director Rose Ann DeMoro, about how to use Schwarzenegger's stardom against him. In the closing weeks of the campaign, Beatty volunteered to be the designated "antagonist."

On the evening of September 22, Beatty gave the keynote address at the California Nurses Association convention in Oakland. In the speech, which was edited by an official of the state Democratic Party, Beatty flirted with the notion that he might run for governor. This was not a serious statement of intent, but served as a way to get TV and press coverage for his real message: criticizing Schwarzenegger and the initiatives.

He suggested Schwarzenegger was more interested in the glory of politics than public service and quoted the poet T. S. Eliot: "Half of the harm that is done in this world is due to people who want to feel important."

"Government is not show business," Beatty declared. "Governing by show, by spin, by cosmetics, by photo ops, fake events, fake issues, and fake crowds and backdrops is a mistake."

The director Rob Reiner, who had run a successful initiative campaign in 1998 and was publicly contemplating a run for governor, joined in. He led a public forum against Prop 75 in San Francisco where a former San Francisco supervisor, Doris Ward, implored him: "I really wish you would one day run for governor because people want movie stars and television stars. The way to beat Arnold is with ..."

"is with a Meathead?" Reiner interrupted.

Schwarzenegger's advisors would have been smart to ignore such attacks. Instead, they publicly mocked Beatty for everything from the poor box office of his recent movies to his age, sixty-eight. Schwarzenegger himself told reporters, "There are some people who are close to him that say that he is just starving for attention and that's the way he gets attention. Other people said, look he's not working and he just feels like he should maybe get involved in politics." Even Maria Shriver offered a public barb in a speech at her women's conference: "When I look in the mirror, I don't just see a first lady, I don't just see a Kennedy or a Schwarzenegger, I don't just see a mother, a daughter, a wife, a sister, and a friend, and thank God, I don't see Warren Beatty." Beatty hit back: "I would think Maria might have some trouble looking in the mirror because she knows and I know that all these right-wing, union-busting initiatives are bad for California."

The counterattacks fueled a media story—the battle of two Hollywood heavyweights—that kept the attention off the initiatives. That was just what the unions wanted.

With Hollywood magic being used against him, Schwarzenegger tried to distance himself from his own persona. In an op-ed published in the *Sacramento Bee* on September 25, the governor offered regrets for his over-the-top antics, and particularly for calling legislators "girlie men" in the heat of the local government battle in 2004. "I made some mistakes and learned many vital lessons along the way that make me a better governor. I've learned that it is a good idea as governor to listen more and talk less, especially lines best left for *Saturday Night Live*," he wrote.

But as his campaign situation grew more desperate, Schwarzenegger reverted to what he knew best: stunts and Hollywood-style gimmicks. Nearly every day, the governor presented his political team with new ideas for TV ads and public events that he thought could turn the tide. He wanted to make an ad that would be called "Lies Lies Lies." In Schwarzenegger's vision, the TV spot would show snippets of the various union ads for a few seconds. Then the governor, in a special effect that would have cost the campaign more than $100,000, would break through the screen. "I break through the lies," he explained. The campaign never made the commercial.

There was not enough money or time. President Bush, showing little loyalty for Schwarzenegger's campaigning during his re-election, made a fund-raising trip to California two weeks before the election to tap some of the same donors the governor was courting. "We would have appreciated if he would have done his fund-raising after the November 8 election, because you know we need now all the money in the world," Schwarzenegger complained at the time. Pressed for cash, the governor accepted donations from trade associations, ending a ban he had imposed on himself during the recall. Schwarzenegger also took contributions from Wal-Mart and the American Insurance Association on the same day he vetoed bills that would have hurt their interests. There was no evidence of a quid pro quo, but a year earlier, the governor might have been sensitive enough to appearances to return the money.

Schwarzenegger added public events to his schedule, but the ABC unions found a way to answer him almost everywhere he went. When he visited a wildfire in the hills on the border between Ventura and Los Angeles counties on September 30, members of the California Professional Firefighters union objected to appearing at the governor's press conference. Fire officers had to order firefighters to stand next to Schwarzenegger. The incident drew national media attention.

The governor seemed to shake up his strategy and messages every day. In his quest for positive TV coverage, he held events that had little to do with the initiatives on the ballot. On October 13, he endorsed a ballot initiative to require sexual predators to wear Global Positioning System devices, even though that measure would not appear on the ballot until November 2006 at the earliest. A week later, Schwarzenegger campaigned for solar energy legislation that the Democrats had effectively scuttled; it was his way of showing how legislators elected in gerrymandered districts blocked progress. On October 10, Murphy's longtime client John McCain flew out to California to do two town halls with Schwarzenegger. But McCain did not know much about the initiatives he was discussing, and the two politicians had little natural chemistry. Next to the pale, blunt McCain, the tanned Schwarzenegger looked more like a movie star than a governor.

The governor considered holding events at which he would confront the unions and union members. For a time, he was obsessed with putting on a "teacher town hall," where he could take questions from educators and address criticism of Prop 76 head on. Despite the widespread anger at the broken education deal, the governor claimed teachers came up to him all the time and said that they liked his reforms, but were afraid to say so openly because of CTA. The governor and his team debated various formats for such a town hall, but the idea died.

SCHWARZENEGGER'S FIRST NIGHTLY tracking poll on October 20 offered a smidgen of hope. Prop 75, the paycheck protection measure, had a lead and Propositions 74, teacher tenure, and 77, redistricting, were within striking distance of 50 percent. Prop 76, the Live Within Our Means spending limit, which he had called the centerpiece of his effort, was dead. More than half of voters had opposed it in every poll since August.

Prop 77, the redistricting measure, would collapse in the days ahead. It faced a barrage of TV ads from two separate No campaigns. One was funded by Democratic members of California's congressional delegation and had received $4 million from the Hollywood producer Steve Bing. That committee produced TV ads starring Judge Joseph Wapner, famous from TV's *The People's Court*, denouncing the initiative for allowing judges rather than legislators to draw districts and "make law."

A second No on 77 committee, formed by legislative leaders in Sacramento, hired the veteran Democratic consultant Bill Carrick to produce ads. Carrick used a casting director to find three TV actors to play judges who, in one spot, cut up a map of California and rearranged it to look like the state of Texas. It was a reference to the middecade redistricting by Congressman Tom DeLay and the Texas legislature that produced more Republican congressmen in that state. Prop 77, by removing redistricting power from the legislature, would prevent exactly the kind of redistricting that had taken place in Texas. But the ad did its job. Prop 77 had a narrow 41 to 38 percent lead in No on 77 polls done in mid October. After the ads with three "judges" had been on the air for three weeks, the measure trailed, with 37 percent saying they planned to vote yes and 58 percent no.

Schwarzenegger could do little to stop the slide. Supporters of 77 even suggested that the governor cancel a San Jose appearance with Common Cause on behalf of the initiative. Wayne Johnson, a Republican consultant who was working independently of the governor on the Yes on 77 campaign, wanted to separate the measure from Schwarzenegger's troubles. He thought Schwarzenegger's decision to list all four measures together in his ads and signs—74 through 77—as part of one slate would bring 77 down. But the governor felt obligated to show up, and other Prop 77 supporters reluctantly agreed. "We ended up coming to the conclusion that without the governor, we're not going to get the media," Poizner said. "So it was really a classic rock and a hard place."

JUST AS HIS CAMPAIGN SEEMED to be falling apart, Schwarzenegger rallied. He piled up newspaper endorsements for his measures, including the support of thirty-five of the thirty-six largest papers in California for Prop 77, the redistricting initiative. And on October 24, two weeks before the election, he appeared at the first televised forum on his four initiatives, in Walnut Creek in the Bay Area. Rose Ann DeMoro, the executive director of the California Nurses Association, and Don Perata, the Democratic leader of the state senate, spoke against the governor's four initiatives for the first forty-five minutes of the debate, then left the stage to Schwarzenegger for the second half.

The governor bantered naturally with audience members over everything from their jobs to their love lives. To a woman who asked why cops and firefighters were mad at him, Schwarzenegger quipped: "Sometimes when I listen to those TV ads, I'm mad at myself." The governor benefited in particular from the contrast between himself and his opponents. Perata came off as a caricature of the out-of-touch politician. In describing why he opposed Prop 77, the redistricting measure, the senator declared: "We are politicians and we do have the interests of incumbents at heart."

Schwarzenegger's performance drove two days of positive TV and newspaper coverage. He might have gotten a bigger bang, but his team, in an excess of caution, declined an offer to have the forum broadcast statewide. Instead, the forum appeared on only one TV station in the Bay Area. Prop 75, which had been dropping in the polls, inched upward in two nights of tracking after the Walnut Creek forum.

SCHWARZENEGGER'S TURNAROUND briefly rattled the unions. In the view of Democratic pollster Mark Mellman, who worked for CTA and the ABC unions, 76 and 77 were dead, but both 74 and 75 still had a chance to win. Those two measures had less than 50 percent support, but Mellman was troubled by the low number of undecided voters—less than 10 percent in most polls. In typical initiative elections, the overwhelming majority of undecided voters chose to vote no. But the ABC unions worried that undecideds would split 50–50, providing Schwarzenegger with two narrow victories.

ABC convened a conference call on Wednesday, October 26. One union official suggested bringing in Chris Lehane, a former operative for Al Gore. Outside the union alliance, leading liberal thinkers suggested that the unions adjust their attacks. George Lakoff, a UC Berkeley linguistics professor whose advice had become fashionable in Democratic circles, sent word that ABC should link Schwarzenegger to President Bush and Karl Rove. But the ABC unions did not change personnel or tactics. To portray Schwarzenegger as a Bush acolyte was to make a two-step argument (the Bush agenda is bad, and Schwarzenegger is his servant) instead of the effective one-step argument: the governor broke his promise to California schools.

As WAGNER'S "RIDE OF THE VALKYRIES" played over the speaker system, a man dressed in stage makeup and a black cape emerged in front of a giant mock tombstone inscribed "Car Tax RIP 2003" that had been constructed at the Pick-a-Part auto junkyard in the Southern California city of Ontario. "I am Count Cartaxula," said the man, Walter von Huene, Schwarzenegger's dialogue coach. At a signal, a black 1957 Ford Fairlane was lifted up from behind the tombstone, as if the vehicle were rising from the dead. A skeleton sat in the driver's seat. The governor appeared from offstage to argue that if his initiatives failed, Democrats and unions would try to raise taxes, perhaps even reviving the car tax increase from 2003.

The Count Cartaxula spectacle accomplished little. That same Halloween night, his own tracking polls turned decidedly against the two measures, Propositions 74 and 75, that had the best chances of success.

Schwarzenegger did the event out of what he said was his obligation to entertain the public and himself. "How do you make sure that you don't get bored? How do you make sure it's always exciting?" he explained. The week before the election, he invited reporters onto a bus decorated with his picture and the numbers of his initiatives and rode slowly down the 405 freeway in rush hour, from Sherman Oaks to Long Beach, to show the need for infrastructure investment in the state.

Each day, Schwarzenegger had more ideas for events or ads. He wanted to do appearances in a number of ethnic communities, so those were combined into a day-long sprint through Southern California. He demanded that billboards showing nurses, teachers, and law enforcement officials who supported him be put up along major freeways. He wanted a last-minute newspaper ad with one hundred union members saying, "We love Prop 75," but the campaign didn't pull it off. "The last ten days, I'd go home at night and think, 'Thank goodness one more day is over and that's one less day for him to come up with more ideas,'" said a Schwarzenegger advisor.

The governor hit as many as seven cities a day to give press conferences, attend house parties with supporters, and raise money. Schwarzenegger aides even figured out they could neutralize the unions by pointing giant speakers in the protesters' direction and playing the Southern California band War's "Why Can't We Be Friends?" at ear-splitting decibels.

Still, no one, not even his wife, would ride to his rescue. The governor suggested Shriver might announce her initiative choices in a speech at her annual women's conference in Long Beach. But in Long Beach, she praised her husband without detailing her views. "Even in the face of attacks and criticisms, he's an eternal optimist," said Shriver. "We may not agree on every single thing," she added, but "I have to give him credit, no matter how tough it gets ... he has the strength and courage to press on."

Schwarzenegger appeared in televised forums with voters nearly every day. On November 3, he hit two in the same evening. The governor acquitted himself well, but never recaptured the magic of the first forum in Walnut Creek. A debate in Los Angeles, sponsored by the local TV station KNBC, turned into a minor disaster when Democratic activists, posing as regular voters, managed to get into the audience and ask questions. One repeatedly interrupted Schwarzenegger, telling the governor, "I'm not going to let you finish." Schwarzenegger handled it well enough, warmly praising the activist for his commitment to his beliefs. "This is really great," he said. "I like it when you're passionate."

At times, the forum exchanges sounded like a debate about direct democracy and its uses. Speaker Núñez, speaking in opposition to the initiatives at the November 3 KNBC forum, declared, "We need to put an end ... to the governor wanting to use the initiative route to govern." Schwarzenegger said his only regret was that he had not pushed for more reforms. "Don't look at this like this is all we need," he said of the four measures he supported. "I could have put fifteen more ideas on the ballot, but people are already saying we've done too much."

On November 4, the day after the KNBC forum, Schwarzenegger's consultants debated Hail Mary strategies. Perhaps they could let union members who disagreed with the governor ride along on his campaign bus. If he did well in tough exchanges, he might get good press. Randle suggested the governor challenge CTA president Barbara Kerr to a debate, but the consensus among advisors was that such a move would look desperate.

As the governor and the unions battled to the end, each side claimed to represent the need for change and reform in the state. Both the union alliance and Schwarzenegger's campaign thundered against the capital. "Don't let Sacramento bureaucrats steal our future," warned one union ad. "Stop Sacramento," said the Schwarzenegger spots. At the end of the costliest election battle in state history, California seemed trapped in a giant movie full of explosive special effects. The suspense was whether Californians would be stuck with the status quo once the lights came back up.

CONTINUING HIS OWN TRADITION, Schwarzenegger devoted the final Saturday of the campaign, November 5, to a bus tour. The governor's goal was to create political momentum. The California Nurses Association had decided to charter its own bus and chase after the Schwarzenegger coach as it made its way north from San Diego to Irwindale, an industrial Los Angeles County city.

The ABC unions, which were working with the nurses, asked Warren Beatty to join the countertour and provide rapid response to the governor. The actor initially balked, and Gale Kaufman, the top political consultant for the unions, spent part of Friday evening talking the star into it. Kaufman explained that the unions needed some way to compete visually with the TV pictures that would be generated by Schwarzenegger. Beatty agreed, and brought along his camera-friendly wife, the actress Annette Bening.

Reluctant though he was, Beatty deftly stole the show from Schwarzenegger. He drew camera crews to a union rally in front of the San Diego offices of the CTA, and then boarded the California Nurses Association bus with more than a dozen reporters in tow for the short ride to Schwarzenegger's first rally inside a hangar at a small San Diego airfield. This rally, while boisterous, was limited to several hundred guests, invited by Republican and business groups, who had to pass by security guards posted at the airport gate. The union bus, with Beatty and Bening on board, parked about 150 yards away, on the other side of a tall fence.

Just as the rally was about to begin, the security guards left the gate to help one audience member who was having difficulty walking. Beatty and Bening, trailed by CTA president Barbara Kerr and nurses' union executive director DeMoro, made their move. They got through the gate and within about thirty yards of the hangar entrance when Darrel Ng, a young press aide with the best manners of any member of the Schwarzenegger operation, sprinted over to intercept them.

"Are you on the list?" Ng asked pointedly.

"Do you have to be on a list to see the governor?" Beatty asked, with Bening silent behind him.

Ng walked over to a table to retrieve a clipboard with the list of invited guests. "Let me see if you guys are on the list," Ng said. He asked how their names were spelled.

Why don't you spell our names? Beatty asked.

B-E-A-T-T-Y, Ng said, scanning the list.

B-E-N-N-I-N-G?

"You've got an extra n," the actress said, with a look that could kill.

"I'm sorry. Neither of you is on the list."

"Do you have to be on the list to go in and listen to the governor speak?" Beatty asked again. "I'm a citizen. I'd like to hear the speech."

After a brief exchange, Beatty declared, "We're going to go ahead anyway," and he and Bening headed for the hangar entrance. They were ten feet from the door before Ng and a group of other aides stood directly in the couple's path.

"I'm sorry. We're going to have to ask you to leave," Ng said.

"I know you've asked, and I've turned you down," Beatty said.

"I'm turning you down and telling you to go back outside," Ng said.

"Can we listen to the speech?" Beatty asked again. "We'll be very quiet. We won't make any noise."

Beatty smiled. He had already won this round of celebrity political warfare. Reporters and cameramen left the hangar to cover the stand-off between Ng and the two movie stars. Todd Harris, a consultant who worked with Murphy, appeared and told Beatty and Bening that he would love to let them in, but the unions had been protesting Schwarzenegger's events for most of the year. Didn't the governor deserve to have his voice heard?

The argument was briefly halted by the playing of the national anthem. At the first notes, Beatty and the Schwarzenegger aides put their hands over their hearts and stood silently.

Schwarzenegger's aides debated whether to close the door to the hangar and lock out Beatty and Bening. The doors closed for a few minutes. But when law enforcement officials objected to shutting the main exit to a crowded hangar, the doors reopened. From just outside the open door, Beatty and Bening listened quietly to the speech as Schwarzenegger aides held signs that obstructed their view of the governor and the TV cameras' view of the couple. Schwarzenegger made no reference to the rally crashers, though Roger Hedgecock, the radio talk show host who introduced the governor, could not stop talking about the uninvited guests. "*Dick Tracy* was a terrible movie, just terrible. That was celluloid abuse. It's time for some people to retire," said Hedgecock, who couldn't help but add: "How much fun would it be if he actually ran against Schwarzenegger?" The suggestion drew a loud cheer. Beatty would give a press conference after the stand-off that was his only misstep of the day. Reporters looked puzzled as he quoted Hubert Humphrey, who had been the Democratic presidential nominee in 1968, and said the state legislators were "heroes" for standing up to Schwarzenegger. (Lawmakers were even less popular than the governor.) The governor's bus, with a police escort, beat the Beatty counter–bus tour to the next stop, Anaheim, and there would be no repeat of the stand-off there or in Riverside. Beatty and Bening had already done their job. News coverage of the tour focused on the battle between the stars, not on the initiatives.

SCHWARZENEGGER HAD PLANNED the biggest rally of the bus tour for last. It was to be modeled on the final event of the recall tour, when Dee Snider had sung "We're Not Gonna Take It" live in front of the capitol. Murphy had fallen in love with the Fifth Dimension tune "Let the Sun Shine In," and the campaign tried and failed to book members of the original Fifth Dimension. A local band performed the song instead.

More than one thousand people, most of whom had learned of the event from a talk radio show, crowded into a warehouse in Irwindale. Schwarzenegger's team had arranged for banners that read "Let the Sun Shine In" to be hung from the ceilings. Children were given yellow beanies to wear. It would be the most electric crowd of the campaign. But, since the event did not start until past 6 p.m., long after newspaper reporters and TV producers had filed their stories, only the people in the room would see it.

As the band struck up the chords of "Let the Sun Shine In," a giant door opened on one side of the warehouse, and the campaign bus approached. Schwarzenegger appeared in the front of the bus, next to the driver, and the crowd gave a deafening roar.

The bus was supposed to make a sharp turn and park immediately behind the stage, serving as a backdrop. But the bus failed to negotiate the tight left turn all the way into the building. Schwarzenegger stayed in full view, his smile fixed in place, for five minutes, before he finally hopped out and ran to the stage himself.

In spite of all the snafus, Schwarzenegger had given the public an enormous show. More than $325 million was spent on campaigns for and against the eight measures on the special election ballot. The unions spent $164 million against him and his initiatives, while Schwarzenegger and the various committees affiliated with his initiatives would spend $74 million. (Most of the rest of the money was spent by the pharmaceutical industry to beat back the union initiative on drug prices.) At $238 million, the total spending on the governor's four measures was greater than the domestic box office gross of any Schwarzenegger movie. (*Terminator 2* came closest with $204 million.)

This was blockbuster democracy. California's system turned the making of laws into a contest that the people could follow. But a contest wasn't the same as real action. Schwarzenegger, his special election, and his governorship had shined the brightest of lights on the state and its government. In doing so, he had changed—perhaps forever—the look and feel and scale of politics. But blockbuster democracy would not produce the reforms he sought.

The band played "Let the Sun Shine In" once, twice, ten times in a row. Each time, the song sounded sadder. Schwarzenegger's bus tour was over. While the music still played, the governor headed out into the night.

On the way home, the governor made a recording of his thoughts about the day. He was blocking out the prospect of defeat. "I always visualize success," he said on the recording. "Visualize us winning all of the reforms passing and creating the reforms. So I'm not planning on losing any of those initiatives."

THE GOVERNOR AND HIS SUPPORTERS gathered on election night at the Beverly Hilton Hotel in the same ballroom that hosted the Golden Globes. His initiatives on teacher tenure (Prop 74), the Live Within Our Means spending limit (Prop 76), and redistricting (Prop 77) quickly headed to defeat.

Prop 75, the paycheck protection measure, took a ten-point lead in early returns. Once a bargaining chip that the governor hoped to trade away in a giant enchilada compromise, it was now his only hope for a win. Prop 75's lead declined steadily as the vote was tallied in Los Angeles and the Bay Area. With less than half the votes counted, Prop 75 slid under 50 percent. It would never rebound.

Schwarzenegger came down to the ballroom after 10 p.m. He looked beaten, but, with the Prop 75 numbers still close, he did not concede defeat officially. "I want to thank those who voted for our propositions and I want to thank those who did not vote for our propositions . . . and most of all I want to thank the people who were so passionately against us. I guess I didn't do a good enough job to convince them otherwise."

That was how the governor saw it. He was a salesman who had not made the sale, not a politician whose ideas had been rejected. He concluded by telling the crowd, "I feel the same tonight as that night two years ago when I was elected governor."

Could that possibly be true? The recall had been a triumph for Schwarzenegger and for direct democracy. This was the greatest defeat for ballot measures supported by a California governor since all of Hiram Johnson's propositions went down in the 1915 special election. The most popular of Schwarzenegger's four measures, Prop 75, received 46.5 percent and lost by more than 500,000 votes out of nearly 7.9 million cast. Prop 74 had finished with 44.8 percent. Prop 77 had received 40.2 percent, and Prop 76, the spending limit, tallied just 37.6 percent. That initiative was a direct casualty of Schwarzenegger's political Waterloo: his education funding deal with

CTA. The rest of his reform agenda was collateral damage. A post-election survey would find that 44 percent of those who had voted no on Prop 77 agreed with the following statement: "I supported redistricting reform but I did not want to vote with the governor of California."

The other four initiatives on the ballot lost, too. The union counter-measures on prescription drugs and energy won just 39.3 and 34.4 percent of the vote respectively. Prop 78, the pharmaceutical industry's counter to the unions' counter, did little better, with only 41.5 percent. The closest any measure came to winning a majority was the 47.2 percent of the vote received by Prop 73, the initiative requiring parental consent before minors have abortions. Californians had said no to all eight propositions on the ballot.

SCHWARZENEGGER WOULD ACCEPT defeat two days later in a press conference at the capitol. He still felt the state needed reform. But he had damaged the prospects of his proposals by drafting them too quickly and calling an extra election that the public did not embrace. "If I would do another *Terminator* movie," he said, "I would have Terminator travel back in time and tell Arnold not to have a special election."

Schwarzenegger had mistaken his ability to stir interest in ballot contests for a talent to convince people to adopt his plans. In the final days of the election, more than 80 percent of voters told pollsters they were following the contest at least somewhat closely. And when asked which initiatives they knew and cared most about, voters listed the four Schwarzenegger measures first. Turnout for the election had surpassed 50 percent, about 10 percentage points higher than what had been predicted. But many of those voters saw Schwarzenegger as the villain of the story and showed up to vote against him.

"What I should have done is nurtured everything along, brought more people along, and got more and more people to become part of a movement for the reform," Schwarzenegger would say of the reform push. "Then you create kind of a momentum, the kind of momentum we created with workers' comp reform or the momentum that was created with the recall where the people slowly buy in and say, 'Yes, we need that change.' But I did not do it."

Californians still wanted big changes. And they still liked direct democracy and distrusted their elected leaders. The ballot would remain a tool for politicians and others who knew how to draft measures that told stories that appealed to the public.

But Schwarzenegger's initiatives for the special election had failed the movie test. None of the measures told a story so new or compelling that they caught fire with voters. The governor might have drafted measures that explicitly offered the public new ideas or programs in education and health care. He could have included provisions in his spending limit that gave the public the ability to lift the cap by popular vote. Instead of his discredited pension measure, he could have put together an initiative to require a vote of the people before the pensions of public workers were increased.

While many explanations and excuses would be offered for his defeat, Schwarzenegger's inability to produce initiatives the public could support did not result from a lack of intelligence, ambition, time, money, or good intentions. The governor had plenty of all those things.

The political defeat of Schwarzenegger, the man who had lived an unimaginable life, was a failure of imagination.

SCHWARZENEGGER HAD USHERED IN a new era of politics, but the era would not belong to him. Although California's system of ballot measures fit the governor as well as anyone, it was a mechanism too big, too complex, and too unwieldy for any one person—no matter how smart, famous, or wealthy—to make entirely his own.

Blockbuster democracy was an imperfect machine, but it was still the people's.

"The Reality of It"

On a chilly Sacramento evening in March 2006, four months after the special election debacle, Governor Schwarzenegger took a seat by an outdoor fireplace in a dark hotel patio. Before starting our interview, he lit a cigar, the flash of light illuminating new lines in his face and hands. His hair looked more natural and far less orange than when he'd been running for the office. A few gray hairs were visible.

He appeared to be a different governor. After the defeat of his four ballot initiatives, Schwarzenegger spent weeks privately seeking advice from friends and critics, Democrats and Republicans, on where he'd gone wrong. This self-examination spurred Schwarzenegger, usually reluctant to let employees go, to replace much of his divided staff. Big players such as Clarey and Stutzman were out. Tom Campbell went back to Berkeley to run the business school, and Murphy, while staying on as a "volunteer" advisor, gave up his formal role to pursue his Hollywood work. The governor had a new communications director, a new cabinet secretary, a new finance director, and new consultants for a re-election campaign that appeared far more daunting than it did a year before.

Shriver, who had privately opposed the special election, helped with the reshuffling. The new chief of staff, Susan Kennedy (no relation to the First Lady's extended family), was a Democrat who had been cabinet secretary in the administration of Gray Davis. Shriver's own new chief of staff was a former Davis policy advisor and close friend of Kennedy's. Their appointments made it official: the recall was finally over.

Much of the Posse, the left-leaning aides who were personally close to the governor, remained, but the Cabal was gone. When Republicans protested Schwarzenegger's decision to hire Kennedy, the governor didn't budge. In a meeting to soothe leading Republicans, he suggested conservatives didn't like Kennedy because she is gay. He also called Shawn Steel, the former party chair who was one of the earliest supporters of the recall. The meeting did not reassure conservatives, some of whom openly wondered if they would have been better off leaving a wounded Gray Davis in office.

Schwarzenegger was more concerned with satisfying his larger audience, the voters. He interpreted the special election results as a message from the public to cool the rhetoric. He knew better than anyone how his own persona had been used against him, and he began using public appearances to present himself as a slightly more conventional governor. Instead of mall rallies and junkyard stunts, he gave policy speeches in and around public buildings.

Rather than challenge the establishment again, Schwarzenegger sought accommodations as he fought for political survival. By the spring, he had made a new agreement with the California Teachers Association that not only restored his original funding deal but also provided billions more to schools. Schwarzenegger reappointed CTA's political director, who had been one of the architects of the unions' campaign against him, to the state school board. He also reached out to the hard-line Indian tribes whom he had battled in the Prop 70 fight. And he even courted the prison guards' union, another part of the labor coalition that had so successfully opposed the special election, and abandoned an effort by his own appointees to reform California's abysmal prison system. In public, Schwarzenegger talked less of ballot initiatives and more of compromise. He would move more slowly, more deliberately. He would not repeat the mistakes of 2005.

"At the end when the dust is settled and done, the only one that I blame for this is myself," he told me. "That's the reality. We can go and say, 'So and so said this or did this.' That's really all mechanical stuff. I'm not sure it would have changed things in one way or another. The reality of it was that you can't go and say, 'This year, this has to be done,' when in fact, it might take two or three years to do it. Reform was a huge undertaking. And I feel responsible for the whole thing."

THAT SOUNDED LIKE A sober concession to the power of the status quo. But when he talked about old friends from Austria, his time as chairman of the President's Council on Physical Fitness and Sports, and his years of unorthodox preparation for his current job, his old bonhomie returned. He shared a few stories from the recall campaign and his ballot measure victories on Propositions 57 and 58, local government, and Indian gambling. And even in the shadow of popular rejection of his proposals, he couldn't stop talking about the people. He wanted to go to the people again, this time in pursuit of a giant, history-making $222 billion project to rebuild the state.

Infrastructure was popular with the public, and the state's establishment had yearned for a major investment for years. But the scale of Schwarzenegger's ambitions dropped jaws. His plan called for 1,200 miles of new highways, 600 miles of mass transit, more than 2,000 new schools, two new prisons, a new crime lab, 40,000 new classrooms, 101 new courts, and new levees to protect the Central Valley from floods. He envisioned voters approving

$70 billion in infrastructure bonds over five election cycles to leverage $222 billion in projects.

For all his talk about learning the lesson of patience, Schwarzenegger was in a hurry again. He used the March 16 deadline for adding measures to the June 2006 ballot to try to force lawmakers to agree to bonds that could be put before voters. In these talks, the governor was, of course, weighing all his options, using multiple channels, changing his mind and talking directly to the various legislators on right and left. He made two deals, but each fell apart. "Can you believe that they called it a failure on infrastructure?" Schwarzenegger said as he sipped hot tea on the hotel patio. "We'll get there. It's a big, big thing."

The governor resolved to put the bond on the November ballot instead. Negotiations would be underway again by April. This time Schwarzenegger played a less direct role, allowing legislative leaders to handle much of the deal-making. Schwarzenegger also had a familiar ally in forcing the legislature's hand: a ballot initiative. The state's transportation lobby gathered enough signatures to qualify an initiative to prevent the legislature from raiding gas tax money, which was supposed to be spent on roads.

The transportation lobby threatened to file its signatures by May 6 unless the legislature passed a bond package that included legal protections for the gas tax money. After midnight on Friday, May 5, the legislature voted to place four infrastructure bonds on the November ballot: $20 billion for transportation, $10.4 billion for schools, $4.1 billion to repair levees, and $2.8 billion for affordable housing. Lawmakers added a fifth ballot measure, limiting how often they could raid gas tax money, and the transportation lobby dropped its initiative.

The $37.3 billion package of infrastructure bonds would be the largest in state history, and would leverage $116 billion in new spending. That was a little more than half what Schwarzenegger had sought, but still a substantial political victory. Schwarzenegger would be campaigning for multiple measures on the November ballot. Because the bonds had bipartisan support, Democrats would find themselves campaigning with Schwarzenegger—at the same time they campaigned against him.

If the measures won and he secured re-election, he would likely return to the ballot for more infrastructure bonds. Perhaps he would revisit some of the reforms that failed in the special election. "I made mistakes," he said of 2005, "but there was no mistake on policy, because we were right on the money with the policy. We have to take more time, do it a different way."

His political standing was different. His advisors were different.

He was the same governor.

HAD SCHWARZENEGGER'S POLITICAL method been a flawed experiment or a glimpse of the future? It could prove to be both. In the aftermath of the special election, some commentators railed against ballot initiatives. But the state's industry of signature gatherers, consultants, and pollsters readied for another big season of democratic shows.

Schwarzenegger was not the only player in California's blockbuster democracy who was dreaming of more campaigns. Rob Reiner, working with many of the same people who helped Schwarzenegger with Prop 49 in 2002, had qualified Proposition 82 for the June 2006 ballot. Reiner's initiative was an audacious plan to raise taxes to pay for a massive expansion of preschool programs, and he launched a campaign too large for its own good. A state commission Reiner chaired—which had been established through a successful ballot initiative the movie director had sponsored in 1998—paid for TV spots about the value of preschool. The use of public dollars to benefit a political campaign, in this case Prop 82, was a no-no, and Reiner resigned from the state commission. The Prop 82 campaign would continue, with Reiner and his family giving more than $4 milllion to the effort. The measure would lose, with 61 percent voting no, but Reiner would vow, "I am not going away."

As many as fifteen measures were expected to appear on the November 2006 ballot. Schwarzenegger was already championing "Jessica's law," an initiative that would require more extensive monitoring of sex offenders. Two wealthy Silicon Valley stalwarts, Netflix Inc. CEO Reed Hastings and venture capitalist John Doerr, were gathering signatures on an initiative to create a $50 tax on nearly every real estate parcel in the state to raise $500 million for schools. This promised another big fight with taxpayer groups, whose leaders argued the initiative was a back-door attack on Prop 13. The California Nurses Association, which had denounced Schwarzenegger's use of the ballot as illegitimate during 2005, was now sponsoring its own ballot initiative to reform campaign finance.

No one made plainer the extent to which Schwarzenegger's tactics ruled the day than the two men who fought for the Democratic nomination to run against him. The state Controller Steve Westly, who had made a fortune as an early executive of eBay and used it to fund his political career, was best known to California voters for serving as co-chairman for Schwarzenegger's campaign for Propositions 57 and 58. Detractors dubbed him Arnold's Mini-Me. His rationale for running was that Schwarzenegger, despite a good initial direction, had lost his way and become a partisan.

State Treasurer Phil Angelides, the candidate backed by the Democratic establishment, was running as the self-proclaimed "anti-Arnold," an opponent of everything Schwarzenegger had ever done. But even the anti-Arnold would not run away from blockbuster democracy. In an interview with the *Sacramento Bee*, Angelides said that if the legislature refused to go along with his plans to raise taxes and boost education spending, he would turn his proposals into ballot initiatives and go to the people. Getting action, Angelides explained, "is a matter of a moral imperative." After a nasty primary battle with Westly, Angelides would narrowly win the Democratic nomination and face the governor in the fall.

Schwarzenegger had risen to political power at a moment in history when the reach of both popular entertainment and democracy had never been greater. There were nearly 150 democratic countries on the planet by the early twenty-first century. Entertainment was becoming, in form if not necessarily in substance, more democratic, as viewers chose from an expanding menu of channels and films. The Internet made it far cheaper for unknowns to create and distribute popular entertainment. The top-rated TV show "American Idol" allowed viewers at home to determine the outcome. And democracy had become steadily more entertainment-oriented. Politicians routinely sought celebrity backing and appeared as often as possible on entertainment-oriented shows as part of a never-ending contest to get the attention of their constituents. Parties turned to celebrities with little preparation for office—the latest, sportscaster and former football star, Lynn Swann, was the Republican nominee for governor of Pennsylvania in 2006—in hopes of turning star cachet into real power.

Schwarzenegger had combined democracy and entertainment more thoroughly than anyone. He also demonstrated—inadvertently—the difficulties of using star power to govern. Celebrity had its own checks and balances.

IF SCHWARZENEGGER COULD REBOUND and win re-election, he would be in a stronger position to use the ballot to pursue other changes in his second term, and his example would have deep implications for the rest of the country, particularly those twenty-four states that had the initiative. (Twenty-seven states have some form of direct democracy.)

In the 1990s, American states had set a record for the number of measures reaching the ballot, a record that was likely to be broken in the first decade of the twenty-first century. Politicians in initiative states were using the ballot as a tool of political communication and governance. Schwarzenegger liked to point out that many other countries allowed national votes on issues. European countries voted on whether to join the European Union and signing its new constitution. During the 1990s, referendums were conducted in eighty-four sovereign states around the world, according to the Initiative & Referendum Institute. In addition, more than fifty other countries have the referendum or initiative intheir constitution, but do not use it. The total number of ballot measures worldwide roughly doubled in the past decade.

In the United States, Schwarzenegger said, a national initiative, referendum or recall "is something to study. Other countries have it . . . You have to re-evaluate the system every so often and just see where it needs some updating." Direct democracy at the federal level was not a new idea. Late in the Civil War, there was talk of a national vote on whether the fighting should continue. In 1939, the Wisconsin senator Robert LaFollette, Jr. championed a proposal to require a vote before America went to war. In Los Angeles County, the 1978 ballot that included Prop 13 also had the following advisory question: "Should we have a national voter initiative?" By a two-to-one margin, Angelenos said yes. A plan for a national referendum was introduced by Congressman Richard Gephardt in 1980.

As President Bush made the cause of spreading democracy a central tenet of national security policy, the United States opened itself up to the charge of hypocrisy. The American government had long argued for national votes—in Nicaragua in the 1970s, in the Philippines in 1987, and in Iraq in 2005—to settle difficult questions in foreign countries, without ever permitting its own citizens to vote directly on national issues.

SCHWARZENEGGER ALLOWED THAT one day he would like to advocate nationally and internationally on issues. But first, he had to avoid the ignominy of lasting just three years in office (shorter, a few Democrats pointed out, than Jesse Ventura's four-year term in Minnesota). No incumbent California governor had failed to win a second term since Culbert Olson, an atheist who refused to say the entire oath of office and lost his re-election bid to Earl Warren in 1942. Even if Schwarzenegger pulled out a victory, as many commentators believed he would, he would likely never return to the popular heights he had enjoyed in late 2004, when he chewed on his cigar at 71 percent and thought he could turn California upside down.

Politically, Schwarzenegger found himself in an unusual predicament. By most measures, the state had recovered somewhat from the electricity, budget, and other crises that prompted the recall. Even without the Prop 76 spending limit he had said was necessary, the state was projected to end the 2005–06 budget year with a surplus. The structural deficit, projected at more than $16 billion when he took office, was less than half that. Revenues had grown so quickly that Prop 49, his after-school initiative from 2002, was finally scheduled to take effect. But Schwarzenegger had talked so forcefully about the state's problems and the need for reform that most voters did not give him credit for this progress.

SCHWARZENEGGER SAID HE didn't intend to hold another elected office after 2010, when he could complete a second term as governor. "I don't see myself building a political career," he said. "I think I owe it to my family to go and get back to normal life." The U.S. Constitution's requirement that presidents be "natural born citizens" made him ineligible for that office. Schwarzenegger believed the provision should be eliminated but that any change was unlikely to come soon enough to benefit him.

Many of his friends did not believe him when he professed disinterest in national office. Joe Weider and Reg Park, longtime associates from bodybuilding, said his goal was the presidency. Werner Kopacka, an Austrian journalist who had known Schwarzenegger for years, said: "I'm sure his ultimate dream is the White House. He'll protest in public. But when the cigar is lit and you're talking to him, you feel it." (A 2005 poll by a market research firm found that 37 percent of Austrians believed the sitting governor of California would become president of the United States.)

An amendment to the constitution would require a two-thirds vote of both houses of Congress and ratification by three-quarters of the state legislatures. Since members of Congress, many of whom saw themselves as presidential timber, were unlikely to vote to expand the pool of potential competitors, a change was unlikely to come without outside pressure. Strong supporters of such an amendment—who included immigrants' rights advocates and the families of children adopted overseas—suggested bypassing Congress and using another feature of the Constitution to eliminate the "natural born" requirement: a constitutional convention.

Article V of the Constitution provides that a convention may be called to consider amendments when two-thirds of the state legislatures demand it. Any amendment produced by that convention would have to be ratified by three-quarters of the state legislatures. No such convention had ever been held. But the threat of a convention worked as leverage in the case of the Seventeenth Amendment, which stripped legislatures of the power to pick U.S. senators and instead allowed the people to vote directly. When that amendment's backers, who included Progressives such as Theodore Roosevelt and Hiram Johnson, convinced eleven state legislatures to demand a constitutional convention, Congress responded by voting for the amendment in 1912. It was ratified by the states the following year.

DIRECT DEMOCRACY MIGHT POINT Schwarzenegger in the direction of the states. With nearly half of the states allowing the initiative, he had considered using direct democracy in a national way earlier in his political career. After the victory of his after-school measure Prop 49, his team had produced a plan that suggested a campaign to pass after-school initiatives in other states. Supporters of term limits for politicians and legal rights for animals had sponsored successful initiatives in multiple states.

Schwarzenegger had indicated there were a number of causes he would be happy to promote, from global environmental issues to political reforms such as redistricting. Perhaps advocacy for initiatives in multiple states would match his political history and his action persona. He could argue that he was not an ambitious office holder but merely a concerned citizen with an idea. Out of elected office, he would be free to make movies and pursue other money-making opportunities, producing cash that he could to donate to these campaigns. This would be blockbuster democracy on a national scale.

Schwarzenegger's presence in so many state capitals would create media attention and likely fuel the debate about changing the U.S. Constitution. He could develop political committees and networks of allies in enough states to make himself a political kingmaker. Members of Congress seeking his endorsement might be more likely to support an amendment to the "natural born" citizens' clause. State legislatures under the sway of his allies might do the same.

SCHWARZENEGGER CORRECTLY DISMISSED such notions as fanciful. But then again, so was his political career thus far. The lure of blockbuster democracy—and of California—was that anyone could find a way around insurmountable roadblocks and established institutions, if only he or she could gather enough signatures or raise enough money or somehow get the story out to the public. Such dreams often proved to be illusions. But such dreams were irresistible to the people. Just ask Arnold Schwarzenegger. He's a people person.

Notes

I covered the Sacramento Memorial Auditorium speech for the *Los Angeles Times*. Reaction quotes came from interviews conducted that day. I later reviewed the speech on DVD, as recorded by CSPAN. Some of the language about Schwarzenegger's dualities was drawn from a profile I wrote in the *Los Angeles Times*, October 8, 2003. The descriptions of Johnson were based on my review of the papers from his governorship on file at the Bancroft Library at the University of California Berkeley. The Carey McWilliams quote was taken from his classic book, *California: The Great Exception* (New York: Current Books, 1949, p.25).

In describing the Sacramento Memorial Auditorium and its history, I relied on the book, *Sacramento's Memorial Auditorium: Seven Decades of Memories*, by Bonnie Wehle Snyder and Paula J. Boghosian (Sacramento: Memorial Auditorium Book Project, 1997). A building manager also provided a tour in 2004. Johnson's speech at the dedication was quoted in the *Sacramento Bee*, July 16, 1925.

Facts about the choice of venue, political advice, and the ignorance of the building's history came from interviews with dozens of staffers and advisors to the governor's campaign, as well as campaign documents and an interview with Schwarzenegger.

CHAPTER 1

The description of the shooting of Heney was from newspaper articles of the time and from the "1909 Report on the Causes of Municipal Corruption in San Francisco, as Disclosed by the Investigations of the Oliver Grand Jury, and the Prosecution of Certain Persons for Bribery and Other Offenses Against the State." Johnson's summation was from newspaper accounts and his papers. (He wrote out the speech by hand.)

Details on Johnson, including his campaign film and offer of a job working as a lawyer for Hollywood, were from his papers at the Bancroft Library. I also consulted Sitton's *John Randolph Haynes* (Stanford: Stanford University Press, 1992); George Mowry's *The California Progressives* (New York: Quadrangle, 1951); *Hiram Johnson*, by Michael Weatherson and Hal Bochin (Lanham,

Maryland: University Press of America, 1995); as well as Spencer Olin's work. I conducted phone interviews that informed the chapter with Olin, Bill Deverell, and Joel Fox. The Hichborn quote about the value of newspapers appeared in a June 23, 1911, letter to Johnson. I visited Johnson's grave in Colma, California.

My description of direct democracy, the Southern Pacific, and its history was informed by the Johnson papers; *Direct Democracy*, by Thomas E. Cronin (Cambridge: Harvard University Press, 1999); *The Initiative and Referendum in California*, by John M. Allswang (Stanford: Stanford University Press, 2000); *A Government by the People*, by Thomas Goebel (Chapel Hill: University of North Carolina Press, 2002); *Paradise Lost*, by Peter Schrag (Berkeley: University of California Press, 1998); and *Democracy Derailed*, by David Broder (San Diego: Harvest, 2000). In Switzerland, I observed the Swiss referendum elections in June 2005. I also consulted *Direct Democracy in Switzerland*, by Gregory Fossedal (New Brunswick, NJ: Transaction Publishers, 2002). My description of the early days of movies and the Edison Trust was from Robert Sklar's *Movie-Made America* (New York: Vintage Books, 1994), *Edison: A Biography*, by Matthew Josephson (New York: History Book Club, 2003), and David Thomson's *The Whole Equation* (New York: Knopf, 2005). The quote from Karl Brown appeared in Tom Shone's *Blockbuster* (New York: Free Press, 2004). The DeMille quote was from Kevin Starr's *Inventing the Dream* (New York: Oxford University Press, pp. 1985, pp. 310–311).

The information on Robinson & Company, the early signature-gathering firm, was from Carey McWilliams, *California: The Great Exception* (Berkeley: University of California Press, 1947, p.207).

The Clem Whitaker quote appeared in *Banana Republicans: How the Right Wing Is Turning America Into a One-Party State*, by Sheldon Rampton and John Stauber (New York: Tarcher/Penguin, 2004). I also used information on Whitaker and Baxter from Goebel. Sandow was described in detail in Schwarzenegger's own *New Encyclopedia of Modern Bodybuilding* (New York: Simon & Schuster, 1985). The information on Haynes, including the quote from his unpublished autobiography, was from Tom Sitton's *John Randolph Haynes: California Progressive* (Stanford: Stanford University Press, 1992).

CHAPTER 2

This chapter used material from interviews with, among others, Governor Pete Wilson, Joel Fox, Charlotte Parker, Jim Lorimer, Jon Coupal, Larry Gerston, Shelley Zalis, Bruce Friend, Joe Farrell, John Mockler, Rick Claussen, Mike and Bill Arno, Fred Kimball, Angelo Paparella, Rick Arnold, Gerald Uelmen,

Ted Costa, Lewis Uhler, Wayne Pacelle, George Gorton, Ron Unz, and Tom Laughlin. The Schwarzenegger material came from interviews and conversations for the book and for the *Los Angeles Times*. Other quotations came from his speeches and published interviews: a September 3, 1989, *Los Angeles Times* interview by Jack Mathews ("I wanted to make sure that if . . ."); an interview in the *Buffalo News*, June 27, 1993 ("What I always like to do is let the audience tell us the way they feel . . ." and "In the end we have to make movies not for the press but for the people"); and an interview in the *New York Times*, June 24, 2004. The James Cameron quote was from a *Rolling Stone* interview published in 1991. The quote, "in our business . . . ," first appeared in *Premiere* magazine in 1993.

Other details were from previously published work, including a profile in the *Washington Post* magazine on June 23, 1991, and an interview with *Playboy* published in 1988. The quote, "When people see one of my movies . . . ," was from the *Playboy* interview. The story of Franklin giving Washington his crab-tree walking stick was from "The Writings of Benjamin Franklin," as reported in Joseph J. Ellis's *Founding Brothers* (New York: Knopf, 2000). Ed Koupal's story was from Dwayne Hunn and Doris Ober, *Ordinary People Doing the Extraordinary: The Story of Ed and Joyce Koupal and the Initiative Process* (People's Lobby: 2001). The Jarvis material was from his autobiography *I'm Mad as Hell* (New York: Times Books, 1979), and Joel Fox's *The Legend of Proposition 13* (Philadelphia, Penn.: Xlibris, 2003).

Material on the less-than-direct impact of initiatives was first suggested to me by the work of Elisabeth R. Gerber and D. Roderick Kiewiet; *Stealing the Initiative*, by Gerber, Kiewiet, Arthur Lupia, and Mathew D. McCubbins was particularly valuable (Upper Saddle River, NJ: Prentice-Hall, 2001). I consulted dozens of books about direct democracy, among them Schrag's *Paradise Lost*, Broder's *Democracy Derailed*, John Allswang's *The Initiative and Referendum in California*, Cronin's *Direct Democracy*, and reference material from the Initiative & Referendum Institute at the University of Southern California. T. Anthony Quinn's declaration in the 2005 legal case, *Citizens to Save California vs. California FPPC*, was also helpful. The Reiner material was from published interviews, public records, and an interview with a consultant to Reiner.

Tom Shone's *Blockbuster* was quoted on the need for actors who can work with special effects, and on the quality of *Last Action Hero*. Shone's book was one of several relatively new works on blockbuster moviemaking that I consulted in putting the chapter together. The others were Bing and Hayes, *Open Wide* (New York: Miramax Books, 2004), and Edward Jay Epstein's *The Big Picture* (New York: Random House, 2005). The definition of blockbuster came from the *American Heritage Dictionary of the English Language* and from William Safire in the *New York Times*, March 13, 2005.

CHAPTER 3

The information on Austria was based on two trips I made there, one in July 2004 and the other in May and June 2005. I interviewed Alfred and Heidi Gerstl, Josef Krainer, Albert Kaufmann, Peter Urdl, Werner Kopacka, Reinhold Lopatka, Oliver Rathkolb, Michael Steiner, Kurt Marnul, Martin Eichtinger, Ernest Kaltenegger, Heinz Anderwald, Herwig Hösele, and aides to Chancellor Wolfgang Schüssel. Graz Mayor Siegfried Nagl and his aide Gert Haubenhofer provided some guidance. My interviews with the Gerstls, Kaltenegger, Mayor Urdl, and Kurt Marnul were conducted in German with a translator. Urdl gave me a tour of Thal and introduced me to citizens there. The Fröbel School, which Schwarzenegger attended, hosted me for a morning.

Christian Jauschowetz and Werner Kopacka's book, *Arnold Hautnah* (Arnold Up Close), was an invaluable resource (Munich: Herbig, 2004). Alfred Gerstl shared speeches, correspondence, and records of Schwarzenegger's endorsements. Gerstl recalled his comment, "paved the way for forces . . .," in a 1998 speech. "Arnold is an American . . ." and "Democracy is the way . . ." were from an interview with Gerstl. Regarding Austrian politics, I relied upon several books, including *Contemporary Austrian Politics*, edited by Volkmar Lauber (Boulder, Colo.: Westview Press, 1996); and *From World War to Waldheim*, part of a multi-volume project of the Center for Austrian Studies at the University of Minnesota (New York: Berghahn, 1999). The anecdote about Haider and Schwarzenegger was first reported by the *Los Angeles Times* on December 11, 1997. Gustav Schwarzenegger's records were on file at the Vienna State Archives, where I reviewed them.

I interviewed Reg Park at the Arnold Classic in March 2004. For the bodybuilding section of the book, I interviewed Rick Wayne by phone. Jim Lorimer sat for interviews in Columbus. The anecdotes about Schwarzenegger's arrival in the country and meeting John Kerry were recounted by others and confirmed by Schwarzenegger. The Charles Gaines quote was from his piece in *Men's Journal*, January 2004. The purchase agreement from *Pumping Iron* was first disclosed by thesmokinggun.com.

For the section of the chapter on *Free to Choose*, I interviewed Milton Friedman, Bob Chitester, and George Shultz. Schwarzenegger's quote was from volume one of the five-tape set, "Free to Choose" (Idea Channel, 1990). Material on the Reason Foundation came from newsletters of the foundation and from interviews with, Robert Poole, Lynn Scarlett, and George Passantino.

The transcript of the *Pumping Iron* interview was released during the Schwarzenegger gubernatorial campaign. Schwarzenegger's own speeches, particularly the addresses on September 21, 2001, and June 9, 2004, were crucial. The governor also granted me an interview in Austria in July 2004, and we discussed Austria in November 2004 and March 2006 "I didn't want a safety net . . ." was from the March 2006 interview. Austrian journalists provided me with translations of several stories on and interviews with Schwarzenegger. Particularly helpful were interviews with the *Kronen Zeitung* in August 2003 and with *Die Presse* in September 2004.

Much of the Shriver family material was from the interviews with Schwarzenegger. For quotes and the history of Sargent Shriver, I drew heavily on *Sarge*, a biography by Scott Stossel (Washington: Smithsonian Books, 2004). The Maria Shriver quote, "I would say certainly the biggest influence . . ." was from *Sarge*, p. 670. Sargent Shriver's quote, "It was about to break up . . ." was from *The Courier Mail*, December 24, 1999. The "showman's desire to entertain" was from *Sarge*, p. 239, and "we're going to write Head Start . . ." was from *Sarge*, p. 422. "The sponge" quote from Schwarzenegger was from a November 2005 interview, and "Eunice was always probably hoping that her children . . ." was from March 2006. The anecdote about Schwarzenegger designing an exercise program for Rose Kennedy was recounted by Schwarzenegger in his book, *Arnold's Bodyshaping for Women* (New York: Simon & Schuster, 1979, p.23). Maria Shriver's quote about marrying her "authentic self" was from *Vanity Fair*, January 2005.

The University of Wisconsin at Superior section came from materials on file at the Jim Dan Hill Library there. I viewed videotapes of Schwarzenegger's lectures. Schwarzenegger described his education in detail in a speech at Santa Monica City College, June 14, 2005.

Material on his citizenship was from his speeches, including remarks on September 16, 2003, in Los Angeles as well as a 1983 news report. Schwarzenegger's quote "when you promote a movie . . ." was from a March 22, 2006, interview. "People listen much more . . ." was from his autobiography, *Arnold: The Education of a Bodybuilder* (New York: Simon & Schuster, 1977, p. 109). "I didn't get the credit alone . . ." was from the book *Pumping Iron* (New York: Simon & Schuster, 1974, p. 23). "I find out which poses . . ." was from *Pumping Iron*, p. 195. "Let's create a villain . . ." was from a Schwarzenegger interview for the DVD of the twenty-fifth anniversary of *Pumping Iron*. Schwarzenegger's comments about Knaur were from the March 2006 interview. His work selling wood was mentioned in an interview with *After Dark* in 1977 and in the book *Arnold Hautnah*. "I am familiar with . . ." was from an interview published in the *Kronen Zeitung*.

CHAPTER 4

This chapter drew from interviews with Lorimer, John Cates, Kopacka, Danny Hernandez, Jim Pinkerton, Greg Payne, Judy Young, Pete Wilson, Parker, Bonnie Reiss, Gary Moody, Craig MacNab, and two longtime associates of Schwarzenegger. The quote from the 1988 rally in Columbus was from reports in the Associated Press and *Houston Chronicle.*

All available records on Schwarzenegger and the President's Council on Physical Fitness and Sports were obtained from the George Bush Presidential Library in College Station, Texas. The memoranda, history of the council, and letters quoted in the chapter were from the library collections. I also viewed Schwarzenegger's speeches in which he mentioned his council work, on September 21, 2001, and September 7, 2003. In describing the summits with physical education advocates, I relied on a profile of Schwarzenegger in the *Washington Post* magazine in June 1991 and an interview with Cates.

Some fitness council records were held secret under the Presidential Records Act. I appealed the denial of access to several records, and every appeal of mine was denied.

Some of the rallies, meetings, and appearances with governors were videotaped, including the one in Utah. I viewed several tapes and local press reports. Former Arizona Governor Fife Symington and former Wisconsin Governor Tommy Thompson were interviewed by phone. The detail on cigars was from an interview with Werner Kopacka, who said that during this period his photographer had to put his camera away when Schwarzenegger took out a cigar.

The speeches at the teachers' alliance and at Jack LaLanne's birthday party were videotaped. I also reviewed tapes of Inner City Games events, including fund-raisers, the games themselves, and meetings. I examined Inner City Games IRS Form 990 tax filings and attended ICG and After-School All-Stars events. (A note regarding Planet Hollywood: the restaurant chain later declared bankruptcy, with some investors claiming too many resources had been spent courting celebrity partners such as Schwarzenegger.) Published reports on the Inner City Games in the *Los Angeles Times* and in *Youth Today* also informed the chapter.

CHAPTER 5

This chapter was based on polls, contemporaneous notes taken by participants, schedules, memoranda, email, and other records, as well as interviews with Schwarzenegger in September 2003, July 2004, November 2005, and March 2006. Among the people interviewed for this chapter were Garry South, Moody, Lorimer, Joe Rodota, Keith Richman, Reiss, Shawn Steel, and six political consultants.

The description of Schwarzenegger's political meetings were based on the star's schedules and news reports, including an August 14, 2003, report in the *Los Angeles Times*. The description of the March 17, 2001, meeting was based on interviews, a printed agenda, and notes taken by participants. "Authenticity" quotes were based on videotape of the interview.

The material on Schwarzenegger's health and the death of his mother was from published reports. Several quotes—"It was not clear to me . . . ," "It was politically motivated." "It was like wherever you turned . . . ," "I was really testing . . . ," "I knew my life hasn't yet in the movie . . . ," and "I thought they were going to say . . ."—were from a March 2006 interview.

Details of the *Terminator 3* contract were first reported by Epstein in *The Big Picture*. Hayes and Bing in *Open Wide* (New York: Miramax Books, 2004) reported on the survey showing the need for Schwarzenegger to star in the movie. Schwarzenegger described his decision-making about the movie and a 2002 campaign for governor, as well as his conversations with *Terminator 3*'s producers, in a March 2006 interview with me and in an August 2004 interview with the *Los Angeles Times* and *Sacramento Bee*. He also talked about the decision in an April 2001 interview with Werner Kopacka. The quote, "world needs new political heroes . . ." was from that interview. Kopacka also recounted Schwarzenegger's decision in the book *Arnold Hautnah*.

CHAPTER 6

This chapter was based on interviews with Schwarzenegger, Bill White, An-Me Chung, Steve Fowler, Chip Nielsen, Maryann O'Sullivan, Brian Lee, Bill Kolender, Mike Carona, Gorton, Richard Riordan, Danny Hernandez, John Hein, Jim Brulte, John Mockler, Joel Fox, five political consultants, a GOP pollster, and two former Wilson administration officials.

Descriptions of focus groups, speeches, and other scenes were based on videotapes, written reports, e-mails, and schedules. The description of the September 21, 2001, speech was based on a videotape. The Enron meeting was described in publicly released emails from Enron records. Campaign finance numbers were from the California Secretary of State. CTA's total initiative spending was compiled and reported by the *Los Angeles Times*, September 28, 2005.

CHAPTER 7

The description of the campaign kick-off was based on a videotape and news reports. The chapter included material from interviews with Schwarzenegger, Paul Folino, Larry Higby, Tom Tucker, Mark Chapin Johnson, Chris St. Hilaire, John Campbell, Russ Bogh, Shultz, Carona, Kolender, Lee Baca, O'Sullivan, Mike Jimenez, Bill Simon Jr., Steve Frates, Rick TerBorch, Hernandez, Jim Brulte, Reiss, and five political consultants.

The Spago meeting was described through notes, e-mails, interviews, and the list of talking points with questions and answers. Dates were based on Schwarzenegger's schedules, his own web site Schwarzenegger.com, and news reports. Other information came from campaign memos, polls, a Rose Institute study of after-school costs, and Walsh's earned media plan. Many campaign papers were in a booklet distributed to supporters in September 2002.

Schwarzenegger's *Terminator 3* contract was first disclosed by Epstein in his book, *The Big Picture*. The quote "All my life I tried to make money . . ." was from a September 2003 interview. "Building a political organization for the future" quote was from a March 2002 campaign memo. "I came home that night . . ." was from a March 2006 interview. The discrepancy between Schwarzenegger's views on Vancouver (expressed in a promotion for *The Sixth Day* in 2000) and his stand on runaway movie production (from a September 2003 speech in Orange County) was pointed out by my *Times* colleague Robert Salladay in *Emmy* magazine in December 2004. The outlines of the endorsement battle with law enforcement were partially described in a June 7, 2002, letter from Chief McDonell to Maryann O'Sullivan.

CHAPTER 8

This chapter drew from more than one hundred interviews. Among those interviewed were Ted Costa, Mark Abernathy, Kevin McCarthy, Bill Thomas, Sid Novaresi, Bill Simon Jr., Riordan, South, Darrell Issa, Dale Neugebauer, Lynn Schenk, Steve Maviglio, Melanie Morgan, Roger Hedgecock, Pat Caddell, Grover Norquist, Sal Russo, John Hein, David Binder, Howard Kaloogian, Buck Johns, Scott Taylor, Phil Paule, Duf Sundheim, Rob Stutzman, Ken Khachigian, Ray Haynes, Mike and Bill Arno, David Townsend, Rick Arnold, Fred Kimball, Tom Bader, Angelo Paparella, George Gorton, Rod Paige, Bill White, Chung, David Dreier, Art Laffer, Steve Moore, Kevin McCarthy, Russ Bogh, Steve Weir, and Dave Gilliard.

The chapter also drew on e-mails and memoranda from the recall effort, People's Advocate, the California Republican Party, and Schwarzenegger's gubernatorial campaign. Issa's and Schwarzenegger's schedules were reviewed. Dan Weintraub also shared some of his reporting on the recall's origins.

The state library provided copies of its records of the recall, including daily signature logs. In a March 2006 interview, Schwarzenegger recalled the Thomas meeting and his view that his ties to the recall should not be too obvious. Extensive records of the after-school funding fight, including reports and schedules, were from the C. S. Mott Foundation.

The figures on signatures were from a variety of sources, including Tom Bader's logs, People's Advocate records, and county clerk records. The description of Schwarzenegger's meeting with Rove was from interviews with three people familiar with the meeting and from reports in *USA Today* (August 11, 2004), the *Washington Post* (August 14, 2003), and the *New Yorker* (June 28, 2004). I also relied upon the reporting of John Fund of the *Wall Street Journal*, particularly his piece on July 25, 2003, and of Bill Bradley of the *LA Weekly*. Davis said he would fight "like a Bengal tiger" at a July 23 press conference in San Francisco.

I reviewed a DVD of Schwarzenegger's speech at the Prop 13 anniversary. The consideration of a "Terminator for Governor" campaign was reported in the book *Open Wide*, page 235. The *Terminator 3* box office estimate was from Box Office Mojo, a web site that tracked the movie business. Similar figures appeared in published reports.

Quotes from Sean Walsh and from George Gorton (with regards to Schwarzenegger's comment that the *Los Angeles Times* did not believe the recall would qualify) were taken from a post-election forum at UC Berkeley on October 18, 2003. Don Sipple's comments in that forum also informed the chapter. Steve Smith, a leader of gray Davis's political team, said at the same event: "If you read the tea leaves the way they should have been read, we probably should have lost in November of '02. The only reason we didn't is because we had a hapless opponent and a horrendous campaign against us." Reaction quotes from moviegoers were from the *Los Angeles Times*. Schwarzenegger's trip to Baghdad was described in news reports. His quote that Iraq was "pretty much like California" was from the Associated Press.

CHAPTER 9

I began covering the Schwarzenegger campaign for the *Los Angeles Times* as soon as he announced his candidacy, and I observed each of his public events first-hand, including his New York trip, his economic recovery press conference on August 20, and his visits to Norwalk to pull and file papers. Much of this chapter was based on reporting conducted in the course of that coverage, including conversations with Gorton, Sipple, Walsh, Stutzman, Joe Weider, Bill Lucia, Karen Hanretty, Tamminen, and Arnold Steinberg. After the recall, I conducted interviews with, among others, Riordan, Costa, Issa, Ken Khachigian, Scott Taylor, Tom McClintock, John Stoos, Peter Urdl, Milton Friedman, Pete Wilson, Frank Luntz, Folino, Lorimer, Keith Richman, Dreier, Kopacka, Jim Brulte, Mike Murphy, Fox, Reiss, Pat Clarey, Marty Wilson, Garrett Ashley, Jan van Lohuizen, John Cogan, Shultz, Laffer, John Campbell, Rodota, David Crane, George Borjas, Wayne Johnson, Bill Simon, Jr., six Republican consultants, two Democratic consultants, three former Davis administration officials, and three pollsters. Warren Buffett responded via e-mail to written questions.

Schwarzenegger described the process by which he chose to run in several speeches, press conferences, and public interviews. In a March 2006 interview, he added considerably to that description. His comments about his discussions with Riordan, his talk with his wife, his thinking throughout those final hours of decision-making, and his quotes—"Everyone wanted to call whoever . . . ," "I tried to play . . . ," "Finally, I said to myself . . . ," "I said, 'Dick, you've got . . . ," "She knew I was going to say . . . ," "Whenever people said it can't be done . . . ," and "Inside, I was thinking . . ."—were from that interview. Shriver explained the decision-making process publicly several times, including in an interview with *Vanity Fair* (January 2005). Shriver recounted her mother's comment, "Don't complain . . . ," during an April 8, 2005, appearance on *Oprah*.

The description of the scene offstage at *The Tonight Show* was from interviews with five people who were there. The Sargent Shriver letter was quoted in Scott Stossel's biography, *Sarge*, p. 669. Robert F. Kennedy Jr. wrote about the weekend in Cape Cod and his conversation with Schwarzenegger about the environment in *Crimes Against Nature* (New York: HarperCollins, 2004, pp. 42–43). The account of the New York fund-raising lunch was based on interviews with three participants.

Schwarzenegger's home price and size were reported by Ruth Ryon in the *Los Angeles Times* and disclosed in public records.

The account of the deal with American Media and Weider was based on reports in the *New York Daily News*, *Los Angeles* magazine, and the *Los Angeles Times*. The meeting between Pecker and Schwarzenegger was first reported by Ann Louise Bardach in *Los Angeles* magazine in 2004. The $20,000 contract between Goyette and American Media was first disclosed by author Laurence Leamer in the *Los Angeles Times* on July 10, 2005. In an interview for Leamer's book *Fantastic*, Goyette was quoted as saying she and Schwarzenegger had an occasional relationship that did not include intercourse. On August 12, 2005, my colleagues Peter Nicholas and Carla Hall disclosed further details of the contract and the existence of a contract between American Media and one of Goyette's friends.

Polling reports were based on the actual surveys presented to the campaign by John McLaughlin and Jan van Lohuizen. McLaughlin summarized his results in an online column. Newspaper polls were performed by the Field Poll and the *Los Angeles Times*. I also reviewed polling done for the California Teachers Association.

Schwarzenegger's comment about being careful what he put in his mouth was from news reports. Feinstein described her decision-making in a conference call with journalists.

Art Laffer described his conversation with Schwarzenegger in an interview and in a newsletter produced by his company. (The quote was from the interview.) Maslin's memo was quoted in the UPI, August 6, 2003. Gorton's quote about the Buffett episode, "It was a disaster," was from an interview in October 2003. Accounts of Schwarzenegger University, the economic recovery summit, and other internal campaign deliberations were based on interviews, campaign schedules, e-mails, memoranda, and a policy binder.

CHAPTER 10

I observed most of the events in this chapter myself, including the Huntington Beach chaos, the Fresno rally, the Long Beach State speech, various "Ask Arnold" town halls, and scenes outside his fund-raisers. I also drew on the work of my *Times* colleagues and my competitors, including Margaret Talev and Dan Weintraub of the *Sacramento Bee*, Erica Werner of the Associated Press, Dion Nissenbaum of the *San Jose Mercury News*, and Robert Salladay, then of the *San Francisco Chronicle*.

Other details in this chapter were based on interviews and conversations with more than one hundred people, among them Clarey, Stutzman, Ashley, Parvin, Hanretty, Reiss, Todd Harris, Rodota, Hedgecock, Fred Beteta, Jeff Randle, Cassandra Pye, Allan Zaremberg, van Lohuizen, Brulte, Shawn Steel, Sundheim, McClintock, John Stoos, Sipple, John Campbell, a former Schwarzenegger aide, and five Republican consultants. I reviewed campaign polling, polling from other candidates and interest groups, e-mail, memoranda, and schedules.

My description of von Huene's career was based on his resume, and the account of his duties came from my own observation of his role. The

Mickey Kaus episode was from his blog and from a *Los Angeles Times* account of how *Oui* magazine made news. The description of the McLaughlin polling was based on the polling itself and an online column written by McLaughlin.

CHAPTER 11

This chapter was based on my coverage of the campaign for the *Los Angeles Times*. I attended nearly all the public events, including the railroad museum speech, town halls, rallies, the TV debate, and the Dana Carvey press conference. I have since reviewed videotapes and DVDs of events I missed.

I conducted interviews with more than one hundred people whose observations informed this chapter. Among them were McClintock, Beteta, Steel, Ray Haynes, Coupal, Fox, Stoos, South, Laffer, Steve Moore, Morgan, Dreier, Tom Tucker, Folino, Johns, Ron Nehring, Sundheim, Tom McEnery, Reiss, Costa, Rodota, Burton, Colleen McAndrews, Stutzman, Harris, van Lohuizen, Walsh, Lynn Valbuena, Jacob Coin, Doug Elmets, Sharon Runner, Caddell, Anthony Pico, Bonnie Garcia, Issa, Paula Lorenzo, Robert Smith, Deron Marquez, Richard Milanovich, Gene Raper, Don Novey, Curt Pringle, Campbell, Ashley, Clarey, Parvin, two pollsters, six Republican consultants, a longtime advisor to the candidate, and two state legislators. I also drew on the campaign coverage by the *Los Angeles Times*, *Sacramento Bee*, *San Francisco Chronicle*, *San Jose Mercury News*, *San Diego Union-Tribune*, *Bakersfield Californian*, *Fresno Bee*, and *New York Times*.

The fact that Schwarzenegger's team was behind some attacks on Bustamante was confirmed by interviews. I based my description of the debate over Indian gambling on campaign email, schedules, and other records kept by participants, and interviews with parties to the discussions. The CNIGA memo declaring war against Schwarzenegger was first reported by the *Wall Street Journal*. The figures on Indian gambling were based on estimates by gambling industry analysts and have been widely used in press reports. The figures on Indian campaign donations, vote totals, and Schwarzenegger expenditures were from the California Secretary of State. Schwarzenegger's suspicions about the power of Indian gambling interests were from conversations with him.

The description of the debate preparation was based on notes of two participants and multiple interviews, including an April 2006 interview with Schwarzenegger. The quote, "Mike Murphy thought, 'No, Arnold is Arnold . . . ,'" was from that interview. His state of mind during the debate was from an interview with him and from his remarks to reporters on September 25, 2003. The account of the Republican county chairmen's meeting was based on interviews with four of the county chairs as well as notes of the meeting kept by a participant.

The descriptions of the investigations facing the Schwarzenegger campaign were based on campaign documents and interviews. The campaign made Joe Weider available to me on October 2, 2003, to respond to the Butler book proposal. The quote was drawn from that interview. Butler's retraction was from a statement he issued.

George Gorton disclosed that more than 90 percent of those surveyed had heard about the allegations in the *Times* story during a forum at UC Berkeley, October 18, 2003. The transcript of the forum was published in *California Votes: The 2002 Governor's Race & the Recall that Made History* (Berkeley: Berkeley Public Policy Press, 2003). Gorton's statement appeared on p. 247.

CHAPTER 12

Much of this chapter was derived from my coverage for the *Times*. I attended many of the events mentioned here, including the swearing-in, the chamber of commerce party on inauguration day, his first press conference as governor, and his rallies at Galpin Ford and at the malls.

Dozens of interviews informed this chapter. Among them were conversations with Dreier, Parvin, Costa, Arduin, Cogan, Moore, Reiss, Riordan, Rob Stutzman, McEnery, Pete Wilson, Richard Costigan, Keith Richman, Joe Canciamilla, Gilbert Cedillo, Fabian Núñez, Dan Savage, John Mockler, Burton, Brulte, Hernandez, Shultz, Panetta, Sharon Runner, Garcia, Campbell, Hein, Barbara Kerr, Kevin Gordon, Scott Plotkin, Kevin McCarthy, three Democratic lawyers, a top administration official, a department head in the Schwarzenegger administration, two Republican legislators, an education lobbyist, and four Republican consultants. Several interviewees provided some information on the condition that it not be attributed directly to them.

Some details on the genesis of the inaugural speech were provided during background briefings by officials of Schwarzenegger's administration. For the section about Schwarzenegger's use of malls as his setting of choice for speeches, I drew on reporting conducted for my pieces in the *Los Angeles Times* on December 8, 2003, and on March 5, 2004. The transition description was based on documents and e-mails, as well as interviews. The story of how

Dreier was recruited to lead the transition was first reported by David Drucker in the *Daily Bulletin*. The American Media contract was disclosed in a 2005 filing with the SEC. The quote, "Everything is psychological . . ." was from a 2004 conversation with Schwarzenegger.

The existence of DVD sales projections depending on the outcome of the governor's race was first reported in *Open Wide*. Schwarzenegger discussed his feelings about Cedillo and the driver's license legislation with reporters on September 2, 2004. The description of the meeting with Cedillo at Oak was based on the accounts of four participants. The governor's quote, "They want me to have a little problem in Sacramento because they know I go out to the shopping malls and help their business," was from an August 2004 interview with the *Los Angeles Times*.

Schwarzenegger's brief consideration of Tim Shriver was first disclosed by Laurence Leamer in his book, *Fantastic* (New York: St. Martin's Press, 2005, p. 326). The description of the chief of staff search was from interviews with six participants in the deliberations. "I chose who I chose . . ." was from an April 2006 interview with Schwarzenegger.

The story of the negotiations to put Propositions 57 and 58 on the ballot came from interviews conducted after the fact as well as my reporting for the *Times* during the negotiations. I drew in particular from a story I wrote with Peter Nicholas for the *Times*, December 13, 2003. Shriver's remarks on December 9 were from a transcript provided by the governor's office. Warren Buffett, by e-mail, confirmed that he urged a longer time period for the bond.

The section on the education funding deal was based on notes of two participants, schedules of Schwarzenegger, and interviews with officials of CTA, other education lobby groups, and the Schwarzenegger administration. I also relied on Schwarzenegger's public statements on the subject, as well as a conversation with reporters on January 8, 2004, and an April 15, 2006, interview. The quote, "I missed that because this was more a conversation . . . ," was from that April interview.

CHAPTER 13

Much of this chapter was drawn from my coverage of the 57 and 58 campaign for the *Los Angeles Times*. I attended every public event, including the Fresno town hall, the Feinstein press conference, the state Republican convention, the Shriver-Burton press conference, the bus tour, his "grip-and-grin" at the Pantry restaurant, and election night. I also covered his trip to Washington and New York in late February 2004, and was present for events with governors and his visit to the White House.

The account of the campaign's strategy was based on Schwarzenegger's public statements, three conversations with him in February 2004, campaign memoranda, e-mails, talking points, and polling performed by van Lohuizen, John McLaughlin, and the CTA. I also reviewed polls by the Public Policy Institute of California and the Field Poll. This chapter drew from interviews with, among others, Lucas, Stutzman, Harris, Murphy, Randle, Eric Person, Steve Westly, Kevin McCarthy, Brulte, Burton, Darry Sragow, Warren Hellman, David Crane, Shultz, Lorimer, Pulaski, Alan Autry, one Democratic consultant, and three Republican consultants.

The depiction of the December 30, 2003, meeting was based on interviews, a printed agenda, notes taken by participants, and a copy of McLaughlin's slide show.

Questions about Schwarzenegger's non-profits emerged in news reports in 2005. I reviewed the work of Robert Salladay and Peter Nicholas in the *Los Angeles Times*, particularly a story published on August 24, 2005. Schwarzenegger's quote about Burton, "When I met him . . . ," was from a story by Nicholas in the *Los Angeles Times*, May 21, 2004. The anecdote about Burton signing the $100 bill first appeared in a *Los Angeles Times* story by myself, Nicholas, and Virginia Ellis, on April 14, 2004. I also consulted a profile of Burton by Jordan Rau in the *Los Angeles Times*, November 27, 2004.

Van Lohuizen's quote in which he suggested slapping around the legislature was from talking points for the 57 and 58 campaign from January 2004. The detail about von Huene telling Schwarzenegger about his use of Armageddon was from interviews.

Records of the California Recovery Team, including its initial board and budget, were available from the California Secretary of State. CRT's priorities and the consultants it employed were disclosed on Schwarzenegger's political web site, joinarnold.com.

CHAPTER 14

This chapter was based on day-to-day coverage of Schwarzenegger during this period. I attended all of Schwarzenegger's public events but two—a press event in Sacramento and a rally in Torrance. I listened to audiotapes of his remarks in both places.

This chapter contained material from interviews with Schwarzenegger, Bob Grimm, Jeff Green, Sean McNally, Frank Luntz, Stan Harper, Fox, Chris George, Tom Hagerman, Costa, Núñez, Brulte, Ackerman, McCarthy, Chuck Poochigian, Costigan, Clarey, Burton, Gale Kaufman, Stanley Zax, Zaremberg, Tom Rankin, Beth Miller Malek, Frank Neuhauser, Richard

Alarcon, Barry Broad, Angie Wei, Haynes, Mike and Bill Arno, Frank Schubert, Marty Wilson, Gorton, Rick Claussen, Randle, David Schwartz, Suzanne Guyan, Christina Hernandez, Joe Alarcon, Beteta, and Stutzman. Warren Buffett confirmed by e-mail the detail about his signing a candy box. Schwarzenegger's staff made available three administration officials who provided details of the negotiations. Another administration official, two political consultants, two legislative staffers, a lobbyist and two lawyers familiar with the workers' comp negotiations also provided their recollections and records.

Schwarzenegger made extensive public remarks about workers' comp both during and after the negotiations. I interviewed him on March 1, 2004, and spoke with him about workers' comp on March 12 and April 19, 2004.

Stan Harper allowed me to spend a day in his office in Bakersfield during the processing of the workers' comp petitions. The management of the Costco store in the city of Hawthorne, near LAX, permitted me to spend two days following around employees who were gathering signatures. (The Teamsters filed a complaint alleging that Costco was coercing employees to collect signatures. The attorney general's office investigated but found no evidence of any violation.) Throughout this book, I regularly spent Saturdays with signature gatherers who worked outside shopping centers in the South Bay and San Fernando Valley sections of Los Angeles. Jonathan Renner of the government law section of the attorney general's office explained how initiative titles and summaries are written.

The governor's senior advisor overseeing events, Fred Beteta, permitted me to follow the advance team in the week leading up to the signing of the workers' compensation bill on April 19, 2004. I was given full access to meetings and materials for the workers' comp event and another public event. Those materials informed this chapter.

I also relied upon schedules of Schwarzenegger and others involved in the initiative effort, e-mails, and counts of signatures. Campaign finance records were from the web site of the California Secretary of State.

The details of the governor's preliminary deals with Burton and the Democrats were from e-mails and documents. One staffer with knowledge of the talks provided extensive notes of the negotiations' progress. Schwarzenegger told the story about Burton and his brother during an April 2006 interview. I relied heavily on the coverage of my colleague Marc Lifsher. The work of John Gittelsohn and Jim Hinch in the *Orange County Register*, particularly their articles on April 16 and April 18, 2004, thoroughly laid out key moments in the negotiations. Burton's quote about a "shit sandwich" was from the *Regis-*

ter's April 18 piece. Hinch and Gittelsohn, in the April 16 piece, first disclosed the meeting between Rankin and Clarey.

The Art Azevedo comment was from a story in the *San Francisco Chronicle*, April 15, 2004. The Luntz comment on ties was from interviews with Luntz, Green, McNally, and Grimm. The description of the meeting at Nielsen Merksamer between different initiative proponents was reconstructed from interviews with a dozen people. Schwarzenegger made his comments that "we had to make decisions very quickly" and that he liked "the carrot and stick" method on April 16, 2004, and to me in a 2006 interview. Burton's quotes that he was "fucked" in workers' comp and that "I should have asked for that deal" were from an interview in April 2005.

The figures on workers' comp costs and on the reductions in average payments to permanently disabled workers came from a January 2006 report of the California Department of Industrial Relations, Division of Workers' Compensation, "A Study of the Effects of Legislative Reforms on California Workers' Compensation Insurance Rates." I reviewed several other reports on workers' comp, including a UC Davis study from 2004 and a Public Policy Institute of California report from 2005.

The description of growing conditions and Grimmway's history was from a company history and interviews.

CHAPTER 15

This chapter was based on my *Times* coverage and interviews conducted with, among others, Ron Loveridge, Cassandra Pye, Lucas, Reiss, Carona, Chris McKenzie, Steve Szalay, John Campbell, Darrell Steinberg, Pringle, Autry, Burton, Núñez, McCarthy, Ackerman, Shultz, Gerstl, Josef Krainer, Valtraud Klausnic, Herwig Hosele, Arduin, H.D. Palmer, Mike Genest, Robert Dynes, Reed, Jimenez, Kerr, a top administration official, two education lobbyists, four Republican consultants, and four other mayors. Two consultants familiar with Proposition 1A also provided assistance. I discussed the local government negotiations with Schwarzenegger in interviews on July 10, 2004, November 2, 2005, and April 15, 2006. I also relied on his extensive public statements on the budget and local government, particularly speeches given on June 17, July 3, July 17, July 18, July 29, and July 30. The governor's schedules, e-mails of local government officials, drafts of the possible alternative ballot measures, and polling on Prop 1A also informed the chapter.

The description of the "girlie men" scene was from a recording of the event, and the account of my colleague Peter Nicholas in the *Los Angeles Times*.

I attended the other public events referenced in the chapter, including the June 17 speech in Chino, the library dedication in Pomona, the July 3 speech at the Valley fire station, the July 5 campaign stop in Dixon, the Austria trip, the July 29 meeting of the League of California Cities in Monterey, and the Prop 1A campaign events. On the Austria trip, the Krainer and Schwarzenegger comments were made in English. I relied on Austrian journalists to translate interviews given in German.

The account of the phone call to the league of cities board was from the recollections of five participants, including Schwarzenegger, and the notes of one participant. Schwarzenegger's line about the need to be organic and flexible was from a phone conversation in January 2004. The Burton comment, "What the fuck is he doing?" was made in my presence.

Schwarzenegger's routine was from observation, conversations with aides, schedules, Secretary of State records, his own public statements, and a Schwarzenegger interview with the *Los Angeles Times* on March 30, 2004. Much of the material appeared first in an April 14, 2004, piece I wrote with Peter Nicholas and Virginia Ellis for the *Times*. Some of the material on Clay Russell's role was from Gary Delsohn's profile in the *Sacramento Bee*, June 2004. Charlie LeDuff described Schwarzenegger's Sunday motorcycle rides in *The New York Times*, February 13, 2004. Schwarzenegger's financial and tax information was from a briefing for reporters in April 2006.

Negotiations on the alternative ballot measure were described in detail in a May 10, 2004, memo distributed among local government groups. The polling done for Schwarzenegger was from a May 6, 2004, survey by John McLaughlin. The Jackie Speier quote, "the governor is trying to make the legislature meaningless," appeared in the *Los Angeles Times*, May 12, 2004. Ann Marimow first wrote about press aides and their use of Blackberrys in the *San Jose Mercury News*, July 22, 2004.

The Núñez comment, "We are not on a movie set here," was from an interview with the *Los Angeles Times*, July 5, 2004. The background information on Núñez was drawn from interviews and press reports, particularly a profile in the *Los Angeles Times* on August 1, 2004. Reaction from Romero and Núñez was from the *Sacramento Bee*. The *Wall Street Journal* op-ed was written by author Joseph Epstein and published on July 21, 2004.

Schwarzenegger discussed Teddy Kennedy and jokes on the Doug McIntyre radio show, October 27, 2004. "We cannot just hang" was a comment to reporters, June 24, 2004. Dion Nissenbaum reported the complaint that Republicans were being treated like a "potted plant" in the *San Jose Mercury News*, July 3, 2004. "I never walked away from the negotiating table" was from a

Schwarzenegger interview with NPR, broadcast August 4, 2004. "There was a line drawn" was from a November 2005 interview.

CHAPTER 16

This chapter drew on reporting I did for the *Los Angeles Times* in 2004, as well as subsequent interviews. I attended the June 21 compact signing and all No on 68 and 70 events at which Schwarzenegger spoke. Details on the convention speech were from my own reporting at Madison Square Garden, as well as interviews and drafts of the speech.

I visited the Pala, Viejas, and San Manuel reservations. Among the people interviewed for the chapter were Anthony Pico, Deron Marquez, Jacob Coin, Dreier, Paula Lorenzo, Robert Smith, Richard Milanovich, Gene Raper, Bill Lockyer, Jack Gribbon, South, Don Novey, Burton, Núñez, Ackerman, Kevin McCarthy, Haynes, Stutzman, Harris, Vince Sollitto, Garcia, Parvin, Clarey, Lorimer, Gale Kaufman, Maviglio, Pete Wilson, Schenk, David Townsend, Baca, Kolender, Howard Dickstein, and Doug Elmets. Information for this chapter also was provided by a lawyer familiar with the compact negotiations, a lawyer who was active in the campaigns against 68 and 70, a lawyer who had done work for the governor, a senior Schwarzenegger administration official familiar with the passage of the first five compacts by the legislature, a Democratic political consultant involved in the campaign, six Republican consultants, and three advisors to the governor.

Schwarzenegger himself made extensive comments on Propositions 68 and 70 to reporters on September 2, October 14, 18, and 19, and November 3, 2004. "I let it hang out . . ." quote was from an April 2006 interview. I also questioned him on this subject in November 2004. His desire for more offense on reform was recounted to me by his aides and was supported by the notes of one participant in an August 5, 2004, meeting with the team. I also reviewed a memorandum that described that meeting and a similar session on August 6.

In addition, Schwarzenegger explained his state of mind about the Republican National Convention and tribal gambling (and offered the joke about his wife denying him sex for two weeks) during an October 18, 2004, forum with Leon Panetta in Monterey. Schwarzenegger made his comment—"It's Democratic leaders, okay? They said to me, 'Have you ever heard of the word *jamming*?'"—at the Panetta forum.

For information on Indian gambling in California, I used the background material available from Institute of Governmental Studies Library at UC Berkeley. My colleague Dan Morain of the *Los Angeles Times* shared his work and

wisdom. On the history of California tribes and of tribal gambling throughout the country, I consulted A. L. Kroeber's *Handbook of the Indians of California*,
published in 1925 (New York: Dover); *Tribes of California*, by the nineteenth-century adventurer Stephen Powers (Berkeley: University of California Press,
1976); Brett D. Fromson's *Hitting the Jackpot* (New York: Atlantic Monthly Press,
2003); *Indian Gaming & the Law*, edited by William R. Eadington (Reno, Nev.:
Institute for the Study of Gambling and Commercial Gambling, 1990); *New
Capitalists*, by Eve Darian-Smith (Belmont, Calif.: Wadsworth/Thomson,
2004); and *The Nations Within*, by Vine Deloria Jr. and Clifford M. Lytle (Austin:
University of Texas Press, 1984). The estimates on Indian gambling revenue in
California have varied. The Institute of Governmental Studies put the figure at
$5.1 billion in 2004, though gambling industry analysts and California newspa-
pers, including mine, used the $6 billion figure. The Marybel Batjer detail was
from interviews I conducted with her and Steve Wynn for the *Los Angeles Times*.
The numbers on tribal donations were from the California Secretary of State.

Among the polls I cited in this chapter were a Field Poll, June 9, 2004;
John McLaughlin polls of December 29, 2003, and May 6, 2004; and surveys by Moore Information from May, June, and September 2004. Among
other documents that were useful were the No on 68 and 70 campaign
plan, an October 3, 2003, open letter from Paula Lorenzo of the Rumsey
Band, and a letter from state Treasurer Phil Angelides to Schwarzenegger,
December 22, 2004.

The reporting of David Drucker in the *Los Angeles Daily News*—particularly his stories from February 4, April 1, and June 1—was helpful. James P.
Sweeney of the Copley News Service was the first to break crucial details of
the negotiations, in a March 31, 2004, piece. Bill Bradley revealed important
news on the talks in his column in *LA Weekly*, "Rolling Campaign Dice," June
10, 2004. My colleagues Peter Nicholas and Dan Morain first reported the
governor's comments to Republican legislators at a fund-raiser near Palm
Springs. Schwarzenegger spoke out against Measure U, the local referendum
on Agua Caliente's development plan, in comments published October 27 in
the *Press-Enterprise*. Schwarzenegger's comment about John Kerry was from a
radio interview with Tony Snow on August 12. Schwarzenegger's comments
from the late March meeting with tribes were based on interviews with tribal
leaders and one gubernatorial aide.

CHAPTER 17

This chapter was based on coverage of Schwarzenegger's campaign for the
Los Angeles Times, including a story I wrote on November 7, 2004. I witnessed

the Ontario press conference for No on 66, the campaign event attended by former governors, Schwarzenegger's speech in Columbus on behalf of Bush, the October 30 bus tour for the ballot measures, the November 1 fly-around, and election night.

The chapter relied on information from interviews with, among others, Schwarzenegger, Ed Jagels, Greg Totten, Jimenez, Randle, Stutzman, Richard Temple, Ray McNally, Lucas, Henry Nicholas, Sipple, Ryan Shuck, Sandy Harrison, David Paulson, Pete Wilson, Don Novey, Sundheim, Burton, Frank Schubert, Lorimer, Bill Thomas, Lissa Morgenthaler-Jones, Shultz, three Republican consultants, and several consultants involved with Propositions 62, 64, 71, and 72. I also used Schwarzenegger's remarks to reporters about Prop 66 on October 20, November 1, and November 3. His quote, "The wisdom says . . . ," was from an April 2006 interview. And I reviewed records of a court dispute over the number of convicted felons who would have been eligible for early release if Prop 66 had passed.

A *Sacramento Bee* story, by Dan Smith, on October 17, 2004, was the first to report that the prison guards' union "may be throwing in the towel" and "conceding victory" for Prop 66. Some of the details on the effort to amend the U.S. Constitution to allow foreign-born citizens to serve as president first appeared in a story of mine in the *Los Angeles Times*, February 2, 2005.

CHAPTER 18

This chapter was informed by several interviews, including those conducted with Reiss, John Campbell, Shultz, Pete Wilson, Pringle, Costa, Abernathy, Bill Thomas, Dreier, Fox, Parvin, Stutzman, Roman Buhler, Chellie Pingree, Zaremberg, Bill Hauck, Larry McCarthy, Rex Hime, Jeff Miller, Garcia, Tony Strickland, Keith Richman, Dan Pellissier, Lew Uhler, George Passantino, Rose Ann DeMoro, Terri Carbaugh, Chuck Idelson, Hein, Mockler, Kerr, Riordan, Tom Campbell, Dave Gilliard, Gale Kaufman, Kevin Gordon, two Democratic legislative staffers, a real estate executive, two Republican pollsters, three Democratic pollsters, six Republican political consultants, two former Schwarzenegger administration officials, four administration officials, three education lobbyists, a Schwarzenegger campaign official, and two CTA officials.

The description of the November 18 meeting came from interviews with eleven participants, as well as memoranda, schedules, notes, and a copy of McLaughlin's slides and poll, completed November 14. The accounts of the August 5 and 6 meetings were based on interviews and notes, as well as an August 7 memo summarizing the meeting. The account of the cabinet retreat was based on interviews and a conversation the week after the meeting with

Schwarzenegger. "I mean we know if I cannot change it . . ." was from a Schwarzenegger interview with the *Orange County Register*, January 24, 2005.

Schwarzenegger's state of mind, optimism, and frustrations were described on the basis of his public statements as well as interviews on November 2, 2005; November 5, 2005, March 22, 2006, and April 15, 2006. In the November 2 interview, he said: "It's a fight that I have decided to take on. I just deep inside was motivated by what I promised I would do when I get to Sacramento. I had the choice to go in and enjoy the high approval rating and not to rattle the cage, to just move along smoothly with the changes. Then we would never have had any changes. We would have had the same system the way it was. Or to go and get in there and potentially make it a war because people are very intense about holding onto the status quo." He explained his thoughts on pensions to reporters on April 7, 2005.

I reviewed the two-volume CPR report, "A Government for the People for a Change," as well as assessments by the Little Hoover Commission and coverage in the *Los Angeles Times*.

The description of the dispute over nurse ratios was from interviews with Rose Ann DeMoro and other union officials, as well as court records of the lawsuits over the ratios. The American Nurses Association and hospital industry aired criticism of the California Nurses Association in several forums. I consulted an article in *American Nurse*, January/February 2005, and a profile of DeMoro in the *Los Angeles Times*, April 17, 2005.

The descriptions of the CTA deal were based on documents released January 8, 2004, when the deal was announced, as well as other notes and documents from five participants in the negotiations. The deal was also codified in the legislation suspending Prop 98, SB 1101. The extent of CTA's partnership was described to me by senior administration officials and four CTA officials, and confirmed by e-mails. The CTA provided a copy of the videotaped message that Schwarzenegger made for the NEA. The account of the January 5, 2005, meeting among Riordan, Reiss, Campbell, and the education lobby was from interviews with six participants and notes kept by two members of the education lobby. Schwarzenegger discussed his decision-making on the education deal in a number of conversations, most extensively in the April 2006 interview. Many of his quotes—including "I thought, 'The only way you can find out . . .,'" "You have to understand, it's nothing personal with me . . . ," "I had a choice . . .," "I tried to make it work . . . ," "I always recognized that we owed them money . . . "—were drawn from that interview.

I reviewed the Legislative Analyst's work on Prop 98, particularly its "California Fiscal Outlook" of November 2004.

CHAPTER 19

This chapter was based on interviews and conversations with, among others, John Russonello, Maviglio, Fabian Núñez, Kaufman, Ackerman, Hein, Kerr, Lou Paulson, Carroll Wills, Jimenez, Bob Baker, DeMoro, Dave Low, Rob Feckner, Bob Balgenorth, Richman, Pellissier, Costa, Bill Mundell, Mark Abernathy, Peter Welch, Zaremberg, Hauck, Reiss, Clarey, Tom Campbell, Larry McCarthy, Fox, John Campbell, Dave Gilliard, Stutzman, Claussen, Baca, Lockyer, Peter Siggins, Parvin, H.D. Palmer, a Republican lawyer, a Republican Congressional staffer, three senior Schwarzenegger administration officials, two CTA officials, two Democratic staffers, two Democratic pollsters, seven Republican consultants, as well as dozens of union members who protested the governor. Dick Morris replied to a question by e-mail.

Schwarzenegger's views were culled from his public statements and media interviews, as well as interviews on November 2 and 5, 2005, and in March and April 2006. "Exactly the way you rewrite the script . . ." was from an interview on Fox News Sunday, May 8, 2005. "I even gave them the budget . . ." was from the November 2 interview. "I was unhappy about that" was from the April 2006 interview.

I attended many of the events in the chapter, including the "red ink" news conference and the late April and early May signature gathering events. Schwarzenegger's "close the borders" comment came during a speech in April that I did not attend. The quote was from a transcript and press reports. I relied on recordings and transcripts in describing the Sacramento Press Club speech, and the San Diego armored truck event. Carla Marinucci broke the story of the San Jose pothole in the *San Francisco Chronicle* on May 27, 2005, and reported more details on August 7, 2005.

The description of the January CTA strategy meeting was based on interviews with five participants. The Kerr-Schwarzenegger meeting in February was described by five participants. Descriptions of Schwarzenegger's fund-raising were from fund-raising schedules, minutes, and notes of conference calls with donors. I reviewed several memoranda, including the January 23, 2005, memo written by Sipple. My account of the February focus group was based on interviews and e-mail. The phone call on February 19 was based on interviews with seven participants.

The pension strategy memo of the public relations firm working for the Los Angeles police union was first disclosed in the *Los Angeles Times*. I also reviewed documents—including schedules, e-mails, talking points, and other memoranda—of the unions that challenged the governor's pension proposal.

The quotes about the pension negotiations between the administration and unions, including the April 19 walkout, were from union e-mails.

The account of the negotiations between CTA and the Schwarzenegger staffers was from interviews, notes taken by participants, schedules, and an expense report. The account of the Public Opinion Strategies research was based on the polls themselves, as well as an internal report on the March focus groups in Concord. I also reviewed polling by McLaughlin, the Field Poll and PPIC, particularly a survey released January 27, 2005, on the state budget.

I consulted Jesse Ventura's *I Ain't Got Time to Bleed* (New York: Signet, 2000) and *Do I Stand Alone?* (New York: Pocket Books, 2000). Murphy's "Any advantage the Democrats thought they'd have" quote was from the *Sacramento Bee*, March 30, 2005. One of Schwarzenegger's consultant's suggested, in an email, starting over with a reform commission.

My colleague Robert Salladay reported on Steve Kram's hiring the *Los Angeles Times* on March 19, 2006, and Bill Bradley, a columnist for *LA Weekly*, reported on Schwarzenegger's political spending in his blog, *New West Notes*. Schwarzenegger said that he looked at the spending and found no wrongdoing. "It was not like someone ripped us off or someone misused money," the governor told Salladay.

In writing about the legislative Democrats' tax proposal, I referred to reports published June 1 in the *Los Angeles Times, Sacramento Bee,* and *Orange County Register.* The *San Jose Mercury News* and the *Sacramento Bee* reported on the family atmosphere and the Schwarzeneggers' spending time with Nunez's children in articles on July 10 and July 11, 2005.

CHAPTER 20

This chapter was based on day-to-day reporting of the campaign events, as well as documents, interviews, and newspaper reports. The documents included schedules of the Schwarzenegger and ABC efforts, e-mails, memoranda from both sides, as well as polling conducted by Binder, Mellman, McLaughlin, Luntz, and Newhouse. I watched video footage of events I did not cover myself, such as the the Beatty speech in Oakland.

This chapter drew from interviews conducted with, among others, Reiss, Fabian Núñez, McPherson, Stutzman, Clarey, Tom Campbell, Margaret Fortune, Siggins, Lucas, Kerr, Maviglio, Pete Wilson, Shultz, Harris, Bill Mundell, John Laird, Steve Poizner, Wayne Johnson, Costa, Uhler, Fox, Claussen, Bill Carrick, Art Pulaski, DeMoro, Art Torres, Hannah-Beth Jackson, Kaufman, Ron Nehring, three senior administration offi-

cials, four Democratic legislative staffers, a GOP pollster, three Democratic pollsters, a former state office holder, a Republican Party offical,
and six Republican consultants. I drew heavily from interviews with
Schwarzenegger in November 2005 and March and April 2006, as well as
from his public statements throughout the summer and fall of 2005. Particularly helpful were his remarks to reporters on August 18 and his speech
of October 6. Warren Beatty was interviewed on board the California
Nurses Association bus on November 5. Beatty's quote, "I would think
Maria . . . ," was from the *Associated Press*, October 27, 2005.

The description of the focus groups in Orange was drawn in part from interviews and an e-mail report. The Enchilada Chronicles and participant interviews provided the account of the enchilada meetings. Stu Spencer's quote to
Shriver was from Steve Lopez's column in the *Los Angeles Times*, January 8, 2006.

The strategy of putting together public events that highlighted Schwarzenegger's governing was first disclosed by Gary Delsohn in the *Sacramento
Bee*, July 26, 2005. The American Media contract was disclosed in an SEC filing and in the *Los Angeles Times* and *Sacramento Bee* on July 14. The account of
the Prop 77 dispute was from court papers. The account of the July 22 conference call, during which the cancellation of the special election was discussed, was based on notes, interviews, e-mails, and Delsohn's story of July
23 in the *Sacramento Bee*. Gorton's suggestion of polygraph machines was made
by e-mail to other advisors.

Accounts of the negotiations mediated by Hertzberg were from interviews with participants, schedules, notes, and a review of multiple versions
of the "ROAD MAP TO PEACE IN OUR TIME" document. "We added
and added . . ." comment was recalled during a November 2 interview with
Schwarzenegger. Schwarzenegger also described the negotiations in some detail in interviews on November 5, 2005, and April 15, 2006. The governor's
comment about Núñez, "He came back and said . . . ," was from the April
2006 interview. The details on the history of deadlines for adding measures
to the ballot was drawn in part from a four-year-old memo of Rick Simpson
that was sent to Hertzberg on October 24, 2001.

Schwarzenegger described his conversation with his mother-in-law, in
which she urged him to talk more about himself, on several occasions, including in the October 6 speech. My colleague Bob Salladay wrote about the
"micro-targeting strategy" employed by Schwarzenegger and the Republican
party in the *Los Angeles Times*, on November 1. The figures on Schwarzenegger's
own donations, as well as the timing of donations by Wal-Mart and the
American Insurance Association, were from the California Secretary of
State. The California Professional Firefighters provided a DVD of the test

"Yes on 75" ads. Schwarzenegger's ad buy numbers were from news reports and public records. The scene with Rob Reiner was reported in the *Sacramento Bee*, on September 30.

Schwarzenegger's quote about Beatty—"There are some people who are close to him that say that he is just starving for attention . . ."—was from an interview with the Associated Press, published September 21. His comment about President Bush's fund-raising was made to reporters on October 19. I reviewed coverage of the Count Cartaxula event in the *Mercury News* and the *Los Angeles Times*. Two quotes—"How do you make sure you don't get bored?" and "Don't look at this as all we need . . . "—were from November 2005 interviews. The governor's ideas for events and ads were described in interviews. The Schwarzenegger recording the night of the bus tour was done for a podcast that played briefly on his Web site. The quote, "What I should have done . . ." was from an April 2006 interview.

The post-election poll that found support for redistricting was conducted by Lake Research Partners, November 8 through November 10.

EPILOGUE

The epilogue drew heavily on interviews with Schwarzenegger in November 2005 and spring 2006, as well as his public statements in the first half of the year. Three quotes—including "At the end when the dust is settled . . . ," "I made mistakes . . . ," and "Can you believe . . ."—were from spring 2006 interviews. The comments about national initiatives and his future—"I think I owe it to my family" and "is something to study . . ."—were from November 2005. My description of the meeting with Republicans was from e-mails of participants and from interviews with two Republican officials. The accounts of the infrastructure bond and education deal were based, in part, on my own reporting, some of it published in the *Los Angeles Times* on May 8 and 9, 2006. The first set of negotiations on infrastructure was described by Robert Salladay and Jordan Rau in the *Los Angeles Times*, on March 17, 2006. I also relied upon the coverage of the *Sacramento Bee*, *Orange County Register*, and *San Francisco Chronicle*.

Angelides's comments about taking his proposals to the people were published in the *Sacramento Bee* on April 12, 2006. The estimates on the budget were from the Legislative Analyst's Office. The information on the prison guards was based on reports by Jenifer Warren in the *Los Angeles Times*, as well as stories in the *Sacramento Bee* on February 27, and the *San Diego Union-Tribune*, April 24, 2006. Schwarzenegger's outreach to tribes was reported by several papers, including the *Bee* on May 15, 2006. The list of ballot measures was from the Secretary of State. The description of Reiner's troubles was from multiple news reports. Laura Mecoy's coverage of Prop 82 in the *Bee*, particularly her June 11 piece, was helpful.

The information on direct democracy nationally and internationally was drawn from material from the Initiative & Referendum Institute, as well as books including Cronin's *Direct Democracy*, Hunn and Ober's *Ordinary People Doing the Extraordinary* and Fossedal's *Direct Democracy in Switzerland.* Culbert Olson's story was from accounts of the time. I reviewed the written plan outlining what Schwarzenegger might do after Prop 49. Joe Weider and Reg Park both talked about Schwarzenegger's presidential ambitions in interviews at the Arnold Fitness Expo in March 2004. The Werner Kopacka quote was from an interview in Graz in 2005. The material on amending the U.S. Constitution was from reporting I did for a *Los Angeles Times* story on the subject in February 2005.

Index

PublicAffairs is a publishing house founded in 1997. It is a tribute to the standards, values, and flair of three persons who have served as mentors to countless reporters, writers, editors, and book people of all kinds, including me.

I.F. STONE, proprietor of *I. F. Stone's Weekly*, combined a commitment to the First Amendment with entrepreneurial zeal and reporting skill and became one of the great independent journalists in American history. At the age of eighty, Izzy published *The Trial of Socrates*, which was a national bestseller. He wrote the book after he taught himself ancient Greek.

BENJAMIN C. BRADLEE was for nearly thirty years the charismatic editorial leader of *The Washington Post*. It was Ben who gave the *Post* the range and courage to pursue such historic issues as Watergate. He supported his reporters with a tenacity that made them fearless and it is no accident that so many became authors of influential, best-selling books.

ROBERT L. BERNSTEIN, the chief executive of Random House for more than a quarter century, guided one of the nation's premier publishing houses. Bob was personally responsible for many books of political dissent and argument that challenged tyranny around the globe. He is also the founder and longtime chair of Human Rights Watch, one of the most respected human rights organizations in the world.

For fifty years, the banner of Public Affairs Press was carried by its owner Morris B. Schnapper, who published Gandhi, Nasser, Toynbee, Truman, and about 1,500 other authors. In 1983, Schnapper was described by *The Washington Post* as "a redoubtable gadfly." His legacy will endure in the books to come.

Peter Osnos, *Founder and Editor-at-Large*